The French Canadians *1760-1967*

THE FRENCH CANADIANS

1760-1967

MASON WADE

Revised edition, in two volumes

VOLUME TWO

1911-1967

Macmillan of Canada
A Division of Gage Publishing Limited
Toronto, Canada

This is a revised edition, in two volumes, of *The French
Canadians, 1760-1945,* which was first published in 1955.

First published in paperback 1968

First published in the Laurentian Library 1976

Reprinted 1983

ISBN 0-7715-9855-6

Revised paperback edition originally
published in 1968 by The Macmillan
Company of Canada under ISBN 0-7705-1485-5.

Manufactured in Canada by Webcom Limited

FOR
JOHN BARTLET BREBNER

ABBREVIATIONS

AAQ: Archives of the Archdiocese of Quebec

APQ: Archives of the Province of Quebec

ASL: Archives seigneuriales de Lotbinière, Leclercville, Québec

ASTR: Archives du Séminaire des Trois-Rivières

Bib. St. Sulp.: Bibliothèque Saint-Sulpice, Montréal

Can. An. Rev.: The Canadian Annual Review

CAR: Canadian Archives Report

CHAR: Report of the Canadian Historical Association

CHR: The Canadian Historical Review

CJEPS: The Canadian Journal of Economics & Political Science

I.O.A.P.Q.: Inventaire des Œuvres Artistiques de la Province de Québec

LOC: The Library of Congress

NYPL: New York Public Library

PAC: The Public Archives of Canada

PIB: Press Information Bureau, Montreal

QLHS: Quebec Literary & Historical Society

QLHST: Transactions of the Quebec Literary & Historical Society

RAPQ: Report of the Archives of the Province of Quebec

RHAF: Revue de l'histoire de l'Amérique Française

TRSC: Transactions of the Royal Society of Canada

CONTENTS OF VOLUME TWO (1911–1967)

CONTENTS OF VOLUME ONE (*to* 1911)
(*bound separately*)

MAPS

ILLUSTRATIONS

PREFACE

THIS BOOK is essentially an attempt to explain why the French Canadians live, think, act, and react differently from English-speaking North Americans. It is also an account of what French Canadians call *le fait français en Amérique* — the French fact in North America — for only by tracing the intellectual and cultural history of French Canada from its beginnings can present-day Quebec be understood. French-Canadian culture is an intricate amalgam of the French heritage, the North American environment, and Roman, British, and American influences. The unifying thread in French-Canadian history is the spirit known as 'nationalism', which is actually an intense provincialism mingled with ethnic and religious factors. Therefore somewhat disproportionate attention will be devoted to the extremists of a generally placid and easy-going people, who possess a singular devotion to the golden mean as a rule of life; for this is an attempt to explain differences, not to stress resemblances.

This book is also the story of the ceaseless struggle of a minority group to maintain its cultural identity in the face of all manner of conscious and unconscious pressures to conform to the dominant civilization of other ethnic groups and another culture. The French Canadians are the *Sinn Feiners* of North America, for their strong group consciousness and cohesiveness arise from a basic loneliness and insecurity. It is the sense of 'ourselves alone' that motivates efforts at enhancement by stressing French Canada's peculiar ties with France and Rome. The attitudes of minority groups can often be explained only in psychological terms, and French Canada is no exception to this rule. Sir Wilfrid Laurier, one of the most eminent French Canadians, who had a profound understanding of both French and English Canadians,* once formulated this fact in the observation that 'Quebec does not have opinions, but only sentiments.' So this history will be in some measure a psychological study, whose findings may have some general validity for other minority groups.

Intellectual and cultural history is one of the broadest forms of non-specialized science. This book will be based on constitutional and political history, though by no means confined to it. It will use economic history and sociology, which do much to explain intellectual developments in this instance; it will employ literary and artistic history for illustrative pur-

---

* These terms are used for 'French-speaking' and 'English-speaking' throughout, and do not necessarily refer to ethnic origin.

poses. In so broad an attempt at synthesis in a field far from covered by adequate special studies, comprehensiveness or finality is not to be expected, but it is hoped that this book may lead to a better understanding of French Canada than previous histories largely concerned with political events unrelated to economic and social developments. So far as possible, this study is based upon primary sources, since many of the supposedly standard works proved inaccurate and unreliable upon detailed investigation. But it has not proved feasible to carry this policy as far as the author would have liked, largely because of the inadequacies of Canadian archives and libraries and the wide dispersion of materials.* Considering its scope and the immense amount of work that remains to be done in the field, this book had to rely largely on the secondary sources which proved trustworthy. Crucial episodes have generally been investigated in these sources, and recourse has been had to the basic materials whenever the secondary works were obviously unsatisfactory. This method has provided a basic for critical judgement of earlier works, and the author has not hesitated to differ with them. This book could not have been written without critical use of previous work, for scholarship is a cumulative process, with an ungrateful tendency on the part of the laborer of the eleventh hour to disparage earlier workers in the vineyards. But historical truth can only emerge through continual sifting and winnowing of facts and theories in the light of new knowledge and new perspectives.

This process has been particularly necessary, for until very recently it has been the tradition in Canada to write history from a certain partisan position: French or English, Catholic or Protestant, Liberal or Tory. This tradition has had the unfortunate result of making the standard French and English histories of Canada so dissimilar as to suggest that they are the histories of two different countries. Such a situation, when members of the two chief Canadian ethnic groups are largely educated in separate school systems and different cultures, and are rarely thrown together until their minds are formed, can have and has had tragic consequences. It is hoped that this book will dispel some of the misunderstandings that are the basis of much needless friction between Canadians of different cultural backgrounds. The author has sought to use and correlate all available French and English sources, many of which are not available even throughout Canada, and as a disinterested outsider to interpret them objectively in a broader way than would be possible for a Canadian, subject to conscious or unconscious bias and preoccupied with the national scene.

The author is committed to neither side in the ancient ethnic conflict in Canada, and sympathetic to both, for his own ethnic and cultural heritage is Scots and English, while he shares the faith of French Canada and is a native of New England, a region whose history has many analogies with

---

* This situation has since vastly improved, thanks largely to the leadership of the Dominion Archivist and National Librarian, Dr. W. Kaye Lamb.

that of Quebec and one which within the last century has become almost as French as Quebec has become English. He claims freedom from ethnic prejudice; and he believes that the Catholic historian's duty is best summarized by Leo XIII's dictum that the first law of history is not to lie, and the second not to be afraid to tell the whole truth. In the course of this book it has been necessary to state some hard truths; this has been done without malice and without any other design than to do justice to the facts. The ancient tradition of diplomatic relations between the French and English in Canada has been outmoded by Canada's national development, and frankness is now the best and most useful approach to their differences.

It doubtless seems presumptuous of the writer to take it upon himself to write the history of a country of which he is not a native and whose mother tongue is not his own. There are advantages, however, in such a course; and perhaps particularly in this instance, where there has existed at times an almost unbridgeable abyss between two peoples with a common history, and where ancient quarrels have a fatal way of entering into the thinking of each group about the other. The writer has devoted ten years to this work; he lived in Quebec for two years, thanks to the Guggenheim Foundation, and has made many extended visits there for research purposes, thanks to the Rockefeller Foundation and the Carnegie Corporation of New York. The Corporation, through a grant to the Canada Foundation, has made publication possible. He has traveled through almost all parts of the province, which is larger than France and Britain combined, meeting and talking with all classes of its people, and learning some of the things which are not to be found in books. He has taught in a French-Canadian university and lectured on French Canada both in Quebec and the other provinces, and through discussion learned much of both French and English attitudes towards the matters with which this book is concerned. He is vastly indebted to many Canadians who undertook his education in their history, and is grateful for the light they have shed upon the problem with which he was concerned. He trusts that in these pages they will find no cause to regret their courtesy and kindness to a stranger in search of knowledge, who now seems to intervene in a family quarrel.

But the matters with which this book is concerned are not exclusively Canadian in nature. While there are 5,500,000 French Canadians in Canada, there are at least 2,000,000 Franco-Americans of Quebec and Acadian stock in the United States. While their history, and consequently their attitudes, like those of the French Canadians of the Maritime Provinces, Ontario, and the West, differ from those of the French Canadians of Quebec, the old province on the St. Lawrence remains to various degrees their cultural homeland, and they have deeply felt its influence. This book is primarily concerned with Quebec, the heart of French Canada; but it also deals with the history of the outlying groups when this has affected Quebec, and the far-flung French-Canadian people have been re-united, regardless of provincial or international frontiers. It has been impossible for the author, with the time and means at his disposal, to tell this broader story in detail, or even to sketch it fully. But the history of Quebec is essential to the understanding of these outlying minority groups, which in the past have shown varying tendencies to follow the Quebec tradition of standing apart and preserving their separateness from English-speaking North Americans; and there are common patterns, as well as significant differences, in the behavior of all minority groups. These are of concern to all North Americans, whether citizens of Canada or the United States, and indeed to all mankind, for only by the acceptance of diversity, through the understanding and reconciliation of cultural differences, can the great world problems of our time be solved.

It is unfortunately impracticable for reasons of space to acknowledge in detail all the obligations incurred by the writer in the course of ten years' work. Among many libraries the Dartmouth College Library offered extraordinary facilities for research throughout the undertaking. The staffs of the Public Archives of Canada and of the Quebec Provincial Archives were unfailingly helpful. The author is particularly indebted for criticism of the first draft to Professors J. B. Brebner of Columbia University, and Jean-Charles Falardeau and Jean-Charles Bonenfant of Laval University, who read the entire manuscript. Others who criticized one or more chapters include Professors E. R. Adair, J. I. Cooper, and F. R. Scott of McGill University, A. L. Burt of the University of Minnesota, G. F. G. Stanley of the Royal Military College of Canada, Miss Elizabeth Armstrong, M. G. Ballantyne, Dr. Pierre Dansereau, Dr. Eugene Forsey, the late J. K. Howard, and Major Gustave Lanctot. The late Paul Rainville, Gérard Morisset of the Quebec Provincial Museum, and A. J. H. Richardson of the Public Archives were of great assistance with the illustrations and maps. To these individuals and many others the writer wishes to express his gratitude, while absolving them of any responsibility for the views which he finally adopted after considering divergent points of view.

MASON WADE

Cornish, New Hampshire
  April 1954

PREFACE TO THE REVISED EDITION

In preparing a revised edition of this book, concluded in 1950 and first published in 1955, I have added a new chapter, carrying the narrative down to 1966; I have sought to remedy factual errors in the older chapters; and I have added references to the major works published since that time. I have not attempted major revisions for two reasons: I do not find it necessary to change the basic interpretations or the main outlines, and while at the present time I might be inclined to write another and different book on the same theme, because of other commitments I could not attempt to write this one over again. Rereading my views of 1950, before beginning to write the new chapter, I was forcibly reminded of the warning of my historical father-in-God, J. Bartlet Brebner, about the dangers of writing contemporary history:

As we approach the present our inferences grow more and more subject to distortion. Circumstances which bear one kind of fruit in tranquility yield another kind in days of apprehension and still another in times of war. Secrecy and censorship veil huge areas of behavior so thoroughly that the same group of known events can be put together in half-a-dozen explanatory patterns, none of which will remain completely valid twenty-five years from now, and some of which will appear ridiculous. Any attempt to make the course of events intelligible, therefore, is like an exercise in algebra where the values of many of the components are unknown and where even time-tested formulas produce at best tentative results.*

Brebner was writing in time of war, but many of the same considerations have operated in the stormy post-war years of French Canada. Much of the evidence is simply not available to the historian, who in any case may have been too close to events to achieve a proper detachment. The best that one can do is to summarize developments in the light of one's personal knowledge and such documentary and other evidence as is available. There can be nothing definitive about contemporary history, since all the returns are not in, and a single new revelation may call for complete revision of one's judgements. But it still may be useful to attempt to find the pattern in the tangled skein of events, and, in order to aid the reader who wishes to make more detailed investigations in the period which I have attempted to summarize, a rather full bibliography of the wealth of materials available has been appended.

The publishers have supplied a new and much improved index, and

* J. Bartlet Brebner, *North Atlantic Triangle* (New Haven and Toronto, 1945), 304.

Major C. C. G. Bond has added greatly to the usefulness of the work with new maps. I am grateful to those individuals who were kind enough to make suggestions for revision of the older portion of the work and to those who offered criticism of the new chapter: F. R. Scott, Michael Oliver, Gérard Pelletier, G. V. Ferguson, M. Adelard Saudie, and Pierre Dansereau.

University of Western Ontario
London, Ontario   MASON WADE

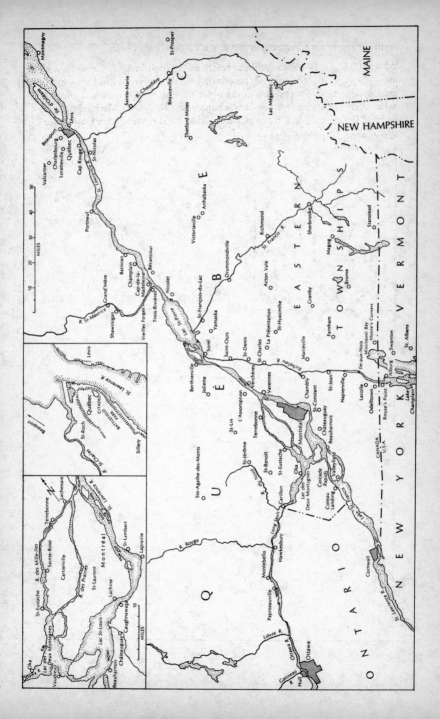

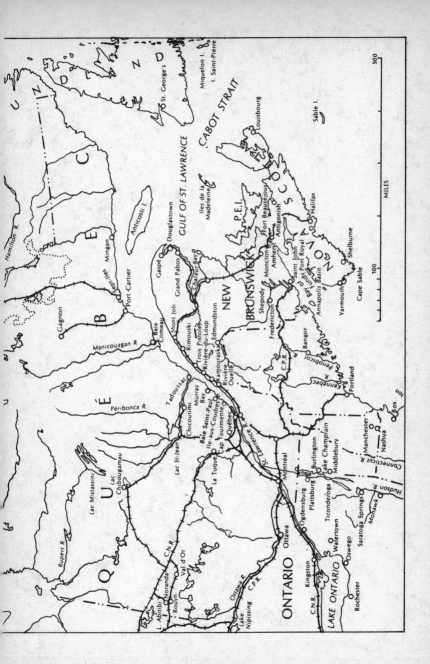

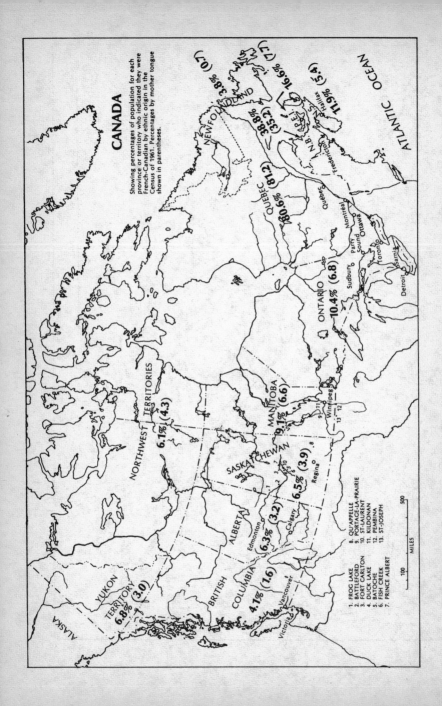

CANADA

Showing percentages of population for each province or territory who indicated they were French-Canadian by ethnic origin in the Census of 1961. Percentages by mother tongue shown in parentheses.

YUKON TERRITORY 6.8% (3.0)

NORTHWEST TERRITORIES 6.1% (4.3)

BRITISH COLUMBIA 4.1% (1.6)

ALBERTA 6.3% (3.2)

SASKATCHEWAN 6.5% (3.9)

MANITOBA 9.1% (6.6)

ONTARIO 10.4% (6.8)

QUEBEC 81.2% 80.6%

NEWFOUNDLAND 3.8% (.7)

38.8% (35.2)

16.6% (.7)

11.9% (5.4)

ALASKA

Vancouver
Victoria

Edmonton
Calgary

Regina

Winnipeg

Sudbury
Parry Sound
Sarnia
Detroit
Toronto
Ottawa
Montréal
Québec
Fredericton
N.B.
Halifax
P.E.I.

ATLANTIC OCEAN

1. FROG LAKE
2. BATTLEFORD
3. FORT CARLTON
4. DUCK LAKE
5. BATOCHE
6. FISH CREEK
7. PRINCE ALBERT
8. QU'APPELLE
9. PORTAGE-LA-PRAIRIE
10. ST-LAURENT
11. KILDONAN
12. PEMBINA
13. ST-JOSEPH

MILES
100   500

The French Canadians *1760-1967*

CHAPTER XI

STRIFE IN ONTARIO AND WAR IN FRANCE
(1911–16)

I T WAS A new and greater Quebec that in 1911 faced the future in somewhat lonely isolation after bringing about the defeat of Canada's first French-Canadian prime minister. Its population had increased since 1901 from 1,648,898 to 2,005, 776; a region which had been nearly two-thirds rural in 1891 was now nearly half urban. [1] These changes were caused largely by the rapid growth of greater Montreal, which now included a quarter of the population of the province. And they reflected the impact of the industrial revolution upon Quebec, since Montreal's growth was due to the fact that it was the financial and industrial capital of the Dominion. The city was the headquarters of eight banks, holding two-thirds of all Canadian bank capital, and of two great railway systems. [2] The great Angus Shops of the Canadian Pacific, the rapidly developing shoe and dress industries, and the port which held an ever-tightening monopoly of the St. Lawrence trade, all combined to make Montreal a magnet for the surplus rural population. Despite the movement from country to town, farm production doubled from 1895–1910 as agricultural methods improved. [3]

Montreal had become cosmopolitan, rather than more French. Its English minority, which controlled most of the great industrial and financial institutions, built the English sub-city of Westmount, where they could forget that they lived in one of the largest French cities of the world. The French upper-classes abandoned the Place Viger and Saint-Denis districts for the new suburb of Outremont. The working-class suburbs of Maisonneuve, Verdun, Lachine, and Montreal-Est expanded or began their rapid development. Meanwhile the older portions of the town became centers for immigrant groups: Jews, Poles, Chinese, and Italians. Among the newcomers, only small numbers of French and Belgians assimilated to the French Canadians and hence were welcome; there was growing feeling against the Jews, whose school population had risen from 1,500 in 1901, to 5,900 in 1911, [4] partly because they took over a growing share of the dress industry and of the small business which had been left to the French Canadians by English and American dominance in big business. For by 1907 there were 150 American branch plants established in the province, and much American capital there.[5] Big business, largely integrated into a continental economy regardless of its ownership, tended to give the city an increasingly American air.

Quebec City had not matched Montreal's growth. Its population increased only by 10,000 during the first decade of the century,[6] and its 78,000 would have been lost among Montreal's half million. Its shipbuilding industry was dead. With the improvement of the St. Lawrence channel and of port facilities at Montreal, shipping tended to bypass Quebec in favor of Montreal. Quebec's shoe industry was largely transferred to Montreal, and its cotton industry to Trois-Rivières. G.-E. Amyot's Dominion Corset plant burnt in May 1911, but was replaced before the end of the year by a larger and more modern one, the single exception to the general picture of industrial stagnation. Hull, the industrial capital of the Ottawa and Gatineau Valleys, thrived on its wood industries and increased its population by half in the first decade of the century. Sherbrooke, the industrial center of the Townships, did the same, thanks to its textile factories. Trois-Rivières, largely burnt out in 1908, nevertheless increased its population by a third and became the capital of the rapidly developing Saint-Maurice region. Its pulp and paper industry supplied a notable share of the Canadian contribution of 10 per cent of American newsprint. Prohibition of the export of pulp caused the establishment of paper mills at Trois-Rivières, and a thriving cotton industry also grew up there. Up the Saint-Maurice the ten-year-old industrial town of Grand'Mère, doubled its population, and to its pulp mills added foundries, shirt factories, and woodworking plants. Still farther upstream, the little town of La Tuque was founded. The Lake St. John region, fifty years after its first colonization, was turning towards industry, with great pulp mills at Chicoutimi, and the Dubuc and Price interests struggling for control of the vast waterpower resources of the region. The slow-starting colonization of the Abitibi region in the far northwest of the province was stimulated by the discovery of mineral deposits uncovered by the construction of the Canadian Northern from North Bay to Quebec, which opened up this distant and inaccessible region. But colonization activity had lagged behind, the orphan child of a provincial government much more concerned with the rapid industrial development of the province.

At the turn of the century Errol Bouchette had proclaimed the coming of the industrial age in a pamphlet, 'Emparons-nous de l'industrie,' whose title echoed Ludger Duvernay's outmoded slogan of 'Emparons-nous du sol.' Bouchette foresaw that industry would become more important than agriculture, which was not 'the exclusive need of our people.'[7] He pointed out that the ground the

French Canadians gained by colonization, they lost in the established centers of the province, where others were founding industries. The new age called for skills acquired through education, and he deplored the fact that there were only 722 French lay university students in the province, out of a population of 1,293,000, while the English students numbered 1,358 out of a population of 196,000. The most serious weakness of the French Canadians was reflected by the fact that there were only 27 students of the applied sciences at Laval, compared to 250 at McGill and Bishop's. He predicted 'foreign control of our industry' unless the provincial government, like the German one, became a patron of science, protected the workers, and financed industries.

Bouchette repeated his warning to the Royal Society in 1901, urging that Quebec stood on the eve of an industrial revolution which would have effects as profound as those of the French Revolution: 'We can approve or disapprove of such movements, but no people can escape them; to dam them out is impossible.'[8] The American trusts, seeking new conquests, would invade Quebec, raising new problems and creating a new industrial population. 'We should welcome the forces which may come from beyond our frontiers, but we should await them in a good strategic position, in order to remain, whatever happens, masters in our house.'[9] He claimed that the French Canadians had the same aptness as any other people for business and industry, though hitherto they had largely followed other paths. He deplored, as Arthur Buies had done many years before, the absence of professional and technical schools, which prevented the French Canadians from making use of their natural dexterity and mechanical ingenuity in industry, in other than subordinate and unskilled positions. The Ecole Polytechnique had few pupils, because primary technical and trade schools were lacking.

Bouchette urged the extension of the cooperative principle, already successful among cheese and butter makers, to industry, to overcome the lack of French-Canadian capital. The colonists of new areas could form such syndicates for the making of pulp, thus avoiding speculative exploitation of the forests by foreigners and making later large-scale agriculture possible. He urged that the French Canadians should become 'an industrial people without ceasing to be an agricultural people,' thus exploiting all their resources:

A people is never safe when it leaves the resources of its country unexploited. If it does not exploit them itself, others will come to exploit them for it, and thus give themselves a pretext for intervening in its affairs. Or yet again an industrial oligarchy will arise, which is not less to be feared.[10]

But this warning of Bouchette was largely disregarded until Bourassa began his campaign against the Gouin government's administration of natural resources.

Chiefly at the instigation of Honoré Gervais, in 1907 the provincial government added an architectural course at the Polytechnique, and in 1910 a department of decorative arts, forerunner of the Ecole des Beaux-Arts. Then, too, came the opening of the Ecole des Hautes Etudes Commerciales for which Gervais had long agitated, and technical schools in Montreal and Quebec, aided by federal subsidies. The English industrialists of Shawinigan established a technical school there to meet their own need for trained workmen, and the Collège de Sherbrooke opened a two-year industrial course. The new technical schools suffered, however, from criticism on the grounds that they were not under the direction of the Church, and because of this criticism the commercial academies hesitated to introduce the industrial courses for which subsidies were offered by business. The province still lacked trade schools to fill the gap between primary and technical education, and most French Canadians remained unskilled workers, while the more lucrative posts of technicians and managers were filled by non-French Canadians who had the training the natives lacked.

The province's educational system continued to produce too many lawyers, journalists, and would-be politicians, while industrial development went on apace. The result was a dangerous division between English, English-Canadian, or American management and French-Canadian labor, which was soon exploited by the nationalists, who drew their following largely from the economically insecure intellectuals. J.-E.-A. Dubuc of Chicoutimi, Rodolphe Forget of Montreal and Quebec, and G.-E. Amyot of Quebec were almost the only great French-Canadian industrialists and capitalists of a period which saw a tremendous development of industry and finance in Quebec. The cooperative movement founded in 1902 grew slowly, chiefly among farmers, and the Lévis *Caisse Populaire* of Alphonse Desjardins, established in 1901, now mustered a capital of $40,000, with a record of 3,800 loans without a single loss.[11] Desjardins and his disciples, the Abbé Philibert Grondin, the Abbé Joseph Hallé, and Cyrille Vaillancourt, spread the cooperative gospel through the countryside, once they were convinced that the system worked. The fifty *caisses populaires* of 1911 became sixty-five by 1912. Bourassa, Monk, and Lemieux favored the movement; and Desjardins was received at Rideau Hall by Lord Grey, who was an enthusiastic disciple of the cooperative movement.

Intellectually Quebec was also making rapid advances. Its illiteracy rate, the highest in Canada in 1901, dropped during the decade from 17.71 per cent to 12.73 per cent, with the improvement most

marked among the younger age groups.[12] In 1901 Quebec had 97
French newspapers for its 1,300,000 inhabitants, and 97 English
papers for its 300,000 English inhabitants.[13] During the decade
journalism progressed on one hand from pure politics to the discussion of general ideas by such able pens as those of Bourassa, Omer
Héroux, Georges Pelletier, Olivar Asselin, and Jules Fournier; on
the other it imitated American mass journalism so successfully that
La Presse possessed the largest circulation of any Canadian daily.
Beginning with the Ecole Littéraire de Montréal of 1895 poetry
showed notable improvement, abandoning the romantic echoes and
patriotic themes of the School of Quebec for more original and artistic
expression of emotion.

The most brilliant talent uncovered by the Montreal group's
soirées at the Château de Ramezay was that of Emile Nelligan, who
owed his inspiration to Verlaine and Baudelaire, but achieved an
orginal distinction. Unhappily Nelligan's feverish and unstable
mind collapsed in 1901, when at 19 he had already produced some of
French Canada's best verse.[14] One of the founders of the group,
Gonzalve Desaulniers, only published his poems in 1930,[15] but
exercised an influence in the tradition of Lamartine upon his con-
temporaries. The painter and poet Charles Gill's unfinished epic
Le Cap Eternité was not published until after his death in 1919. The
invalid Albert Lozeau published three books of lyrics and three
collections of prose poems contributed to the press between 1907
and 1918. Albert Ferland turned from early preoccupation with
sentimental themes to the hymning of the Canadian soil and forests
in his *Le Canada Chanté* (1908–10). Blanche Lamontagne, Englebert
Gallèze, and Alphonse Desilets developed rural themes in the
language of the people, as Paul Morin, Guy Delahaye, and René
Chopin followed the path of the French symbolists and concentrated
on perfection of form.

History, like poetry, showed a marked development, with a more
scientific spirit replacing the propagandist patriotism of earlier
writers. Thomas Chapais, who also took an active role in politics
and journalism, published admirable studies of *Jean Talon* (1904)
and *Le Marquis de Montcalm* (1911), and then devoted himself to the
history of the English regime from 1760 to 1867, which he taught
at Laval and chronicled in eight volumes published from 1919–34.
Though a Conservative in politics, Chapais wrote in the spirit of
British Liberalism. Using primary source material and much more
documentation than earlier writers, he produced an interpretation
more favorable to the British. Alfred De Celles, long parliamentary
librarian at Ottawa, published a study of the United States, followed
by popular lives of Papineau and Cartier in French and English, and
of Lafontaine and Laurier in French. A disciple of Laurier, De Celles

wrote in the spirit of *bonne entente* between French and English. The Abbé Auguste Gosselin devoted himself to the history of the Church in Canada, while Mgr. Amedée Gosselin produced the first substantial study of education under the French regime. Canon H. A. Scott wrote an excellent history of the parish of *Notre-Dame de Sainte-Foy* (1902). Pierre-Georges Roy, founder of the *Bulletin des recherches historiques* (1895) and later provincial archivist, began his torrent of genealogical and antiquarian publications. Léon Gérin pioneered in the social sciences with his monographs in the tradition of Le Play on *L'Habitant de Saint Justin* (1898) and *Deux familles rurales de la rive sud de Saint-Laurent* (1909). These admirable studies, produced while Gérin served as a translator at Ottawa, were completed and united with three others in his *Le type économique et social des Canadiens* (1937), when French Canada at last seriously concerned itself with social studies. The novel was a neglected form, with Laure Conan's *L'Oublié* (1902) and Dr. Ernest Choquette's experiments in psychological studies of the rural environment the most notable efforts of the period.

Mgr. Camille Roy established a critical foundation for Canadian literature with his studies published from 1902 onwards in *La Nouvelle France* and *Le Bulletin du Parler Français* and later assembled in book form in *Essais sur la littérature canadienne* (1907), *Nos Origines littéraires* (1909), and *Nouveaux Essais sur la littérature canadienne* (1914). Like Abbé Casgrain, he sought to foster the development of an independent Canadian literature, and in his enthusiasm for the cause erred on the side of leniency in criticizing such efforts as had been made. More critical if equally sympathetic studies of Canadian literature were produced by the Frenchman Charles ab der Halden in his *Etudes* (1904), and *Nouvelles Etudes de Littérature Canadienne Française* (1907), which represented a tightening of the cultural ties between France and Quebec. French newspapers and magazines circulated more widely in Quebec, and more French-Canadian students went abroad to study in Paris. With the French language under attack in Ontario and the West, the defensive *Société du Parler Français au Canada* was founded at Quebec in 1902 by Adjutor Rivard, who devoted his own studies to French-Canadian speech and folklore.

In general Quebec emphasized the Canadian part of the tradition, while more worldly Montreal, in closer contact with Paris and less suspicious of modern anti-clerical France, emphasized the French tradition. Such artists as the illustrator Henri Julien, the painter Suzor Côté, and the sculptors Philippe Hébert and Alfred Laliberté followed the French schools of the period in technique, while using Canadian subject matter. This revival and intensification of the French cultural tradition became dominant as Quebec was separated from the rest of Canada by political and social developments. It played its part in increasing the division between the two chief peoples of Canada.

2

The wedding of the nationalist and Conservative parties, achieved at the point of the electoral gun in 1911, was soon dissolved. Borden called upon Monk to choose the ministers representing Quebec, and Monk consulted with Bourassa, whom he urged to enter the cabinet. Bourassa refused office, both to prove his personal disinterestedness and in fear of Tory influence in the new Borden government; but urged Monk to accept if Borden would agree to a plebiscite on the naval question, relax the immigration policy, and redress the grievances of the minorities in the West. Monk understood that Borden accepted these conditions, and took the portfolio of public works.[16] Lavergne was offered a cabinet post, but declined in favor of Louis-Philippe Pelletier, who became postmaster-general. Lavergne blocked the desire of Rodolphe Forget for a place, and was consulted by Borden[17] on the remaining Quebec nominations: Bruno Nantel, minister of internal revenue; C. J. Doherty, minister of justice; and George Perley, minister without portfolio. None of the French Canadians represented the nationalist movement, and none exercised much influence in the cabinet. Monk, who would have made a good minister of justice, was lost in the post which fell to him; Pelletier was an old style politician who rejoiced in the rich patronage of his post; and Nantel was a staid nonentity. Pierre-Edouard Blondin, named deputy-speaker of the House, was the only nationalist to be rewarded for his part in the campaign which had defeated Laurier. The rest of the cabinet was not of a complexion to make Quebec rest easy, Robert Rogers, Sifton's successor in Manitoba, became minister of the interior; Sam Hughes, minister of militia; and George Eulas Foster, minister of trade and commerce. Dr. Sproule, the leader of the Orangemen, became speaker of the House. In Philippe Landry, chosen president of the Senate, the nationalists counted an admirer of Bourassa and a friend of Lavergne, an old ultramontane of *Castor* tendencies. But the Senate, appointed for life, remained Liberal in majority. The need for alliance with the nationalists having passed, Hugh Graham gave orders for the *Star* to cease its support of Bourassa and to launch a new campaign for Canadian participation in the defence of the empire.[18]

In his public appearances after the election Bourassa asserted his independence and his readiness to judge the government by its acts. He called once more for a plebiscite on the naval question. His new friendship with C. H. Cahan, who replaced the late Goldwin Smith as a sympathetic English-Canadian ally, led Bourassa to support Cahan's principle that Canada should make no contribution to imperial defence without a part in the government of the empire. But Bourassa's followers wanted no participation in imperial affairs under any conditions, while Borden's supporters favored contribution without any consideration in exchange. While the candidates supported by Bourassa in the election transferred their allegiance to Borden, the nationalist chief deplored the ruthless use of patronage by the new government. At Saint-Hyacinthe on December 1, 1911, he presented the nationalist program: emancipation from party spirit; no participation in imperial wars but concentration on internal development and defence of Canada; an appeal to the people for approval of any change in this policy. He sketched out a theory of participation in imperial expenses in exchange for a share in imperial government, but aroused no enthusiasm for it. Once more he argued that he was not anti-British, and merely sought to awaken British pride in the French Canadians: 'The ambition of my life, which has sustained and animated me in my battles, when I was isolated, when the *Rouges* did not love me and the *Bleus* mistrusted me, is to make my compatriots understand that they ought to observe in their provinces, with regard to minorities, the great lesson of justice, tolerance, and charity.'[19] Bourassa soon found occasion to assert his independence and his doctrine by attacking Sam Hughes for his imperialist declarations and for purging French Canadians from the militia department. In its final issue of the year *Le Devoir* asserted his independence in regard to the new government.

Questions on which Bourassa, like his grandfather Papineau, might exercise his talent for opposition soon arose in parliament. In a series of articles in *Le Devoir* from February 1 to 21, 1912—reprinted in pamphlet form in English—he discussed imperial problems, calling for a repeal of the Navy Act. He took advantage of Sir Edward Grey's declaration on January 29, urging a policy of non-interference in the imperial ventures of other powers, and of Lord Charles Beresford's arguments in *The Betrayal* against recent naval policies, to support his own stand against the Navy Act and to urge its repeal. The revelation after fifteen years of the Colonial Defence Committee's memorandum of 1896 on imperial defence—it was laid before the House in January 1912—also furnished justification for the nationalist position. He concluded:

Let the Navy Act be repealed.
Let our militia be thoroughly reformed.
Let the defence of our harbours and shores be organized.
Above all, let our system of transportation, by land and by water, be completed without a minute's loss. While we are talking 'Dreadnoughts' and 'Niobes', populations, drawn to Western Canada by alluring advertisements, are clamouring for the means of selling and shipping their wheat. If our politicians lose their time in endeavouring

to displace Imperial statesmen and save the British fleet and the motherland in spite of the British people, they may suddenly awaken from their
magnificent dreams of Imperialism, and be confronted with serious
troubles occasioned in Canada by their neglect to secure Canada's
economical safety and national unity.

Let Canada be looked after first. Not only is it the country which Providence has given to all Canadians; it is also *the part of the Empire* committed
to our care by the Crown of England and Imperial Parliament. If in
order to do other people's work we neglect our own, neither the British
nor the Australians will come and help us in setting our house in order. [20]

In the House, Sévigny presented a motion for the repeal of the Navy
Act, and in the Senate, Choquette and another dissident Liberal
moved in a similar sense. But Sévigny's motion stood at the end of a
long list, with Borden showing no anxiety to consider it.

The government found a more pressing problem in the annexation
of the Territory of Keewatin to Manitoba, in fulfilment of an election
promise to Robert Rogers. Though there was only a small population in the region, it included Catholics among both whites and
Indians, and separate schools existed. Once again the question of
the right of the minority to separate schools was raised. The Vicar
Apostolic of Keewatin, Mgr. Ovide Charlebois, O.M.I., and Archbishop Langevin of Saint-Boniface insisted that the existence of these
schools should be guaranteed. Rogers and Sam Hughes, in the
tradition of Sifton, opposed in the cabinet Doherty and Nantel, who
supported the schools. Borden yielded to Western pressure and the
measure presented by the government on February 19 carried no
guarantee of the educational rights of the minority.

Debate on the Keewatin question coincided with that on a bill
presented by Edward Arthur Lancaster of Ontario, invalidating any
provincial or canonical law against mixed marriages performed by
any authorized person. The measure was the fruit of agitation against
the application in Quebec of the papal *Ne Temere* decree by annul-
ment of the Hébert-Clouâtre marriage. The Catholic thesis was that
the provincial law merely gave civil force to a religious marriage;
while the Protestants held that the *Ne Temere* decree had no civil
force. [21] The government appealed to the Supreme Court to decide
the question. The apostolic delegate conferred in Montreal with the
archbishops of Canada and adopted the position that the federal
authorities should not interfere with the provincial law in the case of
the *Ne Temere* affair. But he decided not to press opposition to the
Keewatin decision, to the relief of Quebec members of the government. Meanwhile the Superior Court of Quebec heard the Hébert-
Clouâtre case anew, and decided that the *Ne Temere* decree had no
force in law, but only on the consciences of Catholics. In the provincial
legislature Bourassa protested against federal intervention in the

matter, and urged the Quebec government to defend provincial rights when the case was heard by the Supreme Court. Gouin agreed, and appointed Aimé Geoffrion, who had served on the Alaska Boundary Commission, and Robert Cooper Smith, like Geoffrion a law professor at McGill, to represent the province. [22]

While the *Ne Temere* question aroused agitation chiefly in English Canada, where John Ewart labored in vain to clarify the question in another 'Kingdom Paper', [23] the Keewatin question stirred Quebec. The two Western prelates were both natives of the Montreal district, and Archbishop Langevin was the idol of the A.C.J.C., which launched petitions in favor of the Keewatin schools. The Quebec members warned Borden that feeling was aroused in Quebec, but Borden refused to hold back a measure urgently desired by the Manitoba government and to reopen the school question, 'which the French Canadians had settled in 1896, by voting for Mr. Laurier, against their own interest.' [24] Lavergne visited Ottawa to muster the opposition, and found only Senator Landry and young P.-E. Lamarche willing to make a fight against the bill. In the cabinet the suggestion that the four Catholic Quebec ministers might resign on the issue had no great effect, and Borden argued that the Roblin government of Manitoba had promised concessions on the order of the Laurier-Greenway agreement. Monk was skeptical, after 1896, of Quebec's real interest in the minorities of the West; [25] Pelletier did not believe in the effect of a mass resignation and was not willing to be more intransigent than the hierarchy. The apostolic delegate expressed his willingness to accept the law, if it were accompanied by a written guarantee of concessions.

The Liberals were delighted by the division of their opponents, and taunted the nationalists with their failure to secure repeal of the Navy Act and separate schools in Keewatin. Choquette's motion in the Senate in favor of repeal of the Navy Act was crushed by the declaration of the government leader that the administration would take no action on the question during the session, pending consultation with the Admiralty and maturing of a new proposal. Laurier moved an amendment opposing the 'unjust conditions' of the Keewatin bill, and Lamarche pleaded with the French Conservatives to support the amendment. But only five of the rank and file voted against the government. Lamarche defended his vote in a moving speech which won admiration from the English members, but Monk and Pelletier eschewed any revival of the Manitoba school question. The bill was about to enter upon its third reading when Bourassa broke his previous silence upon the question at a meeting at the Monument National in Montreal on March 9. He was supported only by Lavergne and Garceau, all the nationalist M.P.s having been rallied to support of the government.

Bourassa spoke for three hours, first sketching the history of educational legislation in the North-West and repeating the arguments he had adopted in 1905 in the case of Saskatchewan and Alberta. Then he criticized the government's defenders. Hushing the disapproval expressed by the crowd for Monk, he criticized his friend's stand more in sorrow than in anger, citing the opinions of Blake and C. H. Cahan against Monk's legal stand. With more vigor he disposed of Pelletier's speech in favor of the bill. He emphasized that the Manitoba government had given no written guarantee to protect minority rights, and he expressed his disillusionment with the Laurier-Greenway agreement. He argued on historical grounds that only statutory guarantees had lasting value. As for the argument that the hierarchy had not spoken against the new law, he proclaimed: 'It is not the business of bishops and priests to make laws, to support them, and to apply them.'[26] He paid tribute to the bishops and to their authority in religious questions, but quoted Daniel O'Connell's saying, 'I take my theology at Rome, but I take my politics at home.'

Then he evoked the spirit of Confederation: the duality of race and language guaranteed by equality before the law. If Confederation were to be respected, the French Canadians had to fight always and everywhere for the maintenance of their rights and of all minority rights. 'And we should not pursue this fight by invoking the authority of the Church, nor by appealing to the voice of our blood, but in the name and with the strength of our rights as British subjects, of taxpayers of our country.'[27] He warned: 'If the Canadian constitution is to last, if the Canadian Confederation is to be maintained, the narrow attitude towards minorities which increasingly manifests itself in the English provinces must disappear, and we must return to the original spirit of the alliance.' He described the French Canadians as a rampart against annexation to the States or separation from England: 'We are as British as any other race in Canada. We are not British by blood and language, but we are British by reason and tradition.'[28] British institutions were the heritage of the French Canadians from the Norman conquest of England, as well as from the English conquest of Canada:

To these institutions no one is more attached than we; but we are not submissive dogs; we are not valets; and after a hundred and fifty years of good and loyal service to the institutions that we love, to a Crown that we have learned to respect, we deserve better than to be considered like the savages of the old reservations and to be told: 'Remain in Quebec, continue to stagnate in ignorance, you are at home there; but elsewhere you must become English.'

No, we have the right to be French in language; we have the right to be Catholics in faith; we have the right to be free by the constitution.

We are Canadians before all; and we have the right to be as British as anyone. And we have the right to enjoy these rights throughout the whole expanse of Confederation. [29]

He called upon his audience to invoke these rights and make its voice heard by supporting resolutions calling upon parliament to safeguard the rights of the minority in Keewatin. When a standing vote was taken, the entire audience supported the resolutions, despite Bourassa's plea for respect for difference of opinion.

Seeing Cahan in the hall, Bourassa called upon him to speak. Cahan rebuked the French Canadians for expecting the English to defend French-Canadian rights more vigorously than their own representatives had done, citing the stand taken by Quebec's representatives in 1896 and at the present time. If the French Canadians tried to abolish the English schools of Quebec, the whole English population would protest by acts as well as words. 'But you, people of Quebec, you are content to come and hear fine speeches, and then return to your homes without doing anything, often disposed to belie by your acts the words you have applauded with frenzy . . . If you do not succeed in making yourselves respected, you have only to blame yourselves and your chiefs, in whom you cannot have faith when it is a question of your national interests.' [30] Lavergne thanked Cahan for emphasizing what Bourassa and he himself had preached for seven years: that lack of energy was the worst enemy of the French Canadians. He said that the question of schools was not settled anywhere, and if one day it was necessary to provoke a crisis, 'We shall know how to prove that we are not helots or pariahs in this land which is our own.' [31]

The meeting greatly stimulated the movement of protest against the Keewatin bill. John Boyd appealed to the press of the entire country in favor of the minority, while the *Star* warned the majority against abusing their strength and leaving the minority with the lasting impression that they had been wronged. But the amendment jointly presented by A.-A. Mondou and P.-E. Lamarche, guaranteeing minority rights, was defeated by 160 to 24 votes—seven Conservatives and seventeen Liberals. The bill was passed by the House on March 12. In the Senate the resistance headed by Philippe Landry and John Costigan was quickly overcome. Once more Quebec added another defeat to the long list compiled since 1867. The younger generation, with its newly awakened national pride, did not forget the fact. And Bourassa became more determined than ever to remain free of party ties while undertaking the formation of a new national mentality. [32]

Having outraged Quebec feeling in the matter of Keewatin, the Borden government appeased it by authorizing the annexation of Ungava, once part of Rupert's Land, to the province. This step, which nearly doubled Quebec's area and extended its northern limits to Hudson Strait, represented an old dream of Mercier, supported by the Gouin government in 1909, and arranged by Gouin and Laurier, though it was carried through by the Borden government. Quebec gained little for the moment, for this New Quebec was a deserted wilderness known only to a few Indians, Eskimos, and fur traders. But it was believed to contain forest, mineral, and water-power resources which might later be developed. The annexation of Ungava chiefly benefited Lomer Gouin, who now appealed to the people on the platform that his government 'had made Quebec richer, better educated, and greater.'[33] Thanks in part to a reaction in favor of Laurier and the Liberals after the nationalist-Conservative alliance had failed to realize its promises, the Gouin government retained its majority of forty-five in the elections of May 15. Lavergne and Jean Prévost were the only nationalists to be re-elected, and Lavergne's majority was considerably reduced. Bourassa had re-fused to run, and had gone to Europe, where he spent most of his time in France. The Liberal press proclaimed the end of nationalism, and even *Le Devoir* admitted, on the occasion of a banquet in honor of Laurier at Montreal, that he was still 'the great figure of Canadian politics.'[34]

3

While the Supreme Court decided that the federal government could not supplant the matrimonial legislation of Quebec (though recognizing that the *Ne Temere* decree had no civil effect) and the federal government took an appeal to the Privy Council, the province was preoccupied with preparations for the first Congress of the French Language at Quebec, from June 24 to June 30. This event celebrated the tenth anniversary of the *Société du Parler Français au Canada*, founded by the Abbé Lortie and Adjutor Rivard, who had also collaborated with Bishop Paul-Eugène Roy, the auxiliary of Quebec, in the establishment of *L'Action Sociale*. Bishop Roy's program of Catholic Action included defence of the French language and of national traditions, as well as unionization of the workers, and he wished to assemble in a single organization all the Catholic social movements of the province. But the age-old rivalry of Montreal and Quebec had asserted itself with the foundation of the Ecole Sociale Populaire in Montreal in 1911, under the direction of the Jesuit Père Hudon and Arthur Saint-Pierre. The clergy had shown a growing distrust of the international unions and had become partisans of the Catholic syndicate movement launched at Quebec and Chicoutimi in 1902. The Fédération Ouvrière of Chicoutimi, founded in 1902, took on new life in March 1912 when Bishop

Labrecque recommended that all diocesan social and labor movements should be grouped within it.[35] The congress was to sanction this trend and the campaigns of the A.C.J.C. in favor of the French language, and to consolidate the efforts of the outlying French-Canadian groups in defence of their educational and language rights.

The assembly organized by the Abbé Lortie, Rivard, and Bishop Roy himself was a national gathering. There was a contingent from the West headed by Archbishop Langevin, another from Ontario led by Senator Belcourt and Judge Cousineau; an Acadian group headed by Senator Poirier; and Franco-Americans led by Bishop Guertin. There was a delegate from Louisiana, and a French mission headed by the academician Etienne Lamy. The apostolic delegate and most of the Quebec bishops were on hand. To greet the guests Quebec's notables assembled in force, without distinction of party: Laurier, Gouin, the Lieutenant-Governor Sir François Langelier, Senator Landry, Thomas Chapais, Sir Adolphe Routhier, Boucher de la Bruère, the superintendent of public instruction, and a host of ministers, M.P.'s, and other French-Canadian leaders.

Archbishop Langevin opened the congress with the ringing declaration: 'We do not recognize the right of anyone to stop the French Canadians at the border of Quebec and to say: "Beyond this point you are not at home." We are at home everywhere in Canada.'[36] The French consul, C.-E. Bonin, won an ovation, as did Lamy and the Abbé Thellier de Poncheville, who stressed Quebec's bonds with France. Senator Dandurand and the young Abbé Lionel Groulx differed widely in the ideas they expressed, but Dandurand was sympathetic to Groulx's concluding slogan, 'France quand-même.' A statue of Mercier by a French sculptor was unveiled, reviving the memory of one who had sought to link Quebec with France once more. The Franco-Ontarian spokesmen won warm applause, although Bishop Roy vetoed Père Charlebois' plan to announce to the congress that the Ontario government had just decided to restrict French teaching to the point of virtual suppression. Senator Belcourt exercized a moderating influence by urging that Quebec's support for the minorities should not draw down reprisals upon them. Mgr. Paquet invoked theological support for the preservation of the mother tongue and identified the French language with the Christian apostolate, thus supporting Bourassa's argument at Notre-Dame in 1910.

Bourassa, just returned from France, spoke at the close of the congress on 'La Langue française et l'avenir de notre race.' He treated not only the role of the French language in the survival of the French Canadians, but also its role in the relations between the French Canadians and the other races of America. Citing the example of

the Irish and the Scots, he declared that 'the conservation of the
language is absolutely necessary for the conservation of the race,
its genius, its character and its temperament.'[37] If the French
Canadians lost their language, 'we would perhaps be mediocre
Englishmen, passable Scots, or bad Irishmen, but we would not be
true Canadians.' He maintained the moral right of the French
Canadians to use their mother tongue from Halifax to Vancouver,
because of their defence of Canada in 1775-6 and 1812, their fight
for British rights in 1837, and the work of Lafontaine and the
French fathers of Confederation. If the two languages were official
in Canada, both had the right to exist in every aspect of Canadian
public life. There were two ways to preserve the French language in
Canada: through the schools, despite those who betrayed the spirit
of Confederation; and through nourishment drawn from the source
in France.

Bourassa discounted fear of modern France, and warned that
'if for fear of poison one ceased to eat, one died of hunger, which is
just as sure a way of going to the cemetery.'[38] In French literature
there was much remedy for poison, as well as the poison itself. Then
there was no more danger that the French Canadians would
become less Canadian by seeking intellectual stimulation in France
than of the Americans becoming English by drawing their culture
from England. But he urged that the French Canadian's language
should 'give birth to a Canadian literature; it should serve us in
writing and reading the history of Canada; it should teach us to
draft and plead Canadian laws; and to make us understand the spirit
and the letter of the Canadian laws and constitution'—with
'Canadian' understood in the broad sense. 'We should, with the aid
of this perfected and living French language, search out the origins
of English and American civilization; we should study the history of
England and the United States, we should learn to know the English
and the Celts better, and to make ourselves better known by them.'[39]
He warned of the double danger of isolation from and of fusion with
the other races of Canada. French culture held no more dangers
to Catholicism than English, the language of Protestantism, of
materialism, and of ' the most enthusiastic worshippers of the golden
calf.'

Despite D'Alton McCarthy's arguments, bilingualism was not a
danger to national unity. The French Canadians had been charged
with being more French than Catholic, but they believed that their
language was the human element most essential to the conservation
of their faith. He called the preservation of the French language
'the sole true moral guarantee of the unity of the Canadian
Confederation and of the maintenance of British institutions
in Canada,'[40] in warning of the penetration of Americanism,

particularly in Toronto and Winnipeg. The national school principle was borrowed by the West from the States. If the anglicizers succeeded in their projects, they would make Americans and not Englishmen of the French Canadians, who then would have no more reason to remain British.[41] French groups in all the Western provinces would be the best obstacles to Americanization, for they would not share American ideals.

Mentioning the protest of an Ontario Anglican against the importation into that province of the 'France of Louis XIV,' Bourassa pointed out that Quebec had adopted the civil code more than fifty years ago, while the English Canadians had remained content with the outmoded laws of England; that Quebec had freedom of religion and worship while England still discussed exempting the non-conformists of Wales from payment of the tithe; that Quebec had abolished seigneurial tenure sixty years ago, while in England a third of the people starved because the great landowners held half the country; that Quebec had enfranchised the Jews before England did the Catholics. While Ontario worried about imaginary perils, English Canada was becoming in habits, language, and mentality more American than if reciprocity had made it an 'adjunct of the United States.' Knowledge of French was demanded by Canada's growing world trade; its universality would help Canada to the heights of civilization.

In an eloquent peroration Bourassa recalled his recent presence at the beatification of Joan of Arc at Rouen, and urged:

Let us ask of Joan of Arc that she consummate the alliance between the conquered and the conquerors of other days, and that she permit that her tongue, this tongue so beautiful and clear, which enabled her to unknit the subtleties of casuists and repel treason and cowardice, that this French language preserved by us, the French of America, instead of being an element of discord between the two great races should become on the contrary the vehicle of the most beautiful and noble thoughts, generous thoughts, thoughts of union, by which Anglo-Canadians and French Canadians, Saxons and Celts, should cause to triumph in the northern part of the American continent the best traditions of the two great races which have given birth to the nation of Canada.[42]

Though the congress adopted resolutions favouring the maintenance and spread of the use of French language in the home, school, commerce, and public life, Bishop Roy discouraged a proposal by a young disciple of Lavergne, supported by Senator Choquette, for a message of sympathy to the Franco-Ontarians in their struggle for their schools. The congress took no significant action, but by rallying the forces of French Canada it supplied evidence of their vitality. It also revealed the important part played by the clergy as national leaders of the French Canadians. An interesting light on the ultramontanism of French-Canadian Catholicism was supplied by criticism of the modernism of the French Abbé Thellier de Poncheville by Paul Tardivel of *La Vérité* and the Abbé J.-G.-A. D'Amours of *L'Action Sociale.*

4

While French Canada mustered its forces at Quebec, Borden had gone to England to consult the imperial authorities on the naval question. He had sought the company of Monk, but the latter refused to go; so the ministerial delegation consisted of Doherty, Hazen, and Pelletier. They were subjected to the usual imperialist pressure, and on Borden's first day in London, Winston Churchill, the First Lord of the Admiralty, warned him of the pressing danger of German aggression. Borden had already been in correspondence with Churchill, who had offered his assistance in drafting a Canadian naval policy.[43] Borden also conferred with Asquith on the question of Canada's having a share in imperial policy in exchange for its naval collaboration. He visited the fleet at Spithead and attended a meeting of the Defence Committee at which Sir Edward Grey spoke on the foreign relations of the empire, and Churchill again stressed the German menace and urged Canadian collaboration.

A series of conferences at the Admiralty then began, which were interrupted by a brief visit to Paris, where the French government besought the Canadians to support the *Entente cordiale*, upon which France relied for protection against the German menace. After Borden's return to England and during his visits to various ship-building yards, Churchill prepared a memorandum on the naval emergency, which was revised at Borden's request and finally took form in the dual shape of one secret memorandum for use in the Canadian cabinet and another which could be submitted to the Canadian parliament.[44] Earlier, in exchange for Borden's willingness to commit Canada to a naval program, Asquith modified his stand of 1911 and spoke in parliament of 'the duty of making such response as we can to the Dominions' obviously reasonable appeal that they should be entitled to be heard in the determination of the policy and the direction of imperial affairs.'[45] Borden conferred with Asquith, Grey, Harcourt, and Walter Long on how this might be achieved. But though the British pressed for speed in naval contributions, they urged that imperial representation should not be hurried.

During Borden's extended visit to England, the imperialist press in Canada, headed by the *Star*, made much of the German menace and urged Canada to save England. *Le Devoir* took a skeptical attitude toward the danger, maintaining that if it were not wholly imaginary, it was exaggerated by the jingoes. Bourassa commented:

It seems absurd that Canada should and ought to 'save' England and France, preserve the neutrality of Belgium, annihilate the German fleet in the North Sea, and hold Austria and Italy in check in the Mediterranean, when so much remains to be done to put her own house in order, and years of intense effort and the expenditure of fabulous sums are required to complete, on her own territory, the essential works with which England has been provided for centuries.[46]

According to Bourassa, Canada's true danger was from American economic, intellectual, and moral penetration. In a series of articles which appeared in *Le Devoir* from July 16 to 26 and were reprinted in pamphlet form in French and English,[47] he dealt with this danger in reply to the *Star*, which had raised the 'spectre of annexation' by the United States if Britain fell before Germany. He pointed out that the French Canadian, with his rights restricted to Quebec as an Indian's were to his reservation, and with his Church less attacked in the States than in Canada, was now more disposed to favor annexation than ever before. Under the Tenth Amendment of the American Constitution, Quebec would enjoy more autonomy in the American union than under the Canadian constitution. Bourassa stated that this was neither a plea for annexation nor an argument that the French Canadians were ready to accept it. He professed to be 'still more British and less American than the majority of my fellow citizens, either of British or of French origin.'[48] But such was the impression he had formed of a growing sentiment. He recalled Elgin's statement that assimilative efforts might americanize the French Canadians, but would never anglicize them. The French Canadian was still essentially Canadian and profoundly British, but would remain the latter only if the English Canadians put Canada's interests first and treated the French Canadians as equal partners. He pointed out to the English Canadians that they were already American 'by your language, your nasal accent, your common slang, your dress, your daily habits; by the Yankee literature with which your homes and clubs are flooded; by your yellow journals and their rantings; by your loud and intolerant patriotism; by your worship of gold, snobbery and titles.'[49] Most American of all was the principle of the national school. He also deplored adoption of corrupt American political practices, American economic penetration of Canada by both capital and labor, and discrimination against French Canadians in the West and Ontario. To this indictment of the English Canadians he added a confession of partial French-Canadian responsibility for the decline of politics and journalism to a low level and the degradation of public spirit.

x

The English press promptly accused Bourassa of advocating annexation and illustrated the charge with incomplete quotations from his articles. His friend Cahan protested, in a letter published in the *Montreal Gazette* on August 3, that 'Mr. Bourassa, who is thoroughly Canadian and British in sentiment, and who, of all Canadians, is most antagonistic to those regrettable tendencies which so frequently find expression in the social, political and commercial life of the United States . . . who so frankly expounds and so fearlessly condemns all tendencies which might possibly lead to annexation, should be so falsely and flagrantly misrepresented and so boldly and even brutally censured as an alleged advocate of annexation to the United States.'[50] But Bourassa had been represented as a traitor in New Brunswick, Ontario, Manitoba, and Alberta, while the *Quebec Chronicle* accused him of a desire to drive the English out of Quebec.

Bourassa's habit of mustering in the scholastic tradition the arguments for and against the policy he was discussing lent itself to this sort of misrepresentation, as did his sudden changes of opinion. When asked by the *Canadian Courier* whether he favored imperial federation, to which he had lately seemed to incline, he approved it in theory but denounced its impracticality. And the same Bourassa who insisted upon the necessity of drawing cultural support from France denounced *La Patrie's* campaign for aid to Britain as aid to her ally France: ' The French Canadians are no more ready to exhaust their resources for France than for any other country.'[51] *La Patrie's* campaign, soon taken up by the *Star*, was instigated by Sir Rodolphe Forget, who derived much capital for his enterprises from France and sought a place in the Borden government. But *Le Devoir* assigned it to bribery by armament manufacturers in search of contracts.

When Borden returned from England on September 6, Monk was already under pressure from *Le Devoir* to maintain his stand against a navy or to resign. At a Montreal banquet in honor of the first anniversary of the triumph of 1911, Borden spoke vaguely of calling parliament in November to discuss imperial defence questions, and said that with cooperation in defence must come cooperation in policy.[52] At another banquet in Toronto the following night, he subordinated the theme of Canada's great heritage and future, which he had stressed at Montreal, to that of the greater heritage and future of the empire. He expressed the view that the people of Canada would come as one man to the defence of the empire if the need arose : ' For the preservation of its unity, for the preservation of its power and influence, for the maintenance of its work, the Motherland and the Dominions are one and are indivisible.'[53] Bourassa took alarm at the possibility of the quick passage of an imperialist measure in the midst of the German scare aroused by the press, and warned that its authors would be denounced. Monk was warned that he was obliged 'in honor and conscience, first to demand a plebiscite on any policy of imperial contribution, then to resign from the cabinet and fight against this policy, until the majority of the Canadian people had decided to accept it.'[54] Borden exercised pressure on Monk to remain in the cabinet; but when the latter's insistence on a plebiscite was overruled and the government's proposal of an emergency contribution of $35,000,000 to Britain for naval purposes was announced, Monk resigned on October 18, on the grounds that such a measure, without consultation of the people, violated his electoral promises and went beyond the scope of the constitution. Borden sought to modify the terms of Monk's resignation, and induced him to keep it secret.

Meanwhile Laurier held two meetings in Quebec, minimizing the emergency and taunting the nationalists for their failure to keep their promises. Monk's resignation was promptly rumored in the press. Despite the fact that the young nationalists of Quebec were ready to hail him as a hero, he kept his promise to Borden and went to the States for a rest. Meanwhile the Liberals won a by-election at Sorel on October 24, though by an indecisive margin. Louis Coderre of Montreal was chosen to replace Monk in the cabinet, and the by-election was set for November 19. Borden carefully prepared the ground for his naval proposal, submitting it to a press conference and stressing the emergency as seen by the Admiralty. He passed on the secret Admiralty memorandum to Laurier, and held a special caucus of the Quebec members, most of whom approved the proposal, although some of them declared themselves pledged to vote against it. Laurier decided not to oppose a Liberal to Coderre; but Lavergne and his friends supported an independent candidate. Monk broke his silence to explain to one of the independent's sponsors that he had resigned because the government refused a plebiscite and that he favored an expression of the people's will in this election. This confirmed the suspicions of Bourassa, who opposed Coderre and all those who had accepted a policy contrary to their engagements. But on November 19 Coderre was elected by the solid English vote of Westmount, after winning the three French quarters of the district by a slight majority over his opponent. The death of nationalism was once more proclaimed by *Le Canada*, *Le Soleil*, and *La Patrie*.[55]

Meanwhile the educational situation in Ontario, with its growing French population in the Ottawa Valley, Northern Ontario, and the Windsor-Essex area,[56] had complicated the situation by arousing racial feeling. The Provincial Department of Education had adopted in June 1912 and amended in August 1913 a regulation (Instruction No. 17), which imposed English as the sole language of instruction in the elementary schools, with minor exceptions, and placed the bilingual Catholic schools under English Protestant inspectors. The study of French was confined to an hour a day.[57] This step was taken as a result of Dr. F. W. Merchant's highly critical report on the English-French schools of the Province.[58]

The French members of the Ottawa Separate Schools Commission, under the leadership of Samuel Genest, immediately protested. *Le Devoir*, *L'Action Sociale*, and *Le Soleil* (which had no objection to embarrassing a Conservative government) supported the Franco-Ontarians. Senator Landry requested Borden's intervention with the Ontario government, and raised the question of federal disavowal of the legislation. But no action was taken by the Ontario authorities to halt enforcement of the new regulations. Bourassa sent a questionnaire on Regulation 17 to a number of distinguished English Canadians of Quebec, and their replies, generally recognizing the injustice done to the Franco-Ontarians, were published in *Le Devoir*.[59] But Ontario remained determined to realize a program reminiscent of that of the Protestant Protective Association, and feelings mounted so high there that Laurier made a concession to it by not opposing Coderre, lest the ethnic tension be heightened by a campaign against the naval proposal in Quebec.

Before Borden introduced his proposal on December 5, calling for an emergency contribution of $35,000,000 which would enable Great Britain to build three dreadnoughts in a situation too grave for the delays demanded to build ships in Canada, A.-A. Mondou moved a resolution, revised by Bourassa,[60] refusing all contribution while Canada was barred from imperial councils. The motion was crushed after Borden and Laurier had made professions of loyalism and the House had sung 'God Save the King.' It was supported only by P.-E. Lamarche and two other French-Canadian Conservatives.

Borden argued that he sought to combine cooperation with autonomy: 'When Great Britain no longer assumes sole responsibility for defence upon the high seas, she can no longer undertake to assume sole responsibility for and sole control of foreign policy, which is closely, vitally and constantly associated in that defence in which the Dominions participate.'[61] This principle had been accepted by the leaders of both parties in England during his visit. The crucial situation called for immediate aid to Britain, but if Canada later established a navy, the three dreadnoughts might be recalled to form part of it. The question of a permanent navy would be referred to the people. But Borden indicated that he had been won over by Churchill to the Admiralty policy of outright contribution by stressing the difficulties and expense of building up a Canadian Navy. The Admiralty promised to construct small vessels in Canada, stimulating the shipbuilding industry and justifying Canada's outlay for the dreadnoughts. For the present, the British government would welcome the presence of a Canadian minister at meetings of the Imperial Defence Committee and would consult with him on important questions of foreign policy. Borden concluded with an evocation of the coming storm in Europe and the need for immediate action:

Almost unaided, the Motherland, not for herself alone, but for us as well, is sustaining the burden of a vital Imperial duty, and confronting an overmastering necessity of national existence. Bringing the best assistance that we may in the urgency of the moment, we come thus to her aid, in token of our determination to protect and ensure the safety and integrity of this Empire, and of our resolve to defend on sea as well as on land our flag, our honour and our heritage.[62]

Borden won an ovation, and the House adjourned after singing 'God Save the King' and 'Rule Britannia.'

In his reply on December 12 Laurier rejected the idea that England was in need of immediate aid. She was rich and not in danger. 'If there were an emergency, if England were in danger— no, I shall not use that expression, but simply say if England were on trial with one or two great European powers, my right honorable friend could come and ask us not for $35,000,000 but twice, three times, or four times $35,000,000. We should put all the resources of Canada at the disposal of England; there would not be a single dissentient voice.'[63] But the Admiralty's memorandum showed there was no immediate or prospective danger, though the armament race in Europe had compelled England to concentrate her forces in home waters. Laurier claimed that everything in the memorandum had been discussed four years ago, when it had been agreed that the best way for Canada to discharge her duty was not by contribution but by the creation of a Canadian Navy. Borden had abandoned this stand, but the Liberals had not. The Conservatives had been forced to take a new position because of their 'unholy alliance' with the nationalists. He taunted the Conservatives with their willingness to give to England only 'two or three dreadnoughts, to be paid for by Canada, but to be equipped, maintained and manned by England,' save for such Canadian officers as might volunteer to serve on those ships:

Oh, ye Tory jingoes, is that the amount of sacrifice you are prepared to make? You are ready to furnish admirals, rear-admirals, commodores, captains, officers of all grades, plumes, feathers, and gold lace; but you leave it to England to supply the bone and sinews on board those ships. You say that these ships will bear Canadian names. That will be the only thing Canadian about them. You hire somebody else to do your work; in other words, you are ready to do anything except the fighting. Is that, sir, the true policy? It is a hybrid policy; it is a cross between jingoism and nationalism.[64]

He urged that the Canadian people would not be content without a contribution of money and men as well, as provided in the Laurier naval plan. He accused Borden of having abandoned the idea of a Canadian Navy before he went to England.

Once more Laurier asserted that 'when England is at war, we are at war; but it does not follow, because we are at war, that we are involved in the conflict.' Canada would decide as to whether her forces would take part, if she had her own navy. The government's proposal settled nothing; it provided no permanent policy, and he foresaw a succession of contributions, which would leave no trace behind them. Borden said that a permanent policy must wait upon a voice in questions of peace or war, but Laurier found objections to that plan. Consultation with all the dominions would be unwieldy, and would involve Canada in many questions in which she had no interest. To Borden's argument that the empire's existence hung upon the dominions' having a voice in imperial affairs, he opposed his own convictions:

The firm basis of the British Empire, is, next to the British Crown, the local autonomy of the different dependencies; that is to say, their working out of their own destinies to the central end of Empire. The Crown is the great bond, the cement which binds together the scattered continents over the whole world. The Crown is a purely sentimental bond; but that bond, though purely sentimental, had proven itself stronger than armies or navies; has shown itself to be equal to all occasions. I do not believe the Empire is in danger; I do not believe it can be cemented by the means suggested by my right honourable friend. I believe the relations of the different parts of the Empire to the Mother country are not perfect, but that essentially they are perfectible. You can discuss problems of improvement; there is no occasion to discuss problems of existence.[65]

He concluded by moving an amendment in favor of the construction of two fleet units, to be stationed on the Atlantic and the Pacific, rather than a direct contribution of money or ships to Britain. In short he stood on the terms of the Navy Act of 1910, and Borden judged that his rival hoped to provoke an appeal to the people on the two proposals.[66] On this occasion Laurier displayed his old powers and won an ovation. Again the House sang 'God Save the King.'

Bourassa accused Laurier of wishing to add a human tribute to the tribute of gold requested by Borden. He predicted that the

principle, 'When England is at war, Canada is at war,' would lead
to the sending of a hundred thousand or more young Canadians to
die on foreign battlefields. He fought both measures, and published
the names of M.P.s elected with nationalist support, challenging
them not to support either project without a plebiscite. But party
discipline was effective, and Bourassa found himself attacked by both
Conservative and Liberal organs. Pressure was even brought to bear
on the backers of Le Devoir.[67]

Meanwhile the debate continued vigorously in the House until
adjournment on December 18. Both parties took advantage of the
holiday recess to expound their policies to the people. In Quebec
the Borden spokesmen explained that by the contribution of
$35,000,000 Canada could avoid the construction of a navy and rid
herself of the whole question once and for all; while in Ontario the
measure was presented as a temporary one, since in the emergency
England could not wait for the creation of a Canadian Navy.
Laurier's supporters criticized this 'tribute,' without the promised
consultation of the people, as an abdication of autonomy. Lavergne
privately urged Monk to resume his seat in parliament, where only
Lamarche was left to fight the measure on nationalist grounds.
Bourassa deplored the rivalry between the two parties to be 'the
most "loyal," the most "jingo," the most "imperialist,"' without
regard to Canada's interests.[68] On February 13 Laurier's amendment and that of Alphonse Verville in favor of a plebiscite on the
gift to Britain were defeated by straight party votes, with all the
Quebec Conservatives siding with the government. Borden's
resolution in favor of his proposal were carried by a majority of
thirty-two, with seven French Canadians breaking party lines. Once
more the House broke into 'Rule Britannia,' 'God Save the King,'
and 'O Canada.'

During the debate on the second reading Joseph Guilbault and
Lamarche offered an amendment in favor of a plebiscite, while
Western Liberals moved for suspension of the debate until redistribution according to the census of 1911, which would give the West
fourteen more seats, and until the people had been consulted.
Laurier supported the latter amendment but rejected Guilbault's,
calling upon Borden to appeal to the people in an election. Guilbault's motion was supported by only eleven votes, and the bill
passed its second reading by a vote of 114 to 83. Bourassa prevailed
upon Monk to announce that his 'convictions were unchanged';[69]
and then made two speeches in Toronto, where he maintained that
Canada, having no authority save in her own territory, had no duty
to defend anything except that territory. By organizing her own
coastal defences and completing the public works necessary to her
development, she would contribute to the defence of the empire in

better fashion than by giving dreadnoughts. In the future he foresaw a development either towards imperial federation or independence, and favored the latter. In this argument he concurred with John S. Ewart, who had already advanced much the same ideas in *The Kingdom Papers*;[70] and for them he won the support of Ernest Charles Drury, head of the Dominion Grange, who wrote to the *Globe*: 'It is perhaps humiliating for a man who belongs to the same race as Pym and Hampden to admit that it is Frenchmen and not Englishmen who have taken this position. Honor them all the same!'[71]

On third reading the Liberals had resort to obstruction. Their resistance had been stiffened by Borden's revelation of his correspondence with Churchill, in which the latter maintained that the Canadians could not build dreadnoughts nor man cruisers nor maintain an efficient navy, and argued for perpetual use of British shipyards and for permanent Admiralty control. In March Churchill announced in the British Commons an Admiralty plan—on which Borden had been consulted—for the formation of an imperial squadron to be based on Gibraltar and made up of ships supplied by the dominions. This squadron could reach any portion of the empire before an equal force of any European power. The dominions would be consulted about movements of the squadron, in which officers and men from the participating dominions might serve. The dominions were to provide the necessary base facilities and auxiliary craft to enable the squadron to operate in any part of the empire.[72] After two weeks of night and day debate, the House recessed for Easter, and when it reassembled Borden decided to force the bill through by closure, rather than to dissolve parliament and make the appeal to the people which Laurier sought. The bill finally passed on May 15 by a majority of 101 to 68 after the most strenuous parliamentary battle in Canadian history, with five Quebec Conservatives voting against it. Laurier bitterly suggested that the three dreadnoughts should be named the *Pelletier*, *Nantel*, and *Coderre*.[73]

But the bill still had to pass the Senate, controlled by a Liberal majority led by Sir George Ross, an enthusiastic imperialist. Laurier had held a meeting at Toronto on May 5, calling for an appeal to the people and representing himself as the defender of liberty and autonomy. The Conservatives' recourse to closure at the expense of Laurier himself had strengthened the old leader's standing with his Ontario followers, and he received an enthusiastic reception. Borden held a rival meeting at Toronto on May 19, for which imperialist feeling had been carefully stimulated by the Tory organizers. Addressing an audience equipped with small Union Jacks, Borden reviewed his naval policy, emphasized the gravity of England's situation, and threatened to reform the Senate if it rejected the bill. Bourassa, who had already enjoined the Senate to kill the bill, denounced this threat:

It is neither the statesman nor the honest man who has offered this threat; it is the chief, or rather the instrument, of an arrogant faction moved by jingoism and the gold of the armaments trust. The Senate would be unworthy of its functions; it would deserve public scorn, if it yielded to this audacious attempt at blackmail.[74]

Meanwhile Lavergne busied himself with influencing Senators Landry and Legris against the bill.

The government had already negotiated privately with Sir George Ross about a compromise. Ross objected to a contribution without establishing a Canadian Navy, and proposed to couple the two plans. But neither the Liberal Senators nor Laurier supported this compromise which Borden would have accepted. The bill was presented by Senator Lougheed on May 20 and attacked by Ross, who stated that the Naval Act of 1910 was preferable to the present plan. The government bill sent only empty ships, not men, to fight; it made no appeal to national feeling; it would lead to cleavage rather than unity of public opinion. The will of the people should prevail; therefore he proposed in the very words used by Borden in 1910 'that this House is not justified in giving its assent to this bill until it is submitted to the country.'[75] Ross' motion was adopted by a vote of 51 to 27 on May 29, and the Conservative Naval Bill was killed.

But Borden did not give up hope for its eventual passage, either through the death of Liberal senators or the creation of additional senatorships under Section 26 of the B.N.A. Act. On June 1 he suggested to Churchill that Britain lay down three ships with the assurance that Canada would pay for them before completion.[76] Churchill agreed to anticipate the construction of three ships, and Borden proposed to introduce in 1914 a provision for the grant of ten or fifteen millions for that purpose. Senator Ross expressed sympathy with such a scheme, but his death in the following March, financial depression, and the lessened emphasis on dreadnoughts combined to cause abandonment of the plan. The defeat of Borden's Naval Bill was attributed to the influence of Bourassa by the *Montreal Star* and the press in England. Bourassa did not hesitate to point out himself his 'moral triumph without precedent'; after four years of agitation the nationalists had succeeded in defeating all imperialist proposals: a Canadian navy, dreadnoughts for Britain, or a money contribution.[77]

5

While the naval question dragged on to its inconclusive end, the educational conflict had grown more bitter and had strengthened Bourassa's role as unofficial leader of French Canada. In Manitoba the government's promises of better terms to the Catholic minority were not fulfilled, and Philippe Landry was charged with presenting a petition from the Catholics of the West to the government. At Rome the appeal of the Franco-Americans who had been excommunicated by Bishop Walsh was rejected, but they remained patriots to the French Canadians. In Ontario attempts to enforce Regulation 17 were resisted by the Franco-Ontarians, who now numbered about a tenth of the population and were concentrated in the Ottawa Valley, in the railroad, lumber, and mining centers of the center and northern parts of the province, and around Windsor. Under the leadership of Samuel Genest Franco-Ontarian teachers refused to sign the declaration required by the authorities, and students left the schools when the inspectors arrived. A newspaper was needed to rally and direct the resistance, and a group of priests and civil servants of Ottawa founded *Le Droit* on March 27, 1913. The French Canadians of Saskatchewan had already established *Le Patriote de l'Ouest* and those of Winnipeg launched *La Liberté* in May 1913. *Le Droit* followed the pattern of *Le Devoir* and *L'Action Sociale*, and maintained close relations with them and its Western colleagues.

Ontario priests sought support for the venture in Quebec; and Olivar Asselin, now president of the Saint-Jean-Baptiste Society of Montreal, was induced to sponsor a collection for the Ontario schools, actually intended for the support of *Le Droit*. With all his usual vigor Asselin urged the cause of '*Le Sou de la Pensée Française*,' and renounced in its favor the customary parade and fireworks of June 24, with some acid remarks about his predecessors. The Quebec Saint-Jean-Baptiste Society and the Societé du Parler Français, with the usual Quebec distrust of Montreal initiatives, refused to renounce their customary celebrations but launched collections of their own. Asselin dealt with the opposition which succeeded in dislodging him as president in an interview in Fournier's *L'Action* of July 26, later reprinted as the third of his '*Feuilles de Combat*,' which were designed 'to serve the truth and make the morons rage.'[78] He pointed out that the celebration of Saint-Jean-Baptiste Day was primarily a national rather than a Catholic one; that nothing had been done in the past for the cause of French culture on this occasion; and that French culture must be renewed at its source, as Bourassa had advised at the 1912 Congrès de la

Langue Française, regardless of those who feared modern France. He mocked the customary procession of 'ridiculous' historical floats, which cost far more than real contributions to French-Canadian culture, and the choice of a lamb, the '*Bête Nationale*,' as an unfortunate national symbol. Asselin's suppression of the traditional symbol was not anti-religious, as some of his critics had chosen to deduce from Archbishop Bruchési's Saint-Jean-Baptiste sermon on the Lamb of God, nor evidence of a Masonic intrigue. He also defended the right of Gonsalve Desaulniers as a French Canadian to take part in the celebration, though Archbishop Bruchési had barred the poet from the university as a Freemason. The obstacles raised by 'stupid right-thinkers' had reduced the collection to $15,000, although $50,000 was customarily spent on the parade.

A series of articles by Père Joseph-Papin Archambault, S.J. (under the pseudonym of 'Pierre Homier') provoked the organization at Montreal of the Ligue des Droits du Français, a more nationalist version of the Societé du Parler Français. The founders were all friends or disciples of Bourassa: Omer Héroux, Dr. Joseph Gauvreau, Léon Lorrain, Anatole Vanier, A.-G. Casault, Henri Auger, and Père Archambault himself. Their program included the defence and promotion of the French language, insistence on its use in trade and the public services, and an effort to 'give once more to the exterior of our social life an appearance revealing the French soul of our race.'[79] The undertaking was encouraged by Cardinal Bégin, Bishop Roy, and Archbishop Langevin.

At Ottawa on June 22 the Franco-Ontarians held a meeting for a crowd of 7,000. Their spokesman, Senator Belcourt, who a year earlier had counselled moderation, proclaimed: 'Our decision is irrevocable and irreducible. We have resisted and we shall continue to resist the odious attempt to proscribe our mother tongue, despite all threats, at the price of all sacrifices.'[80] Asselin, Adjutor Rivard, and Armand Lavergne promised Quebec's support. Bourassa would have been on hand if he had not begun a tour of the West, during which he had made some twenty speeches at Edmonton, Calgary, Regina, Saskatoon, Winnipeg, St. Norbert, Fort William, Port Arthur, Sault Ste. Marie, and Sudbury, more often in English before Canadian Clubs than in French before audiences of his compatriots. He expounded his views and took advantage of the opportunity to study Western problems, becoming convinced that national sentiment must be developed if the West and East were not to part.

Bourassa's own true nationalism was enhanced by the journey, but his Quebec disciples increasingly tended to narrow down theirs to a provincialism. The A.C.J.C. held its fifth general convention at Trois-Rivières at the end of June. For a year its study groups had considered the educational question, but reached no more startling conclusions than resolutions supporting control of primary education by the Church and parents, and the control of all educational institutions by the Council of Public Instruction. The A.C.J.C. condemned as 'inopportune' all the reforms urged for ten years by the freethinker Godefroy Langlois and other less suspect revisionists. But Abbé Lionel Groulx, in discussing the congress in *La Nouvelle France*, praised the society and proclaimed: 'Those who come after will have only to will it to become the masters of the future.'[81] And to this end Abbé Groulx sought to give a nationalist bent to the teaching of literature and history. Religion and nationalism became curiously intermingled as the clergy took a leading role in the nationalist movement. This development led to such incidents as the differences between the extremist Asselin and the moderate Archbishop Bruchési, and the censuring of Bourassa for his criticism of the apostolic delegate's role in the Keewatin school question. Intervention of the clergy in politics also had unfortunate repercussions among the English Canadians, whose loyalism was further disgruntled by the decision of the A.C.J.C. to celebrate the memory of Dollard des Ormeaux on May 24, long honored as Victoria Day by the English.

Laurier exploited the defeat of Borden's Navy Bill and the growing inflation at a meeting at Saint-Hyacinthe on August 16. He attacked the nationalist movement which had brought Borden to power, and then had become a 'movement toward the manger,'[82] renouncing its pledges in favor of the perquisites of office. He paid tribute to the Liberal Senate which had maintained its independence by defeating the Navy Bill which the nationalists had accepted in the Commons. Bourassa in turn attacked Laurier in a series of four articles. He treated the defeat of Laurier's former minister Sydney Fisher in Chateauguay on October 11 as another repudiation by Quebec of Laurier's leadership. But Laurier continued his campaign to regain Quebec, emphasizing the rising cost of living under the Borden government rather than the naval question, which had been the chief issue in the Chateauguay by-election. The provincial Liberals under Gouin's leadership maintained provincial rights at the Fifth Interprovincial Conference at Ottawa in October, requesting an increase of the federal subsidy since the federal tax receipts had swollen far beyond those of the provinces, thanks to Canada's growth in population and trade. The Borden government proved less friendly to provincial rights than Laurier's, and the question was left unsettled, with Quebec nursing a new grievance against Ottawa.

The Ontario school question grew ever more embroiled. Dr. J. W. Edwards of Toronto, a Conservative Orangeman, urged that the French language be driven out of Ontario. The provincial department of education suppressed its grants to the Ottawa separate schools in October. The Irish of Ottawa largely separated from the French on the school question, and accused them of neo-gallicanism. Senator Landry again sought the intervention of Borden in vain, and Thomas Chapais was advised by Sir James Whitney that Ontario affairs were no concern of *Québecois* when he urged the repeal of Regulation 17.[83] Bourassa took to the platform before three Ontario Canadian Clubs in support of the bilingual schools, and at a St. Andrew's Day banquet found himself at the same speaker's table with Bishop Fallon of London, the leading opponent of the French schools among the Irish clergy, who in 1911 had denounced 'an alleged bi-lingual school system which teaches neither English nor French, encourages incompetency, gives a prize to hypocrisy, and breeds ignorance.'[84] The A.C.J.C. and Saint-Jean-Baptiste Society of Montreal expressed their sympathy with the Franco-Ontarians, and at a protest meeting under the auspices of the latter at the Monument National on December 15 Bourassa insisted upon the presence of an Irish spokesman, J. K. Foran of Ottawa, and urged his audience to support their protests with those from Irish Catholics and English Protestants.

In the middle of January Bourassa spoke at a congress of the Ontario *Association canadienne-française d'Education*, which was torn by political division in its fight against the Conservative government of Ontario. Again he urged the necessity of interesting Irish Catholics and English Protestants in the movement, for after his Western trip he had become convinced that most English-Canadian prejudice against his compatriots could be dissolved by better acquaintance with them. He had already gained the virtual alliance of Ewart, Boyd, Cahan, and J. C. Walsh, and now he sought to generalize the process. His counsel was followed by the Saint-Jean-Baptiste Society of Montreal in a new sympathy meeting at the Monument National on March 6, when the speakers, in addition to Lamarche and Asselin, were Walsh, the Ontario journalist Thomas O'Hagan, and the English Montrealer W. D. Lighthall. Bourassa himself addressed the Irish of Hamilton on St. Patrick's Day[85] and spoke to the Canadian Club of Oshawa the following day, freely criticizing English ignorance of the French language and English injustice to the French Canadians. In January he had conceived the notion of an English page in *Le Devoir* and asked Ewart to collaborate on it.[86]

When the mayoralty campaign in Montreal between G. W. Stephens and Médéric Martin brought an outburst of the ethnic feeling aroused by the Ontario troubles, Bourassa published four articles in English in *Le Devoir* (March 11-14, 1914), which he later brought out in pamphlet form under the title of *French and English Frictions and Misunderstandings*, prefaced by letters from Cahan and

Walsh. For many years it had been the custom in Montreal to elect alternately French and English mayors, despite the fact that the English only constituted a quarter of the population. To this custom there had been three French attitudes: the majority favored it, a minority grumbled about it, and a third group, to which Bourassa belonged, felt that the best man should be elected regardless of race or creed. But the French were becoming disillusioned about English fair play; for the English always claimed their right when it was their turn, and when it was not, the best man always seemed to be English. *Le Devoir* had supported the successful English candidate in 1910 in its effort to reform municipal affairs. But the English papers of Sir Hugh Graham and Lorne McGibbon did not censure political corruption practiced by the great English companies, and were willing to support a corrupt French candidate rather than an honest English one.

Bourassa deplored the lack of contact and understanding between French and English, who seldom met except in politics and business, where they displayed their worst tendencies. He laid the greater blame on the English of Montreal, who in return for the privileges freely granted them made no effort to understand their French fellow-citizens. He exalted the French-Canadian tradition of tolerance of creed and language, and the habit of electing English Protestants to represent communities in majority French and Catholic —a precedent not followed by English majorities. English businessmen had not proved good public men. They had been reluctant to accept the language of the majority in the public services; they regarded the French Canadian as a 'nuisance'; and they refused to learn the language of the majority, internationally recognized as the language of culture and civilization. Only a few English Quebeckers had deplored the Ontario anti-French educational policy, but if Quebec should adopt a similar anti-English one, all English Canada would be up in arms. Yet the educational rights of the English in Quebec rested on the same basis as those of the French in Ontario. He urged equal justice and equal rights for both groups, and recommended that the English should take a more active part in public affairs, instead of 'living in this city and province as a group of isolated Uitlanders, wealthy, self-satisfied, and self-contained, with no care for their French-speaking neighbours—except on such occasions as when French votes are needed to elect an English-speaking mayor.' Bourassa saw in such conduct 'the most active factor in the growing estrangement between the two races.'[87]

In his comment on Bourassa's articles, Cahan made a distinction between the large number of English Montrealers coming from all parts of Canada or outside Canada, who were uninterested in Quebec, and the native English Quebeckers who appreciated the tolerance of the French, but had little direct representation or parti-cipation in the affairs of the province. He blamed most political corruption on lobbying at Quebec by English business interests which had no direct political representation. Since they had little political influence at Ottawa, they allied themselves to their com-mercial colleagues of Ontario and refrained from criticizing their political actions. Finally he urged that there were many English Montrealers sympathetic with French Canada, but who preferred to speak English rather than to speak bad French to French Canadians who had mastered both languages. J. C. Walsh deplored the gulf between English and French Montreal; praised Bourassa for reveal-ing the French state of mind; and asserted that 'No Canadian will assent to seeing another Canadian wronged.'[88] But despite Bour-assa's support, Stephens was defeated by Martin, backed by the tramway interests and Sir Rodolphe Forget. Bourassa deplored the fact that an explosion of racial feeling aroused by the Ontario struggle had resulted in 'the victory of a man of the fifth order, incapable of a gesture or action suitable to the revindication of the honor and rights of his race, and the defeat of one of the rare English Canadians who had manifested real sympathy for the French Canadians.'[89]

Bourassa did not content himself with telling the English where they were wrong, but also applied himself to attacking French-Canadian faults. On April 12 he gave a lecture on '*Nos défauts et nos vices nationaux*,' which he called 'an examination of the national conscience.'[90] He censured the capitulation to materialism which had led a rural people to overcrowd the cities; the loss of the spirit of simplicity and economy; and the development of dishonesty with electoral frauds, political scandals, and unpunished misdeeds. Turning to the clergy who were present, he censured the hierarchy for its tolerance of politicians in exchange for superficial respect and financial grants to religious institutions. He called upon priests, teachers, and parents to fulfil their responsibilities. This blast, which clearly arraigned Archbishop Bruchési who had made peace with Sir Lomer Gouin, irritated the hierarchy. But a few days later Archbishop Langevin, speaking at a meeting at the Monument National, eulogized Bourassa's 'exemplary Catholicism' and 'con-tagious patriotism,'[91] to vast applause from Bourassa's student followers. Shortly afterward the nationalist leader left for Europe, where he was anxious to study the Irish question, now raised once more by Ulster's resistance to Home Rule, and the minority question in Belgium and Alsace.

With depression at home and a respite in the European war scare, parliament devoted most of its attention to the financially embar-rassed Canadian Northern Railway controlled by Mackenzie and

Mann, and to the proposed Georgian Bay Canal. In the debate on the address, Laurier taunted Borden with the abrupt disappearance of the 'emergency' of which he had made so much in supporting the Navy Bill, and attacked the government for taking no steps to counteract the depression. Borden criticized the Senate's action in killing the Navy Bill as bringing discredit upon Canada and being detrimental to the empire, but announced his intention of withholding further action on the naval question until a satisfactory conclusion was possible. A bill abolishing titles failed to win support from either party. The Redistribution Act, which increased the Senate's numbers from 72 to 96, was supported by both parties; but the Liberals added an amendment that it should not take effect until the termination of the present parliament, thus forestalling any Conservative packing of the Senate in the interests of a naval measure. On the eve of the session Bourassa urged a program of needed public works rather than 'draining the public coffers to enrich the shareholders of Vickers-Maxim, Armstrong-Whitworth, Beardmore, and to swell the heritage of the daughter of the Krupp dynasty.'[92] On January 14, 1914, Monk, too ill to attend the opening of parliament, from which he resigned in March, sketched out in *Le Devoir* a vast program of public works, including the Georgian Bay Canal, favored by Montreal over further development of the Welland Canal and the St. Lawrence route. On February 23 Laurier moved for immediate construction of the Georgian Bay Canal and also the development of the Welland Canal. P.-E. Lamarche, in an able speech in which facts and figures were relieved by occasional bursts of eloquence, supported only the Georgian Bay proposal, expressing distrust for joint development of the St. Lawrence with the United States, which had always emerged from past difficulties with Canada with a piece of Canadian territory. The government promised to study the question, which had always been blocked, according to Bourassa, by the railways, which thanks to their campaign contributions were more powerful than the government.

Quebec took little interest in the new raids upon the federal treasury by the Canadian Northern and the Grand Trunk Pacific. But it did object to a militia budget of $11,000,000, much larger than usual because of Sam Hughes' dream of militarizing Canada. *Le Canada* deplored 'the frenzy of militarism which deflects so many millions of our money—which we need so much for other purposes—to spend it in purchases of arms, cannons, and munitions,' while *Le Soleil* remarked: 'Eleven millions have been sacrificed in the gulf of militarism in order to permit Sam Hughes to play soldier.'[93] Parliament was prorogued on June 12, with a minor cabinet crisis over Sam Hughes' refusal to allow the 65th Battalion of Montreal to take part as usual in the Corpus Christi Day procession. Doherty threatened to resign if the order was not revoked, but Hughes, supported by the Orangemen, remained firm. Finally a compromise was arranged whereby the 65th paraded but without arms. Hughes gained no popularity in Quebec from this incident, or another later in June when he refused to allow the Régiment de Lévis to escort Cardinal Bégin upon his return from consecration in Rome. Quebec buried its political differences to pay honor to the new cardinal, and Laurier, Pelletier, Doherty, Nantel, the lieutenant-governor, the premier, and the chief of the provincial opposition were all on hand for the occasion. Cardinal Bégin's elevation gratified Quebec City's sense of superiority to Montreal, and represented a French-Canadian triumph at the expense of the Irish Catholics, whose role in Ontario heightened the old friction between French and Irish.

For the Ontario school question was now contested on strictly ethnic lines. While Cardinal Bégin was at Rome, urging the cause of the Franco-Ontarians and pleading for a division of mixed parishes, so that the French Canadians might have their own clergy, it was rumored that the Irish bishops intended to issue a pastoral approving Regulation 17.[94] The Irish Catholics of Ottawa were up in arms at the banishment from the French-controlled university of Father James Fallon, who had tried to prevent French Canadians from voting in the election of separate school commissioners. They sought an injunction against payment of teachers opposing Regulation 17. The Ontario government announced that it would take steps not only against the rebelling teachers, but against the parents. Père Charlebois obtained the assistance of Père Roderigue Villeneuve, a young Oblate theologian, in writing editorials for *Le Droit*. He also joined the Montreal *Ligue des Droits du Français*, and kept its members posted on the struggle in Ontario. The Orangemen took up collections to aid Ulster's resistance to Home Rule, and worked off their enthusiasm in attacks on the separate schools. The French Canadians of the West held congresses at Edmonton and Prince Albert, attended by delegates from Quebec. In Montreal the A.C.J.C. met in a congress, at which Abbé Groulx exerted his growing influence. The A.C.J.C. discussed the problems of inflation, immigration, unionization, and unemployment—the latter a novelty in the newly industrialized province. In June the Franco-Ontarians voted against the Conservative government which had introduced Regulation 17; their breaking of party lines aroused English feeling. In Manitoba in July the French Canadians supported the Conservative Roblin government, which by the Coldwell Amendments had shown tolerance to the French minority.

As the First World War drew near, Quebec looked westward to its persecuted compatriots rather than towards Europe. In three of

Canada's nine provinces ethnic feeling had been aroused, and a narrow nationalism predominated in French Canada. These facts played a notable part in the troubled years that lay ahead.

6

War came unexpectedly upon a Canada preoccupied with domestic affairs in 1914, and was met by impromptu measures. Borden, who had been so alarmed by the threat of impending conflict during his European visit of 1912, had attached no great importance to the Sarajevo incident of June 28, and had postponed setting a definite date for Admiral Jellicoe's proposed visit to Canada to discuss naval aid. On July 28, while on vacation at Muskoka, Ontario, he learned that Great Britain would probably be involved if France were attacked.[95] Reassured by his secretary but urged to be ready to return to Ottawa on short notice, he arrived in a virtually deserted capital on August 1. In the absence of the governor-general and most of the cabinet, Borden cabled the British government in Connaught's name a hope for peace and expressed Canada's desire to cooperate in that end, coupled with assurance that 'if unhappily war should ensue, the Canadian people will be united in a common resolve to put forth every effort and to make every sacrifice necessary to ensure the integrity and maintain the honour of our Empire.'[96] On August 2 he asked for advice and suggestions from the imperial naval and military authorities, and offered a considerable Canadian force, to be enlisted as imperial troops to avoid the 'defence of Canada' clause, but to be equipped, paid, and maintained by Canada. In reply, appreciation of the offer was expressed, but the British government postponed 'detailed observations on the proposals put forward pending future developments.'[97]

Meanwhile on August 2 and 3 Borden and the hastily summoned cabinet passed orders-in-council in accordance with the War Book plans drawn up the previous spring by a committee of deputy-ministers and service representatives. Censorship was established; currency regulations adopted to forestall a financial panic; the detainment of enemy ships authorized; and the export of articles useful for war purposes prohibited. The Canadian cruisers *Rainbow* and *Niobe* were ordered manned and put at the disposal of the Admiralty, while two submarines were purchased in hot haste in Seattle and got to sea before they could be detained, in spite of pursuit by U.S. cruisers. The *Rainbow* was ordered south from Esquimalt to escort back two small British craft, the *Shearwater* and *Algerine*, endangered by the presence of German cruisers in the Pacific.

While the cabinet was in session on the evening of August 4, word of England's declaration of war was received. Parliament was promptly summoned to meet on August 18—the two-week limit prescribed by Laurier's Naval Act. The cabinet resisted British pressure to intern German and Austrian reservists in Canada, and granted them protection unless they sought to leave the country. Upon the suggestion of George Perley, who was then in London, on August 6 Canada offered Britain a million bags of flour, a gift which was welcomed by the British government as it steadied prices and relieved distress in England. Sam Hughes, confronted with an opportunity for which his Napoleonic soul had longed, sprang into action. On July 30 he summoned the Militia Council, which decided to send a contingent of 20,000 men if war was declared. A call for volunteers for overseas service was issued on August 3. Mobilization of the First Division was ordered on August 6, when England accepted the offer of troops, by an order-in-council which begged the question of Canada's right to declare war or refrain from it: 'Considering the state of war now existing between the United Kingdom, and the Dominions, colonies, and dependencies of the British Empire on one hand, and Germany on the other . . .'[98] Already many officers had volunteered their own services and those of their units. Sam Hughes ordered the mobilization of two infantry battalions: the 13th, made up of the Royal Highlanders, and 14th, made up of the Grenadier Guards, Victoria Rifles, and Carabiniers de Mont-Royal; and Major Thomas-Louis Tremblay's Field Artillery Battery. A site chosen earlier by Hughes at Valcartier near Quebec was selected as the concentration center, and the first troops arrived there on August 20.

Quebec, with many of its leaders following the growingly popular custom among the bourgeois of European travel, and with its rank and file wholly unconcerned with world events, was taken by surprise by the outbreak of the war. Sir Lomer Gouin was vacationing in Brittany, the speaker of the legislative council was in Berlin, the chief justice and many others in Paris, Dr. Béland in Belgium, and Bourassa in Alsace. Sympathy with threatened France was expressed on August 1 by a crowd which assembled before *La Patrie's* bulletin boards, sang the 'Marseillaise,' and then paraded to the French Consulate under the Union Jack and Tricolor. French and Belgian reservists flocked to their consulates, and were hailed by crowds singing the 'Marseillaise.' Much the same scenes took place at Quebec. Both cities displayed more patriotic enthusiasm than imperialist Toronto.[99] On August 4 the first contingent of French reservists sailed from Montreal, after having been escorted to their ship by an enormous crowd. With the old mother country threatened, French-Canadian suspicion of modern France was disarmed, with the exception of the editors of *La Vérité*, who solemnly warned that France's greatest enemy was not Germany but Freemasonry.[100]

A committee to aid the families of French reservists was organized at
Quebec, and later at Montreal. Newspapers carried the intertwined
flags of Britain and France at the top of the page, and *La Patrie*
appeared with a huge headline: '*Vivent la France et l'Angleterre et Dieu
sauve le Roi.*'[101]

Rodolphe Lemieux, a great lover of France, on August 3 urged
his people to rally first to the defence of Canada's coasts and then to
that of the great empire to which they belonged.[102] Laurier issued
a statement on the morning of August 4, expressing a hope for peace,
but the conviction that 'it is probable and almost certain that
England will have to take her share in the conflict, not only for the
protection of her own interests, but for the protection of France and
the higher civilization of which these two nations are today the
noblest expression.' He proclaimed the Liberal policy of Canada's
rendering 'assistance to the full extent of her powers' to the endangered mother country, and called for a truce to party strife,
cancelling all his political meetings.[103] Lamarche asserted that it
was every Canadian's duty to defend the empire.[104] At Quebec
on August 4 Albert Sévigny glorified England for coming to the aid
of her allies and evoked British loyalty. Armand Lavergne sounded
a discordant note in a following speech, when he stressed that Canada
was bound to defend herself, but herself only; and that if the French
Canadians were to be called upon to die for their country, they must
first be granted the right to live in their country. 'If we are asked
to go and fight for England, we reply: "Let us have our schools!"'[105]

Lavergne's utterance was greeted with both approbation and
disapproval. *La Presse* on August 5 suggested that French-Canadian
volunteers should form distinct battalions and be placed directly at
the service of France. In *Le Devoir* the following day Omer Héroux,
acting as spokesman for the nationalists in Bourassa's absence,
rejected this proposal and all participation in the war overseas:

We persist in believing, along with the great statesmen of the past,
that the proper duty of Canadian troops is to ensure, along with the
defence of our territory for which we are ready to consent to all sacrifices,
freedom of communications and the free export of the wheat necessary
to the life of the English nation.[106]

The following day Héroux urged the repeal of Regulation 17 and
the grant to the Franco-Ontarians of an educational regime such as
that enjoyed by the English Protestants of Quebec as 'the most
efficacious fashion in which to promote the necessary rapprochement between English and French Canadians.' Taken to task by
Fernand Rinfret of *Le Canada* for his 'inopportune claims' when
common duty called for united support of the war, Héroux insisted:
'Whatever be the gravity of European events and the problems they

raise for us, that does not give us the right to shut our eyes on the longstanding injustice in Ontario.'[107] But Héroux's voice was lost in the general enthusiasm in Quebec. *La Patrie* rebuked him by asking: 'If England were conquered by Germany, would not our language and our schools be in danger of being sacrificed?' There was no more hesitation in Quebec to approve Canada's course than among the members of the Ontario Grange and the Western Grain Growers' Association, reflected in August in the *Ottawa Citizen* and the *Winnipeg Free Press*. War enthusiasm was greatest among recent British immigrants, but the wave of patriotism soon carried all before it.

Some feeling was aroused in Quebec not against the war, but against Sam Hughes, who had issued orders for sentries to shoot to kill. As a consequence a French-Canadian soldier guarding the peaceful dock at Rivière-Ouelle killed a French-Canadian tramp on August 9, and an English-Canadian sentry at the Craig Street Arsenal in Montreal killed a French reservist on August 14. Mayor Médéric Martin protested violently, and some Liberal papers called for Hughes' dismissal. *Le Devoir* did not exploit these incidents, but with *Le Droit* continued its campaign against Regulation 17. *La Patrie* deplored it, and *Le Canada* called for the forgetting of all differences in the pursuit of victory. In the latter paper L.-O. David eloquently developed Laurier's theme:

England being at war, Canada, like all parts of the British Empire, is at war. Our destinies are bound to those of England, our duty and our interest command us to aid her to triumph, to protect ourselves and to protect France. Loyalty, patriotism, our most sacred interests make it a duty for us to contribute in the measure of our strength to the triumph of their arms. The defeat of England and France would be a disaster for the world, for Canada, for the province of Quebec especially, for the French Canadians. It would be a mortal blow to our political and national destinies, to our dearest and most sacred interests and sentiments. . . .[108]

Archbishop Bruchési lent the support of the Church to the cause when in a sermon on August 9 he declared that it was the duty of the faithful to give the mother country, dragged into the war in spite of herself, the loyal and hearty support demanded by both religion and patriotism.[109] He added: 'If troops have to be sent to the other side, our brave young men will not hesitate to face the ordeal, and I know that we will find in them the same heroism which characterized our forefathers long ago.'[110]

Parliament met for the special war session on August 18, while this mood of enthusiastic national unity was at its height. Clad in khaki, the governor-general, the soldier Duke of Connaught, delivered the speech from the throne, which called for approval of the measures already taken by the government and others now proposed. Laurier promptly assured the government of Liberal support of all these measures:

If in what has been done or in what remains to be done there may be anything which in our judgment should not be done or should be differently done, we raise no question, we take no exception, we offer no criticism, and we shall offer no criticism so long as there is danger at the front. It is our duty, more pressing upon us than all other duties, on this first day of this extraordinary session of the Canadian parliament, to let Great Britain know, and to let the friends and foes of Great Britain know, that there is in Canada but one mind and heart, and that all Canadians stand behind the mother country, conscious and proud that she has engaged in this war, not from any selfish motive, for any purpose of aggrandizement, but to maintain untarnished the honour of her name, to fulfil her obligations to her allies, to maintain her treaty obligations, and to save civilization from the unbridled lust of conquest and power.

We are British subjects, and today we are face to face with the consequences which are involved in that proud fact. Long have we enjoyed the benefit of our British citizenship; today it is our duty to accept its responsibilities and its sacrifices. We have long said that when Great Britain is at war, we are at war; today we realize that Great Britain is at war and that Canada is at war also. Our territory can be attacked and invaded. . . .[111]

He discounted the danger of invasion, but stressed that Canadian ports might be attacked by enemy raiders, which were loose in both the Atlantic and Pacific. He pointed out, as another proof that Canada was at war when England was at war, that Canadian ships had ceased to sail the Atlantic and Canadian commerce had been interrupted.

As to the government's decision to send overseas a contingent of 20,000 men, Laurier observed:

I have declared more than once that if England were in danger—even engaged in a conflict which would test her power—it would be the duty of Canada to come to her aid in the full measure of her resources. Today England is not engaged in an ordinary contest. The war in which she is engaged will in all probability—nay, in absolute certainty—stagger the world with its magnitude and horror. But that war is for as noble a cause as ever impelled a nation to risk her all upon the arbitrament of the sword. That question is no longer at issue; the judgment of the world has already pronounced upon it. I speak not only of those nations which are engaged in this war, but of the neutral nations. The testimony of the ablest men of these nations, without dissenting voice, is that today the allied nations are fighting for freedom against oppression, for democracy against autocracy, for civilization against reversion to that state of barbarism in which the supreme law is the law of might.[112]

He spoke of how Canada replied to the call to defend England with a 'ready, aye, ready,'[113] and he made a special appeal to his compatriots:

If my words can be heard beyond the walls of this House in the province from which I come, among the men whose blood flows in my own veins, I should like them to remember that in taking their place today in the ranks of the Canadian army to fight for the cause of the allied nations, a double honour rests upon them. The very cause for which they are called upon to fight is to them doubly sacred.[114]

He paid his respects to the German Canadians and said the war was not one against the German people. He anticipated that as a result of the war 'the German people will decide to put a final end to personal government, so that a single individual nevermore can precipitate millions of human beings into all the horrors of modern war.' He paid tribute to the Belgians for their gallant resistance, and expressed his satisfaction that the Irish troubles had ended in union to fight for King and country. The same spirit of union was to be found in Canada, Australia, New Zealand, and even in South Africa, where English and Boers alike were ready to shed their blood for the common cause. He closed with the hope that 'from this painful war the British Empire will emerge with a new bond of union, the pride of all its citizens, and a living light to all other nations.'[115]

Borden congratulated Laurier upon his patriotism and eloquence. After discussing Britain's efforts to preserve peace, he, too, paid tribute to Canada's half a million Germans and urged regard for their feelings. He warned of trials to come, and said: 'Let us see to it that no heart grows faint and that no courage be found wanting.' After describing the government's measures and reading the dispatches from Britain, he came to an unusually eloquent conclusion:

As to our duty, all are agreed, we stand shoulder to shoulder with Britain and the other British Dominions in this quarrel. Not for love of battle, not for lust of conquest, not for greed of possessions, but for the cause of honour, to maintain solemn pledges, to uphold principles of liberty, to withstand forces that would convert the world into an armed camp; yea, in the very name of the peace that we sought at any cost save that of dishonour, we have entered into this war; and while gravely conscious of the tremendous issues involved and of all the sacrifices that they may entail, we do not shrink from them, but with firm hearts we abide the event.[116]

D.-O. Lesperance spoke in French, professing in the name of Quebec and the French Canadians her loyalty and eagerness 'to defend the integrity of the vast Empire which assures them the greatest amount of liberty and happiness that a people ever enjoyed.'[117] But no

French-Canadian voice was heard in the cabinet, since Pelletier was sick and Nantel and Coderre took no active part. In the four-day session every government proposal was ratified; a war appropriation of $50,000,000 was passed in one minute; the suspension of gold payment and other financial measures were approved; a Canadian Patriotic Fund for the relief of soldier's relatives was incorporated; and the War Measures Act, giving the government broad powers of censorship, deportation, and control over trade and transport, was approved. There was not a question raised nor a hint of party feeling.

When Sir Lomer Gouin returned to Quebec from France on August 17, he summoned his ministers and on August 19 cabled to London an offer of 4,000,000 pounds of cheese as an initial war contribution from Quebec. In the district of Montreal 3,443 volunteers had enlisted; 568 in that of Quebec. Confronted with more numerous enlistments in Ontario and particularly in the West, where many recent English emigrants were established, Omer Héroux in *Le Devoir* foresaw conscription to come when there were not enough volunteers. But upon the return of Bourassa, who had found his way on foot across the German and Belgian borders after being caught in Cologne on August 2, Héroux paid tribute to the French greatness of heart in the moment of danger which Bourassa had observed.[118]

With the exception of *Le Devoir*, the French-Canadian press supported the war effort enthusiastically. There were a few echoes of party spirit, with *L'Evénement* regretting on August 5 that Canada was unprepared thanks to the Liberals, and *La Presse* pointing out on August 6 how the logic of events had justified Laurier's contention that Canada was at war when Britain was at war.[119] On August 11 *La Presse* launched a daily column of army and recruiting news. The country weeklies, which generally published little but local news, began to join in the chorus of approval of Canadian participation. Reservations as to sending men overseas were expressed by the Liberal *L'Avenir du Nord* of Joliette and the ultramontane *Le Bien Public* of Trois-Rivières. But *Le Peuple* of Montmagny, despite Lavergne's influence, from the first espoused wholeheartedly the cause of the war, and approved Pelletier's statement there on August 14 that it was the duty of the French Canadians to observe a political truce and to answer the call of their country.[120]

But French-Canadian recruiting did not match the French-Canadian press' enthusiasm for the war. Thanks to Sam Hughes, the army had been largely anglicized, with preference given to English-Canadian officers. English was the only language of command, and there were few French Canadians among the graduates of the Royal Military College at Kingston, who formed an inner circle in the army. The highest-ranking Canadian officer, Major-General F.-L. Lessard, a veteran of the North-West Expedition and the South African War who was adjutant-general, was relegated to the post of inspector-general for Eastern Canada instead of receiving the command of the First Division, as his compatriots had hoped. Colonel Eugène Fiset remained deputy-minister of militia, thanks to his South African War record, but had little influence under Hughes' autocratic regime. Only one French-Canadian officer headed a unit in the First Division, Lt.-Col. H.-A. Panet of the Royal Canadian Horse Artillery. Captains Hercule Barré and Emile Ranger of the Carabiniers de Mont-Royal sought to form a separate French-Canadian battalion, but in the face of official opposition had to content themselves with raising two French-Canadian companies in the new 14th Battalion. There were also scattered French Canadians in the 13th Battalion. On August 23, 300 French-Canadian volunteers of Montreal were blessed by Archbishop Bruchési as they departed for Valcartier. He said to them:

The question cannot be discussed. The French-Canadian people has done its duty. We have given England provisions and gold, and we will give her men . . . we shall prove to England that we are not loyal only in words. . . .[121]

It was also Archbishop Bruchési who inspired *Le Soleil* to write:

Once more, we must grasp all the gravity of the struggle being fought over there, and realize that we must do all that we can, in deeds and not in words, to bring all our aid, under whatever form it may be required, to those who there fight, in the last reckoning, for us and for all ideals that we hold most dear in the world.[122]

But on the whole the French Canadians had long lost the military spirit. Militia officers were more frequently politicians than soldiers, and their service had consisted largely of parades and mess dinners. Quebec's growing isolationism since the South African War left few except its leaders concerned about world affairs, while the anti-imperialist agitation had revived the traditional folk hatred of England. Quebec's rank and file failed to echo with any real feeling the authentic sympathy for France felt by French-Canadian leaders who knew and loved France. The people had been exposed too long to ecclesiastical warnings against irreligious and anti-clerical modern France, particularly stressed by the French religious orders which had taken refuge in Quebec after the anti-clerical laws of 1900-1. Quebec was more concerned with the struggle in Ontario than that in Europe. With Pelletier incapacitated by illness, French Canada had no real leader at Ottawa. The fervent patriotism of Sévigny and

Blondin in 1914 was contrasted with their violent anti-imperalism of 1911, and so lost effectiveness in moving public opinion. But perhaps the major factor in the poor French-Canadian recruiting record was the breaking up of the old local militia units and the refusal of the authorities to form separate French-Canadian units. The French Canadian has a strong group consciousness and likes to be among his own people, especially when called upon to venture into the unfamiliar world outside Quebec. For many, the prospect of being thrown into an English-speaking environment had more terrors than the dreadful fates conjured up by patriotic orators as apt to befall Quebec if French Canada failed to do its part.

Ottawa did not take advantage of the original enthusiasm in Quebec by authorizing French-Canadian units; and it was not surprising that the First Division numbered only some 1,200 French Canadians out of the 5,733 men furnished by Quebec to the total of 36,267. Naturally enough, the first to enlist were the English-born, the second those of British stock, the third the French Canadians, to whom Canada was the sole fatherland. The First Division men were overwhelmingly British-born, 64 per cent according to the official statistics; 25.6 per cent were non-French-Canadian native-born; and 3.7 per cent French-Canadian. Aliens contributed 7 per cent.[123] Most of the British-born came from the Western provinces; most of the Canadian-born from Ontario and Quebec. Quebec made a poorer showing than Ontario in part because of a higher percentage of rural than urban population, and also because of earlier and heavier family responsibilities. Under the recruiting regulations of August 17, preference was given to men who had militia experience or had seen service, and to single men over married men and married men with families.

But a certain share in the quick cooling-off of French Canada's enthusiasm for the war must be assigned to Henri Bourassa, who soon changed his ground on the question. At the Lourdes Eucharistic Congress on July 23 he and Bishop Gauthier, the auxiliary of Montreal, had spoken on the relations between Canada, France, and the Church. Bishop Gauthier had eloquently discussed what the Church and France had done for Canada, while Bourassa still more eloquently dealt with the theme of what Canada had done for France and the Church. He spoke of Canada as 'the oldest son of France,' established by a patriotic act of faith and preserved as a center of intense faith, but become 'the most solid, the most loyal, the most faithful, support of British dominion in North America.'[124] To France the French-Canadian people owed their mentality, their temperament, their family spirit, their love of home, their gaiety and endurance, their apostolic zeal, their idealism, the French soul and genius, and the French language in which they were expressed.

Canada had scarcely known Jansenism, scarcely been touched by liberalism, and modernism was unknown. French Canada had kept French Catholicism untainted and had prevented the missionary work of the Church from becoming an instrument of a race or a government. It had won for the faith a liberty under the British flag which Catholicism did not enjoy in Catholic countries. As a *quid pro quo* French Canada asked only the right that the Gospel should be preached in the language of the people. Three million French Catholics of Canada bore witness to what the French race had done and what it could do. They had preserved the faith and the French language; they represented France's most lasting mark on North America. France's history was also French Canada's history, and Bourassa pleaded that France's love and aid should be given to Canada.

After the Eucharistic Congress, Bourassa had continued in Alsace the study of the bilingual question which he had already made in Wales and Belgium. He found the Alsatians ready to fight for France. At Lourdes, in Alsace, and in Paris on the eve of the war and during the first hours of mobilization, Bourassa found French courage worthy of all admiration and said as much in the first article he wrote for *Le Devoir* on August 27 after his return. He also reprinted letters from such French Catholic leaders as Cardinal Amette, Mgr. Baudrillart, Maurice Barrès, and Albert de Mun, exalting French courage and France's return to the Faith.

But his critical spirit objected to the wholehearted pro-war enthusiasm which swept Canada, explaining everything in black and white terms, and on August 29 he questioned the theory which assigned blame for the war solely to the Kaiser. On September 8 Bourassa took the stand that Canada as a British colony had no direct reason to intervene in the war and had good reasons for remaining neutral; but that Canada as an 'Anglo-French nation, bound to England and France by a thousand ethnic, social, intellectual and economic ties, had a vital interest in the maintenance of France and England, and of their prestige, power, and world influence.' Consequently: 'It is her national duty to contribute in the measure of her strength and by the means of action proper to her, to the triumph and above all to the *endurance* of the combined efforts of France and England. But to render this contribution effective, Canada should begin by resolutely surveying its real situation, making an exact account of what it can and cannot do and assuring its internal security, before lauding or pursuing an effort which it perhaps will not be able to maintain until the end.'[125]

From September 9 to 14 he published in *Le Devoir* a study of the origins of the war based upon the English *White Book*. This study was immediately republished as *La Politique de l'Angleterre avant et après la guerre,* and early in 1915 in English translation under the title of *The Foreign Policy of Great Britain.* It was a searching and able analysis, which reached the conclusion that Sir Edward Grey had been 'faithful to the highest British traditions, he was, before and above all, the man of his country,' intervening in support of France and Belgium only when his country's interests demanded it. Bourassa drew the inference that 'Canada could not better demonstrate her loyalty to British traditions than by imitating the example of the great nation from which she derived her political institutions.'[126] Self-interest was the true and natural policy of all nations; it was patriotic, and neither hypocritical nor perfidious. Bourassa opposed British policy only when Canadian policy was subordinated to it. He deplored the effort made to convince the French Canadians that they had a 'double obligation' to support the war and only 'half the rights' of other Canadian ethnic groups. He urged Canadian statesmen 'to imitate the example of British statesmen, to unite freely the interests of Canada to those of England when their interests were identical, to oppose Canada's interests to those of England when they were contrary, and to separate them when they were divergent.'[127] His demonstration was treated as disloyal and infamous; the moment was ill chosen for objective, logical analysis.

In the English edition Bourassa supported his study against these charges by reprinting an article of H. N. Brailsford which treated the war as 'a cooperative crime,' and its issue as one 'so barbarous, so remote from any real interest or concern of our daily life in these islands that I can only marvel at the illusions and curse the fatality which have made us belligerents in this struggle.' Bourassa contrasted 'the liberty of appreciation enjoyed and practiced in England even in time of war and under the ban of censure, and the grotesque and stupid intolerance manifested in Canada against everyone who dares think and say that there are many aspects to the struggle in Europe....'[128] He also reprinted from the *Ottawa Citizen* of October 26 a study by John S. Ewart, which named as causes of the war national and racial antipathies, huge alliances, and preparedness for war; and singled out militarism as the real enemy. Bourassa particularly deplored the rousing of racial feeling by invocation of the 'double loyalty' of the French Canadians, since Canada's part should be taken for purely Canadian motives; and in case of the future wars against Russia or France which Brailsford and Ewart anticipated, discord might result from the racial feeling now aroused.[129]

If the English press lavished such epithets as 'pro-German' and 'traitor' upon Bourassa for these articles—*Saturday Night* said: 'Every day in Europe, men who have done no more harm are hung as traitors,'[130]—the French press was equally vigorous. *La Patrie* felt his articles would justify the federal authorities in accusing him of high treason; *Le Canada* undertook to answer him by a new interpretation of the *White Book*; *Le Soleil* accused him of having done 'more harm to the French Canadian people than its worst enemies have ever been able to do'; *Le Presse* opposed Archbishop Bruchési's sermon to his articles; *L'Evénement* described him as actuated by 'hereditary hatred of England.' *L'Action Sociale*, now regarded as the inspired organ of Cardinal Bégin, then absent at Rome for the election of Benedict XV, and of Mgr. Paul-Eugène Roy, flatly refuted Bourassa's thesis:

> We have the duty to grant to the mother country, in just and equitable proportions, the cooperation of which she has need from us . . . We owe her this cooperation as every subject owes it to his sovereign and every citizen to his country when it becomes necessary.

> What should be the measure of this cooperation? It should be that demanded by the necessity of conquering. And of this measure, in law and fact, England is the final judge, since from her derives the authority necessary to accomplish this great task, along with the burden of defending the Empire.[131]

And on the same day Archbishop Bruchési, speaking in support of the Patriotic Fund at Montreal, confirmed this expression of the hierarchy's views:

> England is engaged in a terrible war, which she sought to avoid at all costs. Loyal subjects, recognizing in her the protectress of our liberties, we owe her our most generous cooperation. Indifference at the present hour would be on our part a fault, and also the gravest error. Is it not evident that our fate is bound to the fate of her armies?[132]

Aside from *Le Canada's* articles, Bourassa's thesis was greeted only with insults, and was misrepresented to such an extent by the English press that Cahan protested in a letter to the *Gazette, Herald,* and other papers on September 15. Even some of Bourassa's closest followers expressed opposition. Olivar Asselin in *L'Action* on September 16 regretted that Bourassa had 'once more fallen into his customary error of being erudite when it would have sufficed to have entrenched himself in plain common sense,' while he also objected to Archbishop Bruchési's intervention in the political question of whether Canadian troops should be sent overseas.[133]

But against almost unanimous opposition Bourassa maintained his position that Canada should not refuse to aid England and France, but should do so only under certain conditions and within the limits of Canada's own obligations. On September 23 he pointed out that

Canada's contribution was already greater than that of Britain herself, in proportion to national wealth and population. He called for the end of persecution of the Franco-Ontarians and censured the lack of discipline and the drunkenness of the troops at Quebec. Sam Hughes had a Winnipeg journalist arrested for criticizing the administration of Valcartier Camp, but he took no steps against Bourassa. The latter did not hesitate to question the thesis of *L'Action Sociale* that Canada had a moral obligation to support England. He also criticized the Belgian mission, brought to Montreal by the British on September 23 and fêted at the city hall and the Monument National, for not expressing their gratitude to France as well as to England.

With Pelletier sick and the two other French-Canadian ministers nonentities, Charles Fitzpatrick, chief justice of the Supreme Court, was much consulted by Borden on the problem of Quebec. Fitzpatrick urged that the Quebec bishops should preach a holy war through a collective *mandement*, in the tradition of their loyalist stands in 1775 and 1812. Doherty was chosen as the government's intermediary, and set to work through his friend Archbishop Bruchési, who was already won to the cause by personal conviction. Fitzpatrick also urged the journalists of Quebec to preach a holy war. On September 23 the archbishops and bishops of Quebec, Montreal, and Ottawa signed a joint pastoral letter asserting that England 'counts on our help with perfect right and this help we are happy to say has been generously offered her in men and money.'[134] Most of the *mandement*, read in the churches on October 11, was devoted to urging the faithful to subscribe to the Patriotic Fund and to pray for a just peace. But the message clearly approved of the war policy and of the sending of troops, and the bishops were thanked by the governor-general for their action. For once 'clerical influence' in Quebec was welcomed by English Canadians. But Bourassa wrote at once to Archbishop Bruchési, asking whether this was a directive binding in conscience, and was told that he was perfectly free to differ in opinion.[135] Asselin protested in *L'Action* on October 24, when the majority of the French press had taken the attitude that the bishops had spoken and the matter was no longer to be discussed. He said their action was not interested, and perhaps their hand had been forced, but he censured them for exalting the imperialist doctrine of the obligation to send troops abroad into an 'untouchable dogma.'[136]

While Bourassa was making the transition from approval to criticism of Canada's participation in the war, the movement for a separate French-Canadian unit gained strength. Dr. Arthur Mignault, something of a French-Canadian Sam Hughes in his fondness for fancy uniforms and in his blustering militarist enthusiasm, won the assistance of L.-T. Maréchal in the cause and besieged

Borden and Hughes. The proposal was supported by J.-M. Tellier, Senator Belcourt, and Rodolphe Lemieux. Laurier wrote Borden in favor of the proposal, pointing out that 'The War Office at all times has taken advantage of the force of race sentiment in the formation of the army.'[137] On September 30 the government authorized the formation of the 22nd French-Canadian Battalion.

Under the auspices of *La Presse*, a recruiting meeting was held at the Parc Sohmer in Montreal on October 15, with Laurier, Gouin, Lemieux, T.-C. Casgrain, Mathias Tellier, and Belcourt urging their compatriots to enlist. Laurier invoked the memory of Dollard: 'If there are still a few drops of the blood of Dollard and his companions in the veins of the Canadians who are present at this meeting, you will enlist in a body, for this cause is just as sacred as the one for which Dollard and his companions gave their lives.' He made much of the fact that Canada's aid to Britain was given of her own free choice, not as an obligation, and he added: 'If some Canadians were frightened by the monster of conscription in the past, they must now recognize that this monster was a myth.'[138] Fifteen thousand people attended the rally, which had been widely publicized by the press, and students sang the 'Marseillaise.' The battalion was soon recruited to full strength and began training at St. Johns. *La Presse* virtually adopted the 22nd and filled its columns with news of the camp. There was marked popular enthusiasm for 'our regiment,' and Quebec's support was thus gained for the raising of a Second Division, which was decided upon on October 18, three days after the First Division landed in England. Borden virtually took charge of military affairs, after convincing the bellicose Duke of Connaught that he was only nominally commander-in-chief, and after reluctantly allowing the Napoleonic Hughes to follow the First Division to England.

Bourassa, who had sounded the sole dissenting voice to the Parc Sohmer meeting by calling it an 'explosion of empty and sterile chauvinism,'[139] gradually was joined by others in his criticism of the government as the first enthusiasm wore off. He inveighed against false patriots who beat their breasts to send other men to war. He criticized the British government for making purchases in the States which could have been made in Canada, while the Canadian government supplied the troops with razors made in Germany. He defended Montreal and Trois-Rivières, where unemployment was rife, for their poor showing in contributions to the Patriotic Fund; and he criticized the snobs who turned over to the Fund their usual gifts to charity, so that the Montreal Children's Hospital was about to close its doors for lack of money, while the Patriotic Fund had been given $1,500,000 in a few days. French-Canadian shoe manufacturers protested against British orders being placed in the States. *Le*

Patriote de l'Ouest proclaimed: 'It is not the time to discuss what was the extent of our strict obligations in the circumstances; it is manifest that we have exceeded the limits.'[140]

On October 17 Bourassa launched a campaign for a great agricultural reform, which would establish the unemployed of the East on land in the Prairie Provinces returned to the government by the great railway companies, which had received excessive grants. He urged that parliament be summoned to adopt this measure. He attacked the government for permitting the continued export to neutral countries of Ontario nickel, which had already gone into the making of German munitions and arms. He also attacked the proposal of a 'khaki election' to which Robert Rogers won Borden in the middle of October, but which was rejected in the face of the opposition of so stalwart a Conservative organ as the *Montreal Star*, which termed it 'treachery,'[141] and that of the united Liberal press. Borden contented himself with revising the French representation in the cabinet: Pelletier retired to the bench because of illness, and Nantel to the Railway Commission, while T.-C. Casgrain, an old-school Tory, became postmaster-general and P.-E. Blondin minister of internal revenue. The new ministers were re-elected without either Liberal or nationalist opposition.

On October 22 Bourassa gave a lecture on Belgium at the Monument National, under the auspices of the Saint-Jean-Baptiste Society and for the benefit of the Belgian Relief Fund, the French Red Cross, and the St. Vincent de Paul Society. Bourassa cited Belgium's pre-war prosperity as a proof that Catholicism was compatible with modern social organization. But he devoted most of his attention to the Flemings' successful fight for their language and their schools against the dominant French element. Flemish was now established on an equal basis with French, yet Belgian unity had not been endangered. Whatever might be the military result of the current struggle, Belgium would live, as Poland, Ireland, and French Canada would live. 'Justice does not die, because God, creator and guardian of justice, does not die.'[142]

Thus Bourassa took the occasion to support indirectly the rights of the Franco-Ontarians, whose struggle continued to enlist more sympathy in Quebec. *Curés* showed favor for the Ontario cause in the pulpit, and Cardinal Bégin sought support for it at Rome. Philippe Landry renewed his efforts to induce Borden to intervene with the Ontario government in the interests of a truce during the war. Two members of the Association d'Éducation had an interview with Doherty and Fitzpatrick on October 15 and got them to intercede with the Ottawa Irish, who refused to lift the injunction against payment of salaries to the teachers rebelling against Regulation 17. The case of the French-Canadian majority on the Ottawa Separate

School Board was pleaded by Senator Belcourt at Toronto before Judge Lennox, who expressed the view: 'Speak French at home if you like, but not at school.'[143] *Le Devoir* exalted the 'handful of heroes' and said that sympathy for the French and Belgians should not distract Quebec's attention from 'the assassination of a race which is being perpetrated' in Ontario.[144] The French-Canadian clergy followed the question eagerly, but Archbishop Gauthier, the English bishop of Ottawa who bore a French name, considered it a political and not a religious one. The apostolic delegate preserved a discreet silence. Bourassa took to the warpath more openly on November 12 when he gave a lecture on Alsace-Lorraine for the benefit of the French Red Cross and compared the Ontario regime with that of Alsace, showing that the English Ontarians were more Prussian than the Prussians. The whole question was embittered by the stubbornness of both parties, with the French asking for their schools first, and the Ontario loyalists saying 'Enlist first and then we shall see.'[145]

By October 31 Bourassa had so thoroughly swung around to opposition to the government's war policy that he was writing to this effect:

Instead of spending one hundred to one hundred and fifty millions to enlist and maintain for months, perhaps years, a great number of men badly clad, badly shod, and undiciplined, they could have, with a fifth of this sum, organized a suitable contingent of soldiers, well disciplined and perfectly equipped.

Instead of making a gift, at one swoop, to very wealthy England of millions of bags of flour and great piles of cheese—which rot today on the docks of Liverpool because the English do not know what to do with it, while millions of Belgians starve and thousands of Canadians have scarcely enough to eat,—they could have organized with intelligence and method Canada's economic and agricultural production; they could have controlled vigilantly the operation of transport tariffs; they could have watched with care to prevent any cornering of food supplies; they could have directed the export of Canadian products, and even of charitable gifts, public or private, in such fashion as to meet true needs, to aid true misery, instead of giving all to the rich and nothing to the poor; and above all they could have adopted suitable measures to support to the end the endurance of the effort of the nations whose friends they claim to be.

But no, it was necessary at all costs that Canada's aid should take an inflated, noisy, loud form, worthy of the fat-stomached newly rich who dominate high finance, big business, and the high policy of the Canadian nation. It was necessary also that it should profit above all the boodlers, vampires, the furnishers of bribes and electoral funds, the merchants of boots made of uncured cowhide and razors made in Germany.

Glory to the Empire![146]

This bitter blast was all the more effective, since Sam Hughes' awards of contracts to his cronies had already forced Borden to take the supply question under his supervision late in September and to launch an investigation of contracts in October. But Bourassa's intervention was not relished and he was branded as a traitor. The *Star* referred to him as 'Von Bourassa.'

On the whole French-Canadian opinion tended to support him, as the early enthusiasm wore off and English-Canadian scorn of Quebec's enlistment record and the Ontario school question had their effect. But Jules Fournier took objection to Bourassa for not being openly anti-British. Fournier reproduced in *L'Action* all news unfavorable to England and the British Army, thus replying to the English press' habit of making much of the minute B.E.F. in France and ignoring the French Army. He compared the German outrages in Belgium to those of the English in South Africa. He asked Bourassa flatly whether or not he favored the sending of the contingents, and whether or not he still believed in the principles which he had preached for fifteen years.[147] But the better-publicized Bourassa alone won the hatred of English Canadians. He was prevented from speaking at Kingston at the invitation of some Queen's University professors, thanks to the protest of Dr. J. W. Edwards, who called Bourassa 'much more dangerous than the Germans or Austrians interned as prisoners of war.'[148]

The Franco-Ontarians lost the first step in their long legal battle. While Senator Landry sought to interest Casgrain in their plight, Père Charlebois appealed to Quebec for funds to continue the battle. Fear of charges of disloyalty shut several doors, but the A.C.J.C. undertook to raise funds for 'the wounded of Ontario.'[149] This action aroused the Orangemen, and when Bourassa was invited to speak before the People's Forum of Ottawa on November 22, the clamor raised by the loyalists, with the *Journal* at the head of the agitation, resulted in the cancellation of the affair. A committee of nine, including three French Canadians, renewed the invitation for December 16. While incendiary handbills were circulated in Ottawa, calling Bourassa the 'arch traitor of Canada' and urging that 'the skull of rebellion must be smashed,'[150] Bourassa made a lecture tour through the Franco-American centers of New England, where he told the Franco-Americans to be resolutely American, to become naturalized citizens, and to learn English, but to keep contact with Canada and to preserve their religion, their language, and their traditions. 'By remaining French and Catholic, you will be better Americans.'[151] The most notable Franco-American, Governor Aram J. Pothier of Rhode Island, accepted Bourassa's invitation to come to Montreal on December 17. On December 10 a Quebec Dominican priest, Père Pierre Granger, gave a lecture in Ottawa in which he likened the Anglo-Ontarians to the Prussians and paid tribute to Le Devoir's 'happy national and religious influence,'[152] and to Bourassa as the soul of the movement in favor of the Franco-Ontarian schools. Bourassa attended a meeting of school commissioners at Hawkesbury on December 15, and learned of the tense feeling in Ottawa from Samuel Genest, Alphonse Charron, and Père Charlebois. A. C. Glennie, the Scottish secretary of the committee sponsoring Bourassa's appearance, was fired from his job, after influence had been brought to bear on his employer.

Police protection had been promised for the meeting at the Russell Theater on December 16, but from the outset songs and catcalls drowned out the voices of the chairman, Dr. Anthony Freeland, and of Bourassa himself. Bourassa nonetheless continued to speak for the benefit of the newspapermen who surrounded him. His speech, printed in 1915 as The Duty of Canada at the Present Hour, was made up almost entirely of extracts from his editorials in Le Devoir since the outbreak of the War. By giving the context which had been omitted by ultrapatriotic English editors in search of damning extracts, Bourassa hoped to clarify his position. But the speech was not heard except by a few journalists, for the tumult in the auditorium steadily increased. Glennie was manhandled and pushed through the glass entrance door. A sergeant climbed on the platform, handed Bourassa a Union Jack, and ordered him to wave it. The front rows were filled with soldiers ready to support their companion. Bourassa took the flag and laid it on a table, in a momentary hush which allowed the audience to hear his reply: 'I am ready to wave the British flag in liberty, but I shall not do so under threats.'[153] The sergeant repeated his order. Bourassa repeated his reply and eyed him firmly. The audience rose howling to its feet and the soldiers prepared to storm the platform when the curtain was suddenly dropped. Some French Canadians in the audience sang the 'Marseillaise,' while the uproar continued. Bourassa and his party left the theater after the tumult had continued for fifteen minutes, and went to the Chateau Laurier, where he continued the lecture for his friends and the newspapermen.

All Ottawa was up in arms. A French Canadian knocked down an English Canadian who insulted Bourassa in the grill room of the Chateau that evening. The next morning Mrs. Glennie visited the office of the Journal, which had played a leading role in arousing the agitation, and horsewhipped the editor. The French Canadians of Ottawa sent her two great bouquets of roses. The Ottawa Free Press protested at the part taken by the soldiers at the Russell Theater, and censured the prevalence of drunkenness among the troops camped on the Exposition Grounds. The Toronto Globe and Montreal Star described the incident as 'regrettable.' Casgrain replied to a suggestion from Landry—that he appeal in behalf of the Franco-Ontarians to the governor-general—with the observation that the invitation to Bourassa to speak in Ottawa was 'a defiance of public opinion' which would injure their cause.[154] *Le Droit* wildly observed that Bourassa had been attacked less as the champion of certain ideas than as champion of the oppressed minority. The party press of Quebec played down the incident, since it gave too much importance to Bourassa.

But at the Montreal reception for Governor Pothier on December 17, at which Coderre represented the federal government, Cyrille Delage the provincial government, Senator Dandurand Laurier, Wilfrid Gariépy the Alberta government, Senator Poirier the Acadians, and Senator Belcourt the Franco-Ontarians, Bourassa was greeted with wild enthusiasm. He warned that 'If we let the French minorities which are our outposts be sacrificed one by one, the day will come when the Province of Quebec itself will undergo assault.'[155] He called for the preservation of French culture against all traps, all denials, and all treasons: 'We have not the right to abdicate by committing suicide, and committing suicide in dishonor.' The following day Lavergne and Lamarche held a meeting in favor of the French language in Montreal. The next day, the A.C.J.C. issued a manifesto for its meeting on December 21, which was to launch the campaign for 'the wounded of Ontario.' In *Le Devoir* Bourassa urged all patriots to attend:

In the name of religion, liberty, and faithfulness to the British flag, the French Canadians are enjoined to go fight the Prussians of Europe. Shall we let the Prussians of Ontario impose their domination like masters, in the very heart of the Canadian Confederation, under the shelter of the British flag and British institutions?[156]

The meeting was attended unexpectedly by Archbishop Bruchési, as well as by his more nationalist-minded auxiliary Bishop Gauthier, the Jesuit provincial, the rector of the Collège Sainte-Marie, and the secretary of the university. Père Charlebois, Bourassa, and Lavergne sat side by side with Senators Dandurand, Landry, and Belcourt. Party ties were forgotten. Archbishop Bruchési clearly indicated his support of the movement. Senator Landry stressed the importance of the question: 'We wish to have it settled whether Confederation has been for us a pact of honour or an infamous trap.'[157] He appealed to Borden, Laurier, Gouin, Fitzpatrick, and Doherty. Belcourt gave the legal case for the Franco-Ontarians, and Alphonse Charron the history of the movement. Bourassa, not on the program, was called for by the crowd, and once more compared the English Ontarians to the Prussians, to the favor of the latter. Cardinal Bégin later approved Archbishop Bruchési's stand in a letter from Rome: 'If the trial imposed upon our brothers of Ontario must be prolonged, as please God it may not, it will be the noble duty of the French Province of Quebec to support with its influence and all its strength those who fight, until full justice be rendered them.'[158] The A.C.J.C. under the leadership of Guy Vanier organized meetings, publicity, and sought subscriptions. Omer Héroux announced in *Le Devoir:* 'The attention of the public is now fixed on Regulation 17 and we shall try to keep it there.'[159]

7

Quebec entered the year 1915 with far more of its attention and sympathy concentrated on Ontario than on Europe. French Canada still supported generously the numerous appeals for various war funds; but its military enthusiasm cooled as news of illness, mismanagement, and poor equipment came from the muddy Canadian camp on Salisbury Plain in England. However, Dr. Mignault proposed to raise a French-Canadian hospital unit, to match that organized by McGill. Already the bugbear of conscription had been raised. When Borden had assured the Canadian Club of Montreal on December 7 that Canada would send all the men and money necessary to a triumphal conclusion of a 'terrible and protracted struggle,'[160] Bourassa predicted that this policy would end in conscription. Speaking at the Montreal Reform Club on December 12, Laurier characterized conscription as 'repugnant to the British character' and supported the Liberal endorsement of the government's policy:

I have no particular love for the government, but I love my country, I love the land of my ancestors, France. I love the land of liberty above all, England, and rather than that I, in my position as leader of the Liberal party, should remain passive and quiescent, I would go out of public life, and life together.[161]

But Bourassa had a firmer hold on Quebec's heart than Laurier at the end of 1914.

The provincial session opened on January 7, 1915 and soon provided evidence that particularist Quebec was being drawn into a wider world. The speech from the throne included an invitation to Belgian refugees to establish themselves in the province. *L'Action Sociale* and *L'Evénement* had misgivings about thus introducing 'radicals, Freemasons, and socialists' in a country which wished to preserve 'healthy social and religious ideas.'[162] Tellier endorsed the policy of political truce by approving the government's gifts to England, France, and Belgium, and said that regardless of constitutional or civil obligations, he was ready to support any aid that the government proposed to give to England, as a son would fly to the defence of his father's house.[163] But on January 11 Sir Lomer Gouin himself anticipated Armand Lavergne, who intended to present a resolution in favor of the Franco-Ontarians:

While in Europe English and French rival each other in fighting for the triumph of justice, while on the battlefields French and English generously shed their blood in order that there may be no more oppression in Europe, why must their brothers of Ontario be divided on the merits of teaching to the children of a minority the language of the discoverers of this nation. . . .

I cannot forget that it was the English Canadians of Ontario and the French Canadians of Quebec who founded the already potent structure which is the Dominion.

Who would wish to pretend that it was not in their minds to give to the two races equal rights in the matter of language, of property, and person, as Sir John Macdonald put it in 1890? And who could pretend that it was not under the inspiration of such sentiments that the British North America Act was drawn up by the Fathers of Confederation? . . .

It is moved by this sentiment, Mr. Speaker, that I wish, before taking my seat, to address in the name of all the population of Quebec—English, Scottish, and Irish Canadians as well as French Canadians—an appeal to the government and the majority of the Province of Ontario. In the name of the justice and generosity of which England has given so many proofs and which cannot fail to animate every truly British citizen, as well as in the name of the struggles that our fathers waged to open to civilization the rich domains which are our common heritage, I ask that justice be done to the French minority of Ontario, and even, if need be, that generosity be shown to them.

In the name of the sublime expressions which it has given to human thought, I ask, for the French tongue, the right to be heard on the lips of the school children of Ontario who wish to learn it and to speak it.[164]

For once Gouin found something of the eloquence and feeling of his father-in-law Honoré Mercier.

Two days later, at Gouin's instigation, two English-speaking members—W. S. Bullock of Shefford, a former Baptist preacher, and J. T. Finnie of Montreal, born in Scotland—introduced the following motion:

This House, without derogating from the principles of Provincial autonomy and without any intention of advising or intervening in the affairs of other Provinces of the Confederation, views with regret the divisions which seem to exist among the people of the Province of Ontario over the bilingual schools question, and believes that it is in the interests of the Dominion in general that all questions of this sort be considered on broad, generous, and patriotic lines, always remembering that one of the cardinal principles of British liberty throughout the Empire is regard for the rights and privileges of minorities.[165]

Lavergne congratulated Bullock and Finnie, but attacked the tyranny of the Orangemen and Bishop Fallon. He took the opportunity to reaffirm the nationalist principle of no Canadian participation in England's wars, citing Lord Granville's dictum that it was England's duty to defend Canada and not Canada's duty to defend England. Tellier approved the resolution, and deplored Lavergne's irrelevant remarks. Only one English member, C. E. Gault of Montreal, questioned the opportuneness of the gesture. The resolution was passed unanimously. In *Le Devoir* Lavergne stressed the fact that the Liberal government of Quebec had adopted a program which the nationalists had long advanced.

On the following day, January 14, the friends of *Le Devoir* celebrated the paper's fifth anniversary at the Monument National. As chairman, J.-N. Cabana announced that a public meeting had been chosen rather than a private banquet as the means of celebrating the occasion in order that 'examination of conscience'[166] might be made before the public of Montreal. Admission was charged to aid in increasing the circulation of the paper. The chief backer, G.-N. Ducharme, confessed that he had originally supported the paper in the interest of the Conservative Party, but had been converted to Bourassa's view of the necessity of an independent journal to claim and to defend French-Canadian rights. He expressed his perfect confidence in Bourassa and in his disinterestedness. Armand Lavergne retraced the whole history of the nationalist movement and paid tribute to Bourassa, who 'incarnated all the claims of the race.'[167] Bourassa had been accused of treason; so had Lafontaine, Mercier, and Riel. Tomorrow all Quebec and all Canada would thank him, as Quebec's youth did today.

Bourassa himself spoke for more than two hours, giving an account of *Le Devoir's* campaigns and achievements. As for the future:

In fair or foul weather, with or against all comers, *Le Devoir* will continue to fight for the rights of Canada against the foreigner, and even against the contrary interests of Great Britain and the other countries of the Empire; for the rights of minorities, Catholic or Protestant, French or English, and for the equality of the two races and of the two civilizations in each of the Canadian provinces; for the creation of a true national spirit made up of the best elements of these two civilizations; for the colonization of the land by our citizens and against the invasion of the country by foreigners of all races and countries; for the intellectual, moral, and social progress of the Canadian people; for the economic development of all the resources of the country in the interest of the people who inhabit it; for the honest and intelligent administration of the state and of all its provincial and municipal fractions; for the subordination of particular interests and the cupidity of parties to the higher interests of the nation.[168]

He stressed his belief in the bi-ethnic and bilingual character of Canada, and that a moral agreement between French and English was essential to the formation of Canadian nationality:

We wish both elements to conserve the characteristic traits of their race, their traditions, their language, their literature, and all their aspirations which are compatible with the moral and political unity of the Canadian people. We wish that the one should become more Canadian than French, and the other more Canadian than English. Let each group derive from its country of origin the ideas, advances, and developments necessary to the conservation of its particular patrimony, intellectual or moral; but each must also have enough patriotism, intelligence, and generosity to subordinate its particular tastes or prejudices to the exigencies of national unity.

In other words, we oppose equally French colonialism, in the world of ideas, and English colonialism in the world of politics and facts; we wish that both give place to a Canadian nationalism, both English and French, sharply distinct in the elements proper to the two races and their particular genius, but harmoniously united in the research of a common ideal, made up of Canadian traditions, rooted in the Canadian soil, and having no other object than the moral and material greatness of the Canadian fatherland.[169]

Bourassa explained that *Le Devoir* was a Catholic journal, but not the organ of the hierarchy, the clergy, or any group of monks or priests. He stressed its freedom in all national or political matters, but also its conviction that the French Canadians 'would remain Catholic only on condition of remaining French, and remaining French only on condition of remaining Catholic.'[170] *Le Devoir* would continue independent of party politics. Bourassa opposed the formation of a nationalist party on the grounds that party spirit was already too strong; that third parties were only favored by exceptional circumstances for certain immediate ends, while his program of nationalism was too extensive and too far reaching; and finally that the elements of a superior party were lacking after forty years of degrading party strife. 'Instead of seeking to win elections against one or the other party, or against both, we shall seek more and more to create around the parties a barrier which will contain them, supplying beneath them a solid base which will prevent them from sinking too low, and above them a directing master thought which will force them to work for the good of the nation instead of corrupting its spirit.'[171] Bourassa closed with an appeal for financial aid through subscriptions, printing contracts, and advertising.

In his speech Bourassa had mentioned the possible necessity of forming a third party to combat the ostracism of French in Ontario, if it continued and if both parties refused to remedy it; but in fact he had already rallied almost all of Quebec to the cause of the

Franco-Ontarians. The hierarchy now joined the struggle, sub-scribing to the A.C.J.C. fund, recommending it to their clergy, and referring to the struggle in Ontario in their pastoral letters. Laval University in Quebec organized a demonstration for January 25, while the campaign in favor of the Franco-Ontarians continued in the press and on the platform. At Quebec the assemblage included Cardinal Bégin, his auxiliary Bishop Roy, Mgr. Amédée Gosselin, rector of Laval, Gouin and four members of his cabinet, Senator Landry, Senator Belcourt and five or six other senators, the speakers of both houses of the provincial legislature, and Sévigny, the future deputy-speaker of the federal House, the chief justice of Quebec, and a host of other notables.

Only Laurier and Bourassa were missing at what *Le Soleil* called 'the hour of mobilization of the French-Canadian race.'[172] Laurier, who feared the repercussions of the agitation in the other provinces, swept as they were by war hysteria, held himself apart from it. Bourassa spoke on 'The Renaissance of Small Nationalities' at the university in Montreal on January 27 for the benefit of the Franco-Ontarians. He developed the theory of national rights and applied it to the Canadian minorities. He called upon Quebec, the natural protector of all the French of Canada, to make this right respected: 'In the name of our own constitution, of our own dignity, in the name of the conscience of humanity, of which we possess a part which awakens, we have the duty to aid with all our strength the French-Canadian minorities of Canada who fight for the conservation of their rights and their traditions.'[173]

The federal government took alarm at the rising tide of feeling in Quebec, and Borden privately intervened with W. H. Hearst, the premier of Ontario. Afterwards he reported to Fitzpatrick that Hearst desired to do everything possible to remedy injustice, but his efforts were frustrated by interventions from outside the province. In short, if Quebec would quiet down, something might be done by Ontario. Fitzpatrick passed on a copy of Borden's letter to Arch-bishop Bruchési. But Quebec was now animated by a crusading spirit, and feeling continued to rise in all quarters of the province. In a letter to *Le Devoir* Napoléon Garceau censured the growing tendency to set the re-establishment of the Ontario separate schools as the condition of French-Canadian support of the war. But *Le Devoir* dismissed the old nationalist as merely another 'dissident.' Anti-French-Canadian feeling in Ontario rose as Quebec's feeling against Ontario mounted. Neither side would yield, and the way was paved for the later explosion of ethnic feeling.

Rifts in the political truce appeared during the federal session from February 15 to April 15. The address was moved by an Ontario German and seconded by a former Quebec nationalist,

Honoré Achim. Laurier qualified his pledge of full support of the government by saying that expenditures could not be sanctioned without accounting and that such questions as giving 'the Dominion a voice in all questions of peace and war' [174] should be postponed until after the war. He took up the matter of the bad boots supplied to the First Division and urged an investigation, which Borden promised. Borden reported that '31,000 men are today in the British Isles or in France; 1,000 are in Bermuda; and nearly 10,000 are doing garrison duty in Canada.'[175] He also announced that 50,000 men had been enlisted for the defence of Canada. Laurier taunted Blondin, the new minister of internal revenue, with his past nationalist statements; 'the honorable gentleman had filled up the holes in the flag and . . . would now breathe the atmosphere of liberty,' [176] as he had taunted Sévigny upon his rise to the deputy-speakership by supporting a program contrary to that on which he had been elected.

In March Laurier criticized the government for extravagance in the budget, which had not been previously submitted to the opposition, as was done in England. New taxes, bad boots, profiteering on war contracts, and a new measure permitting soldiers to vote were debated. The latter was passed, but in the face of the Senate's opposition to immediate application of the Redistribution Act, Borden accepted an amendment in that sense. On the final day of the session Borden spoke on the report of the Public Accounts Committee which had investigated war expenditures, and severely censured the part of two Conservative M.P.'s in profiteering in drugs and horses. He announced his intention of appointing a committee to supervise the purchases made under parliament's appropriation of $100,000,000 for war purposes. This War Purchasing Commission, to whose establishment Sir Sam Hughes objected, was made up of Edward Kemp, G. F. Galt, and Hormisdas Laporte on May 8. It eliminated many of the criticisms to which the government had been exposed by Hughes' favoritism in awarding contracts.

Soon after the prorogation of parliament, Robert Rogers made a speech in Montreal demanding an immediate election, in order that the government should not be 'handicapped and crippled and interfered with at every turn, tarrying and disputing with an Opposition that . . . has declared a want of confidence in our proposals for the carrying on of our part in this great conflict.'[177] A majority of the cabinet favored a dissolution, but Borden decided against it, after the governor-general had deprecated such a course and adverse public opinion had made itself felt.[178] At Toronto on May 15 Laurier declared that he was a party man in time of peace, but 'I do not care, for my part, so long as the war lasts, to open the portals of office with that bloody key.'[179] Opposition to a wartime election grew as word came across the Atlantic of the tremendous casualties suffered by the First Division in the Second Battle of Ypres.

The Princess Patricia's Canadian Light Infantry had gone into the line in January and by May 7 was down to half strength, and by June only 12 men and one officer, Lieutenant Talbot Papineau, of the original battalion had escaped death or wounds.[180] The First Division reached the front in March. They got their first real baptism of fire in the Battle of Saint-Julien or Langemarck from April 22 to 28. They withstood the first gas attack of the war, losing about 6,000 men in killed, wounded, and missing as they held a gap left in the line by the panic-stricken French Turcos and Zouaves against four enemy divisions. Withdrawn from the front line on May 3-5, they returned to it on May 19 at Festubert and Givenchy, losing about half their strength by June 30. Sam Hughes was bitterly critical of British command, and urged the replacement of the British General E. A. H. Alderson by the Canadian General R. E. W. Turner. The Second Division arrived in England by installments in March, April, and May. It did not go to France until September, though in August it supplied reinforcements to the First Division. The Canadian Corps was then formed under the command of the British General Alderson, but with the divisions commanded by the Canadian Generals A.W. Currie and Turner.

The recruiting of 150,000 men was authorized on July 8, 1915 by order-in-council, and in October the limit was raised to 250,000. By the end of the year 212,000 men were under arms, of whom 180,000 were raised in 1915; and early in the new year an attempt was made to bring the force up to 500,000 men. The ceaseless demands for more manpower occasioned by the heavy losses in France resulted in an intensification of the recruiting campaign in Canada. In the House on February 25, 1915 Sam Hughes had boasted that he 'could raise three more contingents in three weeks if necessary.'[181] But he was not given to weighing his words, as an utterance in Montreal on May 4 gave evidence: 'Canada has sent one contingent, a second is on the way and a third will be going in a week or two. A fourth is almost ready, and if necessary we will send a fifth, a sixth, a tenth, or a twentieth.'[182] In the face of such unrealistic enthusiasm a French-Canadian reaction made itself evident. In the Commons on March 9 the Liberal Roch Lanctôt and the Conservative Adélard Bellemare declared their belief that Canada was doing too much and that increased production would be Canada's best contribution.[183]

Of the 32,070 men asked for the third contingent, only 22,738 were raised, according to the Militia Department's figures of March

26, with only one military department (Kingston) enlisting more than its quota and with all the others short of their goal, gravely so in the Maritimes, British Columbia, Manitoba and Saskatchewan, and Quebec.[184] By the end of 1915 only 212,000 had been enlisted out of the 250,000 goal set on November 1. The official figures of February 15, 1916 showed that of a total of 249,471 then enlisted, 62 per cent were British-born, 30 per cent Canadian-born, others 8 per cent.[185] The increasing difficulties encountered in recruiting were due to the facts that the British-born of military age had largely enlisted in the early days of the war, the unrooted urban population had largely been absorbed, native Canadians still showed a reluctance to fight for 'civilization' or 'the empire' as the recruiting cries went (no specifically Canadian appeal was made), and the rural regions remained apathetic to the war.

Early in 1915 the raising of a second French-Canadian battalion, the 41st, was authorized, and Lt.-Col. Louis H. Archambault left the 22nd to recruit the new unit, based at Quebec but drawn largely from Hull and Montreal. Dr. Mignault was allowed to organize the French-Canadian hospital unit which he had proposed should be put at the service of the French government. But early in the session Hughes returned a vague answer when questioned by a Quebec member as to whether the government intended to form the French-Canadian brigade desired by many patriotic Québecois. In reply to a whispering campaign against Quebec's enlistment record, and to a direct question about the number of French Canadians in the first contingent, Hughes said that Quebec had done its duty and set the number as between 3,000 and 6,000. This statement encouraged the over-optimistic estimates of French-Canadian patriots, while its vagueness did not quiet English-Canadian detractors. Another French battalion, the 57th, was authorized later in the spring, under the command of Lt.-Col. E.-T. Paquet. A fourth, the 69th, was recruited in June by 24-year-old Adolphe Dansereau, a wounded veteran of the 14th Battalion and a son of Arthur Dansereau of La Presse. By midsummer these units were at full strength, and together with the 22nd, totaled more than 4,000 men, in addition to the French Canadians scattered throughout the forces.

But the group spirit aroused by the formation of exclusively French-Canadian units was weakened by the refusal to let French-Canadian members of the 13th and 14th Battalions transfer to the 22nd, the only French-Canadian unit at the front, and by drafts on the 41st and 57th for the reinforcement of English-Canadian units. There were also other developments which dampened enthusiasm. Dr. Mignault's hospital unit, raised for service in France, was ordered to the Dardanelles; but after vigorous protests the order was cancelled and in November the unit was established at Saint-Cloud near Paris as General Hospital No. 8. Colonel J.-P. Landry, a Permanent Force officer, was relieved of the command of the 5th Brigade of the Second Division on the eve of its departure for France in September, and relegated to the post of inspector-general of camps in England. He was replaced by Colonel David Watson of the First Division, a personal friend of Sam Hughes, who was promoted to the rank of brigadier. The highest ranking French Canadian in the whole Canadian Army Corps was Colonel F.-M. Gaudet of the 22nd. The replacement of Colonel Landry, which was considered to be Hughes' revenge on his father Senator Landry for the latter's role in the Ontario school quarrel, confirmed the growing French-Canadian opinion that Hughes kept the higher commands for English Canadians. Recruiting lagged in Quebec, thanks to these factors and to events at home. An English Canadian was appointed chief recruiting officer for Quebec, and the choice was no more popular because of the fact that he was a Baptist clergyman. Officers of the French-Canadian units complained that their units were kept too long in Canada, and that it was difficult to maintain discipline when their men were sent home on harvest leave and thus tempted to desert.

But the major factor in the deteriorating war spirit of Quebec was unquestionably the Ontario school question. Most English Canadians did not realize the importance attached to the matter by the French Canadians, and the few sympathetic English-Canadian voices found little hearing in the midst of the concentration of English opinion upon the war. Father M. J. Whalen of Ottawa replied to Cardinal Bégin, Archbishop Bruchési, and Sir Lomer Gouin in an open letter to the *Toronto Mail and Empire* on February 14, in which he blamed the Ontario war of races on a conspiracy on the part of Archbishop Duhamel, the Association d'Education, and *Le Droit* to favor a French invasion of the province. He urged that ecclesiastical provinces should be realigned to coincide with the boundaries of the civil provinces, thus depriving the French clergy of the opportunity to intervene in Ontario. In Manitoba a movement also arose among the Irish clergy in opposition to Archbishop Langevin. Meanwhile in Quebec Héroux supported the Franco-Ontarians in *Le Devoir* and the A.C.J.C. extended its campaign for funds to the classical colleges and primary schools, thus focussing the attention of French-Canadian youth on Ontario rather than on Europe. On March 7 Senator Landry, Thomas Chapais, P.-E. Lamarche, Dr. Baril, and Senator Belcourt took part in a mass meeting of protest against Regulation 17 at the Théâtre Français in Ottawa. The presence of Conservatives, Liberals, and nationalist spokesmen indicated compliance with Landry's injunction: 'Before we are Liberals or Conservatives, let us be French Canadians.'[186]

Three days later Senator L.-O. David presented a motion urging settlement of the school question in accordance with the spirit of the constitution, recalling the aid given to the Irish by French Canadians in the past. An Irish senator, George McHugh, supported the resolution. On the same day the Orange Grand Lodge met, with Sam Hughes in attendance, and called for the suppression of all teaching of French in Ontario. A Conservative M.P., H. B. Morphy, proclaimed: 'Never shall we let the French Canadians implant in Ontario the disgusting speech they use.'[187] This utterance was echoed in the Senate, where Senator Choquette called Morphy a 'brutal maniac and ignoramus.'[188] Senator Poirier of New Brunswick urged conciliation and a truce. Senators Béique, Dandurand, Legris, and Boyer defended the Franco-Ontarians. Senator Power of Halifax, an eminent Irish Catholic, proposed a sub-amendment which destroyed the force of David's motion. Senator Pope of the Eastern Townships supported Power, and reproached the nationalists with subordinating the French-Canadian military effort to the settlement of the school question. Senator Landry, as speaker, sought to bar Power's amendment on grounds of procedure, but his effort was defeated by an ethnic vote. In the face of the opposition of the English members, Senator Landry ceased to preside over the Senate on April 8 and offered his resignation to Borden, who refused it. Landry resumed his seat for the final session on April 15, after accepting the presidency of the Association d'Education the previous evening. The debate on the David resolution was cut short by the prorogation of parliament, but it had already produced a minor division between French Liberals and Conservatives, both in parliament and in the press.[189]

Quebec continued to grow more aroused about the school question. Père Villeneuve of Ottawa was invited to preside over the March meeting of the Saint-Jean-Baptiste Society of Montreal. On March 19 Bourassa gave a lecture on 'La Langue française au Canada, sa necessité, ses avantages,' under the auspices of the same society for the benefit of the Franco-Ontarians. At Quebec the curé of Saint-Sauveur presided over a protest meeting against the attitude of the Ontario Orangemen.

Bourassa hailed the initial manifesto of Landry, which urged that the school question should not be made a political one. He stressed the overriding importance of the question:

The whole problem of the French language and of French survival is being raised in Ontario. For Canada, for all America, it is not on the battlefields of Europe that this survival will be maintained or extin-guished.   Let France be victorious or defeated, let her retake Alsace-Lorraine or lose Champagne, it is not the Prussian armies of the Kaiser or German culture which will decide our fate.   It is ourselves.

The enemies of the French language, of French civilization in Canada, are not the Boches on the shores of the Spree; but the English-Canadian anglicizers, the Orange intriguers, or Irish priests.   Above all they are French Canadians weakened and degraded by the conquest and three centuries of colonial servitude.

Let no mistake be made: if we let the Ontario minority be crushed, it will soon be the turn of other French groups in English Canada.[190]

The French Canadians carried on the war for the defence of their language on many fronts, insisting on the use of French in business and the public services of Quebec.

Ethnic feeling was evident in the hockey games between French and English teams, and also in the sports at military camps.   Even the small boys of Montreal, Quebec, and the urban centers of the Townships waged war upon each other on racial lines.   The 22nd, transferred to Amherst, Nova Scotia, for final training before embarkation, was greeted on arrival by empty streets, closed shops, and cold looks.   But thanks to the battalion's contributions to the poor of the town and its good behavior, Amherst declared a holiday to allow the people to escort the troops on their departure, and the mayor accompanied them to Halifax.[191]   The news of the Canadians' gallant behavior at Ypres and of the heavy losses brought a momen-tary lull, with even *Le Devoir* paying homage to the heroic dead; but a reaction soon set in upon the ground that French Canada was not bearing her fair share of the war burden.   The loss of one or more sons in the small average English-Canadian family was felt perhaps more strongly than in the larger French-Canadian families.

On May 19 Bourassa delivered at the Monument National an expanded version of his earlier lecture on '*La Langue française au Canada, ses droits, sa necessité, ses avantages,*' under the auspices of the A.C.J.C. and for the benefit of the Franco-Ontarians.   Senator Landry acted as chairman and assured the large audience that French would continue to be spoken at home and at school in Ontario, since 'we wish it, you wish it, God wishes it.'[192]   Senator David appeared on the platform.   In a careful constitutional analysis Bourassa reviewed the natural rights of the French Canadians to their language, the rights derived from the capitulations, the Treaty of Paris, the Quebec Act, and the Constitution of 1791.   He pointed out that provision was made for a French version of the laws when Upper Canada was established, that Egerton Ryerson had approved of the teaching of both languages in the Ontario schools, and that many French schools were established in Ontario before Confederation and were given government subsidies. He cited Macdonald's interpretation in 1890 of the B.N.A. Act as assuring 'equal rights of every kind, of language, of religion, of property, and of person.'[193] He argued that rights acquired under the federal constitution overrode those acquired under provincial law, and that French Canadians in Ontario had the same rights to their language as English Canadians in Quebec. But he counseled against seeking revenge by reprisals in Quebec.

Bourassa pointed out that the great majority of British subjects were not English-speaking, and that in many quarters of the empire other languages than English enjoyed a larger place than that of French in Canada. He denounced the Prussian and American doctrine that national unity must be based upon one language; he defended bilingualism by citing its success in Wales, Ireland, Belgium, Switzerland, and Alsace, pointing out that the Ontario oppression was worse than that of the Germans in the latter region. The French language was necessary for the preservation of the French Canadians' faith; it was a barrier to Americanization; it was useful in trade and diplomacy; it was the language of superior civilization. He defended Quebec's right to intervene in Ontario, urged contributions to the cause, and the development of a cult for the preservation of the language in its purest form: 'Let us be defenders of the French language, not only against others, but against ourselves.' In a passage omitted from the printed text, he attacked the Irish clergy:

It is time, high time, that Rome should know that in supporting the cause of the oppressed, our bishops accomplish not only a duty of justice and charity. Inspired by the example of St. Paul, they protect in America the catholicity of the Church against the insidious or declared attempts of those who wish to make religion the weapon of domination of a race. . . .

As to the prelates and priests who unite themselves to the worst enemies of the Church to snatch from the French Canadians the free enjoyment of their natural rights, guaranteed by history, civilization, and the practice of civilized nations, they fail in their double duty of Catholic pastors and British subjects . . . Instead of persecuting the oldest and most faithful people of America, why do they not apply their ardor for fighting to saving the millions of English-speaking Catholics whom mixed marriages, attendance at neutral schools, and Protestant or materialist literature throw each year into the immense army of unbelievers, worshippers of the Golden Calf?

I hope this declaration will scandalize no one. I make it without anger, in the spirit of the father of a Catholic family who knows that God has given him the right and imposed upon him the duty to preserve for his children the unreckonable treasure of the faith and of national traditions . . .

The acts from which we suffer, whatever be the character of their authors—and I do not incriminate the good faith of these authors—do not derive from episcopal authority or the priestly character. These are individual acts, outside their apostolic rule, but which constitute a peril for the faith of a number.

It is time that Rome, mother and protector of all Catholics, should know it clearly.[194]

Bourassa gained prestige by this open appeal to Rome, which no other French-Canadian lay leader had yet dared to make. His audience unanimously ratified resolutions affirming the right of the French Canadians to speak their language and to teach it to their children in all the provinces of Canada; claiming respect for the federal pact and Macdonald's interpretation of it; and expressing the hope that the Ontario minority would receive the support of all Canadians, Catholic or Protestant, French or English, 'desirous of preserving in America the benefits of French civilization and causing to triumph in Canada the precepts and practice of the *entente cordiale* which united England and France on the battlefields of Europe.'[195] These resolutions were reprinted by most of the provincial weeklies. Some days later Archbishop Bruchési and Sir Adolphe Routhier devoted their Royal Society papers to the rights of the French language in Canada.[196] And when Archbishop Langevin died in Montreal on June 15, his funeral was virtually turned into a nationalist demonstration. In every French-Canadian community along the way from Montreal to Winnipeg, troops of kneeling schoolchildren greeted the funeral train as it carried the body of the 'hero of the West' to his last rest.[197]

Bourassa spoke in Montreal again on June 23 for the benefit of the Franco-Ontarians; Lavergne at the Monument National on June 24; and Landry addressed 5,000 people at the Ottawa Arena on the same day, saying that he would appeal to Rome and London after vainly interceding with the Archbishop of Ottawa and the premier of Ontario: 'We shall ask the mother country if our children have no other rights than to go and be killed in the service of the Empire.'[198] *L'Action Sociale*, now known as *L'Action Catholique*, urged a truce, at the instigation of T.-C. Casgrain, who was alarmed by the Ontario reaction to the charges of 'Prussianism.' But in Quebec feelings had mounted too high to be calmed. Bourassa replied that 'Mgr. Latulipe was not wrong in considering the proceedings of the Ontario Boches as execrable as those of the Pomeranian Boches.'[199] He warned of the probable extension of the struggle to Saskatchewan and Alberta, where the teaching of French was subjected to new restrictions.[200] After *L'Action Catholique* and Archbishop Bruchési had counseled moderation, *Le Canada*, *La Patrie*, and *La Presse* criticized the turning over to *Le Droit*, which had taken readers from them, of part of the money raised by the A.C.J.C. for the Ontario schools.

On July 12 the Appelate Court of Toronto approved Regulation 17. The Ontario government promptly dissolved the Ottawa Separate School Commission, which was two-thirds French, and replaced it by a new commission of three members, with only one French-Canadian representative. These actions, violently protested by *Le Devoir*, coincided with a new recruiting campaign. Their repercussions were soon evident.

Sam Hughes, now promoted to the rank of general, saw no conflict between further recruiting and the continued expansion of war industry. But 250 factories were now engaged in making munitions in Canada, employing at high wages all the men they could find. Industry thus drained off most of the potential urban recruits, while the farmer remained as attached to his land and as indifferent to the war as ever. Bourassa made much of the 'business as usual' spirit of British industrialists, of British opposition to conscription, and of British labor's unwillingness to speed up the production of munitions urgently needed by the army. Shortage of ammunition had in part accounted for the heavy Canadian losses in April and May. Bourassa hailed the role of John Redmond, the Irish nationalist, in insisting upon Home Rule as a condition of Irish participation in the war, and contrasted it with the servility of Canadian leaders. Aroused by these Irish references, the Duke of Connaught urged Borden to censor *Le Devoir*. But Borden had the wisdom to reply: 'Bourassa would like nothing better. I would not be so foolish. Besides, Campbell Bannerman and Lloyd George were far worse in the South Africa War, and Carson respecting Ulster.'[201] Even *Le Soleil* protested against the attitude of British business and labor, when Canadians were being called upon to make greater sacrifices.

But both the government and the military neglected this new factor in French-Canadian public opinion, as well as that of the Ontario school question, in launching a new recruiting drive. Casgrain made a speaking trip through the lower St. Lawrence region, urging total support of England. Colonel Wilson, commander of the Montreal military district, predicted and hoped for conscription in an interview to the *Star* on July 12. A campaign for the purchase of machine guns was launched, amid objections from the French press that this was hardly a matter for public charity, and open-air recruiting meetings were begun in Montreal. On July 15, two English-Canadian industrialists, C. C. Ballantyne and A. D. Dawson, warned that they would not employ men of military age, who should be at the front.[202] At McGill the following day the ex-nationalist N.-K. Laflamme came out in support of conscription, while a

Protestant minister, clad in uniform, proclaimed that Christ would be at the front, if He were on earth.[203] Napoléon Garceau, who believed in wholehearted support of the war, nevertheless protested in an open letter to the minister of justice against the intimidation practiced by Ballantyne and Dawson:

> If military service should be obligatory, let it be so for all, rich as well as poor, but under laws passed by the parliament of the country, and not because of the authority or power that money may give to certain personages . . .[204]

At a recruiting meeting at the Parc Sohmer on July 22, at which Laflamme, Blondin, and Colonel Paquet spoke, there was heckling. And on the following day at Parc Lafontaine a recruiting meeting was broken up by a crowd of workers, clerks, and students, who then paraded to the Champs de Mars crying 'Down with Conscription!' Recruiting posters were torn down by crowds singing 'O Canada.'[205] *La Patrie* blamed the nationalist papers for denouncing recruiting and preaching sedition, and urged the adoption of censorship. Censorship was indeed established, but not often invoked. Bourassa was careful to use the statements of British public figures to support his charges. *L'Action Catholique* pointed out that the best way for French Canadians to avoid conscription was by enlistment in large numbers, and stressed the moral obligation to aid England and her allies.[206] The young men of the Groupe de l'Arche, headed by Roger Maillet, Ubald Paquin, and Olivar Asselin, made anti-conscriptionist speeches from the steps of the university. On July 26 L.-N.-J. Pagé, a barber with oratorical talent, and other popular figures made violent speeches against recruiting at the Champs de Mars. The speakers' platform was stormed by soldiers, and the police had to intervene.

But this explosive state of feeling, aroused by the threat of conscription, soon quieted down, under assurances from French-Canadian leaders that the government had no thought of conscription. On July 8 Casgrain's organ *L'Evénement* and Blondin's *Semaine* accused the nationalists of frightening the people with an imaginary danger. On July 28 Casgrain issued a statement that 'there will be no conscription,'[207] while Liberal leaders continued to back the recruiting campaign. On August 4 Rodolphe Lemieux proclaimed at Montreal that 'it is, I consider, not only a question of duty, it is a question of honour, for our sons and our brothers to enlist bravely and voluntarily in His Majesty's service.'[208] In spite of ill health the 74-year-old Laurier addressed a crowd of 8,000 at his birthplace, Saint-Lin, on August 7, stressing the double duty of the French Canadians and urging unity with the English Canadians in support of the war:

In Montreal there are to be found men who would prevent recruiting. I claim for my country the supreme honour of bearing arms in this holy cause, and if I support the government, it is because I have the heart to do my duty. . . . The fear of conscription in Canada is as groundless now as it was in 1911. . . . My fellow-countrymen, I envy you your youth and your uniform, but above all your chance to fight for such a cause. If I were a younger man, I would be in the firing line.[209]

Colonel Dansereau claimed that this speech doubled the daily rate of enlistment in his battalion. Again at Sherbrooke on August 12 Laurier urged Canadians of all origins to rally to the armed forces, and speaking particularly to French Canadians he added:

I affirm with all my strength that it is the duty of Canada to give to Great Britain in this war all the assistance that is in the power of Canada. . . .
What is the duty of our young men? If I were a young man and had the health which I have today and did not have when I was young, I would not hesitate to take the musket, and to fight for freedom, as so many of our fellow-countrymen are doing. I cannot do that now. But there is one thing I can do; I can use my voice, such as it is, in the great cause in which we all have such a supreme interest. This is the message that I bring to you upon this occasion. The peril is at present great. . . . If we want to win, we must be worthy of freedom, we have to be prepared to fight for freedom.[210]

At Napanee on September 2 he collapsed while addressing a recruiting meeting, and after an operation had to give up public appearances until late in the fall. But other Liberal leaders carried on. At Quebec City on September 8 a recruiting meeting was held under the chairmanship of the mayor, and Sir Lomer Gouin declared his belief that 'the French Canadians should be ready to do all in their power to assist the Allies.'[211] A Citizen's Recruiting League was formed in Montreal on September 17, with a French committee including Senators Dandurand, David, and Béique; Charles Beaubien, L.-T. Maréchal, Hormisdas Laporte, N.-K. Laflamme, Joseph Ainey, and Edouard Fabre-Surveyer, and others. On September 25 at Longueuil Lt.-Col. Hercule Barré, a returned veteran engaged in organizing a new battalion, urged emphatically: 'Don't sit around here and criticize . . . Get out and do something yourself. Remember that Britain is at war, Canada is at war, and you, you are at war.'[212]

Bourassa, who did not let the swelling tide of provincial feeling distract him from international events, took advantage of Pope Benedict XV's appeal for peace, as he had of the sinking of the *Lusitania* to censure England for objecting to the neutrality of merchant ships, and of Italy's entrance into the war to point out that she had acted in her own interest and not out of chivalry. The latter observation cost *Le Devoir* some windows broken by the Montreal Italians, but Bourassa's support of the Pope's plea for peace reinforced his influence with the clergy. *Le Canada* reminded Bourassa that the bishops had supported the contribution of men and money to the war, and asked whether he was trying to censure them. *La Presse* stressed that the war was accepted by the Church and that it was youth's Christian duty to rally to the colors.[213] *L'Action Catholique* began a new series of articles, warning the clergy that they would fail in their duty and injure the Church if they gave 'the least pretext to those who could question their loyalty and their attachment to the British mother country.' It urged Bourassa not 'to anticipate the Pope and the bishops in the defence of Catholic interests' and not 'to admonish those whose advice or orders he ought to take, instead of giving advice and orders to them.'[214] The hierarchy was beginning to take alarm at the evident conversion of the lower clergy to 'Bourassism' and at its silent opposition to conscription, which was beginning to attract attention in Ontario.

Olivar Asselin at once took issue with *L'Action Catholique* in a series of four articles which appeared in *L'Action* from September 11 to October 9 and were reproduced in pamphlet form, like his earlier criticisms of the ecclesiastical organ, as '*Les Evêques et la propagande de l'Action Catholique*'—'a little plea for the freedom of thought of the lower clergy and Catholic laity in political matters.'[215] He accused the 'organ of the Cardinal Archbishop of Quebec'—which fluctuated between being official and unofficial, according to circumstances—with 'seeking to make the French-Canadian bishops popular at London and at Rideau Hall,'[216] by adopting a mild attitude on the Ontario question and censuring Bourassa. Asselin attacked the editor of *L'Action Catholique*, the ex-Jesuit Abbé D'Amours, as 'one of those little jesuitical and Italian abbés such as there were four centuries ago and such as there are, alas, hardly any more left, who wield with equal cleverness the canons of the Church and the pen, and for whom no task is ever too hard, too wicked, or too vile.'[217]

Asselin asserted with his customary vigor that the Cardinal and Bishop Roy had exactly the same authority in politics as his friend Phidime Phidimous of Terrebonne—'and even a little less, since by their cloth they are less free to express their whole thought.'[218] He defended the right of the clergy to their own political opinions, and pointed out that thousands of Protestant ministers had turned their pulpits into political platforms. But he declared that the bishops had gone beyond the loyalist tradition of the Church by approving the sending of men and money overseas in 1914; that their *mandement* was an unjust interference with the rights of citizenship; and that it had paved the way for 'the avalanche of "cretinotheological" bad prose which *L'Action Catholique* had since launched upon the adversaries of the imperialist policy.'[219] He opposed Archbishop Bruchési's support of the Franco-Ontarians to *L'Action Catholique's* lukewarmness in the matter, and denied that the paper was truly the spokesman of all the bishops. He accused Bishop Roy of being its real master, with 'the ex-Jesuit d'Amours, born Damours at Trois-Pistoles'[220] as its Grey Eminence. He ended with a vigorous warning to the bishops that if *L'Action Catholique's* coursé were approved, they would lose the support of the people and the lower clergy. Asselin followed this attack up with three more articles in *L'Action* on October 24, 30, and November 6. In these he made a detailed analysis of Abbé D'Amours' editorial opinions since the outbreak of the war, and accused him of merely playing politics.

8

Borden spent the summer in Europe, trying to iron out some of the problems raised by friction between Sam Hughes and the British authorities, which had led to complaints from the governor-general. Before his departure from Canada in June the prime minister had launched a further investigation under Sir Charles Piers Davidson of Montreal into war purchases. In the company of R. B. Bennett, he crossed on the *Adriatic*, acting as a courier for the British Ambassador in the United States. In London he conferred with Sir George Perley, a member of the Canadian cabinet who had been acting as high commissioner since the beginning of the war, and New Brunswick-born Max Aitken, who played a growingly important role under the curious title of 'Canadian Eye-Witness'. Borden urged upon Bonar Law that Perley, as a member of the Canadian government, enjoyed a higher status than other dominion high commissioners, and discussed constitutional relations between the United Kingdom and the dominions. Law opposed having dominion ministers resident in London in peacetime, but said Perley's presence had been of advantage during the war. He also warned that a voice in foreign affairs for the dominions might involve higher military and naval expenditure than they cared to make, while Borden argued that population, wealth, and internal needs must be considered in such contributions.

Borden was received by the King, who praised the Canadian troops for having saved the day at Ypres, and expressed the view that the dominions should have a voice in foreign policy. From Kitchener, Borden learned that the war was expected to last a long time. He was invited to attend and take part in a cabinet meeting on July 14, the first time that a dominion representative enjoyed that privilege. He had an interview with Sir Edward Grey, and learned from other sources that the coalition government formed in May was shaky. Borden reviewed the Second Division and visited the Canadian wounded as much as possible. Then he went to France late in July, reviewing Canadian troops and visiting hospitals, before returning to England for a Privy Council meeting. He stayed with the King and Queen at Windsor, and was lunched and dined by many groups.

In an interview with Sir James Bryce, who favored giving the dominions a voice in foreign policy, Borden asserted that either they would have it or each would develop a foreign policy of its own. Finally, having vainly sought from various cabinet ministers the information which he desired about Britain's war plans, he warned Bonar Law that he would return to Canada 'with no definite intention of urging my fellow-countrymen to continue in the war work they have begun, or with the extensive preparation which I am sure they are ready to undertake if I inform them that the British Government takes the war seriously, realizes the immensity of the task, is making preparation accordingly, and there is no more cry of "Business as Usual." '[221] Having thus forced a clear picture of the situation out of Bonar Law and Lloyd George, Borden made up his mind that it would be at least eighteen months before the British Empire would be able to throw its whole force and power into the war. He so reported to his colleagues and to Laurier as leader of the opposition when he returned to Ottawa, after receiving a warm welcome at Montreal on September 3.[222]

Upon his return Borden was faced with political problems. George Foster urged a reorganization of the Militia Department so as to deprive Sam Hughes of virtually all authority, while Senator Lougheed, who had administered the department in Hughes' absence abroad, expressed the conviction that Hughes was an incapable administrator. Senator Landry and Alexandre Lacoste, father and brother-in-law of the Colonel Landry so summarily dealt with by Hughes, complained to Borden. But the latter had found Hughes useful in standing up for Canada with the War Office and Max Aitken thought well of him, so for the time being the troublesome general remained in office. Casgrain demanded a reorganization of theFrench section of the cabinet, complaining that Coderre was useless.[223] Consequently Blondin was named secretary of state and Esioff Patenaude minister of internal revenue, with Coderre retiring to the bench. Patenaude was re-elected without opposition, except from the independent Tancrède Marsil, who was disqualified on a technicality.

Patenaude and Casgrain sought vainly to arouse enthusiasm for the war with such statements as Casgrain's 'It is our war; it is my war; it is the war of everyone of us; it is the war of every man who is attached to the free British institutions under which we live.'²²⁴ Blondin and Patenaude multiplied their appeals for wholehearted support of the war during the remainder of the year at Grand' Mère, Valleyfield, Drummondville, and Nicolet, taking the view that Canada's first line of defence was in Belgium and that French Canada should not isolate itself by insisting upon its rights, which would be granted when it had done its part for the defence of the Empire. Charles Beaubien and Napoléon Garceau aided this campaign, but the words of Tories associated with the same party as the Ontario assimilators and of ex-nationalists who had once been violently anti-British had little effect on the people. Casgrain, the only French-Canadian minister who had stood by his lifelong imperialist convictions, was the only one to make the gesture of offering his military services—at the age of 63. The gesture would have had more effect if it had been made by the younger men, Blondin, Patenaude, and Sévigny; and the Liberal and nationalist papers did not hesitate to say so.

The Ontario situation grew more embroiled with the opening of the new school year. Landry had sent two memoranda to the Papal secretary of state, one in the name of the Ottawa Saint-Jean-Baptiste Society, accusing the English bishops of Ontario of persecuting the French population, and the other a personal one, drawn up in even more energetic terms. Archbishop Bruchési and Thomas Chapais accepted Casgrain's view that French intransigence would increase the difficulty of a satisfactory settlement in Ontario. At the call of Landry, the Ontario teachers refused allegiance to the new commission and consequently received no pay. Archbishop Bruchési visited Ottawa at the request of Archbishop Gauthier and urged moderation upon the Franco-Ontarians, while he besought the Ontario premier to avoid taking action against Diane and Beatrice Desloges, teachers at the Ecole Guigues, who had been barred from the school and who had opened classes in a nearby chapel. The striking teachers were aided by contributions from the French parishes of Ottawa and by gifts from Quebec. There were rumors of new restrictions upon French schools in New Brunswick which drew from even *Le Soleil* the observation that the French Canadians could not be expected to fight German tyranny, if the same tyranny was applied in Ontario and New Brunswick. In Quebec there were street rows between students and soldiers and new complaints of prejudice against French Canadians in the public services. With French Canadians everywhere in Canada in an angry mood, the recruiting campaign lagged.

Sam Hughes, who had not spared glowing tributes to the French-Canadian soldiers when he received a civic reception at Quebec on September 14 upon his return from England, decided upon a gesture towards Quebec which misfired. In October he offered the command of a battalion to Armand Lavergne, who was to raise it himself. Lavergne refused the offer in an open letter to Hughes, printed in *Le Devoir* on November 2:

. . . I have always opposed, in the press and on the platform in the provinces of Quebec and Ontario, all Canadian participation in foreign wars, save for the defence of our territory.

Since I have been in public life, that has always been the well-known policy of the nationalist party to which I belong and I have seen the same principles shared and defended forcibly by several of your cabinet colleagues, such as M. Monk, who remained faithful to them until his death, and MM. L.-P. Pelletier, Bruno Nantel, Louis Coderre, and the new Minister of the Interior, M. Patenaude.

To accept your flattering offer and induce my compatriots to enlist for the present war would be to disavow myself, for which you, with your high sense of honor, would blame me.

Let me repeat to you here that I consider it unwise and even criminal to put Canada in danger for a war over which we have not had and will not have any control. I am opposed to, and shall oppose with all my strength, the contribution of a man, a ship, or a dollar until England believes she must share with us not only the dangers, but also the full control and responsibility of the Empire's affairs. It is not for us to defend England, but for England to defend us . . .

I bring you another reason. My compatriots of French origin in Ontario, Canadians like you, sir, are now undergoing a regime worse than that imposed by the Prussians in Alsace-Lorraine, because they do not wish to abandon their mother tongue. Until they have been completely freed of this persecution, I cannot consider for an instant the idea of deserting their cause for a somewhat interesting adventure in a foreign country. I wish to see the reign of liberty and justice well established and maintained in our country, before imposing it upon other nations . . .[225]

Lavergne explained his stand at a public meeting on November 7 in Blondin's county of Champlain. It was approved by the nationalists, cited as clear proof of French disloyalty in Toronto, and accepted by Hughes as that of 'a man of honor' who 'had the same right to his opinions as everyone.'[226]

Lavergne himself had written Asselin on November 3 that he expected conscription, at least for militia officers, within six months, and 'we then can combine the taste of adventure, our principles, and *douce France* . . . I have faith that the future and circumstances will enable me to clear myself of an accusation which may seem founded until then. If this chance is refused me, I shall still believe that one owes everything to one's country, even honor.'[227] Lavergne's gesture focused English-Canadian attention on French

Canada's growing reluctance to support the war effort whole-heartedly. As a result patriotic French Canadians redoubled their efforts in order to clear Quebec's name. It was at this time that Casgrain offered his military services and that the other French-Canadian ministers undertook a speaking campaign in favor of recruiting. One priest, Abbé Tetreau of Drummondville, joined in this campaign, but the great majority of the lower clergy were opposed to enlistment. They had been converted to anti-imperialism by Bourassa, and they saw a danger to the faith of young men who left their homes for military camps and foreign service.

During October and November Borden conferred with Laurier about extending the life of parliament, which expired on October 7, 1916. He proposed that it should be extended until one year after the conclusion of peace, to avoid a general election during the war and to allow time for the men overseas to return home. In the mean-time there was to be a suspension of party warfare. As an alternative to this proposal, Borden suggested an extension of one year. Laurier favored the latter scheme as more definite, but insisted on being informed about Borden's legislative plans, particularly as regarded the railroads. The negotiations broke down because of Laurier's insistence that 'The Canadian Parliament cannot be expected to abdicate its functions.'[228]

During Laurier's illness Rodolphe Lemieux had borne the brunt of backing recruiting as the acting Liberal leader; but on December 9 Laurier and the whole Liberal high command appeared before a packed audience at the Monument National in support of the war effort. In war as in peace, Laurier said, the Liberals stood for the cause of the weak and oppressed, for justice and liberty, and in opposition to absolutism. To the extreme attitudes of the im-perialists who wanted Canada to fight in all wars and called for conscription, and of the nationalists who would fight in no war, he opposed the Liberal doctrine of voluntary participation in a noble cause, reserving Canada's autonomy. He censured the doctrine that Canada should only defend her own soil: 'For a noble cause, we must do more than our duty.'[229] He was happy to see France and England united on the battlefield, but the *entente cordiale* was not yet complete in Canada: 'They who have real patriotism are they who are working for reconciliation, who are helping to sweep away the old divisions, who are working to restore harmony among the people on a basis acceptable to all.'[230] After the war, when the soldiers of both races had mingled their blood on the battlefields, the majority would surely do justice to its com-panions in arms.

But Bourassa continued to link persecution in Ontario with the question of participation in the war, and Lavergne's stand, that

Quebec should not support the latter until the former ceased, found wide favor with French Canadians. On December 16 Bourassa gave a lecture at the Monument National on 'Cartier, Macdonald, and Our Military Obligations,' in which he concluded that Canada had no military obligations outside its territory. Simultaneously he put on sale a book, *Que devons-nous à l'Angleterre?*, which was an extensive historical and legal development of this thesis. He pointed out how the Fathers of Confederation and the imperial authorities had agreed to limit the new dominion's military obligations to defence of Canadian territory. This agreement had been observed until the development of imperialism at the time of the South African War:

This was for Canada a very clear backward step. Laurier, chief of the Canadian government, resisted instinctively. Then, under the double pressure from London and Toronto, his resistance weakened. And we had successively the African expedition, the Navy Act of 1910, the 'emergency contribution' of 1912, and participation in the present war as a dependency of England. So many breaches in the established order, so many knife-blows in the treaties concluded between Great Britain and Canada, so many illegal, unconstitutional measures. Until the agreements of 1867 are broken by mutual consent, England has no right to impose such obligations upon us.[231]

Bourassa's book had a rapid sale, but the press protested against his conclusions. *Le Canada* regretted to 'find him in direct rebellion against the religious and civil authorities of his country,' and advanced the thesis that 'to go and attack the enemy where he could be conquered was to defend Canada, and it is ridiculous to pretend that we must wait until he comes to land on our shores.'[232] The *Daily Mail* accused Bourassa of preaching 'treason to the Empire and to the Sovereign.'[233] The Ontario press demanded prosecution of 'Herr Bourassa.' Principal Peterson of McGill did the same, accusing Bourassa of sowing disunion and hindering recruiting.[234] Unquestionably Bourassa did hinder recruiting, for many of his followers drew no other conclusion from his elaborate anti-imperialist arguments than that they should not enlist. Bourassa was not dismayed by the storm of abuse which greeted him; on December 23 he urged the government 'to cease to send Canadians to the butchery so long as the English workers do not decide to yield to the humble plea of the imperial authorities and to furnish the Empire's soldiers with the arms and munitions which they absolutely need to fight under reasonable conditions.'[235]

One of Bourassa's most notable followers, Olivar Asselin, had meanwhile decided to enlist. In his reply to Lavergne, under whom he had offered to serve when he learned of Hughes' offer, Asselin had stated his belief that 'the man who wishes to serve as a soldier in France—or England—and who because of his poverty or for other reasons can do so only in the Canadian Expeditionary Force, can very well enlist without thus approving the official participation of Canada in the European conflict in Europe.'²³⁶ He approved Lavergne's stand as reasonable, but said that as for himself, 'If I wish to go, it is because I should rather die than see France conquered and powerless.' He added: 'I sometimes think that the greatest need of our race is still to learn to despise life, when necessary; not to attach itself too much to well-being, to purely material comfort; to be hard on itself, and to be prodigal, on occasion, of its blood. . . . I wish that we were in our manner Spartans, not Nazarenes who turn the other cheek like slaves.'

Three new Quebec battalions, including a French-Canadian one, the 150th, under Lt.-Col. Hercule Barré, wounded veteran of the 14th Battalion, had been authorized in November. Asselin now undertook to raise another, the 163rd, refusing the colonelcy offered by Sam Hughes and contenting himself with the rank of major, while securing the command of the battalion for Henri DesRosiers, a former lieutenant of the 14th. Asselin had no wish to class himself with some of Hughes' honorary colonels whose military exploits were confined to recruiting speeches.

His nationalist friends were at a loss to explain Asselin's action, but at a public meeting at the Monument National on January 21, 1916 he revealed his reasons in a speech which was later printed as *Pourquoi je m'enrôle*. He revealed that as early as October 30, 1914, he had sought through Philippe Roy, the Canadian Commissioner in Paris, to enlist in the French army, and failing that, to secure an administrative job to replace a soldier.²³⁷ In the early spring of 1915 he had tried through Casgrain, Fiset, and Sam Hughes to obtain a post as interpreter with the 22nd Battalion or with any other Canadian, British, or French unit. When Barré sought permission to raise a French-Canadian unit, Asselin had asked to serve as a lieutenant under him. He maintained that while condemning the government's policy, he had always admitted the right of the individual Canadian to serve voluntarily in the war. He took up the question of whether the French Canadians were doing their duty, and cited such heroes as Desrosiers, DeSerres, Roy, and others. He pointed out that 90 per cent of the French Canadians of military age could not hope for advancement in the army because English was the only language of command, and that even in the French-Canadian units the highest ranks would be barred to them. He also pointed out that the French Canadians were more attached to Canada than those who had more recently emigrated from Europe. He criticized the fact that so few decorations had been given to the 8,000 French-Canadian soldiers whose fighting qualities had been praised so highly by Sam Hughes and General Meighen. He did not believe that the Ontario situation would improve if French Canada furnished several more battalions, and he did not withdraw his censure of the pro-war attitude taken by the hierarchy.[238]

But aside from all these considerations, he thought British institutions, Belgium, and France worth fighting for. He, like Péguy, was a man of 1793 and gloried in it, and had not been as shocked by modern France as most of his compatriots. But he asserted that the world could not get along without France, which after the war would be more necessary than ever to humanity. He added that the French of America could remain French only through France. He summed up his reasons for enlisting thus:

And so we march for British institutions, because by themselves and independently of the half-civilized persons who apply them today in Ontario, they are worth fighting for.

And we march for Belgium, because in this war she incarnates violated justice, the scorned liberty of small peoples.

And we march for France, because her defeat, while marking a regression of the world towards barbarism, would condemn us, her children of America, to drag out henceforward diminished lives.[239]

He called for a rehabilitation of the French Canadians in their own eyes by fighting, after 'the epoch of capitulations' from 1873 to 1911. Asselin's reasons were too personal to convince many of his followers, and those who listened to him quietly prevented Rodolphe Lemieux from speaking by cries of 'Enlist!' Lemieux came equipped with letters endorsing Asselin's effort from Borden, Laurier, and Sam Hughes[240]—strange supporters for a nationalist whose ardor had once surpassed Bourassa's.

Asselin's unit was but one of a number of French-Canadian ones authorized by Hughes in an effort to overcome Quebec's reluctance to enlist. Lt.-Col. Onésime Readman of Lévis was charged with raising the 167th, and Lt.-Col. P.-A. Piuze of the lower St. Lawrence the 189th, Lt.-Col. Tancrède Pagnuelo of Montreal the 206th, and Lt.-Col. René de Salaberry of Hull the 230th. Sir William Price undertook, with the aid of Onésiphore Talbot and Thomas Vien, to raise a mixed French and English battalion, the 171st, in Quebec; while Lt.-Col. L.-J. Gilbert sought to raise the 117th in the Townships, Lt.-Col. A. A. Magee the 148th at Montreal, and Lt.-Col. H. J. Trihey the 199th (Irish Canadian Rangers) at Montreal. But recruiting went slowly, particularly in the rural districts, and none of these battalions reached full strength.

In all, eleven French-Canadian battalions had been authorized. The 22nd was in France, with the 41st acting as its depot battalion in England. The 57th remained at Quebec, but had furnished reinforcements to the 41st. Colonel Dansereau's 69th sailed for England in April, while Colonel Barré's 150th went to Nova Scotia for further training. Colonel Piuze met with fair success in raising the 189th in the lower St. Lawrence region, and Asselin labored valiantly to fill the ranks of the 163rd. Most of the other colonels failed to raise the necessary number of recruits, and their battalions remained skeleton units in which discipline was lacking. French Canada remained more concerned with the battle for cultural survival in Ontario than with the course of the war in Europe.

9

The school question was now indeed a battle. The two Desloges sisters had been reinstalled in their classrooms at the Ecole Guigues in Ottawa by an army of women, who mounted guard over the school with hatpins as weapons, defying all efforts at interference from the authorities. Bourassa came to Ottawa to speak in a parish hall under the auspices of the A.C.J.C. on January 4, 1916, linking conservation of the French language with conservation of Catholicism, and praising the heroism of the Franco-Ontarians. Philippe Landry called upon Quebec to continue its support during the new year. He sought vainly during January to arrange a meeting of the French-Canadian ministers with Doherty, the minister of justice, and Fitzpatrick, the chief justice of the Supreme Court.

Bourassa mentioned the Ontario question at the sixth anniversary dinner of Le Devoir on January 12, and predicted the triumph of the minority. Then he turned to the question of imperialism, linking his anti-imperialism with the defence of Catholicism against Anglo-Protestant agnosticism. He asserted his conviction that he was in accord not only with the political tradition, but with the religious tradition of Canada. He pointed out that the French Canadians were the best insurance against the annexation of Canada to the United States, and concluded: 'We love France, we admire England; but we believe that our first duty is to the homeland where God ordained we should be born, where six generations link us to the land.'[241] This utterance followed by a few days another statement by Archbishop Bruchési strongly supporting the Canadian war policy and observing 'There has not been conscription, there is still no question of it in the country, and I hope there never will be question of it.'[242] A student journal, L'Escholier, edited by Jean Chauvin, protested strongly:

Monseigneur has said: 'You must enlist, it is your sacred duty to participate in this war.' Monseigneur, we do not believe you. It is not a question of dogma, a truth of religion, an article of morality.[243]

Lavergne also expressed the same attitude at the *Devoir* banquet when he refused to aid the English: 'Not a man, not a penny, not a cannon, until you concede to Canada the right to be represented in the councils of the Empire. . . . If someone wishes to make me undergo a trial for treason, I am ready for it!' And in reply to the threats against Bourassa Lavergne said: 'Let them come and arrest Bourassa if they dare! . . . I have in my county 3,000 farmers ready to protect him with their lives.'[244] Lavergne was just as vigorous the following day in the provincial legislature, asserting that Canada owed nothing to England and the French Canadians had no duty to enlist:

If we must conquer our liberties, it is here we should stay. It is not in the trenches of Flanders that we shall win the right to speak French in Ontario, if we have not been able to obtain it here, we who saved Canada for England when the English merchants of Quebec fled to the Island of Orleans. . . . I say, and I am not afraid to have my words repeated anywhere, that every French Canadian who enlists fails to do his duty. I know that what I say is high treason. I may be thrown into gaol tomorrow, but I don't care. . . . They tell us it is a question of defending liberty and humanity, but that is nothing less than a farce. If the Germans are persecutors, there are worse than Germans at our very gates. I'll go further. I'll say that every cent that is spent in Quebec to aid enlistment of men is money stolen from the minority in Ontario. . . . I am not afraid to become a German subject. I ask myself whether the German regime might not be favorably compared with that of the Boches of Ontario.[245]

Lavergne's outburst was greeted with silence, and followed by a vigorous plea from L.-A. Taschereau that French Canadians should enlist. Tellier called Lavergne a rebel and *Le Soleil* endorsed the Conservative leader's remark. *La Presse* published so hostile an account of the speech that Lavergne brought suit. The English press demanded that Lavergne be cashiered from the militia, and a Toronto minister devoted his sermon the following Sunday to the pious topic: 'Should Armand Lavergne be hung for high treason?'[246] Again on January 17 Lavergne declared that Conservative leaders had in the past expressed nationalist views similar to his, and that monuments had been built to such 'rebels' as Papineau and Lafontaine. Sam Hughes refused to deprive Lavergne of his militia rank, on the ground that militia officers had the right of free speech when not on active service, but the Garrison Club of Quebec did expel him.

When parliament met on January 12, Sévigny replaced Dr. Sproule as speaker. Laurier taunted him with rapid conversion from his extreme nationalist views of 1911, but assured him of support in his new office. Borden defended the increase of the armed forces and announced that the government did not intend to adopt conscription. He reported on his English visit, and proposed that parliament's life should be extended for a year. Laurier agreed to the proposal, and announced that he would support all the government's war measures, but 'to all wrongs, to all frauds, we shall offer determined opposition.'[247] Bourassa protested against this joint agreement 'to promote the cooperation of Canada in the defence of the Empire,' and asserted: 'The truth is that Canada, with more motives to be careful of its strength, has already made more sacrifices than any other country of the Empire, and that apparently these sacrifices will remain without any compensation.'[248] Both Laurier and Casgrain attacked the nationalists and belittled their significance. Casgrain urged that Quebec should not be judged 'by the dreams and exaggerations of a little group of men who have been led astray.'[249] Lemieux asserted that Bourassa no more represented popular opinion in Quebec than Bernard Shaw did that of England. In the Senate, however, Choquette criticized participation in the war and particularly the stepping-up of recruiting. Belcourt, Bolduc, Dandurand, and J.-P.-B. Casgrain censured their colleague, while the *Mail and Empire* called for his expulsion from the Senate. The *Toronto Telegram* classified all French Canadians as disloyal, lumping Bourassa, Lavergne, Choquette, and Laurier together. Ernest Lapointe assured the Commons that Choquette did not represent Liberal opinion, and blamed the poor recruiting results in Quebec on the anti-French-Canadian campaign of the Ontario press, rather than on the nationalists.

The ever-mounting indignation of Quebec over the Ontario school question made itself felt both at Ottawa and Quebec. The French-Canadian *curés* of Ottawa refused to transmit to their parishes an appeal for the Patriotic Fund, pointing out that their parishioners' savings were being exhausted to keep the bilingual schools going. At Sainte-Agathe a *curé* interrupted a recruiting meeting by raising the Ontario school question. The A.C.J.C. held a meeting in honor of the Franco-Ontarians at the Monument National two days after Asselin's recruiting meeting there. Bourassa was unable to be present because of illness, but the presidents of the A.C.J.C. and of the Saint-Jean-Baptiste Society promised to continue their support of the Ontario struggle, and Philippe Landry moved the crowd with his account of Ottawa mothers guarding the doors of the schools in midwinter. On the same day, at a dinner in support of the Patriotic Fund, Archbishop Bruchési thus explained the Ontario difficulties to an audience largely made up of wealthy English Canadians:

What is the basic situation? Two hundred thousand men, proud of their title of British subjects, faithful to their king and country, making it a point of honor to speak English, simply ask to speak also the tongue of their ancestors, the beautiful and sweet French language, and to teach it freely to their children. That is all. The answer belongs to men of goodwill. [250]

On January 25 in the provincial legislature Alexandre Taschereau asserted Quebec's willingness to give its sons and its resources generously to the Allies, but maintained that it was becoming 'profoundly tired and impatient' [251] of the failure of Ontario to pay heed to the message sent last year on the motion of one of its English representatives. Taschereau's observation won long applause. A few days later the *Quebec Chronicle*, managed by Brigadier Watson who commanded the brigade which included the 22nd, urged settlement of the Ontario school question in the name of British fair play. Earlier, J. C. Scott, a Quebec contractor, had paid tribute to the French Canadians in a letter to the *Mail and Empire*, which had been reprinted in the *Chronicle* along with another approving it by J. C. Sutherland, the inspector-general of Protestant schools in Quebec.

But Ontario was unmoved by these interventions, particularly since the man in the street had the notion that the French Canadians wished to impose the study of French upon English-speaking students. The new Ottawa School Commission got control of the school funds, and vainly sought to install its own teachers in schools guarded night and day by embattled mothers. On January 31, 3,000 separate school children, presented themselves at the Ottawa City Hall and presented an address to the mayor, petitioning for the payment of their teachers from the school taxes held by the corporation.

Bourassa was accused of being responsible for this demonstration, and in the House Orangemen called for his arrest and the suppression of *Le Devoir*. Dr. Edwards proposed exchanging Bourassa and Lavergne for Dr. Béland, who had been held prisoner in Germany since the outbreak of the war. In an anti-imperialist speech on February 1 Paul-Emile Lamarche defended his compatriots as merely advocating the doctrine that Canada's obligation was confined to the defence of her own territory, a doctrine which had been supported in the past by both parties and was based on the constitution. When interrupted by former nationalists, Lamarche replied to them thus: 'If it is true, Mr. Speaker, that two of my compatriots deserve to be put up against a wall and shot, I ask equal justice for all. It is just that their accomplices should undergo the same punishment.' [252] The 'accomplices' were the twenty Quebec

z

members elected on the nationalist platform in 1911 who provided the government with its majority. Charles Marcil followed him with a plea for English-Canadian generosity towards the Ontario schools, if only to help recruiting in Quebec. On February 11 the school children paraded to parliament, then sitting in the Victoria Museum as a result of the fire which had destroyed the Parliament Buildings, and presented petitions to Borden and Laurier. Four M.P.'s, Achim, Boulay, Lamarche, and Paquet, spoke at a meeting in the St. Anne Parish Hall on February 14.

The following day the third congress of the *Association d'Education* opened, with the three French-Canadian bishops of Ontario present. Bishop Beliveau said that the Franco-Ontarians were asking only for their rights, and would continue to do so until the flag of justice flew over the schools. Bishop Latulipe told how he had gone to Rome to explain the school question, and how the Pope and the cardinals had agreed with his views. He denounced Regulation 17 as 'a monument of iniquity and injustice.' Bishop Charlebois called Senator Landry the 'Joffre of Ontario.'²⁵³ Landry, Belcourt, and Genest also spoke, announcing their plans to obtain federal disavowal of the Ontario law and to boycott Ontario products. Bourassa likened the heroic school teachers to Joan of Arc.

Quebec sought new means to aid her compatriots in Ontario. Bishop Blais of Rimouski ordered a special collection in his diocese for the cause. The municipalities wanted to contribute, but could not do so without authority from the provincial legislature. Antonin Galipeault prepared a bill to that effect, while Lavergne intervened in a debate on the Montreal Bill, which permitted that city to contribute to the Patriotic Fund, and urged the substitution of a measure permitting it to contribute to the Ontario schools. Lavergne was censured for his criticism of the Patriotic Fund by Gouin and Taschereau, who announced that Galipeault's bill would permit all municipalities to contribute to the Ontario struggle. The Conservative leader Cousineau objected that the English minority would be irritated by the French majority's voting of public funds for the purpose; and as a result of his intervention, the permission to contribute was transferred from municipalities to school commissions, which were exclusively French-Canadian. The Assembly then approved the bill unanimously. Montreal gave $5,000, and other towns contributed according to their means.

This Quebec development aroused new indignation in Ontario, and Mayor Thomas Church of Toronto observed that Quebec would do better to send more soldiers to the war. In Manitoba and Saskatchewan further restrictions on the teaching of French were urged, with John Dafoe crusading in the *Free Press* for a Manitoba Regulation 17 and with the government withdrawing the privileges of the Laurier-Greenway Agreement. In Manitoba Judge Prendergast headed an organization to defend the French schools, at the request of Bishop Beliveau. *Le Devoir* foresaw 'a grave danger for the future of Confederation,' and asked whether the 'Boches of Ontario and Manitoba would suspend the war they wage on our language' because of the lives sacrificed by the 22nd.[254]

The Ontario situation grew daily more tense. On February 22 no less than five public meetings were held in Ottawa, with French-Canadian M.P.'s from Quebec and the Maritimes as well as Ontario appearing on the platform. Two days later Casgrain and Blondin presented a Franco-Ontarian delegation to Borden, who promised to consider transmitting their petition to the Ontario government. Having avoided an encounter with a delegation of 5,000 persons by insisting upon receiving only a committee of twelve, Borden returned the petition to its sponsors two days later.[255] The A.C.J.C. circulated in Quebec a petition for federal disavowal. Mgr. Paquet of Laval supported the struggle on Thomistic principles. Abbé Groulx, who had inaugurated a new chair of French-Canadian history at Laval of Montreal with a course on '*Nos luttes constitutionnelles*,' [256] tracing the struggle for cultural survival from 1760–1867, drew a large and enthusiastic audience for a lecture on educational liberty, which was attended by Archbishop Bruchési. Bishop Larocque of Sherbrooke issued a circular calling for a special collection in his diocese for the Ontario cause. A Quebec boycott of Ontario manufacturers began to make itself felt, with the great Toronto mail order houses of Eaton's and Simpson's finding their catalogues returned unopened.

Borden managed to postpone a raising of the school question in the House by Charles Marcil, while Laurier contented himself with defending the cause privately among his English-Canadian followers. But in the House Lemieux called for justice and generosity to the Franco-Ontarians, and Roch Lanctôt flatly coupled the question of recruiting and the schools. In answer to the charges of the Ontario press that the French Canadians were not enlisting in sufficient numbers, Lanctôt replied: 'I find that too many of them enlist, considering the treatment which is inflicted upon them in the school question by the majority of this country.'[257] He was supported in this view by Calixte Ethier.

In the face of this united support of the Franco-Ontarians, the *Mail and Empire* denounced French-Canadian 'aggression' at a time when 'all the citizens of Canada should be united against the common enemy.' The *Montreal Star* took issue with its Toronto colleague on the grounds that the French Canadians were assaulted, not aggressors, and added: 'If the Ontario government had not, by the unjust and ungenerous suppression of the educational privileges of the French Canadians, created a profound discontent among the Quebec majority, there would be no cause to complain of recruiting in this province.'[258] Ex-Mayor Andrews of Winnipeg supported this view in a letter to the *Winnipeg Telegram*; while Sir Joseph Pope sent a new letter to the *Ottawa Citizen* criticizing the attitude of the Ontario government as playing into the hands of Bourassa and Lavergne, as did E. R. Cameron, clerk of the Supreme Court. W. H. Moore presented the case for the Franco-Ontarians in the *Canadian Courier*, and J. J. Foran supported it on the platform. But in general the Ontario press, led by the *Toronto News*, continued to refuse any concession to the 'ignorant French,' and proclaimed that Ontario was an English province and would remain so.

On March 2 Bourassa began an important series of six weekly lectures on Canadian policy, which were later published in pamphlet form as '*Hier, aujourd'hui et demain.*' In the first he discussed the principles of the British and Canadian constitutions and pointed out that in the past Canada's political and religious leaders had rejected participation in foreign wars. In the second he discussed the 'imperialist revolution' since the South African War, stressing the fact that his anti-imperialism was a reaction against this development. In the third and fourth he dealt with Canadian participation in the present war, saying that a crusade for France and Belgium could wait until French-Canadian rights were won at home. In a later letter to a French correspondent, published in *Le Devoir* on June 23 when his lectures appeared in printed form, Bourassa expressed more clearly his opinion of the official appeal to come to the aid of France:

We have here a little coterie of Tory and imperialist priests who invoke the interests of religion in order to serve the ends of England and of the Canadian imperialists. These same people also exploit the French-Canadians' love of France, after having denounced her for years as the most impious and corrupt country in the world. It is to this coterie that are particularly addressed the pages devoted to the argument of religion and the episcopal tradition in Canada.[259]

In the fourth lecture Bourassa predicted the dire economic, social, and political consequences to be expected from the war. In the fifth he discussed the possible solutions: independence, imperial federation, or annexation, with independence 'the only true solution of the problem of our destinies.'[260] In the sixth, dealing with Canada's foreign relations, he urged a defensive alliance with the United States as less costly than the British connection. The whole thesis was argued with his customary mastery of historical and legal argument, and his usual eloquence. It offered much food for discussion by the élite; the people gathered from it merely that Bourassa was opposed to enlistment.

During March, while the Canadian troops suffered heavy losses in the Ypres salient, enlistments began to decline. On March 14 Brigadier James Mason, a Conservative senator, presented in parliament an analysis of the recruiting situation and called for national registration or conscription. His figures, compiled with the aid of the census and the military authorities, showed that 249,000 men out of a total of 1,500,000 of military age had enlisted. He estimated that 63 per cent of the recruits were British-born, 30 per cent Canadian-born, and the remaining 7 per cent foreign-born. Of the Canadian-born he estimated that 85,000 (28.5 per cent of the total enlisted) were English-speaking, while 12,000 (4.5 per cent of the total enlisted) were French-speaking. The French Canadians, who constituted 40 per cent of the population of military age, had thus supplied only 4.5 per cent of the recruits. But Brigadier Mason was careful to point out that the native-born of both races were not doing their full duty, and urged adoption of the English Derby scheme of national registration to determine whether men could best serve the country in the army or in industry, coupled with an urgent appeal for volunteers for active service.[261] He added: 'There can be no question that the additional 250,000 to bring our quota up to 500,000 and the 300,000, if required, annually to keep it at that figure, will not be obtained under the present system of enlistment.'[262] Lord Shaughnessy, head of the Canadian Pacific, had already publicly stated on March 9 in the presence of Sam Hughes that he believed the raising of an army of 500,000 was impracticable when more than 300,000 were already employed in war industry, and many were needed in agriculture to 'help feed the British nation.' He urged: 'We must go slowly about recruiting, and carry out the best plans for the country in a sane, methodical and business-like way.'[263]

With enlistments particularly heavy among clerical and manual workers, business and industry began to take the attitude that no more of their men could be spared; and through the Canadian Manufacturers' Association they pressed for a plan of national service. These developments tended to confirm French-Canadian belief in Bourassa's view that Canada had already done too much, and henceforward should concentrate on sending supplies rather than men overseas. Recruiting slumped in Quebec, but it also slumped throughout Canada, and only 127,000 men were enlisted between January 1 and June 1, 1916. On a proportional basis, Quebec had raised only one-quarter her share, the Maritimes only one-half and Ontario seven-ninths, while the Western provinces had exceeded their shares. Quebec, of course, had much the lowest proportion of

British-born men of military age.[264] The factors that caused the recruiting decline all over Canada were the exhaustion of the supply of British-born volunteers, and the demands of industry and agriculture for manpower to meet the war boom. In Quebec indignation over the Ontario school question was an added major factor, supplemented by the opposition of the rural clergy to enlistment.

10

Landry and his colleagues now sought publicly to win the concessions which they had previously pursued through private channels. The Ontario government refused a renewed offer of a truce until the Privy Council had rendered its decision on Regulation 17 in the MacBell and Ottawa Separate School Board cases. Landry spoke under the auspices of the A.C.J.C. at meetings organized to gain signatures for the petition for disavowal. Senator Pope censured him for organizing and speaking at 'seditious assemblies.' Choquette defended him, and the wonted calm of the Senate was broken by an angry dispute. Archbishop Bruchési, once so moderate, compared the Franco-Ontario resistance to that of the French on the Marne. Bishop Larocque of Sherbrooke and Bishop Ross of Rimouski supported Landry's appearances in Quebec. A few English Canadians expressed sympathy with the cause. Dr. Finnie urged a peace favorable to the Franco-Ontarians in a Montreal Reform Club speech, while his colleague W. S. Bullock proposed the suspension of Regulation 17. The Canadian Club of Quebec invited Senator Belcourt to expound the bilingual question, and applauded and approved him. John S. Ewart wrote a letter to the *Ottawa Journal* supporting the legal rights of French in Ontario. But on April 2 the Ontario Supreme Court rejected the Franco-Ontarians' appeal, which now went to the Privy Council.

From mid-March to mid-April the seventy-year-old Landry journeyed back and forth between Quebec and Franco-Ontarian centers, pleading his case eloquently despite the rigors of travel at this season which wore out his younger collaborators. He sought the support of the Quebec bishops for the petition in favor of disavowal. But Casgrain and Thomas Chapais persuaded Archbishop Bruchési that the French language had little legal standing outside Quebec and that a disavowal would produce a sharp conflict between the federal government and the Ontario one, with the latter subsequently renewing its stand without a legal basis. Bishop Emard of Valleyfield and Bishop Gauthier, the Montreal auxiliary, followed Archbishop Bruchési in adopting the alternative policy of appealing to the governor-general.

It was known that Paul-Emile Lamarche intended to raise the question in the House. Laurier, who so far had stood officially apart from the question, proposed a conference at the rectory of his Ottawa pastor, the Abbé Myrand, with Belcourt, Lemieux, Lapointe, Lamarche, Patenaude, and Landry on April 6. Laurier foresaw the danger of provoking the English Protestant majority by a request for intervention in provincial affairs, which someday might serve as a precedent for action against the French Catholic minority. He proposed that a resolution should be offered in the House, appealing to the goodwill of the Ontario legislature. The interview was inconclusive. Meanwhile Landry presented to the secretary of state a request for disavowal signed by all the French-Canadian bishops except Archbishop Bruchési, and Bishops Emard and Gauthier. Casgrain, Blondin, and Patenaude put pressure on Borden to intervene with the Ontario government, which replied that any government yielding to the French Canadians would lose power in twenty-four hours. Then, on April 22, the three French-Canadian ministers presented a long request for an examination of the whole language question by the Privy Council, accompanied by a threat not to attend cabinet meetings until satisfaction was obtained. Borden, pressed by the English members of his cabinet, refused the request, and put pressure on the French ministers to remain in office in order to avoid a 'national calamity.'[265] Blondin yielded first, followed by Patenaude, and finally Casgrain, after a week of secret cabinet crisis.

Meanwhile Choquette had set the Senate raging once more by announcing that it was a crime to enlist young farmers, and by reading a letter from Robert Hazelton of Ontario, to the effect that the British-born volunteers were a crowd of undesirables. The Tory journals declared that Choquette expressed Laurier's views, but Laurier replied in the House that he did not share them and that the Senator spoke only for himself. When the *Globe* refused to publish Choquette's corrections of its account, the senator made them in the Senate, renewing his protests against overzealous recruiting. In this troubled atmosphere Landry presented to the government the petition for disavowal, signed by 600,000 persons. Doherty, the minister of justice, decided that the question should be settled by the courts, after the precedents of the New Brunswick school question of 1872, the Manitoba one of 1890, and the North-West ordinances of 1892. His commentaries indicated a preference for the Ontario government's thesis.[266] All the Ottawa bilingual schools were now closed. Senator Belcourt, as a large Ottawa taxpayer, initiated a movement to refuse to pay school taxes to the new commission.

With Quebec on the eve of provincial elections, Bourassa announcing his return to federal politics, and Lavergne resigning from the provincial legislature for the same purpose, the Ontario school

question at last came before the House of Commons. Landry had
sought to get the French-Canadian ministers to present a resolution,
and in the face of their refusal had turned to Borden himself, warning
that he would have recourse to Laurier if turned down. Borden
advised him that Laurier, torn between his English and French
followers, would do nothing, nor would he. But on May 8 Laurier
warned Borden that Ernest Lapointe would introduce such a
resolution, and overrode Borden's objections on the grounds that he
himself was alarmed by conditions in Quebec and that he must have
'some sheet anchor with which to fight Nationalists.'[267]

On the following day Lapointe introduced the following resolution:

That this House, especially in this time of universal sacrifices and
anxiety, when all energies should be concentrated on the winning of the
war, would, while fully recognizing the principle of provincial rights and
the necessity of every child being given a thorough knowledge of English
education, respectfully suggests to the Legislative Assembly of the
province of Ontario the wisdom of making it clear that the privilege of
the children of French parentage of being taught in their mother tongue
be not interfered with.[268]

He was supported by Emmanuel Devlin, after Borden had sought
to avoid debate by invoking a point of order. Laurier refused
Borden's appeal:

Let us discuss this question like free men, like British subjects. Out of
this discussion will come a more complete knowledge of the situation and
of the rights of the minority in this country, and the minority, of which
I am a part, will accept the settlement that is proposed, if this settlement
is reasonable.[269]

Before the debate opened on May 10, the Conservative and Liberal
spokesmen of Ontario affirmed the uselessness of all federal intervention: Regulation 17 was untouchable. Lapointe appealed to
Ontario's sense of justice and generosity rather than making a legal
or constitutional argument. He closed in the tradition of Laurier:

My greatest desire is that this resolution and that this discussion, instead
of dividing more profoundly the two races of this country, should bring
them closer together and cement their union for the defence of liberty
based upon law. I ask my compatriots to proclaim with Gladstone the
equality of the weak and the strong. We ought to try and impregnate
Canadian public spirit with high and generous sentiments; we should
protect the rights of all citizens, and above all, raise on this Canadian
soil a solid wall against the attacks of violence and prejudice. To reach
this goal, we should ask our fellow citizens to make concessions, to respect

the opinions of others. And I hope that in this fashion we shall succeed in creating the harmony so necessary to the well being of the nation and of the individuals who compose it.[270]

Borden made a constitutional argument against the resolution, quoting Blake and Laurier's statements against federal interference with provincial legislation, and warning Quebec of the danger of encouraging federal interference with education. He thought the resolution would do mischief: 'It can hardly fail to intensify feelings already sufficiently aroused and to strain the relations between the two great races in this country.' He asserted that 'no one is more anxious than I am that these good relations should be maintained and improved,' and in the interests of the country as a whole and particularly of Quebec he called for rejection of the resolution.[271]

Laurier made one of his great speeches in reply, recalling the constitutional rights of the French language but appealing particularly to the spirit of justice, 'not of the justice which clings to the cold letter of the law, but the justice which rests in the heart of every man, whatever his nationality.' He did not question Ontario's right to pass final judgment on the question, and did not propose to advise or admonish that province:

I rise to plead before the people of Ontario, in behalf of His Majesty's subjects of French origin in that province, who complain that by reason of a statute passed by the province they have been deprived of rights in the matter of education which they have enjoyed themselves and their forefathers before them, ever since Canada became a possession of the British Crown. . . .

I know there is in the province of Ontario a sense of irritation at the position taken by some of my fellow-countrymen of French blood in the province of Quebec, who have from the first deprecated the participation of Canada in the present war, and who have exerted their influence to attempt at least to prevent enlistment. Alas, it is true; it is only too true. It is deplorable, and to me as unintelligible as it is deplorable. It is true, alas, that there are in my province men of French origin who, when France is fighting the fight of heroism which stirs the blood of mankind, remain with their blood cold, who tell us: 'No, we will not lift a finger to assist Britain in defending the integrity of France, but we want our wrongs to be righted in Ontario.'

Wrongs or no wrongs, there is a field of honour; there is a call of duty.

Sir, I am not prepared to say that my fellow-countrymen of French origin have no rights in Ontario; but I am prepared to say this, and I want my words to be heard throughout the length and breadth of this land. Whether my countrymen have rights or no rights in Ontario, whether those rights are granted or denied, these considerations are no bar to the duty which the French Canadians owe to themselves and to the honour of their race to come forward in their fullest numbers and take part in the great struggle that is going on to-day in the land of their ancestors for the cause of freedom, and of the civilization of mankind . . .[272]

He denounced the Toronto theory of 'one language and one language only' as opposed to the traditions of the Britsh Empire: 'It is because British institutions everywhere have carried freedom and respect for minorities that England is as strong as she is today.'

Then Laurier appealed to the sense of justice and fair play of the people of Ontario, who were determined that every child in that province should have an English education. With that aim he fully agreed:

I want every child in the province of Ontario to receive the benefit of an English education. Wherever he may go on this continent I want him to be able to speak the language of the great majority of the people on this continent. I want it, I say, not only because it is the law of the province, but because of merely utilitarian considerations. No man on this continent is equipped for the battle of life unless he has an English education. I want every child to have an English education. . . .

When I ask that every child of my own race should receive an English education, will you refuse us the privilege of education also in the language of our mothers and our fathers? That is all that I ask to-day; I ask nothing more than that. I simply ask you, my fellow-countrymen, British subjects like myself, if, when we say that we must have an English education, you will say: 'You shall have an English education and nothing else.' There are men who say that in the schools of Ontario and Manitoba there should be no other language than the English language. But, sir, when I ask that we should also have the benefit of a French education, will you refuse us that benefit? Is that an unnatural demand? Is that an obnoxious demand? Will the concession of it do harm to anybody? And will it be said that in the great province of Ontario there is a disposition to put a bar on knowledge and to stretch every child in the schools of Ontario upon a procrustean bed and say that they shall all be measured alike, that no one shall have the privilege of a second education in a single language? I do not believe it; and, if we discuss the question with frankness, as between man and man, in my humble opinion, it can yet be settled by an appeal to the people of Ontario. I do not believe that any man will refuse us the benefit of a French education.[273]

This eloquent appeal was Laurier's swansong. The Quebec and Maritime Liberals backed him, but the Ontario Liberals only supported the measure after Laurier threatened to resign as leader, and the Western Liberals flatly opposed it. John Dafoe, who criticized the Lapointe motion in the *Manitoba Free Press*, accounted for it on the grounds of Laurier's fear of being supplanted in Quebec by Bourassa and of his desire to become once more in Quebec's eyes 'the greatest French Canadian.' But Georges Pelletier of *Le Devoir*, no friend of the Liberals, paid homage to Laurier's sincerity in his last great stand.

Casgrain opposed the motion on the ground that it was a Liberal manoeuver to arouse feeling against the Conservatives on the eve of elections in Quebec. Lemieux and Charles Marcil supported it eloquently. Dr. Edwards denounced Quebec as a province peopled by illiterates, and his Orangeman colleague Morphy went farther in abuse. R. B. Bennett called for unity of language in the name of unity of the Empire. Lamarche proclaimed his political independence, and said he was not 'afraid to extend a loyal hand to the public man courageous enough to undertake the defence of his tongue and his race.'[274] Speaking in English, he infused his constitutional argument for liberty based upon respect of law with great eloquence, and in conclusion revealed that J.-P.-O. Guibault, a Conservative then in hospital, had asked to be brought to the House at the risk of his life in order to support the motion. But on May 11 the Lapointe resolution was rejected by a vote of 107 to 60, with eight Quebec Conservatives supporting it.

The *Free Press* rejoiced: 'Let our Quebec friends thoroughly understand the situation. We shall not allow them to impose their will on the rest of Canada.'[275] N. W. Rowell, chief of the Liberal opposition in Ontario, had failed to yield to Laurier's arguments in a long correspondence which ended, as Laurier put it, in 'a line of cleavage which—I so judge from the tone of your letter just received —is final and beyond redemption.'[276] Laurier had urged upon an Ontario Liberal editor that 'We, French Liberals of Quebec, are fighting Bourassa and Lavergne; will the English Liberals in Ontario fight Howard Ferguson and the extreme Orange element?'[277] But in the face of the opposition of the Ontario Liberals to his stand, and the rebellion of the Western ones, he grew discouraged, and suggested to Fielding and Graham that it had been a mistake for a French Canadian to accept the leadership of the party and that it was time he resigned. Outside the House, he was attacked by English Conservatives as an ally of Bourassa and as the man responsible for Quebec's poor recruiting record.

With the bilingual question being raised once more in Manitoba, Laurier gave this discouraged counsel to a French-Canadian leader in Winnipeg:

We have reached a critical period in the development of Confederation, with regard to the rights of the French language. Unfortunately, the B.N.A. Act contains only one article on this subject, and the rights which are conferred upon us are very restricted alike in letter and spirit . . .

It is a historical fact that without the French population of Quebec the union of the provinces of British North America would have been a legislative union; the French population of Quebec would never have consented to such a form, since that would mean its disappearance as a distinct element. It is Quebec that suggested the federal form, and it must be accepted with all its consequences. For the French population of Quebec the advantages have been immense; outside Quebec, in face of the positive terms of Section 133, the French tongue has nothing to look for, aside from whatever sentiments the justice of the cause may arouse, and whatever influence may be brought to bear upon the majority.[278]

He did not believe in remedial legislation, and his only hope lay in persuasion and moderation, which might bring in Manitoba and Ontario the regime of tolerance which existed in Nova Scotia and New Brunswick. He had no confidence in the violent methods of Senator Landry, 'whose zeal I respect, but who is of too fiery a temper to be a safe guide.'[279]

The debate on the Lapointe resolution intensified feeling in Quebec. *Le Soleil* spoke of breaking the 'insupportable and odious'[280] tie which bound Quebec to Ontario. *La Patrie* stressed the fact that Western Liberals as well as the Conservatives had defeated the motion, but several Quebec Conservatives gave up the fight and only seven won seats in the provincial elections, three of them English Canadians. The Conservative party in Quebec had been killed by the Ontario school question. Bourassa appealed on May 30 to the provincial government to make a grant to the Franco-Ontarians, to enable them to carry their appeal to the Privy Council and to reopen their schools under the auspices of the Association d'Education. Landry resigned on May 22 as speaker of the Senate in protest 'against a collection of measures which tend to constitute the death sentence of the French race in the Canadian Confederation.' He announced his intention of devoting himself wholly to the Franco-Ontarian cause, and of campaigning against Casgrain, whom he called a devil's advocate, and the other French-Canadian ministers, who had become 'men dangerous to our race and to the rights it wishes to conserve.'[281] When Landry's letter was published on June 2, Bourassa paid tribute to his 'act of courage and honor,' which gave new courage to 'all those who fight for the justice and the respect of "pieces of paper" . . . in Canada.'[282] *Le Soleil* made political capital of Landry's resignation and was rebuked by *L'Action Catholique*, which maintained that the question should remain above parties. But the Abbé D'Amours did not approve the Landry-Bourassa alliance, and waited eleven days before eulogizing the senator for his gesture.

After a triumphal reception from a crowd of 10,000 at the Parc Lafontaine on June 19, Landry and Belcourt went to England, where the latter was to appear before the Privy Council. The Irish bishops of Ontario appealed to Rome in the hope of forcing acceptance of their offer to buy the University of Ottawa from the Oblates, which had been refused and which had aroused great indignation among the Franco-Ontarians. *L'Action Catholique's* attitude led many priests to transfer their subscriptions to *Le Devoir*; it was rumored that Cardinal Bégin and Archbishop Bruchési had become subscribers of the latter organ, to the scandal of the Ontario press.

The usual celebrations of Saint-Jean-Baptiste Day were extended for a week, with all parties making common cause with the Franco-Ontarians. School commissions exhausted their funds in gifts, while school children renounced their prizes that money might be sent to Ottawa. Others supplied prizes for the Franco-Ontarian children, who on their commencement days invoked the aid of Joan of Arc in remaining French. The *Toronto News* informed its readers that the French Canadians wished to impose the supremacy of their language in Canada, as a preliminary to driving out the English;[283] and Robert Sellar brought out a new edition of his *Tragedy of Quebec*, which urged Ontario to stand firm before 'a conspiracy devised by French priests to absorb her soil, violate her laws, and undermine her independence.' For him, the question was 'Whether this Canada of ours is to be British and nothing but British, or whether it is to be a mongrel land with two official languages and ruled by a divided authority? . . . Every Canadian has a deep interest in Ontario's answer, for upon it depends whether our country is to have two official languages fastened upon it and its legislatures pass under the lordship of French clericalism.'[284]

Bourassa had found plenty of ammunition for attacking the government in the charges of munitions profiteering and Conservative favoritism made by William Pugsley, Frank Carvell, and G. W. Kyte, which led to a motion by Laurier on March 7 calling for a parliamentary investigation. With the charges continuing, Borden finally appointed a Royal Commission early in April, and ordered Hughes home from England, since he was personally involved through his close connection with Honorary Colonel J. Wesley Allison, who acted as his 'adviser, counsellor and guide' in munitions purchases. The Commission's report, issued on July 20, cleared the government, the Shell Committee, and Hughes, but censured Allison for conduct which 'could not either be justified or excused.'[285] The investigation shook Hughes' position—Borden administered his department during the inquiry, and subsequently appointed a parliamentary secretary to administer it during Hughes' frequent absences—and left a nasty suspicion in the public mind that many of the most vocal patriots were profiteering on the side. The charges had been brought by Liberals, and the whitewashing report was generally accepted or rejected on Conservative or Liberal grounds. The political truce ended, just as the war entered its most crucial period.

Notes

[1] *Canada Year Book 1922–3*, 145, 170, 171–3.

[2] Rumilly, XVI, 156.

[3] M. Q. Innis, *Econ. Hist.*, 281.

[4] Rumilly, XVI, 159.

[5] Innis, 290.

[6] *Canada Year Book 1922–3*, 171.

[7] E. Bouchette, *Emparons-nous de l'industrie* (Ottawa, 1901), 16.

[8] *RSCT 1901*, Sec. I, 117–44, E. Bouchette, 'L'Evolution économique dans la Province de Québec.'

[9] *Ibid.*, 119.

[10] *Ibid.*, 135.

[11] Rumilly, XVI, 171.

[12] *RSCT 1901*, Sec. I, 169–70, L. Gérin, 'Notre mouvement intellectuelle.'

[13] *Ibid.*, 168.

[14] See L. Dantin, *Emile Nelligan et son oeuvre* (Montréal, 1903).

[15] G. Desaulniers, *Les Bois qui chantent* (Montréal, 1930).

[16] Rumilly, XVI, 123; Lavergne, *Trente ans* 205.

[17] Lavergne, 209.

[18] Rumilly, XVI, 131.

[19] *Ibid.*, 143.

[20] H. Bourassa, *Why the Navy Act Should Be Repealed* (Montreal, 1912), 46.

[21] Rumilly, XVII, 42.

[22] *Ibid.*, 45–8.

[23] J. S. Ewart, *The Kingdom Papers* (Ottawa, 1912), I, 187–93, No. 7, 'Ne Temere Decree.'

[24] Rumilly, XVII, 51.

[25] Lavergne, 213.

[26] H. Bourassa, *Pour la justice* (Montréal, 1912), 30.

[27] *Ibid.*, 32.

[28] *Ibid.*, 33.

[29] *Ibid.*

[30] Rumilly, XVII, 74.

[31] *Ibid.*

[32] Bourassa, *Justice*, 41–2; *Le Devoir*, 14 March 1912.

[33] Rumilly, XVII, 100.

[34] *Ibid.*, 123.

[35] *Ibid.*, 132.

[36] *Ibid.*, 140.

[37] H. Bourassa, *La Langue française et l'avenir de notre race* (Québec, 1913), 4.

[38] *Ibid.*, 11.

[39] *Ibid.*, 12.

[40] *Ibid.*, 15.

[41] *Ibid.*, 18.

[42] *Ibid.*, 22.

[43] *CHR XXVIII* (March 1947), No. 1, 1–30, G. N. Tucker, 'The Naval Policy of Sir Robert Borden, 1912–14.'

[44] Borden, *Memoirs*, I, 365.

[45] *Ibid.*, 361.

[46] Rumilly, XVII, 154.

[47] H. Bourassa, *Le Spectre de l'annexation* (Montréal, 1912); *The Spectre of Annexation and the Real Danger of National Disruption* (Montreal, 1912).

48 Bourassa, *The Spectre*, 18.

49 *Ibid.*, 23.

50 *Ibid.*, vi, Cahan, *Montreal Gazette*, 1 Aug. 1912.

51 Rumilly, XVII, 163.

52 Borden, I, 372.

53 *Ibid.*, 373.

54 Rumilly, XVII, 163.

55 *Ibid.*, 180.

56 The 1911 census figure of 202,442 French Canadians in Ontario is probably 50,000 short of the mark. C. B. Sissons, *Bilingual Schools in Canada* (Toronto, 1917), 92.

57 Sissons, 13-5; G. M. Weir, *The Separate School Question in Canada* (Toronto, 1934), 157-8. The full text of Regulation 17 is given in Weir, Ap. VI, 286-9.

58 F. W. Merchant, *Report on the Condition of English-French Schools in the Province of Ontario* (Toronto, 1912).

59 Rumilly, XVII, 173.

60 Rumilly, XVIII, 12.

61 Borden, I, 404.

62 *Ibid.*, 409.

63 Skelton, *Laurier*, II, 398.

64 *Ibid.*, 401-2.

65 *Ibid.*, 405.

66 Borden, I, 410.

67 Rumilly, XVIII, 16-7, 36-7.

68 *Ibid.*, 20.

69 *Ibid.*, 33; *Montreal Gazette*, 3 March 1913.

70 Ewart, *Kingdom Papers*, I, 243-89, No. 9, 'A Revision of War Relations'; 291-331, No. 10, 'Differences, Dangers, Duty.'

71 Rumilly, XVIII, 35; *Toronto Globe*, 8 March 1913.

72 *CHR 1947*, 17-18, Tucker.

73 Rumilly, XVIII, 45.

74 *Ibid.*, 46; *Le Devoir*, 22 May 1913.

75 Skelton, II, 413.

76 *CHR 1947*, 19, Tucker.

77 Rumilly, XVIII, 50.

78 O. Asselin, *Feuilles de Combat III: Le Sou de la pensée française* (Montréal, 1913). According to a typical note, this pamphlet had not been deposited for copyright at the ministry of agriculture, the federal department oddly charged with that function, because 'we are not steers' and in order 'not to deprive *La Croix* and *La Vérité* of the pleasure of copying it without compunction.'

79 Rumilly, XVIII, 62.

80 *Ibid.*, 63.

81 *Ibid.*, 68; *La Nouvelle France* (September 1913), 416.

82 *Ibid.*, 87.

83 Rumilly, XVIII, 136-7.

84 Sissons, 80.

85 H. Bourassa, *Ireland & Canada* (Montreal, 1914).

86 Rumilly, XVIII, 167, Bourassa-Ewart, 29 January 1914.

87 H. Bourassa, *French and English Frictions and Misunderstandings* (Montreal, 1914), 22-3.

88 *Ibid.*, 7, J. C. Walsh, 15 March 1914.

89 Rumilly, XVIII, 177.

90 *Ibid.*, 178.

91 *Ibid.*, 179.

92 *Ibid.*, 189.

[93] *Ibid.*, 201.
[94] *Ibid.*, 218.
[95] Borden, I, 451.
[96] *Ibid.*, 452.
[97] *Ibid.*, 452-3.
[98] Rumilly, XIX, 20.
[99] *Canadian Annual Review 1914* (Toronto, 1915), 142-3.
[100] Rumilly, XIX, 14-8.
[101] E. H. Armstrong, *The Crisis of Quebec*, 1914-18 (New York, 1937), 56.
[102] *Can. An. Rev. 1914*, 141.
[103] Skelton, 11, 428.
[104] Armstrong, 57.
[105] Rumilly, XIX, 21.
[106] Rumilly, XIX, 22; *La Presse*, 5 August; *Le Devoir*, 6 August 1914.
[107] *Ibid.*, 23, 27; *Le Devoir, Le Canada; La Patrie*, August 1914.
[108] *Ibid.*
[109] *Can. An. Rev. 1914*, 287.
[110] Armstrong, 58; *Montreal Gazette*, 8 August 1914.
[111] Skelton, II, 432-3.
[112] Descelles, *Discours*, II, 79-80.
[113] *Ibid.*, 82.
[114] Skelton, II, 434.
[115] Descelles, II, 86. The full text is in Descelles, *Discours*, II, 76-86.
[116] Borden, I, 461.
[117] Rumilly, XIX, 30.
[118] *Ibid.*, 32; *Le Devoir*, 22 August 1914.
[119] Armstrong, 68.
[120] *Ibid.*, 69-75.
[121] Rumilly, XIX, 33.
[122] *Ibid.*, 33.
[123] J. Michel, *La Participation des Canadiens français à la Grande Guerre* (Montréal, 1936), 16.
[124] H. Bourassa, *Le Canada à Loudres* (Montréal, 1914), 16, 27.
[125] H. Bourassa, *Le Devoir et la guerre* (Montréal, 1916), 44-5.
[126] H. Bourassa, *The Foreign Policy of Great Britain* (Montreal, 1915), 26.
[127] H. Bourassa, *La Politique de l'Angleterre avant et après la guerre* (Montréal, 1914), vi, 'Avertissement.'
[128] Bourassa, *Foreign Policy*, 37-47; *Contemporary Review* (September 1914).
[129] *Ibid.*, 2.
[130] Rumilly, XIX, 42.
[131] *Ibid.*, 45; *L'Action Sociale*, 14 September 1914.
[132] *Ibid.*
[133] O. Asselin, 'L'Action Catholique,' les evêques et la guerre (Montréal, 1914), 5-7.
[134] Rumilly, XIX, 62, joint pastoral, 23 September 1914.
[135] *Ibid.*
[136] Asselin, 'L'Action Catholique,' 8-12.
[137] Skelton, II, 436.
[138] *Ibid.*, 437.
[139] Rumilly, XIX, 64.
[140] *Ibid.*, 64-5.
[141] *Ibid.*, 68-9.
[142] *Ibid.*, 76.
[143] *Ibid.*, 85.
[144] *Ibid.*, 89.
[145] *Ibid.*, 85.

[146] *Ibid.*, 81.

[147] *Ibid.*, 83, *L'Action*, 31 October 1914.

[148] *Ibid.*, 84.

[149] *Ibid.*, 92.

[150] Reproduced in H. Bourassa, *The Duty of Canada at the Present Hour* (Montreal, 1915), [3–4].

[151] Rumilly, XIX, 93.

[152] *Ibid.*, 94.

[153] *Ibid.*, 97–8.

[154] *Ibid.*, 100, Casgrain-Landry, 17 December 1914.

[155] *Ibid.*, 102.

[156] *Ibid.*

[157] *Ibid.*, 103–4.

[158] *Ibid.*, 110, Bégin-Bruchési.

[159] *Ibid.*, 111.

[160] *Ibid.*, 95.

[161] Skelton, II, 438.

[162] Rumilly, XIX, 132.

[163] *Ibid.*

[164] *Ibid.*, 134.

[165] *CAR 1915*, 565.

[166] *Le 5ᵉ Anniversaire du Devoir* (Montréal, 1915), 9.

[167] *Ibid.*, 19.

[168] *Ibid.*, 67.

[169] *Ibid.*, 67–8.

[170] *Ibid.*, 69.

[171] *Ibid.*, 72.

[172] Rumilly, XIX, 144.

[173] *Ibid.*, 145.

[174] Skelton, II, 443.

[175] Borden, I, 532.

[176] *Ibid.*, I, 535.

[177] Skelton, II, 445.

[178] Borden, I, 483; *CAR 1915*, 283–6.

[179] Skelton, II, 446.

[180] *Can. An. Rev. 1915*, 366–8.

[181] *Ibid.*, 186.

[182] *Ibid.*, 189.

[183] *Ibid.*, 296.

[184] *Ibid.*, 218.

[185] *Ibid.*, 219.

[186] Rumilly, XX, 22.

[187] *Ibid.*, 28.

[188] *Ibid.*, 29.

[189] *Ibid.*, 28–34, 42–3.

[190] *Ibid.*, 45; *Le Devoir*, 20 April 1915.

[191] *Ibid.*, 24, 62.

[192] *Ibid.*, 57.

[193] H. Bourassa, *La Langue française au Canada* (Montréal, 1915), 28.

[194] Rumilly, XX, 58–9.

[195] *Ibid.*, 60.

[196] *RSCT 1915*, Ap. A, xlvi-xlvii, Mgr. Paul Bruchési, 'Le Dualisme Canadien'; Sec. I, 5–11, A. Routhier, 'Le Problème des races au Canada.'

[197] Rumilly, XX, 66–7.

[198] *Ibid.*, 69.

[199] *Ibid.*, 70, *Le Devoir*, 29 June 1915.

[200] Weir, *Separate School Question*, Ap. III, 268–73, *Saskatoon Daily Star*, 8 and 11 May 1916.

[201] Borden, I, 493.

[202] Rumilly, XX, 81; *Montreal Gazette*, 15 July 1915.

[203] *Ibid.*

[204] *Ibid.*, 82.

[205] Armstrong, 111.

[206] *Ibid.*, *L'Action Catholique*, 26 July 1915.

[207] *Can. An. Rev. 1915*, 258.

[208] *Ibid.*, 291.

[209] *Can. An. Rev. 1915*, 276.

[210] *Ibid.*

[211] *Ibid.*, 291.

[212] *Ibid.*

[213] Rumilly, XX, 95–6; *La Presse*, 21 August 1915.

[214] *Ibid.*, 97–8.

[215] O. Asselin, *Les Evêques et la Propagande de 'l'Action Catholique'* (Montréal, 1915).

[216] *Ibid.*, 13, 20–1.

[217] *Ibid.*, 21.

[218] *Ibid.*, 22.

[219] *Ibid.*, 55, 62.

[220] *Ibid.*, 75.

[221] Borden, I, 508.

[222] *Ibid.*, 496–510.

[223] *Ibid.*, 512.

[224] Rumilly, XX, 109.

[225] *Ibid.*, 117.

[226] *Ibid.*, 118.

[227] O. Asselin, *Pourquoi je m'enrôle* (Montréal, 1916), 9–10, Lavergne–Asselin, 3 November 1915.

[228] Borden, I, 513–21.

[229] Skelton, II, 448–50.

[230] *Ibid.*, 450.

[231] Rumilly, XX, 134.

[232] *Ibid.*, 136–7; *Le Canada*, 17 December 1915.

[233] *Ibid.*, *Daily Mail*.

[234] *Ibid.*, 137; *Montreal Gazette*, 20 December 1915.

[235] *Ibid.*, 138.

[236] Asselin, *Pourquoi*, 10, Asselin-Lavergne, 6 November 1915.

[237] *Ibid.*, 11.

[238] *Ibid.*, 11–12.

[239] *Ibid.*, 39.

[240] *Ibid.*, 48–50. Borden's and Hughes' letters were originally written in French.

[241] H. Bourassa, *Le Devoir et la guerre; le conflit des races* (Montréal, 1916), 40.

[242] Rumilly, XXI, 17.

[243] *Ibid.*, 18.

[244] *Ibid.*, 20.

[245] *Ibid.*, 23; *Can. An. Rev. 1916*, 344.

[246] Rumilly, XXI, 24.

[247] Skelton, II, 455.

[248] Rumilly, XXI, 25.

[249] *Ibid.*

[250] *Ibid.*, 32.
[251] *Ibid.*, 34.
[252] *In Memoriam: Paul-Emile Lamarche* (Montréal, 1919), 117.
[253] Rumilly, XXI, 45.
[254] *Ibid.*, 54.
[255] Borden, II, 573–4.
[256] Abbé Lionel Groulx, *Nos luttes constitutionnelles* (Montréal, 1916).
[257] Rumilly, XXI, 57.
[258] *Ibid.*, 59–60; *Toronto Mail and Empire, Montreal Star*, 13 March 1916.
[259] *Ibid.*, 63–4.
[260] H. Bourassa, *Hier, aujourd'hui, demain* (Montréal, 1916), 150.
[261] Armstrong, 121–2.
[262] *Can. An. Rev. 1916*, 312–3.
[263] *Ibid.*, 319; *Montreal Gazette*, 10 March 1916.
[264] *Ibid.*, 303.
[265] Borden, II, 538.
[266] *Parliamentary Documents 1916*, No. 28, Doc. 271a.
[267] Borden, II, 588–9.
[268] *Ibid.*, 589.
[269] Rumilly, XXI, 114.
[270] *Ibid.*, 114–5.
[271] *Ibid.*
[272] Skelton, II, 479–80.
[273] *Ibid.*, 41–2.
[274] Rumilly, XXI, 117.
[275] *Ibid.*, 118.
[276] Skelton, II, 477.
[277] *Ibid.*, 485.
[278] *Ibid.*, 487–8.
[279] *Ibid.*, 490.
[280] Rumilly, XXI, 119.
[281] *Ibid.*, 128–9.
[282] *Ibid.*, 129.
[283] *Ibid.*, 138, *Toronto News*.
[284] R. Sellar, *The Tragedy of Quebec* (Toronto, 1916), 327–8.
[285] Borden, II, 565–6.

CHAPTER XII

THE CONSCRIPTION CRISIS
(1916–19)

IT WAS in a Canada already sharply divided along racial lines by
the bilingual school question that the conscription crisis arose.
In June 1916 enlistments had dropped to half the April total,
and they continued to fall until in December they were only half
the June figure.[1] Of the 250,000 additional men sought in 1916,
120,000 were raised in the first six months of the year, but only
40,000 in the last.[2] Meanwhile Canadian losses continued to
mount. The Canadian Army Corps, composed of three divisions
and commanded after May by Sir Julian Byng, lost 2,759 men in
the Battle of Saint-Eloi in April, and 8,490 in the Battle of
Sanctuary Wood in June. Under these circumstances the training
of the Fourth Division was speeded up in England and in Canada
reinforcements were embarked.

I

Of the French-Canadian units, Asselin's 163rd, raised only to two-
thirds strength despite his tireless efforts, was sent to do garrison
duty in Bermuda, to his great disgust. Lieutenant-Colonel Paquet's
57th, which had already supplied several detachments of reinforcements for overseas, sailed for England on June 2. Five incomplete
French-Canadian battalions were assembled at Valcartier under
Major Emile Ranger, the largest units being Lieutenant-Colonel
Piuze's 189th and Lieutenant-Colonel Barré's 150th. A demand
arose for the organization of a French-Canadian brigade, under the
command of General Lessard or Lieutenant-Colonel Leduc, but Sam
Hughes opposed the plan. With the demand for reinforcements,
men were drawn from other battalions to reinforce the 189th and
150th, which were to go overseas in the fall, and in some cases men
were transferred from French-Canadian units to English-Canadian
ones. These measures destroyed the regional nature of the original
battalions, and aroused much ill will, for French-Canadian regionalism is strong. It was one thing to serve with neighbors under their
own leaders and another to be thrown into an unfamiliar English-
speaking world under officers who knew no French. Desertions

increased, while during July there were disturbances in two French-Canadian battalions at Valcartier. When the officers of the 206th were dismissed, Lieutenant-Colonel T. Pagnuelo told his battalion:

> . . . it is a revenge because we are French Canadians and because of small errors here and there. As far as you are concerned, they are shipping you to Bermuda, where you will undergo hardship and suffer misery from the heat. Now, military law prevents me from speaking, but if you are wise enough to read between the lines, you will know what to do. I will give passes to everybody, and be sure that the little money that your friends have subscribed to the Regimental fund will not be used to run after those who will not come back. [3]

Colonel Pagnuelo was later courtmartialed for his extraordinary speech, and sentenced to six months' imprisonment. Officers of the 167th were accused of irregularities and relieved of their commands, though later acquitted. Such incidents did grave harm to recruiting in Quebec, although French-Canadian leaders renewed their appeals for volunteers.

Ontario and English Canadians at large began to call for conscription, which represented a threat to the individualistic French Canadians who could be led to support the war by their own leaders but not driven into it by their hostile compatriots of English speech. Laurier, who assigned Quebec's poor record in enlistment to its small numbers of British-born, its few urban centers (to which recruiting so far had largely been confined), and to the nationalist movement, once more exerted himself to clear Quebec of the charge of disloyalty. At the Monument National on June 3 he urged an *entente cordiale* between English and French based upon common service, and urged his young compatriots to join those 'brave young men who offer their services—their lives—that France may live again, that Britain may continue her noble and generous rule, and that heroic Belgium may be restored to her standing as a nation.' [4] He maintained that the defence of the French language in Ontario should not interfere with the defence of France at the front.

Le Soleil supported Laurier's contention on June 5: 'It is by enlisting in large numbers and forming good French-Canadian battalions that we shall succeed in resolving in friendly and fruitful fashion the Ontario question.' *L'Evénement* on May 26 had admitted that recruiting in Quebec was a fiasco, and blamed it on the lack of military spirit among the French Canadians and on the antipathy of the bourgeoisie and lower clergy to England. *Le Canada* suggested on July 21 that *L'Evénement* might better blame the ex-nationalist ministers who had preached anti-imperialism in 1911 and were now beating the drum for enlistment. *La Presse* continued, like all the major French-Canadian papers except *Le Devoir*, to support recruit-ing ardently, urging that the French-Canadian position would become worse after the war if they did not do their part in a war which might seem to be solely in British rather than Canadian interests.[5] *L'Action Catholique* on June 5 noted Ferdinand Roy's tribute to France upon his return to Quebec from Europe, and warned: 'If we are proud to be French and British subjects, and we have ample reason to be so, despite the wrongs committed against our race, it is not enough to acclaim France and England; we must, in just and equitable proportions, march with them and not refuse them the testimony of our attachments.'[6] Bourassa mocked *L'Action's* new attachment to France; but at Brome on July 1, Laurier insisted on the alliance between the 'two mother countries' and replied thus to those who preached against fighting for England until the Ontario question was settled: 'Everywhere where there are rights to enjoy, there are duties to fulfil. Do your duty and you will obtain your rights.' At a Limoilou Saint-Jean-Baptiste dinner the following day, Laurier said that 'the French Canadians are in the Confederation to stay,' to which Armand Lavergne added the reservation in a following speech, 'on condition that they are not dishonoured.'[7] But in Ontario, where a by-election was being contested, the Toronto *News* called for a 'solid Ontario' against a 'solid Quebec' and proclaimed that 'A vote for Laurier is a vote for Bourassa.'[8]

On June 11 Sir Sam Hughes, bound for Valcartier, called upon Cardinal Bégin at Quebec. Ostensibly he sought chaplains for the French-Canadian battalions, but actually he wanted the Cardinal's support for recruiting. It was evident from the communiqué issued by the archbishop's office that this doubtless painful pilgrimage by the Orangeman had been well received. Possibly there was a con-nection between this visit and the launching on June 17 of a series of weekly anti-Bourassa articles in *La Presse*, under the title of '*Où allons-nous?*', by the Abbé D'Amours writing under the pseu-donym of 'Un Patriote.'[9] *L'Action Catholique* had been obliged to suspend its pro-war campaign because of opposition from the lower clergy, but the Abbé D'Amours now rejoiced in the freedom of anonymity and attacked Bourassa savagely.

On the other hand, Arthur Hawkes, an English-born journalist of Toronto, published an intelligent interview with Bourassa in the *Toronto Star* on July 14 and 15, in which he maintained that the nationalist leader was neither a firebrand nor a fool; paid tribute to his knowledge of Canadian and international affairs and his courage; and asserted that Bourassa favored Canadian independence but would accept imperial partnership along the lines suggested by Lionel Curtis and the Round Table group. Hawkes likened the nationalist leader to Lloyd George and anticipated that he would become 'the undisputed champion of the French-Canadian people when the time has fully come.'[10] For many English Canadians, this was the first honest account of Bourassa and his ideas, which had been grossly misrepresented by the English press. Bourassa declared in a letter to Hawkes that he was not anti-British, but anti-imperialist:

One point I did not make clear in our conversation is the motive of my desire for the disruption of the British Empire. It is not because it is British, but because it is Imperial. All Empires are hateful. They stand in the way of human liberty and true progress, intellectual and moral. They serve nothing but brutal instincts, and national objects: All that is good in British ideals, and there is much of it, would be better served by the free action of several independent British communities than by the common action of a monstrous Empire, built up by force and robbery, and kept together for no other purpose than allowing one race and one nation to dominate one fifth of the human race. But nations have to choose between British ideals and British domination. I stand for ideals against domination. I may be hanged for it in the name of British liberty, but that does not matter.

2

Bourassa figured largely in another role in the summer of 1916. On July 28 most of the Montreal, Quebec, Ottawa, and Toronto papers, both French and English, published an open letter to him from his cousin Captain Talbot Papineau, dated from the front in France on March 21.[11] The letter had been sent to Andrew Ross McMaster of Montreal, Papineau's law partner, who sent it on to Bourassa on July 18 and published it ten days later when no reply was forthcoming in Bourassa's absence from the city. Captain Papineau, like Bourassa, was a grandson of Louis-Joseph Papineau, but belonged to an anglicized branch of the family and had been educated at Oxford and Paris. At the outbreak of the war he had enlisted in the largely English Princess Patricia's Regiment, and was one of the few original members of that unit still surviving. His letter was addressed to his 'dear Cousin Henri,' and was purportedly personal, but was clearly intended as an appeal to the great mass of French-Canadian followers of the nationalist leader, who gained some of his prestige from being Papineau's grandson.

Captain Papineau regretted that he had not had an opportunity to discuss with Bourassa the issues raised by the war before leaving for the front, and paid tribute to the honesty and sincerity of Bourassa's disinterested views, though he deplored them. He was disappointed that events had not modified them: 'Deeply involved as the honour and the very national existence of Canada has become, beautiful but terrible as her sacrifices have been, you and you alone of the leaders of Canadian thought appear to have remained unmoved and your unhappy views unchanged.' He wrote because he feared Bourassa's influence upon a minority of the French Canadians, and because Bourassa's views might be taken as typical of the French Canadians. Then he marshaled the arguments with which he hoped to convert his cousin. As a matter of international law Canada had become involved in the war by Britain's declaration of war upon Germany. Any discussion of the justness of Canada's participation was an 'idle and pernicious' academic discussion. He dismissed the argument that Canada might have remained neutral until it was attacked by saying that if the Allies had been defeated, the unaided strength of Canada could not have prevented German domination. He added: 'By the time you are within fifteen yards of a German army and know yourself to be holding about one yard out of a line of five hundred miles or more, you are liable to be enquiring very anxiously about the presence and power of British and French forces.'

Papineau dismissed the argument of American protection by saying that Canada would have been subdued before the Americans aided her, since the United States had a record of only going to war for a national principle. If the Allies had not been defeated, 'You might still have edited untrammeled your version of *Duty* and Colonel Lavergne might still, publicly and without the restraining fear of death or imprisonment, have spoken seditiously (I mean from the Prussian point of view, of course).' But would nonparticipation have satisfied a nationalist? 'Can a nation's pride or patriotism be built upon the blood and suffering of others or upon the wealth garnered from the coffers of those who in anguish and with blood-sweat are fighting the battles of freedom?' If Bourassa were a true nationalist, he would have felt that 'in the agony of her losses in Belgium and France, Canada was suffering the birth pains of her national life. There, even more than in Canada herself, her citizens are being knit together into a new existence because when men stand side by side and endure a soldier's life and face together a soldier's death, they are united in bonds almost as strong as the closest of blood-ties.' Papineau felt that Canadians had had a call to fight for Canada in Europe, and gave thanks that 'that question had been answered not as you would have had it answered but as those Canadians who have already died or are about to die here in this gallant motherland of France have answered it.'

As a second argument, Papineau exalted the 'spiritual union' of the self-governing portions of the empire, and their civilization and standards, as 'the highest and noblest to which the human race has yet attained and jealously to be protected against destruction.' The uniting bonds might be readjusted, but they must not be broken. He repudiated Canadian nationalism if it meant antagonism to the spirit now uniting the empire. His third argument was a French-Canadian one. 'I may not be, like yourself, "*un pur sang*" [a pure-blooded French Canadian], for I am by birth even more English than French, but I am proud of my French ancestors, I love the French language, and I am as determined as you are that we shall have full liberty to remain French as long as we like.' But in order to preserve this liberty, concessions must be made to the majority, if the latter was to make concessions to the minority. The war had offered the French Canadians an opportunity to demonstrate to the English Canadians 'a common love of our country and a mutual wish that in the future we should unite our distinctive talents and energies to create a proud and happy nation.' But despite the whole-hearted support given by many French-Canadian leaders, and despite the heroism of the French-Canadian battalions, the French Canadians had not rallied to the colors in the same proportion as other Canadians, and the impression had been created that French Canada was not bearing her share of the burden. 'For this fact and this impression you will be held largely responsible.' For the time being, nationalism had been made a stench in English-Canadian nostrils without any furthering of Bourassa's aims, and after the war 'whoever bears a French name in Canada will be an object of suspicion and possibly of hatred.'

Papineau argued that Bourassa should have supported a war for France and French civilization and a fight for the freedom of the world. He closed with a warning of a 'heavy day of reckoning' when the soldiers returned 'for those who, while we fought and suffered here, remained in safety and comfort in Canada and failed to give us encouragement and support, as well as for those who grew fat with the wealth dishonourably gained by political graft and dishonest business methods at our expense.' Finally, he made a plea for Bourassa to play his share in realizing an ideal which he equally shared: 'At this moment, as I write, French and English Canadians are fighting and dying side by side. Is their sacrifice to go for nothing, or will it not cement a foundation for a true Canadian nation, a Canadian nation independent in thought, independent in action, independent even in its political organization—but in spirit united for high international purposes to the two Motherlands of England and France?'

Bourassa replied to McMaster on August 2,[12] casting doubt upon Captain Papineau's authorship of this 'political manifesto' written in English and presented four months after it was written. He minimized the relationship between himself and his cousin, and expressed the opinion that 'the whole thing has the appearance of a political manœuvre executed under the name of a young and gallant officer who has the advantage or inconvenience of being my cousin.' He reviewed his early attitude to the war and termed it analogous to that of his cousin. He summed up the reasons for his change of views: '"free" enlistment is now carried on by means of blackmailing, intimidation and threats of all sorts'; advantage had been taken of war emotion to assert imperial solidarity, and the Liberal leaders had abandoned their nationalist principles, while the Conservative spokesmen who denounced him as a traitor had exploited anti-imperialism to the full in 1911. Captain Papineau had backed his change of opinion by his deeds, but others had not.

Bourassa defended French Canada's recruiting record on the grounds that enlistment throughout Canada was 'in inverse ratio to the enrootment in the soil and the traditional patriotism arising therefrom':

The simple truth is that the abstention of the French Canadians is no more the result of the present attitude of the Nationalists than the consequence of the Liberal campaign of 1896 or the Conservative appeals of 1911. It relates to deeper causes: hereditary instincts, social and economic conditions, a national tradition of three centuries ... strengthened by the constant teaching of all our political and social leaders from Lafontaine, Cartier, Macdonald, Mackenzie, to Laurier inclusively.

He maintained that he had always distinguished between support of the war and the school question, but 'to speak of fighting for the preservation of French civilization in Europe while endeavouring to destroy it in America appears to us as an absurd piece of inconsistency.' He said that Captain Papineau was 'utterly unqualified to judge of the feelings of the French Canadians,' since he was separated from them by religion, mother tongue, and upbringing. As for Captain Papineau's threat, 'To propagate systematically national discord by quarrelling with all Canadians, either French or English, who hold different views as to the theory and practice of their national duty would be a misuse of time. Moreover, it would be a singular denial of their professions of faith in liberty and civilization.' He pointed out that the war profiteers were not to be found in the nationalist ranks: 'They are all recruited among the noisiest preachers of the Holy War waged for "civilization" against "barbarity," for the "protection of small nations," for the "honour" of England and the "salvation" of France.' He added an ironical postscript: 'I hope this will reach you before you leave for the front: no doubt you have been the first to respond to the pressing call of your partner.' In reply McMaster denied that he had either written or inspired the letter, and asserted that 'the idea of writing to you and the letter itself are the work of my partner.' He said that he had also striven for national unity, and would not return bitterness for bitterness when 'kindly thoughts and kindly words and kindly deeds should unite all those who call Canada their common duty.'

Whatever the inspiration of Captain Papineau's letter—and that question can scarcely be settled, since Papineau died in France—the propaganda honors of the exchange were won by Bourassa, who focussed national attention on Quebec's dislike of the war and the reasons for it. He had appealed to the instincts of his people and brilliantly analyzed their reasons for dislike of active participation in the war. The exchange of letters attracted more attention than the mass meetings held at Montreal, Quebec, and Sherbrooke on the second anniversary of the declaration of war, with official spokesmen proclaiming Canada's resolution to fight to the end. *La Patrie*, which had first published the Papineau letter, accused Bourassa of going off on a tangent to escape a direct answer. *Le Soleil* charged that he remained entrenched, after two years of a crisis such as humanity had never known, in the position that 'Nothing exists outside the province of Quebec which is worth Quebec's attention from the moment that it requires the least effort or sacrifice on the part of the province of Quebec.' *Le Canada* held that Canadian participation in the war had been decided with the full consent of the people of Canada, and its national liberty remained as intact as individual liberty. Casgrain and Lemieux besought Archbishop Bruchési for an utterance which would deprive Bourassa of the role of interpreter of French-Canadian feeling. On August 8 the archbishop spoke thus:

It is not possible to doubt on which side justice and right are in this terrible war. On one side are our enemies, who have been the aggressors, the violators of treaties and honour, while on our side are the defenders of harmony among nations and the champions of right and justice. It is not men and cannons which will have the last word, but God Almighty, and as God is the God of justice and right, he will ordain that in the end right and justice shall triumph.[13]

The Abbé D'Amours rejoiced at this utterance, and *La Patrie* interpreted it as the refutation of those 'who have openly and laboriously preached the denial of all duties in our province.'

3

In August the Fourth Division landed in France, and recruiting was pressed in Canada. The war factories began to employ women rather than men, in order to promote enlistment. The recruiting sergeants warned that if sufficient volunteers were not forthcoming, conscription would follow. On August 23 L.-N.-J. Pagé broke up a recruiting rally at the Place d'Armes in Montreal by protesting against the insults of the recruiting sergeants of the Irish-Canadian Rangers: 'We shall perhaps allow ourselves to be crushed, but we shall never accept conscription. Our people are insulted every day. French Canadians, it is time to make ourselves respected, and no longer allow ourselves to be crushed as in Ontario.' The recruiting rally turned into an anti-conscription meeting, since the crowd backed Pagé. The following day the French-Canadian crowd forced the soldiers to withdraw from the Place d'Armes. The English press demanded that the hecklers of recruiting rallies be punished, but the *Herald* admitted that the recruiting sergeants had been insulting. *Le Devoir* warned that blows were to be feared if the recruiters behaved like ruffians, though no one would bother them if they behaved honorably. The rallies at the Place d'Armes were given up for the time being.

Laurier, dreading racial differences arising out of the enlistment question, renewed his support for recruiting at an outdoor meeting at Maisonneuve before a crowd of 15,000 on September 21.

There are people who say we will not fight for England; will you then fight for France? I speak to you of French origin; if I were young like you and had the same health that I enjoy to-day, I would join those brave Canadians fighting to-day for the liberation of French territory. I would not have it said that the French Canadians do less for the liberation of France than the citizens of British origin. For my part I want to fight for England and also for France. To those who do not want to fight either for England or for France I say: Will you fight for yourselves?[14]

But Bourassa renewed his warnings that conscription was inevitable, since the raising of 500,000 men by the volunteer system was becoming impossible.[15] At Papineauville on September 3, speaking with Senator Landry in the interest of the Franco-Ontarians, he said that 'England and its Empire, Anglo-Saxon civilization, its guiding principle, its worldwide action, together constitute the most formidable coalition of anti-Catholic forces which exists.'[16] Such statements did more harm to recruiting than the perfervid loyalist speeches of Casgrain, Blondin, and Patenaude did good during the fall.

In September the Canadian Corps saw action again in the Somme. Between September 15 and 18 the Royal 22nd lost a third of its strength in the Battle of Courcelette. The courage shown by the French Canadians, who had led the Canadian attack, was hailed in the French and English press. Again at Regina Trench on October 1, the 22nd lost another third of its strength. Total Canadian casualties for September were 9,051, and even during the uneventful months of July and August had run over 3,000 a month. The problem of reinforcements became serious. Two French-Canadian battalions, Barré's 150th and Piuze's 189th, sailed on September 27 for England, where they became depot battalions for the 22nd. The unruly 206th Battalion was broken up, with its men being sent to Bermuda to fill out the ranks of Asselin's 163rd, which was sent to England later in the fall. Colonel de Salaberry's 230th was transformed into a forestry battalion. All hope of a French-Canadian brigade thus perished.

Faced abroad with the task of supplying reinforcements at an unanticipated rate, and with contradictory demands at home for conscription and for selective enlistment to protect industry, the government decided in August to set up a National Service Board to hold the balance between the manpower needs of army and industry. The director-general, Sir Thomas Tait of Montreal, was not chosen until late in September, however, and the subordinate directors for each of the twelve military districts were not selected until early in October. The board was to be under the direct supervision of the prime minister, not of the minister of militia, and according to Borden its purpose was 'to identify and keep within Canada those who could give better service at home, and to identify and induce to service in the field those who could and ought so to serve.'[17] On October 14 R. B. Bennett was named director-general in place of Sir Thomas Tait, who resigned when the government refused to appoint G. M. Murray, secretary of the Canadian Manufacturers' Association, as secretary of the board. Since the great majority of the directors were Conservatives, Laurier refused to accept Borden's offer to name five Liberal members of a cooperating parliamentary committee of twelve members.

On October 23 Borden issued an appeal to the people of Canada for national service:

To men of military age I make the appeal that they place themselves at the service of the State for military duty. To all others I make appeal that they place themselves freely at the disposition of their country for such service as they are best fitted to perform.[18]

The government and Director-General Bennett reiterated that conscription was not in question, though Bennett proposed to Borden that the proposed registration card for every male citizen of Canada should carry a question as to conscription, as well as questions regarding willingness to change present work for war work, and willingness to move to some other part of Canada to do war work. Borden advised against the conscription question.[19] But the Quebec press showed considerable mistrust of the National Service scheme. *Le Soleil* congratulated Laurier for refusing to serve in connection with it, while *Le Bien Public* of Trois-Rivières hinted that it was a plan for raising soldiers rather than war workers.[20]

National registration was set for January 1917, and early in December the government began a campaign for full support of it. On December 6 in Montreal Borden, accompanied by Casgrain and Doherty, explained the plan to Archbishop Bruchési, who was 'very friendly and denounced Bourassa.'[21] Then he addressed a mass meeting, which gave him an attentive hearing, but heckled Patenaude and Bennett by cries of 'Why don't you enlist?' and would hardly allow the former to speak. Students were largely responsible for the disorder. At Quebec the following day Borden called on Sir Lomer Gouin and Cardinal Bégin, who promised their support; and then addressed a mass meeting, backed by Casgrain, Gouin, and Bennett. A group of students cheered Gouin, but called for Bourassa and Lavergne when Casgrain was speaking, and left in a body when Bennett began to speak.[22] On the following day Laurier and Gouin spoke at a recruiting meeting in Quebec, while Borden set out westward to carry his campaign as far as Victoria. Throughout the fall the three French-Canadian ministers had made many speeches in favor of recruiting, while Laurier, Lemieux, and Charles Marcil had done the same.

But the nationalist opposition had also made itself felt, and won an ever larger hearing. Paul-Emile Lamarche resigned from parliament on September 21, the fifth anniversary of the last elections, in protest over the unprecedented prolongation of its life. On the following Sunday he addressed his electors at Nicolet, supported by Bourassa. Lamarche attacked the government's willingness 'to mortgage the blood of the nation to the amount of 500,000 men,' and defended his record, excusing himself for having obtained for the county few bridges, wharves, and post offices, 'which would have had to have been bought with pieces of my conscience.'[23] Bourassa took the opportunity to reply to Laurier's Maisonneuve speech of eight days before, blaming on him the initial responsibility of participation in the war, and taunting him with not having gone to the rescue of France in 1870, when he was thirty years old. He ended his attack on Laurier's career since the South African War by calling him 'the most nefarious politician of Canada, a traitor to his mission.'[24]

On this same Sunday Armand Lavergne and Tancrède Marsil supported Roch Lanctôt at Napierville, where the latter promised to oppose conscription and denounced the government's policy of excessive participation in the war, as leading to bankruptcy for which the farmer would have to pay. Lavergne refuted the argument of protecting France by enlistment by saying that France was being attacked in Ontario and it was there that the fight must be won. French was the first language spoken in Canada; it would be the last, or there would be no more Canada. He invoked the memory of Montcalm, Lévis, the nuns who had sacrificed their lives to teaching, the Jesuit martyrs, and the *Patriote* martyrs of 1837.; and called upon the dead to aid the living in the maintenance of French-Canadian traditions. And on this same Sunday Blondin summoned the people of Batiscan to their predominant duty, to aid France and England, since the liberties and even the existence of Canada were at stake. Of all these various declarations Bourassa's attack on Laurier excited the most comment in the press. *Le Soleil* announced that he had 'arrived at the last stage of the brain fever which has been consuming him for some years,' and explained his psychology in terms of his phobias for England and for Laurier. *Le Canada* took the same line. Lamarche was accused of pushing nationalism to the point of anarchy by *L'Evénement*, and others criticized him for retiring from parliament to a well-paid post as counsel of the City of Montreal.[25]

Meanwhile Bourassa criticized Lionel Curtis' recently published *The Problem of the Commonwealth*, in a series of articles in *Le Devoir* from September 28 to October 9, later reprinted in French and English pamphlet form.[26] The Round Table groups, which had been started in 1910 in Canada, Australia, New Zealand, and South Africa, and later in the United Kingdom, India, and Newfoundland, had been studying imperial affairs in a new spirit, with their quarterly, *The Round Table*, serving as a medium of information on imperial questions. Shortly before the war, their study had been concentrated on 'how a British citizen in the Dominions can acquire the same control of foreign policy as one domiciled in the British Isles.' A draft drawn up in the fall of 1915 served as the basis of Curtis' book. Curtis saw the war as a struggle for liberty against autocracy, and hence parallel to the Seven Years' War in which 'Had France prevailed . . . the principle of self-government would have perished, not merely in America, but also in the British Isles.'[27] This thesis could not but be intriguing to Bourassa, whose interest in control over foreign policy had grown to such an extent that it alarmed Laurier, who through Dandurand warned his former disciple that he was 'playing with fire.'[28]

But Curtis' veiled 'Anglo-Saxon' racism, with its implication of a people chosen to bear the white man's burden, irritated Bourassa, who was beginning to disparage the 'Anglo-Saxon' character:

To his hereditary pride, which marks his cousinship with the northern German, have come to be added the obtuseness developed by insular isolation and alcoholism, and above all infatuation with his immense wealth and pride of domination over weak peoples. As a result, in spite of his remarkable faculties for government, and the general humanity of his proceedings—when cupidity and the desire of domination do not push him to brutalities—the Anglo-Saxon does not know how to gain the confidence, much less the affection, of the peoples that he dominates nor even of those with whom he associates. Now when confidence and love are missing, good understanding is difficult.[29]

Bourassa found himself in complete accord with Curtis, however, on constitutional principles, though he favored dominion independence rather than equal partnership with the United Kingdom as the solution of the present situation, which Curtis called 'intolerable.' Bourassa was willing to accept the latter alternative though, if the majority preferred it to independence, since he believed that it would lead to independence in any case. He reaffirmed his conviction about imperialism as expressed to Arthur Hawkes, and again warned that the anglicizers and the Tory imperialists might drive the French Canadians into the third alternative of annexation to the United States. In the English translation of these articles Bourassa developed at greater length his arguments in favor of independence, and removed the indictment of 'Anglo-Saxon' alcoholism. But there were few English Canadians in the mood for academic analyses of constitutional problems at this period. When Montreal students, on their way to the cathedral for the Mass celebrating the opening of the academic year, tore down recruiting posters and became involved with the police, who made some arrests in the church itself, Bourassa was blamed by the press of Ontario and the West. As in the old song of 1837 which proclaimed '*C'est la faute de Papineau*,' every untoward incident in Quebec was now blamed on Papineau's grandson Bourassa, whose hanging was called for continually by the English press.

4

With French-English relations growing worse every day, Arthur Hawkes conceived the notion of an exchange of visits between representative men of Ontario and Quebec. Two Toronto friends, a Methodist lawyer, John Milton Godfrey and Colonel Mulloy, a blind veteran of the South African War, helped Hawkes to organize the project. Bourassa declined Hawkes' request for aid. But early in October some fifty leading Ontarians began their goodwill pilgrimage through Quebec at a dinner at the Club Saint-Denis in Montreal. Senator Dandurand asked only that the French Canadians be taken as they were, the most Canadian of all Canadians. Paul-Emile Lamarche said the French Canadians were Canadian above all, and that he preferred Canada to the empire. He illustrated two rival concepts of national unity with two gestures: 'Some want national unity like that,' laying one hand on top of the other; 'We wish it like this,' laying one hand beside the other. Charles Beaubien protested that it took more courage to urge others to enlist on the platform than to speak thus to English guests. Lamarche retorted: 'I should not wish to urge others to enlist before putting on the uniform myself,' and was greeted with a 'Right you are' from one of the visitors.[30] With the ice thus broken, the visitors regretted the absence of Bourassa.

The Ontario pilgrims continued on to Trois-Rivières and Quebec, where *L'Action Catholique* greeted them in an English article and urged a permanent *bonne entente* committee. At Sherbrooke Colonel Mulloy received an ovation, and he tried to give Lavergne the accolade in the French manner. More impressive in enlightening the visitors about Quebec than the flood of speeches were their visits to Montreal's port facilities, the factories of Trois-Rivières, the Quebec Ecole Technique, the asbestos mines of Thetford, and the bilingual schools of Sherbrooke. They were also impressed by such distinguished men as Senator Dandurand, Sir Georges Garneau, and Dr. Pantaléon Pelletier, Quebec's London agent. Upon his return to Toronto, S. R. Parson, vice-president of the Canadian Manufacturers' Association, gave an objective lecture on his impressions. But he did not fail to point out that while the bishops supported the war effort, the priests supported Bourassa, which was an index of popular feeling. Some of the visitors also persuaded Joseph Flavelle, the head of the Imperial Munitions Board, that two new war factories should be established in Ontario rather than Quebec, since such a step would 'recompense this population for not having done its duty toward the Empire, and deprive Ontario whose young men have so generously offered and given their lives.'[31]

The Ontario school question continued to set French against English. The Association d'Education opened the bilingual schools in the fall, but was scarcely able to pay the teachers and had no money to buy coal. A campaign was organized for the latter purpose. Abbé Groulx spoke at Ottawa on October 15, and was introduced by Landry and thanked by Laurier, who both saw victory as the eventual result of the scholastic struggle. The meeting was symbolic of Quebec's unity on the question, with a young nationalist supported by the Conservative and Liberal elder statesmen. There was fresh alarm at the new school regulations in Manitoba, seemingly inspired by Regulation 17. Bishop Béliveau spoke on the Western situation at Laval in Quebec on October 17. The province was stirred by various benefits and collections for the Ontario schools.

But on October 27 Benedict XV's encyclical 'Commisso divinitus' was published in Canada, leaving the decision of the school question 'to the bishops, and particularly to those who preside over dioceses where the struggle is most ardent.' It added counsels for calm and unity among all Catholics. La Patrie hailed it in triumph, calling upon 'the fomenters of discord, the exploiters of race and religion,' to give way to 'men of goodwill, to the moderates, to the true friends of progress, peace, and harmony among the different nationalities which compose our population.'[32] L'Action Catholique implied that the encyclical was a rebuke to the nationalists. Le Devoir at first refrained from all comment. Le Canada made common cause with L'Evénement to censure a 'certain politico-religious school' justly reprimanded by the Pope for 'violently pleading a good cause under the mantle of religion.' L'Action Catholique rebuked the journalists who presumed to usurp the bishops' role as interpreters of the Pope's thought.[33] The encyclical at first dismayed the chiefs of the Franco-Ontarian movement. But they drew some comfort from the Privy Council's decision of November 2, which in effect confirmed the validity of Regulation 17, but disavowed the new school commission set up by the Ontario government. Samuel Genest at once claimed the documents and the funds held by the commission, while Mgr. Paquet, Père Rouleau, and Père Villeneuve—two future cardinals—held a theological consultation at Ottawa on the interpretation of the encyclical. Mgr. Paquet stopped in press a new edition of his Cours de droit public de l'Eglise to alter his interpretation of the encyclical. He saw in it an assertion of the principle that the French Canadians had the right, in a province of English majority, to have their language taught and to defend it, and that the faithful also had the right to worship and receive religious teaching in their mother tongue. He infered an implied condemnation of Regulation 17, since the encyclical urged that Catholics should work with zeal and charity to improve the situation. In an interview in Le Droit, Mgr. Paquet said that the papal injunction to avoid discord among the faithful did not preclude efforts to defend the French language.[34] The brash young men of the Arch group in Montreal published two articles on the encyclical and the Privy Council decision in L'Escholier under the headline 'Nous n'irons pas à Canossa.' In an editorial Jean Chauvin recalled Bourassa's words in the Keewatin affair: 'Holy Father, the Catholics of Canada venerate you, but in matters exclusively political, we, British and Canadian citizens, claim from you the liberty the Church has always recognized in these matters for its faithful.'[35] Landry, Belcourt, and Père Charlebois accepted the papal decision, but the young nationalists thus supplied evidence that they had become more French than Catholic. Within a few days, Chauvin renounced his editorial chair and enlisted in the field artillery, giving explanations more complicated than those of Asselin for his enlistment after long opposition to the war. A possible conclusive factor may have been the patriotic feeling aroused by the impressive tribute paid to the dead of the 22nd at Notre-Dame on October 26, when all the regiments of Montreal paraded to the church and Archbishop Bruchési told a congregation which included Sam Hughes, Patenaude, Doherty, and many other notables that 'Quebec has done its duty.'[36]

On the day before this service the *Gazette* published a letter from Gustave Lanctot, who had originally been in Asselin's 163rd Battalion, but on being sent to England on a special mission, had had himself transferred to an English-speaking unit at the front. Writing to a friend in Canada, Lanctot reported that while England and France lavished praise on the 22nd Battalion, they were astonished at Quebec's indifference to the war and at the fact that some French-Canadian papers were actually carrying on anti-Allied propaganda. Lanctot wondered whether public opinion in Quebec had yet awakened to its duty, and appealed to his compatriots to realize that they were fighting for Canadian liberty and to prevent German domination on the shores of the St. Lawrence.[37] But Lanctot's letter, like Papineau's, came too late to reverse the swelling tide against enlistment in Quebec.

In October *La Presse* began a series of articles, issued as a pamphlet, *Our Volunteer Army*, early in December, which was a defensive analysis of the recruiting problem, and also an attempt to encourage further enlistments. It claimed that Quebec did not lag very far behind Ontario in the number of native-born volunteers, with 16,000 or 1 per cent of her eligible male population enlisted as compared to Ontario's 42,000 or 2½ per cent. It declared that more than 9,000 of Quebec's 16,000 were French Canadians. Quebec's poorer showing was blamed on indignation over the Ontario school question, on English control of the recruiting system, on the lesser chance for French Canadians to win promotion or decorations, and to the breaking up of French-Canadian units. It was pointed out that Ontario had more unmarried men and a much larger urban population. It was also argued that French Canadians enlisted only in combat battalions, while in Ontario many joined service forces. According to the *Toronto Globe's* figures, that district had recently supplied only 181 infantry recruits, as compared, to 3,219 enlistments in artillery, engineering, medical, forestry, and other special branches. On July 17 *Le Canada* had claimed a total of 50,000 French Canadians in the army: 5,000 in the First Contingent; 7,200 in the six French battalions subsequently recruited; 7,000 in English Quebec units; 1,200 in the 165th Acadian Battalion, with 3,000 others scattered through other Maritime units; 4,000 in Ontario and Western units; 12,000 in hospital, service, pioneer, and forestry units; and 10,000 French and Belgian reservists. On August 21 the *Orange Sentinel* had rejected these figures as grossly exaggerated, saying that no more than 5,000 French Canadians had ever enlisted, and also charged that the French-Canadian battalions 'enlist in retail and desert wholesale.' *La Presse* contented itself with a claim of 16,000 French-Canadian volunteers in October. And significantly it admitted, despite its effort to produce patriotic statistics, that Quebec had not done its part and appealed to the French Canadians to equal Ontario's war effort.[38] It was now generally recognized that Quebec's recruiting record was bad, but the lack of authoritative figures and the wide disparity of various claims made the situation worse.

The provincial legislature met on November 7, but was largely concerned with local affairs, save for the announcement of the gift of $1,000,000 to the Patriotic Fund by the province, and a Conservative request for the grant of assistance to the Franco-Ontarians. Gouin evaded the latter request as inopportune after the encyclical. Athanase David, Senator L.-O. David's son, made his maiden speech, which revealed the influence of Bourassa even on the son of a staunch Liberal. He defended Quebec against attacks on its enlistment record by urging those who wanted the French Canadians to save France on European battlefields to show the same sympathy for France to those in Canada who were attached to the French language. He asserted the rights of the French Canadians and their place in Confederation.[39] Another proof of the growing rift between the races was a letter written to Bourassa by John S. Ewart on December 1:

I am afraid that we view present circumstances from a different angle and perhaps you will permit me to say that I have very much regretted the course which you have, I have no doubt, conscientiously adopted.

I should not think it at all right, at the time to say anything that would tend to distract our people during the stress of war. To me, the first requisite is solidarity and for that purpose necessarily the subordination of the many conflicting things and ideas which would effect that solidarity. After the war is over, all those interested not only in its cause or purpose, but in the history of wars in general, will have much to engage their attention and quite possibly I shall not be among the silent ones when the right time arrives. Meanwhile I would hope that we would all contribute to the success of what our country—yours and mine—has almost unanimously agreed to adopt.[40]

With this letter their correspondence was broken off until December 1917, when Ewart sought Bourassa's advice on how the government might mend matters in Quebec. But in December 1916 the division between the races had become so sharply marked that the leading English-Canadian nationalist broke off long existing relations with the leading French-Canadian nationalist.

For most English-speaking Canadians the war came before all else; for the French it was subordinated to certain national interests. The French press devoted more attention to the Ontario question than to the struggle in Europe, and the nationalist agitation had reached into the farthest backwaters of the province, leaving Quebec ill-disposed towards measures for furthering a war effort which it already considered too great. A sharp increase in the cost of living affected more people in Quebec's marginal economy than the high wages paid in war plants. How differently Quebec conceived its duty from the other provinces was revealed by Bourassa's speech on 'Le Devoir National' on the same night that Borden supported the National Service plan in Montreal. Bourassa thus defined the national duty of the French Canadians: 'Let us be intensely Catholic and French. In default of the superiority of numbers or of wealth which no doubt we shall never have, our faith will insure us a moral superiority, if we know how to live by it; our civilization will insure us an intellectual superiority, provided that we know how not to degrade it.'[41]

The Abbé D'Amours had continued his attacks on Bourassa and his ideas in La Presse, and late in 1916 they were reprinted in pamphlet form as Où allons-nous? Le Nationalisme canadien. Lettres d'un 'Patriote' and given wide circulation. D'Amours declared that Bourassa's principles were false and that Bourassa was a 'partisan of Kantian subjectivism and of the egotism of the Nietzschian superman.'[42] He asserted that Bourassa had tried to group the French Canadians outside the jurisdiction of the Church and had taught that its opinions on political matters need not necessarily be obeyed, so that the forces of French Canadianism and Catholicism had been divided. D'Amours dismissed independence as being contrary to the will of the majority of Canadians and as leading to the submission of French-Canadian rights to the will of the English majority. Annexation would mean the political and ethnic end of French Canada, as it had that of Louisiana. Belittling Bourassa's fear of imperialism, D'Amours called for the preservation of Confederation and the British connection. The French-Canadian patriot should seek to make friends and allies, rather than to isolate French Canada by a policy of national egoism.

The abbé warned of the dangers of forming a Catholic or nationalist party which would expose French Canada to dangers in a predominantly Protestant country. French Canadians were strongly urged to be loyal to the British Crown and the empire. He denounced as neither legitimate or prudent the nationalist attempt to dispute the decision of the Canadian parliament to participate in the war and Britain's right to be supported by Canada. He condemned Bourassa's views as being contrary to the tradition of the Church in Canada, which had always upheld loyalty to Britain, and which had provided a bulwark against assimilation, Americanization, or contamination by French revolutionary ideas, as well as protection for the Church's teachings on faith and morals. On December 7 Bourassa replied to the abbé with a blast in *Le Devoir* which destroyed him in a few paragraphs.[43] D'Amours' views had long been unpopular, but they had been held to represent the opinion of the hierarchy. But now Archbishop Bruchési criticized him for contributing to a Montreal journal without obtaining the permission necessary for a priest of another diocese. This disavowal by the hierarchy was a highly revealing index of the changing mood of French Canada. Panic-stricken, the abbé excused himself on the grounds of having in the past been encouraged by the archbishop in his opposition, in the interests of the Church and the country, to the 'disastrous campaign of the nationalists,' and of his desire to avoid embarrassing the archbishop.

5

A measure taken by the government in the fall of 1916 removed one ground of nationalist opposition to the war effort, but it came too late to be effective on public opinion in Quebec. Canadian control of the Canadian forces overseas was assured in November by the appointment of Sir George Perley as minister of overseas forces, with Sir Edward Kemp replacing Sam Hughes as minister of militia at home. Hughes had been a constant thorn in Borden's flesh because of his erratic behavior. He had quarrelled with the Duke of Connaught when the latter attempted to be more than nominal commander-in-chief, and he had frequently made trouble with the War Office in London. General Alderson's resignation as commander of the Canadian Corps had come as a direct result of differences with Hughes. The latter had attempted to direct military affairs in the field as well as at home, and his frequent trips to England and France had resulted in poor administration of military affairs in Canada. His connection with the munitions and supply scandals, his notorious favoritism in appointments, and his unwariness in dealing with the sensibilities of Quebec had provided much political embarrassment for Borden. The prime minister allowed his colleague to go his way, however, despite increasing protests both from England and other members of the cabinet, until September 1916, when Hughes set up a Canadian Military Council in London without consultation with the cabinet. Borden at once ordered him home, and announced to him the impending appointment of Perley to the post of minister of overseas troops. Hughes protested violently against Perley's appointment and urged that his friend Sir Max Aitken should have the post.

On November 9 Borden replied to a letter from Hughes, which accused him of making inaccurate statements and referred sarcastically to other 'lovely' commissions appointed by the government, with a demand for Hughes' resignation based upon consultation with his colleagues, among whom Thomas White and George Foster had long favored Hughes' dismissal. Borden referred to Hughes' desire 'to administer your department as if it were a distinct and separate Government in itself' and to his repudiation of the principle of cabinet responsibility.[44] After his resignation had been requested, Hughes made a speech at the Empire Club in Toronto attacking English control of Canadian troops overseas, English rejection of Canadian supplies, and English administration of hospitals. Hughes subsequently intrigued against the government. Lord Birkenhead told Borden of the general's plan to overthrow the administration.[45] Hughes explained his resignation on the grounds of 'interferences and conditions imposed on the administration of this Department' in a farewell speech to his staff on November 15. The English-Canadian press gave him credit for organizing the First Division so rapidly, but spoke freely of his 'weird incompatibility of temperament' and his unwillingness to bear the restraints imposed upon responsible ministers 'with his temperament of a military dictator.'[46]

Hughes had done much to turn French Canada against the war by his Methodist, Orangeman, and Masonic prejudice against French Catholics, by his refusal to appoint French-Canadian officers to high commands, by his unwillingness to exploit fully French Canada's early enthusiasm for the war, and by his association with the war profiteers. During his period in power Hughes kept his opinion of the French Canadians largely to himself, though in laying the cornerstone of the new arsenal which he had secured for his home town of Lindsay, Ontario, on July 15, he had said: 'With all due regard to the Province of Quebec, in this great war it has not done its duty as it should and would if the young manhood of the

Province had been taken in hand by the proper people, who have benefitted so much from British institutions in days gone by.'[47] In 1918, during the conscription debates, he made far more violent charges against the French Canadians, which probably echoed his secret opinions while minister of militia. The kindest possible verdict on Hughes' administration as far as Quebec was concerned was supplied by the recognition of the 'tactless blunders' made during the First World War in Brigadier Maurice Pope's confidential study in 1941 of 'The Recruiting Problem in the Province of Quebec.'[48]

T.-Chase Casgrain died on December 29; and Borden added Albert Sévigny to the cabinet as minister of inland revenue, with Patenaude receiving the postmaster-generalship. The cabinet thus had no strong French-Canadian representative as it entered the stormy year of 1917, which saw Quebec aligned against the rest of Canada on the question of conscription. Late in December the prime minister, who had earlier assured Cardinal Bégin and Archbishop Bruchési that there would be no conscription in seeking their support for the National Service scheme, told labor representatives: 'I hope conscription may not be necessary, but if it should prove the only effective method to preserve the existence of the State and of the institutions and liberties which we enjoy, I should consider it necessary and I should not hesitate to act accordingly.'[49] At the same time, however, he issued a public statement that National Service registration was called for in order that there might be no conscription. Relying upon Borden's good faith, Cardinal Bégin and Archbishop Bruchési strongly supported the registration, the former in a circular letter to his clergy on January 4 and the latter in a public statement.[50] But the thesis of the nationalist press that registration was a prelude to conscription was echoed vaguely in some other journals.

After the January registration was concluded, Director-General Bennett announced that 80 per cent of the men between 17 and 45 had replied. Quebec had only 79,700 men classified as military prospects, compared to Ontario's 186,252, possibly because of the prevalence of early marriage and large families. The classification took account of marriage and dependents, as well as employment in war industry.[51] Nothing was done at once with the inventory thus taken, and enlistments continued at a low rate. Throughout Canada opposition to the registration was strongly expressed by labor groups. The farmers of Ontario and the West were also hostile to registration, in so far as they interpreted it as a step towards conscription. There was renewed pressure for conscription from Tory sources and the recruiting leagues, while the Liberals remained generally opposed to it.

In January 1917 the *bonne entente* movement renewed its efforts to reconcile Quebec and Ontario, with a French-Canadian group visiting Toronto and Hamilton. Sir Georges Garneau was given an honorary degree by the University of Toronto, and on this occasion paid tribute to the men fighting in France and Flanders and to the British Navy. Sir Lomer Gouin urged unity in Canada, when Frenchmen and Englishmen were fighting for the sacred things common to both, 'mingling their blood on the battlefields of right and justice and for the aid of the defenceless of the community.'[52] The visiting Quebec delegation also included L.-P. Pelletier and Charles Beaubien. But this movement involved only certain leaders of French Canada who were already committed to the Allied cause; it did not affect the rank and file.

The attitude of the latter was revealed in the by-election in Dorchester on January 27 in which the new minister of inland revenue, Albert Sévigny, sought re-election. The Liberals nominated Lucien Cannon, the provincial member for the constituency, and denounced Sévigny for his disloyal and unpatriotic statements in the 1911 campaign and criticized his nomination to the cabinet. At Saint-Prosper on January 19 and at later meetings the two candidates discussed once more the Navy issue, participation in the war, and the possibility of conscription. Sévigny admitted his former opposition to participation in imperial wars, but urged support of the government's war policy, the National Service scheme, and the abandonment of partisan politics. Cannon accused him of betraying his nationalist colleagues of 1911 and his constituents, and declared: 'National Service is preliminary to Conscription, and with the chief of my party I am against Conscription.'[53] Stating that he was not against a participation in the war which would not bankrupt Canada in manpower and wealth, he warned that the election of Sévigny would indicate Quebec's support of conscription and of endless Canadian sacrifices for England. Each candidate claimed the backing of his party chief, but while Patenaude and Blondin energetically supported Sévigny on the platform and with the full resources of the Conservative machine, no Liberal leaders appeared in Cannon's behalf.

The electoral meetings grew violent in tone, with Cannon, who was partially of English descent, telling Sévigny that he would 'rather be a half-breed than a pure French Canadian who had betrayed his people.'[54] The government was attacked for graft and profiteering, and for tolerating the Ontario persecution of French Canadians. Sévigny regretted the Ontario situation, but pointed out that the Liberal government of Manitoba had broken the Laurier-Greenway Agreement. Blondin accused Cannon of wanting to start a revolution by raising the province of Quebec against the other provinces. Sévigny was asked what he had done for recruiting, for the Patriotic Fund, and for the Red Cross, and why he didn't enlist. Cannon said the issue was the record of the government and of Sévigny, and whether the people favored National Service in Canada, when in England it had been followed in six months by conscription. The Conservatives were charged with flooding the constituency with liquor, and the Liberals with conducting a seditious house-to-house campaign. Much was made of the bilingual question by both sides. The vote gave a majority of 297 for Sévigny, a slight decrease since 1911. *Le Soleil* flatly accused him of having bought the election.[55] This election showed that Quebec opinion had not yet solidified against the government, though the bitterness with which French-Canadian grievances were aired was not encouraging for the future.

6

The long and eventful 1917 session of parliament opened on January 19. Borden announced the government's intention of extending parliament's life for a year to avoid a wartime election, and the British Government's invitation to the dominion prime ministers to attend as members of the British War Cabinet a special Imperial War Conference to be held late in February. J.-H. Rainville was named deputy-speaker in Sévigny's place. Laurier criticised the government's lack of unity of purpose, thought, and action in its war policy, and its belated assertion of Canadian control over the Canadian forces overseas. Privately he agreed to an adjournment of the session so that Borden might attend the Imperial Conference, though he raised a constitutional question as to how Borden could become a member of the War Cabinet without being a member of the British Parliament. Borden defended his government's war record, and listed Canadian casualties to date as 70,263, out of 392,647 enlisted for overseas service and a total manpower contribution of 413,279.[56] He emphasized the need for the extension of parliament's term, but the question was not debated until later in the year, as it promised to be a highly controversial one. The government was unpopular, and Liberal stock was rising. The Liberals now controlled seven of the provinces, with a total of 336 seats to the Conservatives' 180.[57] There was a growing movement for a coalition government in which the Liberals would have a voice, without the strong Quebec representation that would be involved if the Liberals should win outright power at Ottawa.

The Liberal press of Toronto and Winnipeg favored coalition, with the exception of the *Toronto Star* and the *Manitoba Free Press*, while the Conservative press largely opposed it. But J. W. Flavelle,

Conservative chairman of the Imperial Munitions Board, had urged a coalition government in an address to the Ottawa Canadian Club in December, in order to avoid an election fought on a racial basis and to permit postwar revision of the empire by English Canadians, for 'it is inconceivable to me that a government sustained by the vote of a section of this Dominion which, no matter for what reason of conscience, were unwilling to bear their share in this struggle, would be permitted without civil strife to determine what part Canada should take in the Imperial Council which must follow the war.'[58] Borden had sought to prevent Flavelle from making this proposal.[59] Laurier had had coalition proposed to him by N. W. Rowell and other prominent Liberals, but lacked confidence in that form of government and had faith in a Liberal victory in an election, though he inclined to the belief that the Liberal leader should not be a French Canadian.[60] But pending the Imperial Conference, Laurier agreed to pass the War Appropriation Bill and a portion of the normal estimates, and parliament was adjourned on February 7 until April 19 by joint agreement. On the eve of Borden's departure for England, it was decided to postpone application of the Militia Act for home defence purposes, while Bennett proposed disenfranchising those who had failed to register for national service. The shadow of conscription loomed larger, with enlistments still declining, casualties rising, and a labor shortage in the West.[61]

Accompanied by Douglas Hazen, minister of marine, and Robert Rogers, minister of public works, Borden left Ottawa on February 12 and reached London on the 23rd. Borden at once had a consultation with the colonial secretary, Walter Long, with whom he had corresponded about the conference. He heard the new prime minister, Lloyd George, speak in the Commons, and had an audience with the King. He conferred with Admiral Jellicoe on the problems raised by the intensification of the German submarine campaign, and with the colonial secretary. The opening of the conference was delayed until late in March by the difficulties experienced by the Australian delegation in reaching England, so Borden spent the intervening weeks in visiting the Canadian troops at the front and British and French headquarters, as well as the Canadian base at Shorncliffe in England and many hospitals. On March 2, he attended the first meeting of the War Cabinet set up by Lloyd George, who had acted on Laurier's challenge of 1897, 'If you want our aid, call us to your councils.' For the first time department heads, experts, and other non-members of the cabinet were in attendance, in addition to the dominion representatives.

Borden developed an immediate friendship with the South African representative, General Jan Smuts, and the two evolved a new concept of the imperial relationship which was foreshadowed in their speeches at the Empire Parliamentary Association luncheon on April 2. It was embodied in the mutually drafted Resolution IX, which Borden moved and Smuts seconded in the conference on April 16, calling for the readjustment of the constitutional structure of the empire at a special Imperial Conference after the war:

> They deem it their duty, however, to place on record their view that any such readjustment, while thoroughly preserving all existing powers of self-government and complete control of domestic affairs, should be based upon a full recognition of the Dominions as autonomous nations of an Imperial Commonwealth, and of India as an important portion of the same, should recognize the right of the Dominions and India to an adequate voice in foreign policy and in foreign relations, and should provide effective arrangements for continuous consultation in all important matters of common Imperial concern, and for such necessary concerted action, founded on consultation, as the several Governments may determine.[62]

In his speech in support of this resolution, Borden stressed the importance of the Crown as the tie linking the Dominions with the United Kingdom, and of the acceptance of the general principle by the British Government in establishing the Imperial War Cabinet. Smuts stressed that in the future 'the Governments of the Dominions as equal Governments of the King in the British Commonwealth will have to be considered far more fully than that is done today.' To him the resolution implied the rejection of the ideas of an imperial parliament and an imperial executive, and favored the development of the empire along the old loose lines with still more freedom and equality for the constituent parts. The resolution had been produced in consultation with Australia, New Zealand, and Newfoundland, and was previously approved by the British War Cabinet. The inclusion of India was made at the suggestion of Austen Chamberlain, then secretary of state for India.

Resolution IX was passed unanimously by the conference, and the way was thus paved for the establishment of the British Commonwealth of Nations in 1926, confirmed by the Statute of Westminister in 1931.

In his public addresses in England and Scotland during the remainder of his stay Borden emphasized the great constitutional development which had taken place, thanks to the stress of events, British flexibility and pragmatism, and the power of the prime minister under the British constitution. Lloyd George was, in fact, as Walter Long told Borden, virtually a dictator; and he was a dictator who favored Borden's constitutional views and was willing to take his advice on dominion matters. Borden upheld Canada's interests strenuously in the meetings of the Imperial War Cabinet, where matters of common imperial concern were discussed, while the British War Cabinet dealt with day-to-day questions chiefly concerning the United Kingdom. Before the Conference closed on May 2, it unanimously accepted the principle that each part of the empire should give special favorable treatment to the produce and manufactures of other parts of the empire, but this was the only concession to Chamberlain's imperial dream. It was agreed to hold imperial war cabinets regularly, annually or more often. In the new imperial council Great Britain presided, but was merely *primus inter pares* in Borden's favorite formula.

Upon his return to Canada Borden submitted a report to parliament on his English visit, and stressed the importance of this new 'cabinet of governments rather than of ministers.'[63] Laurier put his finger on a major difficulty by pointing out that the imperial cabinet was merely a consultative body, whose conclusions might or might not be adopted by the various parliaments of the empire, each the proper advisor of the Crown in the country in question. In a letter to the editor of the *Manchester Guardian*, who had requested his views on the conference and on future imperial relations, Laurier said that he thought discussion of the subject inopportune during the war, but stated his opinion that since foreign affairs could not be divorced from the domestic policies of the United Kingdom, the dominions could have no real voice in questions of peace and war. To have such a voice, they would have to back it with permanent defence contributions. He was opposed to this on the grounds of Canada's need to devote her wealth to internal development and her unwillingness to participate 'in such a senseless war as the Crimean War.' He regarded imperial federation as impracticable at present, and the present loose connection as 'the safest and the most promising.'[64]

7

But the constitutional questions raised by the Imperial Conference of 1917 were overshadowed by the conscription crisis which arose in Canada at this time. The enlistment figures for the early months of 1917 were dwarfed by the casualty figures:

	Enlistments	Casualties
January	9,194	4,396
February	6,809	1,250
March	6,640	6,161
April	5,530	13,477
May	6,407	13,457 [65]

The conquest of Vimy Ridge in April had cost the Canadians particularly dear, but with four divisions at the front there were continual losses which threatened to exceed the supply of reinforcements. In March the new militia minister, Sir Edward Kemp, made a last vigorous effort to obtain volunteers. On March 16 he called for the enlistment of 50,000 men as a Canadian Defence Force, so that troops still in Canada might be released for overseas service. It was hoped that the men so enlisted might later be induced to go overseas, though for the time being they were only asked to drill three times a week and to attend a summer camp. Disliked by the army and by conscription enthusiasts, this effort was a recognized failure by May. Meanwhile revolution-torn Russia was virtually out of the war; submarine warfare was proving far more effective than anticipated; and though the United States had declared war, it was felt that it would be a long time before American military strength was exerted in France.

In the same speech on May 18 in which he reported on his London visit, Borden stressed the need for reinforcements and announced his reluctant conviction that the selective conscription of 50,000 to 100,000 men was necessary. The announcement was timed to coincide with the day that the American Select Draft Bill became law at Washington. Previously there had been rumors of considerable numbers of young Canadians crossing the New Brunswick, Quebec, and Ontario borders to the States, in order to avoid pressure to enlist. Laurier reserved comment on the proposal which he had so long dreaded, stating that Canada was in the war to the end, but the method of carrying on the war to the end must be carefully considered before the established policy of the country was set aside. He promised due and fair consideration of the government's proposals, and that his Liberal colleagues would do their duty to the best of their judgment. Privately he stated that he was opposed to conscription by his commitments and by his conviction that, as in England, it would bring in only a tiny number of slackers, since 'the number of men who can be spared from agriculture and industry is infinitesimally small.'[66] To Lomer Gouin he wrote on May 28:

As to conscription, there can equally be no hesitation. After the agitation which has been carried on upon this subject, if we were to hesitate at this moment, we would hand over the province to the extremists: instead of promoting national unity, it would open up a breach, perhaps fatal.

As for myself, the situation is clear, but I doubt whether I will succeed in inducing our friends from the other provinces to accept it. The Eastern provinces will be nearly solid with us; Ontario solid on the other side, and the West perhaps divided; there is some ground for hoping for a fairly solid vote, but I am far from being sure.[67]

The *Montreal Gazette* and the English press in general favored conscription from the start. *La Patrie* and *L'Evénement*, the government organs, accepted it unenthusiastically as a necessity. *Le Canada* on May 21 attacked the government for going back on its promises of no conscription, on May 24 urged a referendum on the question, and on May 26 came out flatly against conscription. On May 28 *La Presse* also urged a referendum, though on May 16 it had asserted that if conscription had been adopted at the beginning of the war 'it would be working well today,' and that if found necessary, 'it will be religiously accepted by the Province of Quebec.'⁶⁸ But the rural weeklies at once expressed opposition, and popular feeling in Montreal was indicated by the fact that mobs broke the windows of *La Patrie* on May 23 to the cry of 'Down with conscription!' and again the following night, when *La Presse* also suffered the same attentions. Mass meetings were held on the night of May 23 at the Champs de Mars and at Parc LaFontaine. In Quebec City on May 21, a crowd of 10,000 heard Oscar Drouin say that he would fight conscription to the death, while on May 25 a crowd roused by a fiery speech by Armand Lavergne smashed the windows of the *Chronicle* and *L'Evénement*. On May 29 there was a great anti-conscription meeting at Hull, followed by others in other towns during June. As early as May 28 *Le Devoir* urged the French Canadians to remain calm, and to beware of agents-provocateurs inciting them to violence so as to make them seem rebellious to the laws of the land. They were asked to listen to the voices of their religious leaders and to oppose conscription in a calm, disciplined manner.

But Quebec was in no calm or disciplined mood at the long-expected appearance of conscription, which had so long been used in the province as a political bugaboo. Enthusiasm for the war was at a low ebb. In March Blondin had resigned from the cabinet to raise the 258th Battalion among his compatriots for overseas service, 'deeply convinced that the most imperious duty of the present hour for me is to practice what I have preached to you for the last three years and to devote myself entirely to the rallying of the French Canadians.'⁶⁹ Despite support from General Lessard and two returned officers of the 22nd, and an elaborate organization which scheduled fifty-eight meetings throughout Quebec between May 1 and July 15, the Lessard-Blondin effort brought in only 92 recruits. In Montreal on May 7 the crowd refused to listen to any of the political leaders, veterans, or the recruiting officers. An effort was made to invoke the influence of the *curés*, but the recruiting campaign was cancelled on May 20 with the announcement of impending conscription. In April and May troops passing through Quebec were pelted with rotten vegetables, ice, and stones when they taunted

French-Canadian youths with not being in uniform. At the National Unity Convention, which met in Montreal from May 21 to 25, as a development of the *bonne entente* movement, Bishop Gauthier made a passionate defence of French Canada's war efforts, rather than a plea for national unity.

Bourassa was not surprised by the coming of conscription. He had long anticipated it, particularly since the United States declared war in April. For a year he had followed American affairs closely, and from May 7 to 19 he published in *Le Devoir* a series of articles on causes, ends, and consequences of American intervention in the war, which he published in pamphlet form at the end of the month, with a new section on the consequences for Canada.[70] American neutrality had furnished support for French-Canadian nationalism, as it was to do again in the Second World War. Bourassa admired Wilson as a sincere partisan of peace, but blamed his insistence on the right of Americans to travel and trade freely across the seas as compromising his hope for peace. He laid much stress on the influence of German philosophy and educational ideals on both Americans and English Canadians to explain American neutrality, supported by the Irish hatred of England and Jewish hatred of Russia. Sympathy with and against France seemed to him to be about equal in the States, while English legal and financial influences had counteracted pro-German influences. The invasion of Belgium, the heroism of France, the submarine campaign, the swaying of the press by the Morgan interests, and the sinking of the *Lusitania*, cunningly exploited by English and American financial interests deeply committed to the allied cause, had done much to bring about American support of the war. The Russian Revolution had aroused democratic sympathies, as Wilson's peace program became his war program.

Bourassa approved of the immediate adoption of selective conscription in the United States—'the only practical and just means to organize an effective army while reducing to a minimum the dangers of economic disorganization'—as opposed to the so-called voluntary system in Canada, which he characterized as 'enlistment by blackmail, intimidation, seduction, and the grotesque methods of circus advertising, without any regard to the needs of agriculture and industry, as essential to victory as a great number of soldiers.'[71] In Canada there had been 'the triumph of militarism under its most dangerous and stupid form'; in the United States 'the subordination of military organization to the supreme needs of the nation.'[72] The United States had also applied the agricultural measures which Bourassa had long called for vainly in Canada. He cited the difference as that between the concrete applications of nationalism and of colonialism to the solution of vital national problems. The United States was now torn between the immediate contribution of money and supplies, and the eventual contribution of a vast army, with England calling for supplies and France for soldiers. Bourassa indicated his belief that English influence would be the most influential on American policy. He anticipated that the American entry into the war would shorten the conflict; would drain American capital, bring about a postwar depression, and promote a return to the land. He feared permanent militarism and a peace based upon power politics rather than Wilson's 'peace without victory.' In a curiously prophetic passage he foresaw a postwar Anglo-American alliance which would force Japan into an Asia-for-the-Asiatics policy. In considering the consequences for Canada of American intervention, he stressed the fact that Canada was a North American country whose future was tied to that of the United States. He foresaw immediate economic advantages, but eventual disadvantages for the weaker partner. American emigration to Canada would be halted, while state socialism, continuing militarism, and eventual absorption of Canada by the United States would be promoted, barring Canadian independence.

Bourassa did not discuss conscription in *Le Devoir* until May 28, when he published a series of articles which ran until June 6, and were immediately printed in pamphlet form in French and later in English.[73] The title-page carried the quoted assurances of both Laurier and Borden on January 17, 1916 that there would be no conscription. Bourassa explained his silence since May 18 on the grounds that calm consideration would have been impossible in the first explosion of popular opposition. His belief since the South African War that Canada had entered upon the road leading to conscription was now justified by events. He called for the signature of the anti-conscription petitions of the *Ligue Patriotique des Intérêts Canadiens*, but warned of the danger of mass meetings which might lead to excesses of language or acts of violence. He argued that now Canada had done enough, though he said he would have favored a policy of selective conscription at the outset of the war. He pointed out that proportionately Canada's military effort was greater than that of England and France, and that proposed by the United States. He warned of the dangers of national bankruptcy, of the labor crisis, and of famine in England; and urged that slackers be conscripted for agricultural service, and that wealth and industry also be conscripted. He supported Laurier's argument of 1916 that conscription would be a bar to postwar immigration.

Bourassa then turned to the racial cleavage created by the war, pointing out that differences were inevitable, but stressing the advantages of racial partnership. He reviewed the nature of French-Canadian patriotism, with its devotion to Canada as the only homeland, with its affection for France and its reasoned sense of duty to

Britain. But this latter view of Canada's obligations to Britain, once held by English Canada, had been transformed by massive British immigration and imperialist propaganda, leaving few unhyphenated Canadians. He stressed the fact that Canada was divided when it entered the war, and had become more so as time went on. Many French-Canadian leaders had sought to win the support of their compatriots for participation by appeals to British loyalty and to duty toward France, and when these efforts failed, sought to prove that French Canadians were supporting the war as vigorously as English Canadians. To Bourassa this second mistake was worse than the first, since it could only end 'in acrimonious explanations, in bitter disillusionment and extremely dangerous reactions'—the present situation. He considered the 'system of mutual deception' practiced by the leaders of both races in recent years the greatest danger to national unity, and called for absolute frankness.[74]

Bourassa stated that the vast majority of French Canadians had long concluded that Canada had gone beyond reasonable limits in its participation in the war. As long as enlistment was voluntary, they had largely kept silent. But when Borden broke the pledges of both himself and his Quebec colleagues, the French-Canadian reaction was first amazement, then anger, and finally determination to oppose conscription by all legitimate means: 'Two million French Canadians are opposed *en masse* to conscription.'[75] He warned that 'everything in the application of compulsory service—however impartial it may appear to be—will tend to irritate the French Canadians, and generally all Canadians who are Canadian before all.'[76] Conscription would bear more heavily upon young French Canadians than upon the English. Bourassa did not mention the main reason: that more young English Canadians had already enlisted; but rather laid the blame on the exodus of young English Canadians to the States. He criticized the presence in Canada of many young Englishmen who had fled conscription at home, and warned that since the large number of unnaturalized aliens could not be conscripted, true Canadian influences at home would be lessened. He censured the government's willingness to exempt from service on religious grounds the Mennonites, Doukhobors, and Quakers, while refusing to recognize the French-Canadian sentiment against military service except in the defence of Canada.

Bourassa warned that the adoption of conscription would 'soon transform the most peaceable, perhaps the most orderly, population of the two Americas into a revolutionary people.'[77] He stated that English-Canadian workers and farmers were anti-conscriptionist, and urged a national referendum to settle the question, 'the only safety valve to prevent a dangerous explosion.'[78] Calling attention to Borden's and Laurier's pledges against conscription in 1916, renewed at the National Service registration and in the Dorchester election, he blamed Borden's adoption of conscription on English pressure exerted at the Imperial Conference and on an effort to prevent American draft-dodgers from taking refuge in Canada, as so many British and Canadian slackers had done in the United States before that country entered the war.

He opposed coalition government and the extension of parliament's life: 'To prevent the designs, by no means established, of William the Autocrat, shall we permit Robert the Headstrong— even with the cooperation of Wilfrid the Conciliator—to play with our lives and also with the constitution and the established order?'[79] He saw Borden's program as an effort to avoid the control of the government by the people, and warned that Laurier had no right to lend himself to the manœuvre. He opposed to the analogy with England, which had adopted coalition and conscription, the fact that Canada had neither the right to declare war nor to make overseas service compulsory without the people's consent. Neither Australia nor South Africa had adopted conscription or coalition government. He called for an immediate dissolution of parliament, and a referendum on conscription. He considered that coalition, followed by an election and then conscription if the government were sustained, would, by making anti-conscriptionists run against both parties, be 'a formal and definitive incitement to insurrection.'[80] He claimed that he had done his best to calm the present excitement, would do his best to maintain public order, but would not be responsible for popular anger if this course was followed. Resolutions denouncing conscription and in favor of a referendum were unanimously passed at a meeting organized by Bourassa at the Monument National on June 7.

As feeling mounted in Quebec, Laurier was invited by Borden on May 25 to join a coalition government in which each party would have equal representation, apart from the prime minister. Laurier expressed his opposition to the conscription proposal and warned of the consequences in Quebec if it were adopted without a referendum or an election, the latter course being the one he favored. Borden expressed strong opposition to a wartime election, and Laurier promised to consider the coalition proposal and consult his supporters. On May 29 Borden yielded to Laurier's insistence on an election, and suggested coalition government and passage of the Military Service Act, with the understanding that it should not come into effect until after an election. On June 4 he added his willingness to make the Conservative wing of the coalition government acceptable to Laurier. But on June 6 Laurier declined to enter into coalition, on the grounds that he could not join in carrying out conscription, whose principle had been previously adopted and to which he was opposed. He told Borden that he would be in a stronger position to oppose Bourassa and his propaganda outside the government, and promised his support for the Military Service Act if it should be adopted by parliament. An exchange of letters summarizing the negotiations was published on June 7.[81]

Laurier's private letters of this period indicate that he was opposed to coalition even if conscription were not involved, having no confidence in the stand of some of Borden's colleagues on economic, railway, and other questions.[82] In a letter to Rowell on June 3 he gave his reasons for opposing conscription, which would 'create a line of cleavage in the population, the consequences of which I know too well, and for which I will not be responsible.' He was convinced that there was an undercurrent of opposition to conscription in every other province, as well as Quebec's solid opposition, thanks to the government's repudiation of its no-conscription pledges. Because of his stand on the Navy Bill in 1911, Laurier had been attacked in Quebec as a supporter of conscription and had been led to make many pledges against it. 'Now if I were to waver, to hesitate or to flinch, I would simply hand over the province of Quebec to the extremists. I would lose the respect of the people whom I thus addressed, and would deserve it. I would lose not only their respect, but my own self-respect also.' To him the only solution of the question was an immediate appeal to the people, either by a referendum or an election: 'Let the people decide, and if they decide in favor of conscription, as it seems to me they will, under present circumstances, from the attitude of our friends in Ontario, whatever influence I may have will be employed in pleading to the Quebec people that the question is settled by the verdict of the majority, and that all must loyally accept the issue and submit to the law; and this will be no light task, but a task to which I will devote myself with all my energy.'[83] During this period Clifford Sifton was assuring Borden that he favored coalition, and assuring Laurier that he was opposed to it, but favored an extension of parliament's life. His motive has been variously assigned to a desire for successful prosecution of the war and a desire for assuring an amenable government in the pending crisis of the affairs of the Canadian Northern and Grand Trunk Pacific railways.

Borden introduced the Military Service Act, which he had previously submitted to Laurier, on June 11. He emphasized the need for reinforcements, and to offset his pledges against conscription quoted his statements of January 1, 1916 ('By the greatness of the need, our future efforts must be measured') and of December 27, when he refused to give labor any assurance against conscription. He denied that conscription was being introduced at the request of the British Government, and maintained that the principle of compulsory service had been embodied in Canadian law for half a century. Instead of the selection by ballot already provided by the Militia Act, he proposed selection according to the country's needs, with exemptions provided for essential war work, serious individual hardship, or conscientious objections. Tribunals were to be set up to deal with exemptions and to hear appeals. He made an eloquent plea for keeping faith with the men overseas, and said he was more concerned about their reaction when they returned home, if the bill were not passed, than about the 'disunion, discord, and strife' foreseen as results of its passage. [84]

Upon second reading on June 18, Laurier moved an amendment providing for a referendum before further consideration. He said that the law of the land had long provided for compulsory military service only for the defence of Canada, and denied Borden's claim that Canada's first line of defence was in France and Flanders. He claimed that there never had been any danger of a German invasion of Canada. He argued that parliament's life would not have been extended in 1916, if the government had announced that it contemplated introduction of conscription; and since parliament no longer represented the people, and labor and the French Canadians were opposed to conscription, he urged a referendum. He blamed the comparative failure of recruiting in Quebec on the fact that the French Canadians were the oldest Canadians, and lacked the close relationship with France which so many English Canadians had with Britain; on the absence of military organization in Quebec since 1760; on Bourassa's attitude since 1903; and on the government's ineptness in dealing with Quebec recruiting. He argued on Colonel Blondin's testimony that the French Canadians would have responded if they had been recruited from the start for French-Canadian battalions by such men as General Lessard, Captain Papineau, and Colonel Barré. [85]

The debate lasted for three weeks, with growing Liberal support for conscription from Ontario, Maritime, and Western members. Hugh Guthrie, George Graham, F. F. Pardee, F. P. Carvell, and Michael Clark led the Liberal revolt against Laurier's stand, while Frank Oliver, Charles Murphy, and all the French-Canadian members except four supported the Liberal leader. Sam Hughes attacked both Laurier and Borden, saying that the latter was responsible for the failure of voluntary responsibility. Solicitor-General Arthur Meighen bitterly told Laurier that the only reason that he believed Canada was not in danger of invasion and could sit safely in his seat was because he knew the Allies would hold the line in France. Laurier was also accused by Dr. Edwards of being responsible for Quebec's anti-British bias by preaching independence and separatism, and his younger followers with interfering with the recruiting campaign in Quebec. J. A. M. Armstrong insisted that the only reason conscription was necessary was because Quebec had failed to do her duty. Patenaude resigned from the cabinet on June 9, leaving Sévigny as the only French-Canadian representative. Deputy-Speaker Rainville and Dr. Paquet, government whip for Quebec, also resigned; while Sévigny said he saw no reason to resign because most French Canadians opposed conscription, and blamed the comparative failure of Quebec's war effort, which he defended, on faulty organization. Conscription was also backed by Dr. J.-L. Chabot of Ottawa and F.-J. Roubidoux of New Brunswick, while a group of nine French Conservatives supported J.-A. Barrette's amendment for the six months' hoist, made on June 20.

A solid bloc of French-Canadian members, with the above exceptions, supported Laurier's stand, and many a Quebec member was heard for the first time. Since most of their speeches were in French, they were neither effective upon the majority of the House at the time, nor did they reach English readers of *Hansard* until some months later, when translations were published in the revised edition. But they expressed French Canada's bitter resentment and foreshadowed the violence which was to come. L.-J. Gauthier warned that 'my people are willing to go to the limit if you impose upon them such a piece of legislation.' Joseph Demers said the sending of 200,000 men would have been sufficient for the needs of the Allies, while Canada should concentrate on the production of food, ships, and munitions. Jacques Bureau resented slanders on the French Canadians: 'We do not want to fight for liberty in Europe and create a condition of slavery in Canada.' Hermenégilde Boulay gave four reasons for French-Canadian opposition to conscription: the traditions, constitution, and colonial status of Canada; the sufficient number of men already sent overseas; the fact that such a step was not justified by the 1911 mandate from the people without a referendum; the lack of fair treatment from the English majority; and opposition to overseas service created in 1896 by the Liberals and in 1911 by the Conservatives.

Alphonse Verville, a Labor Liberal, threatened a general strike. Georges Boivin felt that Canada had done more than the other Allied nations and the other dominions; J.-A.-C. Ethier felt that Canada had done enough and conscription would destroy autonomy, remove liberty, and lead to ruin. Honoré Achim said disruption of the country would not come from Quebec but from Ontario, where capital crushed labor, where manufacturers sought to restrain freedom of trade, and where Jingoes sought to strangle freedom of conscience. Roch Lanctôt said Canada had no trenches to defend in Europe but that the French Canadians must fight the Boches of Ontario and Manitoba. He was not alarmed at the prospect of

Canada's having a third European master. L.-J. Papineau asked whether Canadian troops were sent to the most exposed positions, and warned that many more than 50,000 or 100,000 men would be called for in the future. D.-A. Lafortune said that it was Canada's war only in the mind of the government and its friends: 'They may say that we should give our last cent to save the Empire; as for me, I shall say I have no more to give.' J.-E. Marcile called upon the British Army to display its mettle and relieve the colonial troops of the major burden they had borne since the beginning of the war. Médéric Martin warned of the end of Confederation and civil war, if English and French continued to insult each other and if conscription were adopted. Quebec believed that the best way to aid the empire and the Allies was through supplying food and ammunition. Dr. Paquet supported a referendum but denounced the Liberals for having advocated nationalism, and non-participation in imperial wars before 1909. Major Gustave Boyer expressed lack of confidence in the government, urged that parliament had no mandate from the people, and declared that more men were essential for home production. A.-A. Mondou opposed conscription, although he admitted that the future of the empire was at stake and Britain was fighting for a just cause, and announced his future support of Laurier. [86] At five o'clock on the morning of July 6 Laurier's motion for a referendum was defeated by a majority of 59, and the Military Service Bill was supported by a majority of 63.

The bill came up for third reading on July 19. It was advocated by J. C. Turriff, a Western Liberal, who also supported the proposal made by Hugh Guthrie a month earlier in favor of conscription of wealth. Guthrie and Pardee reiterated their support of the bill. Laurier regretted the estrangement of his former colleagues, but said he had not sought to impose his views upon his followers. He warned that 'We are face to face with a cleavage, which, unless it is checked, may rend and tear this Canada of ours down to the very roots.' He defended his attitude in refusing to join a coalition which had already accepted conscription. He concluded:

I oppose this Bill because it has in it the seeds of discord and disunion; because it is an obstacle and a bar to that union of heart and soul without which it is impossible to hope that this Confederation will attain the aims and ends that were had in view when Confederation was effected. Sir, all my life I have fought coercion; all my life I have promoted union; and the inspiration which led me to that course shall be my guide at all times, so long as there is a breath left in my body. [87]

Arthur Meighen, who was taking a leading role in the Conservative forces as Borden's health declined, replied to Laurier, pointing out that the bill had been supported on second reading by an overwhelming majority. The bill was carried on July 24 by 102 to 44.

In the Senate the government was sharply criticized by Quebec members, after Cardinal Bégin had opposed the measure for not exempting theological students. Senator Landry accused the authorities of having systematically ignored rural Quebec in recruiting, and stressed resentment of the breaking up of French-Canadian battalions and of the failure to form a French-Canadian brigade. Quebec's indignation over the school issue was frequently assigned as a cause of its poor recruiting record. Senator Dandurand argued that the nationalists had exploited this issue so successfully in 1915 and 1916 that they had brought recruiting to a standstill. He urged organization of agriculture and industry for war purposes. Senator Beaubien admitted the need for reinforcements, but refused to follow his party in supporting conscription, since Quebec feeling was so strong against it. The bill reached second reading in the Senate on August 3. An amendment offered by the Liberal leader, Senator Bostock, that the bill should not come into force until after a general election, was defeated by a vote of 44 to 35, with the Conservative Senators Landry, Beaubien, and Montplaisir supporting it. Senators L'Espérance and Beaubien espoused conscription on the second reading, and were supported by Senators Poirier and Bourque of New Brunswick.

On August 3 Brigadier Mason offered in the Senate a summary of recruiting statistics, stating that out of a total of 424,456 men Ontario had supplied 184,545 and Quebec 46,777. He estimated that there were 162,092 British-born volunteers amounting to 49.2 per cent of the men overseas; 132,265 English Canadians constituting 40.2 per cent of the men overseas; and 14,684 French Canadians constituting 4.5 per cent of the men overseas. Laurier questioned the French-Canadian total, expressing the opinion that 20,000 was more nearly correct, while Senator Choquette asserted that the figure ran as high as 25,000 or 30,000. Senators Bourque and Poirier urged their Quebec colleagues to emulate the Acadian example, but told their English colleagues that Quebec would do as well as any other province if she were appealed to in the proper way. The bill passed the Senate by a vote of 54 to 25, with nine English Liberals supporting the government. [88]

On August 9 Borden organized a conference at Government House with Laurier. The governor-general spoke of the dangers of a wartime election and Borden of those of incomplete victory or defeat. Laurier stood firm for an election to clear the air. Lord Shaughnessy and Clifford Sifton proposed postponement of an election. Sir Lomer Gouin backed Laurier and refused to form the government. Borden made a final offer of coalition, with suspension of conscription

for six months, extension of parliament for the same period, and a
united appeal for recruits; but this offer was refused.[89]

8

The English-Canadian press gradually united in support of conscription, after the *Toronto Globe* had backed and filled over the
question during the first month of discussion. The French-Canadian
press, with the exception of *La Patrie* and *L'Evénement*, was almost
solidly opposed to conscription. *Le Canada* and *La Presse* at first
urged a referendum, and then on July 25 the former said the government had passed the death verdict of 100,000 young Canadians
and the latter pressed for an election as the only means to calm
racial passions. On July 28 *L'Action Catholique* published an interview with Cardinal Bégin in which the prelate stated that the
failure to exempt lay brothers and theological students constituted
a grave interference with the rights of the Church and one which
should be opposed by all good churchmen. On August 8 Archbishop Bruchési said that racial and religious war was near, since
'incontestable rights have been violated.'[90] After conscription was
announced in May, the archbishop had urged his people 'to use
their rights as free citizens with calm and moderation,' and on
June 6, expressing resentment of the government's change of policy,
he explained that he had supported National Service because
Borden had assured him that there was no question of conscription
and that he was opposed to it.[91] *Le Devoir* continued to oppose
conscription, and on June 28 proclaimed that if Canada were to
survive enlistment should stop altogether. On July 26 it censured
parliament for criminal neglect of the rights of the people and the
needs of the nation, saying that Canadian soldiers were fighting
for the empire in the same manner as the Senegalese were forced
to fight for France.[92]

Ferdinand Roy, a distinguished Quebec lawyer and member of
Laval's law faculty, issued a pamphlet, '*L'Appel aux armes et la réponse
canadienne-française*,' in which he pleaded with his compatriots to
reverse their anti-war stand, to enlist, and to submit gracefully to
the Military Service Act when it became law. He appealed for
reason, tolerance, and a new view of French Canada's duty lest
French Canada be swept away altogether by the mounting tide of
racial hatred. He warned of the danger of isolated opposition to
Canada's war policy, which he blamed on the school question, the
unfortunate policy of the Borden government, the unskilful Liberal
maneuvers, nationalist errors, and French anti-clericalism. He
insisted that the Allied cause was the cause of civilization, and urged
that the French Canadians should not desert a cause which they had

espoused in 1914. Stating his own firm opposition to conscription, he urged the French Canadians to cease protesting against a *fait accompli*, a course which could only end in civil war. The time had passed for sterile discussion, which now might only increase the trouble; the French Canadians should sacrifice their opinions, their pacific tastes, and their blood in the interest of the future well-being of their race. Roy censured Bourassa for preaching 'sacred egoism' in a land where compromise between the races was essential, and for saying that French Canada had no call to fight for France, the mother of her civilization. [93] The altered attitude of the hierarchy was reflected by an editorial on Roy's pamphlet in *L'Action Catholique* on July 31, which said the French Canadians' only duty was to safeguard their country, which was now being asked to undertake an effort beyond its strength. Senator Dandurand and Sir Georges Garneau supported Roy's stand, while Armand Lavergne rejected it and said that if a referendum were not granted it would be necessary to call the people to arms to defend democracy in Canada.

The hierarchy's opposition to conscription was made evident by Archbishop Bruchési in an interview with Borden on July 7, when the archbishop expressed his doubts about good results from further recruiting, his opinion that exemption of French Canadians would make them despised, and favored an election. Cardinal Bégin also put pressure on Minister of Justice Doherty at the end of July to modify the act's provisions about clerics. [94] On July 7 the Quebec ecclesiastical weekly *La Vérité* published an article by one 'Louis Romain,' thought to be Mgr. Paquet, the rector of Laval University, which by elaborate theological arguments demonstrated that the bishops' pastoral of 1914 had not made participation an absolute obligation. This utterance by an unofficial spokesman of the hierarchy reflected the shift in the higher clergy's attitude.

Evidence of the lower clergy's views was contained in *Halte là*, '*Patriote*,' a pamphlet refuting the Abbé D'Amours and arguing with 'Louis Romain' by one 'Jean Vindex,' thought to be Père Hermas Lalande, S.J. The pamphlet frankly admitted the division of opinion between the pro-war upper clergy of the cities and the anti-war *curés* of the country parishes. It combated the doctrines of the 'New School of Imperialists' to which the hierarchy belonged and defended the nationalists from D'Amours' charges. 'Jean Vindex' accused Abbé D'Amours and the imperialists of misrepresenting the attitude of the hierarchy and twisting the pastoral letter of 1914 to suit their convenience. [95] There can be no doubt that 'Jean Vindex' truthfully expressed the attitude of the lower clergy, whose opposition to the war was completed by the adoption of conscription. The country clergy were in closer touch with the people and less affected by outside influences than the hierarchy and city clergy. They at once reflected public opinion and exercised a strong influence upon it. Through them Bourassa's influence reached into the backwaters of the province. The depth of their anti-war feeling may be judged by the fact that they dared to oppose their superiors' views, despite the strict discipline of the Church.

Feeling soon mounted high in Quebec and continued so. As early as June 15, *La Croix* of Montreal, an ultramontane journal, discussed the possibility of Quebec's secession from Confederation. Lavergne, who had declared in 1915 and 1916 that he would enlist if conscription ever came, announced on May 25 that: 'I will go to jail or be hanged or shot before I will accept it.' At Loretteville on May 27 he urged disobedience to the law if parliament passed it, and evoked the spirit of 1837. To a mass meeting of 15,000 people at Quebec on July 15 he said: 'If the Conscription law is enforced, Canadians have only one choice—to die in Europe or to die in Canada. As far as I am concerned, if my body is to fall in any land, I want it to be on Canadian soil.'[96] Tancrède Marsil, whose anti-war *Le Réveil* had been discontinued in March after a warning from Ottawa, issued the equally violent *La Liberté*, which thought 'revolution a hundred times better than slavery'[97] and was suspended on July 24 after urging a general strike, withdrawal of money from the banks, and revolution if necessary.

Night after night in June, July, and August anti-conscription meetings were held in Montreal, with crowds marching through the streets yelling '*A bas Borden!*' and '*Vive la révolution!*' and breaking windows and shooting off blank cartridges. One Elie Lalumière boasted that he was drilling 500 men for active resistance to conscription. The disturbances came to a head on the nights of August 29 and 30, when the crowds were urged to clean their old guns and to contribute for the purchase of other arms. The police attempted to break up the meetings, with one man shot and four policemen injured as a result.[98] During the conscription debates Borden and his French-Canadian followers also received threatening letters from Quebec.

The verbal violence of the anti-conscription orators produced the first major incident of real violence on August 9 when the Cartierville home of Lord Atholstan (Hugh Graham), whose *Montreal Star* vigorously supported conscription, was dynamited. Lalumière and eleven others were tried for the crime, and the former made a written confession of plots to blow up the offices of the *Star* and *Gazette*, the Mount Royal Club, and Senator Beaubien's home, and to kill Borden and other public men who supported conscription. Paul Lafortune approved the Cartierville crime at a public meeting on August 12, but Bourassa censured it in an editorial on 'Sterile

Violence' on August 11. He warned that the agitators were providing deadly weapons for the foes of French Canada, and deprecated talk of passive resistance. Instead he called for the election of anti-conscriptionist candidates to seek the repeal of the law. He censured acts of violence as illegimate and inexcusable. The rural press, appalled by the violence in Montreal, enthusiastically echoed Bourassa's appeal.[99] But the agitation in Montreal continued with unchecked violence until four of the leaders, Villeneuve, Lafortune, Côté, and Mongeau, were arrested after a public meeting on September 12, in which Villeneuve called for annexation or independence, saying: 'We have had enough of the Union Jack,' while the other speakers condoned the attempt on Atholstan. The agitators were released on bail, and continued their work with less violent words.

9

Meanwhile the government had introduced on July 17 a proposal for the extension of parliament's life for a year, with Borden promising not to act upon it if the opposition opposed it as a party. Laurier did not support the motion, and George Graham moved that consideration of extension should be postponed until conscription of wealth was introduced. This amendment was supported by all the Liberals except Dr. Clark and was defeated only by a majority of seventeen. After Laurier had attacked government administration of the war effort and Dr. Clark had supported Borden, the motion for extension was carried by twenty votes. Borden, however, announced that extension would be abandoned, since it had been approved by so small a margin. The British Government had previously indicated that it would provide the necessary imperial legislation to authorize extension only if the proposal received practically unanimous support.

Negotiations for the formation of a coalition government had continued steadily since Laurier's refusal of the proposal on June 6. To facilitate matters, Foster presented Borden with the resignations of all the ministers on June 12. Coalition was made difficult by the division into many different camps of the Liberals as the conscription debates went on. Borden began overtures to the Conscriptionist Liberals of Ontario headed by N. W. Rowell through Sir John Willison. On June 25 he called C. C. Ballantyne of Montreal into conference and received his assurance of support for conscription and coalition. On the following day he discussed coalition with Rowell and Sifton.[100] When Rowell learned that Laurier would not aid the formation of a coalition government under any circumstances, he urged coalition upon the Ontario Conscriptionist Liberals, while Sifton worked upon the Western ones. On July 20 a meeting of

Liberal members and candidates at Toronto supported Laurier's leadership, opposing coalition and the application of conscription until after another voluntary recruiting effort. On July 26 the Liberal editors of Ontario favored coalition on a platform of conscription of men and wealth, though they refused to accept Borden's leadership of such a government.

Meanwhile, on July 3, Sifton had issued a manifesto in favor of union government and conscription, with an extension of parliament if possible. He later called a convention of Western Liberals at Winnipeg on August 7. In a letter to Premier Martin of Saskatchewan, who had assured him that Sifton's alliance with Borden was resented in the West, Laurier expressed approval of the convention, but denounced Sifton's attempt to split the Liberal party along racial and religious lines.[101] In a whirlwind campaign to enlist Western support, Sifton said that an electoral victory under Laurier's leadership would mean that Canada would quit the war. Laurier replied in the House that he was in the war to the end, but on a basis of voluntary enlistment and not of conscription.[102] The convention was a fiasco from Sifton's point of view, since the Alberta and British Columbia Liberals strongly supported Laurier's leadership. Resolutions were passed condemning the Borden government, calling for vigorous support of the war but rejecting an amendment supporting compulsory service, and paying tribute to Laurier as 'the greatest of all Canadians.' Sifton nonetheless continued his efforts for coalition, with the support of the *Manitoba Free Press*, and by August 20 had lined up Western support for a coalition government including his brother Arthur Sifton of Alberta, J. A. Calder of Saskatchewan, and T. A. Crerar of Manitoba. A second Liberal conference at Winnipeg on August 24–5 agreed to coalition, but refused to accept Borden as prime minister, suggesting Sir George Foster, Sir William Mulock, Sir Adam Beck, or F. B. Carvell for the post. A Conservative caucus on August 29 declined to accept Borden's resignation. For the time being coalition efforts were deadlocked.

Meanwhile the government carried on August 29 the Military Voters Act introduced on August 13, which enfranchised all British subjects in the Canadian forces as well as those who had enlisted in certain British forces while in Canada, and made provisions for taking a vote overseas. A further War-Times Election Bill was introduced by Arthur Meighen on September 6 during Borden's illness. This highly controversial measure provided for the enfranchisement of female relatives of soldiers, the disenfranchisement of enemy aliens naturalized since 1902 and of conscientious objectors, and the preparation of new electoral lists upon this basis. Meighen, who had framed the bill, excused the enfranchisement provisions on the grounds that many soldiers could not vote, and the disenfranchisement of aliens on the grounds that they had been barred from enlistment. The majority of the newcomers, however, were Liberals, since they had found prosperity under the Laurier regime. The women were counted upon to support conscription both in gratitude for the privilege of voting and in the interest of their relatives overseas. The measure was obviously a colossal gerrymander, and was attacked by the whole opposition. It was forced through under closure on September 14, with Guthrie as its only Liberal supporter.

This measure broke the back of Western Liberal opposition to coalition on Borden's terms. Rowell conferred with the Western Liberals at Winnipeg on September 20, the day parliament was prorogued, and they resumed negotiations with Borden early in October in Ottawa. Borden had already added several Liberals to his government: Ballantyne as minister of marine, General Mewburn as minister of militia, and Hugh Guthrie as solicitor-general. The Westerners, faced with the prospect of being left out of the government, dropped their objections to Borden's leadership and their insistence on four places in the cabinet; and on October 12 A. L. Sifton was sworn in as minister of customs, Crerar as minister of agriculture, and Calder as minister of immigration and colonization. Rowell was made president of the Privy Council, and later on Carvell was named minister of public works, and G. D. Robertson and A. K. Maclean ministers without portfolio. Sir George Perley was named high commissioner to London—a post he had long coveted —and dropped as a member of the cabinet, which now included thirteen Conservatives and ten Liberals. A ten-man war committee, with equal Conservative and Liberal membership, was set up on October 16, and a reconstruction and development committee, with six Conservative ministers and four Liberals. Blondin and Sévigny were the only French-Canadian ministers, and they were admittedly without influence in Quebec.

Canada now faced a wartime election with Quebec almost completely isolated from the other provinces. An attempt was made early in October by the Conscriptionist Liberals to induce Laurier to resign in favor of an English-Canadian leader, but the party as a whole refused to accept his offer to withdraw. The government made arrangements to avoid Conservative opposition to Liberal-Unionist candidates, and in only two constituencies did the Conservatives rebel and run a candidate against their new allies. Laurier sought to make the government's record of incompetence and corruption the issue, but the government forces insisted that it was a question of going on with the war through conscription or quitting, of supporting the men at the front or deserting them. This plea was all the more effective because of the loss of 30,741 men in

November, in the costly victory of Passchendaele. Losses from July through October had amounted to 38,057, while enlistments had only totalled 18,471.

The first conscripts were summoned under the Military Service Act on October 13 to report in January 1918. But 57 per cent of the men between 20 and 45 who were called had claimed exemption by November 10. The final figures for the year showed that out of 125,750 men registered in Ontario, 118,128 had claimed exemption; while out of 117,104 registered in Quebec, 115,707 had claimed exemption. The Ontario tribunals disallowed 19,148 claims and did not deal with 4,783; the Quebec tribunals disallowed 3,711 claims and did not deal with 22,421. In almost all the provinces a similarly high proportion of men claimed exemption, and in most cases were granted it.[103] In November La Presse defended Quebec against the Ontario charge that the local boards in Quebec were exempting men wholesale, and pointed to the general situation throughout the country.[104] The whole conscription question was debated once more during the campaign, and this fact interfered with the effectiveness of the attempt to put the measure into force.

English Canadians, regardless of political affiliation, were loud in their lipservice to conscription, if not much more willing in fact to accept it than the French Canadians, who in overwhelming majority were opposed to it. Of the French press only L'Evénement remained faithful to the government, with La Patrie wavering in its support. La Presse evoked solid French-Canadian support for the old leader Laurier, abandoned by most of his English-Canadian supporters. Le Canada made much of a supposed plot to isolate and discredit French Canada. L'Action Catholique appealed for calm, but expressed unmitigated opposition to conscription and accused the government of stirring up English Canada against Quebec to win the election. The government had almost the entire English press behind it, as well as the organization of both parties in most of the provinces. A Victory Loan campaign in November, violently opposed by Bourassa as leading to national bankruptcy, fitted in with the government's cause.[105] On the Sunday before the elections of December 17, three out of four Protestant pulpits appealed for support of the government as a sacred duty, in response to a Unionist circular.[106] The soldier ballots provided only for a vote for the government or against it.[107]

Bourassa's decision early in November to urge support of Laurier and the Liberals as the lesser evil for the moment played into the government's hands. He pointed out that there were 4,000,000 men of military age in Britain still not called for service, and argued that Canada had done more than enough without conscription. The press of Ontario and the West conducted a violent campaign against Quebec and Laurier. The *Toronto Mail and Empire* on December 10 announced that Laurier was undoubtedly favored by the Kaiser, and on the following day carried an election advertisement declaring that a united Quebec sought to rule Canada. On election day the *Mail and Empire* called a vote for Laurier and his followers a vote for Bourassa, a vote against the men at the front, the British connection, and the empire; and a vote for Germany, the Kaiser, Hindenburg, von Tirpitz, and the sinker of the *Lusitania*. Laurier was depicted as the hope of Quebec, a menace to Canada, and as satisfactory to the Kaiser. The *Toronto Daily News* printed on December 14 a map of Canada with Quebec in black, under the caption 'The Foul Blot on Canada.' Laurier was represented as having capitulated to Bourassa. On December 7 the *Manitoba Free Press* told its readers that the choice was between union and the war or Laurier and disunion. A Toronto Citizen's Union Committee filled the English press with inflammatory advertisements declaring that 'Quebec must not rule Canada' and that 'a Laurier victory will be the first Canadian defeat.'[108] The Unionist publicity committee under Sir John Willison constantly linked Laurier, Bourassa, and Quebec, and roused ethnic feeling against French Canada.[109] Conservative leaders warned that 'Quebec was the spoiled child of Confederation,' 'the plague-spot of the whole Dominion,' and that if Laurier won the election Bourassa would rule Canada.[110]

In Quebec the government hoped for little beyond the elections of Doherty, Ames, Ballantyne, Sévigny, and Blondin. Sévigny ran in both Dorchester and Westmount, arguing that by refusing to accept coalition, Laurier had brought disgrace upon Quebec and prevented the settlement of the Ontario and Manitoba school questions. But his meetings were systematically obstructed and he was burnt in effigy in Montreal, while his colleagues Blondin and Rainville were coupled with him as the 'triumvirate of traitors.' The meetings of Ballantyne, Doherty, and Ames were also broken up by rioting mobs, as were those of lesser Unionist candidates. Feeling mounted so high that for a time Unionist meetings were abandoned. Sévigny and Joseph Barnard of *L'Evénement* were threatened with lynching. Violence was evident all over the province, in Montreal, Quebec, and Sherbrooke, and in the rural constituencies as well. Reports of it in the English press reacted against the Liberals and Quebec, though Borden was howled down by a crowd at Kitchener, Ontario. Laurier in his election manifesto condemned the coalition government as being purely Conservative in its program, attacked the War-Times Election Act and the government purchase of the railways, and denounced conscription of men without conscription of wealth and without a referendum. He pledged himself to carry out the will of the majority as expressed by a referendum, and to make a strong appeal for voluntary recruiting, which 'especially in Quebec did not get a fair trial.' If called upon to form a government, he would include representatives of business, labor, and agriculture so that the masses would be protected 'against organized privilege, which has heretofore had far too much control over the Government of the country.'[111]

At his first electoral meeting on November 9 at Quebec Laurier said: 'We began with the voluntary system; it is our duty to continue with it,'[112] but called for support of the army with more men. Sir Lomer Gouin denounced the attempt to isolate Quebec, and endorsed Laurier's plea for enlistment. At Ottawa on November 27 Laurier pointed out that conscription had been defeated in Australia, though there was no Quebec or 'racialism' there; stressed his differences with Bourassa; and stated that the way to get men to win the war was 'by appealing to the soul, not to coercion of the conscience.' Leaving Quebec to Lemieux and Gouin, and Ontario to his faithful supporters H. H. Dewart and Sir Allen Aylesworth, Laurier devoted the final weeks of the campaign to the West, where he won a wide hearing but evidently did not influence many votes. Both in the West and in Ontario much agrarian support for Laurier was lost when General Mewburn, minister of militia, promised on November 25 that farmers' sons engaged in the production of food would be exempted from military service. The recruiting leagues, the churches, and the newly enfranchised women threw their support behind the Union government. Labor launched a third party movement, but was not actively hostile to the government. The soldiers were strongly appealed to by the government and the Unionist Liberals, while W. T. R. Preston conducted a one-man campaign for support of Laurier by advertisements in the English papers.[113]

The result was an overwhelming victory for the Union government, with a government majority of seventy-one. Quebec returned only three government supporters, Doherty, Ballantyne, and Ames, in predominantly English Montreal constituencies, while Sévigny was defeated in both Dorchester and Westmount, and Blondin rejected by a huge majority in Champlain and a lesser one in Montreal. In the Maritimes the Liberals won only ten seats, to the government's twenty-one; in Ontario only eight to the government's seventy-four; in the West only two to the government's fifty-five. The soldier vote went twelve to one for the government. Only one French-Canadian supporter of the government was elected, Dr. J.-L. Chabot of Ottawa, who defeated Laurier in that constituency by a majority of over 5,000, though the Liberal leader was returned in Quebec East by the usual triumphant majority. French Canada was left without representation in the government, since Blondin took refuge in a senatorship and Sévigny resigned on March 7, paying tribute to Borden's goodwill to French Canadians.[114]

Bourassa described the result of the election as a victory for independence: 'The French Canadians resisted *en masse* because they are *en masse* and by instinct Nationalist.' He anticipated a postwar breakup of parties, with a new political alignment on the questions of settling accounts with England and the readjustment of Canadian economic equilibrium, in which the French Canadians would play an important role on the nationalist side against imperialism.[115] Arthur Sauvé, the provincial Conservative leader, agreed that the election was a triumph for Bourassa and his ideals, but *L'Evénement* warned the province that 'Under a leader in whom you have so long placed your confidence, and who has conducted you into so dangerous a position by placing you in opposition to almost all the rest of Confederation, you are now really isolated and alone in your corner, unable to do anything for yourself or for anyone else.' *Le Soleil* assigned Laurier's defeat to fanaticism and the racial cry, but consoled itself with the thought that he would have more followers in the new parliament than he had had since 1911. *La Presse* said Quebec had been true to its national obligations, but urged a revival of the *bonne entente* movement. The *Montreal Herald* proposed a new invitation to Laurier to enter the cabinet, and was strongly criticized for it in the Ontario and Western press.[116] Laurier, who felt at first that his lifelong effort for unity had ended in ruin, soon regained confidence in a postwar restoration of a 'fair and respecting partnership.'[117] He blamed his defeat on the gerrymander in the West and on the alliance of press, parsons, and women in Ontario.[118]

10

The isolation of Quebec, admitted by its own press and underlined by the *Toronto Star* and the *Manitoba Free Press* in their comments that 'we in Ontario and the West regard the War as a Canadian question and Quebec does not' and that the only reason for racial cleavage lay in Quebec's refusal to 'walk beside the rest of Canada along the road of national duty and sacrifice,'[119] bore heavily on the French-Canadian mind. The long-heralded cleavage between French and English in Canada, which some had desired and more had dreaded, had at last arrived in all earnest. Sore in heart at being overridden on the conscription question and weary of being the butt of English-Canadian abuse, the province showed much interest in a motion tabled by J.-N. Francoeur before the end of the year in the provincial legislature, that Quebec 'would be disposed to accept the breaking of the Confederation Pact of 1867 if, in the other provinces, it is believed that she is an obstacle to the union, progress, and development of Canada.'[120]

The Francoeur motion was much discussed by the press and public before it came up in the legislature on January 17, 1918. Asserting its belief that Quebec did not wish to secede, *La Presse* said on December 24 that it might be better to terminate an alliance no longer based on the principles upon which it was founded, if the English provinces felt that Quebec was interfering with their freedom of action. But it professed Quebec's loyalty to Britain and her desire to remain under the British flag whatever happened. *La Patrie* on December 22 refused to take the resolution seriously. *Le Canada* on December 24 urged its readers to remain calm and not to be carried away either by English-Canadian jingoes or French-Canadian extremists. *L'Action Catholique* on December 27 admitted that Quebec should not remain in Confederation if the other provinces no longer desired her presence, but opposed secession and characterized the resolution as inopportune. In later articles *L'Action* took the position that Quebec's isolation was not to be dreaded, since the French Canadians were united as never before and Quebec's position was impregnably strong; but it held that the resolution would lead to further persecution by extremist English Canadians. In *Le Devoir* late in December Bourassa also held that isolation was no cause for alarm. There was no possibility of conciliation from the Union government, and no honorable French Canadian could enter the government or co-operate with it. He urged French Canadians to remain aloof and to be the champions of right, truth, and real Canadian interests. The *Courrier de Saint-Hyacinthe* warned the French Canadians against losing their heads because the Liberals had lost the election, while *L'Etoile du Nord* saw no harm in secession if Quebec were not wanted in Confederation. The Montmagny *Peuple* opposed the resolution.[121] Sir Georges Garneau rejected the motion as inopportune and called for support of the *bonne entente* movement. Ferdinand Roy warned in *L'Evénement* that it was dangerous to play with loaded weapons and opposed the resolution.

Meanwhile the eloquent young nationalist leader Abbé Groulx was influencing large audiences by his lectures at Laval University in Montreal on Confederation, in which he made much of the forebodings of the French-Canadian leaders that Confederation spelled danger to their faith and national existence—forebodings which, the abbé made abundantly clear, had been fully realized by 1917. Confederation had resulted in vastly increased parliamentary corruption, the loss of the original ideals of religious liberty and racial equality, and the destruction of the Canadian national soul, torn by racial conflict and menaced by cosmopolitan European immigration.

The abbé later indicated that he was opposed to secession, which would mean abandoning the French Canadians outside Quebec, but his argument encouraged separatism and opposition to the Military Service Act.

In introducing his motion, Francoeur said it was demanded by the flood of bitter criticism of Quebec in the last three years. He saw evidence of a conspiracy to ruin the reputation of Quebec, quoting defamatory statements from the *Orange Sentinel*, the *Kingston Standard*, the *Toronto News*, and the *Winnipeg Telegram*. He also cited the election propaganda of the Citizen's Union Committee, evoking the 'menace of French-Canadian domination' and accusing Quebec leaders of stabbing Canadian soldiers in the back. He cited the attacks upon Quebec of H. C. Hocken and Isaac Campbell, and threw particular stress upon N. W. Rowell's statement of December 6 that 'There is a Nationalist, clerical, and reactionary movement at work in the Province of Quebec which today dominates the political situation in that province and is using this hour of great national peril to dominate the political situation throughout the Dominion of Canada.'

To all these charges Francoeur replied:

Her [Quebec's] only crime is that she interpreted the Constitution in a different manner from her fellow-citizens of different origin, that she denounced certain acts which in her opinion not only did not contribute to the success of the war and the safety of the Empire, but rather interfered with the issue of the one and the attainment of the other. It is because her people have shown themselves first of all Canadians, because they believed that the first thing to do was to develop this country in the interest of the Empire itself, that the greater its prosperity is, the greater is the possibility of achieving our destiny, because above all they demanded that the people be consulted before conscription was accepted.[122]

But there were also deeper reasons. Confederation was a compromise, which had not eradicated conflicts arising from differences of language, faith, and tradition. Dorion, Perreault, Taschereau, and Joly had foreseen trouble. Quebec had never shrunk from any duty nor evaded any responsibility arising out of Confederation; it had gone to 'the extreme limit of conciliation and of concessions . . . at the sacrifice of our acquired rights and our race pride.' But it had not got credit for it, and was maligned instead of being treated as an equal partner.

The only result could be the breaking of the Confederation pact, since 'Nobody can seriously argue that if the spirit of the constitution is not respected, the mere letter of the contract is enough to maintain the association.' The resolution expressed the sentiment of 'the very great majority of our people, who are tired of being treated in this manner, and who think that the time has come to stop these futile struggles or to accept their logical consequences.' Quebec did not want secession, but she would not falter at the prospect if it were thrust upon her. The desire of the French Canadians was to live and let live:

> To live observing not only the letter of the constitution but its spirit more particularly; to live according to our tastes, our temperament, and our mentality; to live as free citizens, conscious of our duties and careful of our responsibilities; to live working for the progress and development of our province, convinced that in this way we are assuring the progress and development of the country; to live preserving our language, our faith, our traditions, our institutions, and our laws; to live, in a word, as loyal Canadians devoted to the British Crown. Let live; to respect among others those things that we demand they respect among us; to recognize the liberty they wished to enjoy in the exercise of their acquired rights; to let them speak and teach their language, retain their faith and their traditions, and even to struggle with them, if it is necessary, for the defense of the heritage which they hold as dear as we . . . It is in this way that we will become in real truth a Canadian nation . . . We will then have not only the outward semblance of a nation whose material interests are its only bonds, but we will form a nation by the true union of hearts and souls.
>
> Why not realize this ideal? While our soldiers on the soil of France are fighting heroically for liberty and civilization, respect of treaties and constitutions, the independence and autonomy of nations, we here should cease to give the spectacle of struggles that have their origin in the negation of these principles. We must be worthy of the supreme sacrifice of these heroes. Their death is the greatest lesson in patriotism. Let us profit by it.[123]

Arthur Sauvé, the Conservative leader, said that all Tories were not anti-French fanatics, and opposed the resolution as inopportune. He blamed the racial feeling on the school question and on anti-conscriptionist feeling. He defended Quebec's record for obeying the law by producing figures which indicated that the province had the lowest percentage of men failing to report when called for military service. He had suggested to Sir Lomer Gouin an amendment to the resolution, petitioning for disallowance of the Military Service Act, but the premier had refused to present it.[124]

Athanase David reviewed the history of Confederation, pointing out that it was necessary from the economic and commercial points of view and at first tended toward the development of a common Canadian mentality. But political-religious problems arose, and with them the specter of French domination, as the imperialist mentality replaced the Canadian one in the English provinces. He defended Quebec's behavior since the outbreak of the war as 'animated purely and simply by a desire to avoid placing in danger the economic future of our country, the national future of our race.'[125] He asserted French Canada's reasoned loyalty to the British flag, but admitted that there was no love for it, and such love could not be evoked by insults. He blamed discord on the introduction of the imperialism of Dilke, Chamberlain, and Milner, who were willing to 'plunge Canada into bankruptcy if necessary to save the Empire.'[126] He asserted that imperialism of any kind, whether German, English, or American, was a danger to the world, and acceptance of it would be a backward step for Canada. He looked forward to full Canadian autonomy and eventual independence. Urging that 'only those who believe in the destinies of Canada'[127] should be entrusted with the solution of Canadian problems, he criticised the provisions of the War-Time Election Act.

But David anticipated the day when, the present crisis passed, the relations between the various provinces would once more be renewed in the tradition of Confederation. He believed that even today there was a strong minority of English Canadians who wished that Canada should remain mistress of her destiny, and that 'the doctrine for which we stand should resume its sway over the Canadian people.'[128] As in every national crisis in the past, men who did not share the faith and blood of French Canada would arise to join hands with the French Canadians. He had no fear of Quebec's temporary isolation, since it was a market which the English Canadians could not neglect. The English Canadians of Quebec would be the greatest sufferers from isolation, which might benefit the material and financial development of French Canada. He did not regret or fear Quebec's political isolation, since it arose from the refusal to betray an ideal which sixty-two members of the assembly had received a mandate to sustain. Good sense and logic would prevail in the end over prejudice and fanaticism. He was confident that:

, Our Confederation will arise from this chaos like all the peoples of the world, taught by suffering, enlightened by a new experience, and finding her pathway, and needing the effort of each group and each race, will issue the appeal that will serve to rally all groups and races. Freeing herself then from the grip of the autocracy in which she herself will deem she has remained too long, and understanding the dangers of the future if she does not consolidate at once all her force, energy, and will, she will unite in a great ideal of Canadian political democracy all those who under her aegis wish to continue to live to assure her greatness.[129]

Hector Laferté defended Quebec's loyalty and rejected the insults to which it had been subjected. He thought French Canada was not ready for independence; he was opposed to annexation; but he supported the resolution. T.-D. Bouchard opposed the English fear of domination to the French fear of persecution by citing attacks of the Quebec press on the Ontario fanatics, and called for a spirit of brotherhood to ensure the continuance of Confederation. A.-M. Tessier condemned the 'systematic campaign organized against the province of Quebec, accentuated by fanaticism and hatred of everything that is French.' But he did not believe that this represented the opinion of the English-Canadian majority, who in Ontario had given Laurier more support in the last election than in 1911. The fanatics might rave; but 'they cannot prevent the French nationality not only from continuing to exist, but from living, spreading, and increasing its influence in strength and number.' As proof that Quebec could weather this crisis as it had others, he cited history. He condemned the infringement of constitutional rights by the federal government, and he reminded English Canadians of the words of an Ulster leader: 'All we want is fair ground and no favor. We ask for no more and are determined to take no less. We believe you have the same tolerance and the same sanity as we have.'[130]

Lawrence Cannon urged the study of Cartier's career for an understanding of Confederation, and recommended following Laurier's leadership in the solution of the present problem. He rejected the motion because Quebec was the essential center of Confederation and had the right and the duty to remain at the head of Confederation. Louis Letourneau approved the resolution, stressing Quebec's growing industrial self-sufficiency and discounting the dangers of isolation.

Charles Ernest Gault warned that Montreal would secede if Quebec separated from the rest of the dominion, and that tariff barriers would ruin the province. Independence was unthinkable and would be ruinous. Annexation would mean the end of the French language and denominational schools. Gault blamed much of Ontario's bitterness on the feeling that the Catholic Church was not sympathetic to the Allies, and urged that this misapprehension should be cleared up. He paid tribute to the Canadian soldiers, and urged everyone to do something to help them, criticising the number of young men of military age present in the galleries who should be at the front. He blamed the Ontario school question for causing trouble between the provinces and said it would have been settled fairly if it had not been for the war. He censured extremists in both Ontario and Quebec, and deplored the lack of free speech in the last campaign, which had seen assaults on ministers of the Crown. He regretted that Gouin had refused an invitation to enter the federal government, a step which would have helped to remove the causes of the ethnic trouble. In a fiery speech Dr. Georges Grégoire replied to Gault that Quebec wanted peace, but Ontario seemingly sought to break up Confederation. He opposed French pride of race to British pride of race, and asserted that Quebec had done its part and did not deserve the stigma of cowardice.

Sir Lomer Gouin closed the debate, supporting the motion by citing the precedent of Nova Scotia, which in 1886 had adopted a resolution approving the separation of that province from Confederation and had almost unanimously voted in favor of it at a subsequent election. He asked why Quebec alone should be condemned for voting against conscription, when New Brunswick, Nova Scotia, and Prince Edward Island had also returned a majority against it. He had opposed Sauvé's proposed amendment because it would be ineffective. He expressed his belief in Confederation, which had made possible great development and progress in Quebec, and asked whether it would be in the interest of the half-million French Canadians in the other provinces for Quebec to leave Confederation. The school questions in the other provinces would have arisen without Confederation. He pointed out the plight Quebec would be in if it left Confederation, with no winter port, no defences, burdened by a share of the national debt and forced to pay customs duties to other provinces. He cited the example of union provided by the United States and closed with an eloquent appeal to preserve Confederation.[131]

After the premier's speech Francoeur withdrew his motion on January 23, stating that he was satisfied with the results obtained and defending his resolution's opportuneness.[132] Without question the Francoeur Resolution debate had provided a safety valve for Quebec's pent-up resentment at English-Canadian attacks at a crucial moment. It was clear that Quebec had no serious desire to quit Confederation, but had only been driven to consider it by English Canada's intransigent and insulting attitude.

11

Late in December 1917 John S. Ewart reopened his correspondence with Bourassa and sought an interview with him in the hope of improving the strained relations between English and French Canadians. The overture was not particularly welcomed by Bourassa, and in several exchanges of letters the two nationalists thrashed out their differences on the war. Ewart thus summed them up in a letter of January 21:

At the commencement we agreed upon the necessity for suppression of home differences with a view to production of war solidarity. Imperialistic war propaganda induced you to change this attitude. To me that change seems illogical. In my view, imperialism is a domestic question and has no relation to our attitude towards Germany. I therefore see in

Sir Robert Borden's excessive imperialism not a reason for alteration of Canada's opposition to her external enemies, but a reason for attack upon the imperialists.[133]

Then he revealed his purpose in seeking an interview with Bourassa.

Profoundly regretting the present political situation, and seeing in it a menace and danger to our political institutions, I have earnestly sought for some method by which our English-speaking and French-speaking peoples can be brought, if not to perfect harmony, at least to the relations which existed before the conscription act. I recognize that bilingual and other questions have always presented difficulties, and have confined myself to the recent acerbation of feeling due to the conscription act. It has occurred to me [to wonder] whether some modification of the statute would not relieve the tension, and I have thought of suggesting that every conscripted man should have the right of choice between service in the army and such other service in Canada as might be assigned to him. I have thought that such an amendment would meet, to a very large extent, the objections which you and your friends have raised against the act, and I desired to ascertain how the suggestion would appeal to you. I have not as yet said anything to Sir Robert Borden or any of his colleagues. It would probably be useless for me to do so without being able to give them some assurance that the proposed amendment would be welcomed in Quebec. May I ask if you will be good enough to let me know whether you think my proposal is practicable? If you should reply in the affirmative, I should then ask you whether I might be permitted to pass on your view to Sir Robert Borden, either in confidence or for such other use as you might think best.

Knowing you as I do, and appreciating your love of Canada, I feel sure that you will lend your assistance to any proposal which, in your judgment, will tend to the creation of sympathetic relations between the provinces.

For some unexplained reason—possibly his wife's illness—Bourassa delayed for two months in answering this request, which was in the great tradition of relations between leaders of the two main Canadian racial groups, and which took considerable courage to make at a time when Bourassa had become the most hated man in Canada. On March 29, 1918 he finally replied:

It is probably too late now for any useful answer to your inquiry, with regard to what might be done to alleviate the hostile feeling in Quebec against the Government and their war policy. I do not wish, however, to leave you under the impression that I had the slightest objection to write you in all open frankness on this or any other matter.

Your suggestion, if honestly and effectively put into execution, would do a great deal to appease the feelings of our people. But I could not leave you under the delusion that it would be sufficient to restore the

confidence of the French Canadians either in the Government or, generally, in the good faith and fair spirit of the English-speaking majority.

With regard to the Government, the representatives of Quebec in the
Cabinet and Sir Robert Borden himself, have so deceived and disgusted
the people, that nothing coming from Ottawa would be accepted in
confidence. Any announcement such as suggested by you, but coming
from the Government, would be taken as a new claptrap, as a new form
of deception, soon to be followed, as former assurances were, by measures
of coercion. It would take some time and a prolonged application to convince the people that the offer was made in good faith; and till the war
is over most people would remain convinced that those conscripts turned
on the farm would be liable to war service, the moment the Government
would change their mind on the matter.

As to racial misunderstanding in general, and lack of national unity
and spirit, it will take a very long time to convince our people that
British fair play is not a mere shibboleth and a pharisaic stock-phrase.

It would take too long a letter to explain fully the reasons and causes
of that feeling, and the obstacles to a prompt and decisive reaction. When
the occasion and the pleasure will be given to me of meeting you, we will
talk these matters over. We will also try to fully dispel the past misunderstanding on our respective attitudes on the war. I cannot quite accept
your last word upon it.[134]

During the early months of 1918 Bourassa had urged a negotiated
peace in *Le Devoir*. On February 22 he described Confederation as
'in fact prejudicial to the French Canadians,' and on March 26
he urged anti-conscriptionist members of parliament to refuse to
vote any more money for the war.[135] He also continued his bitter
denunciations of British policy.

12

There was much bitter feeling in Quebec early in 1918. Abbé
Groulx continued to intensify popular indignation about the Ontario
school question, and on March 16 the Montreal Saint-Jean-Baptiste
Society moved a resolution congratulating the Franco-Ontarians
'who had learned to oppose a persistent resistance to iniquitous
laws.'[136] In response to a query from Toronto as to what Quebec
wanted, *La Presse* gave this summary on February 20:

1. That the French language, recognized as an official language in the
Canadian Parliament, should be similarly treated in all parts of the country, because it has rights acquired in virtue of treaties and of the Constitution.

2. That the Ontario Government, in place of making regulations to
ostracize the French language and to prevent by the submission of a
shameful oath the French Canadians from establishing themselves in that

Province, should apply itself to treating our people as brothers: that is to say, as the Anglo-Protestant minority of Quebec is treated by the French.

3. That the Roman Catholic religion should be more respected by the Ontario press.

4. That the treatment of minorities should be based henceforth on justice, fraternity, and the intentions of the Fathers of Confederation, rather than on the very letter of the law.

5. That the other races should not seek a quarrel with us for any cause or no cause; that they should cease to discredit us abroad, because in doing so they discredit the whole of Canada.

6. That there should be an end of the belief that national unity can be secured only by unity of language; that the law of the strongest should no longer be enforced against us.

7. That good understanding between the two great races which predominate in Canada should be established on the basis of a knowledge of the two official languages.[137]

Article 2 referred to the new practice of making French-Canadian settlers in northern Ontario sign an oath to obey Regulation 17, under penalty of losing their land and the money paid for it. This was a measure adopted at the instance of the Orange Order, which on March 13 called upon 'the loyalists of Canada' to secure by changes in legislation the ideal of 'one flag, one school, and one official language from Coast to Coast.'[138]

The enforcement of the Military Service Act aroused difficulties in Quebec, despite *L'Action Catholique's* injunction on January 7 to submit to the law cheerfully and *La Presse's* urging on the same date of 'a courageous and worthy submission to the law.'[139] Exemptions were claimed on a wholesale scale, as they were throughout Canada, with local tribunals in Quebec refusing 4.1 per cent of the claims as compared to a refusal rate of 10.1 per cent in Ontario. But many Quebec cases were appealed by the military authorities, with the result that the total percentage of Quebec claims refused was 9 per cent while in Ontario it was 8.2 per cent.[140] Attention was focused on the operation of the law in Quebec, because of the province's solid opposition to conscription; and it was widely rumored in English Canada that many Quebec defaulters and deserters were seeking refuge in the bush or in the States. When deserters were rounded up in Montreal, the French press asked whether similar zeal was being shown in Ontario.

By the end of February conscription had only put 22,000 men in uniform, of whom 2,000 were from Quebec. Measures were taken to speed up some 30,000 appeals still pending in the province. The resistance of the Western farmers to conscription was also determined, and pressure was brought to bear on the government for the exemption of farmers' sons. An order-in-council of December 31, 1917 provided for the discharge by the militia minister of agricultural draftees whose claims for exemption had been rejected; while on February 8 the militia department issued instructions for special attention to such claims. By the end of March only 31,000 had been ordered to report for duty, with 5,000 of the number defaulting. It was generally agreed that conscription was a failure, as Laurier had maintained it would be. The woods were rumored to be full of armed defaulters ready to resist arrest.

Anti-draft riots were anticipated in Montreal, long a center of violent opposition to conscription, but instead they broke out unexpectedly in Quebec City on the night of March 29, when the federal police arrested a French Canadian named Mercier who was unable to show his exemption papers. After he was able to produce his papers, he was released, but a mob of several thousands gathered and burnt the federal police station. The police appealed to the military for assistance, but were referred to the civil authorities. Mayor Lavigeur sought to get the crowd to disperse, but did not read the Riot Act or call in the troops. The crowd got out of hand, and marched to the tunes of 'O Canada' and the 'Marseillaise' to the offices of the *Chronicle* and *L'Evénement*, which they sacked. On the following evening the crowd gathered after dark and attacked the office of the registrar of the Military Service Act, seeking to burn it with its records. The city police were reported to have refused adequate protection to the building, and to have looked on passively. An attempt was also made to free imprisoned draft-evaders.

The commanding officer, Brigadier Landry, asked for reinforcements, which the government tactlessly supplied in the form of a Toronto battalion. On March 30 the troops charged the crowd with fixed bayonets, and aroused a fury which found expression in one continuous riot the following day, March 31, which was Easter Sunday. Cavalry drove back the crowd with improvised bludgeons made of axe-handles, while feeling grew ever uglier. That evening Armand Lavergne addressed the crowds, claiming that he had an agreement with the military authorities that the troops would be withdrawn if the rioters dispersed to their homes. Brigadier Landry at once denied such an agreement. Lavergne then demanded that the troops be withdrawn and that 'reputable men' be used to enforce the Military Service Act; otherwise he promised to put himself at the head of the mob and to fight the authorities without mercy.

On April 1, despite placards posted ubiquitously requiring the citizens to remain at home under orders from General Lessard, who had been sent from Ottawa to take charge, and despite admonitions from Cardinal Bégin and the press for the populace to refrain from violence and to remain at home, the rioters opened fire on the troops from housetops, snowbanks, and other hiding places. After several soldiers had been wounded, they returned the fire with both rifles and machine guns. Cavalry charged the mob with drawn swords, while infantry picked off snipers. Order was restored by one o'clock in the morning of April 2, but five soldiers had been wounded and four civilians killed, with many wounded and fifty-eight arrested. On April 4 the government suspended the *habeas corpus* and provided for the immediate conscription of rioters by order-in-council.[141]

There was much criticism of these actions and of the sending of a Toronto battalion to restore order in Quebec, as well as of the allegedly brutal pursuit of slackers by the military authorities which had aroused the riots. But a Quebec which has always had a deep regard for law and order despite its tendency to verbal violence was horrified by the outbreak; and the Church and press promptly called for the re-establishment of order. The riots were represented as not being typical of public feeling. In a debate in the House on April 5 half-hearted and ineffective enforcement of the Military Service Act in Quebec was sharply criticized by English Canadians, while Laurier blamed the riots upon the men chosen to enforce the Act and upon a secret association drawn from the 'scum of Montreal.' But he joined Borden in calling for submission and obedience to the law. On April 13 a Quebec coroner's jury returned a verdict that 'considering the persons killed on that occasion were innocent of participating in the said riot, which owed its origin to the tactless and grossly unwise fashion in which the Federal police in charge of the Military Service Act did their work, it should be the duty of the Government to reasonably indemnify the families of the victims who have been found innocent and unarmed, and to pay indemnities to all who suffered damages from that riot.'[142]

French Canada blamed the riots on maladministration of the conscription act, while English Canada considered them the outcome of Quebec's resistance to the act. Misled by French-Canadian verbal violence, English Canada overestimated Quebec's rebelliousness, while Quebec made too much of 'Anglo-Saxon brutality' in enforcing conscription and repressing the riots. But since the French press had long been critical of police brutality and tactlessness in enforcing conscription, and had even brought definite charges that notorious criminals and strongarm men were used for the purpose, it seems clear that some blame for the riots must be attached to the way in which the Military Service Act was enforced in Quebec.

Discussion of the Quebec riots in parliament revealed the full extent of racial cleavage. Colonel Currie called for martial law in Quebec, with the internment of Bourassa and Lavergne and the suppression of *Le Devoir*. Borden refused, pointing out that 'a man behind the bars sometimes has more influence than outside the bars.'[143] Sam Hughes, who had often officially professed friendship for French Canada, attacked it savagely. He told of French-Canadian officers who had failed to enlist battalions, and of units which deserted as soon as they were enlisted. He accused the Catholic clergy of opposition to participation in the war, and asserted that Quebec had been perverted by German propaganda. But other English Canadians pointed out that the underlying cause of the riots was that Quebec was no longer under the control of Laurier and the moderates, but rather under that of Bourassa and the more fanatical members of the clergy. Growing opposition to conscription in the farming districts of English Canada led to a more indulgent attitude toward Quebec than during the election, though wholesale exemptions in Quebec were criticized. This criticism was disarmed by an order-in-council of April 19 cancelling exemptions, on the grounds of the emergency presented by the German break-through late in March, which had caused Canadian troops to be sent to reinforce British units. Laurier criticized the measure as a departure from the principles of the Act and of constitutional government, and urged the continued exemption of farmers' sons. General Mewburn declared that urban conscripts would be called first, while farmers would be permitted to finish their planting and would not be called till the last possible moment.

The cancellation of exemptions created intense excitement in Ontario and the West, as well as in Quebec. On May 14 a delegation of 5,000 farmers arrived in Ottawa under the joint leadership of J.-E. Caron, Quebec minister of agriculture, and of the United Farmers of Ontario. The *Toronto Globe* estimated that 3,000 of the delegation came from Ontario.[144] When the delegates were refused permission to wait upon parliament in a body, it was rumored that they were prepared to do so by force. Finally the farmers held a mass meeting at the Russell Theater. Borden addressed the meeting and stood firm by the order-in-council which had been approved by parliament. Protest meetings were held in Ontario and the West and petitions dispatched to Ottawa without effect; and on June 9 the United Farmers of Ontario, meeting for their annual convention at Toronto, censured the government and threatened an appeal to the Privy Council. This action was supported by the United Farmers of Alberta, and later by the Canadian Council of Agriculture meeting at Winnipeg. Criticism of the farmers became as common with ultra-patriots as criticism of the French Canadians. F. B. Carvell admitted in the House on April 19: 'There are thousands and tens of thousands, yes, hundreds of thousands, of people in the rest of Canada who have tried assiduously to evade military service.'[145]

After cancelling exemptions, the government adopted the policy of conciliation rather than coercion of Quebec which Laurier had urged. Bishop Mathieu played a notable role in quieting Quebec feeling, while Gouin was once more urged to join the government. Borden asserted his willingness to support formation of the French-Canadian brigade which was urged by Quebec members, and revealed plans for building up exclusively French-Canadian units by using French-Canadian reinforcements for battalions containing many of their compatriots. But he concluded with the statement that the government was inclined to think the mixing of the races in the army a good thing—which confirmed the fear of some French Canadians that it was sought to anglicize them through the army. General Mewburn visited Montreal and Quebec, and at the latter city on June 5, when welcomed by a formal address from the bench and bar, stated:

I for one have never for a moment doubted the loyalty of Quebec and its people; and from the wonderful things I have seen during my visit, my firm conviction has been strengthened . . . Permit me to say that I am putting forth every effort that recruited French Canadians be kept together in distinct units, commanded by officers of their own race and tongue.[146]

General Mewburn had also admitted that the recruiting results might have been much better if Sir Sam Hughes had allowed the old militia units to go overseas and to recruit on a territorial basis. Rodolphe Lemieux hailed the government's new policy. Laval University took the lead in the new recruiting effort, as the German threat to the Channel Ports became serious, and by June 21, 9,970 men from Montreal and 2,848 men from Quebec had enrolled. On that day *Le Soleil* urged immediate steps by the authorities to quell disturbances in rural communities blamed on defaulters. Quebec's new willingness to cooperate was noticed even by so long-standing an opponent as the *Toronto Mail and Empire*, which on April 30 commented on the gratifying way in which young men were answering the call to arms under the new order-in-council. The validity of the order-in-council was tested in numerous court cases all over Canada. It was denied by the Alberta Supreme Court, and finally upheld by the Supreme Court of Canada on July 20.

In an effort to make the Military Service Act effective, heavy penalties were provided for defaulting or desertion, and manhunts were held in public places for those without exemption papers. These measures were bitterly resented in Quebec. But on August 2 an amnesty was proclaimed for defaulters if they reported for duty before August 24; and some 10,000 took advantage of it. There were many others who hid out in the Laurentian wilds of Quebec and Ontario, the forests of British Columbia, or fled across the American

border. A group of young Nova Scotians sailed away with the fishing
fleet in June, while in other provinces men took refuge in remote
lumber camps where no questions were asked. In the end conscription yielded a total of 83,355 soldiers actually enlisted, of whom
47,509 actually went overseas, about 11 per cent of the total sent from
Canada and the equivalent of two divisions. Quebec provided 19,050
men under the Act, while it had 18,827 defaulters out of the country's
total of 27,631, with 40.83 per cent of the men ordered to report
failing to do so. Nova Scotia with 16.72 per cent defaulting,
Ontario, and Saskatchewan had the next highest percentages of
defaulters.[147] At a cost of three and a half millions for administration, conscription provided fewer men per month than the voluntary
system, while it bitterly divided the races and provinces and aroused
religious feeling. The latter issue was brought to a head in June by a
police raid on the Jesuit College at Guelph, Ontario, which the son
of the minister of justice had recently entered. The *Orange Sentinel*
and the *Toronto Telegram* demanded investigation and action on
charges that Catholic students received preferential treatment under
the act. Colonel H. A. C. Machin, head of the Military Service
Branch of the Department of Justice, denounced the charges with the
observation that 'The greatest menace to the Province of Ontario is
the Methodist Church, which seems to make us in Ontario the most
hypocritical body or class of people in the Dominion of Canada.'[148]

But the triumphs won by the Canadian Corps, in constant action
after the Allied break-through at Amiens on August 8 until the
Armistice on November 11, at the cost of more than 30,000 casualties, served to unite Canada once more. The 22nd played a
notable part in this final struggle, with all its officers casualties at one
point, and the fighting qualities of the French Canadians were
recognized all over Canada. Two members of the 22nd won Victoria
Crosses and two of its commanders became brigadier-generals,
F.-M. Gaudet, C.M.G., and T.-L. Tremblay, C.M.G., D.S.O.
When the troops came home, French and English alike received a
triumphant reception in Quebec and Montreal. About 15,000
French Canadians saw service at the front, 15,000 more were in
training in England and Canada, and some 4,000 or 5,000 served in
the naval forces.[149] The total of 35,000 thus arrived at represents
only the most accurate possible guess, as no official figures were
supplied after March 1918, in an effort to let the vexed question of
French-Canadian participation die. The fact that the French
Canadians contributed only 5 per cent of the Canadian total, as
compared to English Canada's contribution of something less than
50 per cent of Canadian-born soldiers,[150] remained to embitter the
relations between the races in Canada. English Canada soon lost
most of its bitterness against Quebec as time passed, but French

Canada never forgot the troubles of 1917-18, which served to nourish a new nationalist movement which was distinctly provincial and sometimes separatist in outlook.

13

Bourassa seemingly underwent a change of heart after the events of 1917 had split Canada along ethnic lines and made impossible the larger nationalism which he had always professed. He largely abandoned politics for religion. He had little to say about the Francoeur Resolution, and took the attitude that secession had never seriously been contemplated. Late in January 1918 he collected some of his utterances from the beginning of the war and coupled them with the Papal pronouncements on peace in book form, under the title of *Le Pape, arbitre de la paix*, in an effort to prove his adherence to the Papal program throughout. He likened Wilson's attitude to that of the Pope, and urged the presence of the latter at a peace conference which would seek for a Christian peace and thus avoid social revolution. This publication was approved by most of the Quebec bishops, although Archbishop Bruchési dryly observed that some of Bourassa's judgments on men and events were open to discussion, and that he himself would not have dared to make pronouncements on many of the questions with which Bourassa dealt. During the Quebec riots Bourassa's only comment was a strongly worded admonition to the populace to keep cool; and the application of strict censorship in April produced no blast from *Le Devoir*.

Under the auspices of the *Action française* movement launched by Abbé Groulx, Bourassa delivered a lecture on 'La Langue, gardienne de la foi,' on November 20, 1918 at the Monument National. He rejected the charges that the French Canadians were more French than Catholic, too French and not British enough, and traitors to the empire and ungrateful to France. He asserted that the faith had other safeguards, but the French language, necessary for the preservation of the faith, could only be preserved by vigorous efforts on the part of the French Canadians. He reviewed the principles of social order and natural law which justified the preservation of the mother tongue, and pointed out that the Church had always protected and adopted the language of its adherents. He saw French as the language of Catholicism *par excellence*, and urged his audience to 'fight for our language in order to better preserve our faith.'[151] His second public address of the year was a review of the missionary work of French-Canadian orders, given at the Monument National on December 5 under the patronage of Archbishop Bruchési. This was published in March 1919 in enlarged book form as *Le Canada Apostolique*, with a prefatory appeal for the writing of mission history as 'an excellent manner to react against the singular state of spirit, born of colonial abjection, which leads so many Canadians to remain ignorant of the beauties of their history while according all their admiration to foreign works.'[152]

A pastoral letter, issued by the Pope on June 7 and published in Canada on October 24, had settled the school question with the following injunctions:

The French Canadians may justly appeal to the government for suitable legislation as to the above-mentioned law [Regulation 17], and at the same time desire and seek further concessions. Such are, undoubtedly, that the Inspectors of their Separate Schools should be Catholics; that during the first years of tuition the use of their own language should be granted for the teaching of certain subjects, chiefly and above all, of Christian doctrine; and that Catholics be allowed to establish training schools for the education of teachers. But all these advantages and others which may be useful must be invoked and sought for by Catholics without the least appearance of revolt and without recourse to violent or illegitimate methods; and let them employ peacefully and moderately all such means as are legally or by lawful custom permitted to citizens seeking advantages to which they consider themselves entitled. . . .

Thus, while confining themselves within these limits and to these proceedings, the French Canadians are free to seek for school legislation the interpretations or changes which they desire. In this matter which concerns all Catholics, let no one venture, nonetheless, in the future to appeal to the civil courts or to promote litigation without the knowledge and consent of his Bishop, and in such questions let the latter not decide anything without consultation with other Bishops immediately interested . . . Let all priests endeavor to acquire the knowledge and use of both languages, English and French, and setting aside all prejudices, let them adopt one or the other according to the needs of the faithful.[153]

The pastoral included injunctions to the bishops to avoid division by language or race, and to the laity to show charity to one another. It desired that severe warnings should be given to any among the clergy or laity who in the future should dare to nourish or excite 'the animosities which have divided Canadians up to this day.' Commentaries on the encyclical by Père Rouleau, Mgr. Paquet, and Père Leduc were published in Le Droit, L'Action Catholique, and La Revue Dominicaine, and reprinted with the text of Bourassa's address. Active and violent agitation of the school question duly came to an end, though not until the adoption of the Merchant Report of 1927 was the Ontario policy of coercion abandoned in favor of one of cooperation, with the equal importance of the teaching of French and English in bilingual schools recognized. The bilingual school question remained vexed enough throughout Canada for Abbé Groulx to make capital of it in 1933, when nationalism regained strength under the pressure of economic crisis, a condition which, like a time of war, always favors the development of ethnic feeling in Canada.

The development of English-Canadian nationalism during the war, made evident in the closing months of the conflict and during the peace conference, doubtless had an appeasing effect on French Canada, whose opposition to the government's war policy had been based on the grounds that Canada's interests were subordinated to Britain's. Borden, accompanied by three ministers—Calder, Meighen, and Rowell—sailed for England on May 24, 1918 to attend the second Imperial War Conference. Prompted by Sir Arthur Currie, the first Canadian commander of the Canadian Corps, Borden was frankly critical of the War Office and of the Admiralty, and denounced incompetency, disorganization, and confusion at the front in a meeting of the War Cabinet on June 13. As a result, a sub-committee of the War Cabinet was set up, consisting of the British and dominion prime ministers and thus exemplifying the principles of equal status and autonomy for which Borden had striven. The Imperial War Cabinet remained in almost continuous session during the summer, with Borden and Rowell in attendance, while Meighen and Calder represented Canada in the Imperial War Conference. Borden visited the Canadian troops in France and England in intervals between meetings. He backed the resolution proposed by Hughes of Australia in favor of direct communication between the dominion and British prime ministers, and the right of the dominions to be represented continuously in the Imperial War Cabinet by ministers serving as representatives of the dominion prime ministers. This motion was adopted unanimously, confirming the decline of the authority of the Colonial Office and of the governor-general.

The Imperial War Conference closed on July 26, after dealing with the problems of empire communications, statistics, and news services, in addition to war problems. Ballantyne and Mewburn replaced Calder and Meighen in London, while plans were evolved for a Canadian contingent in the proposed Siberian expedition. Speaking at a luncheon on July 31, Borden made clear that the British government's announcement of the policy of imperial preference was made in behalf of the United Kingdom, while Canada retained the right to control its own fiscal policy. He also rejected the Admiralty's proposal of a single imperial navy under British control in war and peace. Lloyd George suggested that Canada should take over the West Indies and Borden agreed.[154] Borden sailed for Canada on August 17 and on Labor Day at Toronto reported on the work of the conference, emphasizing the fact that no great constitutional changes had been made.

Lloyd George had expressed the desire that Borden should return to England when the war ended, and on October 28 he cabled him to be prepared to start on short notice. It was agreed in cabinet at Ottawa to continue the Union government after peace came; and a Canadian peace mission was formed, composed of Borden, George Foster, and A. L. Sifton, with Doherty to come later, and additional representatives from various government departments, the labor unions, and John Dafoe as press representative. Borden sailed on November 10 and was met in London by Lloyd George and a representative of the King. It was at once proposed that Borden should represent the dominions as one of a five-man British delegation to the peace conference. Borden held that all the dominion prime ministers should have equal status, and agreed to confer with General Smuts. He offered to keep two Canadian divisions overseas during the peace negotiations, but said Canadian public opinion would not permit compulsory service in an army of occupation. In December Borden met General Louis Botha of South Africa for the first time, and like Laurier before him, found that Canada and South Africa held similar imperial ideals and positions. Both believed 'that upon the basis of equal nationhood and adequate voice in external relations the salvation of the Commonwealth could be worked out most surely.'[155] Late in December Borden refused an urgent suggestion from his colleagues that he should return home for the opening of the session in a month's time, as the Union government was under fire and Liberal activity was marked. Borden maintained that his duty lay rather in guarding Canada's interests at the peace conference.

In a meeting of the War Cabinet on December 31 Borden strongly urged that each dominion prime minister should have a turn at representing the empire in the peace conference, and warned that Canada's desire for representation in the making of peace might lead to regrettable consequences if not gratified. Borden was backed by Hughes and Cook of Australia, and Lloyd George agreed. Under the system finally adopted, each dominion was to have the same representation—two delegates—as the smaller Allied nations, and in addition the five representatives of the British empire were to be drawn from a panel including all the dominion prime ministers. This measure caused horror in the Foreign Office, and encountered severe opposition from President Wilson at the first meeting of the Big Four on January 11–12; but was subsequently adopted with the modification that New Zealand only had one representative, while Canada, Australia, South Africa, and India each had two. Borden urged upon Lloyd George a South African proposal drafted by Smuts, limiting the governor-general's status to that of the King in Britain and advocating that governors-general should be chosen from eminent men of the dominion to which they were appointed. Lloyd George rejected the latter suggestion as removing the last link between the dominions and Britain, with Borden replying that 'if the Empire's unity depended upon that link, it was not very secure.'[156] Non-British governors-general were soon appointed in the other dominions, but Canada still waited until 1952 for her first Canadian governor-general.

Borden took so active a role in the peace conference that there were several attempts, seemingly, to kick him upstairs by making him British representative at a proposed meeting of Russian governments at Princes Island in the Sea of Marmora on February 15, or British ambassador to Washington, while the equally independent Botha was named president of the Polish Commission. Disregarding these offers, Borden stood firm, insisting upon the right of dominion representatives to sign the peace treaty as plenipotentiaries, and to be recognized in the League of Nations and in the International Labor Bureau. In the end Borden represented Britain in the Council of Five and also presided over the British Empire delegation, while Canadian representatives took influential parts in committee work. In May Lloyd George urged Borden to delay his return to Canada, which was demanded by the political crisis created by the One Big Union general strike and by differences between Liberal and Conservative cabinet members over tariff matters. But having seen the peace treaty through, Borden was forced to return home to ensure his remaining in power.

14

The general strike in Winnipeg in May, coupled with later strikes in Toronto, Ottawa, Calgary, Vancouver, and elsewhere, was virtually broken late in June 1919, after violence had been suppressed by the use of armed police and soldiers. The Winnipeg disorders were much more severe than the Quebec anti-conscription riots of 1918. Quebec was unaffected by the labor troubles of 1919, since the international unions were not as strong there as in English Canada, and since Quebec labor was moderate in sentiment. Borden took a firm stand, recognizing the rights of labor but refusing to allow interference with public services. Reconstruction of the government became necessary in June as the Unionist Liberals led by Calder, who resigned from the cabinet, supported free trade. The government was unable to pass a measure for setting up a peacetime purchasing commission. Before the session closed on July 7, Borden held a caucus, proposing a continuance of the present government with the formation of a Unionist Party. The caucus adopted a notably vague platform, and authorized Borden to reconstruct the government, from which Sir Thomas White, the finance minister and acting prime minister in Borden's absence, had also now resigned.

Borden was conscious of the necessity of winning Quebec back from its isolation by French-Canadian representation in the cabinet. Early in July he made overtures to Sir Lomer Gouin, the titular leader of French Canada since Laurier's death in February. Gouin suggested that Borden visit Quebec and consult Jacques Bureau, Rodolphe Lemieux, and Ernest Lapointe. Borden did not get far with Bureau at Trois-Rivières, but at Quebec he conferred with Sir Charles Fitzpatrick, the lieutenant-governor, and Cardinal Bégin, stressing his desire that Quebec should take her due share in the government of the country. In a conference with Lapointe at Rivière-du-Loup, Borden offered to resign if that step would ease the situation, but Lapointe held that public opinion in Quebec would prevent French Canadians from taking part in a Union government in any case. He was sympathetic to Borden's ideas, but regarded them as impracticable.[157] At Murray Bay Borden got the same reaction from Gouin and Lemieux, with Gouin urging the prime minister to settle the Ontario school question. In final consultations at Quebec and Montreal Borden found that Fitzpatrick thought Gouin was willing to enter the federal government, but feared he could not be elected; while Lord Atholstan felt that Gouin would be a strong representative of Quebec. In August Borden accompanied the Prince of Wales on his visit to Quebec, and used the French which he had acquired in Paris in conversation with Lady Gouin. But his railway car was stoned at Chaudière Junction when he left for Ottawa.[158]

Under pressure from Borden the British government delayed ratification of the peace treaty until it had been submitted to the Canadian parliament at a special session in September. The treaty was approved on September 12, after a debate in which Fielding contested Borden's theory that Canada's ratification was necessary and proposed a resolution, seconded by Lapointe, to this effect:

In giving such approval, this House in no way assents to any impairment of the existing autonomous authority of the Dominion, but declares that the question of what part, if any, the forces of Canada shall take in any war, actual or threatened, is one to be determined at all times as occasion may require by the people of Canada through their representatives in Parliament.[159]

There was a sharp conflict over Article X of the League Covenant in parliament. C. G. Power, an English Liberal from Quebec, urged that Canada's policy for the next century should be based upon Washington's principle of 'absolute renunciation of interference in European affairs' and Laurier's doctrine of 'freedom from the vortex of European militarism.' Rodolphe Lemieux declared:

'In military matters we are governed also by and from Ottawa, and not by and from London; and we do not want to be governed by and from Geneva.' L.-T. Pacaud stated that by the adoption of Article X, 'we are placing the Canadian people at the beck and call of a council not responsible to the voters for its actions.' The coalition majority in parliament triumphed, however, over the opposition which came from both parties.[160]

After this final struggle for ratification of the peace treaty, Borden's health began to collapse, but he continued to work until October 3. On that date he forwarded to London a dispatch calling for the appointment of a Canadian minister to Washington to carry on the work of the wartime Canadian mission and to conduct all negotiations between Canada and the United States. This epoch-making proposal was accepted by the British government and announced in 1920, but not carried into effect for seven years.

Borden then went to the States on a vacation recommended by his physicians, though he conferred with his ministers there on several occasions. He sought to aid passage of the peace treaty in the United States Senate by waiving the right of the dominions to vote in the settlement by the League of a dispute in which any part of the British Empire was involved. He returned to Ottawa on November 26, but early in December announced his decision to retire, on grounds of health, to his cabinet colleagues and the governor-general. Under pressure from his colleagues he agreed to defer his resignation until he had sought restoration of his health by a prolonged vacation, which lasted from January 2, 1920, to May 12. Then, on the occasion of prorogation on July 1, he announced his definite decision to resign. After Sir Thomas White had refused to form a government, Arthur Meighen succeeded Borden as prime minister on July 10, with the Unionist Liberals Calder, Guthrie, Ballantyne, and Sifton remaining in the government and with Senator Blondin as the only French-Canadian minister.

In the years that followed Borden came to occupy the position of Canada's elder statesman which Laurier had held after his defeat in 1911. By his lectures and writings on constitutional problems he did much to formulate the new English-Canadian nationalism which he had helped to crystallize in the latter part of a career which had begun in the imperialist camp. In the end he had led in the realization of many of Bourassa's ideals for Canada. With the slow postwar development of English-Canadian nationalism, French Canadians were left less isolated politically, though the chasm between the races remained deep, thanks to the bloodshed in Quebec in 1918.

Laurier, the greatest advocate of unity in Canada, had died in February 1919, and Quebec was left without a federal leader. Laurier's health had failed gradually during 1918; though near the end it revived, and in November and January he made vigorous speeches to Liberal gatherings. In November at London, Ontario, he made a notable plea which summed up his philosophy:

As for you who stand today on the threshold of life, with a long horizon open before you for a long career of usefulness to your native land, if you will permit me, after a long life, I shall remind you that already many problems rise before you: problems of race division, problems of creed differences, problems of economic conflict. Problems of national duty and national aspiration. Let me tell you that for the solution of these problems you have a safe guide, an unfailing light, if you remember that faith is better than doubt and love is better than hate.

Banish doubt and hate from your life. Let your souls be ever open to the promptings of faith and the gentle influence of brotherly love. Be adamant against the haughty, be gentle and kind to the weak. Let your aim and purpose, in good report or ill, in victory or defeat, be so to live, so to strive, so to serve as to do your part to raise ever higher the standard of life and living.[161]

Still in harness at seventy-eight, faithful to the end to the politics which he loved and of which he was a great master, Laurier suffered a slight stroke in his office on the eve of the opening of the session in February. Next morning, as he was dressing for church, a second stroke came, from which he failed to rally. The end came the following day, with the whispered words, ' *C'est fini.*'

There was a week of national mourning, with tributes voiced in parliament by Sir Thomas White, the acting prime minister, and Rodolphe Lemieux, Laurier's loyal lieutenant. Borden issued a statement that 'all Canada will mourn his loss and those who differed from him will be profoundly conscious that his death leaves in the public life of our country a blank that cannot be entirely filled.'[162] There was a state funeral at the Basilica in Ottawa, with Bishop Mathieu and Father Burke paying tribute in French and English. The King sent his sympathy to Lady Laurier, with assurance of the friendship and esteem he and the Queen had felt for Sir Wilfrid for seventeen years; and to the governor-general the King expressed his regret, with the assurance that 'Canada will mourn for one who dearly loved his country and will remember with pride and gratitude his great powers of administrative genius.' A Canadian friend called Laurier 'the best man I have ever known. His instinctive honour, his kindliness and forgetfulness of self, that shining out of nobility and distinction of character which men call magnetism, made every man who entered his presence a better man for it.'[163] Though he was replaced in the leadership of the Liberal Party by his disciple Mackenzie King, who worshipped Laurier's memory and by alliance with Ernest Lapointe sought to remedy his own deficiencies in understanding Quebec, no statesman rose in postwar Canada who, like Laurier, could lead both races in Canada and be equally respected by both.

Notes

1 *Can. An. Rev. 1916*, 304.
2 Lucas, II, 31; Armstrong, 121.
3 *Can. An. Rev. 1916*, 353.
4 Skelton, II, 468.
5 Armstrong, 131-3.
6 Rumilly, XXI, 146.
7 *Ibid.*
8 *Ibid.*, 147.
9 These articles were published in pamphlet form under the title of *Où allons-nous? Le Nationalisme Canadien. Lettres d'un 'Patriote'* (Montréal, 1916), with a note of Cardinal Bégin's observation to the priests of his diocese during their annual retreat in August: 'It is very important that you should not oppose recruiting, and even that you should favor it' (73).
10 A. Hawkes, *Canadian Nationalism and the War* (Montreal, 1916).
11 *Montreal Gazette*, 28 July 1916, T. Papineau-Bourassa, 21 March 1916.
12 *Le Devoir*, 5 août 1916, Bourassa-McMaster, 2 Aug. 1916.
13 Rumilly, XXI, 155.
14 Skelton, II, 468.
15 Armstrong, 141; *Le Devoir*, 18 août, 7 sept. 1916.
16 Rumilly, XXI, 163.
17 Borden, *Memoirs*, II, 609.
18 *Can. An. Rev. 1916*, 329.
19 Borden, II, 611.
20 Armstrong, 124; *Le Soleil*, 23 oct. 1916; *Le Bien Public*, 30 nov. 1916.
21 Borden, II, 613-14.
22 *Can. An. Rev. 1916*, 330.
23 Rumilly, XXI, 173.
24 *Ibid.*, 175.
25 *Ibid.*, 173-8.
26 H. Bourassa, *Le Problème de l'Empire: Indépendance ou Association Impériale* (Montréal, 1916); *Independence or Imperial Partnership* (Montreal, 1916).
27 L. Curtis, *The Problem of the Commonwealth* (London, 1916), 7.
28 Skelton, II, 467.
29 Bourassa, *Problème*, 25.
30 Rumilly, XXI, 181-3.
31 *Ibid.*, 185; Col. Thomas A. Duff-General Hughes, 19 June 1917.
32 Sissons, *Bilingual Schools*, Ap. III, 222-7.
33 Rumilly, XXI, 191.
34 *Ibid.*, 196-7.
35 *Ibid.*, 193.
36 *Ibid.*, 198.
37 Armstrong, 139-40; *Montreal Gazette*, 25 Oct. 1916.
38 *Our Volunteer Army* (Montreal, 1916).
39 Rumilly, XXI, 221-2.
40 Ewart Papers: J. S. Ewart-Bourassa, 1 Dec. 1916.
41 Rumilly, XXI, 226-7.
42 *Où allons-nous?*, 30.
43 Rumilly, XXI, 231.
44 Borden, II, 570.

[45] *Ibid.*, 571.

[46] *Can. An. Rev. 1916*, 268.

[47] *Ibid.*, 263.

[48] Rumilly, XXI, 158. See *CHR 1950*, 1–27, D. M. R. Vince, 'The Acting Overseas Sub-Militia Council and the Resignation of Sir Sam Hughes'; *CHAR 1950*, 30–70, S. H. S. Hughes, 'Sir Sam Hughes and the Problem of Imperialism.'

[49] Borden, II, 617.

[50] Armstrong, 163.

[51] *Ibid.*, 162.

[52] *Can. An. Rev. 1916*, 476.

[53] *Ibid.*, 484.

[54] *Ibid.*

[55] Armstrong, 167; *Le Soleil*, 29 Jan. 1917.

[56] Borden, II, 660.

[57] Skelton, II, 492.

[58] *Ibid.*, 498.

[59] Borden, II, 619.

[60] Skelton, II, 497.

[61] Borden, II, 663.

[62] *Ibid.*, 668.

[63] *Ibid.*, 666; Skelton, II, 501.

[64] Skelton, II, 503–4; Laurier-C. P. Scott, 13 Feb. 1917.

[65] *Can. An. Rev. 1917*, 307.

[66] Skelton, II, 509–11; Laurier-Aylesworth, 15 May 1917.

[67] *Ibid.*, 512.

[68] *Can. An. Rev. 1917*, 490.

[69] *Ibid.*, 492.

[70] H. Bourassa, *L'Intervention américaine: ses motifs, son objet, ses conséquences* (Montréal, 1917).

[71] *Ibid.*, 27.

[72] *Ibid.*, 28.

[73] H. Bourassa, *Conscription* (Montreal, 1917).

[74] *Ibid.*, 25.

[75] *Ibid.*, 26.

[76] *Ibid.*

[77] *Ibid.*, 28.

[78] *Ibid.*, 29.

[79] *Ibid.*, 38.

[80] *Ibid.*, 42.

[81] Borden, II, 720–7; Skelton, II, 512–17.

[82] Skelton, II, 514.

[83] *Ibid.*, 515–16; Laurier-Rowell, 3 June 1917.

[84] Borden, II, 701.

[85] Descelles, *Discours*, II, 129–70.

[86] *Can. An. Rev. 1917*, 486–9.

[87] Borden, II, 705.

[88] *Can. An. Rev. 1917*, 347.

[89] Borden, II, 740.

[90] *Can. An. Rev. 1917*, 506.

[91] *Ibid.*, 505-6.

[92] Armstrong, 195–6.

[93] F. Roy, *L'appel aux armes et la réponse canadienne-française* (Québec, 1917).

[94] Borden, II, 733–4.

[95] 'J. Vindex' (R. P. Hermas Lalande, S.J.), *Halte là, 'Patriote'* (Rimouski, 1917).

[96] *Can. An. Rev. 1917*, 480-1.

[97] *Ibid.*, 481.

[98] Armstrong, 196-7.

[99] *Ibid.*, 198; *Etoile du Nord*, 16, 30 août; *Le Peuple*, 6 sept. 1917.

[100] Borden, II, 730-1.

[101] Skelton, II, 524.

[102] Dafoe, *Sifton*, 416-17.

[103] *Can. An. Rev. 1917*, 351.

[104] Armstrong, 210; *La Presse*, 23 nov. 1917.

[105] H. Bourassa, *L'Emprunt de la 'Victoire'* (Montréal, 1917).

[106] Skelton, II, 536.

[107] Armstrong, 202.

[108] *Can. An. Rev. 1917*, 610.

[109] *Ibid.*, 610-11.

[110] *Ibid.*, 611.

[111] *Ibid.*, 598-9.

[112] *Ibid.*, 600.

[113] *Ibid.*, 600-1.

[114] Borden, II, 782.

[115] *Can. An. Rev. 1917*, 642-3.

[116] *Ibid.*, 642.

[117] Skelton, II, 543.

[118] *Ibid.*, 544.

[119] Armstrong, 209.

[120] A. Savard & W. E. Playfair (*trans.*), *Quebec & Confederation: A record of the Debate of the Legislative Assembly of Quebec on the Motion proposed by J.-N. Francoeur* (n.p., 1918).

[121] Armstrong, 210-11.

[122] *Quebec & Confed.*, 16-17.

[123] *Ibid.*, 22.

[124] *Ibid.*, 65.

[125] *Ibid.*, 47.

[126] *Ibid.*, 49.

[127] *Ibid.*, 52.

[128] *Ibid.*, 59.

[129] *Ibid.*, 65.

[130] *Ibid.*, 73-4, 80.

[131] *Ibid.*, 117-36.

[132] *Ibid.*, 136.

[133] Ewart Papers: Ewart-Bourassa, 21 Jan. 1918.

[134] *Ibid.*, Bourassa-Ewart, 29 March 1918.

[135] *Can. An. Rev. 1918*, 639.

[136] *Ibid.*, 640.

[137] *Can. An. Rev. 1918*, 641; *La Presse*, 20 feb. 1918.

[138] *Ibid.*, 600.

[139] *Ibid.*, 640-1.

[140] Armstrong, 226 n.

[141] *Ibid.*, 227-30; *Can. An. Rev. 1918*, 462-4.

[142] *Can. An. Rev. 1918*, 463-4.

[143] Borden, II, 789.

[144] *Can. An. Rev. 1918*, 411.

[145] *Ibid.*, 466-7.

[146] *Ibid.*, 454.

[147] C. P. Stacey, *The Military Problem of Canada* (Toronto, 1940), 79-80; Armstrong, 238.

[148] *Can. An. Rev. 1918*, 458.
[149] Armstrong, 249.
[150] *Ibid.*, 250.
[151] H. Bourassa, *La Langue, gardienne de la foi* (Montréal, 1918), 51.
[152] H. Bourassa, *Le Canada apostolique* (Montréal, 1918), 9.
[153] *Can. An. Rev. 1918*, 645-6.
[154] Borden, II, 844.
[155] *Ibid.*, 879.
[156] *Ibid.*, 901.
[157] *Ibid.*, 984.
[158] *Ibid.*, 987.
[159] *Ibid.*, 999.
[160] J. B. Brebner, *North Atlantic Triangle* (New Haven, 1945), 280.
[161] Skelton, II, 554-5.
[162] Borden, II, 914-15.
[163] Skelton, II, 588.

CHAPTER XIII

NATIONHOOD AND INTERNATIONALISM

(1920–39)

QUEBEC's wartime retreat into a narrow provincialism, as a result of its bitter differences with the other provinces over the treatment of their French-Canadian minorities, and as a result of the ethnic cleavage brought about by the conscription crisis, predisposed French Canada toward a more rigid isolationism in the postwar world than otherwise probably would have prevailed. The years between 1920 and 1939 on the national and international scene were characterized by Canada's increasing involvement in international affairs, and by its gradual shift from economic and political dependence upon Britain to a greater economic but lesser political dependence upon the United States as its wartime industrial development continued in the booming 1920's. Both historic processes represented a threat to French-Canadian cultural survival, and hence reinforced Quebec's tendency to turn inward upon itself which did not yield to the new internationalism until the mid-1930's.

French Canada's long conditioning against imperialism resulted in some postwar years of battling against a British political imperialism that was fast dying, while the lack of an economic point of view among most of the humanistically educated élite long' blinded French-Canadian spokesmen to the new American economic imperialism, which offered an even greater challenge to a minority determined to maintain its separate way of life. The threat was finally recognized as a result of the simultaneous American cultural penetration of Quebec, which was vigorously fought by the élite and generally welcomed by the masses, to whom industrialization brought a higher standard of living than they had previously known.[1] Towards the end of the period American isolationism reinforced traditional French-Canadian isolationism, as the newer nationalist leaders adopted Henri Bourassa's tactics of quoting British and American public figures to the embarrassment of Canada's own leaders. These leaders were themselves torn between the pull of a new English-Canadian nationalism which went largely unrecognized in a Quebec turned in upon itself, and the sometimes conflicting pressures from London and Washington. Before the vitally important social and cultural developments in Quebec itself can be explained, the national and international political scene against which these developments occurred must be summarized. Henceforward this account must be tentative, like all histories of the recent past, for though facts are here recited, other facts now unknown may upset the interpretation here advanced.

I

Both federal and provincial leaders sought to heal the split between Quebec and the rest of Canada, when Arthur Meighen replaced Sir Robert Borden as head of the Union government and Alexandre Taschereau replaced Sir Lomer Gouin as premier of Quebec in a double changing of the old guard in July 1920. Gouin announced his retirement on July 8, after his return from a tour of France and England, where he was honored by the French president and the King and Queen. Taschereau, long Gouin's chief aide and frequent spokesman, announced that he would follow the same policy as his predecessor had done for fifteen years: continued development of Quebec's natural resources and wealth, and the maintenance of the province as a sanctuary of peace and tolerance. In a speech on July 27 he expressed regret at Quebec's isolation:

Since Quebec is so necessary to Confederation, is it not deplorable to note its isolation. Some people see good in this isolation; others regret it, and I am of the latter class. . . . We did not enter Confederation to form a band apart, and like new Robinson Crusoes to live alone and separated on our own island . . . Quebec is not the only one to suffer thereby; all the country feels the effects and I shall welcome the day when our Province takes the place in the Canadian household which it deserves by reason of its riches, its geographical position, and all its other elements of greatness. [2]

This same conciliatory attitude was reflected in Taschereau's advice to the students of the Quebec Commercial Academy, whom he urged to learn English well while young, since 'Quebec is not surrounded by a Chinese wall.'[3] The provincial government gave $1,000,000 to both McGill and the new Université de Montréal, which became independent of Laval in this year, with five times as many students as the parent institution. Of the total of $4,000,000 raised to endow the new institution, the Séminaire de Saint-Sulpice supplied $1,000,000, while *bonne entente* sentiment was given substance by gifts of $50,000 by the Canadian Pacific Railway, $20,000 by the Ontario government, and smaller gifts from other English-Canadian sources.[4] The new wealth of French Canada as a result of wartime industrialization was indicated by the ease with which the endowment fund was raised.

The National Liberal and Conservative government formed by Arthur Meighen after Borden's resignation on July 10 included only one French Canadian, Senator Blondin, who was named postmaster-general. His wartime role had left Blondin virtually without support in Quebec, and Meighen's ardent Conservatism made him highly unpopular in Quebec. Only four of the sixteen members of the new government had Liberal antecedents, and it was a coalition government only in name. Bourassa characterized the new prime minister thus in *Le Devoir*: 'Mr. Meighen represents in person and temperament, in his attitudes and in his past declarations, the utmost that Anglo-Saxon jingoism has to offer in the way of brutality, all that is most exclusive, most anti-Canadian.'[5] Yet in his first important speech as prime minister, at Portage la Prairie on August 2, Meighen went out of his way to appeal for French-Canadian support:

We have two great races. The fundamental institutions of Canada are just as dear to the one race as to the other. The peril of every nation has been a tendency to divide on lines of race, on lines of religion, on lines of social caste—If we do not come together to reach a better understanding and a better unity on things that are vital and essential to the state, there will be a heavy penalty paid.[6]

This plea, echoing Taschereau's recent utterances, was approved by both the *Toronto Globe* and the Montreal *La Presse*, and was taken up by the *Mail and Empire*, which on August 9 urged:

Quebec ought to be exercising her full and vigorous influence in national affairs. She has everything to lose by remaining in a state of isolation. It cannot but be the wish of the new Premier of the Dominion to have Quebec duly represented in his Cabinet.[7]

In Montreal on September 10, Senator Blondin denounced isolation as suicide for Quebec and called for an end of exploitation of racial and religious prejudices.[8] During that month, after the prime minister had joined Taschereau and Cardinal Bégin in unveiling a statue of Cartier at Quebec, there were rumors of overtures to E.-L. Patenaude and Georges-H. Boivin, and later to L.-J. Gauthier, but Quebec Conservatives and Liberals alike refused to join the new government.

The new leader of the Liberal Party, William Lyon Mackenzie King, fared better than Meighen in wooing Quebec, since he already had some standing there as a favorite disciple of Laurier and was strongly supported by the old leader's lieutenants, Rodolphe Lemieux and Ernest Lapointe, the latter of whom was rising rapidly in influence among the Quebec delegation at Ottawa. During the session King conducted a vigorous attack on the government, denouncing the War-Time Election Act as 'one of the most infernal pieces of legislation which was ever perpetrated,'[9] and criticizing the fact that Quebec had no proper share in the administration. Conservative attacks on him for having deserted Canada during the war in favor of the Rockefeller interests—he had been a consultant on industrial relations to the Rockefeller Foundation—did him no harm in Quebec, nor did his denunciation of the government's naval proposals.[10] During the summer King toured Ontario and the West, supported by Quebec members, and in December made two speeches in Montreal, building his political fences for the election made inevitable by Meighen's failure to win backing in French Canada.

The immediate postwar period saw a revival of the old Canadian conflict between imperialism and nationalism, but no longer along ethnic lines. English-Canadian nationalism had developed tremendously during the war years, thanks to pride in Canada's war effort and to friction with colonial-minded Britishers, and tended to grow into an independent nationalism as a result of Borden's struggle for autonomy in the making of the peace treaties. But Britain neglected no means to hold its shaken empire together in the postwar years, and imperialist propaganda was largely concentrated on Canada, the most important dominion. In 1919 the Prince of Wales and Admiral Lord Jellicoe were sent to Canada to strengthen imperial feeling by evoking loyalty to the Royal Family and pride in the Royal Navy. The Prince won wide popularity, but even the most modest of the four alternative schemes which Jellicoe drafted for the postwar Canadian Navy was rejected by the Conservative government.[11] Lord Atholstan, Montreal's leading imperialist, was responsible for the Imperial Press Conference which met at Ottawa on August 5, 1920 and called for an imperial cable service after touching upon other imperial questions. The delegates subsequently toured Canada, spreading the gospel of imperial unity as they went. The Empire Chambers of Commerce also met in congress at Toronto in September 1920, and passed resolutions calling for strengthened imperial commercial ties, organization of imperial resources, an imperial preferential tariff, and the improvement of imperial communications and transportation.

These gatherings were intended to smooth the way for the first postwar Imperial Conference, which was summoned to meet at London in June 1921. Its agenda included preparatory discussion of the constitutional revisions urged at the 1917 Conference, a review of foreign relations, the question of renewal of the Anglo-Japanese Treaty, and discussion of methods of attaining a common understanding on foreign policy affecting all parts of the empire. On February 16 Lloyd George told the Commons that imperial defence should be an imperial concern. He was supported on April 27 by Sir Robert Borden, who argued that: 'We cannot assume or accept the status of nationhood without accepting also its responsibilities . . . whatever the burden may be, I believe it will be less upon this country as a nation of the Empire than if we stood separate as an independent nation.'[12] Mackenzie King replied in the House that the present was no time to settle some of the large questions which had been raised, and proposed a resolution that there should be no change in Canada's relations to the empire and no new expenditure for naval or military purposes. His motion was defeated by 96–64, after Meighen had made a plea for freedom to discuss whatever questions might arise at the conference.

But the strength of the new Canadian nationalism had been made evident. The Canadian correspondent of the *Round Table* reported its program thus:

> . . . separate diplomatic representation for the Dominions at the capitals of all foreign nations; separate navies under national control, abolition of appeals to the Imperial Privy Council, and complete judicial independence; nomination of the Governor-General by the Canadian Cabinet, and the appointment of a Canadian to the office if the Cabinet so wills, and recognition of the Sovereign as the only actual or official link between the Dominions and the Mother Country . . . complete independence under the Crown is the natural and inevitable ultimate relation between the overseas British countries and the ancient seat and centre of the Empire.[13]

Meighen subscribed to Borden's view of the future empire as 'based upon equality of nationhood,' with each nation preserving 'its absolute autonomy' but also having 'its voice as to those external relations which involve the issue of peace or war.'[14]

When the conference met in secret session in London on June 20, Mr. Massey of New Zealand was the only dominion spokesman to echo the Chamberlain ideal of imperial federation, with all the others favoring cooperative action on the basis of equality. On June 27 Meighen urged in the tradition of Laurier and Borden that the dominions should be kept informed on all questions of foreign policy concerning the British government directly, while they must be consulted on those concerning the empire as a whole. He argued that no treaties should be entered into by Britain without consultation with the dominions; that such treaties should be subject to approval by the dominion parliaments; and that upon all Canadian-American questions the advice of the Canadian government should be accepted as final.[15] English opinion was sympathetic to the first three points, while the last had long been conceded. On June 29 Meighen, a newcomer to imperial affairs, flatly opposed the demand of the veterans Hughes of Australia and Massey of New Zealand that the Anglo-Japanese Alliance should be renewed, since it was incompatible with the League and opposed by the United States. In the first assertion of Canada's new role as the interpreter between Britain and the United States, Meighen declared that good Anglo-American relations were 'the touchstone of British policy and the hope of the world.' Despite the vigorous objections of Hughes, Lloyd George was won over to Meighen's views and adopted his idea of a Pacific Conference of Britain, the United States, and Japan to determine Pacific policy.[16] On July 6 Meighen expressed regret that all cable news reaching Canada came from New York 'censored from the American standpoint,' and as a result had 'an undesirable influence.' But no steps were taken to create an imperial cable service, despite strong representations by Winston Churchill, the colonial secretary, and W. M. Hughes of Australia. As a result of these developments President Harding called the Washington Naval Conference on July 10, in the midst of the London meeting.

The Imperial Conference of 1921 put an end to imperial federation by renouncing the idea of a constitutional revision of imperial relations. It agreed upon a policy of continuous consultation and direct communication between the prime ministers of the United Kingdom and the dominions, with meetings 'annually, or at such longer intervals as may prove feasible.'[17] It supplied the first notable instance of a dominion determining imperial policy, and thanks to Meighen decision upon British Pacific policy was postponed, pending the meeting of the Washington Conference. There is no doubt that Meighen represented a Canadian public opinion which cut across party lines. In a debate in the House on April 27 Lapointe had called for Canada's exclusion from the Anglo-Japanese Treaty, while another French-Canadian member maintained that Canada should be guided by American policy and should form a defensive alliance with the United States. British Columbia also was opposed to renewal of the treaty.[18]

Although the conference had proved inconclusive, upon his return to Canada on August 6 Meighen spoke of the value of such meetings: 'Great Britain is the greatest factor in the world today for preserving peace . . . The influence of British statesmen in the councils of the world is greater because the Dominions and India are within the Empire and because she reflects, or wants to reflect, their views as well as her own . . . We must walk with the nations of the Empire or walk away from them . . . I believe in the British Empire.'[19] But on October 7 Sir Robert Borden observed in his lectures at Toronto: 'The foreign policy of the Empire remains under the same direction and influences as before the War, and that is not what we intended should be the case when we took our stand in 1917; it is imperative that the old conditions should not go on.'[20] There was little popular opinion on the question, although Bourassa, John S. Ewart, and Lindsay Crawford urged Canada to assert its independence. There was some feeling that a strengthened imperial organization might conflict with the League of Nations, at the first meeting of whose assembly in November 1920 Sir George Foster, C. J. Doherty, and N. W. Rowell had represented Canada. Dr. O. D. Skelton had already advanced the opinion that Canadian nationhood was dependent upon 'recognition of the fact that foreign affairs are not something that can only be discussed abroad, but matters, so far as they concern us at all, to be debated first in our own Parliament or considered in a parliamentary committee.' He also called for 'clear evidence to the world that the British Empire of other days is now not one state, but many.'[21] Meighen himself maintained that Canada had a right to intervene in the Anglo-Japanese Treaty, and to press for its abrogation in view of British and Canadian relations with the United States, which opposed it.

The fact that the invitation to Great Britain to participate in the Washington Conference had not specified representation of the dominions was a sore point with such pioneers of the new empire as Smuts and Borden, who protested against the American view that the voice of the empire in world affairs should be that of Britain alone—the same stand taken in connection with the League of Nations. The British government named four dominion representatives to its delegation of seven, but at Smuts' insistence the dominion representatives were finally given the same status as at the peace conference. T. A. Crerar, leader of the Western Progressives, declared that 'we should be represented at Washington in our own right or not at all,' while on August 11 the *Montreal Star* warned of the responsibilities of the assumption of separate nationhood.[22] Sir Robert Borden served as the Canadian representative on the British delegation to the Washington Conference, which met on November 12, 1921. Mr. Balfour, the leader of the British delegation, went to Washington by way of Canada, and upon landing at Quebec paid tribute to Borden and admitted Canada's immediate interest in the Pacific question.[23] Borden took an important part in the conference and signed the resulting treaty on behalf of Canada. In his report to the Canadian government upon his return Borden traced out the procedure by which both the diplomatic unity of the empire and the autonomy of the dominions were preserved.[24]

After the Washington Conference the tide of English-Canadian nationalism continued to rise steadily. It was argued that by representation at the Peace Conference, in the League, and at Washington Canada had given evidence of her growing independence. Internationalism was set up as the antithesis of imperialism, and much was made of the fact that Canada's interests, particularly in the Pacific, were closer to those of the United States than those of Britain. There were calls for the establishment of a Canadian diplomatic service, the choice of a distinctive Canadian flag, and the replacement of 'God Save the King' by 'O Canada.' John S. Ewart, who had come out in favor of a Canadian republic in 1920, joined Lindsay Crawford, the editor of the *Statesman*, in calling for Canadian independence. A Daughters of Canada organization was formed in Toronto as a rival of the Imperial Daughters of the Empire. Armand Lavergne told a Kingston audience on February 5, 1921 that 'So long as we are a colony, until the glorious day when we fulfill the promise made in 1867 of making this country a sovereign and independent country, we must not forget that "eternal vigilance is the price of liberty."' At a Quebec dinner to Lavergne on December 23, Bourassa observed: 'Confederation has lived. I do not know how long it will continue—perhaps twenty, perhaps thirty years, perhaps longer—but it is fatally wounded.' Therefore he held that the nationalists should not fight against Britain, but against 'Anglo-Saxonism,' whether British or American. [25]

Abolition of appeals to the Privy Council was generally favored by English-Canadian opinion at this time, with some French-Canadian support, although the right of appeal was generally regarded in Quebec as a safeguard against English-Canadian dominance. The appointment of Lord Byng of Vimy, the first commander of the Canadian Corps in France, as governor-general was hailed with satisfaction as having been made with the approval of the Canadian government. The Irish troubles provided the French-Canadian nationalists with new allies; and Lavergne, Bourassa, and Lucien Cannon took part in the work of the Self-Determination League founded by Lindsay Crawford in 1920. At a meeting in Montreal on May 16 Lavergne called England 'the greatest murderer of small nations,' [26] while Bourassa addressed the national convention of the League in Montreal on November 7 for three hours on the Irish question, which he claimed to be primarily a religious question and secondarily a minority one, which could be solved if the principle of majority rule were applied. This alliance provided new fuel for Orange hatred of French Canada, and gave new support to the old English-Canadian suspicion of French-Canadian loyalty.

2

Upon his return from the Imperial Conference of 1921, Meighen faced the fact that his government must be reorganized and run the risk of election. In September he had added three French Canadians to the cabinet—Louis-de-Gonzague Belley as postmaster-general,

Rodolphe Monty as secretary of state, and Dr. Louis-Philippe Normand as president of the Privy Council. These new ministers were undistinguished—only Belley had previously been a member of parliament—and they added little to the strength in French Canada of a government whose leading Quebec member was C. C. Ballantyne, who was unpopular with French Canadians because of his break with Laurier in 1917 and his support of conscription. Later André Fauteux was named solicitor-general, but he shared with his other French-Canadian colleagues a lack of parliamentary and ministerial experience. With the elections set for December 6, Meighen opened the campaign in Montreal in September, supported by Ballantyne, Belley, Monty, and Normand. He held that the protective tariff was the main issue, maintaining that the government's stand on the question was that of Laurier. He made an appeal for racial conciliation and concord, and urged Quebec to bury the past and to vote for the future.

Mackenzie King had also set the tariff as the main issue at Windsor on August 20, calling for revision of it; while Rodolphe Lemieux, the Liberal leader in Quebec, attacked the government's administration of the railroads and supported Lord Shaughnessy's plan for returning them to private ownership. Ernest Lapointe took an active role in the campaign, supporting King in Ontario and the Maritimes, as well as aiding Lemieux in Quebec. The keynote for the campaign in the latter province was sounded at a Montreal banquet for Lemieux on September 21, with Sir Lomer Gouin in the chair and King as the chief speaker, supported by Premier Taschereau, Lapointe, Charles Murphy, and Jacques Bureau. Gouin, who was being urged to enter federal politics, likened the present situation to that of 1896, and called upon Quebec to put its trust in the Liberal party. King echoed the comparison, and declared that Laurier's policy of racial conciliation was bearing fruit in South Africa as well as in Canada. Lemieux came out strongly for Canadian autonomy, saying that 'every interference in the foreign policy of the Empire leads us towards imperialism,' while 'it is here in Canada, not in any distant adventures, that our destiny is fixed.' He wanted no voice in British councils, trusting to the traditional policy of Macdonald, Tupper, and Laurier. King raised the question of autonomy again at Charlottetown on October 5, hailing Laurier as the first Canadian to demand that Canada be recognized as 'a nation within an Empire,' and characterizing Meighen as merely a follower of Laurier in this respect.[27]

On October 20 Gouin accepted the Liberal nomination in Laurier-Outremont, with the declaration: 'I want to go to Ottawa to make Quebec better known, better respected, better loved. I want all the sister provinces of Confederation to treat Quebec as

nothing more nor less than their equal.'[28] His decision to enter the
federal field was hailed by the Conservative *Montreal Gazette* with
the observation that he had 'the respect, the confidence of all classes
in Quebec,' and that he was 'solid and steady and sane in matters
political.'[29] It was anticipated that a large Quebec delegation would
enable Gouin to command the situation at Ottawa. This Conservative support was undoubtedly due to the fact that Sir Lomer
had close connections with the financial powers of Montreal, as a
director of the Bank of Montreal, the Royal Trust Company, and
many other leading institutions. Throughout the campaign the
traditionally Tory *Montreal Gazette* and *Star* failed to support Meighen,
chiefly because he favored continued government ownership of
railroads.

Lemieux took a leading part in the campaign, accusing the
government of betraying public confidence, robbing the soldiers
of votes in 1917, trying to establish divorce courts, bankrupting
Canada, putting imperialism before Canadianism, and inviting
annexation by extravagant policies. He made much of the conscription question, and revealed that Borden had offered Laurier the
dominant role in the coalition government if he would accept
conscription. Mackenzie King aided his Quebec lieutenant's efforts
by charging the government with militarism, stressing certain recent
shipments of surplus British munitions to Canada. Meighen
defended his foreign policy at Montreal on November 4, arguing
that 'matters which appertain to our relations with the world and
the Empire should be treated by Canadians as a whole nation, and
should not be made the subject of divisions.' He declared that at the
Imperial Conference 'this country was committed to nothing whatever beyond what it has always stood committed to, nor was there
anything said or done which went a hairsbreadth beyond the pale
of what I said to Parliament.'[30] Bourassa, prevented by ill health
from running, announced that he and *Le Devoir* would support
independent candidates. He found all three parties unsatisfactory,
and opposed both Meighen and Gouin. Finally he came out in
support of the new Quebec United Farmers' Party, founded in the
Eastern Townships, which ran twenty-five candidates but found
little support. Lavergne ran as a Liberal in Quebec County, proclaiming at Charlesbourg on November 6: 'I am fighting today, as
I did in the past, for non-participation in the wars of the Empire,'
and declaring his sympathy for 'suffering Ireland crushed under the
iron heel of Engand.'[31]

The outcome of the elections was a crushing two-to-one defeat for
the government, with Quebec, Nova Scotia, and Prince Edward
Island going solidly Liberal, and the three Prairie provinces favoring
the National Progressives, the new farmers' party. All the French-

Canadian ministers were defeated, while the Laurier Liberals, Gouin, Lemieux, Lapointe, Béland, and Bureau won large majorities. *La Patrie* held that the government was defeated 'because, being a war government, it remained autocratic after peace was restored; because, having no mandate, it made no progress towards reconstruction; because it was antagonistic to Quebec. The Province of Quebec is splendidly vindicated.' *La Presse* hailed the great Liberal victory as proof that Quebec could again take her rightful place in the government of the country. With the new Liberal government dependent upon Quebec's bloc of sixty-five seats, the *Toronto Mail and Empire* on December 10 revived an old question by asking: 'Are we to be governed on Canadian lines or just French-Canadian lines?' The *Manitoba Free Press* commented sourly that 'the Montreal district went solid for Sir Lomer Gouin, high protection, the right of the Business Interests to control and administer the country, and "Down with Government ownership of railroads."' The *Orange Sentinel* on December 20 deplored the fact that 'French Canada is on top now, with a vengeance.' On the same day *La Presse* observed: 'Quebec asks that there be given to her representatives in the Federal Parliament their fair share, their whole share, of influence.'[32]

Meighen resigned on December 29, and Mackenzie King was sworn in as prime minister, announcing that 'In the formation of the government I have aimed above all else at national unity. This end I have felt would be served, and the federal spirit of our constitution most acceptably recognized, by according representation in the cabinet, so far as might be possible, to all the Provinces of Canada.'[33] After her virtual exclusion from the government since 1917, Quebec now had a lion's share. Senator Dandurand became the government leader in the Senate, while Lemieux was named speaker of the House. Gouin became minister of justice; Lapointe, minister of marine and fisheries; Bureau, minister of customs and excise; Béland, minister of soldiers' re-establishment; and Dandurand, minister without portfolio. Quebec thus had five places in a cabinet of nineteen members, and its influence was even greater than that fact indicated, thanks to its solid Liberal delegation in the House. But the Liberal government, lacking a working majority, was dependent upon Progressive support.

3

Canadian nationalism continued to make itself strongly felt, with a tendency for withdrawal from European involvements. The new government's bent towards autonomy was indicated by Prime Minister King's negotiations in Washington for a definitive treaty confirming the Rush–Bagot Agreement and settling several outstanding Canadian–American questions. When Sir Robert Borden reported to parliament on the Washington Conference, it was pointed out that the treaties would not be ratified by the King until approved by the Canadian parliament. The Chanak Crisis in the Near East, precipitated by Kemal's advance on Constantinople in September 1922, brought up once more the old question of Canadian participation in imperial wars. Without any previous warning the dominions were suddenly informed by cable on Friday, September 15, that a crisis existed and were invited to send contingents to aid Britain in resisting Turkish aggression. The press carried the news of the appeal before the official dispatch could be considered by the government. This timing was taken as an English attempt to influence Canadian public opinion and aroused wide opposition. New Zealand and Australia, at whom the appeal was primarily aimed, promptly agreed to supply the desired aid if required; but a special meeting of the Canadian cabinet on Monday, September 18, decided that nothing could be done without the sanction of Parliament, which was then prorogued, and raised the question of whether a special session was justified. In response to Conservative attacks Mr. King subsequently declared that he had offered to hold daily sessions of the cabinet while the crisis lasted, but had been informed by the British government that there was no need to summon a special session of parliament.[34]

In certain English-Canadian circles there was a quick traditional emotional response to the imperial appeal for Canadian aid, which was echoed in Protestant pulpits on Sunday, September 17, and by most of the press in Ontario and the West. Mr. Meighen, who interpreted the despatch as a desire for a declaration of solidarity rather than for the actual sending of a contingent, urged at Toronto on September 23: 'When Britain's message came, then Canada should have said: "Ready, aye ready, we stand by you."'[35]

The French press was generally opposed to any Canadian participation. *Le Droit* held that 'the duty of Canada in this issue is clear— to reply to England's request by a refusal.' *L'Evénement* observed: 'As a party to the League of Nations and a member of the British Empire, Canada cannot be indifferent to any danger which may threaten the Empire on any side, but otherwise the Canadian nation has no interest in a war on Turkey.' *La Patrie* urged the government to keep cool and weigh its action carefully, while *La Presse* declared that the matter should be settled by parliament. Bourassa took a firm stand in *Le Devoir*: 'The motives for opposing any intervention by Canada in the Near East imbroglio are multiple and peremptory. Some that come naturally to mind are: (1) Canada has no interest, direct or indirect, in the region concerned; (2) Canada is in no way morally responsible for the situation which has precipitated this peril; (3) the European nations have at their disposal ten times the force necessary to crush the Kemalist invasion; (4) why should Canada, with a new outpouring of blood, consummate its ruin so as to expiate faults and obstinacy for which it is not responsible?' On September 29 the Saint-Jean-Baptiste Society of Montreal adopted a resolution that 'Canada, a North American country, should refuse all participation in the Near East.'[36]

Though the *Montreal Star* urged faith in Britain's leaders and the *Quebec Chronicle* held that the government would repudiate Laurier's principle that Canada was at war when Britain was at war if it refused participation, the *Montreal Gazette* was lukewarm about intervention. The *Toronto Star*, the *Manitoba Free Press*, and the *Farmer's Son*, organ of the United Farmers of Ontario, opposed intervention. Prime Minister King, irritated by the British government's failure to respect the new status of the dominions, took advantage of this divided state of public opinion to advance Canadian autonomy. He denied Mr. Meighen's charges of September 22 and 28 that Canada was bound by the Treaty of Sèvres, by pointing out that it had never become operative. The crisis evaporated early in October, but the constitutional issue continued to be discussed in Canada.

John S. Ewart produced a vigorous tract on *Canada and British Wars* which raised the questions:

Are we to engage when our parliament says so, or merely when requested by a British government? Like bull-terriers, are we to fight when whistled for? Or, like intelligent human beings, are we to investigate and for ourselves determine (1) whether the stated cause is just; (2) whether, from Canadian point of view, it is worth a war; and (3) whether war is unavoidable.[37]

Ewart summed up his constitutional and historical argument with the following conclusions:

That Canada, without hesitation or investigation, ought to hold herself in readiness to engage in war merely because so requested by the British government, is an assertion unsupported by reason and incompatible with the interests, the self-respect, and the dignity of Canada....

If Canada may, in any true sense, be said to be still a part of the British Empire, the relationship implies protection by the dominant of the subordinate, and not, contrariwise, foreign-war assistance of the dominant by the subordinate. If Canada is not really a part of the British Empire, but a nation enjoying a status equal to that of the United Kingdom, obligation can be created only by treaty. And there is none.

Canada's status with reference to foreign affairs is in process of rapid development. Recent practice indicates that the statement 'When the United Kingdom is at war, Canada is at war' is not now unqualifiedly true.

Canada is situated in the North American continent. Her foreign policy ought to be based upon that indisputable fact. She ought to abstain from engulfment in the affairs—now more than ever perturbed—of Europe and the Near East. She ought to give no pledges with regard to future actions.

While Canadians will refuse to accept this last statement, I trust that there are very few who would agree that our government should have the power to commit Canada to participate in war without the authority of parliament.[38]

Ewart's views were radical in the Canada of that time, but they came to be held by an increasing number of Canadians as the years passed. The effect of Prime Minister King's handling of the Chanak Crisis was to leave the government committed to consultation of parliament before declaring war.

When parliament met in February 1923, the issue was raised again by the Conservatives, who called for the production of all papers dealing with the Chanak affair. Mr. Meighen made a plea against selfish isolationism, while one of his followers called for Canadian representation in the councils of the empire.[39] Prime Minister King blamed his failure to produce the documents on the British government's unwillingness to permit their publication. He explained his actions in the matter, and declared that the British appeal had been primarily intended for Australia and New Zealand. He concluded with a statement of general policy which reaffirmed Laurier's stand on the question.

. . . if the relations between the different parts of the British Empire are to be made of an enduring character, this will be only through a full recognition of the supremacy of Parliament, and this particularly with regard to matters which may involve participation in war. It is for Parliament to decide whether or not we should participate in wars in different parts of the world, and it is neither right nor proper for any individual or for any group of individuals to take any step which might limit the rights of Parliament in a matter which is of such great concern to all the people of the country.[40]

The prime minister's attitude was heartily endorsed by Robert Forke, leader of the National Progressives who held the balance of power in parliament, and by J. S. Woodsworth.[41]

An advance rather than a reassertion of Canadian autonomy characterized the episode of the Halibut Treaty, signed at Washington on March 2, 1923. This treaty dealt with the halibut fisheries of the North Pacific, and thus concerned only Canada and the United States. The Canadian government sought to have it described thus, rather than as a convention between Great Britain and the United States, but failed to win its point. It was successful, however, in having Ernest Lapointe, minister of marine and fisheries, named plenipotentiary with full powers to sign the treaty; and in insisting that he should sign the agreement alone, rather than in association with the British ambassador at Washington, on the grounds that 'The Treaty, being one of concern solely to Canada and the United States, and not affecting, in any particular, any Imperial interest, the signature of the Canadian Minister should be sufficient.' This marked a considerable advance upon the precedent of the Franco-Canadian Commercial Treaty of 1907, which had been signed by a Canadian representative in association with the British ambassador. The United States Senate, however, showed its failure to recognize Canada's new status by ratifying the treaty on March 4, with an added reservation covering the nationals of 'any other part of Great Britain.'[42] This reservation turned a Canadian treaty into an imperial one.

When the treaty came up for ratification in the Canadian parliament on June 27, Meighen objected to the government stand as emphasizing to the world a desire to dissociate Canada from the empire, while Lapointe took the ground that his objection to signature by the British ambassador had been based upon the principle acknowledged at the Peace Conference. The treaty was described as having been 'signed on behalf of His Majesty, acting for Canada, by the plenipotentiary therein named.' Probably because of Meighen's criticism of this formula, it subsequently became 'in behalf of his Majesty in respect of Canada by the plenipotentiary therein named'[43] in the Canada–United States Boundary Treaty of 1925. Prime Minister King's followers held that the treaty had been signed on the advice and responsibility of the Canadian government alone. Bonar Law, the Canadian-born British prime minister, declared that it was on the advice and responsibility of both the British and Canadian governments. Despite criticism from both Conservative sources and older Liberals[44] the treaty was duly ratified, and passed by the United States in its original form in the following year.[45]

Prime Minister King, who had steered such a nationalist course in the Chanak and Halibut Treaty episodes and was following the same line with regard to the Lausanne Treaty, issued a statement reassuring the imperialists before leaving for the Imperial Conference of 1925:

It is my privilege to go to the Imperial Conference in the name of the people of Canada without a single grievance, to say that our relations with Great Britain and with all parts of the Empire are of the best, and that we have only the most cordial feeling towards all concerned. So long as this happy condition prevails, friends of Canada and friends of the British Empire need have no concern for the future of either. To make it prevail at all times must be our supreme endeavour.[46]

With the tide of dominion nationalism rising high, there was no question in London of closer imperial union. The precedent afforded by the Halibut Treaty was extended to the whole empire, with the formulation of specific principles for the negotiation, signature, and ratification of treaties relating to the empire.[47] International treaties were to be dealt with on the basis of the Paris and Washington precedents, bilateral treaties affecting more than one part of the empire were to be based upon the fullest possible exchange of views; while bilateral treaties affecting only one part of the empire might be made solely by the government concerned. It was also decided that each dominion should make its own arrangements for defence and such contributions to imperial defence funds as it saw fit.[48] Canada objected to a proposed Imperial Economic Committee, responsible to all the governments involved, and not much was done to foster imperial preference. Sir Lomer Gouin and G. P. Graham, who had accompanied Mr. King to London, also represented Canada at the Geneva Conference of the League of Nations in September, with Gouin pressing for an interpretation of Article X of the Peace Treaty and playing a leading part in the deliberations. Philippe Roy was the Canadian representative at the Fifth International Labor Conference at Geneva in October. This participation by French-Canadians in international affairs helped in some measure to break down Quebec's traditional isolationism.

The question of Canada's national status was again brought up late in March 1924, when J. S. Woodsworth moved that the Canadian parliament 'ought to possess, under the British Crown, the same powers with regard to Canada, its affairs and its people, as the Parliament of Great Britain possesses in regard to Great Britain, its affairs and its people.'[49] The resolution implied that Canada should have the right to amend its constitution, the B.N.A. Act, which as an imperial statute could only be altered by vote of the British parliament. Reform or abolition of the Senate, in which a lingering Conservative majority hampered the carrying through of Liberal or Progressive measures, was also involved. Quebec's reliance upon British support against English-Canadian dominance was once more revealed when Charles Marcil and Thomas Vien reminded the House that Confederation was a compact, and that Quebec and perhaps other provinces would oppose any change in the *status quo* by which provincial rights might suffer from increased federal power.

At this same time the Lausanne episode, which was the third post-war crisis in imperial relations in which Canada took a notably nationalist stand, was coming to a head. On March 24 the Canadian government declined the British invitation to ratify the Lausanne Treaty by refusing to submit it to parliament. In a statement to the House on April 2 Prime Minister King objected to Prime Minister Ramsay Macdonald's assertion on the previous day that Canada had agreed to concur in the outcome of the Lausanne Conference. He took the stand that 'not having been invited, not having been represented directly or indirectly, and not having signed, Canada has no obligations. Therefore we do not feel it necessary to submit the matter to Parliament for approval; nor for that matter, to signify concurrence in ratification to the Treaty.'[50] In his government's correspondence on the matter with the Baldwin and Macdonald governments since October 1922, Mr. King had taken the line that the Canadian parliament would decide the extent to which Canada was bound by the agreements made by the British plenipotentiaries. When pressed for Canadian signature of the agreement, the King government insisted that the four essential features of the Paris and Washington precedents for such action did not exist. Canada had not been directly represented at Lausanne, nor had she signed the treaty, and hence approval by the Canadian parliament and assent by the Canadian government to ratification by the King could not be supplied.[51]

During the debate at Westminster in April and June the British government was censured for not inviting the dominions to confer on the treaty, with Lloyd George characterizing the course followed as 'a very grave departure' and 'a reversal of the whole process by which the unity of the Empire has been advanced during and since the War.'[52] On June 9 Prime Minister King informed the House that the reasons for not inviting the dominions had been given him in confidence—it was subsequently revealed that France had threatened to match a British Empire delegation by a similar one from her own empire—and declared:

I have been taking my stand from the point of view of Canada a nation within the British Empire, not Canada a Colony, not Canada in any inferior or subordinate position, but Canada a country which has gained and which merits equality of status with other Dominions and with the Mother Country in these inter-Imperial relations.[53]

Mr. King held the view that while Canada would be legally bound by the treaty, it would not be morally bound, as it was by the Treaty of Versailles in whose making it had participated. Meighen criticized him for having acquiesced in a return to colonial status and for his unwillingness to cooperate with the British government.[54] The practical result of the incident was to leave Canada and the other dominions free to decide whether or not they would participate in any British action which might arise under the treaty.

Undoubtedly as a result of the criticism of the Lausanne procedure, the British government proposed on June 24 that a preliminary conference of United Kingdom and dominion representatives be held early in July to decide upon dominion representation at the London Conference on Reparations. In his statement to the House on July 17, Mr. King revealed that the Canadian government had insisted upon the Versailles and Washington Conference precedent being followed, and had requested full powers for Senator Belcourt as Canadian member of the British Empire delegation. He criticized with heat the fact that the press was better informed about how the question of representation was to be settled than he was. On the following day the colonial secretary announced the adoption of a panel system, whereby the British delegation was to consist of two United Kingdom representatives and one from the dominions, the latter to change from day to day. Dominion representatives would also be entitled to be present at the conference on days when they were not serving as active members of the delegation. The plan was characterized as a special one for the purpose of this conference, and not to be taken as a precedent.

Bourassa vigorously denounced the panel plan as absurd, and argued that if the British Empire were several nations, it could not act as one or six or seven at choice. L. M. S. Amery and Lloyd George also censured the plan in the British House, declaring that the world must take the empire as it found it, and that the status of the dominions could not be diminished merely to suit the convenience of other powers.[55] The question was to be discussed at a proposed Imperial Conference in October, but that gathering was indefinitely postponed by the new British government early in December after the dominions had shown reluctance about setting a definite date. With the naming of Colonel Amery to the Colonial Office in the new Baldwin government, a broader concept of imperial relations became dominant in Britain.

4

The concessions made to the free-trade views of the Western Progressives, who remained essential political allies of the King government, played a part in bringing about the resignation in 1924 of one of the most prominent members of the cabinet, Sir Lomer Gouin, and later of W. S. Fielding. Ernest Lapointe succeeded Gouin as minister of justice, and P.-J.-A. Cardin of Sorel took Lapointe's portfolio of marine and fisheries. Though the Liberal-Progressive alliance was strengthened by tariff cuts, higher freight rates lost the government Western support, while Quebec Liberals showed a developing protectionism. The government called elections for October 29, 1925, in an effort to break the increasing political deadlock. The outcome made the situation worse rather than better. The Liberals won 101 seats, with the prime minister and eight of his cabinet colleagues failing of election. The Conservatives took 116 seats, more than doubling their membership in the House, but the balance of power remained with 24 Progressives, 2 Labour and 2 Independents. Prime Minister King decided against calling another election or turning over the task of forming a ministry to Meighen, on the grounds that the Progressives were more apt to support him than they were the Conservative leader. His course was denounced by Meighen as 'usurpation of power and contempt of the public will.'[56] The defeated ministers resigned, with their colleagues taking temporary charge of their departments until parliament should decide the fate of the government when it reassembled in January 1926.

During the campaign Meighen had sought to woo Quebec by French speeches in favour of protection and development of natural resources. E.-L. Patenaude ran as an independent Conservative, backed by the *Montreal Star* and befriended by the *Gazette*, but criticized by *Le Devoir* for establishing a Quebec party to guard vested English interests. Bourassa returned to political life as an independent with Conservative backing, and was elected for his old constituency of Labelle. Lavergne served as chief lieutenant to Patenaude, but was himself defeated in Montmagny. The wartime curse still hung over the Conservatives in Quebec, and they won only four seats in Quebec, all in English constituencies.

At Hamilton on November 16 Meighen attacked the Liberal tactics in Quebec during the campaign, where he had been branded as a believer in conscription and a supporter of new wars. He declared: 'I believe it would be best, not only that Parliament should be called, but that the decision of the government, which of course would have to be given promptly, should be submitted to the judgment of the people at a general election before troops should leave our shores. This would contribute to the unity of our country in the months to come, and would enable us best to do our duty.'[57] And in the Bagot by-election in Quebec during December Meighen repeated these statements, which were criticized by his fellow Conservative C. H. Cahan and also by the Liberal Cardin, who found it strange that Meighen favored the policy of consultation in time of peace while he had opposed it in time of war. The Liberal candidate was elected, and the *Toronto Globe* pointed out that 'Meighen has bartered his birthright for a mess of pottage,' while the *Winnipeg Tribune* commented that Quebec had not been won by the new Conservative war policy.[58]

When parliament met in January 1926, Lapointe acted as government leader in the House in the absence of Mr. King. A no-confidence motion was defeated on January 15 by a vote of 123–120, with most of the Progressive members joining the labor and independent members in support of the government. In February H. H. Stevens made charges of serious irregularities in the Customs and Excise Department, in connection with the smuggling of liquor into the United States and of various American products into Canada. A parliamentary committee was appointed to investigate the charges. The House adjourned for two weeks early in March for reorganization of the government, and when it met again on March 15 Mr. King was back in his seat, having won a Prince Albert by-election.

On March 18 J. S. Woodsworth introduced a motion, occasioned by the Locarno Pact in which Canada had not participated, that 'Canada should refuse to accept responsibility for complications arising from the foreign policy of the United Kingdom.' Four days later Bourassa made a long review of Canada's imperial relations in support of the Woodsworth motion, which the latter had defended as not anti-British but anti-imperialist. Bourassa maintained that he did not long for secession and that he prized the association with Great Britain, but that he objected to a policy of 'servile worship of everything English':

On the contrary it is by standing up in the face of Great Britain, not in a defiant attitude, but in an attitude of self-respect and virile admiration, asserting to Great Britain that there are certain matters upon which we can agree with her, and that there are other matters upon which we cannot agree, because they have interests which are not the same as ours and because we have trusts to perform and to hand over to generations still to come with which neither the Englishman nor the Australian can deal for us. We have a duty to perform by Canada; the Australian has a duty to perform by Australia; and the British have a duty to Great Britain, which no other country can perform. If we can only revive these principles, these elementary truths, in the minds of the people of this country or in other portions of the Empire, I am quite sure that this great problem of inter-imperial relations will soon be solved.[59]

Bourassa concluded by announcing that he would not vote for the Woodsworth resolution, which he thought rather narrow in its wording, but that he would not associate himself with those who denounced Woodsworth for raising it. He suggested referring it to a committee which should invite J. S. Ewart, Sir John Willison, Sir Robert Falconer, and Dr. O. D. Skelton to examine the imperial, national, and independent alternatives for Canada's future. He stressed that 'Canada was not bound by any obligation assumed by the government of the United Kingdom in matters of foreign policy, unless and until the government of Canada, duly authorized by Parliament, expresses its adherence thereto.'[60]

The gradual merging of English- and French-Canadian nationalism was revealed by the fact that Bourassa was now able to name four distinguished English Canadians who were at least sympathetic to the views he had long held. In fact he was not very far from the position taken by Mackenzie King at Wiarton, Ontario, during the campaign:

Just as we have gained self-government in domestic affairs, so in foreign affairs, which are of direct and immediate concern to ourselves, we contend that they should be managed by our own people. In foreign affairs in which we have no immediate or direct interest, we believe these questions should be left to the parts of the Empire concerned. If questions arise which are of a character likely to affect all of us, then we say where our interests come in touch with those of other parts of the Empire, we should take our part in shaping the policy and having our voice heard.[61]

The thinking of both Bourassa and King on these matters had felt the common influence of Laurier upon his bright young men.

This became evident in a second debate on Locarno on June 21, when Prime Minister King announced the government's intention to defer any action on the pact until after the Imperial Conference that fall. He did move, however, that parliamentary approval should be obtained before the government ratified 'any treaties affecting Canada or involving military or economic sanctions.'[62] Bourassa, who had earlier in the session called for the production of the communications between Britain and Canada on Locarno, expressed approval of the prime minister's motion, but said it had already been violated in spirit by the withholding from parliament of these despatches. Arguing that one imperial foreign policy was impossible, he reminded the House that Sir Esme Howard, Lord Grey, and Lord Fisher had recognized that the Monroe Doctrine must be the basis of Canadian policy, since Canada was British by historical accident but American by geography. Bourassa revived the old slogan of Canada First:

From a Canadian point of view, or from a British point of view, let us serve notice to the world at large, not in any spirit of animosity toward Great Britain, but in full consciousness of what we owe to our people, that Canada is prepared to uphold morally any real move for peace which may be taken in Europe or anywhere, but that Canada is not prepared to arm her youth and to spend her millions for the sake of any foreign policy with which we are not connected by necessity and from which Canada is disconnected by all the exigencies of her natural situation . . .

If we are to save Canada from internal dissention, from the turmoil of European politics or from American absorption, it will be by bending our energies . . . to make the different sections of this country one united people for Canada . . . To subscribe to undefined and unlimited engagements, or even defined and limited engagements which go beyond the sphere of our action . . . is wrong. There, I say, British, yes, but Canadian first; if necessary secession from Britain rather than sacrifice of Canada; Canada alongside of Britain so long as it is possible, but Canada first and forever.[63]

This speech was more forthright than the government's expressed attitude, but undoubtedly reflected it. The Western Progressive attitude was even more isolationist.[64]

The question of autonomy on the domestic rather than the international level was raised by King's adroit handling of the Byng incident in the summer of 1926. After several close escapes from votes of no confidence in June, debate on the customs inquiry precipitated the resignation of the King government on June 28. When it became apparent that the Progressives would no longer support the government, Mr. King asked the governor-general to dissolve parliament and call an election. Lord Byng refused to do so, on the grounds that the opposition should be given a chance to form a ministry. Mr. Meighen accepted the task of forming a government, but was faced with the awkward fact that the slender Conservative majority would become non-existent if he and his cabinet colleagues resigned their seats, pending re-election after accepting office under the Crown, according to constitutional custom. Meighen postponed taking the oath of office until he could get guarantees from the Progressives not to oust his government, and appointed a cabinet of six acting ministers to avoid the necessity of re-elections. Mr. King maintained that the government was illegally constituted, and on July 2 the Meighen government was driven from office by a single vote on a want of confidence motion. Meighen promptly sought a dissolution, which was granted by the governor-general, and elections were called for September 14.

The new Meighen government announced on July 13 included only two French Canadians, E.-L. Patenaude, who was named minister of justice, and Dr. R. Morand; but Eugène Paquet was subsequently named minister of public health and André Fauteux solicitor-general. Meighen sought to wage the campaign on the issue of the customs scandals, and mercilessly exposed the maladministration of the department under Jacques Bureau and G.-H. Boivin. King insisted that the unconstitutional conduct of the governor-general in refusing a dissolution to a Liberal government while granting one to a Conservative one was the vital issue, and declared that the election would determine whether Canada would remain a self-governing country or would be reduced to the status of a Crown colony. He denounced Meighen's course as unconstitutional. Both parties trimmed their stand on the tariff to meet sectional sentiment. Meighen was vigorously attacked in Ontario for his efforts to win support in Quebec by his Hamilton and Bagot speeches, and for his refusal to discuss at Toronto the issue of consultation before sending troops abroad.

Bourassa asserted at Papineauville on July 18 that 'either Mr. Meighen has odiously fooled His Excellency or His Excellency has made himself the election agent of Mr. Meighen.'[65] Denouncing his old Conservative allies as the 'Tory-Orange clique,' he later adopted the Liberal view that self-government was at stake: 'It is the slow but gradual conquest of our liberties which is in peril; it is the work of Macdonald and Cartier; it is the very spirit of Confederation in its relation with the metropolis of the empire which is being sapped at the present moment by those who falsely claim for themselves the traditions of the Conservative Party.'[66]

Patenaude supported Meighen vigorously in Quebec, asserting that stable government and a protective tariff could only be achieved through the Conservative Party, and giving his leader credit for reviving the party in Quebec. The Liberal spokesman Lucien Cannon and Raoul Dandurand charged Patenaude with forgetting his pledges and putting too much faith in Meighen's Hamilton speech, which had been repudiated by his lieutenants. Bourassa defended King, who was attacked in the English provinces for not having served in the war, though neither Meighen nor Patenaude had done so either:

The crime of Mr. King is that he did not work to send our sons to the slaughter. In the eyes of those who consider that it is the duty of Canada to ruin herself for the glory of England, that is perhaps a crime. In the eyes of true Canadians it ought to be a reason for supporting Mr. King, to permit him to carry to the next Imperial Conference in London the expression of our sentiments and to speak there the clear language of the Canadian nation, faithful to the King of England, but faithful also to herself, to her sons, to her future, to her mission as a people in America.[67]

The disintegration of the two-party system was evident in the fact that 528 candidates contested 244 seats, with the Conservatives naming 233, the Liberals 199, the Progressives 20, the Independents 25, Labor 18, the United Farmers of Alberta 12, and the Liberal-Progressives 21. In forty-eight constituencies the Liberals supported Independent, Labor, or Progressive candidates to avoid three-cornered contests.[68]

The elections resulted in a Liberal gain of seventeen seats, a Conservative loss of twenty-five, while the Progressive, Labor, and

Independent groups gained eight more seats. Though the Conservatives polled more votes than they had in the last elections, Meighen and five of his ministers were defeated, including the four French-Canadian ministers. The final results gave the Liberals 118 seats, the Conservatives 91, and the new parties 36. Meighen's defeat was blamed by the Ontario press on his desperate efforts to win the Quebec vote, while *Le Devoir* saw in it 'a decisive, emphatic condemnation of the *coup de force* and abuse of power suggested to Lord Byng by Mr. Meighen or vice versa . . . It will be a long time before another Governor-General will do violence to the constitution and established custom.'[69]

Mackenzie King took office on September 25, with a cabinet which included six French Canadians. French Canada, which had proved the backbone of Liberal strength, had five places: Lapointe as minister of justice, Cardin as minister of marine, Lucien Cannon as solicitor-general, Fernand Rinfret as secretary of state, and Raoul Dandurand as minister without portfolio. An alliance between the Manitoba Progressives and the Liberals was sealed by the inclusion of Robert Forke, the former Progressive leader, in the cabinet. This step broke up the cohesiveness of the Western agricultural bloc which had held the balance of power at Ottawa for five years. Meighen resigned as head of the Conservative Party, with Hugh Guthrie replacing him as House leader until R. B. Bennett was chosen as the new head of the party in the following year.

5

The verdict of the Canadian people on the constitutional issue raised by the Byng episode had an important bearing on the Imperial Conference of 1926, whose meeting had been delayed until October 19 because of the election. On his way to London Mackenzie King, who was accompanied by Ernest Lapointe, issued a statement in which he said that he favored the development of responsible self-government and disapproved of the interpretation of the conference as an imperial cabinet. But he stressed that Canada's course at the conference would be one of goodwill. On the eve of the conference, at a dinner of the Canada Club of London to Lord Byng, whose term as governor-general had just ended, both King and Byng sought to demonstrate that there had been no serious difference of opinion between them on imperial unity.[70] It was General Hertzog of South Africa, reviving the long-standing South African-Canadian alliance in imperial affairs, who raised the question of dominion status early in the conference, calling for 'in principle unrestrained freedom of action to each member of the Commonwealth; in practice, consultation with a view to cooperative action wherever possible.'[71] But it was known that Mr. King and President Cosgrave of the Irish Free State would prove at least as vigorous champions of dominion nationhood. A committee of dominion prime ministers under the chairmanship of Lord Balfour was formed to report on future inter-imperial relations, and the result of their deliberations was a document drafted in the main by Lord Birkenhead, the secretary of state for India.

The Balfour Report[72] was ratified by the conference on November 19. It was noteworthy for its new definition of the relations between Great Britain and the dominions, which has since become classic:

They are autonomous Communities within the British Empire, equal in status, in no way subordinate to one another in any aspect of their domestic or external affairs, although united by a common allegiance to the Crown, and freely associated as members of the British Commonwealth of Nations.[73]

As a consequence of this definition, the governor-general ceased to be a subordinate of the colonial secretary, and was newly defined as 'the representative of the Crown, holding in all essential respects the same position in relation to the administration of public affairs in the Dominion as is held by His Majesty the King in Great Britain, and ... he is not the representative or agent of His Majesty's Government in Great Britain or of any Department of that Government.'[74] Communications between Great Britain and the dominions now took place directly between the prime ministers, or between departments of the two governments by way of the new Dominions Office established in 1925 and the governor-general. This latter vestige of the governor's functions as a servant of the imperial government was abolished by the provision that the official channel of communication should be between government and government directly, with the provision that the governor-general should be kept informed and supplied with copies of important documents. No change was made in the method of appointment of the governor-general, already virtually made by the dominion government concerned in consultation with the imperial one. After the conference closed, Mr. King stated in the House at Ottawa that Lord Willingdon had been appointed to Canada after consultation between the British prime minister and himself.[75] This extensive readjustment of the theory of imperial relations, which realized the promise of 1917, was worked out in detail at the 1929 and 1930 Imperial Conferences and given legal force by the Statute of Westminster in 1931, which sanctioned the transformation of the second British Empire into the British Commonwealth of Nations.

This great constitutional development was very largely due to Mackenzie King's insistence that the governor-general should confine himself to the position whic.. Sir Robert Borden had already assumed he occupied.[76] The right of each government to advise the Crown in all matters relating to its own affairs was recognized, while legislation affecting the interests of other self-governing parts of the Commonwealth was to be subject to previous consultation with the parties concerned. As for foreign relations, the principle adopted in 1923 was reaffirmed: each government proposing to make a treaty should give notice to other interested parts of the Commonwealth. Treaties were to be signed in the name of the King, as a symbol of the relationship between the parts of the Commonwealth, while 'it was frankly recognized that in this sphere the conduct of foreign affairs, as in the sphere of defence, the major share of responsibility rests now and must for some time to come, continue to rest, with His Majesty's Government in Great Britain.'[77] Lapointe, whose role at Washington in 1923 had raised so many questions, served as chairman of the subcommittee on treaty procedure. The appointment of Canadian and Irish Free State ministers to Washington was approved, though it was recommended that in the absence of dominion representatives, the foreign relations of the dominions should be carried on through the British representatives.

Canada took a very negative attitude towards defence questions at the conference, while on February 5, 1927, Mr. King rebuked Prime Minister Bruce of Australia for criticizing Canada's stand in speeches at Toronto and elsewhere on his way homeward.[78] Economic relations were hardly touched upon at the conference, thanks to the emphasis on constitutional problems. Mr. King replied to Prime Minister Baldwin's official farewell to the dominion prime ministers at a London dinner on November 27, observing: 'The charter of the liberties we individually and collectively enjoy may, to appearances, have been enlarged. In reality, there has been, as respects British political institutions, natural development along inevitable lines.'[79] And in a press statement upon his return to Ottawa on December 8, Mr. King declared that all doubts as to whether Canada had the proper authority to negotiate and sign treaties and whether or not Canada had a nationhood of her own were at an end. He held that the ties which bound Canada to Great Britain and the empire had been made closer rather than shattered by a larger measure of self-government.[80]

The outcome of the conference aroused mixed comment in Canada. The *Manitoba Free Press* observed:

The heart of the declaration by the Conference upon the question of status ought to be clear enough to make it evident, even to the most skeptical nationalist on the one hand and the most purblind colonial on the other, that a new system by which the British Empire is to be made over into an alliance of free and equal nations has been established, and that other conceptions of the Commonwealth are out of date. . . .[81]

But the *Ottawa Journal* minimized what it regarded as a mere crystalization of advances made since the close of the World War: 'We are no freer today than we were this day last week or this time last year, and for the simple reason that this time last year we were completely unfettered and free.' The *Toronto Globe* commented:

The most cursory glance at the statement made public forces the conviction that no effort whatever has been made to increase the bond of union, while every clause in every article of the Report contributes to rob the Mother Country of any directing power as head and forefront of the Commonwealth. Everywhere it is equality of the Dominions that is stressed, it is the autonomy of these States, not their partnership in a common cause and with common aims that is emphasized.

The *Montreal Gazette* also harked back to an earlier day with its declaration:

It is still the opinion of a great many Canadians that there can be no equality within the Empire without corresponding equality and responsibility expressed in adequate provision for the safety, not of the Empire, but of the Dominion itself. As things are now, Canada's dependence on British seapower is practically as great as it ever was, and that dignified and creditable condition seems likely to continue.[82]

Under their new leader the Conservatives sought to repudiate the Balfour Report. When parliament met in December, Guthrie suggested that the new principle that Canada had 'absolute control in every domestic and external matter' gave the Canadian parliament power to alter the constitution and to abolish bilingualism, 'sweeping away those safeguards which the Fathers of Confederation placed in our constitutional act in 1867.' He suggested that the Report might have to be amended when the government received the opinion of Quebec. He also maintained that equality of status conflicted with the facts: Canada could not declare war without Great Britain doing so, yet she would be involved 'as a belligerent the moment Great Britain made the declaration.' He closed with another warning of the future disaster for minorities involved in the Report.[83] Though Prime Minister King replied to some of Guthrie's points at this time, the main debate on the conference did not take place until March 29, when King reviewed its work. The Conservative leader opposed the government plan to commit the country to approval of the Report by tacit acquiescence, and moved a resolution of formal dissent. Ernest Lapointe discounted Guthrie's reiterated fears for minority rights:

We must rely upon ourselves for the safeguard and protection of those rights, working in cooperation and understanding with our fellow Canadians in this country. It would not be possible to secure the permanent adhesion of any section of the Canadian people to any plan whereby there would be any political force superior to their own government and their own constitution which would, even indirectly, have authority to control their actions.[84]

He added that in his opinion no change in the B.N.A. Act could be made without the consent of the parties to that pact.

Bourassa also discussed the Report, asserting that Britain still claimed the right to initiate and conduct foreign relations, since the dominions were supposed to have acquiesced in all treaties which they did not immediately protest. He criticized British foreign policy, but dissented from the view that 'Imperial partnership is not a fair proposition.' He argued that 'we cannot remain within the Empire and at the same time be a full-fledged independent nation. We might as well attempt to square the circle as to try and carry on a permanent policy at once imperial and national along these lines.' But he agreed with Lapointe as to the absence of danger to minorities:

We are manly enough to be prepared to discuss in the future with our fellow citizens of Canada, whether Protestant or Catholic, whether French or English, whether from the West or the East, every one of those rights which we claim to be ours, not because they are contained in a few articles of law in a printed book, but because we know that in the hearts of all right-thinking Canadians there is a desire to see that justice is done, and if we are to maintain that unity of which the leader of the Opposition has spoken, it is not to be done by declarations of law or the adjudication of a tribunal either in Ottawa or London, but by the desire of all thinking Canadians to maintain the spirit of Confederation and the constitution of Canada.[85]

J. S. Woodsworth, speaking for the labor group, warned of the danger of committing Canada to common action for defence, 'lest we lend ourselves to the manipulations of a group of Imperialists which is largely composed of exploiters.' He cited as an index of inequality Canada's inability to amend its own constitution. The Guthrie motion was lost on April 5 by a vote of 122–78, with the Liberal-Progressive and Labor members voting with the government.

The question of abolition of appeals to the Privy Council, which was raised in the debate on the Balfour Report, was brought to the fore by a judgment of March 1, 1927, in which that body settled the long-standing Canada-Newfoundland boundary question in favor of Newfoundland. The decision gave Newfoundland 120,000 square miles of disputed territory in Labrador, including much valuable spruce forest and water-power totaling half that of Quebec. The decision was of particular interest to Quebec, since the territory in question formed an important part of Ungava, the hitherto un-exploited northern Quebec region which was becoming of increasing interest as pulp and power interests expanded their operations in the province. The decision provoked some agitation for abolition of appeals to the Privy Council, and a resolution to that effect in the legislature. But the motion was withdrawn after it had been repudiated by Premier Taschereau, who had helped to present Quebec's case in London. The premier held that the Privy Council was an indispensable safeguard of the constitution and of provincial rights in particular. Both he and the leader of the opposition, Arthur Sauvé, expressed the view, in connection with the imperial conference, that the constitution must not be altered without the consent of the Province of Quebec.

6

The celebration of the Diamond Jubilee of Confederation on Dominion Day 1927 centered in Ottawa and did not evoke much enthusiasm in Quebec, which traditionally made more of its own Saint-Jean-Baptiste Day (June 24). The Saint-Jean-Baptiste Day parade in Montreal this year, however, celebrated Confederation and included allegorical floats devoted to episodes of Canadian history. In Ottawa, after the inauguration of the carillon in the Peace Tower of the Parliament Buildings, Sir Lomer Gouin, Thomas Chapais, and Senator Dandurand joined the governor-general, Prime Minister King, L. P. Tilley, Hugh Guthrie, and George Graham in speeches commemorating the anniversary. The Fathers of Confederation were represented by two sons, Chapais and Tilley, and the daughters of Sir George Cartier and W. H. Pope. Speeches were made in both languages, and both French and English music was played. Similar ceremonies were held at the provincial capitals, with Saint-Boniface commemorating the landing of La Vérendrye while Winnipeg on the other side of the Red River celebrated Con-federation. Only in Nova Scotia, where one town flew its flags at half-mast and a Halifax newspaper continued its refusal to recognize Dominion Day, was the general enthusiasm lacking. The bicultural status of Canada was recognized in the recommendation that the French and English versions of 'O Canada' should be used in cele-brations of the occasion, and by a special issue of bilingual postage stamps.

The Dominion-Provincial Conference which met at Ottawa early in November provided evidence, however, that all was not well with Confederation on its sixtieth anniversary. The conference discussed reform of the Senate, the amendment of the B.N.A. Act, provincial subsidies and representation, immigration, and company law. The result was largely an exchange of views between federal and provincial ministers, with no action taken and no resolutions adopted. Justice Minister Lapointe proposed that Canada, in view of the equality of status she had attained with Britain, should have the power to amend her own constitution after consultation with the provincial legislatures, with majority consent in ordinary cases and unanimous consent in cases affecting provincial and minority rights and questions of race and creed. There was a sharp division of opinion on this proposal, and the King government promised careful consideration of all the views that were expressed. The *Manitoba Free Press* on November 7 approved Lapointe's stand, urging that Canada should not remain 'in the anomalous and humiliating position of being the only country on earth claiming to be a nation, which has to have its constitution patched up for it from time to time by an external parliament.'[86] There were requests from the Western provinces for the return of their natural resources by the federal government and from the Maritimes for special financial treatment, while Ontario protested its heavy share of the financial burden of Confederation and Premier Taschereau of Quebec called for a clearer delimitation of the powers of taxation between federal and provincial authorities.

Public discussion of Canada's national status was renewed by election of Canada to the Council of the League of Nations on September 15, 1927. Senator Dandurand, Canada's representative to the League, who had served as president of the Assembly in 1925, expressed his belief that the election recognized Canada's nationhood in the fullest sense. He decried American comment that Canada was the puppet of Downing Street, and called her 'the spokesman of the North American continent's ideals.'[87] Prime Minister King interpreted the event as definite recognition of Canadian nationhood and an indication of international esteem for Canada. In an address on September 17 Lapointe observed: 'Canada has grown into full nationhood and now takes her place in the international Council of Nations while still proud to retain her position as an autonomous community within the British Empire.' The issue of whether Canada's obligations as a member of the League conflicted with her duties as a member of the Commonwealth continued to be discussed.[88]

When parliament met in January 1928 the question of status was again raised by the government's announcement of its intention to appoint ministers to France and Japan. The Conservatives were reluctant to see Canada assume new international obligations. R. B. Bennett, who had replaced Hugh Guthrie as leader of the opposition in the previous October, decried the doctrine of equality with Britain upon which the appointments were based: 'As long as the

Colonial Laws Validity Act remains on the statute book of Great Britain, we have no equality of status.' Bennett evaded a question from Lapointe as to whether he would join in an effort to secure repeal of this statute, but asserted his willingness 'to use every effort to see to it that this country shall maintain a status of parnership within the British Empire on an equality with other partners in the Commonwealth.'[89] In response to a question from Mr. King, he declared: 'Nationhood . . . involves . . . complete independence. I am not prepared for the complete independence of Canada.'[90] King questioned this interpretation of nationhood, and said: 'The reason that I welcome the equality of status as between the different Dominions of the Empire and Great Britain is that I believe it is the only basis on which the British Empire can continue and endure, and for that reason and not from any desire of independence in the sense to which my honorable friend refers, I am a strong supporter of the recent position of the British Empire as laid down at the Imperial Conference of 1926.'[91]

The two major party leaders continued their debate on Canada's status on the platform during the summer of 1928. At Oshawa on July 22 Bennett asked: 'What port is Mr. King bound for? If he wants to make this an independent country let him say so. Let us have a well-defined expression from Premier King as to where he is heading, what his chart is, and what his port.'[92] On a Western tour Mr. King replied to Bennett at Davidson, Saskatchewan:

The ship of state is safely anchored in the port of unity, prosperity, and amity. I have designated the port to my anxious friend. Let him no longer be afraid. May I tell him that my chart is the development of the British Constitution throughout the entire course of its history, and my compass is the guiding principle of responsible government.[93]

In August Mr. King went to Paris to sign the Kellogg Peace Pact, and then to Geneva, where he was elected a vice-president of the League of Nations Assembly in September. After the close of the Assembly he returned to Paris, where at a banquet commemorating the opening of the Canadian Legation he expressed the hope that 'a Canadian Legation in France may stand not only today, but always, as a symbol, not to Europe alone but to the world, of that union of French and British minds which has made Canada what she is, and of a never-ending friendship between the two races, alike in the old world and the new.'[94] Later, in London, he indicated Canada's desire for British immigrants. Upon his return to Canada he defined Canada's international role at a Toronto banquet on November 22: 'To do our part in maintaining the unity of the British Commonwealth of Nations and to further to the utmost of our ability friendly relations between the British Empire and the rest of the world, and in particular the three great powers I have mentioned: the United States, France, and Japan.'[95]

During Mr. King's absence abroad Bennett had continued his attacks on the Liberal view of Canada's status and on the Liberal tariff policy. At a Montreal banquet on October 25 Bennett defined the aims of the Conservative Party as 'the maintenance of our integrity as a portion of the British Empire' and 'the safeguarding of our constitution and the rights of minority which are guaranteed thereby.'[96] Arthur Sauvé, the provincial Conservative leader, expressed his agreement with Bennett, while C. H. Cahan blamed the Conservative poor showing in Quebec in recent years on ethnic conflicts in other provinces, which offended the traditions and sentiments of French Canadians. He felt that the recent modifications of separate school regulations in Ontario, New Brunswick, and Nova Scotia had improved the situation.

With an increased American tariff in prospect, Mr. Bennett pressed the tariff question vigorously in 1929. He described the American development as 'a crisis in our economic history' and called for an immediate imperial economic conference. He denounced the fact that the so-called British preference of 1897 had been whittled down by various treaties and had reached a stage in which the average Canadian duties were more favorable to the United States than to the United Kingdom.[97] During the session Prime Minister King repudiated numerous Conservative calls for a retaliatory tariff policy against the United States as a result of Republican high tariff promises during the 1928 campaign, which became law in the Hawley-Smoot Tariff Act of 1930. Dr. R. J. Manion, a rising Conservative leader, called upon parliament to deal in 'a red-blooded Canadian manner'[98] with the American tariff attitude. Mr. King suggested that 'a cool-headed manner' was more appropriate, while Minister of National Revenue Euler deplored talk of 'immediate retaliatory measures.' Ernest Lapointe declared that 'we are going to shape our policies, fiscal and otherwise, at Ottawa' and that Canada would take care of its trade by 'British preference and treaties with other nations of the world.'[99] In reporting to parliament on the Geneva Economic Conference, Lapointe had favored international free trade, and had declared that if the American market were closed, tariff revision would be made 'only in the Canadian interest and not at all as a result of retaliation or tariff war.'[100]

The anti-American agitation aroused by the Conservative Party in its effort to emphasize Canada's British ties took somewhat different grounds in a Quebec whose particularism was irritated by the growing dominance of American industry in the province. Quebec's loss of its potential Labrador resources through the Privy

Council decision in 1927 was offset for the time being by tremendous pulp and power developments in the province, with the investment of over $300,000,000 of English-Canadian and American capital from 1925 to 1927. In fact, the development was so great that expanded facilities and increased competition brought about a decline of prices in 1927 and 1928. The largest single development was that of the Duke-Price and Aluminium Company interests, which spent $100,000,000 in the Lake St. John district. Popular criticism was aroused by the flooding of farmlands, caused by the damming of the lake's outlet, for the benefit of 'foreign' trusts. Premier Taschereau retorted that the creation of additional power at Lake St. John and at Carillon on the Ottawa would promote industrial development, which would keep Quebec's population at home and might even bring back those who had emigrated. At the opening of the new rayon mills at Drummondville on September 11, 1927, Taschereau stated his power policy:

The way of success in this province lies in keeping our material resources at home, so that we can develop them here. The key of success is electrical power, so that those who wish to create industries will come here. Such a policy is eminently Canadian and national.[101]

Despite mounting opposition from nationalist sources, the Taschereau government was returned to office in April 1927 with a larger majority, the Conservatives winning only nine seats. In a statement on the result, Taschereau commented that the people had pronounced judgment on the ultramontane press which had opposed him: 'a judgment which should make them understand that the infallibility that they assume is rather slightly acknowledged by the immense majority of the Catholic and French-Canadian element of our province.'[102] The old *Rouge* spirit was not wholly dead, though it was more commonly evident among the young Liberals than in the leaders of the party.

The provincial Conservatives, with their strong tradition of nationalism, continued to charge Taschereau with being subservient to foreign trusts. During the Sainte-Marie by-election in October 1928, the premier replied to the attacks of Camillien Houde thus:

Yes, there is American money in the province and it is welcome . . . While I and my colleagues are here, we will invite foreign capital to come and help us develop our province. The policy of M. Houde, M. Tremblay, and the others is to close our province, and to say that we will remain like Robinson Crusoe on his island.[103]

Again on December 10 Taschereau told the New York Pilgrims that the North American continent was 'a vast domain open to the spirit of enterprise of every citizen, whether he be north or south of the 45th parallel.'[104]   Houde continued, however, to exploit anti-American feeling among the people successfully by denouncing foreign trusts, and in July 1929 he replaced Sauvé as provincial leader of the Conservative Party. Houde's meteoric rise forced Taschereau to modify his stand in an address to the Quebec convention of the Investment Bankers of America on October 16:

Americans are welcome here. We need their capital. Let it be well understood that when here, they will receive fair treatment and be placed on the same footing as our own people. But they must cooperate with us . . . public opinion will not accept being dictated to, nor our natural resources being imperiled, even for the benefit of a most lovable neighbor.[105]

Houde asserted both his nationalism and his anti-Americanism in a speech at Morrisburg, Ontario, on October 5, in which he maintained that Canada could not bow to the will of any other nation or of any other part of the empire: 'Canada is called upon to play a great role in the not very distant future in world affairs, and the Canadian people . . . must be prepared to be in the future much more than a mere hyphen between the people of the United States and the rest of the British Empire.'[106]   Though the onset of the great depression was felt less in Quebec than in other provinces, unemployment became a problem in Montreal in the winter of 1929, and played its part in the election of Houde, who had become the idol of the masses, to the office of mayor in April 1930. Faced with all the problems that depression brought to Canada's metropolis, where the unemployed tended to congregate to benefit from public works and relief measures, Houde yielded his place as Conservative leader in the provincial legislature to Maurice Duplessis, a clever young lawyer from Trois-Rivières.

The tariff and questions of status continued to dominate federal politics. On November 1, 1929, Prime Minister King announced that an imperial economic conference would probably be held in Canada during the following year. He defended his government's non-provocative course with regard to the proposed upward revision of the American tariff, and justified it by the fact that the special session of Congress had adjourned without taking action on the matter. R. B. Bennett continued his attacks on low duties for American imports, and after the first of the year indicted the government for doing nothing about the rising tide of unemployment which resulted from the market crash of October and November. He coupled the issues at Calgary on January 9, observing: 'Thousands in the United States have been given employment fabricating Canadian goods. They've got the jobs and we've got the soup kitchens.'[107] When parliament met in February, Bennett pressed his attack, protesting against Canada 'being bullied by any power on earth'[108] as to its tariff, and against the government's failure to take steps to meet depression.

In connection with the report of the Conference on Dominion Legislation in London in 1929, he again maintained that there was no true equality of status as long as Canada had to go to Westminster to get its constitution revised. He argued that the constitution could not be changed without the consent of the provinces, and that they should have been represented at the London meeting.[109] Mr. King retorted: 'My honorable friend knows that any time we wish to amend our constitution or to get the power to have the constitution amended of our own right, independently of Westminster altogether, all we have to do is to present an address from both Houses of Parliament to the Parliament at Westminster, and that address will be given effect to in legislation at Westminster.'[110] The budget introduced on May 1 increased the list of British preferences and provided for countervailing duties against countries which raised their rates on Canadian goods. Mr. Bennett criticized the concessions to Britain as meaningless and the countervailing duties as giving control of the Canadian tariff to the United States. On May 6 the prime minister announced a forthcoming general election, in order that the government might have a fresh mandate before the imperial and economic conferences scheduled to take place in the fall. Mr. King's statement in a debate on unemployment on April 3, in which he took the line that it was not a federal problem, and that he 'would not give a single cent to any Tory government for provincial relief'[111] provided much capital for Conservative spokesmen in the ensuing compaign.

The prime minister sought to wage the campaign on the record of his government, the budget, and on representation at the imperial conferences; but unemployment, the St. Lawrence Seaway project on which he had not taken a definite stand, and the so-called 'five-cent speech' were the issues raised by the Conservatives. In Quebec La Presse brought up the old bugaboo of conscription, declaring three days before the election that a Conservative victory would encourage the British imperialists to propose conscription in the dominions at the impending imperial conference.[112] Premier Taschereau characterized Mackenzie King as 'a friend of our race' who 'respects our traditions, reverences all that we hold sacred, and merits your support.' He added that 'I have nothing to say against Mr. Bennett, but I must say I don't like his friends.'[113] Mr. Bennett's aides were somewhat too British-minded for Quebec tastes in the first campaign in which radio played a notable part and sectional appeals found a larger audience than was anticipated.

In British Columbia H. H. Stevens appealed for support of the Conservatives in order that Canada might become 'a unit of the Empire' and go to the imperial conference 'in a spirit of cooperation, unity and trust in the Motherland's statesmen.' Dr. Manion attacked the pro-American Liberal tariff policy, and described the elector's choice as one 'between Mr. Bennett, who is a life-long lover of the British Empire, or Mr. King, who suddenly discovers that there is a British Empire and is going out to save it to make us forget the period from 1914 to 1918 when he had business else-where.'[114]

At Quebec Mr. Bennett replied to the charges that he was an enemy of French Canadians and that he was an Englishman by declaring that he was a Canadian of nine generations' standing, and that he would not be there accepting hospitality if the former charge were true. He urged Quebec to support the Conservatives in order that its representatives might have a voice in the new government at Ottawa.[115] His platform had planks of strong appeal to Quebec. He pledged the Conservative Party to a protective tariff, the improvement of agriculture, the St. Lawrence Seaway, Hudson Bay and Peace River railways, the fostering of inter-provincial and inter-imperial trade, a national old-age pension plan, and federal solution of the unemployment question. On the tariff his slogan was 'Canada first, then the Empire.' Mr. King's defence of the British preference as a solution of unemployment and his denunciation of Bennett's program as mere electoral promises were not enough to stem the influence exercised by Bennett's confident assurance that the Conservatives could check steadily increasing unemployment and his adroit exploitation of Canada's latent dislike for an overbearing United States.

7

In the elections of July 28, 1930, the Conservatives won 138 seats to the Liberals' 87. Under a Western leader who promised effective measures to cope with the disastrous conditions on the Prairies, the Conservatives gained twenty-two seats in that region, largely at the expense of the new farmers' parties. The decisive factor, however, was the unanticipated Conservative capture of 25 seats in Quebec, with the Liberals retaining 39 and Henri Bourassa returned without opposition as an Independent. The new Bennett government formed on August 9 included only three French Canadians: Arthur Sauvé as postmaster-general, Alfred Duranleau as minister of marine, and Maurice Dupré as solicitor-general. C. H. Cahan of Montreal was named secretary of state, while Senator Hardy replaced Senator Dandurand as speaker of the Senate, to which Rodolphe Lemieux had been named by the King government at the close of the session in June.

A special session of parliament, called to deal with the unemployment emergency, opened on September 8, but adjourned on September 22 in order to permit the new prime minister to attend the imperial conferences in London. In the brief debate on the address, Mackenzie King declared that the Conservative victory was 'much more apparent than real,' since it was based on less than half the popular vote, and criticized Mr. Bennett for combining the posts of minister of finance, secretary of state for external affairs, and president of the council with the prime-ministership. J. S. Woodsworth criticized the 'protection craze' as a symptom of 'the postwar recrudescence of nationalism'; while Henri Bourassa declared that Canadian nationalism did not necessarily mean separation from the empire or enmity to Britain. He argued that nationalism was stronger than any party and any man or group of men.[116]

To meet the emergency, the government proposed three measures: $20,000,000 for unemployment relief by public works; a general upward revision of the tariff, with special attention to protecting key Canadian industries; and amendments to the Customs Act which were designed to end dumping in the Canadian market. Mr. King made no objection to the principle of the unemployment relief bill, but objected to giving a blank check to the government, with no time limit to expenditures under the bill. The government amended the bill to meet this objection, setting March 31, 1931 as the terminal date. The tariff measure was criticized as an attempt to coerce the House into passing without discussion the most radical tariff changes in Canadian history. Mr. King protested that increases in the tariff on British goods before the imperial conference were contrary to 'common decency and courtesy' and that such tactics would prove of little avail in winning an empire market. He also warned that the tariff changes would swell the movement of population from rural to urban areas and increase the cost of production and of living.[117] After Mr. Bennett had stated that he did not propose to go to England with this legislation unpassed, the tariff provisions were finally approved on the last day of the special session, with the understanding that discussion might be resumed later. Before his departure the prime minister announced that the office of high commissioner in London, being 'of a political nature,' should be held by a member of the administration; but that the ministers to Paris, Washington, and Tokyo would be regarded as permanent appointees.[118]

The Imperial Conference of 1930, which opened at London on October 1, was called to discuss inter-imperial relations, foreign

DD

policy and defence, and economic cooperation, with inter-imperial trade slated to receive major emphasis. The conference was also to consider the report of the 1929 conference on dominion and merchant shipping legislation. Before Mr. Bennett's departure, the premier of Ontario, Howard Ferguson, had urged upon him that the 1929 conference had ignored the fact that Confederation had been brought about by the joint action of the provinces, and that consequently no alteration of the B.N.A. Act could be made without their consent. Ferguson recommended that consideration of the report on dominion legislation should be delayed until the provinces had had an opportunity to discuss it and consult upon it. The conference adopted the report with few modifications, but its embodiment in the Statute of Westminster was delayed until the Canadian provinces had presented their views. The imperial government was eliminated from the appointment of governors-general, who henceforward were to be appointed by the King on the advice of the dominion concerned. The proposed Statute of Westminster repealed the Colonial Laws Validity Act of 1865; provided that Canada might amend or repeal all British laws forming part of Canadian law, with the exception of the B.N.A. Acts; and declared that any future British statute relating to Canada must contain the declaration that Canada had requested it and consented to it. The right of dominion parliaments to make laws having extra-territorial effect was expressly conceded.

But the chief concern of the conference was with economic rather than constitutional problems. Mr. Bennett, who at the opening of the conference had stressed the importance of economic cooperation, on October 8 proposed a policy of inter-imperial tariff preferences, which was approved by practically all the dominions. He opposed empire free trade, declaring that all that was helpful in it might be attained by imperial preference. His plan offered the United Kingdom and all other parts of the empire a preference based upon the addition of 10 per cent to the prevailing general tariffs. The British government, strongly committed to free trade, long delayed an announcement of its policy; but finally rejected Bennett's proposal indirectly in a statement on November 13, which promised not to reduce the existing preferences accorded empire products for three years or pending the outcome of the imperial economic conference which Bennett had proposed. The recent increase in the Canadian tariff on British goods and Bennett's threat of eliminating such preference as remained unless the United Kingdom accepted his scheme did not predispose the Labor government to abandon its free trade doctrine. The British Conservative opposition under Mr. Baldwin favored the Bennett policy, whose origin might be traced to the Empire free trade agitation conducted for some years by the Canadian-born Lord Beaverbrook in his newspapers. Mr. Bennett was frequently called upon to act as spokesmen for the dominions at the traditional round of social events and military and naval displays; and on such occasions he emphasized that the dominions were now determined to manufacture their own raw materials, though he made much of the possibilities for British trade in Canada and was optimistic about the future of the empire.[119]

After his return to Canada in December, Mr. Bennett made a speech at Regina on December 30, in which he declared that at the conference he had been actuated by the interest of Canada first and had sought a more stable market for Canadian wheat in the United Kingdom, where Russian wheat was impeding Canadian sales. The British government had refused to alter this situation, but France for the first time had undertaken to purchase a large quantity of Canadian wheat. Late in January Mr. Bennett went to Washington with W. D. Herridge, whose appointment as Canadian minister to the United States was announced some months later. The prime minister conferred with the American president and the secretaries of state and commerce, but no statement was issued as to the result of these conferences. Mr. King avenged a long series of Conservative charges that he was under American influence by asking when parliament would meet, and speculating as to 'what would have been said if, before meeting Parliament at a time of serious economic distress, I had, while in office, found it necessary to go to Washington for an interview with the President of the United States, or indeed for any other reason.'[120]

When parliament met on March 12, 1931, Mr. King launched a vigorous attack upon the government's policy at the imperial conference, and upon its failure to fulfil its election promises of remedying unemployment and agricultural distress. He deplored the government's adoption of 'coercion' towards Britain, which had foredoomed the attempt to find a British market for Canadian wheat and had made Canada an ally of the Conservative opposition in England. He dismissed the imperial preference scheme as an attempt to build a Chinese wall around the British Empire, which would arouse the jealousy of other nations and would end in imposing upon the dominions the burden of naval armaments. He charged that the net result of the conference had been to intensify 'the very serious condition' in Canada.[121] Prime Minister Bennett defended himself against the charge of 'one-man government' which Mr. King had made, and declared that his stand at the conference had been the same as that of Laurier in 1902. His election promises could not be implemented in a mere eight months, but the government was endeavoring to fulfil them.

Bourassa crossed swords with his old aide Lavergne in this debate, with the latter arguing that Laurier had betrayed the Province of Quebec in 1896. Arthur Sauvé praised the prime minister for having put Canada's interests first at the conference, and denounced the view that the Conservative Party was 'the deadly enemy of French-speaking Canadians.' He cited with pride the Ontario premier's statement that Quebec reacted more strongly than other provinces against 'the political and social penetration of Americanism,' and Sir William Mulock's observation that it was equally opposed to 'the penetration of the revolutionary ideas of Communist agents who would induce people to look upon the French as strangers in a country founded and opened up to civilization by them.'[122] Later in the session Solicitor-General Dupré, who had accompanied Mr. Bennett to London, protested against the anti-French laws recently adopted in Saskatchewan and expressed the hope that they would be repealed.

The budget presented by Mr. Bennett on June 1 increased taxation, both direct and indirect, and raised the tariff. The Liberals protested that the taxes would fall most heavily upon those least able to bear them, and that the tariff would curtail consumption and exports. Mr. King observed that 'the promises of yesterday are the taxes of today,' and that the new tariff would build up 'an industrial feudalism' in Canada.[123] He called for a Dominion-Provincial Conference on taxation and a conference of business, labor, and public men on unemployment. Throughout the session the Western members pressed the government for a statement of its unemployment policy, which was refused until the Unemployment and Farm Relief Act was introduced on July 29. This merely provided for the expenditure of such sums as might be advisable under orders-in-council, and gave such orders the force of law. Mr. King objected to the bill as a 'complete usurpation of the rights of Parliament'[124] to control expenditure, and finally forced government acceptance of an amendment providing for reports to parliament on expenditure under the Act.

A parliamentary investigation of the Beauharnois power project ended in the revelation that the power company had made campaign contributions amounting to $864,000, largely to the Liberal Party. Mr. King defended his administration's course with regard to the project, and declared that it was no function of a party leader to know who contributed to campaign funds. He professed ignorance of the payments made, and urged an investigation by a royal commission of campaign contributions in the last three elections. Bennett refused to establish such a commission, hinted that the Liberal leader was more deeply involved than he had indicated, and called upon the Senate to judge the actions of its members who were involved in the scandal. Action by a Senate committee of inquiry was suspended until the next session, with the recommendation that provision should be made for penalties against any member found guilty of dishonourable conduct. The federal government took over jurisdiction of the Beauharnois project from Quebec, and authorized the necessary diversion of water from the St. Lawrence.

As an aftermath of the Imperial Conference, a Dominion-Provincial Conference was held at Ottawa on April 8 to consider the report on dominion legislation. It agreed to maintain the *status quo ante* so far as the B.N.A. Act was concerned, while the Colonial Laws Validity Act no longer was to apply to dominion or provincial legislation. A new section to be inserted into the proposed Statute of Westminister was drafted and approved by the conference, but its final acceptance was deferred until the provincial representatives could consult their colleagues about it. Mr. Bennett announced that a future conference would consider how the B.N.A. Act might be amended or modified. On June 30 the prime minister introduced a resolution requesting the enactment of the Statute of Westminster, with the inclusion of the section adopted by the Dominion-Provincial Conference. Mr. Lapointe, who had played a part in drafting the 1929 report, supported the resolution, but urged that all doubts about Canada's right to amend her constitution should be dispelled. The prime minister replied that the provinces had already agreed to deal with the question at a future Dominion-Provincial Conference. Lapointe reiterated his views that 'I do not believe that the rights of the minorities in this country are linked with the legal situation as it exists now' and that Quebec was not the 'last bulwark and safeguard against change and innovation' that it was made out to be. He held that 'Canadians as a whole, in Quebec as well as in the other provinces, would not be satisfied with a condition under which they would be subordinated to another power outside the territory of Canada,' and that 'if Canadians are competent to make their own laws they should be competent to interpret them.'[125]

Armand Lavergne declared that 'equality of status cannot be reached and does not exist—we have to face the facts as they are—until Canada has the right to amend her own constitution.' He suggested that the vexed question of appeals to the Privy Council might be decided by 'having our own privy councillors advise the King on matters of appeal.' Though he reasserted his belief in the doctrine of 'Canada First,' he urged that Canada should recognize its duty 'by taxing ourselves for the maintenance of the king and the royal family.'[126] Henri Bourassa objected to appeals to the Privy Council, which he characterized as 'a semi-political, semi-judicial body,' as 'a brand of inferiority' and as an obstacle to the development of a true national spirit. He declared that 'the time will certainly come when there will be enough wisdom, enough sense of self-respect either in the provinces or the dominion of Canada, to find means of exercising that right of amending our own constitution by cooperation between the Dominion parliament and the provincial legislatures.' He deplored the fact that Canada, which had led the movement for autonomy, now lagged behind Australia and South Africa.[127] The resolution was carried without division, and after the approval of the other dominions had been won, the Statute of Westminster was passed by the British Parliament on December 11, 1931.

The measure shocked many Englishmen who were unaware of the gradual evolution towards autonomy which had been taking place in the empire, and the Labor government was accused of fostering the disintegration of the empire. Winston Churchill, the former colonial secretary, was one of the measure's leading opponents, while L. S. Amery, the dominion secretary who had fathered the measure in the British parliament, declared that the dominions were 'Imperial Nations which have risen gradually to a position and sense of Imperial responsibility like ourselves.'[128] There was a general feeling of regret in the British Parliament that it must abdicate the supreme authority of the empire, but the measure was passed 'to avoid giving offence to our great Dominions,' as Lord Buckmaster observed in the House of Lords.[129] This Magna Carta of the new British Commonwealth of Nations did not result in the disintegration of the empire which pessimists then foresaw, and it was widely hailed in the dominions. For some French-Canadian nationalists like Abbé Groulx, it marked Canada's achievement of independence; and he urged that its date should be commemorated as the national holiday rather than the anniversary of Confederation.[130]

Mr. Bennett, who on the day that the new British National government was elected had issued an invitation to the Commonwealth nations to meet in Ottawa for an economic conference, visited England briefly late in November. Upon his return he declared that the Statute of Westminster marked the passing of the old political empire, and that the forthcoming Ottawa Conference would lay the foundations of 'a new economic Empire in which Canada is destined to play a part of ever-increasing importance.'[131] Mr. King continued his attack on the administration's 'blank-check' legislation and on its shift from a 'Canada First' policy to an 'Empire First' one, which he characterized as a shift from extreme economic nationalism to an economic imperialism or isolationism.[132] Mr. King found fault with the government's failure to give the House an opportunity to discuss the impending imperial economic conference, and suggested that preparations for it had been left in the hands of the Canadian Manufacturers' Association. He gave warning that the Liberals were opposed to any tariff arrangement which would shackle the economic independence of any dominion or of Britain itself in dealing with other countries.

8

Unemployment and farm relief were the main topics of the session which opened on February 4, 1932. The Bennett government sought renewal of its blank-check legislation of the previous year, while the opposition waged a vigorous fight against what it considered a violation of the principle of responsible government by circumventing parliament's right to control expenditure. The prime minister was bluntly told by C. G. Power of Quebec that 'the place for him is in some South American republic where he can be dictator at his will, or better still in Italy or Russia.'[133] The government measure was finally forced through by closure. After an inquiry by a parliamentary committee it was decided to establish a national broadcasting system under the federal government, and a bill setting up the Canadian Radio Commission was passed with the approval of all parties on May 24. As early as 1930 Quebec had declared that the provinces had jurisdiction over the radio, and had never abandoned this claim, which was later revived. The Senate's investigation into the connection of Senators Mc-Dougald, Haydon, and Raymond with the Beauharnois project ended with the censure of the first two men and the resignation of Senator McDougald. The vote had been on party lines.

The Imperial Economic Conference opened at Ottawa on July 21. Mr. Bennett was elected chairman, and in his opening speech renewed his 1930 proposal, calling upon the United Kingdom to extend its tariff preferences on natural products and promising adjustments of the Canadian tariff in return. He also urged safeguards against unfair state-controlled competition. Stanley Baldwin of Britain urged the clearing of the channels of imperial trade, and favored the lowering of tariff barriers between empire countries rather than the raising of them against other nations. Twelve inter-imperial trade agreements were made during the conference, with Canada concluding pacts with the United Kingdom, South Africa, Southern Rhodesia, and the Irish Free State along the lines suggested by Mr. Bennett. The conference passed a resolution endorsing Baldwin's principle as the best means of increasing both imperial and world trade. The conflicting interests of the dominions and of the United Kingdom became apparent, with the dominions seeking preference for their foodstuffs in Britain, and the latter seeking outlets for its manufactures, despite the determination of the dominions to protect their infant industries. No single over-all agreement was thus possible.[134]

At the special session of parliament called in October to consider the Ottawa Trade Agreements, protracted opposition was raised by the Liberal, Labor, and independent members, while the government was also criticized for its failure to find any other remedy for unemployment than the dole. The prime minister described the agreements as 'the first forward step in a definite scheme of closer Empire economic association,'[135] while Mr. King maintained that they were a complete reversal of the trend of imperial evolution for the last fifty years.[136] The two leaders clashed repeatedly on whether or not the agreements were in the Canadian tradition. Bourassa, who termed the measure 'perhaps the most important piece of legislation . . . since Confederation,' attacked it as a 'device to maintain the principle and practice of protection.'[137] J. S. Woodsworth assailed it as 'an arrangement between business-men and those who primarily represented the interests of business-men.'[138] The Ottawa Agreements were finally approved on November 24.

A new political party, born of the depression, was formed at a convention of farmer and labor representatives at Calgary on August 1, 1932. J. S. Woodsworth was chosen president of this Cooperative Commonwealth Federation, an unhandy name which soon gave way in general usage to 'C.C.F.' The C.C.F. program, influenced by the traditions of Fabian socialism and the British Labor Party, called for the establishment of a planned economy, socialization of financial facilities, nationalization of utilities and natural resources, encouragement of cooperative enterprises, and a wide range of social legislation. The United Farmers of Ontario affiliated themselves with the new party in December, and C.C.F. study clubs were formed for those not connected with labor or farm groups. The new party held that the Conservatives and Liberals were unable to make fundamental changes in a bankrupt economy, while the Communist Party was pledged to bring about a new social and economic order through violence, bloodshed, and at least a temporary dictatorship. The C.C.F., on the other hand, in the tradition of Fabian socialism, sought to introduce a new order gradually by peaceful and orderly means. It failed in its first electoral effort in an Alberta by-election in January 1933, but came to national notice in February, when Mr. Woodsworth introduced a resolution advocating the setting up of a cooperative commonwealth in Canada as a remedy for the depression.

Despite Woodsworth's emphatic denials of any link with Communism, the new movement was attacked as Communistic by Conservative spokesmen. Mackenzie King had already deplored the division of anti-Tory forces between the Liberal Party and the C.C.F. in a Toronto speech the previous December, in which he had called for 'humanitarianism' rather than 'selfish nationalism' or 'jingo imperialism.'[139] In the debate on the Woodsworth motion he announced a Liberal program which had clearly been influenced by the growth of the C.C.F. movement. It called for a national unemployment commission, abolition of unwarranted new taxes on imports, promotion of trade with all countries on a reciprocal basis, British preference by reduction rather than increases in the tariff, abolition of artificial price control, regulation of investment, creation of a national central bank, abolition of Section 98 of the Criminal Code which threatened free speech and free association, balancing the budget, and an overhauling of all government costs.[140]

On the eve of the Dominion-Provincial Conference, which had been called to meet at Ottawa on January 17, 1933, to consider economic and constitutional problems, Mr. King attacked the government before a Quebec audience. He charged that there was 'a deliberate manoeuvre to bring about something new in the relations of Canada to the other parts of the Empire,' and declared that 'the real issue is whether we are going to change from the position of national sovereignty into one of imperial sovereignty, with imperial policies instead of national policies governing this country.'[141] Friction between different parts of the empire would follow the adoption of imperial policies. The conference agreed that federal assistance for provincial unemployment relief should be continued. Cooperation in the administration of taxation was agreed upon pending another conference, but no decision was made on the question of unemployment insurance, in the face of opposition from Quebec and Ontario on the grounds of provincial rights.[142]

The session, which resumed on January 30, 1933, gave most of its attention to reorganization of the Canadian National Railways, to the budget, and to redistribution. The government met with vigorous opposition to its stand on unemployment and other matters from the Liberals and the C.C.F., who exploited Western discontent with federal pressure on the Prairie Provinces, which were receiving large loans for relief purposes, to reduce their expenditures. Mr. Bennett indicated that he favored the reviving of Canadian titles, which had not been granted since a vote of the House on May 22, 1919 had opposed them. Quebec members pressed for a bilingual currency, but the debate was without issue.

After conferring with President Roosevelt in Washington in April, Mr. Bennett attended the World Monetary and Economic Conference in London in June. He played an important part in avoiding its breakdown by aligning the dominions with the Scandinavian countries behind the proposals of Cordell Hull, and also induced the British government to abandon its neutrality. He presided over the subsequent World Wheat Conference, and agreed to limit Canada's wheat exports for the ensuing year. Upon his return to Canada he defended his course at both meetings, and declared that Canadians had free entry into the greatest single market in the world, the British Empire. During a fall speaking trip through the West, where Mackenzie King had attacked 'Tory autocracy' during the summer, Mr. Bennett challenged the former to make good his threat to scrap the Ottawa Agreements when he returned to power, declaring that such a step would ruin half of Canadian industry. The prime minister stated that the government had spent $122,552,000 on relief since taking office, and announced a public works program to relieve unemployment. On November 20 he adopted President Roosevelt's practice of announcing government policy in a radio broadcast. He stated that the government's program for the next session would include the public works measure, a proposal for a central bank, and defence of the Wheat Agreement. At a Dominion-Provincial Conference in January 1934, Mr. Bennett vainly sought drastic curtailment of federal contributions to relief, endeavoring to shift the burden to the provinces. Since the provinces found their shrinking revenues inadequate to meet the growing burden, the existing contribution by the dominion of one third of the cost of unemployment relief was continued temporarily. At a second conference in August, federal expenditures for relief were reduced about 20 per cent as the total cost continued to increase.[143]

Mr. King campaigned actively in the three by-elections of 1933, which were all won by Liberals, and continued to attack the high tariff policy and to urge reciprocal trade with the United States. He also opposed the Wheat Agreement and the restoration of titles in Canada. The C.C.F. held its first national convention at Regina in July 1933, and adopted a manifesto calling for the establishment of a socialized economic order, socialized financial machinery, socialization of all industries and services essential to social planning, security of tenure for distressed farmers and the progressive removal of their debts, regulation of external trade, a national labor code, public health, hospital, and medical services; a foreign policy aimed at world peace and international economic cooperation, a new equalized taxation policy; and constitutional changes including the abolition of the Senate, assertion of the rights of freedom of speech and assembly, abolition of the deportation policy, and government responsibility for unemployment and the remedying of it. The Regina Manifesto was drafted by a brains trust of forty, led by six former Rhodes Scholars strongly affected by the ideals of English socialism. The document was denounced as revolutionary and Communistic by spokesmen of the two old parties, and savagely attacked by the press.

The political future of the C.C.F., which had been born of Western depression but was dependent upon Eastern support for national effectiveness, was threatened early in 1934. On February 25 Archbishop Georges Gauthier, coadjutor of Montreal, characterized it in a pastoral letter as a dangerous movement, resting 'upon a materialistic conception of the social order which precisely constitutes the anti-Christian character of Socialism.'[144] Mr. Woodsworth, a former Methodist minister, replied a week later in Montreal to this utterance, asking why it was a sin for a Catholic to belong to the C.C.F. in Montreal, but not wrong for one to do so in Alberta and Saskatchewan. He denied that there was anything Communistic about the C.C.F., which guaranteed full religious liberty, autonomy, and minority rights. But for many years to come the C.C.F. remained under a cloud for French-Canadian Catholics, thanks to a confusion of socialism, in the papally condemned revolutionary European sense, with English socialism. Archbishop Villeneuve of Quebec, who was created a cardinal early in 1933 and thus became primate of the Church in Canada, was strongly opposed to the C.C.F., whose centralizing tendencies ran counter to his nationalist ideas. Henri Bourassa, the old nationalist leader who had often made common cause with Woodsworth in the House, had resigned as director of *Le Devoir* in August 1932, and thereafter that influential nationalist organ took a firm stand against the C.C.F. program under Bourassa's conservative and provincialist successor, Georges Pelletier.

From the opening of the session late in January 1934 Mackenzie King waged a vigorous attack upon the government and its measures, declaring that the recent by-elections showed that it had lost the support of the country. He moved a motion of no-confidence as an amendment to the address. The prime minister replied that the people of Canada were opposed to a general election in a time of great problems, and the no-confidence motion was lost after three weeks' debate. The government launched an investigation into Canadian business and economic conditions by creating the Price Spreads and Mass Buying Committee under the chairmanship of H. H. Stevens, minister of trade and commerce. The hearings aroused great public interest and support, and the parliamentary committee was transformed into a royal commission which continued its investigations in 1935. The resignation of Mr. Stevens as chairman and as minister was forced by the prime minister on October 26, after the former had released a pamphlet giving an account of the results of the inquiry up to the end of the session. Differences between the two men had already become widely known. After his resignation Mr. Stevens charged that he had been thwarted in his efforts to remedy economic abuses by reactionary members of the cabinet.

On April 11 Prime Minister Bennett gave notice of proposals for revising the B.N.A. Act, under which the provinces would relinquish their jurisdiction over social problems connected with industry, old age, illness, working hours and conditions, minimum wages, and so on. Two days later he alluded to political factors which might prevent such amendment of the B.N.A. Act, hinting at possible difficulties with Quebec. The government leader in the Senate, Arthur Meighen, referred to the B.N.A. Act as suited to the horse and buggy days of Confederation but no longer adapted to the vastly altered conditions of the present day.[145] At the end of August the prime minister sent a letter to the provincial premiers giving a tentative agenda for a Dominion-Provincial Conference late in the year, which included duplication of taxation and of health and agricultural organizations, as well as the already indicated social problems, and the vital question as to how the B.N.A. Act should be amended.[146] The proposed meeting was postponed indefinitely, however, after two or three provinces had displayed a 'lukewarm if not hostile' attitude.

The 1934 budget called for a reduction of both the tariff and of government expenditures, while laying a heavy tax on gold production. These proposals were criticized by the Liberals as continuing the economic nationalism which had proved disastrous to Canadian trade during the depression. Much attention was devoted during the session to the Natural Products Marketing Bill, which conferred wide regulatory powers upon a federal marketing board and the governor-in-council. The measure was criticized as dictatorial and leading towards regimentation of business, but finally passed when the government refused to accept a Senate amendment. The government was supported by the C.C.F. throughout the debate on the question, and this alliance between Tories and radicals provided much ammunition for Liberal critics. The unemployment relief measure was passed after the usual bitter opposition on constitutional grounds, supplemented by criticism of wanton expenditure and irregularities in administration. Farm indebtedness and credit extension aided the distressed farmers of the West, while a $40,000,000 public works act offered further relief for unemployment. A central Bank of Canada was established under private ownership, despite Liberal and C.C.F. arguments in favor of public ownership. A government measure to pool the French translators scattered through the various federal departments encountered violent opposition from French-Canadian members as a scheme to curtail the use of the French language. The opposition was led by

E.-R.-E. Chevrier, with some Quebec Conservatives joining the Liberals in attacking the motion. Bourassa and A. W. Neill led the Progressives, and C.C.F. opposition to the motion. There were stormy scenes in parliament, with the Quebec members singing a French-Canadian folksong and thumping their desks in protest whenever a Quebec Conservative voted for the measure. Alfred Duranleau, minister of marine, aided C. H. Cahan, the sponsor of the bill, in defending it.

Five by-elections in the spring and fall of 1934 resulted in five Liberal victories. Mackenzie King, who had actively engaged in these contests, called upon the government to resign since it was obviously losing the support of the people. Mr. King visited Europe in the fall to get a firsthand knowledge of conditions there in anticipation of a return to office, while Mr. Bennett also went abroad to represent Canada in the League of Nations and to discuss a new trade treaty with France. Upon his return the prime minister again defended the Ottawa Trade Agreements, but indicated a willingness to make a trade treaty with the United States. He also announced that the government would introduce legislation to implement the recommendations of the Price Spreads Commission, declaring that 'the policy of *laissez-faire* is no longer sufficient.'[147] In December Mr. King announced that if he were called upon to form a government, he would seek to increase British preference in the Canadian market and to lower tariffs affecting Canada's external trade. He also called for an empire-wide investigation of armament manufacturers, urging Canada to take the lead in a policy of peace by refusing arms, food, and credits to nations which disturbed the peace of the world. He denounced economic imperialism, which he claimed Canadian nationalism was being made to serve.

With parliament's life due to expire in August 1935, the prospect of elections dominated the new year. Mr. Bennett, a lifelong Conservative and capitalist, suddenly became convinced that the traditional remedies for Canada's economic ills were inadequate, and under the influence of American example, observed at first-hand by his brother-in-law, W. D. Herridge, the Canadian Minister at Washington, he determined to launch a Canadian New Deal. In five radio broadcasts early in January 1935 he announced a program of radical reforms which the government intended to introduce during the session. All involved government control over economic enterprise. He declared that the dole was 'a condemnation of our economic system,' and that 'if we cannot abolish the dole, we should abolish the system.'[148] Denouncing those who had taken advantage of faults in the capitalistic system for unscrupulous or greedy purposes, Mr. Bennett said his government intended to remove these faults in order to make such unfair practices impossible.

He accused the Liberals of becoming Tories, and predicted that a continuance of *laissez-faire* methods would lead to Fascism.

The legislation announced in these broadcasts and later in the speech from the throne on January 17 was designed 'to remedy the social and economic injustices now prevailing and to ensure to all classes and to all parts of the country a greater degree of equality in the distribution of the benefits of the capitalistic system.'[149] Mr. King opened the debate by attacking the prime minister's method of announcing his program on the radio before submitting it to parliament as unconstitutional and akin to Fascist methods. He declared that the proposals only touched 'the fringe of some evils of the system,' and did not go to its heart. He denounced control by capitalists of industrial policy, and argued that labor should be given a share of control. He stated that the Liberal Party intended to follow both the policies of state intervention and *laissez-faire*. He blamed excessive intervention in the free course of trade for existing conditions in Canada, with a million unemployed and 'a network of barbed-wire entanglements' hampering trade. Criticizing private control of the Bank of Canada, he argued that a government which had favored such a scheme could not be sincere in a program of state intervention. The government's much vaunted reform measures had long been a part of Liberal policy.[150] In reply the prime minister defended the record of his administration, which had brought Canada through the worst of the depression 'better than any other country in the world.'[151] He forecast a trade agreement with the United States and refuted Mr. King's charges. J. S. Woodsworth, the C.C.F. leader, criticized the government for waiting so long to launch reform, but expressed the hope that since the Liberals were pledged to it, that the measures would be passed during the session.

The Bennett New Deal was embodied in eight legislative acts which were passed by almost unanimous vote after much wrangling in parliament. They established an eight-hour day and a forty-eight hour week and banned child labor. A minimum wage, an unemployment and social insurance scheme, and a national employment service were set up. The Natural Products Marketing Act and the Farmers' Creditors Act of the previous year were liberalized. A Dominion Trade and Industry Commission was established to regulate and control trusts and monopolies, to check unfair business practices, and to adjust merchandising procedures to new standards of trade and production. The Criminal Code was amended to provide penalties for false advertising, for payment of less than the minimum wage, and for unfair business practices. The Companies Act was amended to eliminate speculative high finance from business and industry. A Canadian Wheat Board was established to control exports and prices. Legislation providing for relief, public works, credit for fishermen, rehabilitation of the Prairie Provinces, and a housing program was also passed. The budget contained slight reductions in the tariff and raised the tax on corporation and individual income in the higher brackets. Finally a National Economic Council, consisting of the prime minister and fifteen unpaid advisers, was set up to deal with social and economic problems.

As a result of the resolution by J. S. Woodsworth, a parliamentary committee was appointed 'to study and report on the best method by which the British North America Act may be amended so that while safeguarding the existing rights of racial and religious minorities and legitimate Provincial claims to autonomy, the Dominion Government may be given adequate power to deal effectively with urgent economic problems which are essentially national in scope.'[152] The provincial attorneys-general refused to offer suggestions to the committee, but many experts testified, and the committee recommended the early holding of a Dominion-Provincial Conference to consider the question.

The constitutionality of much of the Bennett New Deal was criticized by the opposition. .The prime minister sought to avoid some of the constitutional difficulties by using the dominion's treaty-making power to ratify the 1921 and 1928 conventions of the International Labor Organization concerning wages, hours, and a labor code. Parliament thus assented to these reforms by resolutions approving the draft conventions of the I.L.O. rather than by specific legislation. Mr. Bennett held that the government was justified in taking emergency measures under the 'peace, order and good government' clause of the B.N.A. Act. His impatient attitude towards the courts under existing emergency conditions was much the same as that of President Roosevelt. Mr. King held that the reforms were *ultra vires* of parliament, but refused to oppose measures which he accepted in principle or to raise an election issue of violated provincial rights. Accusing the government of 'calculated unconstitutionality,' he urged that the constitutional issue be referred to the courts. During the session, from which Mr. Bennett was absent for three months because of illness and attendance at the King's Silver Jubilee, Mr. King exploited the differences between the prime minister and H. H. Stevens, accusing the government of insincerity in its reforms and predicting that most of them would be rejected by the courts.

During the Jubilee celebrations in London Mr. Bennett made an empire-wide broadcast in which he urged greater cooperation between empire nations as a solution of economic difficulties. Upon his return to Canada he denied charges that he had entered upon entangling commitments in England, and that his health would force his resignation from the Conservative leadership in the elections,

which were set for October 14. After the appointment of Arthur
Sauvé to the Senate and Alfred Duranleau to the Superior Court of
Quebec, L.-H. Gendron was named marine minister and Onésime
Gagnon minister without portfolio, while Samuel Gobeil became
postmaster-general. Further reorganization of the Bennett cabinet
was promised after the elections. In a series of broadcasts the prime
minister appealed to the people on the basis of the government's
record. He claimed that his promises of 1930 had been fulfilled, and
stressed the recent reform measures. Others, designed to correct
rather than to destroy capitalism, were promised. During a Western
tour he called for a mandate to renew the Ottawa Agreements and
to make a trade treaty with the United States. In a final speech at
Toronto on October 9 Mr. Bennett urged all members of parliament,
regardless of party, to join with him in the task of putting Canada on
a firm foundation.

Mr. King denounced this proposal of a National government as
another form of dictatorship in a series of campaign speeches on the
radio. He urged a repudiation by the electorate of 'the tendencies
towards dictatorship manifested during the last five years,' and of all
steps in the direction of Hitlerism, Fascism, or Communism.[153] He
advanced once more the Liberal platform of 1933, renewed his
demand for a national commission on unemployment, and pledged
the Liberal Party to an immediate reduction of the tariff rates. After
tours through the Western and Eastern provinces, he spoke at
Toronto on October 8 with eight of the nine provincial premiers
supporting him on a nation-wide radio hook-up. Closing his campaign at Ottawa on October 12, Mr. King denounced an election
circular in which three manufacturers appealed for Conservative
votes on the grounds that Canadian plants would be shut down if a
new government deprived them of protection. He promised that
the government would 'run the plants to find out how much tariff
protection is needed to safeguard the interests of the workers.'[154]

The C.C.F., entering its first general election, campaigned on a
platform which called for extensive socialization and social planning,
and appealed for support from farmers, industrial workers, technicians, and professional men. It declared that capitalism could
neither be reformed nor restored, and demanded a new social order.
Its manifesto closed with the declaration that Canada must not be
allowed to drift into another capitalist war and that Canadian neutrality must be rigorously maintained. It disavowed connection
with the Communists or any other party. The Social Credit movement, which had swept Alberta in a provincial election in August,
entered federal politics, with an active group in Quebec. H. H.
Stevens led a Reconstruction Party which called for opportunities
for youth, a vast public works scheme, a national housing plan, and

fair wages and reasonable hours for all workers. The new party proposed an extensive program of economic reforms based upon the findings of the Price Spreads Commission.

With so many new parties, a total of 894 candidates, the largest number in Canadian history, were nominated, but the bulk of the vote went to the two traditional parties. The Liberals won an overwhelming victory, with a majority of 97 seats over all other parties combined. They held 171 seats, with 56 in Ontario and 55 in Quebec, while the Conservatives only retained 39 seats, with little strength outside Ontario. Social Credit won 17 seats and the C.C.F. 7, while the Reconstruction group only secured 1 seat. Twelve members of the Bennett cabinet were defeated, including all the Quebec members. Mr. Bennett accepted the verdict as an indication that the people wanted a change of government, while Mr. King interpreted it as a response to the Liberal protest against 'all forms of dictatorship' and 'endless and dangerous experimentation in matters of government.'[155] He saw the outcome as a mandate for 'the maintenance of British parliamentary practice and procedure and . . . the end of the superman idea.' The new government which took office on October 23 under Mr. King as prime minister, president of the Privy Council, and secretary of state for external affairs included four French Canadians: Ernest Lapointe as minister of justice, P.-J.-A. Cardin as minister of public works, Fernand Rinfret as secretary of state, and Raoul Dandurand as minister without portfolio. C. G. Power of Quebec was also named minister of pensions and national health.

9

Eight of the Bennett New Deal laws were immediately referred to the Supreme Court of Canada and subsequently to the Privy Council, where only three of them were sustained, the others being rejected as *ultra vires*. New members of the Canadian Wheat Board were appointed, and Vincent Massey was named to replace Howard Ferguson as Canadian high commissioner in London. In November Mr. King went to Washington to discuss the Canadian-United States Trade Treaty, which was signed on November 15. Three large public work projects were cancelled, while the government increased grants to the provinces for direct relief.

The Dominion-Provincial Conference held at Ottawa in December 1935 agreed to a substantial increase of dominion relief grants to the provinces, a census of the unemployed, the establishment of a Dominion Employment Commission, and the seeking of industry's aid in putting more men to work. It rejected a proposal to have the dominion collect and distribute to the provinces mining taxes, and agreed to a new Companies Act, designed to protect the public in new mining stock offers. It agreed that the taxation rights of the provinces should be defined, and that there should be cooperation on taxation between the dominion and the provinces. All governments were to reduce costs and to bring expenditures in line with receipts. It was agreed that Canada should have the right to amend its own constitution, and a continuing committee was to meet later to define a method of doing so. Agriculture was to benefit from dominion farm loans and a reduction of interest. A Trans-Canada Highway was to be built by the dominion and the provinces on a fifty-fifty cost basis. Various measures to promote tourist traffic were proposed, including the establishment of national parks in all provinces lacking them and the improvement of highways.

Parliament met on February 6, 1936, in the midst of mourning for the death of King George V. Pierre-F. Casgrain was named speaker of the House, and Raoul Dandurand government leader in the Senate. The speech from the throne announced that the federal labor camps would be closed as soon as expanding employment permitted, and that inquiries would be launched into the textile and coal industries in the interest of labor and the public. It also announced the government's intention to return to parliament control over taxation and expenditure, to provide for greater parliamentary control over the Canadian National Railways, and to reorganize and consolidate government services. In the debate on the address Mr. Bennett criticized the government's action in repudiating Mr. W. A. Riddell, Canada's representative at Geneva, for his stand in favor of sanctions against Italy. He also attacked its settlement of the Japanese trade dispute and its signing of the Canada-United States Trade Treaty, which his government had refused to sign on the grounds 'that for what we could get we were not prepared to give what was asked.'[156] He protested against immediate and wholesale reference of the reform acts to the courts, and defended the old members of the Wheat Board and their policies. He denied that he had had any thought of a National government in his Toronto broadcast, but maintained that all Canadians must work together to extract Canada from her present situation, which he regarded as 'serious in the extreme.'[157]

The prime minister attacked Mr. Bennett for the use made of the government radio during the campaign, and for burdening the Treasury with obligations amounting to $447,000,000, over the expenditure of which parliament had had no control. He defended the restoration of normal trade between Canada and Japan, and the inquiry into the textile industry. He contrasted the sales record of the new Wheat Board with that of the old one. Both the Japanese and American trade agreements had increased employment in industries and on the railroads. The latter was not a hasty measure, but one which had been arrived at after two years' consideration by the experts of both countries. Mr. King declared that Mr. Riddell had exceeded his authority in proposing the addition of oil and certain other commodities during the discussion in a League of Nations committee of sanctions against Italy for its aggression in Ethiopia. He stated that the government had felt it necessary, in view of the critical situation in Europe, to make it clear that the proposal was an individual one and not that of Canada.[158] He declared that Justice Minister Lapointe's statement of December 2 censuring Riddell had been made after consultation with him while he was vacationing in Georgia. J. S. Woodsworth moved an amendment to the address regretting that the government had not indicated any 'definite and immediate steps to end the prevailing poverty and insecurity of the masses by making available to the people of Canada the great actual and potential wealth of the country.'[159]

The United States Trade Agreement was approved by a vote of 175 to 39 after much discussion. Under it Canada lowered her tariff to the 1930 levels on some 700 items, and received concessions on some 200 items which constituted about half her exports to the United States. In general the United States received most-favored-nation treatment in Canada, except for empire preferences, and Canada got the same treatment in the United States. The export of Canadian raw materials and the import of American manufactures was eased by the agreement, which was to last for three years, and was subsequently renewed in more extended form for another three years. The agreement marked an important economic rapprochement. What began as a return to the basis prevailing before the Smoot-Hawley Tariff and the Ottawa Agreements ended as a radical reorientation of the Canadian economy, with American trade displacing British trade.[160]

The Liberal electoral program was soon carried into legislation. The Bank of Canada was nationalized, and a Canadian Broadcasting Corporation, modelled on the B.B.C., was set up with safeguards for political impartiality. Taxes were raised while the tariff was lowered. Finance Minister Dunning called for a halt in the loans which had maintained the four Western provinces in recent years. Under a government-sponsored amendment to the B.N.A. Act, it was proposed to set up a National Financial Council as a permanent forum for the discussion of financial problems, and to establish provincial loan councils to deal with loans and guarantees. The measure was defeated in the Senate. A National Employment Commission was created under the direction of Arthur Purvis. The federal government provided $75,000,000 for unemployment relief, with a corresponding amount to be contributed by the provinces and municipalities. A National Harbors Board was given jurisdiction over the chief ocean ports. Section 98 of the Criminal Code was at last repealed, as was the 1935 Act providing for a National Economic Council. A motion for a joint resolution for amendment of the B.N.A. Act on matters of taxation and guarantees of provincial debts was lost on a straight party vote in the Senate, with its Conservative majority.[161]

For all its overpowering majority in the House, reinforced by by-elections after it came to power, the King government was faced with the same problem as its predecessor in passing emergency economic legislation within the confines of the B.N.A. Act, which had been drawn up before a centralized economy was dreamed of. Justice Minister Lapointe, Opposition Leader Bennett, and C. H. Cahan all took part in a 1937 debate on the question, and all favored amending the act. Lapointe saw 'nothing sacred' in the document, and was opposed to appeals to the Privy Council, which Bennett still favored despite the unfavorable decisions on his New Deal legislation. In 1937 a Royal Commission on Dominion-Provincial Relations was named, charged with drafting proposals for amending the B.N.A. Act, under the chairmanship of the noted constitutional authority N. W. Rowell, with Thibaudeau Rinfret, John Dafoe, R. A. Mackay, and H. F. Angus as members. It began its hearings in November 1937 and concluded them in June 1939, after Joseph Sirois had first replaced Rinfret on the commission and then taken Rowell's place as chairman. Each province was asked to submit briefs of its position.

Quebec called for decentralization of power, and questioned the right of the dominion to investigate provincial finances. Its brief held that 'Confederation was a compact voluntarily entered into and it cannot be modified except with the consent of all parties.'[162] In addition to taking this uncooperative stand, Quebec's new nationalist premier, Maurice Duplessis, opposed a scheme for federal unemployment insurance in 1937, and at Shawinigan Falls on December 16 called for the formation of a bloc of the five eastern provinces, 'not to be run by Ottawa.'[163] He also cemented a virtual alliance with Premier Mitchell Hepburn of Ontario, already at war with Mackenzie King on the power question. Norman Rogers and C. D. Howe, leading members of the federal cabinet, denounced this 'unnatural' political alliance to oust the King government and to replace it with one controlled by Toronto and Quebec.

The Duplessis régime also won unfavorable notice outside Quebec by its arbitrary Padlock Law, first applied against a Communist paper in Montreal in November 1937, and by its tolerance of Adrien Arcand's *Parti National Social Chrétien*, which held a convention at Kingston on July 3, 1937, and sought to become a national organization under the English leadership of J. C. Farr and William Whittaker. Kurt Ludecke, who had been charged by Rosenberg with representing the political interests of the Nazi Party in the United States, Canada, and Mexico in September 1932, had persuaded Arcand to convert his '*Ordre Patriotique des Goglus*,' which the Nazi agent described as 'a violently anti-Jewish, in the main Catholic folkic movement . . . with three publications, all very demagogic and clever,'[164] into a shirt movement modeled on the Nazi Party. According to Ludecke, Arcand was 'greatly pleased when I gave him an autographed photograph of Hitler. We understood each other perfectly and agreed to cooperate in every way.'[165]

While the C.C.F. sought disallowance by the federal government of the Padlock Law as a violation of civil liberties, thus making new enemies for itself in a Quebec which was eager to crush Communism by any means, the *Toronto Globe and Mail* ran a series of articles on Arcand's group which helped to convince many English Canadians that Quebec was dominated by 'clerical Fascists.' The charges were echoed by the New York *Nation* and other liberal publications.[166] This impression was furthered by the prevalence of pro-Franco sympathies in Quebec, while English Canadians generally sympathized with the Spanish Republicans; and by the prestige of both Mussolini and Franco with the clergy of Quebec, who reserved their highest regard, however, for Salazar, the scholarly dictator of Portugal who had introduced the corporative economic system recommended by the papal encyclicals. These views of the élite had wide backing, as was indicated by the fact that the Liberal *Le Soleil*, the Conservative *La Patrie*, the nationalist *Le Devoir*, and the maverick *La Renaissance* all had opposed sanctions against Italy. Jean-Charles Harvey's *Le Jour* was about the only French paper to adopt the vigorous anti-Fascist line of much of the English press.

Premier Duplessis refused the invitation of Ernest Lapointe to confer on the Padlock Law. The federal minister of justice subsequently made a report on the law, in which he favored neither disallowance nor reference to the Supreme Court of Canada, and observed that most of the protests against it came from outside Quebec. Quebec, which always bitterly resents a bad press outside the province and assigns it to Masonic or Communistic conspiracies, was indignant at this interference in provincial affairs, and also at the publicity given to the Textile Industrial Inquiry, which revealed that wage standards in Quebec were much lower than in the other provinces.[167]

The government did not break its silence on foreign policy until four months after its stand on the Riddell incident had been criticized by both the Conservative and C.C.F. leaders. On June 18, 1936, Prime Minister King made a notable speech[168] on foreign affairs in which he announced the government's decision to end sanctions against Italy—on the same day as Britain took the same step, but as result of an independent decision made earlier. He stressed the need for more discussion of Canada's foreign relations than there had been in the past because of a colonial attitude of mind, relative immunity from the danger of war, internal preoccupations, and 'the unparalleled complexity of our position as a member of the League, a member of the British Commonwealth of Nations and one of the nations of the American continent.' He stated that after the Riddell episode the government had twice instructed its representative at Geneva to vote for the inclusion of oil sanctions if the proposal met general support, but 'collective bluffing cannot bring collective security, and under present conditions most countries have shown they are not prepared to make firm commitments beyond the range of their immediate interest.' As for the future, though Canada was 'fortunate both in its neighbors and in its lack of neighbors' it could not isolate itself from world affairs because international trade was essential to its economy. In view of the League's record, Canada could not make 'binding commitments to use economic force or military force': 'Occasions may arise where military action may become advisable or essential, but so far as Canada is concerned, that would be for the parliament of Canada to decide in the light of all the circumstances at the time.' He warned that 'there is no danger to our national unity and our economic recovery so serious as participation in a prolonged war,' and urged that Canada should continue to work through the League for the ideal of world peace.

J. S. Woodsworth largely agreed with the prime minister's views, but argued that 'we should let Great Britain know now, not later when she may become involved in some war, that she need not count us in.'[169] R. B. Bennett suggested that Canada might have associated herself with South Africa in continuing sanctions; expressed the opinion that the League was a failure; and urged that 'the greatest assurance we have for the maintenance of our peace lies in the strengthening of every tie that binds the commonwealth of nations, the members of the British empire.'[170] Paul Martin, a young Ontario Liberal making his maiden speech, suggested that Canada might participate in the advisory conferences of the Pan-American Union, as well as work to strengthen the League,[171] thus echoing Bourassa's suggestion of April 1, 1935.[172]

Canada's new North American orientation was fostered by events during the summer and fall. Prime Minister King joined Lord Tweedsmuir, the new governor-general, and the provincial authorities in warmly welcoming President Roosevelt to Quebec on July 31. Both Lord Tweedsmuir and Mr. Roosevelt expressed the hope that the friendly relationship between the two countries would serve as a model to the troubled world. It was noteworthy that in his subsequent

Chautauqua speech of August 14, President Roosevelt declared that while the United States desired friendship with all nations, it was prepared if need be to defend itself and its neighbors against aggression.[173]

In September Mr. King represented Canada at the League of Nations Assembly, and in a statement before his departure for Europe called for faith in the League and in the ideal of world peace. He admitted that economic action against aggressors would have to be backed in the last analysis by armed force, but declared that in the latter case, 'that would be for the Parliament of Canada to decide in the light of the circumstances at the time.'[174] He emphasized that Canada desired friendship with all nations. In his address to the plenary session on September 29 Mr. King professed Canada's adherence to the fundamental principles of the League, and to the policy of live and let live as far as doctrines and forms of government were concerned. As for the question of an automatic obligation to use force in international disputes, he cited Canada's attitude in Commonwealth affairs: 'The Canadian Parliament reserves to itself the right to declare in the light of the circumstances existing at the time to what extent, if at all, Canada will participate in conflicts wherein other members of the Commonwealth may be engaged.'[175] He opposed amendment of the League Covenant as neither 'possible nor necessary,' citing the record of broken pledges among League members. After leaving Geneva, the prime minister discussed trade agreements in Paris and London. Upon his return to Ottawa he declared that Canada's greatest contribution to world peace would be to put her own house in order and to maintain friendly relations with other countries. He heartily endorsed on behalf of Canadians President Roosevelt's declaration at the Inter-American Conference at Rio de Janeiro that the United States would oppose any invasion of the New World.

But despite the prime minister's cautious course, Canada was stirred by the darkening European situation. The split between French and English Canadians on the question of sanctions against Italy was widened by the divergence of their views on the Spanish Civil War. Isolationism was generally widespread in both groups, but its basis was very different, as became evident in the foreign policy debate opened by J. S. Woodsworth's neutrality resolution, introduced on January 25, 1937. The English-Canadian isolationists regarded the Abyssinian affair as a clash of rival European imperialisms, in which the League was used merely as windowdressing. They approved Mr. Lapointe's statement on oil sanctions as in accord with true Canadian policy, while they accused John W. Dafoe and N. W. Rowell, the leading advocates of sanctions, of being unconscious 'bell-wethers for British Imperialism.'[176] French-Canadian isolationists dismissed the League as a creation of Freemasons and atheists, dominated by Protestant Britain and anti-clerical France at the expense of Catholic Italy. Italian propagandists, who were active in Montreal, had revived the memory of the South African War, and accused Britain of 'Anglo-Saxon hypocrisy.' According to Jean Bruchési: 'If the Province of Quebec had to make the decision alone she certainly would not have adopted the line of conduct which was actually followed. With practical unanimity our French-Canadian press refused to dissimulate its sympathy with Italy by reason of sanctions; and when Mr. Riddell, at the behest of London we reasonably conclude, demanded severer sanctions against Rome, there arose a veritable storm of protest.'[177] Quebec felt the same sympathy for General Franco's 'crusade' in Spain as it had for Italy; in both instances it saw an alignment of the 'Anglo-Saxon' and Protestant powers against the Latin and Catholic countries with which it felt an increasing bond as a result of the racist views which had dominated the teaching of French-Canadian history since 1917.

Mr. Woodsworth's resolution, which embodied the policy adopted by the C.C.F. at a Toronto convention in August 1936, involved three points:

1. That under existing international relations, in the event of war, Canada should remain strictly neutral regardless of who the belligerents may be.
2. That at no time should Canadian citizens be permitted to make profits out of supplying war munitions or materials.
3. That the Canadian government should make every effort to discover and remove the causes of international friction and social injustice.[178]

The resolution was occasioned by the 70 per cent increase in the defence estimates tabled at the opening of the session. Though the government maintained that increased armament was necessary to protect Canadian neutrality, Mr. Woodsworth feared that Canada might be drawn into another war 'to assist in the defence of the Empire.' He urged that Canada should determine its foreign policy now, rather than await a crisis, since 'the oncoming of a war, which might mean our participation, would split this country from stem to stern.' Since there was very strong sentiment in Quebec against 'being dragged into another war,' he suggested that the French-Canadian members should declare the sentiments of their province and join his party in questioning whether these increased expenditures were being made for Canada's defence or for future participation in a European war. He declared that the League had failed; Canada should have complete control over her foreign policy; and that for defence she could rely for protection upon the United States, since she lived in a fireproof area. The Woodsworth resolution was supported by some Quebec Liberals, headed by Wilfrid Lacroix, Maxime Raymond, and Wilfrid Gariépy.[179]

In his reply Mr. King accepted the third point completely, partially agreed with the second, and totally rejected the first. He declared that the increase in the defence estimates had been made 'only and solely because of what the government believes to be necessary for the defence of Canada, and for Canada alone. The estimates have not been framed with any thought of participation in European wars.'[180] He denied that they had been influenced by the British government. The prime minister objected to the first point on the grounds that 'it binds the hands of Parliament completely.' It was the policy of his government that 'Parliament must be free to decide its attitude in the light of the circumstances as they may exist at the time. Parliament acting for the people is the supreme authority in the state with respect to all matters, and certainly with respect to what is most vital to the nation, namely, the question of whether or not it shall be involved in war . . . in deciding matters of this kind, as the representatives of the people parliament shall be the voice of the nation; parliament shall decide.'[181] In response to Mr. Woodsworth's questions, the prime minister declared that parliament alone could commit Canada to war or authorize the sending of troops out of the country. He expressed the view that most Canadians adhered to a middle way between 'thorough-going imperialism' and 'regardless nationalism': 'They believe in deciding questions relating to defence or foreign policy by reference to what is Canada's interest. Decisions must be made by Canada primarily in the interests of Canada.'[182] He urged the need of national unity, unity with the Commonwealth, and unity among all the English-speaking nations. A declaration of Canadian neutrality at the present time would merely encourage 'those forces that are ready to oppose Canada, to oppose the British commonwealth of nations, to oppose the English-speaking peoples, and that have their hand out against democracy and democratic institutions.'[183]

Miss Agnes MacPhail of the United Farmers of Ontario supported the resolution. She praised the prime minister's Geneva speech, stressed the development of a Canadian national spirit, and regretted that Canada had not attended the Inter-American Conference at Buenos Aires. The prime minister explained that Canada had not been invited. T. C. Douglas of the C.C.F. supported the resolution, criticizing the prime minister's trend towards isolationism and urging collective action against war by economic sanctions. He particularly stressed Canadian sales of nickel to potential aggressors. On February 4 he presented a motion calling for the conscription of finance, industry, transportation, and natural resources in the event of war.[184] Denton Massey, the only Conservative to speak in the debate, opposed both isolation and neutrality, deplored disunity, and speculated as to the price for American protection.[185]

Justice Minister Lapointe opposed the motion because in his opinion it would involve a withdrawal from the League of Nations and the British Commonwealth. He declared that 'Canada should not spend one life or one cent' in support of either Fascism or Communism. But Canada should be ready to defend itself, for 'If international chiefs or gangsters ever come to assail us on a mad impulse—because the world is mad at the present time—we cannot meet them with a declaration of neutrality.'[186] He repeated the statement that he had made during the fight against conscription in 1917: that the French Canadiàns were 'prepared to do anything for the defence of Canada.' He added: 'But I do not think that our people would like to be involved in a war that might be waged between communism and fascism, because they hate both.' He concluded by stating: 'We are not committed; we shall decide when the time comes whether we shall participate or not, and I trust the circumstances will justify Canada in remaining outside any conflict. But we want to reserve our freedom and our independence as free men should and not be committed by any resolution. . . .'[187]

H.-E. Brunelle (Champlain) seconded Miss MacPhail's proposal that Canadians should cultivate a North American rather than a European mentality. He favored neutrality, if it were compatible 'with our obligations, our honour and our national protection.'[188] He felt that Canada was exposed to attack as part of the empire. Separation would increase the cost of defence. Reliance on the protection of the United States would end in annexation. Canada in any case could not defend herself against serious attack, but 'should have some kind of an army, in the same way that every city needs a police force.'[189] Brunelle was more worried about the danger of Communist revolution at home than aggression from abroad. Vital Mallette (Jacques-Cartier) stressed Quebec's opposition to imperialist wars and her opinion that Canada had never involved England in war but had twice been involved in war by her. He expressed lack of confidence in neutrality or in protection by the United States, and supported the prime minister's policy. In closing he belittled the talk about separatism in Quebec, which was merely the expression of discontent by young men without jobs. He cited recent statements by Premier Duplessis and Agriculture Minister Bona Dussault condemning separatism.[190]

Secretary of State Fernand Rinfret condemned the motion as inopportune, binding for an uncertain future, and futile, since the neutrality of Canada was not within her control. He admitted that

French Canadians were not militaristic and not anxious to support participation in European wars, but he found that he was 'too good a Britisher' to hold with the language of the resolution. He hinted that the motion might have been intended to win to the social ideas of the C.C.F. the French Canadians—'a certain class of people they have not the least chance of reaching otherwise.'[191] He rejected the first and second points and favored the third. Mr. Woodsworth in reply censured the 'French logic' of the secretary of state, and defended his own right as an opponent of conscription to appeal to the French Canadians against militarism. He criticized Mr. Lapointe's 'misstatement' of the Spanish situation, and suggested that the minister either 'had the jitters or wanted to give the jitters to the Canadian people.' In closing he warned that 'We have sown the wind and we are reaping the whirlwind, but we are not going to prevent that whirlwind by sowing more wind.'[192] The prime minister, by preparing for war, was playing the game of the British imperialists. Mr. Woodsworth urged collective security as an alternative to traveling 'the road which, throughout the years, inevitably has led to disaster.'[193]

Both the Woodsworth and the Douglas motions failed, but the discussion of them paved the way for another debate on foreign policy when the defence estimates, calling for an increase of $10,000,000, came before the House on February 15. C. G. Mac-Neil and M. J. Coldwell moved a C.C.F. amendment deploring 'the startling increases' for armament expenditure in contrast to 'the inadequate provision for the social security of all sections of the Canadian people.'[194] Mr. King maintained that Canada owed it to her 'self-respect as a nation' to see to her defence but calmed the fears of the anti-imperialists by declaring: 'I think it extremely doubtful if any of the British Dominions will ever send another expeditionary force to Europe.'[195] Defence Minister Ian Mackenzie declared: 'There is no idea whatever of sending a single Canadian soldier overseas in any expeditionary force, and there is not a single cent providing for that in the estimates . . . They are for the direct defence of Canada and for the defence of Canadian neutrality.'[196] He stated in reply to Mr. MacNeil's charges that the government had given a blank check to be written in blood 'There are no commitments, no understandings, no agreements, open or secret, of any kind.' He stressed that the problem was no longer one of local defence, but 'the complete responsibility for defence in consequence of Canada's new sovereign status.' He urged upon the nationalists:

The more you believe in, the more you subscribe to doctrines of Canadian nationalism, the more you must provide for the defence of the Dominion of Canada. You cannot any longer lean upon the alliances or implied alliances of the past; you can no longer lean upon the implications of the Monroe Doctrine. If you are going to profess the virtues and the pride of nationalism, you must face your responsibilities and meet your obligations in accordance with the status of sovereignty.[197]

The C.C.F. amendment brought an unusual number of French-Canadian members into action, with the same three Quebec Liberals who had supported the Woodsworth resolution backing this motion. Maxime Raymond described the question as one of 'the utmost importance, first of all on account of the increase of these estimates over last year, due to war preparations in Europe and following the rather ill-timed statements of some foreign or semi-foreign individuals some of whom have no right to interfere in our political discussions and for whom past experience should have been a lesson.'[198] He attacked the suggestions of 'imperialist pilgrims' and approved Mr. King's attitude at Geneva. He asked what sudden threat had necessitated such an increase in defence expenditure, 'apart from the visit of Lord Elibank following the warning of Sir Samuel Hoare.'

Our boundaries are the same. Our neighbors are the same and are just as peaceful as they were. Our geographical position has not changed and we are still separated from Europe and Asia by oceans, that mean almost an absolute security. We have no enemies that we know of. Moreover, the friction that existed by reason of the sanctions against Italy has disappeared since these sanctions have been removed.

Did the conditions in Europe grow worse? There is not any more talk about war than there was last June, when the estimates were voted; as a matter of fact, there is less talk about it since the Italo-Ethiopian conflict is over. At any rate, our frontiers are not in Europe.[199]

Referring to *L'Action Catholique's* statement on January 14 that the government had a duty to preserve order in the country, even by force, and to prevent the enlistment of volunteers for 'the Red army of Spain' in Canada, he favored any necessary increase of the forces to guard against revolution in Canada. But he declared:

My duty to my electors is to oppose Canada's participation in any war outside of her own territory—the horrors of the last war are still too vivid,—and I will not vote a single dollar increase that will not be spent "wholly and exclusively" for the defence of Canada, and in Canada only.

Since our dominion is now a sovereign state, the obligation rests upon us to see to our own national defence, and we must protect ourselves against dangers from within and without. For that reason, I am willing to vote any amount shown to be necessary to make this country safe.

But again, I say that our army, our air force and our navy must be called out only in defence of Canada and solely within her territory.[200]

Significantly, Mr. Raymond was applauded by Mr. Lapointe, the government leader for Quebec.

Lionel Bertrand (Laurier) agreed that the question was a very important one. He declared:

If national defence meant contribution to the future wars of Europe, then I say undoubtedly I would have to be against national defence. If it meant contribution to European wars, I am sure that the people of my own province would soon ask themselves the question: Is it worthwhile to stay within the British Empire if we have to go to war because South Africa wants its independence recognized, because Germany wants its colonies back, or for any other reason.

But if we have to defend Canadian territory and if it means only the defence of our territory, I am going to vote heartily for this measure of defence. [201]

In closing Mr. Bertrand declared that as a French Canadian, he felt he would be belittling his country and his race if he did not favor provision for proper defence. Deploring the campaign to convince Quebec that national defence meant participation, he cited *Le Devoir's* advocacy of the former in 1914. He declared: 'I am sure that in my own province the leader of the government, whose ancestors suffered for the autonomy of Canada, is going to be looked upon as a true Canadian; the province of Quebec will have faith in him and will not have any trouble in voting for these appropriations. [202]

J.-A. Crète (St. Maurice-Laflèche) wondered whether Bertrand truly expressed the sentiment of Quebec on the question. He criticized the increase in expenditure as unjustifiable in view of Canada's geographical, political, and economic status. He believed in reliance on the Monroe Doctrine and in Canadian cooperation in the Pan-American Union. Economic stability was a better guarantee against internal and external conflict than entering the world armament race. He pointed out that the students of both Quebec and Toronto were opposed to rearmament. [203] Both he and Liguori Lacombe (Laval-Two Mountains) rejected the C.C.F. motion, leaving their vote on the main question undecided. Lacombe opposed Canadian participation in imperial or European wars. As a 1917 conscript, he denounced Canada's participation in the First World War on both moral and economic grounds. He stressed the Communist danger, and expressed the view that the defence estimates might be justified as a means to crush it. [204] Joseph Jean (Mercier) deprecated the importance which had been given to the question. He stressed that the issue was not Canadian participation in foreign wars, and urged the responsibilities of nationhood. He saw the organization of a modest army as a major factor in creating internal peace and developing national unity, if French Canadians were given their share in its ranks.

Jean-François Pouliot (Témiscouata) supported the estimates, but criticized the Defence Department for its red tape, for being more British than Canadian, and for being inefficient. He expressed opposition to federal action against Communism. Oscar-L. Boulanger (Bellechasse) supported the government, warning Quebec against repeating the error of 1911 and maintaining that American imperialism was as bad as British imperialism. He urged Quebec to live up to its glorious military traditions. Charles Parent (Quebec West and South) opposed both the C.C.F. motion and the estimates, stressing Canada's geographical isolation and minimizing the danger from without. He did not think that an army was necessary to deal with Communist agitation and labor trouble at home. Maurice Lalonde (Labelle) opposed the C.C.F. amendment and expressed confidence in the Liberal leadership, while opposing Canadian participation in foreign wars. He, too, stressed the Communist menace. Pierre Gauthier (Portneuf) opposed rearmament and stressed the menace of Communism. Alphonse Fournier (Hull) pointed out that Canada's unpreparedness had not prevented her participation in the Boer and World Wars. He made a plea for faith in the administration and opposed foreign wars. H.-E. Brunelle (Champlain) opposed both the C.C.F. and government motions, but censured the Quebec press for misrepresenting the administration's attitude. L.-D. Tremblay (Dorchester) opposed the amendment and expressed full confidence in the government. J.-A. Verville (Lotbinière) supported the government but condemned the increased expenditure. Wilfrid Lacroix (Quebec-Montmorency) did the same, urging that Canada should join the Pan-American Union. In contrast to the French stand against participation in foreign wars, only four English members took the same attitude.[205] The C.C.F. amendment was defeated by 191 to 17, with a few Social Credit members supporting the C.C.F. On the estimates the opposition mustered 26 votes, with a Manitoba Liberal and a few French Canadians joining the C.C.F.

For all its sympathy with Franco, French Canada approved the government's embargo on sending men or munitions to Spain. In reply to three questions early in the session as to its attitude about Canadian volunteers for the Spanish War—one of which was prompted by Premier Duplessis' statement at Trois-Rivières that Communist recruiting for Republican Spain had been carried on in Quebec[206]—the government announced its intention of proposing Canadian legislation modelled on the Imperial Foreign Enlistment Act of 1870. On second reading on March 19, Mr. Woodsworth criticized the measure for not prohibiting the export of arms and munitions to belligerents, as the United States neutrality law did. This criticism was satisfied by a section in a bill amending the Customs Act which gave the government power to control the export of both arms and provisions.[207] Nationalist and imperialist made common cause in supporting these measures, with the former's distrust of European complications matched by the latter's desire to follow the British policy of non-intervention. Maxime Raymond's comment on the departure of Canadian volunteers for 'the Red army of Spain,' which he hailed as ridding the country of 'undesirable people,' met with applause in the House.[208] There was no reflection in parliament of the sympathy with the Spanish Republicans expressed by a resolution of the Canadian Trades and Labor Congress in the fall of 1937, and by the formation under Communist auspices of a Mackenzie-Papineau Battalion for the Republican Army.[209]

The Conservatives, who had become known as the 'silent party' by their avoidance of involvement in the Liberal–C.C.F. quarrels over foreign policy and defence, broke their silence on March 25 when R. B. Bennett made a plea for close naval cooperation with Britain. He based his argument on speeches made by Laurier before 1914, which tended to confirm the suspicion that Conservative policy was based on the hope of splitting the Liberals on defence, as in 1911. Mr. King replied that the government had always favored the Laurier policy, and evaded his opponent's plea for reaching an understanding with the Admiralty. The Conservative naval plea was echoed in the Senate by Senators Ballantyne, Griesbach, and Macdonell, who urged a policy of 'collective security within the empire.' A French-Canadian senator criticised this 'marathon of flag-waving' by a former marine minister and two generals. Senator Meighen had previously criticized the government's seeming willingness to become 'in fact, if not in law, an adjunct, and a humiliated adjunct, of the American Republic.'[210]

The Imperial Conference of 1937, scheduled to meet in May after the coronation of George VI, was to be devoted to the whole field of imperial policy. Before his departure for London, Mr. King made it clear that no commitments would be made, leaving parliament free to decide on Canadian foreign and defence policy. With Australia and South Africa facing elections and the Irish Free State abstaining from the conference, the gathering served merely the purpose of discussion and review, rather than decision and action, as Mr. King defined its function upon his return.[211] Nevertheless, Neville Chamberlain sought to make capital of the concluding words of Mr. King's speech at the Paris Exposition on July 2 when he said:

We like to manage our own affairs. We cooperate with other parts of the British Empire in discussing questions of economic interest. The fact that we have our own representatives in other countries is evidence of that great liberty which above all we prize, and were it imperilled from any source whatsoever, would bring us together in the defence of it.[212]

Mr. King refused to comment on Chamberlain's interpretation, but declared Canada had undertaken no commitments. British disappointment at the conference's inconclusiveness was apparent. Canadian imperialists were still further distressed in October when the governor-general, Lord Tweedsmuir, told the tenth anniversary dinner of the Canadian Institute for International Affairs: 'A Canadian's first duty is not to the British Commonwealth of Nations, but to Canada and to Canada's King, and those who deny this are doing, to my mind, a great disservice to the Commonwealth.' This utterance of a distinguished graduate of Milner's 'kindergarten' for young imperialists in South Africa was promptly adopted as a permanent heading for the front page of Le Devoir, while C. H. Cahan criticized it in a speech to the Montreal branch of the Royal Empire Society.[213] Conservative criticism and nationalist approval of a governor-general indicated the confusion of public opinion in a Canada divided within herself and uncertain about her role in a world darkened by the shadows of war.

When China, once more invaded by Japan, invoked the League Covenant at the 1937 meeting of the Assembly, Canada continued to follow the 'back-seat' policy it had adopted since the Riddell incident. Senator Dandurand, as Canada's representative on the League's Far Eastern Advisory Committee, refused to vote for resolutions condemning Japan's course until he had received instructions from Ottawa. The Canadian government subsequently declared its approval of the resolutions.[214] Though Canada applied the Foreign Enlistment Act to Spain in August, Senator Dandurand voted in favor of Spain's eligibility for re-election to the League, declaring that 'The sole duty of the Canadian delegation was to think of Spain as an entity, without interfering in its domestic quarrels.'[215] At the Brussels Nine Power Conference in November, Canada followed the American and British lead of merely condemning Japanese aggression and offering to mediate in the Far Eastern struggle. The prime minister subsequently commented on Canada's role: 'It did not think less could be done; it did not urge the great powers represented to do more.'[216] Anti-Japanese feeling was strong in the Canadian West, with an unofficial boycott of Japanese goods, but negligible in Quebec.

For all the discussion of international affairs in 1937, the King government's attention was given primarily to pressing economic questions at home. The economic recovery which began in 1935 received a sharp setback from the business recession of 1937 in the States, while successive crop failures on the Prairies increased unemployment. Canada never really rallied from the 1929 collapse until the war boom began in 1939. The successive budgets after 1935 showed decreased deficits, however, and promised tax relief. A new British trade agreement in 1937 and a United States one in 1938, which formed part of the Anglo-American Trade treaty of that year, were important factors in improving Canadian trade, which became increasingly involved in a triangular pattern with Britain and the United States, despite some expansion in Latin America and the British West Indies. It was significant that Mr. King conferred with President Roosevelt and Secretary Hull at Washington in March 1937 before the Imperial Conference in May at which he urged that 'political tension will not lessen without the abatement of economic nationalism and economic imperialism.'[217] Canadian influence played its part in the subsequent Anglo-American Trade Treaty.

Closer Canadian-American and Anglo-American relations were considerably furthered by the visits of Lord Tweedsmuir to Washington in 1937 and of Mr. Roosevelt to Canada, in 1938. The governor-general shattered all precedent by addressing Congress on April 1, telling the House that 'Your nation and mine . . . are the guardians . . . of democracy,' and the Senate that 'the future lies in the hands of the English-speaking peoples.' And at Kingston on August 18, when receiving an honorary degree from Queen's University, the President referred to the common democratic inheritance of Canada and the United States, and the new involvement of the Americas in world affairs. He then declared: 'The Dominion of Canada is part of the sisterhood of the British Empire. I give to you assurance that the people of the United States will not stand idly by if domination of Canadian soil is threatened by any other Empire.'[218] Speaking at Woodbridge two days later, Prime Minister King cautiously welcomed Mr. Roosevelt's declaration, describing it as one made with no thought of military alliance, and declaring: 'Canadians know they have their own responsibility for maintaining Canadian soil as a homeland for free men in the Western hemisphere.' He added that Canadians should see to it that 'should the occasion ever arise, enemy forces should not be able to pursue their way by land, sea, or air to the United States across Canadian territory.'[219] Mr. King also stressed that the president's statement did not weaken Canada's relationship to other members of the British Commonwealth.

Mr. King's course of action during the Czechoslovakian crisis of September gave evidence, however, that he was less interested in supporting Britain's European policy than either old-school imperialists or enthusiastic supporters of the League of Nations. The government issued no statement until Mr. King telegraphed his congratulations to Mr. Chamberlain after the latter's flight to Berchtesgaden.[220] Despite pressure from the Conservative opposition and the Canadian Legion for support of Britain, the government's statement of September 17 merely declared that it was giving 'unremitting consideration' to the situation and warned against 'public controversy' as a threat to Canadian peace and Commonwealth unity.[221] The cabinet held an emergency meeting on September 23, during Mr. Chamberlain's second visit to Germany, but no statement was issued, despite growing indignation in Tory and imperialist circles. Finally, after the cabinet had considered Mr. Chamberlain's empire broadcast of September 27, a statement was made supporting the British prime minister's stand, promising to summon parliament if war came, and urging the avoidance of 'controversies or divisions that might seriously impair effective and concerted action when Parliament meets.'[222] Upon the news of the Munich settlement Mr. King warmly congratulated Mr. Chamberlain.

The Munich settlement brought a general feeling of relief in a Canada which thanks to its growing North Americanism was more favorable to appeasement than Britain itself. It was significant that in December 1939 Canada recognized King Victor Emmanuel as Emperor of Abyssinia without debate in parliament.[223] As the falseness of the settlement became evident with time, this first feeling of relief changed to a recognition that the Chamberlain negotiations had destroyed the League of Nations. Consequently, as Professor F. R. Scott pointed out, while 'before the Munich settlement there were three main groups of opinion in Canada—imperialist, collectivist, and isolationist or Canadian nationalist—two of which advocated Canada's participation in external affairs, today there are only two groups, only one of them willing to intervene in Europe.'[224] There were campaigns for clarification of Canada's right to neutrality and demands for closer cooperation with the United States and representation in the Pan-American Union. But there was a general, if reluctant recognition that Canada must in any case increase its armaments.

The speech from the throne in January 1939 announced that the defence program launched two years earlier would be pursued vigorously—the defence estimates were nearly double the total for 1938—but that 'While taking the measures necessary to assure the maintenance of our national integrity against the possibility of external aggression, the government have sought in positive ways to strengthen the mutual interests which unite Canada in friendly relations with other countries.'[225] Dr. R. J. Manion, who had won the Conservative leadership after R. B. Bennett's resignation in a disruptive contest with Arthur Meighen, took the opportunity to declare that Mr. King's lieutenants in Quebec would not find it so difficult to win support there for the present defence program, if they had not spent so much time in the past telling the people that the Conservatives were bloodthirsty militarists, when the latter had merely sought to provide half the defence which now existed.[226] For his part Mr. King sought to reassure Quebec by declaring: 'It might as well be said now, at the beginning of this session, because it will be the attitude of this government for its time, that before this country goes into any war, this parliament will be consulted.' He quoted as the formula of past, present, and future Liberal policy, Laurier's declaration in 1910: 'If England is at war we are at war and liable to attack. I do not say that we will always be attacked; neither do I say that we would take part in all the wars of England. That is a matter that must be guided by circumstances, upon which the Canadian parliament will have to pronounce and will have to decide in its own best judgment.'[227]

Nonetheless the Quebec nationalists took alarm, although most of the Liberal members with nationalist leanings were reassured by Mr. King's statement. Liguori Lacombe denied that Canada was necessarily at war because one or more of the equal nations of the Commonwealth was at war:

Canada being according to the statute of Westminster, a self-governing country as regards England, any declaration contrary to this treaty must be considered, in the event of war, as outmoded and false. I need not repeat that I am irrevocably opposed to any increase in defence appropriations so long as they may serve to involve Canada in a foreign war. I go further. In the name of the country's most cherished interests, no decision should be taken as to Canada's participation in an extra-territorial war without an appeal to the people . . . Should a conflict occur in central Europe, in America or elsewhere, I assert that the Canadian people alone would have the right to make a decision in such a serious matter.[228]

He declared that public opinion was opposed to participation, and that 'The supreme folly of another venture in a foreign war would spell the permanent ruin of Canada.' Dr. Pierre Gauthier accepted the necessity of defence measures; hailed King's stand as 'frankly and admirably Canadian;' and warned of the danger of press campaigns for participation and for the defeat of King, which would lead to 'the repetition of what occurred in 1911, 1914, and 1917.' He expressed a basic French-Canadian sentiment with his declaration: 'I stand for Canada above all, for Canada alone, and for Canada forever.'[229] L.-D. Tremblay spelled out the same sentiment in detail:

We, from Quebec, do not claim that Canada should have no defence or armaments; on the contrary, Canada is our only fatherland. We are neither French nor English, we are Canadians, and our only fatherland is Canada. When we are requested to vote for an increase in the estimates of the Department of National Defence for the protection of Canada and the defence of our territory, I say that Quebec is willing to support that, but we do not want to share any longer in foreign adventures . . . Let us think a little more of Canada, our country, than the British Empire.[230]

G.-H. Héon, an able independent Conservative, contrasted Lord Stanley's declaration at Toronto with Mr. King's position. Lord Stanley replied to the question 'Is Canada at war when Britain is at war?' thus: 'Certainly not. Canada has entire responsibility of her own. She is a sovereign state and decides for herself.' Héon declared that the issue of the next election would be 'Colonialism or Canadianism,' and he refused to believe that 'colonialism is the regime under which the overwhelming majority of Canadians want to live today.' He was not opposed to Canadian participation in any war:

What I say is that any war in which we do take part must be a war in which something better than sentiment actuated by prejudiced propaganda is at stake. It must be a war that threatens our very liberty, independence and existence, and the issue of which would be of vital concern immediate to all of us. I say, my country right or wrong, but not fifteen countries.[231]

Héon favored an immediate appeal to the people on the issue.

Wilfrid Lacroix refused to withdraw his resolution for the adoption of the term 'Kingdom of Canada' and for the naming of a Canadian 'Viceroy' with the abolition of the office of dominion secretary. To his mind the best way to protect Canada was 'to create an independent kingdom and officially to proclaim our neutrality, thus placing ourselves on the same footing as the United States as regards any future intervention.'[232] The United States was obliged by the Monroe Doctrine to protect Canada, which should 'keep out of European troubles and complications.'

On March 30, after the German occupation of Czechoslovakia and Mr. Chamberlain's suggestion for consultation by the Commonwealth nations on Hitler's attempt to dominate the world by force, Mr. King again reviewed in parliament international affairs and his government's policies. He reiterated that parliament would decide 'if Canada is faced by the necessity of making a decision on the most serious and momentous issue that can face a nation, whether or not to take part in war.' Echoing Chamberlain's noncommital stand, Mr. King declared:

Speaking as the Prime Minister of Canada, I wish to say that I am not prepared any more than is the Prime Minister of Great Britain to engage this country by new and unspecified commitments operating under conditions which cannot now be foreseen . . .

I cannot accept the view which is being urged in some quarters today, that regardless of what government or party may be in power, regardless of what its policy may be, regardless of what the issue itself may come to be, this country should say here and now that Canada is prepared to support whatever may be proposed by the government at Westminster.[233]

He argued that 'a divided Canada can be of little help to any country, and least of all to itself,' and stressed that 'We are and will remain Canadians, devoted, first and last, to the interests of Canada, but Canadians, I hope, who will be able to take a long range view of what Canada's interests require.' He showed his fundamental sympathy with the French-Canadian nationalists in these words:

. . . we must, to a greater or less extent, choose between keeping our own house in order, and trying to save Europe and Asia. The idea that every twenty years this country should automatically and as a matter of course take part in a war overseas for democracy or self-determination of other small nations, that a country which has all it can do to run itself should feel called upon to save, periodically, a continent that cannot run itself, and to these ends risk the lives of its people, risk bankruptcy and political disunion, seems to many a nightmare and sheer madness.[234]

Mr. King declared that participation in another world war could not be 'passive or formal,' and warned that Canada had to keep its Pacific as well as its Atlantic coast in mind. Altered world conditions had brought a marked decentralization of defence activities within the Commonwealth, and eliminated the need for colonial contingents:

They have brought about a great preoccupation of each part with its own defence, a greater responsibility for that defence, a greater self-containment in the provision of means of defence . . . One strategic fact is clear: the days of the great expeditionary forces of infantry crossing the ocean are not likely to reoccur. Two years ago, I expressed in this house the view that it was extremely doubtful if any of the British dominions would ever send another expeditionary force to Europe.

One political fact is equally clear: in a war to save the liberty of others, and thus our own, we should not sacrifice our own liberty or our own unity . . . The present government believes that conscription of men for overseas service would not be a necessary or an effective step. Let me say that so long as this government may be in power, no such measure will be enacted. We have full faith in the readiness of Canadian men and women to rally for the defence of their country and their liberties, and to resist aggression by any country seeking to dominate the world by force.[235]

Mr. King also pledged that if war came, the government would control war profits and suppress profiteering in general. He amplified his quotation of Laurier on January 16 by saying that he had meant to indicate that an enemy of Britain might force war upon Canada if she chose to do so, but that the Canadian government would not be guided by legalism: 'We would not go into a war merely because of legal uncertainty as to our power to stay out. We would not stay out of a war merely because we had provided technical freedom to do so. Our country's decisions on such vital matters, now or later, will depend on deeper forces, they will depend on the thoughts and feelings of our people.'[236] This clever speech, leaving the way open to neutrality, active belligerency or passive belligerency, offered comfort to isolationist and imperialist alike and deprived the Conservatives and the C.C.F. of any major issue on which to oppose the government.

Dr. Manion, who represented a very different school of Conservatism than Arthur Meighen, and who sought to woo Quebec's sympathies, agreed that Canada should have the right to decide its role in any British war: 'I demand for us in Canada the same right to form and express opinions as is possessed by citizens of the British Isles. I refuse to subscribe to any doctrine of inferiority which would cast us in the role of pawns on the international chess board.'[237] He argued that conscription was dubious in value, since at most only 10,000 Canadians reached the trenches in the First World War as a result of its adoption. Two English Montreal Conservatives, C. H. Cahan and R. S. White, supported their leader by arguing that if Quebec were treated reasonably and courteously she would do her part in any war effort. The C.C.F. and the Social Credit leaders also opposed conscription, though Mr. Woodsworth doubted whether it could be avoided as a war went on and heavy losses occurred in overseas forces.

Justice Minister Lapointe, the recognized Quebec spokesman, won the honors of the debate. First he discussed the legal obstacles to a declaration of neutrality, and concluded that there was no 'possibility of one country being neutral and another a belligerent, when they are not separate sovereignties and when one is linked with the other in respect of its own power of legislation.'[238] A declaration of Canadian neutrality would entail a ban on enlistment by Canadians in the British forces, the closing of the British bases at Halifax and Esquimalt, and the internment of British seamen who sought refuge in Canadian ports. He asked whether anyone seriously believed that these steps could be taken without causing a civil war in Canada.

He quoted with approval the remark of E. J. Tarr that 'the loyalty of French Canadians is concentrated too narrowly, and that of many English Canadians is spread too broadly.' He admitted that bombardment of London would cause a wave of public opinion that would force any Canadian government to intervene, and asked his Quebec colleagues: 'What is the use of closing our eyes to stern realities?' But he also asked English Canadians to pay heed to the sentiments of French Canadians, of whom 'none . . . would say that he is "going home" when he leaves Canada.'[239]

Lapointe ruled out conscription, which he had opposed in 1917, as a frightful blunder whose tragic consequences were still being felt. Even if it had proved effective, 'The best way, the most effective way of helping is not the way that would divide our country and tear it asunder.' Canada was not alone in opposing conscription; Australia, South Africa, and Ireland did so also. He declared solemnly: 'I think I am true to my concept of Canadian unity when I say that I shall always fight against this policy; I would not be a member of a government that would enact it; and not only that, but I say so with all my responsibility to the people of Canada that I would oppose any government that would enforce it.' He agreed with the prime minister that the time for expeditionary forces was past: 'The men will be needed here; and in any event it is parliament which will decide about it.'[240] He closed with a warning against a narrow isolationism by quoting an eloquent editorial of the late Jules Dorion in *L'Action Catholique*.

We are the masters of our destinies. Agreed. But that does not obliterate the fact that we have a neighbour to the south, icebound solitudes to the north, and, to the east and west, much travelled oceans beyond which dwell populous and active nations with which we cannot avoid having relations—with which we have to deal, to negotiate, to agree or to fight.

This is a reality which we cannot ignore without exposing ourselves to a terrible awakening.

We are our own masters. Agreed. But that does not prevent us from asking ourselves what are to be our relations with England, to wonder whether we can do without her or whether it would not be better for us to remain associated with her.

Canada has become a nation. We must, however, recognize the fact that a nation has other obligations, other duties and other cares than a colony has, and place ourselves in a position to meet them. We must remember that nations evolve, and are sometimes faced with situations not of their own making.[241]

Despite all the assurances given to Quebec by the government leaders and the heads of the other parties, six French Canadians—

Lacombe, Lacroix, Lalonde, A.-J. Lapointe, Tremblay, and Raymond—reiterated their opposition to participation in a European war and to a repetition of the experiences of 1914–8. In April Raymond summed up their position with the greatest force and eloquence:

> Every Canadian citizen has the military obligation of defending the soil of his motherland, and those of the province of Quebec have never shirked that duty, nor shall they ever do so, but no one is entitled to ask them to go and shed their blood in Europe, or in Africa or in Asia for the greater glory or power of any other country, even if that country should be England or France.
> And if ever a majority of the people of this country should desire to compel an important minority thereof to take up arms in defence of a foreign land, whichever it may be, that would be the end of confederation.[242]

He concluded by quoting Lapointe's statement at Quebec on December 12, 1938: 'Instead of waging war in a foreign land, we shall remain at home and defend the Canada we love.' In the May debate on the defence estimates as the war clouds darkened, Lacombe, Lacroix, Raymond, Gauthier, Crète, and Gariépy, renewed their protests, which broke the unwonted unity of the House.

The basic isolationism of the King government was in part dictated by a popular mood similar to that in the United States which was responsible for the rejection of collective security and for the adoption of neutrality legislation. In part it was also based upon Mr. King's consciousness of the deep divisions of the Canadian peoples in recent years, their hard-pressed economic position, and his heritage from Laurier of a dread of war setting the two chief peoples of Canada at odds. But it also reflected the growing North Americanism of a Canada which in 1938 had sent 32.3 per cent of her exports to the States and derived 62.7 per cent of her imports thence, as compared with 40.6 per cent of her exports to Britain and 17.6 per cent of her imports from the latter source. This new economic relationship was to grow notably closer after the outbreak of the Second World War, despite the barriers of the American Neutrality Act.

This development did not weaken the old sentimental ties with Britain, as was evidenced by the warmth with which the King and Queen were received when they toured Canada in May and June 1939. Anti-imperialist Montreal spent more money on the royal reception than ultra-loyalist Toronto. On the eve of the Second World War some English Canadians deplored the weakening of the British tie and resented the growing paternalism of the United States towards Canada, while French-Canadian nationalists found reinforcement for their isolationism and anti-militarism in the fact that the United States professedly stood ready to defend Canada against aggression. English and French nationalists alike favored the recognition of Canada's new orientation by entrance into the Pan-American Union and hemisphere defence projects.

Notes.

1 See *Notre Américanisation, enquête de 'La Revue Dominicaine'* (Montréal, 1937) & E. Montpetit, *Reflèts d'Amérique* (Montréal, 1941).

2 *Can. An. Rev. 1920*, 629. Translation revised.

3 *Ibid.*, 631.

4 *Ibid.*, 656.

5 *Ibid.*, 405.

6 *Ibid.*, 413.

7 *Ibid.*, 113–14.

8 *Ibid.*, 495.

9 *Ibid.*, 427.

10 C. P. Stacey, *The Military Problems of Canada* (Toronto, 1940), 90–1.

11 *Ibid.*, 89–91.

12 *Can. An. Rev. 1921*, 211.

13 *The Round Table*, XI, 390–1; cited A. G. Dewey, *The Dominions and Diplomacy* (London, 1929), I, 323.

14 *Ibid.*

15 *Can. An. Rev. 1921*, 78.

16 *Political Science Quarterly*, L (March 1935), 53–5, J. B. Brebner, 'Canada & the Anglo-Japanese Alliance.'

17 Dewey, I, 328.

18 *Ibid.*, II, 73; Brebner, 49–50.

19 *Can. An. Rev. 1921*, 220.

20 *Ibid.*, 221.

21 *Ibid.*, 177.

22 Dewey, II, 83–5.

23 *Can. An. Rev. 1921*, 113–14.

24 *Canada, Sessional Papers 1922*, No. 47, 15 March 1922; cited Dewey, II, 86–9.

25 *Can. An. Rev., 1921*, 171.

26 *Ibid.*, 309.

27 *Ibid.*, 482.

28 *Ibid.*, 486.

29 *Ibid.*, 485.

30 *Ibid.*, 489.

31 *Ibid.*, 488.

32 *Ibid.*, 518–9.

33 *Ibid.*, 522.

34 *Dewey*, II, 116.

35 *Ibid.*, 122.

36 *Can. An. Rev. 1922*, 182–3.

37 J. S. Ewart, *Canada and British Wars* (Ottawa, 1922), 5.

38 *Ibid.*, 86–8.

39 Dewey, II, 123–4.

40 *Ibid.*, 125.

41 *Ibid.*, 125–6.

[42] *Ibid.*, 141.

[43] *Ibid.*, 140 n. 3.

[44] *Can. An. Rev. 1923*, 53.

[45] Dewey, II, 137–47.

[46] *Can. An. Rev. 1923*, 92.

[47] Dewey, II, 169–71.

[48] P. E. Corbett & H. E. Smith, *Canada and World Politics* (London, 1928), Ap. I, 191–4, 'Report of the Imperial Conference of 1923.'

[49] *Can. An. Rev. 1924–5*, 43.

[50] *Ibid.*

[51] Dewey, II, 149–52.

[52] *Ibid.*, 154.

[53] *Canada, Commons Debates 1924*, June 9; cited Dewey, II, 160.

[54] Dewey, II, 161–4.

[55] *Ibid.*, 188.

[56] *Can. An. Rev. 1925–6*, 47.

[57] *Ibid.*, 49.

[58] *Ibid.*, 86.

[59] *Ibid.*, 56.

[60] *Canada, Commons Debates 1926*, 22 March, II, 1806.

[61] C. Wittke, *A History of Canada* (New York, 1941), 349.

[62] Dewey, II, 260–1.

[63] *Ibid.*, 262–3.

[64] *Ibid.*, 264–5.

[65] H. Bourassa, *Le Canada, nation libre* (Montréal, 1926), 18.

[66] *Can. An. Rev. 1926–7*, 40; *Le Devoir*, 10 sept. 1926.

[67] *Ibid.*

[68] Wittke, 366.

[69] *Can. An. Rev. 1926–7*, 55; *Le Devoir*, 16 sept. 1926.

[70] *Ibid.*, 115.

[71] *Ibid.*, 119.

[72] Corbett & Smith, Ap. II, 194–222, 'Report of the Imperial Conference of 1926.'

[73] *Ibid.*, 197–9.

[74] *Ibid.*, 201.

[75] G. Neuendorf, *Studies in the Evolution of Dominion Status* (London, 1942), 23.

[76] R. L. Borden, *Canada in the Commonwealth* (Oxford, 1927), 125–6.

[77] Corbett & Smith, 215.

[78] *Can. An. Rev. 1926–7*, 135.

[79] *Ibid.*, 133.

[80] *Ibid.*, 134–5.

[81] *Ibid.*, 130.

[82] *Ibid.*

[83] *Ibid.*, 62–3.

[84] *Ibid.*, 67–8.

[85] *Ibid.*, 68.

[86] *Can. An. Rev. 1927–8*, 150–1.

[87] *Ibid.*, 140.

[88] Corbett & Smith, 107–30.

[89] *Can. An. Rev. 1927–8*, 55.

[90] *Ibid.*, 56.

[91] *Ibid.*, 56–7.

[92] *Ibid.*, 29.

[93] *Ibid.*, 26.

[94] *Ibid.*, 26.

[95] *Ibid.*, 29.
[96] *Ibid.*, 30.
[97] *Ibid.*, 31.
[98] *Ibid.*, 37.
[99] *Ibid.*, 32.
[100] *Ibid.*, 40.
[101] *Ibid.*, 409.
[102] *Can. An. Rev. 1926–7*, 356.
[103] *Can. An. Rev. 1927–8*, 381–2.
[104] *Ibid.*, 104.
[105] *Ibid.*, 397.
[106] *Ibid.*, 397–8.
[107] *Can. An. Rev. 1929–30*, 30.
[108] *Ibid.*, 32.
[109] *Ibid.*, 31–2.
[110] *Ibid.*, 33.
[111] *Ibid.*, 54.
[112] *Ibid.*, 84; *La Presse*, 25 juillet 1930.
[113] *Ibid.*, 87.
[114] *Ibid.*, 85–6.
[115] *Ibid.*, 100.
[116] *Can. An. Rev. 1930–1*, 32–3.
[117] *Ibid.*, 37.
[118] *Ibid.*, 42.
[119] *Ibid.*, 307–24.
[120] *Ibid.*, 31.
[121] *Ibid.*, 44–6.
[122] *Ibid.*, 47.
[123] *Ibid.*, 46.
[124] *Ibid.*, 731.
[125] *Canada, Commons Debates 1931*, 30 June, 3203–4.
[126] *Ibid.*, 3205–6.
[127] *Ibid.*, 3215–21.
[128] Neuendorf, 292.
[129] *Ibid.*
[130] Abbé L. Groulx, *Directives* (Montréal, 1937), 162–3.
[131] *Can. An. Rev. 1932*, 28.
[132] *Ibid.*, 34–5.
[133] *Ibid.*, 57.
[134] *Ibid.*, 319–25.
[135] *Can. An. Rev. 1933*, 43.
[136] *Ibid.*, 51.
[137] *Ibid.*
[138] *Ibid.*, 46.
[139] *Ibid.*, 33.
[140] *Ibid.*, 34–5.
[141] *Ibid.*, 33.
[142] *Ibid.*, 30–3.
[143] *Can. An. Rev. 1934*, 34–5.
[144] *Ibid.*, 53.
[145] *Ibid.*, 35.
[146] *Ibid.*, 36.
[147] *Ibid.*, 33.
[148] *Can. An. Rev. 1935–6*, 2.
[149] *Ibid.*, 11.

[150] *Ibid.*, 12–3.
[151] *Ibid.*, 15.
[152] *Ibid.*, 50.
[153] *Ibid.*, 63.
[154] *Ibid.*, 64–5.
[155] *Ibid.*, 68.
[156] *Ibid.*, 94.
[157] *Ibid.*, 95.
[158] *Ibid.*, 96–7, 93.
[159] *Ibid.*, 97–7.
[160] F. H. Soward, J. F. Parkinson, N. A. M. MacKenzie, T. W. L. MacDermot, *Canada in World Affairs: The Pre-War Years* (Toronto, 1941), 198–9.
[161] *Can. An. Rev. 1935–6*, 125–7.
[162] R. Rumilly, *L'Autonomie Provinciale* (Montréal, 1948), 106.
[163] *Can. An. Rev. 1937–8*, 157.
[164] K. G. W. Ludecke, *I Knew Hitler* (New York, 1937), 54.
[165] *Ibid.*
[166] *The Nation, No. 145* (6 Nov. 1937), 497–9, J. McNeil, 'Right Turn in Canada'; *No. 146* (12 Feb. 1938), 176–9, E. S. McLeod, 'Slander over Canada'; *No. 148* (26 Feb. 1938) 241–4, D. Martin, 'Adrien Arcand, Fascist.'
[167] *Can. An. Rev. 1937–8*, 92–3.
[168] Canada, *Commons Debates 1936*, 18 June, IV, 3862–73.
[169] *Ibid.*, 3876.
[170] *Ibid.*, 3896.
[171] *Ibid.*, 3384.
[172] *Commons Debates 1935*, 1 April, III, 2287.
[173] Soward, *et al.*, 34.
[174] *Can. An. Rev. 1935–6*, 77.
[175] *Ibid.*, 79.
[176] Soward, *et al.*, 38.
[177] *Ibid.*, 23–4.
[178] Canada, *Commons Debates 1937*, 25 Jan., I, 237.
[179] *Can. An. Rev. 1937–8*, 30.
[180] *Commons Debates 1937*, I, 246.
[181] *Ibid.*, 248.
[182] *Ibid.*, 250–1.
[183] *Ibid.*, 252.
[184] *Ibid.*, 256–61, 564.
[185] *Ibid.*, 261–4.
[186] *Ibid.*, 4 Feb., 550.
[187] *Ibid.*, 551.
[188] *Ibid.*, 552.
[189] *Ibid.*, 554–5.
[190] *Ibid.*, 556–7.
[191] *Ibid.*, 558–9.
[192] *Ibid.*, 563–4.
[193] *Ibid.*, 15 Feb., 876.
[194] *Can. An. Rev. 1937–8*, 32.
[195] *Commons Debates 1937*, 15 Feb., I, 893, 895.
[196] *Ibid.*, 902.
[197] *Ibid.*, 909–10.
[198] *Ibid.*, 911–12.
[199] *Ibid.*, 918.
[200] *Ibid.*, 921.
[201] *Ibid.*, 934–7.

[202] *Ibid.*, 937–40.
[203] Soward, *et al.*, 61 *n.* 4.
[204] *Commons Debates 1937*, 29 Jan., I, 386.
[205] Soward, *et al.*, 64.
[206] *Commons Debates 1937*, 15 Feb., I, 910.
[207] Soward, *et al.*, 64 *n.* 1.
[208] *Ibid.*, 66–8.
[209] *Ibid.*, 70.
[210] *Can. A. Rev. 1937–8*, 4.
[211] Soward, *et al.*, 73 *n.* 1.
[212] *Can. An. Rev. 1937–8*, 5.
[213] Soward, *et al.*, 75–6 & *n.* 1.
[214] *Ibid.*, 76–7.
[215] *Can. An. Rev. 1937–8*, 3.
[218] Soward, *et al.*, 107.
[219] *Ibid.*, 108; *Can. An. Rev. 1937–8*, 32.
[220] *Ibid.*, 114.
[221] *Ibid.*, 114–15.
[222] *Ibid.*, 116.
[223] *Ibid.*, 117.
[224] *Foreign Affairs*, XVII (June 1939), 413; cited Soward, 117–18.
[225] *Commons Debates 1939*, 12 Jan., I, 3.
[226] *Ibid.*, 16 Jan., 23.
[227] *Ibid.*, 53.
[228] *Ibid.*, 23 Jan., 256.
[229] *Ibid.*, 24 Jan., 296–7.
[230] *Ibid.*, 26 Jan., I, 353-4.
[231] *Ibid.*, 30 Jan., I, 472.
[232] *Ibid.*, 473.
[233] *Ibid.*, 30 March, III, 2418.
[234] *Ibid.*, 2419.
[235] *Ibid.*, 2426.
[236] *Ibid.*
[237] *Ibid.*, 2434–40.
[238] *Ibid.*, 31 March, III, 2466.
[239] *Ibid.*, 2468.
[240] *Ibid.*, 2468–9.
[241] *Ibid.*, 2470–1; *L'Action Catholique*, 21 jan. 1939.
[242] *Ibid.*, 3 April, III, 2548.
[243] *Canada Year Book 1945*, 501.

CHAPTER XIV

INDUSTRIALIZATION AND LAURENTIANISM

(1920–39)

IT WAS a new and different Quebec which faced a new and different situation in the postwar Canada of 1920. A region which cherished tradition found itself confronted with drastic political, economic, and social changes which were altering the patterns of the past. These changes brought a basic uneasiness, which showed itself in many ways. As a result of the bitter feeling and isolation of the school and conscription crises, the French Canadians were inclined to question the advantages of a Confederation in whose government they were virtually without representation and of whose population they now supplied little more than a quarter. Despite a remarkably high birthrate, their proportion of the total population had steadily shrunk instead of growing ever since 1867, thanks to immigration into English Canada, and to the exodus from Quebec to the United States.[1] Quebec's population only increased 17.72 per cent from 1911 to 1921, compared to the Canadian average of 21.95 per cent.[2] Emigration to the States once more took on alarming proportions in the postwar years of agricultural and industrial depression.[3]

Population trends showed a profound change within the province, as well as in its position in Confederation. In 1921 for the first time Quebec's population was more urban than rural, and in the following decade the urban population increased 37.13 per cent.[4] Quebec became only slightly less industrialized than Ontario. The agricultural country parishes, the traditional backbone of Quebec society, were sending their sons and daughters to the States or to the cities, where rapid industrialization, brought about by the war and continued in the postwar period, created a vast labor market. Montreal, with its population of 618,506, was the largest city in Canada. One-quarter of Quebec's 10,762 manufacturing establishments were grouped there, representing half the capital invested in industry and employing two-thirds of French-Canadian industrial workers.[5] Though Montreal was the chief magnet for drawing country people, Quebec City's population had increased by one-quarter in the last decade, that of Trois-Rivières had doubled, that of Hull had increased by one-third, that of Sherbrooke by one-half, while Shawinigan had more than doubled in size and Grand'Mère, Chicoutimi, and La Tuque had almost done so. All these towns were industrial centers. Their rapid development was outstripped by the new industrial suburbs of older industrial centers, with Verdun more than doubling its population in the Montreal area and with Cap-de-la Madeleine more than tripling in that of Trois-Rivières. [6]

The wartime industrialization of the province continued in the postwar period at even more rapid a pace, for Quebec felt the depression of 1921 less than any other province of Canada. Though it was affected by the decline of lumber and pulp prices, its leading manufactures—shoes, clothing, cottons, steel, railway rolling stock, tobacco, and refined sugar—found a strong postwar market. [7] This industrial revolution radically altered both Quebec's traditional way of life and the nature of French-Canadian nationalism. [8] It was imposed upon the province largely by English, English-Canadian, and American big business, although a small group of French Canadians proved almost as adroit at exploiting both the natural resources of Quebec and the cheap labor of their compatriots.

Ever since Confederation the provincial government had encouraged the introduction of 'foreign' capital into the province, while only Errol Bouchette at the turn of the century had raised his voice against this process, urging the French Canadians not to neglect industry in their traditional concern with agriculture and colonization. [9] Asselin's and Bourassa's subsequent objections to rapid alienation of Quebec's timber and waterpower resources by the Parent and Gouin regimes had found little popular response, since the French Canadians were not economic-minded, thanks to the neglect of such studies in their traditional educational system and their long exclusion from posts of command in the business world by alien capital and management. The same resources policy, carried on by the Taschereau government from 1920 to 1935, encountered growing opposition as the belated arrival of the industrial revolution upset Quebec's way of life.

With capital and management largely in English-speaking hands, while labor was largely French Canadian, the ethnic feeling aroused by the conscription crisis was heightened by postwar economic developments. The French Canadians were left behind in business and industry, for they lacked both capital and training in economics, engineering, and the physical sciences. They found themselves no longer masters in their own house, and blamed their situation on ethnic discrimination rather than on lack of qualification. The newly industrialized and urbanized *habitant* blamed the trials of his new life not on the industrial system, but on the fact that it was introduced and controlled by aliens. [10] Traditional hatred of *les Anglais*, which had lingered in the folk memory, was thus revived.

This economic invasion of Quebec by cultural aliens produced an economic nationalism. After 1920 the nationalist press came to be characterized more and more by protests against 'foreign exploitation of our natural resources' and agitation in favor of French-Canadian support of French-Canadian business and industry. The old opposition to English Canadians was heightened, while a new anti-Americanism sprang up. During the First World War Canada had become closely integrated into the American economy as Britain was forced to liquidate its holdings in Canada. American capital increasingly replaced English capital, with American management replacing English or English-Canadian management to a lesser extent. In the postwar period this American economic penetration continued until it reached a peak in 1934, with 394 American businesses operating in Quebec, representing one-third of the province's industrial capital.[11] Anti-Semitism also became evident as the Jewish population of the province increased sevenfold from 1901 to 1911, largely in the Montreal area where the new forces were most felt,[12] and as the French Canadians were driven by these newcomers from the small industries and small businesses which had been their economic strongholds, since English and American interests largely monopolized finance and big business.

This new economic nationalism led to the formation of exclusively French-Canadian labor unions, credit unions, farmers' and fishermen's cooperatives, and other efforts to make Quebec's economy more self-sufficient and less dependent upon 'foreign' capital and know-how. It was nourished by bitter opposition to the hitherto prevailing principle that Quebec's commercial exploitation should be conducted upon the basis of as much return as possible for master-race management and as little as possible for subject-people labor. The ethnic division between capital and labor was heightened by management's unwillingness to make concessions to the French-Canadian way of life. Company towns were set up and run on English or American lines in remote parts of the province with a blithe disregard of French-Canadian particularism. The old nineteenth-century practice of paying wages in script good only at company stores where high prices prevailed, so that the worker never got out of debt to the company and labor turnover was eliminated, was abandoned; but other practices were adopted which aroused quite as much resentment, such as demanding work on Sundays and other Church holy days. A host of irritations arising from the friction of two very different mentalities served to keep ethnic feeling alive.

As Quebec belatedly felt the full impact of the industrial revolution, the French Canadians found their minority status intensified. They were now arrayed not only against an English-Canadian majority in Canada, which had imposed its will upon the French Canadians during the war years, but also in opposition to the way of life which prevailed in English-speaking North America, and was now invading Quebec. The French Canadians sought to maintain their own 'Latin' way of life against an 'Anglo-Saxon' materialist one which was favored by great odds. The situation furthered development of the racism involved in nationalist theories imported from Europe by such intellectual leaders as Abbé Lionel Groulx, and almost every French Canadian tended to become in some measure a nationalist. The term 'ultranationalist' will henceforward be used to describe the extremists of the Groulx school; though it must be remembered that the term 'nationalism' is a misnomer for the movement after the First World War, which was an intense provincialism complicated by ethnic and religious factors, rather than the true nationalism professed by Henri Bourassa in his early days, and now largely adopted by forward-looking English Canadians.

The period between the two World Wars was characterized by the growth in Quebec of a narrow nationalism which was increasingly economic rather than political, though the dream of a separate French-Canadian state, 'Laurentia,' haunted some hotheaded minds; while on the other hand a group of deeply patriotic French Canadians sought to meet the challenge of the times by modifying their traditional culture to meet the new conditions brought about by the industrialization of Quebec, and to make common cause with English Canadians upon the basis of a broad Canadian nationalism. From 1917 to 1928 Quebec turned in upon itself; from 1932 onwards it looked more abroad, though still deeply isolationist. The great depression of 1929, from which Canada did not recover until the war boom began in 1939, increased the economic emphasis of French-Canadian nationalism and sharpened the ethnic conflict. Depression, like war, has always set French and English Canadians at odds and strained the structure of Confederation.

I

The new nationalism grew directly out of attacks on the French language in 1905 and 1912 and of the rift between French and English during the First World War. Its chief organ, *L'Action française*, began publication in January 1917 under the editorship of Omer Héroux, who had fledged his pen on *L'Action Catholique*. The new magazine, which described itself as 'a doctrinal and *avant-garde* review, which endeavours to present a comprehensive view of the vital problems of French Canada' and which sought the collaboration of 'all free spirits, all right-thinking men,'[13] was launched by the *Ligue des droits de Français*, which had been founded in March 1913 by the Jesuit Père Joseph-Papin Archambault of the Collège Sainte-Marie in Montreal, after consultation with Omer Héroux and Dr. Joseph Gauvreau. The original group consisted of Père Archambault, Dr. Gauvreau, A.-G. Casault, Henri Auger, Léon Lorrain, and Anatole Vanier. Many of the founders had grown up in the A.C.J.C. movement, with its increasing tendency to inter-mingle political and cultural nationalism with religion, and were disciples of Abbé Groulx, whose zeal surpassed that of their master Henri Bourassa. The group's purpose was to 'assure to the French language the place to which it has a right in the different domains where the French Canadians are active, particularly in commerce and industry.'[14]

Its members bound themselves to use French in business relations, even with English firms, and to give preference to firms which recognized the rights of the French language. Through lectures, pamphlets, a white list of merchants who used French, an editorial and translation service for advertisers, and official protests, the *Ligue* sought to further its end. The founders issued a manifesto:

The movement which we launch is not a movement of provocation, a declaration of war. Our language has its rights, legal and constitutional. We desire that they shall not remain dead letters; above all we desire that our compatriots shall be the first to respect them. And since their abandonment arises most often from indifference, carelessness, and inertia, it is these plagues that the *Ligue* will first attack.[15]

The translation bureau began activity at once, and in June 1913 the *Ligue* published a pamphlet, '*La Langue française au Canada, Faits et réflexions*,' originally written as a series of articles for *Le Devoir* under the pseudonym of 'Pierre Homier' by Père Archambault, with a preface by Dr. Gauvreau. The *Ligue* also issued monthly lists of correct French expressions in various technical fields, and con-stantly intervened with government bodies, business, and individuals in the interest of the French language. Mgr. Paul-Eugène Roy gave his enthusiastic sanction to the work in 1914. In the following year Omer Héroux and Père Guillaume Charlebois, the Oblate provincial, joined the directors of the movement, which found shelter in the Monument National thanks to the Saint-Jean-Baptiste Society of Montreal. Later the *Ligue* occupied larger quarters in the Dandurand Building, with Louis Hurtubise assuming direction of its business affairs and Abbé Groulx replacing Léon Lorrain. Abbé Philippe Perrier took the place of Père Charlebois as the latter became preoccupied with the fight for bilingual schools in Ontario. Gradually the *Ligue's* emphasis shifted from its original attempt to 're-Frenchify' Quebec to a generalized intellectual nationalism.

The guiding spirit of the movement soon became Abbé Groulx, who replaced Héroux as editor of *L'Action française* in the fall of 1920, after taking a leading role in the movement since 1917.[16] In its first three years, under the editorship of Héroux, *L'Action française* published only one provocative article, the Jesuit Père Louis Lalande's '*La Revanche des berceaux*,'[17] which in the midst of the bitter feeling of the time expressed the conviction that the French Canadians would avenge the insults directed against them and their inferior position in that period by their eventual dominance in Canada, thanks to their higher birthrate. This 'revenge of the cradle' idea became a perennial bugaboo for racist-minded English Canadians who saw the surplus French-Canadian population steadily overflowing from Quebec into eastern and northern Ontario and into northern New Brunswick, and gradually becoming dominant there, as they already had in the once English Eastern Townships of Quebec. But for the rest *L'Action française* had published scholarly articles on such topics as 'Our national strength' and on such precursors of intellectual nationalism as Errol Bouchette, Edmond de Nevers, and Jules-Paul Tardivel. A new tone at once became evident when Groulx assumed control of the review, with the publication in September 1920 of Emile Bruchési's '*Si la Confédération disparaissait*,' which envisaged a republic of Eastern Canada in which Quebec predominated.[18] In the three following numbers articles were published opposing the teaching of English on a parity with French in the primary schools, the establishment of a *Maison Canadienne* for both English and French students at Paris, and the attempt to put Canadian history 'on a British footing,' as some disciples of the *bonne entente* movement desired.

Abbé Groulx, gifted with a highly charged eloquence as both writer and speaker, espoused a nationalism very different from that of Henri Bourassa, and sought to divide his compatriots sharply from the English Canadians. During his graduate studies at Fribourg in Switzerland and in Paris he had come under the influence of disciples of the Comte de Gobineau, the eminent nineteenth-century French racist whose doctrines so strongly affected Houston Stewart Chamberlain in England and the Nazi racists who derived from him. Groulx was also greatly influenced by the anti-democratic romantic nationalism of Maurice Barrès and Charles Maurras, and from these sources were borrowed many of the ideas, as well as the name, of the Canadian *L'Action française* movement.

This was a much narrower and headier doctrine than the broad traditional nationalism of Bourassa. Among the bases of this integral nationalism were a cult of the homeland and of the French language, folk hero-worship, Catholicism as a national unifying force, a tendency towards Caesarism or monarchism, and corporatism.

As it developed both in France and Quebec, this nationalism was a breeder of hatred of alien influences: Protestant, 'Anglo-Saxon,' Jewish, Masonic, liberal, republican, and socialist. In France the movement even became anti-papal, after its condemnation by Rome in 1927. In Canada the clerical leaders of the movement were too Catholic for this step—which was a not unnatural development, since Maurras was an agnostic himself, though he believed in Catholicism for the masses. But they carried on the movement in the same tradition, which was a logical development from the old *Castor* ultramontane tradition, continuing to be sympathetic to Maurras' doctrine and merely changing the name of their organ to *L'Action canadienne-française* without shunning the ideas condemned by Rome. The myth of 'Latin' cultural dominance was dear to the French-Canadian minority group which was looked down upon by the dominant English-speaking culture of North America; and bitter opposition to the democratic system came naturally to a people which had been born under French absolutism and which had failed to attain equality with the majority under British parliamentary government.

Groulx himself had grown up a young man when the French language and Quebec itself were under constant attack. He was an early follower of Bourassa, Lavergne, Asselin, Omer Héroux, and a leader of the A.C.J.C.; and when he returned from European studies in 1909 the nationalist tide was beginning to sweep Quebec. Supported by Abbé Emile Chartier, Groulx responded to Bourassa's criticism of French-Canadian history-teaching in *Le Devoir* in 1913. In 1915 he became the first professor of Canadian history at the Université de Montréal. It was almost inevitable, considering his background and environment, that he should see Canadian history as a perpetual struggle between the 'races.' The historical views that he evolved during the bitter war years painted the French Canadians as noble martyrs—unless they were *déraciné* traitors to the 'race'—and the English as harsh tyrants, who seemingly devoted themselves to making a mockery of their professed belief in 'British fair play.' He gradually evolved an heroic myth in which the French Canadians—a proud people—could take pride. He painted the days of New France as a golden age, of which the *habitant* and the *coureur de bois* were the folk heroes. He created the cult of Dollard, the hero of the Long Sault fight against the Iroquois, who became the idol of French-Canadian youth. He maintained that a new French race had been evolved in Canada during the seventeenth and eighteenth centuries, with a providential mission to spread the blessing of Catholicism and French culture.

Groulx's history was dominated by the concept of 'race,' not in an anthropological sense, but in the historical ethnological sense.

To him race was 'of all historical elements the most active, the most absolute [*irréductible*]. When thought to have been drowned, it arises after centuries to vindicate its immortal right. It is more powerful than all other influences combined, save the religious one; it transforms without being transformed; and determines the political, economic, social, and intellectual life of a nation.'[19] He constantly stressed the 'racial' factor, for he believed that 'the reality of our national personality, the profound consciousness of our distinct entity, could maintain our racial instincts, could fortify our will to live.'[20] For him French-Canadian particularism was implied by the facts of history: 'history itself shows it, without preconceived design.'[21] Writing as a passionate partisan, he pictured the development of a singularly pure race which had survived despite the errors of French colonial policy and despite the tyranny of the English conquerors. He made much of the just causes of the Papineau Rebellion, of French-Canadian opposition to Confederation, of the persecution of French-Canadian minorities in educational matters, and of British imperialism. He preached a cult of devotion to history and to the traditions of the race, of racial pride and of opposition to anglo-mania and cultural exoticism.[22]

Groulx summed up his doctrine thus in *L'Action française* in January 1921:

Our doctrine can be contained in this brief formula: we wish to reconstitute the fullness of our French life. We wish to re-find, to reconstitute in its integrity, the ethnic type which France left here and which one hundred and fifty years of history has shaped. We wish to remake an inventory of moral and social forces, which in itself will prepare their flowering. We wish to purify this type of foreign growths in order to develop in it intensively the original culture, to attach to it the new virtues acquired since the Conquest, above all to keep it in intimate contact with the vital sources of its past, in order to let it go henceforth its regular and individual way. And it is this rigorously characterized French type, dependent upon history and geography, having ethnical and psychological hereditary traits, which we wish to continue, on which we base the hope of our future; because a people, like all growing things, can develop only what is in itself, only the forces whose living germ it contains.

This germ of a people was one day profoundly stricken in its life; it was constrained, paralysed in its development. The consequences of the Conquest weighed heavily upon it; its laws, its language were hamstrung; its intellectual culture was long hobbled; its system of education, deviated in some of its parts, sacrificed more than was fitting to English culture; its natural domain was invaded, leaving it only partially master of its economic forces; its private and public customs were contaminated by the Protestant and Saxon atmosphere. A distressing make-up has gradually covered the physiognomy of our cities and towns, an implacable sign of the subjection of souls to the law of the conqueror.

This evil of the Conquest was aggravated after 1867 by the evil of federalism. Confederation may have been a political necessity; it may have promoted great material progress; for a time, it may even have given Quebec a greater measure of autonomy. But it could not prevent the system from turning notable influences against us. Our particular situation in the federal alliance, the isolation of our Catholic and French province amidst eight provinces in majority English and Protestant, the imbalance of forces which ensued, sometimes increased by the hostile policy of some rulers, led federal legislation little by little towards principles or acts which endangered our fundamental interests. The political system of our country, such as it is by way of being applied, leads not to unity but straight to uniformity. The dominant ideas at the present time at the seat of the central government tend to restrict from year to year the domain of the French language, to undermine secretly the autonomy of our social, religious, and even political institutions. It suffices to recall the battles so long waged here to maintain respect for the clauses of the federal pact relative to French, the recently projected laws on divorce, the suppression for federal employees of many of our religious holidays, the attempts to make uniform law and education, and finally the multiple assaults directed against our province and denounced by none other than the premier of Quebec, the Honorable Alexandre Taschereau, in his speech of November 22, 1920 at the Hotel Viger. So many symptoms, so many undeniable facts which suffice to explain the regressions of national personality among us and the very large part which *L'Action française* has given and must long give to works of pure defence.[23]

In addition to this negative program, Abbé Groulx proposed to strengthen French-Canadian culture by drawing upon 'the two greatest sources of life,' Rome and France:

For our intellectual élite we ask Roman culture and French culture. The first will give us masters of truth, those who furnish the spiritual rules, which make shine on high the principles without which there is no firm direction, no intangible social basis, no permanent order, no people assured of its goal. In the natural order, the culture of France, the immortal educator of our thoughts, will achieve the perfecting of our minds. And when we speak of French culture, we mean not in the limited sense of literary culture, but in the broad and elevated sense in which the French mind appears to us as an incomparable master of clarity, order, and subtlety, the creator of the sanest and most humane civilization, the highest expression of intellectual health and mental balance. And equally we mean not an initiation which leads to dilettantism or to alienization, but a culture which serves without servility, which safeguards our traditional attitudes before the truth, which become a real and beneficent force, will permit our next élite to apply itself more vigorously to the solution of our problems, to the service of its race, its country, and its faith.[24]

The élite, like the people, would be saved from alienization by mixing with Roman and French sources those nearer sources which embodied 'the substance of our past and our traditions.'

For emphasis upon history was an essential element of Groulx's nationalism:

By history, which maintains the continuity between the generations, which carries from one to the other, like a river, the accumulated flood of virtues of the race, a people remains in constant and present possession of its moral richness. By history we experience for ourselves, as Charles Maurras says, how 'no living being, no precise reality is worth the activity and latent power of the collective will of our ancestors'; and by it their pressure, their imperious directions, which will push us towards the future. From history we shall learn the aptitudes of our people; it will tell us by the observance of what laws, of what exigencies of the intimate nature of the people, they must today be governed, be initiated to new developments, to evolutions which do not bring ephemeral and false prosperity but which are adapted to life as to teething rings. Finally by history will remain joined to our souls the whole of our traditions, at least those which contain life and are only the prolongment of the soul of our ancestors. Traditions, like language, though less perfectly, are a sign of the race, and by that very fact an element of survival. Must we see there anything except a series of actions by ancestors issuing from their most profound ways of thinking, from their sentimental attitudes before the great objects of life, actions so strongly linked to their intimate and collective soul that they have ended by being established as customs, as permanent gestures? And what is there to say, if not that by history will be restored to us in its fullness the fundamental being of the nationality, which must be sought and which we need to re-find?[25]

As the goal of national action Groulx set the ideal of being 'a Catholic and Latin people, of being absolutely and stubbornly ourselves, the sort of race created by history and desired by God.'[26]

In his watchword of 'rester d'abord nous-mêmes' ('remaining first of all ourselves'), Groulx found nothing in conflict with the spirit of Confederation. 'The more we preserve our French and Catholic virtues, the more faithful we remain to our history and traditions, the more we remain the element impermeable by the American spirit, the strongest element of order and stability.'[27] But the French Canadians wanted no alliance in which they incurred all the sacrifices and all the dangers, while all the honors and all the profits went to English Canadians. Groulx thought his people should conserve their aspirations, sacred rights, and strength, so that if Confederation broke down or was reconstructed on a new basis, and they had to choose between imperial absorption or annexation to the States, or if a French state arose, they would be able to face their destiny.

There was always a current of separatism in Groulx's thoughts despite his repeated denials of the charge. He had been an impressionable adolescent in the day of Mercier and Riel; frequent references in his work to Jules-Paul Tardivel's *Pour la Patrie* (1895) indicate the influence of that exalted separatist novel upon him; and he evolved his views on Canadian history during the bitter war years when Quebec stood opposed to the English-speaking provinces. For him the French Canadians possessed most of the essential attributes of a nation, and their attainment of political independence would be a normal part of their coming of age as a people. In the first postwar years the British Empire seemed to many observers to be breaking up, with the Irish, Egyptian, and Indian troubles and an anti-imperialist Labor government in power for the first time. Meanwhile free-trade Western Canada was at swordpoints with the protectionist East, and the school and conscription questions had arrayed English against French. The breakup of Confederation thus seemed inevitable to Groulx in 1922, when he launched a symposium on '*Notre Avenir National*' ('Our national future') in *L'Action française*, whose conclusion was unmistakably separatist.

The annual symposiums constitute the most valuable and most revealing work of the *Action française* movement, but before turning to them it would be well to examine the early work of the man who inspired them and, amid all the wealth of talent he attracted, remained the dominating influence.

Abbé Lionel Groulx had already made a notable place for himself in French-Canadian life when he became director of *L'Action française* in 1920. He was born at Vaudreuil in 1878 and educated at the Séminaire de Sainte-Thérèse and the Grand Séminaire in Montreal. His ancestors had long lived in the region; his father, who had been a lumberjack and a seasonal worker in New York State, as well as a farmer, died the year he was born, but his mother, thanks to an early remarriage, was able to maintain her family of four. Young Lionel early showed more interest in books than in farming, and was sent to college with the idea of studying for the priesthood.

At college he read widely, becoming an impassioned admirer of Louis Veuillot, Joseph de Maistre, and Montalembert.[28] From Garneau, Ferland, and the *Jesuit Relations* he derived a knowledge of Canadian history, and a patriotism which made him lead a student's revolt against the subject oddly set for competition for the Prince of Wales Prize in 1897: the speech of a Puritan in the General Court of Massachusetts in favor of Shirley's proposed expedition against Louisbourg, 'to promote the interests of the colonies, to humiliate the French name, and above all to combat the hated religion of Papism.'[29]

Torn between the priesthood and the law, the vocations of his idols Lacordaire and Montalembert, the young man decided in favor of the former. His four years at the Grand Séminaire in Montreal were broken by a period as secretary to Bishop Emard of Valleyfield, and by teaching at the Séminaire de Valleyfield, where he first displayed his ability to inspire youth. Maxime Raymond and Jules Fournier were among his pupils in rhetoric. Then in 1906 Groulx went to Rome for further studies, winning his doctorate in philosophy in 1907 and in theology in 1908. His third year abroad he spent studying letters at Fribourg in Switzerland, after passing the summer in Brittany as chaplain to Admiral de Cuverville, who had known Montalembert, Lacordaire, and Veuillot, and was a highly conservative Catholic who thought that Canada should not send its young men to study in a contaminated France.[30]

At Fribourg Groulx acquired an acquaintance with historical techniques from Père Mandonnet, a Dominican church historian, but devoted most of his time to the study of French literature under Pierre-Maurice Masson and to the preparation of a thesis on French-Canadian speech. After a short stay at the Sorbonne and the Institut Catholique in Paris, he returned home, resuming his teaching at Valleyfield in the fall of 1909. There he formed a Catholic Action group, and became known as a radical for his emphasis on lay participation in that movement and for his support of Bourassa. After *Le Devoir* had sharply criticized the teaching of Canadian history, Groulx spent four months at the Ottawa Archives during the winter of 1913–14 with the idea of preparing a new manual of Canadian history.

The following fall he left the diocese of Valleyfield, bailiwick of Laurier's moderate friend Bishop Emard, for that of Montreal, where his nationalist friends sought to secure a post for him in the university's faculty of letters. So far he had published only a tract on social duties, a monograph on Valleyfield (1913), and *Une Croisade d'Adolescents* (1912), an account of the origin of the A.C.J.C. When the lone Frenchman who then constituted the entire faculty of letters at the University was called home by the outbreak of the war, Groulx became professor of history at Montreal, while his friend Abbé Emile Chartier became professor of Canadian literature.

Groulx began his lectures in November 1915 on the topic of '*Nos luttes constitutionnelles*,' the period from 1791 to 1837, winning a wide audience from outside the university thanks to the publicity of *Le Devoir*. He was the first professor of Canadian history in the French universities since the death of Abbé Ferland fifty years before. A supplementary post as professor of history at the Ecole des Hautes Etudes Commerciales led him to attach more importance to economic history than any previous French-Canadian historian had done.

Learning his profession by himself for lack of a master and keeping his researches just ahead of his lectures, he dealt with the constitutional struggle up to 1867 in 1916–17, the Confederation period in 1917–18, the French period in 1918–19 and the immediate post-Conquest period in 1919–20, and that between 1774–91 in 1920–21. His five annual lectures on each topic were published in pamphlet form at the end of each academic year and widely circulated.[31] Their combative tone and stirring eloquence made Groulx the idol of nationalist youth and of many elders who had retreated into nationalism in a Quebec isolated from the rest of Canada by the school and conscription questions.

Olivar Asselin made the first and perhaps the best criticism of Groulx's work in a lecture to students at the Salle Saint-Sulpice in Montreal on February 15, 1923 which was later reprinted as a pamphlet. He singled out the fact that Groulx was the first French-Canadian historian to prefer the French period to the English one, and to exalt its institutions over later British ones. Groulx gave a new emphasis to the well-worn story, seeking in his own words 'to discover, under the pile of facts, the evolution of the young race, the social conditions manifested by it. . . . The least revelations of the old forms of the past, of the *petite histoire* of the ancestors, bring us higher satisfaction than any other discovery.'[32] In '*Les Lendemains de la conquête*,' '*Vers l'émancipation*,' '*Les Luttes constitutionnelles*,' and '*La Confédération*' Groulx subsequently depicted 'the frightful misfortune' which the Conquest had brought upon the French Canadians, destroying education, the *seigneurs*, the system of colonization, and corrupting the system of justice. The English regime, in its partiality for commerce, had neglected agriculture, paving the way for the later exodus to the cities and to the States. In the administration of justice, in legislation, commerce, and industry, a frightful jargon was substituted for French. As the only offsets to these disadvantages the English regime had introduced English criminal law and parliamentary government. The brief period of liberty attained in 1848 was followed by Confederation, which inaugurated an era of abdications and defeats from the point of view of French Catholics.

Asselin criticized Groulx for his unrealistic denial of the charge that the French Canadians had Indian blood, for painting the early French Canadians in too glowing colors, and for his attacks on French policy in the last years of the French regime. Asselin himself held that 'all good that we have we owe to France; all that menaces us comes from Anglo-Saxon societies.'[33] But he defended Groulx's history against Gustave Lanctot's charges of partisanship, preconceived judgments, doctored documents, and faked references. To Groulx historical impartiality was not neutrality:

History is a moral act, consequently not free of the supreme finalities. Our ambition and our right are to write and teach as a Catholic and French Canadian should. The historian ought to work with his whole personality; if he makes it neutral and indifferent, let us say with Bossuet that he abdicates his quality as a man.[34]

Asselin opposed to Groulx's partisan nationalism the serene loyalism of Thomas Chapais. Both historians believed in the intervention of Providence in human affairs, but Providence for Chapais was 'a gentleman who drank ale, ate roastbeef, did much business—a "great, a roaring business"—and occupied his leisure like a good giant by freeing peoples, after teasing them a bit to find out what they were good for.' Chapais had the 'timorous spirit of the men of his generation' in defending his language and his faith, to which he was nonetheless much attached; and since he was the son of one of the Fathers of Confederation, the pact was doubly sacred to him. To Asselin 'the English of Chapais were men we have never seen except in books; those of Groulx, with their Jekyll-and-Hyde double personality, are those that we have known since our childhood.'[35]

Asselin criticized Groulx for faults of style in the shape of anglicisms and barbarisms, for errors of grammar and spelling, and for echoing French authors, particularly Barrès. But he praised him for emphasizing the anonymous figures of history, for his gift of evoking eloquently the atmosphere and background of past periods. For him Groulx's work was 'the finest element among French-Canadian intellectual assets.'[36] He approved Groulx's view of the Conquest as a great catastrophe rather than as a providential happening, as the loyalist historians saw it; his theory of a French-Canadian defeatist psychology arising from the parasitical role then thrust upon the *seigneurs*; and his repudiation of 'the historical imposture of a liberal and maternal England which treated us as the spoiled children of its empire.'[37] Asselin found valid Groulx's analysis of French-Canadian defeatism, with 'its spontaneous faith in the superiority of the conqueror, his customs, his institutions; ... its self-distrust, its doubts of its own strength, its scorn of its fellows and of the ethnic genius; ... its morbid taste for peace without dignity, the easy forgetfulness of injuries which it accepts as the pay of its condition, its valet-like mentality in its own home; instead of the proud movement towards the restorations which efface defeat, the desire to make the defeat complete by total abdication; in short, its likeness to a senseless tree, bent by the storm, which has only the stupid obsession to fall.'[38] To Groulx the French Canadians, alienized by 'political and moral colonialism, reinforced by the dualism of a federated country,'[39] needed to regain consciousness of their racial personality and racial pride.

But he had high hopes for the future:

After a long period of indifference and lethargy, we witness an incomparable awakening of the race . . . Let us leave aside extravagant hopes and fix on solid reality. And the reality is the fact that we are two million French Canadians in the Dominion of Canada. We have an impregnable foothold in the province of Quebec; we occupy a territory with geographical unity, we have all the wealth of the soil, all the channels of communication, all the outlets to the sea, all the resources which assure the strength and independence of a nation. We can, if we wish, if we develop all the powers of our race and our soil, become strong enough to lend vigorous assistance to our dispersed brethren . . . The future and Providence are going to work for us. Joseph de Maistre wrote, on the morrow of the French Revolution, that God made such terrible clean sweeps only to lay bare the bases of the future. Let us believe with firm faith that after the vast disorder of the Great War there will be room for marvellous constructions. We make only this prayer to our leaders and to all the chiefs of our race: know how to foresee and to act. Grant that they may no more abandon the development of our life to improvisation and to incoherent action; that for the vanity of a too largely Canadian patriotism they may not sacrifice us to the dream of an impossible unity; that they may know how to reserve the future; that before concluding and deciding our destinies, they may take account of the premises of our history; and then God will not let perish that which he has conserved by so many miracles.[40]

By his historical work Groulx established himself as an ultranationalist of a radicalism hitherto unknown in Quebec. More realistic and more gifted than Jules-Paul Tardivel, he carried on the ultramontane tradition and gave it a racist, separatist bent. How far this tendency really went was revealed in a novel, *L'Appel de la Race*, which Groulx published in 1922 under the pseudonym of 'Alonie de Lestres.' It was both romantic and written to serve a thesis, and was accused of being a *roman à clef*. It was the story of one Jules de Lantagnac, a bilingual M.P. and ornament of the Ottawa bar, who had become '*déraciné*' thanks to the English atmosphere of Ottawa and to his English-Canadian wife. One of the parliamentary leaders in the fight for the separate schools—while the action takes place from 1914 to 1916, there is no mention of the war, though much of the school conflict—he finally reverts to type, and under the spiritual guidance of an Oblate confessor puts loyalty to his race above loyalty to his family, which he abandons.

The book is a clever tract against anglicization, assimilative influences, and marriages mixed in either blood or religion; as well as a rather good dramatization of the school question in personal terms. It is permeated with intransigent nationalism and racism and with frequent comparisons drawn from the history of other minority peoples. The novel was bitterly attacked by Louvigny de Montigny in *La Revue Moderne*, as spokesmen for the French Canadians of

Ottawa, and by Mgr. Camille Roy in *Le Canada Français*, as spokesman for loyalist Quebec. René du Roure, a Frenchman teaching at McGill, also assailed it in *La Revue Moderne*. But the book was a popular success, and its curious theology was defended in *L'Action française*[41] by none other than the future Cardinal Villeneuve, then a young Oblate theologian who had been Groulx's traveling companion on a trip to Acadia in 1914 and who had taken an active part in the Ottawa school agitation.

Two minor works, *Rapaillages* (1916) and *Chez nos Ancêtres* (1920), were prose poems devoted to hymning the good old pastoral days of French Canada in the manner of the *terroir* school launched by Adjutor Rivard. They were sentimentalizations of a rural life which had no appeal for Groulx himself as a child,[42] but which he, in common with other leaders of the intellectual élite, later idealized as the best life for the masses of French Canada. Groulx's early interest in French Canadianisms led him to dot his text with italicized *patois* expressions, an irritating practice to all but the most narcissistic admirers of French-Canadian culture. As Asselin pointed out, Groulx produced his best regionalist work in the course of his historical writings rather than in these minor efforts.

Finally Groulx exercised a considerable effect by his public lectures on patriotic topics, of which perhaps the most notable in early days were '*Pour L'Action française*' in 1918, '*Si Dollard revenait*' in 1919, and '*Méditation Patriotique*' in 1920.[43] He largely took Bourassa's place as the leading French-Canadian orator on patriotic occasions, and during a year of study in Paris in 1921-2 he won a reputation for eloquence which later gained him an invitation to give a course on the French in Canada at the Sorbonne in 1931. Outraged by French ignorance of Canada, he created a committee in Paris to further relations between the intellectuals of France and French Canada, and gave many lectures on French-Canadian history. The most notable, that of February 2, 1922, was printed as a pamphlet by the French *L'Action française*.[44] Upon his return home, he, like Bourassa before him, undertook oratorical pilgrimages to Franco-American and other outlying French-Canadian minority centers, seeking to promote a reunion of the 'race.'[45]

2

The most solid of the long series of influential annual symposiums conducted in *L'Action française* was the first, that of 1921 on '*Les Problèmes économiques*.' The war, the postwar depression, and the census of that year served to focus French-Canadian nationalist opinion on the economic question for the first time in serious fashion.

Edouard Montpetit, the first thoroughly trained French-Canadian economist, who had pioneered in the inauguration of economic courses at the Ecole des Hautes Etudes Commerciales after his return from Paris in 1910, opened the discussion with an article on '*L'Indépendence économique des Canadiens-Francais*,' the fruit of his fifteen years study of the question. He singled out the fact that, thanks largely to the war, the French Canadians had at last become economic-minded. He argued that it was not a question of sacrificing the intellectual to the material factor. Today the French Canadians had to assure the material basis of a more intense intellectual life; it was time to replace the old cries of '*Emparons-nous du sol*' and '*Emparons-nous de l'industrie*,' by that of '*Emparons-nous de la science et de l'art*.'[46] To the old political threats had been added the new menace of commercial imperialism, and French Canada must adapt itself to the new order or die.

Montpetit maintained that French Canada was richer than it believed, but not rich enough for its needs. History and geography should be taught in the primary schools so as to instill a knowledge of the fundamentals of Quebec's economy. Technical schools should train workers and artisans, while advanced schools produced specialists. These last should give attention to sociology, economics, and political science, as well as to history and philosophy. There should be a provincial minister of commerce and industry to further economic development. In addition to the exploitation of the soil, there should be exploitation of waterpower and the forests. Quebec had the manpower, the capital, and the intelligence required for modern industry. Mines, forests, and waterpower exploitation must be left to great capitalists; but Quebec could produce much more of what it consumed in food, clothing, lodging, and meet its higher intellectual, artistic, and moral needs. Montpetit urged that French Canadians should buy their own products, their own art. French-Canadian credit and financial institutions deserved support, so that they in turn could favor the development of French-Canadian businesses. In short, 'let us enrich ourselves in order to make our innate Frenchness shine forth, so that the money question may no longer retard our will and the satisfaction of our noblest ends.'

In March Olivar Asselin pointed out '*Les Lacunes de notre organization économique*': the alienation by politicians in the past of waterpower and timber resources, the need for colonization of new areas in Quebec and Ontario, the improvement of agriculture, more credit for industry, emphasis on training industrial chemists, development of banks and insurance firms, and above all less defeatism in economic matters. In April Emile Miller, Université de Montréal geographer whose career was cut short by premature death, discussed the natural resources of the province. In June Georges Pelletier of *Le*

Devoir traced the history of Quebec's industrial development, emphasizing the extent to which it was due to English Canadians and Americans and calling for the development of French-Canadian industries to meet the needs of the province. In July Léon Lorrain discussed French-Canadian business; in August Beaudry Leman the banking institutions; and in September Henry Laureys commercial and technical education. Omer Héroux dealt with the insurance companies in October, while in November J.-E. Gendreau urged higher scientific education in the French-Canadian universities.

Abbé Groulx summoned up the symposium in December, calling for an economic nationalism:

It will be the duty of the rising generation, if it wishes to attain the potent fruits of its fortune, to cause it to be admitted that the ethnic being of the Quebec State has been long fixed in irrevocable fashion. A history now three hundred years long, the nearly complete possession of the soil by a determined race, the profound imprint that this race has given it by its original manners and institutions, the special status reserved for it by all the political constitutions since 1791, have made of Quebec a French State that must be recognized in theory as well as in fact. It is this truth which must be replaced on high in order that it may govern the economic order amongst us, as one spontaneously admits it should govern the other functions of our lives. Let us say that we should cease to think like vanquished and conquered people. Together we shall rather raise our thoughts to the reality of the homeland, towards this central idea which will put order and strength into our action. It will give us the noble sentiment of respect that we owe to ourselves; better than all speeches, it will make us prefer the role of architects and builders to that of masons and hired men. And in our own house we shall do otherwise than prepare the lion's share for a rival. [47]

Groulx was never again able to muster so notable a collection of French-Canadian leaders for his annual surveys as in 1921, and younger and more hotheaded writers later replaced some of the distinguished figures who took part in the discussion of '*Les Problèmes économiques*.' The latent nationalism that every French Canadian carries within himself comes to the surface in time of economic or political crisis; in such periods the rampant individualism and back-biting tendencies which are part of the national temperament yield to a 'sacred union,' which temporarily provides a truce in what Mercier called 'our fratricidal conflicts.' In 1921 French Canada was isolated from English Canada by the bitter aftermath of the school and conscription questions, and by a postwar depression which affected French-Canadian labor more deeply than English-Canadian or American capital and management. With the easing of ethnic tension and the rapid improvement of the economic situation,

French-Canadian nationalism once more became a minority radical movement rather than a mass national movement; and Groulx and his followers were criticized by many of the staider leaders of a people which has a fundamental devotion to the golden mean and to moderation as the governing principles of life.

The radical nationalism already implicit in Groulx's earlier work, which found expression in his conclusion to the 1921 symposium, was made clearly evident in *L'Action's* symposium of 1922 on '*Notre Avenir politique.*' In an introduction Groulx stressed that Confederation 'was headed inevitably towards a breakup. . . . The issue appears certain to the most clearsighted minds; only the due date remains still unknown.'[48] Groulx protested that he had no desire to destroy Confederation or to wound anyone's sense of duty. But it was the duty of the French Canadians to prepare for a future announced by 'unmistakable signs.' Then, as a starting point for the symposium, Groulx took Bourassa's prediction of 1901 in *Grande-Bretagne et Canada* that Canada, torn between British and American imperialism, would have to develop sufficient strength to preserve the *status quo*, 'the greatest good fortune for our people,' or be led towards a new destiny, and in any case must be prepared to meet the decisive hour. He carefully defended himself from any charge of desiring to disturb the *status quo*, 'whatever harm colonialism or federalism may do us.'[49] But by all appearances it was going to be shattered in the near future. Europe was declining, while a Pan-American continentalism was developing without Canadian participation. Europe was becoming an economic colony of America. The British Empire, troubled in Ireland, Egypt, and India, was being eclipsed by the United States, whose rivalry with Japan in the Pacific might hasten the breakup of the empire. Groulx asked frankly whether British imperialism was not 'an organization of peoples which has become artificial, an outworn political formula, unable to sustain the shock of approaching realities.'[50]

The Canadian Confederation seemed equally threatened, with free-trade West aligned against protectionist East in the elections of 1921, and racial rivalry, aroused by the war, temporarily subject to a truce dictated by commercial and political interest, and by 'the salutary fear momentarily dictated to yesterday's enemies by the strength of Quebec.'[51] For Groulx the 'saddening truth is that in spite of transitory appeasement, the attitude of the French Canadians to the federal power and the Anglo-Saxon majority remains none the less an attitude of always uneasy and in no way superfluous vigilance.' For twenty years the French language had been treated by the federal government in a fashion which was a most disloyal repudiation of the federal pact, and continued to be so treated despite proclamations of *bonne entente*. In most of the English-

Université de Montréal

The new building on Mount Royal, begun in 1926 and finished in 1941, after plans by Ernest Cormier. The greatest monument of the School of Imitation which began a century before, following French rather than native models (I.O.A.P.Q.)

School Yard

Oil painting (1941) by Jean-Charles Faucher (b. 1907). A Brueghel-like study of the recreation period at a Christian Brothers school. (Quebec Provincial Museum.)

Street Scene

Oil painting (c. 1940) by Jean-Charles Faucher. Another study of city life by one of the best Montreal painters. (Quebec Provincial Museum.)

speaking provinces the government had followed the tendency of all federations by encouraging uniformity by all means, including arbitrary force. Not only was there an absolute opposition between the races on the interpretation of the pact of 1867, but the same opposition existed on the relations of Canada with the empire, with the 'Anglo-Saxons' inclined almost unanimously towards imperialism and the French Canadians 'irreducible autonomists.'

Other forces favored the centrifugal action created by the too vast extent of Confederation: lack of geographical continuity, the Americanization of the Canadian West by immigration from the south, tended to create in Canada 'two peoples sharply separated by geography and by ideals, two states of a civilization as diverse as possible.'[52] Edmond de Nevers had foreseen a reorganization of the United States along ethnic lines, while economists foretold that new federative states would arise on the basis of economic unity rather than of such arbitrary geographic divisions as those of Canada. Groulx cited Premier Taschereau's observation on April 17, 1921, that Canada was at the crossroads between preservation of the *status quo* or the breakup of Confederation, annexation to the United States or independence. Nationalization of the railroads which bound Canada together had saved the Western provinces from bankruptcy, but had thrown a burden which threatened to be too heavy upon the old provinces of the East. It was a question to Taschereau whether this was not the first wide breach in the pact of Confederation. Therefore Groulx argued that Quebec must prepare for the future establishment of an Eastern Canada.

He did not believe in economic or geographical determinism; he held that history was determined by the foresight and the will of men in accordance with the plan of Providence. It was 'a people's duty to seek the historic vocation in which it could collaborate most perfectly with God's designs.'[53] The position which the French-Canadian people occupied on a territory which it had made its homeland by three hundred years of effort seemed to indicate for it a separate destiny. Homogeneous in race and faith, grouped by powerful traditions, and possessor of a territory greater than that of many European states, its very situation seemed to offer a separate future designed by Providence. Its providential mission called it to preserve its soul uncontaminated and unfettered in the nationhood to which aspired all nationalities that wished to be absolute masters of their lives. The dream of a French-Canadian nation was an old one which dated back to the Conquest and had ever since 'haunted the spirit of the race.'[54] To Groulx this dream was no artificial creation provoked by an élite of intellectuals and propagandists, but 'the spontaneous manifestation of a national life maintained to a certain degree of perfection, the soul of a history in which the ardent conflict of races had been prolonged in a chronic state.' Nations grew up where human groups were opposed most violently by their family and social institutions, by the geographical diversity of their territories, and above all by their ethnic differences:

Wherever a human collectivity, conscious of its life and of its moral patrimony, finds itself one day obliged to tremble for the possession or the integrity of its heritage, then a pressing instinct of conservation impels it to put its patrimony out of danger. Of itself, by a force more powerful than its will, it tears itself free from oppressive tutelage, seeks the conditions of existence which will procure its security, organizes itself as a state.[55]

On this reasoning Groulx based his support for the creation of a French state in Eastern Canada if Confederation broke up. He did not invoke the principle of the self-determination of nationalities, but rather the elementary right of a people to prepare a self-chosen destiny with the aid of God. He minimized the danger of such a step for the French Canadians of the other provinces, for whom the *Québécois* felt a solidarity which transcended political bonds. The new state must be based upon political and economic geography; it must safeguard the rights of the ethnic enclaves which would be found within it; much planning and forethought would be necessary. He favored a definitive solution of the problem rather than a transition by way of Canadian independence, American annexation, or adherence to a smaller Confederation. The aspirations of the French-Canadian people must be fixed on the political ideal which was the ultimate goal of its life. 'To be ourselves, absolutely ourselves, to constitute, as soon as Providence wishes it, an independent French state, such should be henceforward the aspiration which should animate our labors, the torch which must no more be extinguished.'[56] Groulx set this goal particularly for French-Canadian youth, 'the architect and worker of great things,' as a principle to guide its action.

Louis Durand saw Canada as a conquered country which had become an autonomous colony, obliged to defend only its own territory and on its way to independence. Then its normal political evolution had been interrupted by Chamberlain's imperialism, which had led it to contribute men and money to the South African War; then to sacrifice legions and millions in the World War; and finally to guarantee the territorial integrity of the empire in the four quarters of the globe. Durand examined in turn the present colonial status of Canada and whether it was worth maintaining; whether the bonds of empire were unbreakable; whether Quebec would be justified in repudiating Confederation if Canada separated from the empire; and what solutions remained for Quebec besides annexation to the States, or the constitution of an independent Eastern Canada with Quebec as the nucleus. He traced out imperial developments since 1910, and found Canada enmeshed in a new imperialism with authority inevitably centralized in London unless the British Empire broke up. But allegiance to the King was now the sole bond of an empire which seemed to be disintegrating at home and abroad, and the 'Anglo-Saxons' of Canada were willing to break that last bond over a simple question of dollars and cents.

Durand was skeptical as to the future of Confederation, in which the new Canadian nationality born at Confederation had been swamped by immigration and crushed by imperialism. French and English were still unable to agree on the interpretation of the basic contract which united them, while the Western provinces were opposed to the Eastern ones on the great questions of free trade, transportation, natural resources, and immigration. A minority constantly on the defensive at Ottawa, which had lost cultural ground decisively in 1872, 1890, 1892, 1896, 1905, and 1912, French Canada had no right to make further sacrifices to prevent the inevitable breakup of Confederation. Annexation and immersion in the American melting-pot were repulsive to 'a people who had three hundred years of existence; its own customs, traditions, language, and religion.'[57] Durand envisaged the formation of an independent Eastern Canada, uniting Quebec and the Maritimes with certain territory to the West, and embracing four or five million inhabitants. This predominantly French state would be linked together by the community of language and faith of the French Canadians and Acadians, and by the tolerance and sincere love of the homeland exhibited by the English Maritimers. It could draw upon the essential resources of wheat, iron, and coal, in addition to its agriculture, fisheries, and timber. All that remained was the task of national organization, defined by Maurras as the ordering of its life and the application of this order to its action.

Abbé Arthur Robert of the Séminaire de Québec provided a theological justification for the 'Aspirations du Canada Français,' demonstrating that 'a people has the right to the development and the perfecting of its nationality,' and that 'a people has even the right to seek complete autonomy, and if possible, the sovereignty of a State.'[58] The abbé maintained that nationality was based upon origin, language, territory, and government, while unity of blood and language were more essential than unity of territory and government. In the event of a breaking of the British connection through no fault of their own, the French Canadians would be justified in either trying to preserve Confederation, in annexing themselves to the United States, or in founding a French state. The question was a moot one, but the abbé concluded that the French Canadians would have a perfect right to found an independent state, 'destined to carry on in America what has so well been called the providential mission of the French race.'

In an article on '*L'Etat Français et les Etats-Unis*' Anatole Vanier urged an alliance of Quebec financiers, merchants, and industrialists with the advocates of a French state. The economic independence of Quebec was a prerequisite of its political independence. The commercial superiority of the United States was due to cheap products; Quebec should seek to produce both cheap and quality goods. The exploitation of Quebec's natural resources by Americans should be prohibited by law; not only exportation of raw materials but their fabrication within the province. With the aid of the government of Quebec, control of its own industry must be won. A new wave of American economic imperialism was threatened by the proposed internationalization of the St. Lawrence, after the inroads already made in the pulp and asbestos industries. He argued that Quebec, with its supply of these raw materials, could obtain an American tariff favoring its agricultural producers, its stock raisers, and its consumers. With its favorable balance of trade, it could maintain favorable foreign commercial relations. The sympathy and racial solidarity of France and Latin America with Quebec would further the development of commercial relations. The establishment of a French state would heighten the prestige of the Franco-Americans, while through cultural relations an old moral alliance could be reasserted for the benefit of French civilization in America. To Vanier the failure of Confederation was complete from the point of view of the French Canadians, and both messianic and economic considerations led him to believe in the eventual establishment of a French state. [59]

Emile Bruchési discussed '*L'Etat Français et l'Amérique Latine*,' taking as a starting point Tardivel's dream in 1895 of the foundation in 1945 of a republic of New France, 'whose mission will be to continue on this American soil the work of Christian civilization which Old France has so long pursued with such glory during so many centuries.' [60] He considered the influence Tardivel assigned to Freemasonry exaggerated, but on the whole he thought Tardivel had seen clearly into a future which was already announced by the breakup of the empire and of Confederation. He pointed out that Alexander Galt had anticipated Canadian independence in 1869, and that hence the French Canadians were free to envisage a French state. Such a state would be welcomed by the United States, which would be glad to see the British flag banished from North America; but against the covetous greed of the 'Giant of the North' French Canada must look for allies in Latin America. In this Latin New World were numerous opponents of the 'Anglo-Saxon' civilization of the United States, 'cousins by blood, by race, by mentality, but unknown cousins who do not know us.'[61] Canada was at last becoming known in Latin America through investments, shipping, and commerce; and thanks to its own industries Quebec could supply manufactured goods which the Latin American countries wanted in exchange for their raw materials. Bruchési urged that cultural and commercial relations with Latin America should be developed by Quebec, which through cultivating its natural allies there could make Tardivel's dream come true.

The Oblate Père Rodrigue Villeneuve considered the problem of the French-Canadian minorities outside Quebec in '*Nos Frères de la Dispersion*,' finding that they had nothing to gain by the continuation of Confederation and that they would remain united by religious and patriotic ties to a French Catholic state, which would be the 'torch of an idealistic and generous civilization in the great whole being shaped by the American future . . . an Israel of the new age in the midst of the Babylon now being formed, an American France, a light and an apostle among nations.'[62]

Georges Pelletier dealt more realistically with '*Les Obstacles économiques à l'indépendence du Canada Français*.' Foreigners of another language and race had taken over most of French Canada's patrimony of natural resources, leaving only agriculture to the natives, who were already deserting their fields to become rootless proletarians in the cities. The English, the Americans, and the Jews prospered in Quebec, while the French Canadians were reduced to serving them. Much of Quebec's forestland was already looted and could not be reforested. Other portions, rented rather than sold outright, might be preserved by regulation of cutting and by reforesting. In remote regions there were still unexploited woodlands, which should be preserved for the future rather than disposed of to foreigners. Quebec's asbestos and other mineral deposits should be protected against exportation in the raw state by foreigners, as wood had finally been, and should be rented only for short periods. The resources of New Quebec (Ungava) should be preserved for future generations of French Canadians. Waterpower should be subject to regulation, and in the future leased only to Canadian companies. An inventory of all natural resources should be made in order that they might be sanely developed in the interests of the people.

Pelletier echoed the conclusions of the 1921 symposium on Quebec's industry, stressing the need of self-sufficiency and the industrialization of agriculture and the soil. By creating a class of French-Canadian technicians and by supporting French-Canadian businesses, Quebec could defend itself against the Americanization already threatening Canadian industry. He singled out the danger of the concentration of capital and transport in non-French-Canadian hands. He did not anticipate that foreign capitalists and industrialists would be frightened from Quebec by the establishment of a French state, since Quebec was widely known for its conservatism and its tolerance of foreigners in the midst of a rising tide of socialism among the governments and labor of English-speaking North America. Quebec owned a share of the railways now under government ownership, having helped to build and maintain them, while the Canadian Pacific would scarcely abandon Montreal and Quebec, the principal ports and storage points of Canada. The new state would control the St. Lawrence, the chief artery of an immense hinterland and a source of incalculable waterpower. Pelletier concluded by expressing his conviction that the economic obstacles to a French state could be overcome by effort, hard work, and planning, after a difficult and modest initial period. He preferred the prospect of independence at such a price to that of national annihilation or of a gilded but perpetual servitude. [63]

Joseph Bouchard dealt with the problem of the foreigners in among Quebec's midst in ' *Le Canada Français et les Etrangers*.' He anticipated that this element, reduced to 20 per cent of the population in a predominantly French state and divided into many different groups, could be assimilated or absorbed, while the higher French-Canadian birthrate would gradually reduce the minority's proportion. He called hotly for an end of the old inferiority complex of the French Canadians in economic matters and the indoctrination of a national pride and patriotism which would quickly 're-Frenchify' Quebec. Bilingualism and mixed marriages would henceforward work for the French Canadians rather than against them; and emigration would be halted. [64]

The Dominican Père M.-Ceslas Forest discussed '*La Préparation intellectuelle*', urging the creation of a French-Canadian intellectual life and its defence against foreign influences. He echoed Edouard Montpetit's call in 1917 for the formation of a trained élite of specialists. But the scientific organization of agricultural, commercial, and industrial life was not sufficient; it must be supplemented by the creation of a philosophy, science, literature, and art, in which the French Canadians, thanks to their heritage of French civilization, might surpass their neighbors. Père Forest urged that the culture of Quebec should be French, preferring that the French Canadians should borrow from a suspect but a Latin and Catholic France rather than from Protestant and materialist England and the United States. Some elements of value, nonetheless, could be drawn from 'Anglo-Saxon' civilization, with due caution to preserve an essentially French culture. The culture of Quebec should be Canadian, a French culture purified of modern corruptions and adapted to

North America, and reflecting the Canadian environment. It should be Catholic, since it was based upon the Catholic French and Canadian traditions, and since it must be Catholic to be fruitful and to endure. [65]

Antonio Perrault discussed '*Le Sens national*,' differentiating between patriotism and national feeling. The latter was a higher, more conscious sentiment, disciplining patriotism and guiding it by the light of the spirit. He judged that it had long existed among the French Canadians, breaking out whenever attempts had been made to crush French Canada. But it must be further developed. The ethnic type evolved in New France must be purified of 'Anglo-Saxon' and American accretions by emphasizing the French Canadians' historic and traditional particularism, by strengthening their attachment to their own customs, and their love of their own corner of the earth. An élite of intellectuals and men of action must exert itself to instil in the masses a greater love of their faith and language, of their culture and law, their traditions and customs. He favored the nationalization of literature, through emphasis on regionalism and patriotism and repudiation of exoticism and cosmopolitanism. 'In the family and at the school, education and instruction must turn the spirit and heart of the child to fix them always on the soul of its race.' [66] Nationalization of education would awaken a sense of national responsibilities, pride of race, and will to serve the race. Abbé Philippe Perrier dealt with '*L'Etat Français et sa valeur d'idéal pour nous*,' asserting that man had a duty to develop his national personality as well as his moral personality. He called for an end of cultural colonialism, and the development of the unity of blood, language, faith, history, country, customs, and interests which, according to Etienne Lamy, were the attributes of a nation. The ideal of a French state would help to complete the attainment of these attributes. [67]

Abbé Groulx summed up the conclusions of the symposium, once more asserting his unwillingness to shatter the *status quo*, and his desire merely to prepare against the impending rupture of Confederation. The foresight of his introduction to the symposium, written in November 1921, seemed to him to have been realized by the deep antagonisms displayed in the federal elections of December, which had led even Bourassa to envisage the approaching end of Confederation. The breakup of the British Empire seemed still nearer than it had at the outset of the symposium. The conclusions of the participants had supported those of the instigator of the symposium; and Groulx made the most of those conclusions which agreed with his own.

He emphasized the fact that for half a century French Canada had laid more emphasis on survival than on its ideal goal of independence, thanks to 'the mixed marriage contracted by our race in 1841,'[68] which had only been saved from a shattering divorce by the worse error of Confederation. Quebec had abdicated its sense of nationality, its patrimony of national resources, its very traditions and customs. Americanization and anglomania had created havoc, while a large part of the bourgeoisie had betrayed the national ideal. The goal of independence would supply a new orientation: 'the duty of the moment is to relight the old torch and prevent it from ever being extinguished.'[69] This torch would be carried on by youth, to whom Groulx once more made a special appeal. To him it was clear that 'the ideal of a French state was going to correspond more and more among us to a kind of vital impulsion';[70] it was a saving principle which would set the French Canadians free from the chaos of their divisions and of their scattered labors. He warned youth that there were decisive hours which did not come twice in the life of a nation, and said that he was unwilling to be a speculative idealist; he had not promised to act, but had begun to act.

3

The frank separatism of this 1922 symposium caused a division among Abbé Groulx' following, as the French Canadians lost their crisis psychology with the return of Quebec to a large share in the federal government. Confederation held together, as the new Liberal leader Mackenzie King achieved a working alliance with the Western Progressives and followed a course leading to fuller nationhood which was in part dictated by his loyalty to Laurier. The British Empire did not crumble, but in 1926 evolved into the British Commonwealth of Nations, in which the old anglo-centric imperialism gave way to self-determination by the constituent nations. In the development of this third British Empire, Canada had taken a leading role, as was pointed out by Alfred Zimmern of Oxford, who further considered that the Constitutional Act of 1791 marked 'a decisive turning point in the history of the British Commonwealth.'[71] On November 23, 1923, Bourassa publicly criticized 'Notre Avenir politique,' calling its separatism 'a dream neither realizable nor desirable' and commenting that 'the tendencies of immoderate nationalism here or elsewhere, are contrary to real patriotism and true nationalism.'[72]

The conclusions of 'Notre Avenir politique' were also criticized by middle-of-the-road French Canadians whose faith in the status quo was gradually being restored. Edouard Montpetit evolved into a preacher of federalism on the basis of equality between French and English,[73] while devoting his energies to the improvement of economic and social studies at the struggling young Université de

Montréal in which he became a major influence. Henry Laureys continued to foster the growth of the École des Hautes Études Commerciales, which long provided the only academic economic training to be had in French Canada. Beaudry Leman became the leading French-Canadian banker, protesting in 1928 in reply to the economic xenophobia of the ultranationalists that 'The most serious menace is not the penetration of money capital, but of the moral and intellectual capital of men better qualified than we to profit from our natural resources.'[74] Léon Lorrain dissociated himself from *L'Action française*. Georges Pelletier succeeded Bourassa in the direction of *Le Devoir* and preached a moderate nationalism. Olivar Asselin became a salesman of stocks and bonds for the two leading French-Canadian brokerage firms, returning to his initial profession of journalism only after the stockmarket crash of 1929, which hit Montreal hard and impoverished some of the religious orders which had large investments. Though he retained his interest in economic nationalism, Asselin was not temperamentally cut out to be a follower of any school of thought except his own, and his devotion to French culture put him at odds with the increasingly provincial nationalism of the Groulx school.

But Antonio Perrault, Anatole Vanier, and Abbé Philippe Perrier remained devoted disciples of Groulx, who also kept his influence in the classical colleges. To this nucleus of veterans were added such young recruits as Jean Bruchési, who had carried on as a student in Paris the work of cementing cultural relations between France and Quebec begun by Groulx in 1921; Esdras Minville, the first Quebec-trained economist, whose nationalism was the more realistic because of the fact that he had risen by his own efforts from a humble fishing family of Gaspé and had never had the classical college training which encouraged a devotion to theory at the expense of awkward facts; Emile Bruchési, Yves Tessier-Lavigne, Harry Bernard, and Hermas Bastien.

In 1923 *L'Action française's* annual symposium was devoted to '*Notre intégrité catholique*,' while the magazine also opposed emigration from the countryside to the cities and to the States, American economic imperialism, and the continued persecution of French in the Ontario schools. In 1924 the symposium dealt with '*L'Ennemi dans la place*,' with denunciations of Quebec's high infant mortality rate, the anticipated decline of the birthrate through urbanization, emigration to the States, American economic imperialism, and American movies. In 1925 there was a return to the original purpose of the movement with a symposium on bilingualism, making the largest possible claims for the rights of the French language and bitterly protesting against violation of the bilingual principle of Confederation. The ebb of nationalist confidence was reflected not only in the renewed insistance on bilingualism, which had been dismissed as impossible in the earlier days when a French state was envisaged, but also in the demand for the establishment of Saint-Jean-Baptiste Day (June 24) as a legal holiday which would unite a race which lacked national independence, a state of its own, its own territory, and its own flag. This new defensive attitude was also reflected by articles supporting the movements for national Catholic unions of workers and farmers. French Canadians were urged to elect only compatriots in the federal elections of October 1925, since their influence in the Commons was steadily declining.

In 1926 there were two chief topics of discussion, '*Défense de notre capital humain*' and '*Doctrines de notre jeunesse*,' with Montpetit, the Jesuit Père Louis Lalande, and Olivar Asselin once more joining the usual contributors in stressing the importance of Quebec's greatest asset, its human capital, threatened despite its strong vitality by infant mortality and tuberculosis, emigration, urbanization, and industrialization. Colonization was as usual advanced as a solution of the social problem, with a new emphasis on public health measures and on the establishment of rural industries. Esdras Minville, Léon Lortie, René Chaloult, Jean Bruchési, Albert Lévesque, and Séraphin Marion responded in the name of the rising generation to the doctrines of L'Action française. A symposium on '*La Doctrine de L'Action française*' was launched in 1927, with a new political emphasis. There were attacks on American economic and cultural influences, the Labrador Award of the Privy Council, the fact that Quebec had more Jews than any other province, and approval for measures taken by Mussolini's government.

A special double number in 1927, published on the sixtieth anniversary of Confederation, constituted the most notable symposium since 1922.[75] As might have been expected, no such idyllic view of Confederation was taken as by most English-Canadian spokesmen upon the occasion; but in contrast to 1922 there was a determination to uphold French Canada's rights in Confederation which implied a reluctant belief in its survival. *L'Action française* had always mocked the *bonne entente* movement, but now it justified its freeness and frankness in speaking of Confederation as the only way to prepare a good understanding.

Groulx discussed '*Les Canadiens Français et l'établissement de la Confédération*,' stressing the primary importance of Quebec's role in making Confederation possible by its third of the total proposed population, its political unity, and its geographical situation. He also emphasized the risks Quebec took by merging its destiny with that of three English provinces instead of one. It had to preserve its provincial autonomy and its national and religious rights and those of the French minorities in the other provinces. It was because of French Canada that Confederation took the form of a federal rather than a legislative union. He made much of the misgivings of A.-A. Dorion, Henri Taschereau, and L.-O. David at the time. Cartier and his associates Langevin and Cauchon persuaded Quebec to accept Confederation, 'relying too much on the good faith of their political associates.'[76] Groulx judged that they would not have prevailed without the support of the hierarchy, and stressed the reluctance of Bishop Bourget to back Confederation. He concluded that the good faith of French Canada's political and spiritual leaders had been betrayed by subsequent events, and that 'after more than half a century of existence, the Canadian Confederation still remains an anemic giant, carrying many germs of dissolution. ...'[77]

He issued a stern warning to the English Canadians:

All that has been attempted for the last sixty years, and all that will be attempted in the future against the security of the French-Canadian race in this country, has been attempted and will be attempted against its interest in maintaining Confederation. It did not enter into Confederation to die, nor even to let itself be tamed, but to live, to survive as a whole. This is not the hour to subtilize or to restrain the federal spirit; it must be fortified and generalized across Canada as the contact of the two races is further extended. The French-Canadian race is no longer limited to the East of the country; despite the barriers raised against it, it has exported men to all the Western provinces, as far as the shores of the Pacific. The reactions of these French groups, as well as those of the present Quebec, against the denials of justice and administrative meannesses should give warning that, if formerly our adhesion to the federative pact could be traded cheaply, the generation of today does not admit that its chances of living, any more than its right to live worthily, have been sold.[78]

Anatole Vanier protested in a brief note against the immigration policy which made it cheaper for a Britisher or an American to come to Canada and to establish himself in the West than for a French Canadian of Quebec to do likewise. Under such circumstances it was no wonder that French Canadians emigrated to the States, as Vanier suggested the English Canadians desired them to do.[79] Olivar Asselin dealt with the topic of ' Les Canadiens Français et le développement économique du Canada,' estimating that the French Canadians held about one-seventh of the wealth of Canada, while they represented two-sevenths of its population.[80] He blamed French-Canadian economic inferiority on the Conquest, on a traditional agriculture which impoverished the land, on emigration, on English dominance in trade and industry, on the imposition of the heavy debt of Upper Canada on Lower Canada in 1841, on the favoritism shown to English Canadians in public works and in nominations to administrative posts, and on the development of the West with public funds for the benefit of English Canadians. He concluded that the French Canadians had not been a barrier to the economic development of the country, but had done as much as they could to further it, while Quebec enjoyed abroad the best credit of any Canadian province. Hermas Bastien rehearsed in a brief note the old French-Canadian grievances against the Irish, who had opposed rather than made common cause with their fellow Catholics.[81]

Montpetit discussed '*Les Canadiens Français et le développement intellectuel du Canada,*' giving the history of educational developments under the French regime, which had been interrupted by the Conquest and by the attempt to establish an English system of schools. Gradually the school system had been re-established by the clergy; and granted autonomy in educational matters by Article 93 of the B.N.A. Act, Quebec alone had fully realized the intentions of Macdonald and Cartier with its system of separate Catholic and Protestant schools, numbering 7,000 schools attended by a fifth of the population and fifteen normal schools. Its twenty-one classical colleges had formed an intellectual élite which had influenced the development of English colonial policy, while maintaining the cause of general culture. Two universities had grown up, providing professional and technical training as well as the four fundamental faculties of theology, law, medicine, and arts. Quebec had led the way by establishing the Ecole des Hautes Etudes Commerciales and technical schools. Its government provided scholarships for studies abroad, and more than half the teachers of the universities and colleges had been trained abroad. Since the visit of 'La Capricieuse' in 1855, cultural relations had been renewed with France, enabling Quebec to be the center of French culture in America. By remaining itself French Canada preserved Canada from Americanization and gave a young country the richness of two great civilizations.[82]

Yves Tessier-Lavigne argued in a note on '*Québec, les chemins de fer, et Confédération,*' that Quebec had at least one reason not to celebrate the sixtieth anniversary of Confederation, since the federal government had done little for its railroad development while doing much for the other provinces.[83] Abbé Philippe Perrier discussed '*Les Canadiens Français et la vie morale et sociale du Canada,*' stressing Quebec's contribution to Canadian morality by its Catholicism which maintained the sanctity of the family and of marriage, had given the country a rich 'human capital,' respected the parent's rights in education, insisted on the teaching of morality in the schools, and supplied an answer to the social question.[84] Mgr. Béliveau dealt with '*Les Canadiens Français et le rôle de l'Eglise au Ouest,*' describing the exploration of the West by the Oblate missionaries and their establishment of the first schools in that region.

But Confederation had brought many grievances to the French Canadians of the West, who saw their pact with Ottawa violated again and again. Mgr. Béliveau called for loyalty to the pact of 1867 and a return to its spirit, with equal civil and religious rights for French and English throughout Canada, so that the work of the French-Canadian pioneers of the West for their faith and their country might not be wasted. [85]

Louis Durand, in considering ' *Les Canadiens Français et l'ésprit national*,' emphasized that Confederation had been founded on the basis of absolute respect for the language and the rights of the two contracting nationalities; and that national spirit must find its source and inspiration in the 'high conception which renders to each race and province the justice due to it and which, uniting them in common aspirations and will beyond material prosperity, gives to each the sense of the possibilities, necessities, and duties of a full and fruitful national life.' [86] He maintained that the French Canadian had best respected the fundamental principle of Confederation, and had remained the firmest opponent of the rival dangers which threatened Canada, Americanization and imperialism. He concluded by observing dryly that on the one hundred and twentieth anniversary of Confederation the number of celebrants might be diminished, if others did not remain as faithful to the fundamental principle of the pact, or sought to disorient Canadian patriotism, or were unjust to their national partners.

In a brief note Esdras Minville protested against the Privy Council's 'political' decision in the Labrador boundary case, which had cost Quebec 110,000 square miles of territory in Ungava and access to the Atlantic on the northeast. [87] Antonio Perrault dealt with Quebec's '*Déceptions et griefs*' under Confederation, advancing the nationalist theory that Confederation was a pact between two races and two religious groups on the basis of perfect equality. [88] He blamed the subsequent injustices which the French Canadians had suffered on the failure to incorporate fully the spirit of the pact in its letter, and on the assimilative tendency of the 'Anglo-Saxons.' He asserted that most French Canadians would agree that the Fathers of Confederation deserved to be shot for not making more definite the guarantees provided by the pact. He recalled the violations of the pact in educational matters in 1871, 1877, 1890, 1892, 1905, 1912, 1916, and 1926, without action by the federal government; the refusal to admit that Canada was bilingual; the refusal to give French Canadians their due share of public offices; and the constant insults directed against Quebec and the French Canadians. He asserted that the French Canadians did not believe that either the British Empire or Confederation would survive, but pending the anticipated breakdown they must loyally support

Confederation, though not at the expense of ethnic patriotism. The Canadian union of two nationalities could only be maintained by the maintenance of ethnic duality and provincial diversity. The French Canadians had two duties: 'To express their grievances frankly and to seek to make Confederation conform to its origins and principles.'[89] He regretted that the French-Canadian members had not amended the resolution of the House commemorating the anniversary by adding a wish that Confederation's spirit and letter be better understood in the future. He concluded with the suggestion that Premier Taschereau, as spokesman of French Canada, should express the grief caused the French Canadians by the unjust interpretation of Confederation and their desire to have its rights fairly applied.

Albert Lévesque closed the symposium as the spokesman of youth in 'La Confédération et la Jeunesse Canadienne-Française.' In contrast to its usual fervent patriotism, French-Canadian youth was apathetic on this anniversary. It was determined, thanks to the nationalist movement since 1900, to make Confederation's spirit effective while developing its own ethnic personality and the prosperity of Quebec. If the English Canadians refused to collaborate, French-Canadian youth would 'organize otherwise its future.'[90]

This symposium of Confederation was practically the swan song of L'Action française. The review was stricken by financial difficulties in its later years and survived thanks to the efforts of Albert Lévesque, who developed profitable complementary activities such as the publication of an almanac, books, and pamphlets. Abbé Groulx was at last given a respectable salary by the Université de Montréal, though at first only on the condition that he sign an engagement to respect Confederation and English-Canadian susceptibilities. Groulx refused to sign, but the arrangement was finally concluded on the basis that he would devote all his time to historical work.[91] He retired as editor of L'Action française in the spring of 1928. In the following December the directors announced their decison to end publication of the magazine and of the Almanach de la Langue française, which had been a sort of annual popular supplement designed to reach the masses, while the magazine sought its smaller audience among the élite.

In January 1928 the title had been changed to L'Action canadienne-française, a full year after the condemnation by Rome of Maurras and his movement in France. The change was announced editorially with the observation: 'We have nothing in common with the royalist movement of Paris. . . . For the rest nothing will be changed either in the direction or spirit of the review.'[92] This was a somewhat bland disavowal of an influence more constantly evident than any other in the magazine, with the possible exception of that of Maurice

Barrès; and the hollowness of the repudiation was indicated by the determination not to change the policy of the magazine. This reaction to the condemnation of Maurras was more or less general in French Canada, with many of his admirers continuing to read his paper. But it added to the distrust already felt for the movement by the new school of *'Canadians tous courts'* ('unhyphenated Canadians'), and helped to bring about the end of *L'Action canadienne-française* in December 1928. In its declining years the review devoted itself to what might be called a nationalism of details, rather than its early integral nationalism, with a rather undistinguished list of contributors deploring the decline of the birthrate, the greater attention being given to the study of English, American influences, and preaching a narrow French Canadianism rather than the broad Canadianism then increasingly in vogue in French Canada. That the review now only expressed the views of a segment of the élite was made evident in 1928 by Beaudry Leman's debate with Minville on economic policy and G.-E. Marquis' with Vanier on national unity.

In 1928, at the age of fifty, Abbé Groulx saw the movement to which he had devoted ten years peter out. The boom of the 1920's had made Quebec prosperous; and those French Canadians who had benefited thought politics had nothing to do with business, and that nationalism was bad for it. Quebec had once more become a potent force at Ottawa, with Lomer Gouin and Ernest Lapointe successively taking important roles in the federal cabinet. Mackenzie King had resisted the postwar imperialistic pressures and continued in Laurier's path, seeking fuller nationhood for Canada within the empire. Lapointe had signed the Halibut Treaty of 1923 as the independent representative of Canada, while the first Canadian Minister to the United States took office in 1927, ending the old complaint that the British ambassador at Washington sacrificed Canada's interests to those of Britain. Senator Raoul Dandurand became president of the Assembly of the League of Nations in 1925, and Canada was elected to the League Council in 1927, thus enhancing her nationhood and French Canada's pride. The old sore of the Ontario school question was partially closed in 1927 by the Merchant Report, which recognized the rights of the French language. A final crippling blow to the survival of British control over Canadian policy through the governor-generalship was the outcome of the Byng incident in 1926, when the governor-general refused a dissolution to the King government and granted one to the Meighen government, and the King government was supported by the people in its stand that the governor-general had no right to play politics.

Despite all the social and cultural problems brought by the rapid industrialization of Quebec, largely under American auspices, in this period, the province rejoiced in a prosperity it had never before known. The new economic nationalism was left without a foundation of popular discontent. Except among the élite and the clergy, nationalism was virtually dead on the eve of the great depression which was to revive it and make it almost as potent a force on the eve of the Second World War as it had been at the close of the First.

In the late 1920's Abbé Groulx found his audience at the university reduced to a bare fifty instead of the great crowds which had hailed him ten years before, while he lacked a journal and received few invitations to give public addresses.[93] At the time of the enforced pledge incident he had thought of giving up his work and becoming a *curé*; but he renounced this idea and contented himself with pursuing his historical researches and counselling those young nationalists who sought him out. His influence on youth continued to be strong. French-Canadian youth is naturally nationalist-minded, as American youth is naturally liberal-minded, and this bent was encouraged by the facts that the classical colleges were largely directed by priests sympathetic to nationalism and that history was largely taught in the schools by former pupils of Groulx. Even at the traditionally loyalist Laval University in Quebec Thomas Chapais' interpretation of Canadian history—essentially that of a nineteenth-century British Liberal—seemed pallid and too imperialist to the rising generation by comparison with that of Groulx.

4

Though the *Action française* movement declined rather than gained strength after its triumphant and confident beginning in the postwar period, its influence was widespread among more moderate men than Groulx and his close disciples. Its emphasis on the development of a well-rounded French-Canadian culture furthered a general movement which had begun about 1900. Edouard Montpetit, fortified by three years' study at the Ecole Libre des Sciences Politiques and the Collège des Sciences Sociales in Paris, carried on after 1910 the effort launched by Errol Bouchette and Léon Gérin to study the French-Canadian milieu in economic and sociological terms and to provide French-Canadian training for industry and business. First as professor at the Ecole des Hautes Etudes Commerciales, in whose founding Honoré Gervais had taken the leading role, and after 1920 as secretary-general of the Université de Montréal and director of its Ecole des Sciences Sociales, Montpetit played a notable part in the economic awakening of French Canada. His duties as professor of law, of political economy, public finance, and

The Artist's Family

Oil painting (c. 1940) by Marie Bouchard. A charming primitive by the daughter of a well-known artist. The scene is typical of a country parlor in the French-Canadian taste. (Patrick Morgan Collection.)

Poem of the Earth

Oil painting (1940) by Maurice Raymond. This Montreal-born-and-educated painter reflects the typical French-Canadian intellectual's idealization of rural life. (Quebec Provincial Museum.)

economic politics left him little leisure for the production of original works, but he used his classic French eloquence on many public occasions to preach the economic approach and to stress Quebec's bonds with French culture.

Marius Barbeau applied his Oxford anthropological training to the study of the Indian and of French-Canadian folklore and artistic history. The Belgian Henry Laureys ably directed the Ecole des Hautes Etudes Commerciales and sought to adapt French economic theories to North American practices. Augustin Frigon sought to broaden the scope of the Ecole Polytechnique, established in 1873 and long devoted to the production of civil engineers, by providing training in the new industrial fields in which non-French Canadians had long supplied the trained leadership. He encountered the resistance of a class-proud élite to any occupation which involved rolling up one's sleeves and getting one's hands dirty—a reluctance born of the strength of the old professional tradition in that class, and not unrelated to the traditional English-Canadian taunt that the French Canadians were a race of hewers of wood and drawers of water.

The secondary schools still failed to provide the scientific training which was the necessary preparation for specialization at the advanced level, but the great work of Frère Marie-Victorin, the founder of Montreal's Botanical Garden, in making French-Canadian youth science-minded and in stressing the importance of observation and experimentation instead of the old tradition of purely dogmatic teaching, helped to make possible the creation at Laval in Quebec of an admirable school of science, under the leadership of Abbé Alexandre Vachon and Adrien Pouliot. This Quebec initiative was soon paralleled at Montreal, and more attention was subsequently given to science in the secondary schools. The teaching standards in a vital and long-neglected field of knowledge were gradually raised to the international level. The provincial government, which underwrote the cost of most of these developments and provided scholarships for graduate study abroad under the intelligent administration of Athanase David, the provincial secretary, also supported agricultural, forestry, and fishery schools associated with the two universities and a wide range of trade, technical, and commercial schools throughout the province.

This intellectual ferment was reflected in literature. Thanks largely to the critical work of Mgr. Camille Roy, many times Rector of Laval University, a French-Canadian literary tradition was firmly established and quickly began to bear fruit in works which were not mere belated echoes of French literary trends. The new literature was largely devoted to glorifying the good old days of the French regime and the obsolescent patriarchal rural world untouched by alien influences, for the privileged clerical and professional élite remained firmly convinced that the national genius was for the hard life of pioneering and tilling the soil, and not for the new industrial life which menaced many of French Canada's traditions and in which the French Canadians were largely left behind by aliens. This *terroir* school, led by Adjutor Rivard with his *Chez nos gens* (1914–19), Frère Marie-Victorin with his *Récits laurentiens* (1919) and *Croquis laurentiens* (1920) and by Blanche Lamontagne with her numerous hymns to Gaspé in both prose and verse, was carried on by the poetry of Emile Coderre and Alfred DesRochers. In 1925 Robert Choquette immediately took first rank among young French-Canadian poets with his *A travers les vents*, whose authentic poetic feeling, eloquence, and precocious power eclipsed earlier work which had suffered from imitativeness of French models, limited themes, and a distrust of realism.

In history, the most popular form of literary expression in French Canada, Thomas Chapais carried on his constitutional study of the period between 1760 and 1867 in volumes published from 1919 to 1934. The Abbé Ivanhoë Caron published a series of scrupulously exact monographs on the colonization of Quebec, based upon the documents provided by the Provincial Archives established in 1920. Aegidius Fauteux and E.-Z. Massicotte carried on tireless archival researches into the past, while Pierre-Georges Roy published a host of antiquarian studies, in addition to supervising the valuable annual reports of the Provincial Archives and the *Bulletin des recherches historiques*. Séraphin Marion, one of the first European-trained historians, published his *Relations des Voyageurs français en Nouvelle France aux XVIIe siècle* in 1923 and a monograph on *Pierre Boucher* in 1927. Gustave Lanctot produced an able critical study of Garneau in 1925 and a notable Sorbonne thesis on *L'Administration de la Nouvelle France* in 1929. The following year saw the publication of Antoine Roy's useful *Les Lettres, les Sciences, et les Arts au Canada sous le Régime français*. A pioneering effort in economic history was Noël Fauteux's *Essai sur l'industrie au Canada sous le Régime français* (1927); while Dr. Arthur Vallée produced an equally novel study in the history of science with his monograph on Michel Sarrazin. The flood of parish histories, evidence of an ancient parochialism undisturbed by new social forces, continued with new vigor. Only Abbé Groulx resisted the general tendency to concentrate attention on the French period and to neglect subsequent history, less glamorous but more significant in its relationship to the present.

The novel first became a popular form of literary expression in this period, after Louis Hémon's *Maria Chapdelaine* (1916), an eloquent picture of pioneer life and French survival in the Lake St. John country, won a notable success first in France and later in Canada.

This young Frenchman was killed in 1913, shortly after finishing his manuscript, but his book had a profound influence on the postwar French-Canadian novel. Harry Bernard carried on the *terroir* tradition under Hémon's influence in a long series of novels of rural life, beginning with *L'Homme tombé* in 1924. His books made use of the popular speech instead of a frozen classical French and were more realistic than earlier novels had been. Robert de Roquebrune published a historical novel, *Les Habits Rouges* (1923), dealing with the events of 1837, and then after a second and unsuccessful effort in this field, turned to the psychological novel in *Les Dames les Marchand* (1937). Léo-Paul Desrosiers renounced an early preoccupation with *terroir* themes, which culminated in *Nord-Sud* (1931), in favor of historical novels, of which *L'Acalmie* (1937) and *Les Engagés du Grand Portage* (1938) are among the best produced in French Canada. Jean-Charles Harvey produced in 1922 a novel, *Marcel Faure*, which mirrored the preoccupation of the time with economic emancipation; and in 1929 with *L'Homme qui va* offered a collection of fantastic and symbolic stories characterized by a fine style, marked realism, and a penchant for melodrama. With *Les Demi-Civilisées* (1934), a sensational novel of Quebec high life and corrupting American influence which is both realistic and fantastic, Harvey caused a small tempest in Quebec which drove him from his editorship of *Le Soleil* to less prudish Montreal. Another collection of short stories, *Sébastien Pierre* (1935), revealed the same qualities and defects as Harvey's earlier work, which remains among the most vital and best-written French-Canadian fiction.

In 1933 Claude-Henri Grignon ('Valdombre') published his *Un homme et son péché*, which became a French-Canadian classic and served as the framework of a most popular perennial French-Canadian radio serial. It is a realistic study of *habitant* avarice, tinted by the romanticism of the *terroir* school. There was a return to the older lyrical idealization of the pioneer in Abbé Félix-Antoine Savard's poetic novel, *Menaud, maître-draveur* (1937), and an abler development of 'Valdombre's' realism in Dr. Philippe Panneton's ('Ringuet') *Trente Arpentes* (1938), which deromanticized the *habitant's* life in convincing and moving fashion. Harvey's *Demi-Civilisées* and Ringuet's *Trente Arpentes* were the first French-Canadian novels to be translated and published in English, and the latter attained almost as much fame abroad as *Maria Chapdelaine*. The nationalist tradition in the novel, inaugurated by Tardivel and carried on by Groulx' *L'Appel de la race* was continued by the Jesuit Père Adélard Dugré's *La Campagne canadienne* (1925), Groulx's *Au Cap Blomidon* on the theme of Acadian survival, and Rex Desmarchais' *Le Feu intérieur* and *La Chesnaie*. These are more convincing as illustrations of nationalist theses than as novels.

There was also a notable development of criticism from the traditional log-rolling level. Mgr. Camille Roy remained the leading French-Canadian critic, presiding over Laval's influential review, *Le Canada Français*, and displaying a remarkable tolerance to all writers who sought to realize his goal of a French-Canadian literature. His prewar critical essays were revised and brought out as *Poètes de chez nous* (1934), *Historiens de chez nous* (1935), and *Romanciers de chez nous* (1935). From exile in New England Louis Dantin, who had launched Nelligan's poetry in 1904, kept a sharp critical eye on the development of French-Canadian literature, while writing some verse himself. His *Gloses critiques* (1931, 1935) contain the most searching criticism since the pioneering volumes of Charles ab der Halden in 1904 and 1907 made Europe aware of French-Canadian literature. Jean-Charles Harvey, in his *Pages de Critique* (1926), produced some of the best and frankest critical writing of the period, and acted as a deterrent to the old tradition of log-rolling. Maurice Hébert, a disciple of Mgr. Roy, became the literary critic of *Le Canada Français* and devoted himself to sensitive psychological studies of new books, which were collected in *De Livres en Livres* (1929), *D'un Livre à l'autre* (1932), and *Les Lettres au Canada français* (1936). Marcel Dugas, an exile in Paris until the outbreak of the Second World War, produced more exacting criticism in his *Littérature Canadienne: Aperçus* (1929) and in his study of *Louis Fréchette* (1934). Dugas became the literary prophet of the *anciens de Paris*, the French-Canadian students who returned from Paris convinced that all wisdom and beauty found its source there. Albert Pelletier in *Carquois* and *Egrappages* (1933) displayed ability and unconventionality in judging current books. Claude-Henri Grignon, in his *Ombres et Clameurs* (1933) and in the later pamphlets signed 'Valdombre,' showed a sound judgment which was somewhat outweighed by the violence of his tone as a polemicist.

The analytical tendency of the classical college discipline was reflected in the fact that French Canada produced more critics than creative writers. In the 1930's, as in the 1860's, more ink was spilt over the question of whether a French-Canadian culture existed or was possible than in efforts to advance it. In 1940 and 1941 *L'Action Nationale* was still conducting a symposium on the question as European culture went down before the Nazi assault. The enforced break with France after June 1940 and the unanticipated wartime role of Montreal as one of the two centers of free French culture both emancipated French Canada from its cultural colonialism and furthered the development of an original culture. French Canada at last came of age, after passing through a long imitative period reminiscent of that of American culture before the flowering of New England.

5

French-Canadian nationalism always comes to a head in periods of economic, as well as political, crisis. It was inevitable, considering the economic bent which Abbé Groulx had given to the movement, that it should revive with new intensity in the troubled 1930's, when French Canada felt the effects of the depression more deeply than English Canada, because its lower standard of living afforded less margin for subsistence. Unemployment reached its peak in Quebec in 1932, with 100,000 persons, largely French Canadians, on relief in Montreal. [94] It was not surprising that January 1933 saw the revival of *L'Action canadienne-française* as *L'Action Nationale*, under the editorship of Harry Bernard. The directors included Esdras Minville, Hermas Bastien, Pierre Homier, Abbé Groulx, Eugène L'Heureux, Abbé Olivier Maurault, Anatole Vanier, Abbé Tessier, Arthur Laurendeau, René Chaloult, Wilfrid Guérin, and Léopold Richer—most of the more extreme elders of the original movement and a group of ultranationalists of the rising generation. The first number affirmed the review's dedication to Catholicism and French-Canadian traditions, and with a foreshadowing of a racism which became more pronounced as time went on, made much of 'our ethnic originality.' Groulx contributed an article calling for aggressive rather than defensive action with regard to French-Canadian rights. It was evident that his nationalism was now more inspired by that of Gonzague du Reynold than by that of Charles Maurras. The editors made an appeal for subscriptions by classical colleges, and it was in these institutions, which usually banned most current periodicals except *L'Action Nationale* and *Le Devoir*, that the new nationalism centered.

It was now primarily a youth movement, for young French Canadians launched themselves into political action when the depression barred them from normal careers and economic opportunities. The war cry of the new nationalism was sounded at a meeting of university students in Montreal on December 19, 1932, which was presided over by Armand Lavergne, the idol of nationalist youth, and addressed by Esdras Minville. Their manifesto, already published in *Le Quartier Latin* in November, called for scrupulous respect of the rights of each 'race' in Canada, and insisted that the French language should enjoy the same rights as English. It referred to the growing indignation of French Canadians at the denial of their rights, and warned: 'We ask today what we shall exact tomorrow.' [95] It pointed out that the French Canadians constituted a third of the population of Canada, four-fifths of that of Quebec, and three-quarters of that of Montreal; and demanded that French Canadians should have a just share of federal jobs. Observing that the French Canadians were becoming a proletarian people, it insisted that this situation should be remedied. The natural resources of the province were not to be used in a fashion which would compromise or lose the heritage of French Canadians, while 'foreign capitalists' imposed upon them 'the worst of dictatorships' and ostracized their engineers and technicians, leaving open to French Canadians only the roles of laborers and servants. The manifesto closed with an appeal to youth:

Therefore we appeal to youth, to the whole youth of our race: university youth, the youth of the colleges and schools, the youth of the factories, of the fields, and of the professions. In all domains of national life let the ardent concern awake to reconquer lost positions, to make the future better. It is a vast task: intellectual, literary, artistic, scientific, economic, national to which we, the young, are called by the necessities of our time. Let us remember that we shall be masters in our own house only if we become worthy of being so.[96]

This 'Manifesto of the young generation' was drafted by André Laurendeau, the son of one of the veteran directors of *L'Action* in its various incarnations, and was approved by the twelve or fifteen other members of '*Les Jeune-Canada*,' as the movement soon came to be called. The majority were students at the Université de Montréal, graduates of the Jesuit Collège Sainte-Marie, and were under the influence of Abbé Groulx.

The movement began with articles in the university paper, *Le Quartier Latin*, and was continued with mass meetings at the Salle Gésu during the winter of 1932–3 and at the Monument National the following winter. It was characterized by Pierre Dansereau in *L'Action Nationale* as a reaction against 'the march of the French-Canadian people towards the abyss.'[97] It sought to transform rather than to revolutionize; to consolidate the effort commenced but abandoned in the past, rather than to destroy. It was impatient with and contemptuous of most of its elders, with the exception of Edouard Montpetit, Abbé Groulx, and Esdras Minville. It was particularly bitter against the politicians, whom it held responsible for the present situation, and whom it considered 'the eternal enemies of our race,'[98] because they promoted party divisions rather than French-Canadian unity. *Les Jeune-Canada* attracted attention by exploiting the growing French-Canadian feeling against the Jews of Montreal, who were becoming politically powerful, as well as driving the French Canadians from the fields of small business which the English-speaking economic overlords of Quebec scorned. And to stimulate national feeling, it organized a pilgrimage on Dollard's anniversary to Carillon, the scene of the folk hero's great fight against the Iroquois, and praised his memory and example at the prompting of Abbé Groulx, who had originated the cult of Dollard. It was also active in the elaborate commemoration of the tercentenary of Jacques Cartier's landing at Gaspé, which was officially celebrated on August 26 in the presence of Prime Minister Bennett, Cardinal Villeneuve, and representatives of France, Britain, and the United States.

L'Action Nationale furthered the *Jeune-Canada* movement while pursuing its own campaigns for 'integral bilingualism,' a back-to-the-land movement, 're-Frenchification' of Quebec, and anti-Semitism. In April 1933 it began to attack the capitalist system in Quebec, which it held responsible not only for the depression but also for the condition of the French Canadians. It adhered to the 'Program of Social Restoration' drafted in May by the Jesuits of the École Sociale Populaire which called for state intervention to end the abuses of the 'economic dictatorship,' and urged the adoption of corporatism and the suspension of immigration. The program also called for restoration of agriculture, support of colonization, and promotion of domestic arts and local industries. Its labor policy included wage and hour laws, social insurance, old-age pensions, and collective bargaining. The program also urged a war on the trusts, particularly those of coal, gas, and electricity. The Beauharnois Power Company was to be investigated, and taken over by the state if necessary. The program of financial reforms called for regulation of business and investigation of holding companies. The proposed political reforms included the elimination of graft, the declaration of campaign funds, and the creation of a provincial economic council, with specialists from various professions and classes. The over-all aim was to bring about 'an order more in accord with social justice' and to preserve the country from the 'upsets to which the present situation exposes us.'[99] The signers included Minville, who became the economic prophet of the new nationalists; Dr. Philippe Hamel, the leading crusader against the power trust; Alfred Charpentier, the elder statesman of the Catholic syndicate movement; as well as Albert Rioux, V.-E. Beaupré, Dr. J.-B. Prince, Anatole Vanier, Arthur Laurendeau, Wilfrid Guérin, and René Chaloult.

In 1934 *L'Action Nationale* published a series of articles on 'L'Education nationale.' Abbé Groulx launched the symposium, calling for a revival of national pride but denying the charge of racism. Jacques Brassier hailed the advent of Dollfuss, with the comment: 'Happy Austria, which has nonetheless found its leader, and with him the way of resurrection . . . What need we also have of a National Front and of a man who, like the young and charming chancellor of Austria, would dare to say these moving words: "I wish to reconstitute my country on the basis of the encyclical *Quadragesimo*

Anno."'[100] This emphasis on the need of a leader ('*chef*') was echoed and re-echoed henceforward, to the tune of citations of Gonzague de Reynold, Barrès, Maurras, and Massis, prophets of the strong-man cult.

In May Arthur Laurendeau repeated Groulx's arguments for the necessity of instilling racial pride, while denying a racism based upon purity of blood: 'We wish to speak of a race refined by a culture, which crossing the Mediterranean, was subsequently transfigured by Christ. It is on the virtue of this civilization that we bolster our defences, and not on a mad pride borrowed from the myths of the Black Forest.'[101] It was the elder Laurendeau who succeeded Bernard as editor in the fall of 1934, and under his direction the review took a more aggressive tone. In an article on 'Language and survival' in September, Abbé Groulx regretted the absence of a national leader, of 'the de Valera, the Mussolini, whose politics are open to discussion, but who in ten years have psychologically remade a new Ireland and a new Italy, as a Dollfuss and a Salazar are re-making a new Austria and a new Portugal.'[102] This '*chefisme*,' re-echoed by Groulx in November in a letter to Jean-Louis Gagnon, director of a new youth magazine called *Vivre*,[103] coupled as it was with a growing anti-Semitism, crusades against Communism and the trusts, and impassioned appeals to youth to save the 'race,' was all too reminiscent of the rise of European fascist movements to English-Canadian and American observers.

Under the influence of a depression which weighed far more heavily upon the underprivileged French-Canadians than upon their English-speaking compatriots, the new nationalism became narrowly provincialist and developed the latent tendency to separatism which has always been implicit in French-Canadian nationalism in time of crisis. *L'Action Nationale* was filled with attacks on the English-Canadian and American trusts which controlled the economic life of the province, and upon the constitution and Confederation. In January 1935 the magazine supported Groulx's call for a national leader, a '*chef*' who would guide Quebec in 'the new order which is evolving, in which the theories by which we live today appear perhaps to have expired.'[104] Confronted with the Bennett New Deal, the editors protested against the centralizing tendency of the program and urged either decentralization or the break-up of Confederation.

There was little respect shown to the older leaders of French Canada. In April Thomas Chapais was attacked for his devotion to the Conservative Party; and in May there was a bitter assault upon Bourassa for his 'lamentable' recent lectures, in which he had warned the young nationalists of the dangers of racial pride, ultra-nationalism, and separatism. While admitting the important role

History of Canada

A satirical picture by Robert La Palme, 1945, which was used as the curtain for Gratien Gélinas' revue, *Fridolins-nous*. (Gratien Gélinas Collection.)

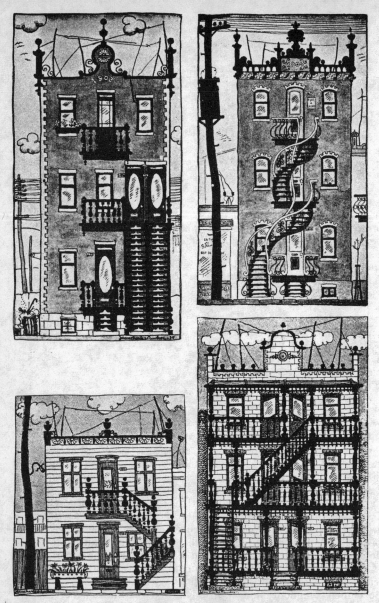

Montreal Architecture

Black-and-white drawings by Jean-Charles Faucher for Oliver Asselin's last journal,
La Renaissance (1935). The artist interprets the atmosphere of different quarters of
Montreal in terms of the distinctive outside stairways.

that Bourassa had played in developing nationalism before 1922, *L'Action Nationale* now formally repudiated his leadership in favor of that of Abbé Groulx, who in February had told the Junior Bar Association of Quebec: 'There is no nationalism in the world more legitimate or more orthodox than French-Canadian nationalism'— a statement sanctioned by the *imprimatur* of Cardinal Villeneuve when the speech appeared in pamphlet form.[105]

Not Bourassa, but Armand Lavergne was the political idol of the new generation of nationalists who found outdated the old nationalist leader's views on the religious and social matters to which he had largely devoted himself since 1920. But just as the Byng episode had roused Bourassa to express his fundamental anti-imperialism, Mr. Bennett's willingness to be guided in foreign affairs by Britain in an increasingly disturbed world provoked an expression of Bourassa's North Americanism, tempered by an international outlook which none of his more provincial disciples had ever equalled. In the House on April 1, 1935 Bourassa made a long speech on the European situation.[106] He moved for re-endorsement of the Kellogg Peace Pact of 1928, urging the government 'to lend its support to all effective measures to ensure the world's peace, either through the League of Nations or otherwise, in cooperation with other governments pledged to the cause of peace.' Bourassa singled out Mr. King—with whom he had a sense of kinship, since they were both grandsons of leaders of the 1837 Rebellion—as 'the Canadian statesman who has done most for peace, not only in words but deeds.' He declared it was Canada's duty to prevent wars or at least to take measures against being engulfed in war. He recommended four 'converging' methods to attain that end: Canada should define its own policy of peace; it should cooperate with Britain if the latter worked for peace; it should cooperate with the peace-loving United States; and it should work for peace through the League.

Bourassa declared that the spirit of Locarno was buried in the tombs of two great men, Briand and Stresemann; and he urged Canada to beware of 'the Locarno of the East': 'Keep aloof, for heaven's sake and for the sake of Canada.' He censured the course adopted towards Russia in 1927 and 1934, a policy 'of kicking and kissing alternately.' As a fundamental principle, he declared: 'There is no great problem of policy, internal or external, which we can solve in Canada without regard to the policy of the United States.' He urged that the government should make it clear to the Americans that Canada stood loyally by Britain as long as Britain stood for peace, and that it should make it equally clear to the British that if the United Kingdom chose war and the United States peace, that Canada also would choose peace. He recalled his conversations in 1914 with Lord Fisher, who found Laurier's and Borden's naval policies 'equally stupid.' The best way to arrange Canada's defence was to go to Washington. In the tradition of his basic anti-militarism and North American isolationism Bourassa urged: 'Let us proclaim to the world that we are disarming, as the best means of defending Canada . . . Why not join the Pan-American Union, in which we would be far more at home than we are in the League of Nations? . . . Canada is a nation in America, and not one in Europe or Asia.' Canada's policy should be based upon its North Americanism. Confidence in the League was now badly shaken, and he deeply regretted that Canada had voted for the admission of Russia into the League.

The extremes to which the new ultranationalism went was witnessed by approving accounts in *L'Action* of the 'Laurentianism' instilled in the young·students of the Collège Sainte-Marie by the Jesuit Père Thomas Mignault, who made history, geology, botany, art, literature and economics center upon the concept of a 'Laurentia,' a separate and unique French Canada.[107] In September Arthur Laurendeau supported the manifesto issued by Paul Gouin when he launched his *Action Nationale Libérale*, a political youth movement, and reprinted the document, which called for the creation of a national '*mystique*.'[108] In October Minville nominated Abbé Groulx as the pre-ordained *chef* of French Canada, paraphrasing Gonzague de Reynold's words of approval for the German National Socialist movement as applicable to Groulx and the directors of *L'Action Nationale*. He hailed the formula expounded by Groulx in his book *Orientations*: 'What we wish is a French people in a French country.'[109] In the same number citations from the Popes and from Cardinal Villeneuve and Mgr. Paquet were presented to support the thesis that nationalism was a virtue rather than a sin. While outside critics deplored the rise of 'clerical fascism' in Quebec, André Marois regretted the efforts of certain priests to eliminate political or nationalist tendencies from the Catholic youth movements. Cardinal Villeneuve settled the dispute by his declaration that 'No social, economic, nationalist action can be undertaken for itself by the groups in question [the clerical youth movements], but only as a means to the ends of Catholic Action.' In January 1936 the editors of *L'Action Nationale* interpreted this statement to suit their own ideas, since for them religion and nationalism were inextricably involved.[110] The extent to which these ideas prevailed was revealed by the publication in April 1936 of the Oblate Père Juneau's *Dieu et Patrie*, a sort of nationalist litany written for performance at a classical college.[111]

In March, in renewing their proposal of the previous year for a French-Canadian flag, the editors expressed their desire 'to create, in our province, a French people and a French State.' The proposed flag, the '*drapeau de Carillon*' which bore a white cross and four fleurs-de-lis on a light-blue background, was to serve as a symbol of 'spiritual unanimity.'[112] Writers in the magazine continued to urge economic nationalism by supporting the *achat chez nous* movement, and political nationalism by opposing suggested centralizing reforms of the constitution. The announcement that the annual *Semaine Sociale* in the fall would be devoted to corporatism was highly approved, while the menace of Communism and the 'treason of the élite' was stressed in editorial comments. In September the magazine supported the political course followed by three of its directors, Dr. Hamel, Albert Rioux, and René Chaloult. In December Arthur Laurendeau re-echoed the call for a French-Canadian '*mystique*,' while his son André was becoming aware as a student in Europe of the dangers of Hitlerism and Italian Fascism, which he later reported in the magazine.

The symposium of 1937 was devoted to '*Une Politique Nationale*,' while the doubled defence estimates of the year roused the old anti-imperialism of French Canada, despite Mackenzie King's assurances that 'the Canadian Parliament reserves to itself the right to declare, in the light of the circumstances existing at the time, to what extent, if at all, Canada will participate in conflicts in which other members of the Commonwealth may be engaged.'[113] In May much was made of the fact that in a speech closing a series of six lectures by Groulx at Quebec on 'New France in Champlain's Time,' Cardinal Villeneuve remarked: 'I have come here this evening to manifest the friendship I have for the Abbé Groulx, to express my gratitude to him, at the risk of scandalizing the weak. Abbé Groulx is one of the masters of the hour; he is one of those to whom our race owes much.'[114] In the same number André Marois held that 'our parliamentary gossips could with profit go and take lessons in Italy, Austria, and Portugal'[115] and expressed particular admiration for Mussolini and Salazar.

But *L'Action Nationale's* admiration for the dictators was checked when in September André Laurendeau became director of the review, after two years' study of philosophy and the social sciences in Paris. Fresh from firsthand contact with the rising tide of Fascism and Hitlerism in Europe, Laurendeau was horrified by the amount of racism he found upon his return to Quebec. In a prefatory note to Emile Baas' '*Introduction à la thèse de Rosenberg*,' Laurendeau observed:

. . . racism, in the strong sense of the word, represents in certain sectors of our intellectual life a menace all the more real because no one yet takes it seriously. In fact the movement, which finds no profound support from us, could not implant itself to a great degree; but it would be already too much if it infiltrated and contaminated the always shaky 'principles' of our nationalists. Knowing the actual source of the error, one will judge more severely its effects, and the division will be made between the conscious racists and the mass of those who are materialists without knowing it.

.   .   .   .   .

To make the National-Socialist doctrine crumble, it suffices to recall that according to modern ethnology there no more exists a pure race in the world, neither Saxon nor Slav nor German. We are confronted with a pseudo-scientific fantasy, whose dynamism must nonetheless not be underestimated. . . .

And to convince oneself that the racists' ideology is essentially anti-Christian, as anti-Christian as Communism for instance, one recalls several major texts of the Gospel and the whole Pauline teaching. Against the predominance of blood, we continue to assert the sovereignty of the spiritual.[116]

And in a long editorial note on the second *Congrès de la Langue française* at Quebec in June 1937, the editors sought to heal the split which had developed between separatists and anti-separatists after Abbé Groulx had on that occasion declared: 'Our sole legitimate and imperative destiny can be only this: to constitute in America in the greatest autonomy possible, this political and spiritual reality . . . a Catholic and French State,' to which he had added: 'Whether or not one wishes it, we shall have our French State.'[117] Bishop Yelle, speaking for the French Canadians of the West, had said on the same occasion: 'When we hear separatism for the Province of Quebec seriously spoken of, we see in it not words of salvation but words of discouragement and defeatism.'

L'Action Nationale hastened to reassure the anti-separatists by quoting earlier pronouncements of Groulx to prove that he referred to a State within Confederation, and that he was not a separatist.[118] But if Groulx was not a separatist at heart—and the whole tendency of his work indicates that he was—many of his followers undoubtedly were, just as Bourassa's followers had gone beyond the limits set by their master. Groulx was severely attacked for his declarations at Quebec, and charged with cultivating a French-Canadian racism. In an editorial note commenting on the papal encyclical '*Mit brennender Sorge*,' which condemned Nazism, André Laurendeau defended Groulx against the charge of racism, while clearly revealing his fear that a racist element had entered French-Canadian nationalism. He observed that 'French Canadians always applaud more willingly anathemas against the extreme left than anathemas against the extreme right. We are too often among those who think, according to the harsh formula of *La Vie intellectuelle*, that God is on the right.'[119] He complained that less publicity than usual had been given in Quebec to this papal utterance, and warned of the dangerous alliances that might be made in the name of anti-communism. In the same number Gérard Plourde of *Les Jeune-Canada* compared the recent lectures of Bourassa and Groulx on the 1837 Rebellion and prefered Groulx' more extreme thesis.

In the January 1938 number the collaboration of the *Jeune-Canada* group with *L'Action Nationale* was hailed, while it was announced that the yearly symposium would be devoted to the problem of corporatist organization. The editors denied the charges that corporatism was a subversive, medieval, fascist system which would mean the end of parliamentary government; they quoted Cardinal Villeneuve's declaration of April 17, 1937: 'We have here and there some bits of social justice, but these appearances of remedies do not suffice. We need more than that: full corporatism.'[120] André Laurendeau belittled Adélard Godbout's anti-fascist crusade against the Duplessis Padlock Law, as he had previously belittled Duplessis' anti-communist stand on the Dominion Textile strike, on the grounds that anti-fascism and anti-communism were mere distractions from the real problems of Quebec, since only a handful really supported Communism or Fascism. The unsuccessful campaign of Paul Bouchard, the editor of the separatist and anti-imperialist *La Nation* in the Lotbinière federal by-election against J.-N. Francoeur, backed by Justice Minister Ernest Lapointe, was hailed by Roger Duhamel as having brought before the people the burning issues of militarization and centralization. It was significant of the strength of extreme nationalism that the French-Canadian federal leader felt it necessary to take part in this by-election. In February the editors called upon the French Canadians to be on guard against centralization, regarding the period as crucial as that of 1867, while the close defeat of Camillien Houde in the Saint-Henri by-election in Montreal was deplored.

In April André Laurendeau replied to recent articles on Quebec fascism in the London *Daily Herald*, the *New York Post*, the Toronto *Magazine Digest*, and the New York *Nation*. He admitted that fascist organizations existed in Quebec, but maintained that they were not taken seriously. He blamed their recent activity and their success in recruiting on a decreasing lack of popular faith in parliamentary government. He denied that the Church was either at the head of or behind these organizations, but admitted that a few well-intentioned clerics might have become propagandists for them. He was convinced that the Church would take a stand against fascism in Quebec, if the latter ever became important, as it had done elsewhere. He admitted the existence of a 'pre-fascist' mentality which might favor the development of fascism if the political, economic, and social disorder continued. Archbishop Gauthier's vigorous pastoral in March against Communism also warned that the journal of Adrien Arcand's National Social Christian Party, *Le Fasciste Canadien*, advanced a watered German Nazism which minimized its anti-Catholic and Caesarist tendencies. But in Quebec, as elsewhere, the Catholic hierarchy was far more voluble about the dangers of communism than about those of fascism.

In May two articles in *L'Action Nationale* were concerned with the question of what the proper French-Canadian attitude should be in the face of gathering war clouds in Europe. Léopold Richer, commenting on the debates in the federal House on the rearmament program, supported the view of Maxime Raymond that Canada should only defend its own territory against aggression, rather than enter into collective security plans or imperial alliances. In September, after the Czecho-Slovakian crisis had passed, André Laurendeau protested against the passive acceptance of imperialist pressure by the French Canadians, and called for a united stand against inevitable attempts to bring about Canadian intervention at the next crisis. Roger Duhamel, who in September had begun a new series of monthly political reviews, hailed President Roosevelt's Kingston declaration as an extension of the Monroe Doctrine to Canada, and suggested that Canada should break its ties with the League of Nations and Britain and fulfil its American destiny.[121] A young nationalist economist, F.-A. Angers, who was making a name for himself as Minville's leading disciple, also launched a series of monthly economic commentaries. In December Laurendeau observed that the principles invoked by Lord Runciman in his report on Czecho-Slovakia might well be applied in Canada, where Confederation's guarantees to the French Canadians were violated by the ruling race.

The annual symposium was devoted in 1939 to 'Canada in the Commonwealth,' with the editors of *L'Action Nationale* obviously alarmed at Canada's close escape from being involved in a European war the previous fall. Roger Duhamel anticipated that the proposed royal visit to Canada would be used to strengthen imperialism, and praised the recent utterance of Professor Percy Corbett of McGill in favor of Canada's joining the Pan-American Union rather than continuing her association with Great Britain. An editorial note hailed the growing number of English-Canadian anti-imperialists, and suggested a 'prudent' alliance with these leftists. Duhamel regarded the election of Camillien Houde as Mayor of Montreal as a sign of popular discontent with the Duplessis *Union Nationale* government which had opposed him strongly. In February an editorial called for the return of Labrador to Quebec, since its possession by the Crown colony of Newfoundland might involve Canada in war, and since its rich natural resources could better be exploited by

Quebec than by bankrupt Newfoundland. F.-A. Angers violently opposed the proposed federal scheme of unemployment insurance as an infringement of provincial rights, while Duhamel expressed sympathy for those who had criticized the heavy military expenses announced in the speech from the throne.

Duhamel was alarmed by the divergence of Liberal opinion evident in the statements of Mackenzie King, who maintained Laurier's doctrine 'When Britain is at war, Canada is at war'; of Lapointe, who assured a Quebec public meeting that 'we shall stay at home and protect our country'; and of Senator Dandurand, who suggested a referendum before Canada participated in a war. Duhamel approved Liguori Lacombe's opposition to participation in any conflict which did not endanger Canadian security, but recognized that this was a minority opinion and concluded: 'It will be a happy day for our country when our representatives resolve, while conserving friendly relations with the old mother country, to limit their activity and efforts to the safeguarding of our territorial integrity and of Canadian unity understood in the bilateral sense.'[122] He also warmly supported the program of the federal nationalist party as formulated at its first meeting in Montreal on November 20, 1938, by Paul Bouchard, with the slogan of 'autonomous provinces in a free Canada,' and a program of Canadian neutrality, to be abandoned only after a provincial referendum. Duhamel favored the nomination of a Canadian governor-general to replace Lord Tweedsmuir, after the precedent established in Ireland and Australia.

During the spring of 1939 *L'Action Nationale* continued to discount the promises of King and Lapointe that they would resign rather than vote for conscription in case of war; to describe the royal visit, that of Stanley Baldwin, and the declarations of R. B. Bennett as parts of an imperialist program to assure Canadian support in case of war; and to express sympathy with Maxime Raymond's declaration in the House of French-Canadian opposition to all extra-territorial wars. But in June the editors exulted in the fact that the King and Queen had spoken French and expressed sympathy for the French Canadians; that the King had formally reasserted the 'free and equal' association of the nations of the Commonwealth; and that the Queen had expressed a wish to see the two great races of Canada linked like the Scots and the English by 'the bonds of affection, respect, and a common ideal.' The old monarchist tradition of French Canada responded to the royal visit; the French Canadians were charmed by the King and Queen—particularly by their use of French—and Montreal spent more money on the royal reception than did ultra-loyal Toronto.

But in the same issue Georges Pelletier warned at the close of an exhaustive analysis of imperialist propaganda:

If we wish to remain Canadians, it is a question of no longer delaying, of reacting and finally organizing ourselves. It is already very late. If we do not act, we will no longer be truly Canadians in 1950. At all events, we will no longer be even 'quality niggers.' We will have become nonentities in the British Empire: propaganda will have melted us, by our own fault, into the great imperial whole.[123]

And Roger Duhamel highly commended the opposition to the military estimates shown in parliament by Maxime Raymond, Liguori Lacombe, J.-A. Crète, L. Dubois, Pierre Gauthier, Wilfrid Gariépy, Wilfrid Lacroix, and Jean-François Pouliot, who had called for an autonomous Canadian policy, free of all subjection to Britain, and had been supported by some English-Canadian M.P.s.

Thus, on the eve of the Second World War French Canada already boasted an anti-war group in the federal House, supported by an embryo nationalist party in Quebec. The Duplessis administration was anti-war but also anti-nationalist, having broken with its electoral allies of 1936 as the federal Conservatives had broken with the nationalists after 1911. The Liberals undoubtedly had a strong hold on Quebec's sympathies, thanks to the anti-war and anti-conscription pledges of King and Lapointe, and the reiterated imperialism of such Conservative leaders as Bennett and Arthur Meighen. Ultranationalists admitted that the King government would be returned to power if it called elections, but remained suspicious of its future course. Two generations of the French-Canadian élite had been raised in an atmosphere of hatred for the English, who were depicted as eternal enemies of everything French and Catholic; of distrust for the Americans, who were painted as materialistic slaves of the almighty dollar and ruthless assimilators of other peoples to their own mediocrity and cultural sterility; and of admiration for the minor prophets of the new cult of the strong man and of totalitarianism which was to engulf Europe in the greatest of its wars. It was under intellectual leaders with this background, and with a tradition of passionate preoccupation with French-Canadian problems rather than international ones, that French Canada faced the outbreak of the great conflict that was to last for six years, during most of which Quebec was cut off from Rome and France, its traditional sources of spiritual strength in the struggle for cultural survival.

Notes

[1] 1871: 31.07 per cent; 1881: 30.03 per cent; 1901: 30.70 per cent; 1911: 28.52 per cent; 1921: 27.92 per cent. *Canada Year Book 1922-3*, 159, Table 20.

[2] *Ibid.*, 141, Table 4. Quebec's loss of rural population by emigration was never less than 50 per cent per decade after 1871. *CJEPS*, IV (1938), 344, E. C. Hughes, 'Industry & the Rural System in Quebec.'

[3] 1920–4: 55,352; 1925–30: 36,096; L. E. Truesdale, *The Canadian-Born in the United States* (New Haven, 1943), 92, Table 35.

[4] *Canada Year Book 1945*, 114, Table 23.

[5] *Canada Year Book 1922–3*, 416, Table 1; 739, Table 16.

[6] *Ibid.*, 171–2, Table 32.

[7] *Can. An. Rev. 1921*, 680.

[8] E. C. Hughes, *French Canada in Transition* (Chicago, 1943).

[9] E. Bouchette, *Emparons-nous de l'industrie* (Ottawa, 1901).

[10] Hughes, 'Industry and the Rural System,' 349.

[11] *CHAR 1944*, 31, M. Wade, 'Relations of French Canada & the U.S.' See H. Marshall, F. A. Southard and K. W. Taylor, *Canadian-American Industry* (New Haven, 1936).

[12] *Quebec Statistical Yearbook 1918*, 128; *Canada Year Book 1922–3*, 164.

[13] *L'Action française* (Montréal), I (jan. 1917), 1.

[14] A. Perrault, Abbé L. Groulx, 'P. Homier' (R. P. J.-Papin Archambault), *Soirées de l'Action française* (Montréal, 1926), 14, '*Consignes de Demain.*'

[15] *Ibid.*, 19.

[16] A. Laurendeau, *L'Abbé Lionel Groulx* (Montréal, 1939), 51.

[17] *L'Action française*, II (mars 1918), 3.

[18] *Ibid.*, IV (sept. 1920), 9.

[19] O. Asselin, *L'Oeuvre de l'abbé Groulx* (Montréal, 1923), 87.

[20] Laurendeau, 47–8.

[21] *Ibid.*, 48.

[22] *L'Action française*, V (jan. 1921), 1.

[23] '*Soirées*,' 7–9.

[24] *Ibid.*, 10.

[25] *Ibid.*, 10–11.

[26] *Ibid.*, 12.

[27] *Ibid.*, 13.

[28] Laurendeau, 20.

[29] *Annuaire de l'Université Laval* (Québec, 1897–8), 156; cited Laurendeau, 22.

[30] Laurendeau, 31.

[31] Abbé L. Groulx, *La Naissance d'une Race* (Montréal, 1919), *Lendemains de la Conquête* (1920), *Nos luttes constitutionnelles* (1916), *Les Patriotes de 1837* (1917—not published), *La Confédération canadienne* (1918), *Vers l'Emancipation* (1921).

[32] Asselin, *L'Oeuvre de l'abbé Groulx* (Montréal, 1923).

[33] *Ibid.*, 27–8.

[34] *Ibid.*, 54–5.

[35] *Ibid.*, 62–3.

[36] *Ibid.*, 67.

[37] *Ibid.*, 86.

[38] *Ibid.*, 91.

[39] *Ibid.*, 89.

[40] *Ibid.*, 90.

[41] *Ibid.*, 93.

[42] *L'Action française*, IX (fév. 1923), 2.

[43] Abbé L. Groulx, *Dix ans de l'Action française* (Montréal, 1926); 43–73, '*Pour l'Action française*'; 74–88, '*Méditation patriotique*'; 89–122, '*Si Dollard revenait . . .*'

[44] *L'Action française* [Paris], VII (mars 1922), 3.

[45] Abbé Groulx' speeches have been collected in *Dix ans de l'Action française* (Montréal, 1926), *Orientations* (Montréal, 1935), and *Directives* (Montréal, 1937), as well as published in pamphlet form in most instances.

[46] *L'Action française*, V (jan. 1921), 4–23.

[47] *Ibid.*, VI (déc. 1921), 706.

[48] *Notre Avenir Politique: enquête de l'Action française*, 1922 (Montréal, 1923), 5.

[49] *Ibid.*, 7.

[50] *Ibid.*, 12.

[51] *Ibid.*, 13.

[52] *Ibid.*, 15.

[53] *Ibid.*, 20.

[54] *Ibid.*, 23.

[55] *Ibid.*, 25.

[56] *Ibid.*, 29–30.

[57] *Ibid.*, 50.

[58] *Ibid.*, 71.

[59] *Ibid.*, 84–5.

[60] *Ibid.*, 93.

[61] *Ibid.*, 107.

[62] *Ibid.*, 113.

[63] *Ibid.*, 141–59.

[64] *Ibid.*, 161–78.

[65] *Ibid.*, 179–96.

[66] *Ibid.*, 216.

[67] *Ibid.*, 219–31.

[68] *Ibid.*, 244.

[69] *Ibid.*, 249.

[70] *Ibid.*, 250.

[71] A. Zimmern, *The Third British Empire* (London, 1926), 24.

[72] *L'Action française*, X (déc. 1923), VI, 350.

[73] Cf. E. Montpetit, *D'Azur à trois lys d'or* (Montréal, 1937).

[74] *Revue trimestrielle* (sept. 1928), Beaudry Leman, 'Les Canadiens-français et le milieu américain.'

[75] *Les Canadiens-français et la Confédération canadienne; enquête de 'L'Action française'* (Montréal, 1927).

[76] *Ibid.*, 12.

[77] *Ibid.*, 20.

[78] *Ibid.*, 20–1.

[79] *Ibid.*, 22–3.

[80] *Ibid.*, 39.

[81] *Ibid.*, 47–8.

[82] *Ibid.*, 49–58.

[83] *Ibid.*, 63.

[84] *Ibid.*, 70.

[85] *Ibid.*, 83–4.

[86] *Ibid.*, 89.

[87] *Ibid.*, 103–4.

[88] *Ibid.*, 107.

[89] *Ibid.*, 120.

[90] *Ibid.*, 142.

[91] Laurendeau, 61.

[92] *L'Action canadienne-française*, XIX (jan. 1928), I, 3.

[93] Laurendeau, 63.

[94] *Can. An. Rev. 1932*, 400.

[95] *L'Action Nationale*, I (fév. 1933), II, 118.

[96] *Ibid.*, 120.

[97] *Ibid.*, I (mai 1933), V, 268.

[98] *Ibid.*, I (juin 1933), VI, 359.

[99] *Ibid.*, II (nov. 1933), III, 210–16.

[100] *Ibid.*, III (jan. 1934), 53–4.

[101] *Ibid.*, III (mai 1934), V, 265.
[102] *Ibid.*, IV (sept. 1934), I, 61.
[103] *Ibid.*, IV (nov. 1934), III, 175–6.
[104] *Ibid.*, V (jan. 1935), I, 4.
[105] Groulx, *Directives*, 52–94.
[106] *Canada, Commons Debates 1935*, April 4, III, 2279–92.
[107] *L'Action Nationale*, V (mai 1935), V, 317; *ibid.*, V (juin 1935), VI, 375.
[108] *Ibid.*, VI (sept. 1935), I, 81.
[109] *Ibid.*, VI (oct. 1935), II, 92–102.
[110] *Ibid.*, VII (jan. 1936), I, 3.
[111] *Ibid.*, VII (avril 1936), IV, 235.
[112] *Ibid.*, VII (mars 1936), III, 129.
[113] *Can. An. Rev. 1935–6*, 79.
[114] *L'Action Nationale*, IX (mai 1937), V, 271.
[115] *Ibid.*, 308.
[116] *Ibid.*, X (sept. 1937), I, 14–15.
[117] Abbé L. Groulx, *Directives* (Montréal, 1937), 234, 242.
[118] *L'Action Nationale*, X (sept. 1937), I, 31–5.
[119] *Ibid.*, X (nov. 1937), III, 181.
[120] *Ibid.*, XI (jan. 1938), I, 25.
[121] *Ibid.*, XII (nov. 1938), III, 262.
[122] *Ibid.*, XIII (fév. 1939), II, 154.
[123] *Ibid.*, XIII (juin 1939), VI, 508.

CHAPTER XV

FRENCH CANADA AND WORLD WAR II

(1939–44)

THE SECOND WORLD WAR came upon a Quebec which had not yet rallied from ten years of economic depression that had gravely shaken its social structure and had also fostered social developments that had made English Canadians and Americans suspicious of French Canada. For some French Canadians, bred in an authoritarian tradition and self-consciously 'Latin' in an 'Anglo-Saxon' North America, felt a certain sympathy for the totalitarian nationalism of Mussolini, Franco, and Salazar which was so antipathetic to English-speaking North Americans. The current of racism which had been running even more strongly in French-Canadian nationalism, thanks to twenty years of Abbé Groulx's teaching and to ten years of being a 'subject people' in a period of economic disorder which did not afflict the 'master race' so sharply, even encouraged a certain sympathy with Hitler in some French-Canadian quarters. It was also difficult for the French Canadians, traditionally anti-imperialists, not to be skeptical of the new anti-imperialism of the English and the Americans as the Germans and Italians sought the empires which the other great powers had long enjoyed.

Preoccupied with its own economic and social troubles, French Canada had not shared the general Western development towards a belief in collective security; and as a world conflagration came ever nearer, French Canada had lapsed more and more into isolationism. The old dream of a separate French Catholic State, a 'Laurentia,' had never been more popular than in the immediate pre-war period, thanks to the provincialist trend of Groulx's nationalism and to fears of the outside world. Some French Canadians envisaged such a state within the British Commonwealth of Nations, another Eire enjoying the privileges but none of the responsibilities of membership in the Commonwealth; others favored Canadian neutrality, no matter what happened in Europe; and still others, whose North Americanism was greater than their sense of kinship with France and Rome, even maintained that annexation to the United States would be preferable to endless involvement in Britain's imperial wars.

I

Considering these trends and the fact that much Italian and German money was spent in Quebec with the aim of embarrassing Britain as the Second World War drew close,[1] it was somewhat surprising that French-Canadian opinion so definitely sided with England and France in the final crisis. The Soviet-German Pact produced a general outburst of violent anger in the French-Canadian press,[2] relieved only by *La Presse's* reflection that it was perhaps not regrettable since the democracies thus avoided an unfortunate alliance with godless Russia. *La Patrie, Le Soleil, Le Canada, L'Evénement-Journal,* and *Le Droit* saw in the Pact only the formal alliance of totalitarian regimes which had the same tyrannical and anti-religious conceptions of life, politics, and power, and the same cynical disloyalty to promises and pledges. Louis-Philippe Roy of *L'Action Catholique* considered it an opportunity for Mussolini to disassociate himself from Hitler, while *Le Soleil* anticipated the day when Italy would line up with Germany and Russia. *L'Evénement-Journal* mocked the Italian army and approved *Le Droit's* campaign against the anti-French articles of *Italia Nuova,* the fascist-inspired Italian weekly of Montreal. Both *La Presse* and *L'Action Catholique,* however, suggested that Mussolini might mediate in the tense European situation, though *La Tribune* of Sherbrooke questioned his qualifications for the role. Adrien Arcand's *L'Illustration Nouvelle* maintained that peace could only be preserved by a four-power pact between the United Kingdom, France, Italy and Germany.

Despite the desire of the French-Canadian press for peace, peace at any price was not favored. *La Presse* admitted during the Polish crisis of August that it might not be well to yield to Hitler's demands. *La Patrie* went farther than any other Quebec paper in condemning Hitler's aims and methods. The Liberal papers, particularly *Le Soleil,* were uncompromising in their stand against another Munich. At the end of August *Le Canada* stated that war depended upon the will of one man, Hitler. The nationalist press was less concerned with the current crisis than with the stand Canada should take in case of war in Europe, but *Le Devoir* credited Chamberlain with having avoided war so far and with attempting to limit its scope if it should break out. *L'Evénement-Journal* blamed Chamberlain for his excessive patience and diplomatic weakness, but threw the whole responsibility for the impending war on Hitler. The editor of *L'Action Catholique,* Louis-Philippe Roy, who always sought to follow papal directives, held that Germany and Italy, the have-not nations, were not wrong in complaining of their needs, since the wealth of the world was unjustly distributed; but he blamed the dictators for their violation of treaties and their attempts to plunder weaker countries. Both *L'Action* and *Le Droit* were convinced that Danzig was simply a pretext and that Hitler sought a complete settlement of the Polish question. Poland, as a Catholic country, commanded much sympathy from these papers.

L'Illustration Nouvelle maintained the official Nazi thesis that Danzig was a German city and that Poland had no more right to determine its fate than did England and France. Hitler was pictured as considering war the greatest of plagues, while big business and the international news agencies were accused of supporting war parties in the democracies. *L'Illustration* also bewailed the encirclement of Germany and Polish persecution of the Ukrainians. The Freemasons were blamed for the resistance of the democracies to Hitler. With the exception of this frankly fascist publication, which was also the chief organ of Duplessis' *Union Nationale*, the French-Canadian press favored the democracies against the dictatorships —though there was some lingering sympathy for Mussolini—and held that the war of blackmail must be ended, once and for all. [3] But there was a strange optimism that once more war would be averted, as it had been in the previous year.

It was doubtless because of this state of opinion in Quebec, upon whose support his government rested, that Prime Minister Mackenzie King continued his ambiguity as the time for decision drew near. On August 23 he announced that the government would, if necessary, use the extensive powers granted under the War Measures Act of 1914, in case of war or apprehended war. [4] On August 25 he re-iterated that parliament would be summoned if war became inevitable in Europe and that the government would submit its policy to parliament. Mackenzie King also cabled appeals to Hitler, the Polish president, and Stalin, urging them to avoid starting a general war. When Germany invaded Poland on September 1, a proclamation was issued that a state of 'apprehended war exists and has existed as and from the twenty-fifth day of August.' [5] Mr. King then summoned parliament to meet on September 7, and declared that if Britain became involved in war with Germany, his government would seek authority from parliament 'for effective co-operation by Canada at the side of Britain.' [6] When Great Britain formally declared war on September 3, Mr. King stated in a broadcast that the government would recommend to parliament 'the measures which it believes to be the most effective for co-operation and defence.' [7] Meanwhile semi-belligerent measures were taken, with the proclamation of the Defence of Canada Regulations, the placing of the armed forces on a war basis, the internment of enemy aliens, the prohibition of trading with the enemy, and the creation of a Wartime Prices and Trade Board to prevent profiteering. [8]

Although a policy of neutrality was incompatible with such

measures as these, the speech from the throne at the opening of the special session on September 7 still left the government's position vague. Parliament was told it had been summoned 'in order that the government may seek authority for the measures necessary for the defence of Canada, and for co-operation in the determined effort which is being made to resist further aggression, and to prevent the appeal to force instead of to pacific means in the settlement of international disputes.'[9] On September 8, under pressure from Dr. Manion, leader of the opposition, the prime minister refused to disclose his views on an expeditionary force and overseas action, while Maxime Raymond presented a petition signed by thousands of citizens against participation by Canada in any foreign war.[10] In seconding the address, J.-A. Blanchette (Compton) declared: 'I have reason to believe that I am expressing the opinion of the majority of electors in my province, in fact in all provinces, when I say that I am in favor of a reasonable and moderate cooperation, consistent with our interests and resources.' He favored voluntary contribution and was 'completely opposed to conscription.'[11]

On the following day Mr. King committed himself to a declaration of war with his announcement that if the House approved the address in reply to the speech from the throne, proclamation of a state of war between Canada and the German Reich would be issued at once. The address was passed on the evening of September 9, and on September 10 the King gave his formal approval to the proclamation.[12]

Though Mr. King later revealed that since the Munich crisis he himself had thought Canada must be prepared to go to war against Germany,[13] his hesitant course in 1939 was dictated by the desire, as he declared on September 8, 'to let no hasty or premature threat or pronouncement create distrust and divisions between the different elements that compose the population of our vast Dominion, so that when the moment for decision came all should so see the issue itself that our national effort might be marked by unity of purpose, of heart and of endeavour.'[14] He was clearly inspired by the example of Laurier, and by his own recollections of the tragic division of Canada in the First World War. In his speech on the address on September 8 he sought to conciliate both French-Canadian nationalists and the left-wing English Canadians who were opposed to full participation. He made much of Canada's dual heritage from France and Britain, the need for unity, and the government's primary concern with the defence and security of Canada. He said little about the possibility of an expeditionary force, and emphatically repeated his promise of March 30 that the present government would not introduce conscription for overseas service.[15] He indicated that Canada's role would naturally be concerned with the defence of her own territory and that of Labrador and Newfoundland, and with economic aid to Britain. In short he left the door open for a policy of aggressive neutrality, such as the United States later adopted, in case public opinion blocked more active participation.

But Ernest Lapointe's eloquence supplemented the prime minister's tactics of caution and persuasion in winning French-Canadian support for the government's proposals. The justice minister reviewed the reasons 'Why it is impossible, practically, for Canada to be neutral in a big war in which England is engaged.'[16] He pointed out that Canadian neutrality could not be 'other than a move favorable to the enemies of England and France.'[17] As for an expeditionary force, no government could stay in office if it refused to do what the large majority of Canadians wanted it to do.' In reply to Raymond, who had taunted him with his refusal at Quebec the previous December 'to fight in behalf of foreign interests,' he declared: 'For the sake of unity we cannot be neutral in Canada.'[18] But Lapointe made a solemn pledge against conscription for overseas service:

The whole province of Quebec—and I speak with all the responsibility and all the solemnity I can give to my words—will never agree to accept compulsory service or conscription outside Canada. I will go farther than that: When I say the whole province of Quebec I mean that I personally agree with them. I am authorized by my colleagues in the cabinet from the province of Quebec—the veteran leader of the Senate (Dandurand), my good friend and colleague, the Minister of Public Works (Mr. Cardin), my friend and fellow townsman and colleague, the Minister of Pensions and National Health (Mr. Power)—to say that we will never agree to conscription and will never be members or supporters of a government that will try to enforce it.

He added a warning, which was probably intended for some of his cabinet colleagues as well as for the Tories to whom it was addressed:

May I add that if my friends and myself from Quebec were forced to leave the government, I question whether anyone would be able to take our place. If my hon. friends in the far corner of the house opposite, if the *Ottawa Citizen*, which just now is waging a campaign for conscription, think they are serving Canada by splitting it at the very outset of the war, then I say they are gravely and seriously wrong.[19]

Mr. Lapointe then appealed to French Canada as he alone could do as Quebec's spokesman at Ottawa:

Provided these points are understood, we are willing to offer our services without limitation and to devote our best efforts for the success of the cause we all have at heart. And those in Quebec who say that we will have conscription, in spite of what some of us are saying, are doing the work of disunity, the work of the foe, the work of the enemy. They weaken by their conduct and their words the authority of those who represent them in the government. So far as the insults and abuses of agitators are concerned—I disdain them! They will not deter me from the path of duty as God gives me light to see it. I will protect them against themselves. I believe the majority in my province trusts me; I have never deceived them, and I will not deceive them now. I have been told that my present stand means my political death. Well, at least it would not be a dishonourable end. But let me assure you, Mr. Speaker, that if only I can keep my physical strength, fall I shall not, and my friends shall not fall, either.[20]

With a foresight that was to be borne out by subsequent events, he warned against 'a Balkanized Canada, a plebiscite by provinces,' in reply to Raymond's suggestion that the issue be submitted directly to the people. And then he closed with a deeply emotional and highly effective variation on the Queen's farewell words at Halifax at the conclusion of the royal tour: '*Dieu bénisse le Canada.*'

God bless Canada. God save Canada's honor, Canada's soul, Canada's dignity, Canada's conscience.

God give Canadians the light which will indicate to them where their duty lies in this hour of trial so that our children and our children's children may inherit a land where freedom and peace shall prevail, where our social, political, and religious institutions may be secure and from which the tyrannical doctrines of nazism and communism are forever banished. Yes, God bless Canada, God bless our Queen, God bless our King.[21]

Lapointe's deeply felt evocation of French Canada's love of country and loyalty to the monarchy won the hesitant Quebec members to the government's program. In vain Liguori Lacombe declared that the sacrifice of neutrality was too high a price for national unity, and called for dissolution of parliament and an appeal to the people.[22] Lacombe moved an amendment to the address, which was seconded by Wilfrid Lacroix, 'That this house regrets that the Government did not deem it fitting to advise His Excellency the Governor General that Canada should refrain from participating in war outside Canada.' But the motion found virtually no supporters. Georges Héon's poll of sentiment in his Argenteuil constituency probably provided an accurate picture of popular French-Canadian sentiment: 15 per cent favored conscription to the last man and dollar, 20 per cent favored complete isolation, 65 per cent were for 'cooperation within our means and resources, preferably by the extension of credits, gifts of provisions and foodstuffs, and the manufacture of planes and munitions,' while there was 'a very strong and earnest sentiment against conscription of manpower,' and opposition to an expeditionary force.[23] The government motion received almost unanimous support on an unrecorded vote in which only one member was noted as having risen in opposition.

2

When Britain went to war on September 3, the French-Canadian press was united in the conviction that the conflict was a righteous one into which the democracies had been forced by Hitler. *La Presse* asserted that Canadians endorsed the attitude taken by the King, the British prime minister, and the French president at the outbreak of hostilities. *La Patrie*, *L'Action Catholique*, and *Le Soleil* used the contemptuous word '*Boche*' on all occasions. The dailies were backed up by the weeklies in condemning Hitler for bringing on the war. *L'Action Catholique* considered Hitlerism the chief danger in Europe, particularly since its alliance with Communism; while *Le Droit* blamed the war primarily on Communism. *Le Devoir* devoted little editorial attention to the war during the first two months, although on September 16 its editor, Georges Pelletier, speculated as to why London and Paris had not taken steps against Lenin and Stalin in Russia, and Négrin in Spain, who had long behaved in the same way as Hitler. *L'Illustration Nouvelle* carefully avoided reference to the war.[24]

The French-Canadian press was somewhat less quick to consider the conflict a crusade than the English-Canadian newspapers, which hailed it as a holy war against the enemies of religion and civilization. *Le Canada* questioned this interpretation; but *L'Action Catholique* characterized the Nazis as the 'enemies of Christianity,' *La Patrie* called Hitler 'an Anti-Christ,' and *Le Droit* spoke of 'the truly Catholic character assumed by the Allies in this crusade against an alliance of Hitlerism and Communism.' There was much sympathy for the plight of Catholics in Poland and Germany. *L'Action Catholique* urged a Christian Front against Bolshevism, embracing the Allies, Italy, Spain, and other neutrals, lest it be forgotten that 'the greatest peril of the hour is Bolshevism rather than Hitlerism.' Repressive measures against the Canadian Communists were recommended. There was no sympathy for Hitler's peace proposals after the rapid overrunning of Poland.[25]

While the French press was almost unanimously anti-German and anti-Russian, it was not pro-war, in the sense of favoring Canadian participation. It urged either neutrality or limited participation, in the interests of Canada, national unity, and Canadian freedom of action in foreign affairs. Louis Francoeur, one of Quebec's most popular commentators on world affairs, held that the British government should assume the cost of the war, since 'though it is the duty of every free, responsible man to do his part in the defence of civilization against the aggressor nations and the powers of brute force, Canada as such was not directly interested in the present crisis in Central Europe.'[26] It was pointed out that under the Neutrality Act the United States would be bound to cease supplying Canada once the latter declared war, with results that would be 'very much felt by every friendly belligerent.' Most papers favored American neutrality, and thought it in the interest of internal peace in Canada.

When it became obvious that Canadian public opinion at large favored participation, the French press hailed the policy of limited participation announced by Mackenzie King and Ernest Lapointe when parliament met in special session on September 1. *La Presse* called on September 6 for 'fair and reasonable' aid to Britain:

> The Province of Quebec is ready to lend its most generous aid within the limits set by the speeches of Messrs. King and Lapointe, i.e., putting our national interests first, and adhering to the voluntary principle. Quebec will not associate itself with a policy that would compromise national interests by leading Canada to economic ruin and causing a division of ideas across the country.[27]

Two days later it approved the cautious course announced by the King government in the speech from the throne as sound and constitutional. *La Patrie* on September 10 observed: 'It is fortunate that we have as the Government of Canada men who can reconcile their duty to the British Empire with their duty to their country.'[28]

The Liberal press was markedly reluctant to back participation wholeheartedly. On September 6 *Le Canada* declared that Canada had the right to assert its neutrality, but that complete neutrality was impossible considering the opinion of the English-speaking majority. It criticized anti-participationist agitators for doing a disservice to the French Canadians by presenting the question as a racial issue. Since Canada derived advantages from the Commonwealth in time of peace, it was logical that it should cooperate with Britain in time of war. *Le Canada* saw Lapointe playing a dual role in the cabinet as a defender of Canadian interests and a protector of the link between French Canada and England. In its September 9 editorial on the government's war policy, it called upon Quebec to support this 'intelligent, reasoned participation,' with no conscription for overseas service, no expeditionary force, and reasonable economic aid. It observed: 'If Canada's effective co-operation should mean economic and financial ruin, it would be a disservice to the Commonwealth and disastrous for the Canadian people.' The defence and security of Canada were set up as the first responsibilities of the Canadian people. *La Tribune* of Sherbrooke warned that 90 per cent of French-Canadian electors were opposed to conscription: 'So let no government in this country ever commit the error of passing a law so pregnant with troubles, and which in the past produced nothing but evil.'[29]

Le Soleil during August had demanded that British and French propaganda for Canadian participation should be checked, and had asserted that there was no reason to believe that popular opinion had changed since the King government won power in 1935 on a peace platform. On September 6 it explained its attitude in detail:

For some years the conflict of ideas and interests has enabled one to foresee the outbreak of a catastrophic European war. *Le Soleil* has strongly urged the Canadian authorities to base their foreign policy on the national interest in relation to the solidarity of the countries of the American continent. It is not our fault if this advice, widely supported by French-Canadian opinion, has not prevailed. But as the majority think otherwise, we would not have the temerity to doubt their patriotism or to encourage any sort of sedition. War is a great calamity, but anarchy is worse.[30]

On the following day it asserted that Canada would stay neutral, following the example of Eire. And on September 9 it noted that Mackenzie King had taken account of the divergences of opinion on the question of participation, and concluded: 'Short of a crisis or a *coup d'état*, the internal peace of Canada will not be disturbed, as in 1917, by a new attempt to raise a levy of Canadian blood for the profit of an imperial power.'[31]

Such independence of attitude in the most widely circulated French Liberal paper indicated the pressure that Quebec brought to bear upon Ottawa at the outbreak of the war. The country weeklies accepted the necessity of participation, since it was favored by the English majority; but they joined the chorus against obligatory service outside Canada. Jean-Charles Harvey of *Le Jour* stood alone on September 2 when he found it 'logical, natural, and right that Canada, a democratic country united to the British Commonwealth by a sort of unwritten treaty, more binding even than the treaties binding France and England to Poland and all the little nations of Europe which wanted to keep their liberty, should join the democratic bloc, participating wisely for the defence and triumph of an ideal which should be that of every man of heart.' But even Harvey favored assistance 'within the measure of our means, for our two nationalities of different origin should remember that the war is not the end of the world and that afterwards we shall have to live side by side, as sons of the same land.'[32]

The nationalist press called for a Canadian foreign policy 'that would take account of geographical realities and our overriding interests.' Canada, as a North American country, should confine its responsibilities to the New World; and since it had no influence on British foreign policy, it was not bound to endorse British commitments. Canada had the right, under the Statute of Westminster, to maintain its neutrality, and should do so; intervention would be a return to colonial status. The example of the United States and the smaller European powers which remained neutral was pointed out, with the comment that they either had greater interests at stake or were closer to the battleground than Canada.

Le Devoir carried on a vigorous campaign against intervention. Omer Héroux saw the crisis as only 'a boundary dispute between Germany and Poland,' into which France and England might be drawn because they promised to stand by Poland. But 'they did not and could not claim to commit Canada,' and Canada had no reason to intervene, either for the survival of Britain, France and Poland, or to restore the balance of power in Europe, or to defend a democracy which for months had sought alliance with Russian autocracy. Georges Pelletier asserted that Canada was not a party to the treaty invoked by the Poles, but that all Canadians were parties to the Confederation pact:

. . . in which it was agreed among other things that Canadians should defend their common country. Their country is in America. Its frontiers are not in the Rhineland, nor on the shores of the Baltic or banks of the Vistula. They are only on the American continent, between the Atlantic and the Pacific and the Arctic. What has become of the sanctity of that treaty, for it is a treaty bearing the most authoritative signatures? It was violated from 1914 to 1918. They are ready to violate it again in September 1939. And supposedly it is in Europe that treaties are endangered . . . Let us think of our own.[33]

Léopold Richer, *Le Devoir's* Ottawa correspondent, gloomily accepted intervention as foredoomed from the first. He maintained that Mackenzie King's theory that parliament would decide the issue contradicted Laurier's theory that 'when Britain is at war, Canada is at war and exposed to attack.' If the Liberal leaders stuck to Laurier's theory, parliament had only to decide the manner and extent of intervention. If the Liberals rejected the idea of Canadian neutrality, it did not mean that Canada had no right to it but that the Liberal government had doubts about it or had decided not to exercise that right. Héroux revived some of Bourassa's old arguments when he proclaimed that 'the people who want to ruin Canada for the sake of the Empire are really the most dangerous promoters of annexation'; and when he argued that intervention now, as in 1899 and in 1914, would constitute a new precedent for later interventions all over the world. He urged that conscription would be the inevitable result of intervention, and 'in any case, whether they fall as conscripts or volunteers, the fallen soldiers are an equal loss to the country, and the costs of war are the same.' As early as August 3 Richer preferred independence to intervention: 'Every Canadian who sincerely wants to save his country the enormous losses of men and money which war requires inevitably, could make no other choice . . . It would be better for the internal peace of the country and for its future to adopt a *modus vivendi* with the nations of the Commonwealth, which would allow us full liberty of action in case of armed conflict in Europe or Asia.' *Le Devoir* saw only two circumstances under which Canada should intervene: if a plebiscite showed that the nation willed it, or if the United States joined the Allies.[34] The nationalists were convinced that a plebiscite would result in a verdict against intervention—a conclusion which seems somewhat dubious.

Le Droit was actively anti-interventionist, asserting that Canadian foreign policy was in the hands of London and that Canada had become a suburb of England. On September 6 it accused Mackenzie King of sabotaging Canadian unity: 'If, supported by the parliamentary majority it counts on, the Federal Government is ready to impose on a part of the Canadian people, by force of numbers, a policy that they do not want, then we have oppression of minorities such as is condemned in Europe by those practising it here.' But on September 8 it admitted that 'the Government would take the attitude which would be least likely to endanger Canadian unity.' Camille L'Heureux seemed to envisage the formation of a French-Canadian party, after he had appealed to French-Canadian members of parliament to put their duty to their electors above party loyalty:

French Canada has no chance of getting a strictly Canadian foreign policy, to say nothing of respect for the Canadian constitution. In each party our presentation is subjected to the dictatorship of an Anglo-Canadian majority which unites every time it sees fit, to oppose with a united front the legitimate aspirations of the French Canadians . . . In the light of recent events one sees more clearly that there will be no safety for us save outside the present political parties. The present attitude of the Federal Government emphasized this conviction among the French Canadians, and strengthens their determination to break the chains binding them to the present parties and to turn to a strictly Canadian party.[35]

L'Action Catholique argued during August that before rushing into an intervention 'more generous than wise,' it should be considered that 'we are an American nation,' that 'our military assistance could only be relatively diminutive,' that 'the warring nations should count on the production of friendly countries almost exclusively,' that 'civilization needs some corners for refuge during the coming carnage,' that 'as far as we participate with military forces, we take the roles of belligerents and attract reprisals,' that 'prudence compels us to organize some defence for our immense territory,' and that 'our people, crushed by the burden of debt contracted in the last war, are unable to pay the costs of a new war infinitely more disastrous than the last.' On September 2 *L'Action Catholique* set forth its principles for a Canadian foreign policy:

Above all, we still wish the maintenance of peace as far as possible. In principle we refuse to accept the doctrine that Canada is at war just because England is, and in practice we strongly oppose any military participation caused merely by that doctrine. However, if a situation should arise that might really jeopardize one or another of the great interests of humanity, above all the interests of Christianity, the Canadian people would then decide that there was a case for joining with other nations to deal with the peril. Even in that case our participation should be voluntary, and should by no means exceed the rigid limits imposed by our resources. These principles should suit all Canadians, of whatever origin, because they arise from the purest Canadianism and take account of our affection for pacific peoples, and our preoccupation with world welfare.[36]

L'Evénement-Journal on September 7 warned French Canada's representatives at Ottawa that they would be held responsible if they violated the peace pledges they had made in the 1935 elections. And on the following day it expressed the hope that Mackenzie King would not develop the habit of facing the country with *faits accomplis.* *L'Illustration Nouvelle* blended nationalist isolationism with fascist inspiration in its insistence on neutrality, since England and France, in taking up arms against Hitler, 'were waging an aggressive war of intervention.'[37] Self-centered nationalism, with its 'sacred egoism' which put French-Canadian rights and sentiments before the will of the majority, and which for years had sought to build a Chinese Wall about Quebec, found it easy to concentrate on the plight of French Canada in the midst of a world struggle. This isolationism, with its long tradition of anti-imperialism, offered a fertile field of exploitation for Italian and German propagandists, who remained active in Quebec until the outbreak of the war, and whose work was later carried on, in some few instances, by French-Canadian converts to the concept of the 'new order.'

Once parliament had endorsed the government's stand in favor of participation on September 9 and had asserted Canadian sovereignty by declaring war on its own account, not as an automatic consequence of Britain's declaration of war a week before, the French press as a whole preached moderate participation and the maintenance of Canadian interests above those of Britain. *La Presse* envisaged Canada's role as that of principal base of supplies for the Allies. It urged that participation should not be allowed to injure Canadian agricultural, industrial, or economic life, and expressed the hope that the war budget would be confined to necessary expenses. It opposed putting pressure on the unemployed to enlist. *La Patrie* showed somewhat more enthusiasm for recruiting, but in general took the same stand. The Liberal press continued its reserved attitude, with *Le Canada* even likening the sending of an expeditionary force 'to complete participation which would ruin our country.' It stressed the gratitude which French Canadians owed to the King government for persuading the country to adopt a compromise policy, and warned of the dangers of rousing antagonism to French Canada by opposing intervention. [38]

The nationalist papers swallowed the pill of intervention with some bitterness, and urged very moderate participation, except for *Le Devoir*, which remained resolute in its opposition and constantly deplored the cost of participation. *L'Action Catholique* proposed a two-fold program: 'First to spread by all Christian and wise means the spirit of "Canadianism" wherever it is lacking, and secondly, whenever the opportunity occurs, to use our constitutional right to discuss the best manner and extent of participation, while avoiding any appeal to disturbing passions, and always following the line of reasonableness.' Both *Le Droit* and *Le Devoir* suggested in the middle of September that Canada should declare its neutrality at the end of the war, since its declaration of war had established a precedent that it was not automatically at war when Britain was at war. The nationalist press harped on the danger of conscription, 'which could not be accepted or applied in Quebec,' and deplored talk of union government, while continually reminding the present government of its pledges. The French-Canadian press outside Quebec, which had taken little part in the earlier debate as to whether Canada should intervene, now joined its Quebec colleagues in taking a firm stand against conscription. [39]

L'Action Nationale's September number was delayed by the establishment of censorship, which was imposed upon some of its articles, thus lessening its influence at the crucial period of the special session. But the views that were expressed may be taken as typical of the nationalist élite, although doubtless diluted by censorship. The editors took the stand that the government should impose no measure contrary to the will of either interventionists or anti-participationists. They opposed both conscription and war taxes. There should be 'no volunteering organized by the Canadian

government at Canadian expense for military operations outside
of Canada,' though 'it is well understood that we accept resolutely
the principle of true national defence, of a rational nature propor-
tioned to our means.' The editors declared that the French Canadians, to do justice to an 'important portion of English-Canadian
opinion,' would accept an embargo on exports to Germany or her
co-belligerents, the freedom of individual Canadians to join the
British Army or to recruit volunteers for the British Army at their
own expense, and the selling to Britain of arms or other needed goods.
The keynote of this highly individualistic program was 'Since
Canada is divided on this question, let Canadian policy be to leave
each individual free to act according to his convictions.'[40] What
these convictions were in the case of the editors was made apparent
by the hailing of Paul Gouin, René Chaloult, Ligouri Lacombe,
Paul Bouchard, and Dr. Philippe Hamel, as well as the leaders of
the Catholic syndicates and the Union Catholique des Cultivateurs,
for organizing protests against conscription and compromise programs, a course which Lapointe had characterized as 'dishonorable,
shameless, ignoble.'[41]

In the face of the *Ottawa Citizen's* campaign for the immediate
adoption of conscription, while the *Montreal Star* made much of the
demands for it by the Conservative and Social Credit parties and
veteran groups, the isolationists of *L'Action Nationale* found comfort
both in American belligerent-mindedness and in American isolationism. Roger Duhamel pointed out that President Roosevelt's
statement in a September press conference, that the United States
would tolerate no domination of Canada by a non-British power,
disposed of the argument that Canada would be the prey of the
victors if it did not help to crush the Germans.[42] *L'Action Nationale*
also quoted with obvious satisfaction Colonel Lindbergh's speech
of October 13, which admitted the United States' duty to defend
the American nations against invasion, but called for freedom from
the 'totalitarian influences of Europe,' and questioned Canada's
right to draw the Western Hemisphere into a European war 'for
the sole reason that it prefers the Crown of England to American
independence.' Lindbergh also urged that the United States
'should not permit any American country to extend the use of its
bases to foreign ships of war, or to send its army to fight abroad
while remaining safe under our protection.'[43] The isolationists of
French Canada, hiding behind their intellectual Chinese Wall,
had more in common with the Middle-Western isolationists, in-
sulated by half a continent, than with other dwellers on the Atlantic
seaboard who faced the possibility that the war might soon be
brought to their doorsteps.

3

The potential opposition and isolation from the rest of Canada latent in this situation was largely dispelled by Quebec's verdict in the provincial elections of October 1939, which were called by Premier Duplessis two weeks after Canada had declared war. He declared that a vote for him would be a vote against conscription and participation, and that the election was 'a battle for the survival of our popular liberties.'[44] But his anti-war, autonomist government was swept from office in an electoral landslide quite as earth-shaking as that which had dislodged the Liberals from office three years before. By its autocratic and extravagant regime which had doubled the debt of the province in three years, *L'Union Nationale* had alienated labor and offended the French-Canadian instinct for the way of moderation. When Ernest Lapointe denounced Duplessis' 'electoral adventure' as 'an act of national sabotage' and threatened that he and his French-Canadian colleagues in the federal cabinet would resign *en masse* unless the province cleaned house and supported the war policy by electing a Liberal government, French Canada responded enthusiastically. The new premier, Adélard Godbout, had declared: 'I pledge myself on my honour to quit my party and even to fight it if a single French Canadian, from now till the end of hostilities, is mobilized against his will under a Liberal regime, or even under a provisional regime in which our present ministers in the King cabinet participate.'[45]

La Presse and *La Patrie* agreed that the electoral verdict indicated that 'Quebec would not allow itself to get into the position of being apart from the other provinces of the Dominion,' though the latter made the reservation that approval of the war policy did not mean approval of obligatory overseas service.[46]

The four federal ministers promised that as long as they held office there would be no conscription for overseas, while the Liberal press interpreted the vote as a ratification of the stand adopted by the French-Canadian ministers and members at Ottawa. In the elections Duplessis was supported by *L'Illustration*, *L'Evénement-Journal*, and somewhat indirectly by *Le Devoir*. On November 4 the latter belittled the result as simply provincial in character, but *L'Illustration* immediately proclaimed that Quebec had pronounced against provincial autonomy. *L'Action Catholique*, which had inclined towards the Liberals before the elections, subsequently expressed fears that Adélard Godbout's victory might be taken as a blank check given to the federal government. It interpreted the electoral verdict thus: 'Messieurs the French-Canadian ministers at Ottawa, Quebec accepts the policy you have obtained, and wants you to stay at your posts and vigorously resist any attempt to go beyond the compromise, lest Canada be ruined.'[47]

The English-Canadian press hailed the verdict as a reknitting of the bond of Confederation and a repudiation of an administration which had been associated with the fascist movements in French Canada. Mackenzie King himself observed that 'nothing since Confederation has contributed more to national unity.'[48] English-Canadian confidence in Quebec was still further restored by the federal elections of March 1940, in which the Liberals won all but one of the Quebec seats in a striking endorsement of Mackenzie King's policies, which had been censured by the Hepburn government in Ontario. *Le Soleil* summed up French Canada's attitude by saying that the King government was 'the living symbol of practical cooperation' in the war effort, while *Le Progrès du Saguenay* observed that there could be no doubt that there were fewer dangers for Quebec in the policies of the Liberals.[49] The placid course of the 'phoney war' had disarmed overzealous English Canadians who would have preferred immediate conscription and economic assistance to the last cent from the outbreak of the war, while French Canada was led to play a modest but respectable part in the war effort on the basis of King's moderate, 'pay as you go' policy. A small Canadian expeditionary force of one division landed in England on December 17, without protest from Quebec. Canada faced the real opening of the war in Western Europe in the spring of 1940 far more united that it had been the year before.

4

The *Blitzkreig* which began with the invasion of Norway in early April and closed with the collapse of France in June brought the war very close to Canada. The internment of Adrien Arcand in May for publishing statements prejudicial to the safety of the state was calmly accepted. Quebec saw the France it loved despite all differences brought under the Nazi yoke; English Canada saw Britain left alone to face the conqueror, with only the remains of an army salvaged at Dunkirk. It was fired with enthusiasm by Winston Churchill's statement to the British Commons on June 4:

We shall go on to the end, we shall fight in France, we shall fight on the seas and oceans, we shall fight with growing confidence and growing strength in the air, we shall defend our Island, whatever the cost may be, we shall fight on the beaches, we shall fight on the landing grounds, we shall fight in the fields and in the streets, we shall fight in the hills; we shall never surrender, and even if, which I do not for a moment believe, this Island or a large part of it were subjugated and starving, then our Empire beyond the seas, armed and guarded by the British fleet, would carry on the struggle, until, in God's good time, the New World, with all its power and might, steps forth to the rescue and liberation of the old.[50]

The English Canadians were swept by an overpowering desire to rush all possible aid to Britain and to step up Canada's war effort. Loyalism was heightened by the prospect that the royal family might be forced to take refuge in Canada. Feeling rose very high in Ontario, with a mass meeting of 10,000 people in Toronto supporting the *Globe and Mail*'s cry of May 24: 'Give us leadership and arms, and Canadians will do the rest.'[51] Mackenzie King's cautious leadership was questioned, and he replied in parliament to the swelling tide of criticism with a warning against hysteria and panic, after recapitulating Canada's war effort to date, which included the sending of 25,000 men to England.

Universal sympathy was expressed by the Quebec press for France after its collapse, which stunned French Canada and produced a certain defeatism. The nationalist *Le Guide* on June 19 observed: 'The heart of New France bleeds for the mother country, but what of our own future? Will it be annexation? Very probably.'[52] And the paper went on to urge the French Canadians to prepare to defend themselves, to bring the Canadian Navy back from Europe to defend Canada, and to enter more fully into the North American orbit. Outrage at the betrayal of France by its own people was also expressed, although *Le Soleil* expressed the general attitude when it observed on June 25: 'Let us not judge too quickly. The least we French Canadians can do for France is to be just.'[53] French Canada felt itself more isolated than ever by the fall of France and by the English-speaking world's attacks on French cowardice and betrayal of the Allied cause. Mackenzie King used the occasion of Saint-Jean-Baptiste Day to declare that 'the tragic fate of France leaves to French Canadians the duty of upholding the traditions of French culture and civilization and the French passion for liberty in the world.'[54]

This message improved French-Canadian morale and helped to make possible acceptance of conscription for the defence of Canada at the end of June. The power given the government under the National Resources Mobilization Act, requiring 'persons to place themselves, their services, and their property' at the disposition of the country 'as may be judged necessary or expedient for securing the public safety, the defence of Canada, the maintenance of public order, or the efficient prosecution of the war,' was carefully limited against requiring 'persons to serve in the military, naval or air forces outside of Canada and the territorial waters thereof.'[55] As a result of this precaution, the limited conscription law was cheerfully

accepted in Quebec and the French-Canadian leaders of both
Church and State urged their compatriots to comply with it.

With France fallen and Britain beaten to her knees, and with the
clear possibility that Canada itself might soon be threatened, the old
objections to compulsory service lost most of their force. In vain *Le
Devoir* on June 20 headlined its announcement of the measure
'Government "imposes" conscription on the country,' and described it as a repudiation of the free, voluntary, and moderate participation promised by French Canada's leaders at Ottawa.[56] There
was little echo of this charge even in the rural regions, where the
necessity of compulsory service for the defence of Canada was calmly
accepted. An anti-mobilization resolution in the provincial legislature, proposed by René Chaloult and seconded by Camillien
Houde, was defeated on June 19 by 56 to 13, despite Chaloult's
claim that the resolution represented the opinion of the vast majority
of French Canadians, and Maurice Duplessis' statement that he had
been right in predicting in 1939 that participation would mean
coercion.[57] Maxime Raymond, the most notable of the French-
Canadian federal M.P.'s who had opposed participation in September 1939, declared in the House that he would support the
mobilization measure, since compulsory service was limited to the
defence of Canada on Canadian soil. Liguori Lacombe, however,
attacked it as being in flagrant contradiction with the promises of
the government, and Wilfrid Lacroix urged that Canadian participation be limited to 'possibilities.'[58] From the outset the Catholic
hierarchy approved the measure, with Cardinal Villeneuve in-
structing his clergy to explain the law from the pulpit in order that
the people might fulfil with exactitude and submission a duty which
the civil authorities were legitimately requiring of them.[59]

The Cardinal's intervention offset Mayor Houde's advice to the
people of Montreal on August 2 not to register as required by the
act, lest the law be used to send their sons overseas unwillingly.
Houde was promptly interned, and the federal government clumsily
sought to suppress news of the incident,[60] but there was no need to
do so. A chorus of disapproval for Houde's action broke out, with
even *Le Devoir* observing that he had acted like a fool and deserved
what he had got, though it maintained his right to appeal against
internment. *La Presse* pointed out on August 6 that the French
Canadians, who had a profound respect for law and order, were
shocked by Houde's defiance of authority. A few days later *L'Action
Catholique* told its readers that they could not choose which laws to
obey, and added that Cardinal Villeneuve had acted in accordance
with the best French-Canadian traditions. A petition for Houde's
release was circulated by René Chaloult, Dr. Philippe Hamel, and
Paul Bouchard, but it did not attract much support. One rural

paper, *L'Eclaireur* of Beauceville, urged that Houde should be released after a short time, lest a reaction in his favor do harm, but it approved the government's action in preventing sabotage of the war effort. The pro-Houde reaction did not come until late in the war, when ethnic feeling had been aroused by a new conscription crisis and he could be exploited as a martyr of the 'race.' Meanwhile the *Winnipeg Free Press* hailed Quebec's repudiation of Houde as an expression of national unity which deserved all Canada's thanks.[61]

On the eve of the national registration, which took place August 15–19, Ernest Lapointe made a broadcast address to his compatriots in which he attacked those who had urged the French Canadians not to register and called attention to Cardinal Villeneuve's stand. He stressed that the purpose of the registration was to obtain an inventory of men and resources for Canada's defence, and that overseas service remained purely voluntary. He reassured his compatriots as to his intention of keeping his promises of no conscription for overseas service.[62] All authorities agreed that Quebec co-operated fully in the registration, and the *Toronto Globe and Mail*, no friend of Quebec or of the Catholic clergy, pointed out with approval that even in remote parishes the *habitants* flocked to register in response to their priests' explanation of the necessity of the measure.[63]

Quebec's acceptance of the National Resources Mobilization Act and her contribution to the war effort in subsequent months led many English Canadians to hold the mistaken idea that the French Canadians would accept conscription for overseas service, which seemed increasingly necessary to the former as time went on. Opposition to such a policy was deeply rooted in the French-Canadian tradition, and had been fostered by the oft-repeated promises of both political parties not to adopt conscription for overseas service. The French Canadian was eager and willing to defend Canada, but he was less concerned with the fate of Britain than his English fellow-citizens and anxious to avoid establishing a precedent for compulsory service in imperial wars. Nationalist spokesmen were not wanting to point out that this was Britain's war and not French Canada's. Among the rank and file in Quebec popular sentiment desired the defeat of Germany, but it was felt that it would do no great harm if *les Anglais* were humbled a bit in the process. There was no popular support for the doctrine that the defence of Canada began in Europe, until the entry of the United States into the war destroyed a prop of French-Canadian isolationism.

When English-Canadian publications proposed conscription or a coalition government which would be free to adopt conscription if necessary, the French-Canadian press repelled both suggestions.

Much use was made of the argument that in the interests of Britain herself, Canada should conserve her manpower, not only to defend her own territory but to maintain the war industries whose products were so badly needed by Britain. Talk of coalition revived the bitter memory of 1917, and *Le Devoir* did not fail to keep that memory alive, while most of the French-Canadian press expressed staunch loyalty to the King government whose policy had been guided by Quebec's sentiments. At the end of February 1941 Ernest Lapointe said that he and his French-Canadian colleagues would resign from the cabinet if a coalition government with a conscription policy was formed. And on June 12 Defence Minister Ralston declared that it was a question of conscription or national unity, and that the wise course was to let well enough alone, since French Canada was giving good support to the voluntary enlistment program. [64]

French Canada's enlistment record in the early years of the Second World War was very different from that of the First War. A French-Canadian unit, the Régiment de Maisonneuve of Montreal, was the first in Canada to fill its ranks with volunteers for overseas service, and General L.-R. Laflèche, the deputy-minister of national defence, estimated that 50,000 French Canadians were in uniform by January 1, 1941. [65] The same authority estimated that 30 per cent of the Royal Canadian Navy was made up of French Canadians, and many French Canadians served in the R.C.A.F., whose famous French-Canadian fighter squadron, '*Les Alouettes*,' was formed in June 1942. Since the Canadian Navy at the outset of the war was largely staffed by British officers and had a strong English tradition, and the R.C.A.F. was at first integrated with the R.A.F., French-Canadian group consciousness favored enlistment in the Army, where French-Canadian regional units were organized at the outset of the war and where a program of bilingual officers' training schools, announced by Lapointe on September 24, 1941, permitted French Canadians to enter all branches of the service and to attain higher ranks. Similar measures were later adopted in the Navy and Air Force, but there remained a popular belief that a French Canadian was handicapped in these services.

At first privately, and later openly, there was much criticism by English Canadians of the fact that there was a higher proportion of French-Canadian enlistments in the Reserve Army units than for overseas service. This criticism neglected the considerations that popular feeling in French Canada was for the defence of Canada rather than for 'overseas adventures,' and that for many a French Canadian who had never been outside of Quebec, service in the Maritimes or in British Columbia, and later in Alaska or Greenland, was indeed 'foreign service.' In addition to its military effort,

French Canada made a notable contribution to war industry, which developed much more rapidly in Quebec than it had during the First World War.

5

After the fall of France the rivalry between the Pétainists and the De Gaullists was a divisive factor in Quebec, although the issue interested a much smaller proportion of the French-Canadian population than English Canadians believed. There was at first much sympathy for the Pétain regime among the élite—particularly among the lower clergy, who were hoodwinked by such pious Vichy slogans as 'Homeland—Work—Family' and by the restoration of religious teaching in the state schools and of the privileges of the religious orders. These measures seemed to indicate a return to the old French values which Quebec cherished and a repudiation of the anti-clerical attitude of French governments since the turn of the century. The De Gaullists were welcomed with intense sympathy by other groups of the élite, who saw in the movement a survival of the French tradition which they cherished, after the capitulation to the Nazis of the Vichy regime. But on the whole the fall of France left Quebec singularly cold, to the astonishment of English-speaking people who had not realized how deep was the isolationism of Quebec and how far its ties with France had been broken. This isolationism was in part a natural result of the long cultivation of a Chinese Wall about the province, so that the French Canadians should not be corrupted either by the surrounding 'Anglo-Saxon' mass or by godless modern France, and in part a parallel of Middle-Western American isolationism.

Both British and De Gaullist propagandists underestimated the new North Americanism of Quebec, and they alienated some of their original sympathizers and the mass of the people by their attempts to pull French-Canadian heartstrings in the interest of the war by invoking Quebec's ties with France. Quebec had not reacted with particular warmth to the French military and cultural missions of the First World War; it was even less pleased by the intellectual refugees and political bagmen of the Second War, who failed to conceal their view that Quebec was a cultural province of France with an unfortunately thin veneer of French culture over its North American barbarism. The fervent de Gaullists in particular alienated sympathy by their view that the French Canadians were un-French, unemancipated, and shockingly unmoved by the tragedy of Europe. On the whole, the De Gaulle-*vs.*-Vichy issue was confined to the press and the élite, while the great mass of the people was unaffected by it.

In July 1940 *La Patrie* asked: 'Why weep over the Third Republic, which confounded liberty with licence?' *L'Action Catholique* and *Le Devoir* displayed strong sympathies for the Pétain regime, with the latter on August 3 commending Pétain for forming the only government possible under the circumstances and defending him against charges of fascism, and the latter paying tribute on September 10 to his efforts to reorganize French life in the Christian tradition and to suppress Freemasonry. But at the same period *L'Action Catholique* expressed its opinions on the relative merits of Pétain and De Gaulle by explaining that though the Vichy government was the only legitimate government of France and Pétain's reforms were to be commended, naturally Vichy functioned under Nazi surveillance; while De Gaulle was to be approved for continuing the fight at Britain's side and for restoring France's credit with her former allies. There was little reaction in the press to De Gaulle's broadcast appeal of August 2 to French Canada, in which he said: 'The soul of France seeks and calls for your help, French Canadians, because she knows your importance in the British Empire, because in you a branch of the great French stock has become a magnificent tree, and above all because your example restores faith in the future.' As *Le Devoir* later remarked, though the French Canadian has a natural sympathy for France, it is absurd to think that he can be rallied to a cause by sentimental appeals to a French patriotism he has not possessed since Canada became his only country more than 175 years ago.[66]

But *L'Evénement* expressed approval of the Free French movement after the British destruction of the French fleet at Oran on July 4; and as Vichy came more and more under Nazi control and as Britain rallied from the disaster of June, there was a growing realization in the Quebec press that France's future hopes lay in the De Gaullist movement. The organization in Quebec City by Madame André Simard and Père Delos, O.P., of the first Free French group outside of Europe helped to turn the tide of opinion against Vichy. While the bishops' Labor Day message echoed Pétain, on October 25 Ernest Lapointe launched the first of many French-Canadian radio appeals to France, in which he urged the French not to turn against Britain. Declaring that 'we have the same language and with it have inherited a portion of the same soul,' Lapointe said that French Canadians still considered France their ally, for they could not conceive of even a completely defeated France renouncing her century-old ideals. The French Canadians could not believe that their ancient mother country would become the enemy of Britain, to which they were bound not only by community of interests but by a French oath of fidelity. Canada, the offspring of both France and Britain, constituted an indissoluble bond between the two countries. *L'Action Catholique*, in commenting on the Lapointe broadcast, expressed the hope that it would prevent complete French subservience to the Nazis and would show other Canadians what an important role Quebec could play in Franco-British relations.[67]

On October 29 *L'Action*, which had been enthusiastically pro-Pétain, admitted under the headline 'France Betrayed' that Vichy was beginning to play Hitler's game, and expressed the fear that the nazification of France instead of its restoration would be the result. When the De Gaullists sent Commandant Thierry D'Argenlieu, a Carmelite monk with a distinguished war record as a naval officer, to plead their cause in Canada in March 1941, he was given a testimonial dinner in Quebec which was attended by Premier Godbout and Mgr. Camille Roy, the Rector of Laval University. Commandant D'Argenlieu's argument that it was a mere mockery to attempt to erect a Christian state within the Nazi framework, and his careful references to Pétain as a great but misguided Frenchman, made many new friends for De Gaulle's cause. Mackenzie King furthered this gradual evolution of French-Canadian sentiment away from sympathy with Pétain by refusing to break off diplomatic relations with Vichy, despite strong pressure from English-Canadian sources. On October 7 *L'Action Catholique*, still unwilling to condemn the Vichy regime, had warned that such a step would seriously endanger national unity. But it was noteworthy that General Georges Vanier, the Canadian Minister to France who had remained at his post until the armistice of June 1940 and who enjoyed great prestige in Quebec as a hero of the Royal 22nd in the First World War, stated that France's will to resist remained resolute, when he returned to Canada on October 4 after a stay in England.[68]

Another development of the fall of France was a new French-Canadian attitude towards the United States, which loomed larger on Quebec's horizon after contact with Europe was largely cut off. The Ogdensburg Agreement of August 18, 1940 was little short of a Canadian-American military alliance, with its establishment of a Permanent Joint Board to 'consider in the broad sense the defence of the north half of the western hemisphere.'[69] *L'Action Catholique* on August 21 hailed it as an act of immense importance, pointing out that if Germany should defeat Britain, only association with the United States and other American nations could preserve the liberty and national personality of French Canada.

But this relief that the defence of Canada was to be supported by the mighty neighbor to the south was mingled with a certain anxiety lest the United States should swallow up Canada. It was pointed out that after the war Canada would be called upon to choose between the British and the American worlds, and it was hoped that she would not lose her independence. *L'Evénement* on August 20 said that Canadians shared with Americans a common heritage, a common way of life, and a common desire to remain free, which had to be protected in concert with the United States. *Le Devoir* showed no great enthusiasm for joint defence, while on November 7 *L'Action Catholique* argued that Canada should be the partner and not the ward of the United States in the defence of the continent, lest the Americans should be led to annex a neighbor who would not provide for its own defence.[70]

The prospect of close cooperation with the United States raised the old specter of annexation for many French Canadians after the Hyde Park Declaration[71] of April 20, 1941, which provided for economic integration for war purposes; and *L'Action Nationale* was led to devote its June number to a symposium on the subject, which was more widely discussed in private than in the press. The symposium opened with an editorial note, headed 'There'll always be an England, but will there be a Canada?' which expressed the belief that France and England would withstand the catastrophe of war but doubted that Canada, lacking its own culture, geographical unity, and national unity, would survive. It envisaged the hypotheses that Canada might become a colony or protectorate of the United States, or that the provinces as units or groups might be admitted to the Union as new states, or that Quebec might become a state, preserving its frontiers and its autonomy. This latter possibility was studied in its juridical, political, economic, cultural, and religious aspects, with a historical note on annexationism by Abbé Groulx and a note on the American attitude towards French Canada by Burton Ledoux. The editorial foreword urged cautious study of the question, concluding: 'You have a thousand reasons for complaining about the Canadian Confederation; but do not conclude that anything is better than the present situation. An evil is not cured by a greater evil. And before launching oneself in an adventure, one must know where it leads.'[72]

In his historical survey of annexationism up to 1849, Abbé Groulx found 'the resistance of our little people to American continentalism, that is, to any form of imperialism, one of the marvellous facts of the history of this hemisphere.'[73] In a legal study Jacques Perrault expressed his belief that French Canada would enjoy more security for its religion, language, and educational rights under the American states' rights system than under the Canadian constitution.[74] But Edmond Lemieux held that despite the fact that the three main Canadian parties were committed to centralizing policies, the trend of centralization was still stronger in the States, and French Canada would have still less influence at Washington than at Ottawa.[75] In an economic study Francois-Albert Angers anticipated that under annexation Quebec would lose its industries and become a reserve in which agriculture and extractive industries would flourish, while many French Canadians would be drawn away elsewhere by higher wages. Even if Quebec became more highly industrialized, the need of more labor would swamp the French Canadians with 'foreigners.'[76] Jean Nicolet expressed fears that annexation would mean the end of the French-Canadian ethnic group, with French becoming a dying secondary language. He rehearsed the old arguments against Americanization by movies, radio, and magazines.[77]

The Jesuit Père Jacques Cousineau held that French-Canadian Catholicism had nothing to gain and everything to lose by annexation, since the United States was less Catholic and Christian than Canada.[78] Burton Ledoux evoked the specter of traditional 'Anglo-Saxon' enmity to the 'Gallo-Roman' culture of the French Canadians, who were considered by Americans to be backward, priest-ridden people given to fascism and anti-Semitism. His opinion was that Quebec would have substantially less autonomy after annexation.[79] André Laurendeau summed up the conclusions of the symposium by saying that annexation would lead either to 'death by immersion' or 'death by inanition.' He saw the annexationist movement as a new defeatism, which would diminish the autonomy of French Canada and its influence. He concluded: 'We ought not to desire annexation,' and if it should be imposed, 'We shall live if we are living'—that is, if the French Canadians stimulated their will to live by becoming creative and building up their culture and sense of nationality.[80]

6

From the outset of the war many English and French Canadians labored zealously to prevent the development of the rift between the races which had been such a tragic feature of the First World War. Mackenzie King, inspired by his loyalty to the memory of Laurier and wisely guided by Ernest Lapointe in all matters affecting Quebec, avoided many of the mistakes which Ottawa had made in the First World War. Though some English Canadians grumbled at the government's 'catering to Quebec,' there was a general appreciation of the fact that national unity must not be imperiled. French Canada was largely left to do what it could or would in the war effort, without overzealous loyalism pointing a pistol at its head. Ottawa made no attempt to impose English Canada's ideas of national unity on Quebec, but left the task of stimulating patriotism to French Canada's own lay and clerical leaders. Ernest Lapointe's important role in insuring Quebec's support of the declaration of war, of participation, and of national mobilization has already been mentioned.

Premier Godbout made a pilgrimage to Toronto on December 4, 1940 to discuss 'Canadian Unity'[81] before a joint meeting of the Empire and Canadian Clubs. He recalled the Toronto speeches of Alexandre Taschereau in the 1920's, which had promoted better English-French understanding, and hailed the Franco-Ontarians as 'a living and a necessary bond between us.' Then he launched into an appeal for strengthening Canadian unity by establishing 'a perfect accord in all that has to do with the basic factors of Canadian problems, to be achieved at the expense of neither the one race nor the other, but to the advantage of all.' He assured his audience that 'In no wise are we sparing of our pennies, our pains, our blood when it becomes a question of Canada, human liberty, the democratic ideal, or honor, which are our very soul.' He stressed the historical fact that the French Canadians were the most Canadian of Canadians and had made many contributions to the achievement of Canadian nationhood. He hailed the *bonne entente* efforts of William Henry Moore, Arthur Hawkes, P. F. Morley, Lorne Pierce, Wilfrid Bovey, Howard Ferguson, Harry Stapells, and F. C. A. Jeanneret; and made a plea for bilingualism: 'When the two master languages of the country are in current use from sea to sea, we will have so multiplied the points of contact between our two races that many of our difficulties will have disappeared of themselves, without the necessity of recourse to persuasion, conventions, press campaigns, and the like.' He urged: 'What we ought to safeguard, what we ought to defend, is the privilege of developing ourselves in our own way.' There could be unity in spirit and heart, while each province preserved its own manners, customs, religious practices, and cultural life.

Godbout declared that the French Canadians were a constituent part of Canada, not only as the majority in Quebec, 'but everywhere they are there present; everywhere they make that presence felt; everywhere they contribute to the effort of the country as a whole; everywhere they enrich by their culture, their language, their toil, their devotion, their sacrifices, the patrimony of Canada as a whole.' He maintained that French Canada was doing its duty just as English Canada was, but urged that 'it is high time to accord to our province and our people an adequate share of the national defence, responsible posts in the army, the administration, and the government.' He described French Canada at war, and with a figure of speech drawn from his early career as an agronomist, he asserted: 'In the national hive there is not a French-Canadian bee but brings forth of its honey, beside that of the English-Canadian bee.' He called for 'unity of purpose, unity in fact, unity in general, fair play all along the line, that is to say unity at the cost of no one of our characteristics or respective peculiarities.'

After paying tribute to the heroes of both races and giving an account of the two French-Canadian winners of the Victoria Cross in the First World War, Godbout pledged Quebec's determination not to break faith with its dead. He closed with these eloquent words:

Separatists, gentlemen, we are not, nor could we be. We have made too many sacrifices for Canada. There is not a foot of the soil of the country which has not felt the tread of our people; not a town, not a village but has given birth to a nation-builder, to makers of men, to a hero illustrious or unsung. We will not renounce a single parcel of our patrimony, for it is identified with us as we with it. Moreover you understand us well enough now to know that we will never abandon our brother French Canadians in the other provinces. We only ask that we be respected as we respect others, and that our concept of the indissoluble unity of Canada in war and peace be taken as coming from a heart that is at once fervent and realistic, whose ideal is to serve the nation with all the strength of its being, in order that the opprobrium and the shame of the Nazi yoke be never ours to bear, and that the British Crown may never cease to find in Canada its brightest jewel.

This frank and courageous utterance, coming at the close of a series of such speeches in Quebec, won enthusiastic approval from both the English and French press without regard to party affiliation.

Cardinal Villeneuve, who on June 5, 1940 had declared that 'our allies have the right to count on our sacrifices to ensure their victory,'[82] and had firmly supported the national registration, on November 22 strongly denied rumors that French Canadians were contemplating separatism under his leadership, and asserted that the French Canadians had shown their true loyalty and 'within the last year had struck the greatest blow of a quarter of a century for national unity, at what had seemed unity's darkest hour.'[83] The Cardinal made his greatest contribution to the cause of national unity with his call for the celebration of Masses for victory on February 9, 1941, in every parish of Quebec. He himself officiated at Notre-Dame in Montreal before a congregation which included Ernest Lapointe and almost every high dignitary of Church and State. After urging the people to emulate British steadfastness and to fight for victory against those conquerors whose false ideas must be defeated at any cost, he closed his allocution on this occasion thus: 'We, the Church, the State, and the people of this province, beseech the Lord of Hosts to help us overcome the forces of evil.'[84] This gesture, without precedent in French Canada since the days of the Masses offered for the victory of Britain over Napoleon, made a tremendous impression on English Canadians who had been led to think of the Church as the root of all disloyal evil in Quebec. It also stimulated Canada's war effort by putting the influence of the Church squarely behind the cause.

On numerous occasions the Cardinal stressed national unity, notably in a speech before the Empire Club of Toronto on April 16, 1941. Once more he denied the charges of separatism, clericalism and Fascism that had been leveled at Quebec:

> Never did I wish that Quebec should become either a clerical or a fascist state. The Church does not admit that patriotism should be love of isolation . . . No, patriotism should extend to the whole of Canada. Divine Providence seems to have destined the English and French-speaking Canadians to co-operate in building a nation based on Anglo-Saxon and French civilization.[85]

The Cardinal declared that the French Canadians were the most stable element of the Canadian population and a bulwark against Communism or other subversive doctrines. He urged that the educational rights extended to the English-speaking minority in Quebec should be granted to the French-Canadian minorities in the other provinces, and warned that Quebec would always stand up for the rights of her separated brethren. In conclusion the Cardinal paid tribute to the heroism of the British people, and calling patriotism the highest of virtues, hailed those Canadians who had enlisted in a righteous cause.

From a small group of ultranationalists there continued to come, however, protests against wartime alterations of Quebec's way of life and invasions of its autonomy. When Senator Athanase David warned his compatriots in August 1940 against the tendency of narrow nationalists to consider Quebec the center around which Canada turned, and against their desire to have French Canadians hate their English fellow-citizens, *Le Devoir* deplored David's tendency to address the French Canadians as a refractory people hesitating to obey the law or even sabotaging it. *L'Illustration Nouvelle* said the David speech would not lessen political animosities and was merely the thousandth edition of the anti-conscription promises of King, Lapointe, and their associates. It observed that the Liberal program of half-truths and reticences created doubt in the leaders and even in the cause itself.[86] When the Dominion-Provincial Conference called to take action on the Rowell-Sirois Report collapsed after two days in January 1941, nationalist circles accused Premier Godbout of having failed to defend provincial rights in order not to offend his chiefs, King and Lapointe. Premier Hepburn of Ontario, who played the major part in preventing any action on the recommendations of the Report, accused Godbout of having deserted the other provinces in their fight for provincial autonomy. Henceforward it became a practice in nationalist circles to brand Godbout as a mere creature of Ottawa, sacrificing Quebec's rights to party loyalty. Party loyalty no doubt played its part in Godbout's policy of cooperation with Ottawa, but he was also strongly convinced of the necessity of national unity and of avoidance of the isolation of Quebec in the First World War.

Maxime Raymond, who had become the spokesman at Ottawa of the ultranationalist group by his stand for Canadian neutrality, his vote against participation, and his reluctant acceptance of conscription for home defence, in May 1941 made another attack on government policy. He urged that the government should stop telling the people that Canada was in danger of an invasion which he considered impossible. He said that Canada's strength and resources were not endless, and asked why Canada should ruin itself in the interests of a Britain which after the war might make friends with Germany. He declared that Quebec was unanimously opposed to conscription, and argued that Britain needed munitions and food, not men. He complained that the French-Canadian laborer was asked to work for low wages and under shocking conditions, and yet he was told that he must fight to free Polish or other European workers from slavery. He concluded with an appeal to the government to remember that a Canadian's first loyalty was to his own land, and to consider the future of Canada in its war policy.[87]

Ernest Lapointe replied to Raymond and vehemently denied that he represented anything but a small minority in a Quebec which had repudiated such isolationist and anti-participationist sentiments in the provincial elections of October 1939 and the federal elections of March 1940. *La Presse* commented that Lapointe's disapproval of Raymond's sentiments was shared by the great majority of French Canadians, while the *Montreal Gazette* pointed out that Raymond represented only a small clique of malcontents.[88]

And despite this undercurrent of nationalist opposition, by June 1941 Quebec was playing a large part in Canada's war effort. She had contributed generously to the war loans and had become a leading center of war industry and of vital raw materials. While she lagged somewhat behind other provinces in voluntary enlistments for overseas service, she fully cooperated in the training of home defence forces. Her early sympathy with Vichy had virtually dissolved, and that issue had ceased to divide her from the rest of Canada.

Then the German declaration of war on Russia on June 22 raised the question of what the French-Canadian reaction would be to cooperation with Soviet Russia. Quebec was notoriously anticommunist, as her Padlock Law, her espousal of Franco's cause in Spain, and her sympathy with the anti-communist crusades of the

German and Italian dictators had given evidence. The hierarchy realized that Quebec must be swung into line with the rest of Canada on the Russian alliance if national unity were to be preserved. On June 25 *L'Action Catholique* declared that although Russia enjoyed little or no sympathy in Quebec, it was only right to wish for continued Russian resistance and heavy Nazi losses. Two days later *L'Action* urged French Canada to rejoice at the sight of Germany forced to fight so mighty a foe and to support Russia against the common enemy, although it liked Communism no better than it ever had. Help from any source was to be welcomed when one was in the right and fighting for a just cause. In still another article on July 11 *L'Action* answered the question whether aid to Russia would help Communism by saying that Germany was the common enemy and Canada and Britain were helping Russia in their own interests. There was no question of helping Communism as distinct from the Russian people, unless suppressed Communist organizations were allowed to function again in Canada.[89]

The provincial press generally followed the lead of *L'Action Catholique*, which was thought to have been inspired by Cardinal Villeneuve, accepting Russian help against the Germans as desirable but echoing Quebec's dislike for Communism. There was none of the uncritical acceptance of Russia as a democratic ally which made many idealistic English Canadians innocent dupes of Communism. A traditionally conservative English Canada developed an enthusiasm for all things Russian, under the spell of Russia's gallant resistance and final turning of the Nazi tide of invasion, and among young intellectuals Communist sympathies became as popular as they had been in the States ten years before. This wave of enthusiasm was ruthlessly exploited by Canadian Communists and Russian diplomatic officials to build a spy ring which was only bared after the end of the war.[90] Quebec's reservations about the Russian alliance, which had been branded as 'disloyal,' were then fully justified.

7

French Canada figured largely in the psychological warfare which was waged by shortwave radio. After the fall of France, Radio Paris beamed a program at Quebec which used 'Alouette' as a musical signature. It sought to keep alive the memory of French rule in Canada by making constant allusion to historic ties; to influence French Canada's attitude towards the rest of Canada, fostering separatism and opposition to conscription; to link Pétainist France and Canada, to magnify Canadian cultural differences so as to incite disunity, and to justify collaboration between unoccupied France and Germany. For these ends it used flattery, inculcated persecution and minority complexes, exploited grievances, and cultivated anti-Semitism and anti-Communism. The Vichy radio also directed broadcasts first to Saint-Pierre and Miquelon, and later to North America as a whole. Its propaganda promoted hostility to Britain, minimized American strength, stressed the virtues of collaboration, attacked De Gaullism, and defended Vichy's policies. Its themes were that France considered the French Canadians to be Frenchmen; that French-Canadian influence in Canada had grown ever stronger since 1763 and would continue to do so; that France was still the mother country of the French Canadians; that the French Canadians were attached to France but not politically disloyal to Canada; that France and French Canada enjoyed a profound cultural identity; that French Canadians were persecuted because of their French views; and that Pétain's France was moving towards the French way of life long cherished in French Canada in the matters of family, land, home, and religious education.[91]

For a year one man took upon himself the task of answering this propaganda barrage. He was Louis Francoeur, a well-known Montreal journalist, who had no love for Germany, having been interned by the Germans from 1914–18 while studying in Belgium as a member of the Benedictine order. His daily radio program, 'La Situation Ce Soir,' acquired great influence in French Canada and was so highly valued that the texts were printed in bimonthly pamphlets[92] from January 1941 until his death in an automobile accident early in the following summer. Francoeur, with his easy erudition, keen psychological sense, and the outlook of a citizen of the world, did much to guide French-Canadian opinion through the confusions of the Vichy-vs.-De Gaulle question and to awaken it to the world-wide and crucial nature of a war which was not merely Britain's, as the nationalists maintained. Francoeur himself was pro-British and a great lover of France and Belgium; he hated Fascism in all its forms but respected differences of opinion on the French question. He protested against the carrying on of France's internecine quarrels in Quebec and against the English-speaking world's confusion of the French Canadians with the French. By his adroit analysis of the news he gradually won French Canada to the cause of De Gaulle.

After his death Mlle. Beatrice Belcourt of the C.B.C. inaugurated a program 'Le Canada Parle à la France,' which was first shortwaved from Boston and later from Sackville, New Brunswick, when Canada constructed its first shortwave station. This series included broadcasts by Premier Godbout, Cardinal Villeneuve, Archbishop Vachon of Ottawa, General Vanier, General Laflèche, and a host of other French-Canadian notables, who stressed French Canada's sympathy for France but also its enthusiastic loyalty to the Allied cause and its determination to free France from German oppression.[93] These broadcasts unquestionably bolstered French morale under the occupation and likewise met a French-Canadian need for reassurance that France would not die. Since relatively few people in Quebec possessed shortwave receivers, the German and Vichy propaganda had little influence except among a small group of the nationalist élite; while French Canada's messages to France won a much wider audience.

8

The death of Ernest Lapointe late in 1941 deprived French Canada of its only representative in the federal government who thoroughly understood his province, who enjoyed its full confidence, and who was a Canadian first and a French Canadian second. It was then, as the war attained ever greater and graver proportions and the United States was finally forced into all-out participation by Pearl Harbor, that the Canadian government determined to consult the people on the question of freeing it from its promises not to invoke conscription for overseas service. A plebiscite on the question was proposed in the speech from the throne in January 1942. The plebiscite was immediately opposed by Maxime Raymond on February 5, in a speech which also criticized the proposed war effort of the year, including a war budget of three billions and a gift of a billion and a loan of $700,000,000 to Britain, as beyond the means of a 'little people of eleven millions and a half, still in the epoch of development.'[94] Raymond accused a hyperpatriotic Toronto group known as the 'Two Hundred' of a desire to impose their will on the country by 'a campaign of propaganda and intimidation, with the purpose of forcing the government to impose conscription for service overseas, in contempt of the pledge given and the popular will expressed on March 26, 1940.' He ironically compared their enthusiasm for defending democracy and punishing the violators of treaties with their desire to make the government violate its pledges against conscription.

Raymond recalled Lapointe's anti-conscriptionist pledges of September 9, 1939 and the compromise then arrived at of participation without conscription, which had been approved by the country in the elections of March 1940. He maintained that only the anti-conscriptionists, toward whom an obligation had been incurred for their consent to participation, could free the government from its pledge. The need for national unity and the ineffectiveness of conscription were even stronger reasons for avoiding conscription in 1942 than they had been in 1939. Raymond held that Canada's war effort could be compared advantageously with that of any Allied country and should not be stepped up:

It is not at the moment when we are asked to augment agricultural production, which calls for a larger labor supply which is already lacking; it is not at the moment when we are asked to augment industrial production, which calls for more workers to equip and arm the soldiers; it is not at the moment when our defence calls for more soldiers to defend our territory, that we should think of augmenting the number of soldiers for service overseas by means of conscription, with a limited population which represents less than 1 per cent of the total population of the Allied countries.[95]

He saw only one purpose to the plebiscite: to free the government of its anti-conscription pledge and to give it a mandate to impose conscription when and how it saw fit. While he admitted that he preferred to see Mr. King at the head of the government rather than any rival, he preferred to see the prime minister bound by his promise and not given a blank check to be filled out at will. He called for the respect of engagements solemnly undertaken, in the name of national unity both during and after the war:

We are not separatists, but let us not be forced to become separatists. We wish indeed to dwell in the same house, but the house must be habitable for all. We are partisans of national unity, but according to certain equitable conditions, and when our conditions have been fixed in advance, we ask that they be observed.

And I fear that the 'Two Hundred' of Toronto, who agitate in favor of conscription for service overseas in violation of the pact of September 1939, are about to forge the nails which will serve to seal the coffin of national unity, and perhaps of Confederation.[96]

On March 3, when the plebiscite bill was in committee, Raymond renewed his attack upon it, pointing out that the clear purpose of the plebiscite was to enable the government to impose conscription at will, and that in any case the measure should be amended to permit young men between eighteen and twenty-one, who would be conscripted, to vote upon it.

Despite the best efforts of the government to convince Quebec that the issue was not immediate conscription, but the right of the government to consider the question of conscription if it should become necessary, French Canada—perhaps more realistically— saw the plebiscite as an opportunity to vote directly for or against conscription. In vain Mackenzie King broadcast over the French network of the C.B.C. on April 7, appealing for a vote which would give the government complete freedom of action in accomplishing its duty of pursuing the war. He declared that the government had the constitutional and legal power to conduct the war as it saw fit, but that the democratic tradition compelled it to consult the people when it sought to free itself of a solemn promise. He recalled the background of the anti-conscriptionist pledge, and its adoption to preserve national unity, but warned that it now endangered national unity:

> You know perfectly well that the preservation of national unity has always been one of my dearest political aspirations. I must say that the situation is no longer the same and that, Canada having played for two years and a half the role in the war that is known, I see no more risk of endangering our unity by making this restriction disappear. On the contrary, I have the firm conviction that in this fashion the germs of irritation and disunity which are being born in our country will be smothered. [97]

As an argument for giving liberty of action to the government, he pointed out that this restriction upon Canada's war effort created misunderstanding in the other countries, which did not realize that 'the fact of not having imposed conscription had in no wise limited our war effort.'

Mr. King explained that the question at stake in the plebiscite was not that of conscription: 'It is a question of establishing whether or not the government should be free to decide the question in terms of all the factors of national interest.' He urged that the government and parliament should have the responsibility of making the decision and judging the question on its merits, since it was essentially a military question and all the necessary information for a wise decision could not be furnished to the public at large. He called for a declaration of confidence in the government by a 'yes' vote. In conclusion he warned that the maintenance of the existence of the nation came before national unity; that the military situation was critical; and that Canada could best defend itself against attack by beating the enemy before he reached her shores. Canada was not fighting to help others, to support some 'egotistical imperial end,' but 'for the preservation of our liberty and national existence, for the defence of our homes and families, against an enemy who ever draws nearer to us,' in the East and in the West.

Two nights later, on April 9, P.-J.-A. Cardin, the veteran minister of transport who was attempting to fill Lapointe's shoes as French Canada's spokesman at Ottawa, also made a broadcast over Radio Canada, calling for a 'yes' vote in the plebiscite. He urged loyalty to King and to his program, and advocated defending Canada by battling overseas, thus warding off an enemy who had quickly overcome other peoples who had waited to defend themselves on their own territory. He also asserted that it was not a question of voting for or against conscription, and that 'Mr. King has on several occasions declared in the House and elsewhere that for the present conscription was not necessary; he has even said that he believed firmly that it would not be necessary to impose it, because voluntary enlistment sufficed and perhaps the present circumstances might change.' He warned that the critics who reproached King with not having at once imposed conscription for overseas service were those who would replace him if the confidence of the majority were not given to him. Cardin reserved his own freedom to decide the question of conscription when it arose, and warned against premature agitation as injurious to the good name of Canada and Quebec in particular.

Cardin said that altered circumstances justified an altered attitude towards conscription, and called for support from all parties of the government which had brought a united Canada almost scatheless through two years of war:

> To my fellow citizens of Quebec, I wish simply to say, without weakness and equally without shame, that it is better not to run the risk of isolating ourselves. We wish that confidence be shown to us; therefore we must show confidence to others. Let us speak not only of rights; let us also sometimes think of the obligations which guarantee them . . .
> Be the first to reply 'yes' to the question of the plebiscite. It is in your interest to act thus, first as citizens and then as members of a minority which has need not only of the law and the treaties to develop according to its ideals, but which must count on the goodwill of all and feel its soul surrounded by the respect and comforting friendship of the great majority of the people of the country.[98]

But thanks to the efforts of the *Ligue pour la Défense du Canada*, headed by Jean Drapeau and supported by most ultranationalists, French Canada answered with a resounding 'no' to the question of the plebiscite on April 27, 1942. There was no differentiation of votes by ethnic origin, as there had been no such breakdown of similar enlistment figures; but Quebec as a whole voted 72 per cent 'no,' while all the other provinces voted 80 per cent 'yes.' The old bitter question of conscription had once more isolated Quebec from the rest of Canada. The plebiscite shattered national unity, and henceforward anti-war sentiment grew in French Canada, as it reacted to English-Canadian charges that it was not doing its part.[99]

The government, feeling that it had been freed from its pledge and under pressure from the Conservatives, did not delay in introducing Bill 80, amending the N.R.M.A. Act for eventual conscription for overseas service. In proposing the second reading in June, King declared that conscription 'was not necessary at the present moment and perhaps never will be.'

The prime minister favored consultation with parliament before putting conscription into force, while Colonel Ralston, the defence minister, insisted on acting by order-in-council without reference to parliament, if and when the time came. Two other ministers, T. A. Crerar and Angus Macdonald, also favored this course; and to end a cabinet crisis Mr. King agreed to action by order-in-council, with parliament to be called to approve the action. Ralston subsequently declared in parliament that he was to be the judge of when conscription was required,[100] and described the government's policy as 'not necessarily conscription, but conscription if necessary.'[101] The Quebec Liberals protested strongly against the measure, and P.-J.-A. Cardin resigned from the cabinet in adherence to his pledges.[102]

Maxime Raymond bitterly attacked the bill in June, recalling all the solemn promises of King and Lapointe against conscription. He maintained that Quebec alone could free the government from the obligation which it had incurred in exchange for Quebec's support of participation. He argued that the two motives for the anti-conscription pledge—the necessity of national unity and the ineffectiveness of conscription—were more valid than ever, with the plebiscite showing Canada's profound division on the question, and with an official statement of June 9 showing that 52,615 men had enlisted in the last five months, more than half the quota for the year. He quoted the statements of King, Defence Minister Ralston, Munitions and Supply Minister Howe, Navy Minister Macdonald, and Air Minister Power to prove the excellent results of the voluntary enlistment policy. He belittled King's statements that the law might never be enforced, and criticized the measure for not providing for age limits, exemptions, and appeal tribunals. He warned that after the war the government would enjoy the greatest lack of confidence ever known, having promised no European expeditionary forces before 1939, having promised moderate participation in 1939, having promised conscription for home defence only in 1940 and then used the National Resources Mobilization Act as a system of 'disguised conscription,' having said that the plebiscite was not on the question of conscription and using its result to justify conscription. He complained bitterly: 'The most solemn engagements are violated in the name of the right of the majority, while we are asked to go and fight to defend the rights of minorities.'[103] He declared that Quebec had not forgotten conscription in 1917 and would not forget the 'infinitely more odious and revolting' conscription of 1942.

When the bill came up for third reading, Raymond on July 23 supported Sasseville Roy's motion for the six months' hoist, complaining that 'for a hundred years national unity has always been achieved at the expense of the Province of Quebec' and that 'there must be a limit to sacrifice always at the expense of the Province of Quebec.' To the argument that the will of the majority should prevail, he replied that the majority 'should not abuse its powers and that an engagement made by the majority to the minority is sacred.' He insisted that the plebiscite had not freed the government from its pledge, since the interested party, Quebec, had voted 'no.' He repelled the charge of disloyalty with two questions: 'Since when is it disloyal to insist that engagements be respected? Is not he who seeks to violate them the one who is disloyal?'[104] But the conscription measure was passed on July 23 by a vote of 141 to 45, largely along ethnic lines.

Raymond also expressed during the July debate on the budget another French-Canadian nationalist attitude which was to find ever more support in Quebec as time went on. He quoted the secretary of state's declaration that 'our country, in proportion to population, is doing more for the war than any other of the United Nations.' He protested that war expenses were heavier in Canada than in England, and taxes consequently higher, and he opposed a billion dollar gift to England at a time when that country was lending money at interest to other allied nations. The French Canadian has always shown a very North American reluctance to pay taxes, since he has been emotionally 'agin the government' ever since the early days of New France, when opposition developed between the Canadians and the officials sent out from France. He was willing to contribute to the defence of Canada and proved it by providing notable support for the war loans, which were often oversubscribed in Quebec; but the prospect of pinching himself for the benefit of Britain aroused the same opposition as the early propaganda for Canada to rally to Britain's side, which evoked an emotional loyalty he did not feel. The Hong Kong disaster of December 1941, which cost Canada two battalions (one of which, the Royal Rifles, came from Quebec and was in part French Canadian), had stimulated his latent anti-English feeling. Unfortunately Winston Churchill had then proclaimed that the loss of Hong Kong, which had fallen in less than a month because of inadequate British preparations, was 'a great imperial disaster.' Thus he reinforced the nationalist thesis that the war was an imperialist conflict in which Canada had no real interest.

By the summer of 1942 various incidents and frictions had produced a marked deterioration in French-Canadian enthusiasm for the war. In the previous six months there had been an extraordinary development of anti-British feeling, which was credited to the Nazi propaganda activities of the Vichy consulates. Admiration for Pétain and Vichy France was used to arouse the traditional latent hatred of England, as well as scorn of the British war effort and opposition to the Canadian one. Reaction to the plebiscite played an important role in the change of public opinion. The individualistic French Canadian resented the pressure brought to bear in what was supposed to be a democratic vote. Some voted 'no,' and then promptly volunteered for overseas service. The plebiscite was seen as the last step before conscription, and most French Canadians remained convinced that their leading representatives at Ottawa were right in their earlier declarations that conscription would be deplorable and ineffective. They judged rationally a question which the English Canadians judged emotionally.

It was felt by young men of military age that the recruiting system was unjust in favoring the well-to-do. They could not find employment in business or industry, and unless they had private means they were forced to enlist. There was a general feeling that Canada had neither the manpower nor the means nor the resources to maintain armies to fight everywhere in Europe. Some individuals talked of French Canada being engaged in two wars: the so-called 'holy war' against the Axis, and the traditional war against *les Anglais*. French refugees were welcome in Quebec, but not English ones. The patriotic activities of the hierarchy had led to the development of anti-clericalism on all levels, with Cardinal Villeneuve's zeal winning him the nickname of 'Kid Villeneuve' and 'Newtown, O.H.M.S.' It was felt that he was true neither to his people nor his cloth. The Wartime Information Board showed a singular lack of understanding of the French-Canadian mentality by making appeals to 'Canada at Britain's side' and using the Union Jack on war posters. A basic factor in the situation was the refusal of many English Canadians to recognize that Canada was a bi-ethnic, bi-cultural, and bilingual country. While there was improvement in mutual understanding among university people, intellectuals, and the younger generation less conditioned by old differences, there remained a fundamental misunderstanding. J.-A. Blanchette (Compton) startled the House in July by proposing to settle it by arranging a golf match between the editors of the *Globe and Mail* and *Le Devoir* and the president of the Saint-Jean-Baptiste Society and the Grand Master of the Orangemen.[105]

9

Quebec's support of the war was momentarily stimulated by the gallant part played by French-Canadian troops in the disastrous Dieppe raid of August 19, 1942. But the growing feeling that Ottawa was betraying French Canada was furthered by the cabinet's decisions of September 4 and September 14 to send home defence conscripts to Alaska, Newfoundland, and Greenland. These steps were taken by order-in-council, without debate in parliament. In October the anti-war *Ligue pour la Défense du Canada* took political form in the *Bloc Populaire Canadien* under the leadership of Maxime Raymond.

This French 'Canada First' party won increasing support as the conviction grew in Quebec that Canada was undertaking too great a war effort which would inevitably lead to application of conscription for overseas service and to national bankruptcy. The *Bloc Populaire* also exploited French Canada's psychological soreness as a result of becoming the target after the plebiscite for all manner of attacks as the home of slackers, traitors, and fascists.

The ill-considered official decision to make it impossible to compare the manpower contributions of French and English gave rise to the freely expressed English-Canadian suspicion that the French-Canadian war record was too bad to be disclosed, while the French Canadians thought it was better than it really was. The result was a passionate clash of unfounded French and English opinion on the question, as in 1917. This intensely irritated a French Canada which was acutely aware, through the maze of family relationships which links people all over the province, that its sons were dying and being wounded in many quarters of the world in a war which it still felt was fundamentally none of its business. Meanwhile Quebec was constantly complimented for its war effort by its own patriotic leaders and by Ottawa spokesmen. English Canada tended to judge war effort exclusively in terms of volunteers for overseas, while French Canada reckoned in service in Canada, its major contribution in war industry, and its notable support of the war loans.

Unfortunately at this difficult period the place of Ernest Lapointe as French Canada's Ottawa leader was not wholly filled, for his successor, Louis St. Laurent, was new to politics and as a successful Quebec corporation lawyer and the son of an Irish mother was popularly considered to be '*anglifié*.' St. Laurent was first elected to parliament in February 1942 in the by-election necessitated by Lapointe's death. He was opposed by Paul Bouchard, who had run against Lapointe in 1940 and on both occasions was supported by the Duplessis machine and various nationalist groups. The newcomer St. Laurent, with all his sincere devotion to French Canada and to the interests of his compatriots, was unable to command the same confidence in his province that the veteran Lapointe had enjoyed.

Quebec rapidly lost faith in the leadership of its Ottawa representatives and turned in upon itself. After three years of war it was gravely disturbed by the shattering of its traditional way of life by mobilization and intensive wartime industrialization, which produced considerable social disorder. Its innate individualism and devotion to provincial rights were irritated by the ever-increasing number of wartime controls ordained by Ottawa; its traditional belief that woman's place was in the home was outraged by efforts to attract young women into the auxiliary army, navy, and air services and into war industry; its national pride was injured by fancied or real grievances as to the lot of French Canadians in the services and in the war agencies. Above all, there was a profound feeling that Canada's real interests were being subordinated to those of Britain and the United States.

Deeply patriotic French and English Canadians labored hard to offset this growing tide of discontent and opposition to the war effort in French Canada. Colonel Dollard Ménard and the Abbé Sabourin, heroes of the Dieppe raid, were brought back to Canada to stimulate French-Canadian pride and support of the war. But Quebec's resentment against the flood of Ottawa propaganda was extended to its own sons who lent themselves to this cause. Abbé Arthur Maheux, the author of a *bonne entente* study of the post-Conquest period who had been slated to become Rector of Laval University, made himself highly unpopular in Quebec by a series of C.B.C. broadcasts from September 1942 to January 1943 on 'Why Are We Divided?'[106] in which he sought to explode the old legends which lay at the base of anti-English feeling in Quebec. But his negative approach to the question of national unity, which denied or minimized certain unpleasant facts, outraged the growing tide of nationalist feeling, which soon made itself felt in personal attacks of a virulence never known before in Quebec in the case of a priest. Abbé Maheux was driven from the lecture platform at Laval, and despite the support of high ecclesiastical authorities he was left in virtual isolation in his own university and among his own people. It was probably an unfortunate decision to delegate a priest to the role of spokesman in the *bonne entente* movement, for his cloth and clerical attitudes— which led him to refer to 'Garibaldi's gangsters' in English-speaking circles which had always idolized Garibaldi—alienated the sympathies of many English Canadians who were vaguely convinced that the Catholic Church was the root of all disloyal and undemocratic evil in 'priest-ridden' Quebec. But Abbé Maheux did succeed in forming an academic axis between Laval and the University of Toronto which enlisted the support of many men of good will on both sides of the ethnic fence and which brought about a better understanding between the élites of French and English Canada, if it failed to have much influence on popular feeling.

F. R. Scott, professor of law at McGill and the son of the beloved Padre Scott of the First World War, made an effort to explain to English Canadians the anti-imperialist and pro-Canadian nature of Quebec's 'no' vote in the plebiscite,[107] which unjustifiably was discounted in the press as an attempt to woo French-Canadian votes for the C.C.F. movement, of which Scott was a national leader. Late in 1942 Emile Vaillancourt published under the title of *Le Canada et les Nations Unies* a collection of his newspaper articles, speeches,

radio addresses, and letters to public figures in which he pleaded for
respect for France, diplomatic relations with Russia, Canadian
support of the United Nations, a second front in Europe, and recognition of Canada's postwar mission as a non-interested country
seeking a better world order.[108] General Vanier, who commanded
the Quebec military district after his return from Europe in October
1941, continued his exhortations to patriotism until February 1943,
when he was named the Canadian representative for negotiations
with the DeGaullists and Canadian Minister to the governments in
exile in London. General Laflèche, who had taken a leading role in
Ottawa since his return from his post as military attaché in France
in 1940, campaigned vigorously for election in Outremont when he
was named war services minister in November 1942, and succeeded
in defeating his opponent Jean Drapeau, the director of the *Ligue
pour la Défense du Canada.*

10

French Canada's enthusiasm for the war had sharply diminished
by the latter part of 1942. The polls of the Canadian Institute of
Public Opinion showed that, in August, 31 per cent of the French
Canadians favored peace if Hitler should offer it on the basis of the
status quo, while 59 per cent felt that Canada would not be at war if
she were completely independent of the British Empire. With 78
per cent of English Canadians favoring conscription, 90 per cent of
French Canadians opposed it. While only 44 per cent of the English
Canadians felt that Canada was doing all she could to win the war,
89 per cent of French Canadians were so convinced. These sentiments found expression in support of the *Bloc Populaire,* which grew
rapidly in strength despite Cardinal Villeneuve's statement of
November 10, 1942, reproving the 'impertinence' of Leopold Richer,
Le Devoir's Ottawa correspondent, in criticizing *L'Action Catholique*
for refusing to support the new party. This reproof was based upon
the ecclesiastical regulation which requires Catholics to make complaints about institutions under the control of the hierarchy only
to the bishops; but it indicated indirectly how the Cardinal viewed
the new party. But if the *Bloc Populaire* found little favor with Cardinal Villeneuve and Archbishops Charbonneau and Vachon of
Montreal and Ottawa, it was clearly welcomed by the lower clergy.
The Jesuits of the Ecole Sociale Populaire had continued their support of the Pétain regime despite the change of popular feeling on
that score. They deplored the effects of wartime industrialization
upon French-Canadian family life and morals. Their monthly
organ *Relations* frequently showed nationalist sympathies, as did
their press service carried by many rural weeklies run under clerical
auspices. The country *curés* expressed fears as to the corrupting

effects of life in the military camps and in the war plants, and winked at attempts to avoid military service.

Fortunately for Canadian unity, the *Bloc Populaire* proved to be anything but a bloc. Its development was beset by differences among its leaders and its history is reminiscent of the shifting combinations which produce the frequent falls of governments in France. The *Bloc* movement, essentially a new phase of nationalist developments since 1933 which had invoked the tradition of Mercier and Bourassa, began with the *Ligue pour la Défense du Canada* in 1941, André Laurendeau's *Bloc Universitaire* of March 1942, and Paul Gouin's call on May 15, 1942, for a French-Canadian congress to channel anti-imperialist and anti-conscriptionist sentiments. Later in May Gouin conferred with Abbé Pierre Gravel, a well-known nationalist orator in Quebec; Emile Latremouille, a collaborator of Paul Bouchard; and Dr. Georges Lambert, a former aide of Adrien Arcand, who was seeking to revive the fascist National Unity movement. But it was Maxime Raymond who assumed the leadership of the *Bloc Populaire* when the party took form in October, while André Laurendeau became its secretary-general. Gouin, Dr. Philippe Hamel, and René Chaloult rallied to the new party, but soon fell into disagreement with Raymond over the question whether its field of action should be primarily federal or provincial.

Meanwhile a Gallup poll of April 1943 showed that the *Bloc* was favored by 37 per cent of Quebec voters, as contrasted with 26 per cent in February, while the Liberals were favored by only 39 per cent. The *Bloc* was originally based upon exploitation of the latent nationalist sentiments of French Canada which had been brought to the surface by the conscription question. But it was shattered by division on economic matters; for Gouin, Hamel, and Chaloult were crusaders for corporatism and nationalization, while their trust-busting speeches were opposed by Raymond, a man of large means derived from big business. The adhesion of Edmond Lacroix, a wealthy lumberman, to the *Bloc* resulted in the departure of Chaloult and Hamel, who as a *Québecois* also maintained the ancient tradition that no good could come out of Montreal. The real difficulty of the *Bloc*, however, was that there were too many candidates for the leadership and too little willingness to cooperate.

Paul Gouin made a vigorous bid for provincial leadership of the *Bloc*. *L'Union*, with its Pétainist motto of 'Work-Family-Homeland,' was his personal organ, and his speech of April 28, 1943 at the Monument National was entitled 'What ought we to expect of the *Bloc*?' and was prefaced by a statement that he could speak objectively as he was somewhat outside the bosom of the party. He denounced both the Liberal charge that a French-Canadian bloc would be disastrous and Duplessis' betrayal of the nationalist cause in 1936-9, accusing

Godbout and Duplessis of being 'merely the two faces of the same sinister Janus: the trust.' He expressed his faith in the success of Raymond and his lieutenants, if they avoided admitting a new Duplessis to their ranks and limiting their program too narrowly. As he saw it, the *Bloc* should not limit itself merely to creating an honest government, to maintaining the rights of the French language and of the French Canadians, and to continuing the campaign against conscription. He urged: 'The *Bloc Populaire Canadien* will succeed in being a true French-Canadian bloc only if it advocates, defends, and realizes a complete social and economic program, a pro-French-Canadian policy.' At Ottawa it should claim 'the integral application of the Statute of Westminster which makes of Canada, in right and above all in fact, a free and adult nation, mistress of its destinies like Ireland.' Gouin called for an end to leaving the initiative in time of war to Downing Street, for decentralization, for assurance to French-Canadian minorities in other provinces of the rights enjoyed by the English minority in Quebec, an equitable French-Canadian share of federal offices, and the adoption of 'O Canada' as the national anthem and of a distinctive Canadian flag.

In the provincial field the *Bloc* should work for a French State: 'the absolute control of our land, our natural resources, our economy and our educational system; a French State which will be the loyal application of the whole B.N.A. Act, in letter and spirit, which a young compatriot has summed up in a happy and very just formula: "Autonomous provinces in a free country".' In an echo of Abbé Groulx's celebrated dictum of 1937, he observed: 'This French State is due us, and we shall have it.' The proposed Laurentian state should have a pro-French-Canadian and an anti-trust policy. It should nationalize outright the production of electricity, gas, mines, and chemical fertilizer. It should strictly control the insurance companies and the textile, forest, distilling, refining, and tobacco industries. It should replace the coal, milk, farm implement, butchering and cold storage, fishing, and chain store trusts by co-operatives. It should establish a provincial bank to head the system of credit unions. Agriculture should be aided and the industrial worker given an equal share of the profits of industry, while corporatism should be applied to correct the evils of capitalism. The family should be protected by workmen's compensation; insurance against sickness, unemployment, old age, and death; family allowances; strict regulation of the labor of women and children; and aid to young couples.

Gouin repelled the charge of isolationism, declaring: 'It is not we who isolate ourselves, it is others who wish to isolate us.' The French Canadians wished to collaborate with the English Canadians on a footing of equality. To counter the existing English-Canadian bloc, a French-Canadian bloc must be established. If Quebec had 'a single leader, a true one like Maxime Raymond, who truly spoke in the name of the French Canadians and behind whom the French Canadians were unanimous, the rest of the country would indeed perceive that it was the authorized voice of Quebec which made its claims.' He urged that the *Bloc* should make its program known among the English Canadians by every possible means to overcome the language barrier. He denied the charges of Valmore Bienvenue, Edmond Turcotte, Jean-Charles Harvey, and Fred Rose that the *Bloc* was a fifth-column movement: 'It is . . . because we want our country to be able to continue the War until the end and then to be in condition to win the peace, that we do not wish it to bleed itself white, to ruin itself.' In a moving peroration he concluded:

The fight for civilization, Christianity, and liberty is not new to us. We have been fighting for just that for three hundred years. We are going to continue this fight until the end, in order that each country may one day know liberty, true liberty, in order that one day Canada may be for the Canadians and French Canada for the French Canadians.

Yes, ladies and gentlemen, the day will come when this Carillon flag that we see this evening, motionless in its strength, motionless in its century-old patience, will fly, flapping in the winds of victory, floating over Quebec, capital of our French State![109]

On this occasion Gouin was introduced by René Chaloult and thanked by Dr. Philippe Hamel. Chaloult assured the audience that he and Hamel would remain at Gouin's side, while Hamel expressed the loyalty of all three to Raymond and discounted talk of dissension in the *Bloc*.

René Chaloult had already become the idol of the ultranationalists for his declaration in May 1942 that 'if the people of Canada ever vote for compulsory military service overseas, let the government face the danger of civil war,' and his subsequent acquittal after trial for violation of the Defence of Canada regulations. As the only *Bloc* leader with a seat in the provincial legislature, Chaloult introduced in February 1943 an anti-conscription motion which no other member would second, and subsequently announced in April that his party stood for nationalization and state ownership. By way of reply to the attacks upon him in the English press, Chaloult brought suit for libel against the *Quebec Chronicle-Telegraph*, the only English paper in the capital, based upon its comments on his role in the fight against conscription the previous year. The trial served to revive the anti-conscriptionist agitation during the end of May and beginning of June, when the *Bloc* was hoping to force a provincial election upon the Liberals. It was exploited in the weekly radio commentaries which *Bloc* orators had been making since April.

French-Canadian public opinion was also aroused at this time by news of a brawl at Sussex Camp in New Brunswick between men of the Voltigeurs de Québec and of the Dufferin and Haldimand Rifles of Ontario, in which fist-fighting led to shooting and the death of one soldier. The commanding officer, Brigadier Topp, denied that the quarrel had been based upon racial or religious prejudices or by animosity between volunteers and conscripts. Nonetheless it was so interpreted by the French press, which was already up in arms at the *Montreal Gazette's* attacks on the conscripts, whom it contemptuously called 'zombies.' The *Gazette* urged that the 'zombies' should be put to work in agriculture and forest industries, since 'under the existing circumstances they will never make good soldiers.'[110] Emile Benoist made a bitter reply in *Le Devoir* on May 20 which admirably expressed the sentiment of French Canada about the home defence forces:

The regimented conscripts are citizens of whom the State has asked the sacrifice of their liberty, who have submitted to the exigencies of the State, even if they consider that this exigency is not opportune nor justified in the present juncture. As conscripts of the State, the sacrifice to which they have consented is more meritorious since they do not consider it justly motivated, and since this sacrifice which is exacted from them comes in contradiction, even in violation, of the promises that have previously been made to them. And they have the right to the respect of all, even to the respect of those who write in the *Gazette*. Let that organ take what tone it will to speak of these good citizens who conform to the law, the fact none the less remains that the conscripts bear the uniform of His Majesty the King of Canada, that they are soldiers of the King of Canada, and that they are ready to defend at any time the sacred soil of the Canadian homeland quite as well as would the editors of the *Gazette*.

'Zombies!' Let the old Tory and Ulster gossip of Saint-Antoine Street learn that it was soldiers of this sort, that is to say sons of the Canadian soil and also of our race, who in 1775 undertook to defend the city of Quebec against the Yankee invader, while Quebeckers of another race prudently retired to the tranquil countryside of the Island of Orleans.[111]

English-Canadian contempt for the 'zombies', who were commonly reputed to be predominantly French Canadian, continued to grow as the Canadian forces overseas saw active service and suffered casualties. On the other hand French Canada never lost its sympathy for those who observed the letter of the law by serving in Canada but refused to volunteer for overseas service, despite browbeating by their superior officers and insults from their fellow soldiers and the general public. It is probable that the effort to make the French-Canadian home defence units 'go active' would have had more success if it had been left in the hands of French-Canadian officers who had won honor overseas. At any rate there was a marked increase in volunteering for overseas service after the Quebec camps were put under the command of such officers as Dollard Ménard late in 1944.

It also was probably a mistake to organize a divided army in the first place. It is possible that a policy of imposing conscription for overseas service might have been better accepted in Quebec after some such crisis in the war as Pearl Harbor, which destroyed the American prop of French-Canadian isolationism, than was the gradual extension of conscription by a series of steps, each one of which aroused an increasingly bitter reaction in Quebec. The extensions by order-in-council of 'home defence' service to the outposts of North America in 1942 led P.-J.-A. Cardin to move for suspension of the Mobilization Act in February 1943, and to resign from the cabinet when Mr. King vigorously denounced the proposal.

In continuing his attack upon the government's war policies, which he characterized as being equivalent to Arthur Meighen's 'to the last man, to the last penny,' Maxime Raymond noted on February 10 Churchill's statement that he could not understand how Canada had been able to make such a war effort and observed: 'If Mr. Churchill does not understand it, we understand it: it is by ruining Canada, by sabotaging all our present and future economy.' He also cited Beaudry Leman's comments in the annual report of the Banque Canadienne Nationale on the dangers of attempting simultaneously to be a 'granary, arsenal, and reservoir of man power' and of taking women from the home for war plants. Raymond quoted King's declaration that 'nothing mattered but victory,' but expressing grave fears for the postwar period, he observed: 'Surely we all want victory over the Axis powers, but we do not want to lose the peace.'

Raymond bitterly repelled King's reproaches to him and his handful of followers for having left the Liberal Party and followed a course which did honor neither to themselves, nor their province, nor their country. He remarked: 'In the matter of honor, I would like to make the Prime Minister observe that we do not all have the same notion of honor. In the Province of Quebec, since it is a question of this province, the man of honor is the one who respects his word, his promises, and his obligations; and when the hour comes to present ourselves before our electors and to submit ourselves to the judgment of the province, we shall not fear the result.'[112]

Once more Raymond recalled King's anti-conscription pledges, and added: 'We have parted from the Prime Minister because we no longer have confidence in his declarations and promises, above all since the plebiscite and since the conscription law ... We have lost confidence because we have been constantly deceived.' He concluded with the declaration that the *Bloc Populaire*, although it had few representatives in the House, represented 'the sentiments of a very great part of the population of Quebec,' and was inspired by truly Canadian interests.[113]

There can be little doubt that Raymond's claim for the *Bloc's* hold on French Canada was true. The war was beginning to weigh heavily upon a Quebec which found its way of life radically altered without its consent, while little attention was paid to its sentiments, which were no longer clearly understood at Ottawa as they had been in Lapointe's day; promises made to it were violated; and outside attacks upon it increased. Particular indignation was aroused by the publication of Fred Rose's pamphlet, *Hitler's Fifth Column in Quebec,* in which the Montreal Communist denounced the secret Order of Jacques Cartier as the mainspring of all nationalist movements and described it as 'anti-Soviet, pro-Vichy, and pro-fascist';[114] and also by an article in *Life,*[115] which depicted Quebec as a backward, medieval region in which fascist youth movements flourished. The gift of a second billion to Britain in 1943, as taxes weighed more heavily upon Canadians, caused *L'Action Catholique* on May 25 to commend as 'true Canadians' those who urged that Britain in return should give up its interest, estimated at $2,900,000,000, in the Canadian economy. By this means it was hoped to end the British economic imperialism which had continued in Canada after the Statute of Westminster had ended British political imperialism. Edouard Laurent concluded his editorial on the question thus: 'Not a Canadian wishes that his country should profit from the present war by acquiring colonies, but there are many who wish that the sacrifices of the present war should be at least in part compensated for by the conquest of our own territory and our economic life.'[116]

The protests made by Quebec members at the end of the federal session in June 1943 against the policy of drafting farm laborers into the army, in defiance of promises to exempt them, were echoed in the provincial legislature when an amendment was proposed on June 9, deploring the shortage of farm labor and the government's failure to fulfil its promises. Duplessis attacked the policy under which 'Farmers and their sons are enlisted, and by virtue of a paradox of the federal administration they are forcibly enlisted voluntarily.'[117] He warned of the danger of a scarcity of food and fuel. Onésime Gagnon declared that farmers' sons were called for military service without regard to their role as essential workers in the war effort, and deplored a published statement that Italian and German prisoners from North Africa would be brought to Canada as farm workers, while young French-Canadian farmers were being conscripted. Premier Godbout explained that farmers' sons were not exempted *ipso facto* from military service, that they must answer when called for service, but would be exempted if they proved that they were essential workers. He admitted that if they failed to report they were made liable for service.

Statistics tabled by Labor Minister Humphrey Mitchell in the federal House on June 23 showed that the Montreal and Quebec districts had the largest number of draft dodgers, 14,932, slightly more than half the national total.[118] John Diefenbaker commented on the figures, and criticized the lenient penalties exacted from defaulters by the courts in Quebec. The manpower question became and remained a political football, with Quebec getting most of the kicks from critics of the government's policies, while French-Canadian nationalists exploited popular dissatisfaction with the regulations. The opposition to the regimentation of men in the armed services and in essential occupations was intensified by the *Winnipeg Free Press's* suggestion on June 10 that women might be drafted into the auxiliary services. On June 18 Omer Héroux pointed out in an editorial in *Le Devoir* that the conscription of women was legally possible and expressed strong opposition to the proposal, while Emile Benoist observed that family life was threatened by the absence of fathers in military service and of mothers working in war plants.

II

Various patriotic French Canadians sought to turn this anti-war and pro-*Bloc* tide of public opinion. In March 1943 Valmore Bienvenue, a member of the Godbout cabinet, told *L'Union Démocratique du Canada Français*:

> It is time, it is more than time, that we said to Canadians in other provinces: 'Do not judge us by the declarations of those whose very existence we deplore.' Before the evil has become irreparable we must put a stop to the work of the wreckers of our country, who discredit us and the prestige of all French Canadians. These demagogues must be stopped from telling the people that our enemies are to be found not in Germany, Italy, and Japan, but in the other provinces of Canada.

He deplored their Utopia: 'a Laurentia surrounded by a very thick, high wall, which will be a French "reservation" into which nothing will enter and out of which nothing will come, a reservation closed to all social and economic progress . . . a sort of museum for lovers of antiques.' Denouncing their charge that Canada was subjugated to England, Bienvenue declared: 'We are the ally of England and not its vassal . . . And if in this struggle unprecedented in history we are at the side of Britain, it is not because we are a colony which blindly espouses London's quarrels, but simply because England, like us, fights on the side of liberty and justice.' He concluded: 'Liberty, like peace, demands solidarity. We cannot keep our liberty in a world in which three-quarters of the population are reduced to slavery. We cannot live alone . . . We cannot alone be free.'[119]

This *Union Démocratique* founded by Jean-Charles Harvey was short-lived, like the earlier *Ligue Pancanadienne*, but the tendency of both groups was carried on by *L'Institut Démocratique* founded by T.-D. Bouchard, provincial minister of roads, on May 8 at a meeting in Montreal. Bouchard was introduced by Senator Léon-Mercier Gouin, who was one of the governors of the new organization, along with Bouchard, Georges Savoy, Dr. Oscar Mercier, and J.-P. Galipault. Bouchard declared that the purpose of the body was 'the progress of French Canadians in all spheres of their public and private activities.' Bouchard described himself as a lifelong disciple of progress, and professed his desire at the close of his political career to establish a society which would permanently group men 'cherishing freedom of thought, believing in science, and having large views on the questions of races and nationalities.' He pointed out that among all peoples two main currents of ideas existed:

. . . that of men who have faith only in the rules established by the partisans of ancient traditions and antique theories; that of those who have the spirit of research, who believe in evolution towards perfection, and who do not fear to experiment with reforms in all spheres of intellectual, economic, and social activity. . . . These are the two opposed poles of the magnetic field of human society.[120]

He observed that Quebec had until recently been dominated by the former spirit, which had cost it dear. But a change in atmosphere had occurred, with laymen free to preach educational reforms, priests exploding the old legend that the English had mistreated the French Canadians and condemning the instilling of racial hatred, and the majority of the bishops recommending compulsory education.

Bouchard warned of a dangerous reaction to the changing times, of a secret society which sought to establish an independent French and Catholic state on the model of Eire. The *Institut Démocratique* had been formed to oppose such isolationist ideas. It was clad with no religious, charitable, or patriotic mantle; it had no political or commercial interests; and all its activities were to be inspired by a healthy democracy, neither demagogic nor plutocratic. It was limited to French Canadians, so that its enemies might not consider it a tool of the English Canadians. It would be inspired by a progressive patriotism, and would seek to develop public spirit and advance the arts, letters, and the sciences. It would seek to give the younger generation a broader outlook by improving education. It would popularize its ideas by means of the press, radio, lectures, and prize contests. It would launch investigations into public problems of a nature not suited to political bodies and in every fashion would seek to assure the triumph of 'modern progress.'

The foundation of the *Institut Démocratique* was warmly hailed by such Liberal organs as *Le Canada* and *Le Soleil*, and denounced by André Laurendeau in a radio broadcast as the *'Institut Ploutocratique'* and as a Liberal front which returned to the original fanatical *Rouge* ideals of the party. *Le Devoir* took alarm at the growing number of anti-nationalist organizations. It bitterly complained when it learned of the existence of a *Bloc d'Entente Canadienne*, which distributed Abbé Maheux's *Pourquoi Sommes-Nous Divisés?*, which had been published under the auspices of the C.B.C., to all classical college graduates of the year. *Le Devoir* linked Harvey, Bouchard, and Maheux; accused the Wartime Information Board of being responsible for the free distribution of the books; and protested against such one-sided airing of controversial ideas at the expense of the taxpayer.[121]

Quebec's leaders of Church and State, however, continued their efforts to stimulate patriotic feeling. Cardinal Villeneuve ordained a *Te Deum* in his archdiocese on May 16 to celebrate the Allied victory in North Africa. In the June debate on manpower in the legislature, Premier Godbout defended the patriotism of the Quebec farmer and attacked those who had misled the people on the question of military service. On July 14 Godbout sent a Bastille Day message to France, hailing the fact that 'France, represented by her troops in Africa, has retaken her fighting place beside her glorious allies.' He concluded his message thus: 'We, the grandsons of France, French Canadians and Acadians of Quebec and all the provinces of Canada, together with the whole French-speaking population of America, and especially our brothers of the United States, have but one thought—to thank God who gives victory and to extol France and her allies who deserve victory.'[122] A special Bastille Day High Mass—an event which would have curdled Bishop Bourget's blood—was celebrated at Notre-Dame-des-Victoires Church in Quebec, attended by French and French-Canadian members of the R.A.F. and R.C.A.F., who were reviewed by Major-General Thomas-E. Tremblay, inspector-general for Eastern Canada and hero of the First World War.

The federal government simultaneously quieted Quebec's protests that the defence of Canada was being neglected and incited patriotism by organizing Gaspé as a defence area under Brigadier Edmond Blais, the new commander of M.D.5. There had been numerous sinkings of freighters in the lower St. Lawrence and the Gulf by German submarines during the summer of 1942, and a renewal of the campaign was feared. From Ile-Verte on the St. Lawrence to Douglastown on the Baie des Chaleurs the Gaspé peninsula was partially blacked out, to prevent shore lights from silhouetting ships, while army, navy, and air defences were co-ordinated under French-Canadian officers. A civilian defence and warning system was set up with the support of the clergy, while a Reserve Army unit, Les Fusiliers du Bas St. Laurent, under the command of Colonel Joseph Pinault, a Gaspesian hero of the First World War, manned a series of anti-aircraft and defence installations. Gaspé was put on a war footing without arousing anything but French-Canadian pride, thanks to an intelligent choice of leaders, adroit publicity, and the fact that the population, which earned its living from the sea, had had the war brought to its door.

French Canada was further wooed by the holding of the first Quebec Conference in August. For two weeks the ancient capital sheltered the meetings of Roosevelt, Churchill, King, and the British, American, and Canadian general staffs. The streets were thronged with detachments of soldiers, sailors, and marines of the Allied nations; anti-aircraft and radar installations dotted the rocky crest on which Quebec stands; and a squadron of Spitfires maintained guard in the air. The populace lined the streets and the entrances of the Citadel and the Chateau Frontenac for hours in order to catch a glimpse of the civil and military leaders of the United Nations. It was widely rumored and believed that Stalin would attend the conference, and even the prospective presence of the Russian dictator was welcomed by a Quebec which was pleased to find itself momentarily the center of the world. Churchill attended a meeting of the provincial cabinet and was given an ovation when he toured the city in the company of Prime Minister King. Although Roosevelt did not make a formal public appearance, he was easily the most popular statesman present in French-Canadian opinion. His subsequent speech at Ottawa, in which he highly praised Canada's war effort, won him many more Canadian friends.

The joint Canadian-American landing at Kiska in the Aleutians on August 16, which was announced during the conference, lent a culminating touch to French Canada's sense of full participation in the war, since the Régiment de Hull, under Colonel Dollard Ménard, was one of the Canadian units involved. The success of the bloodless Kiska episode took the curse off the further extension by order-in-council of 'home defence' service to Bermuda, the Bahamas, and British Guiana; while the successful conclusion of the Sicilian campaign in thirty-eight days cheered French Canada, which in June had taken a gloomy view of the length of the war.[123] But a poll of the Canadian Institute of Public Opinion in August showed that 66 per cent of the French Canadians still favored keeping the conscripts in Canada, while 56 per cent of the English were in favor of sending them overseas. Relief at the prospect of an early peace was responsible for Quebec's enthusiastic celebration of the surrender of Italy. *Le Canada* hailed it as a judgment on Fascism: 'Fascism's failure is an object lesson for the misguided who maintain that it is possible to exhort people into following a leader blindly.' *Le Soleil* commented more soberly:

Italy's unconditional surrender should facilitate entry of the United Nations' forces into Germany. It should soon be possible to render practical assistance to Greek and Yugoslav patriots. Even France's early liberation can now be anticipated. Russia, too, may soon have the opportunity of seeing a long-awaited European second front opened up on an extensive scale. The Italian capitulation is, therefore, a most important development of great political value.[124]

12

But once these milestones in the war were passed, Quebec turned back upon itself. The Godbout government had to call an election within a year, and the opposition parties sought to exploit popular dissatisfaction with the administration and the growing social unrest brought about by the war. In two significant federal by-elections in September, the Communist Fred Rose was elected in a Montreal working-class district by a majority of 1,800 over his *Bloc* rival Paul Massé, while Armand Choquette, the *Bloc* candidate, won the agricultural constituency of Stanstead by a 1,300 vote margin over an English Liberal. This radical trend alarmed Liberal leaders, while the press called for a revision of the Electoral Act which permitted the election of candidates who did not win a majority of the votes cast. *Le Devoir*, with its eye on Eire whose neutral status was envied by the nationalists, favored adoption of the Irish electoral system, while *Le Soleil* and *Le Droit* favored that of France. This agitation was in the main produced by fear lest the existing system should permit one of the new political groups to elect an undue number of representatives. Both the old parties were alarmed by the success of the *Bloc*, the C.C.F., and the Labor-Progressive (Communist) parties in exploiting popular unrest.

Rumors that the *Bloc* might join forces with Duplessis' *Union Nationale* were dispelled on September 1 when André Laurendeau, secretary-general of the group, declared:

We will fight with all our strength against Mackenzie King and Adélard Godbout. We have already given the former a severe jolt; and the latter will not be overlooked. But the first article of our program is not to defeat Mr. So & So. This was the mistake made in 1935 and 1936. True, we succeeded in ridding the province of Taschereau, only to have him replaced by Duplessis, a great deception. However, the people are frequently deceived. To deceive them again might one day throw them into the arms of Socialism or Communism.[125]

Duplessis returned the compliment by denouncing the *Bloc* on September 19, while on the same occasion one of his chief lieutenants, Antonio Barrette, congratulated P.-J.-A. Cardin for leaving the Liberal Party and thus left the door open for an alliance with the new federal party which Cardin was rumored to be forming among such maverick Liberals as J.-F. Pouliot, Emmanuel D'Anjou, and Wilfrid Lacroix, and the Duplessis Conservatives Frédéric Dorion and Sasseville Roy. This group was to adopt a program similar to that of the *Bloc* and would provide a better federal ally for Duplessis than the Conservative Party, which was handicapped in French Canada's eyes by its imperialist and capitalist traditions.

At the base of the confused political situation in Quebec was the labor problem. Wartime industrialization and unionization had produced a tense situation, with a demand by French-Canadian workers for pay rates equal to those of other provinces. The housing problem was acute, with thousands of new workers jamming the industrial centers. While the C.C.F. and Labor-Progressive parties sought to exploit French-Canadian bitterness about poor pay and working conditions, the *Bloc* blamed these evils on 'foreign' exploitation and called for nationalization of Quebec's natural resources. Even traditionally conservative leaders and newspapers favored reforms of a socialist nature. Cyrille Vaillancourt, a director of the Wartime Prices and Trade Board, told the Junior Chambre de Commerce:

It appears at the present time that a planned economy will be necessary when peace comes . . . Sound, methodical, progressive planning is required, however, to assure the best possible development of natural resources, industry, and commerce. . . . State intervention will increase in scope as the march of social reforms gains momentum.[126]

Le Soleil and *Le Droit* strongly supported M. Vaillancourt's statement, which was backed by almost all of the Quebec press except the Tory *Montreal Gazette*. Oscar Drouin, the provincial Minister of Commerce was also applauded when he declared:

As I see it, riches, that is national capital as we understand it, can come from one principal source: the development of our natural resources —hydro-electric energy, mines, forests—through economic planning along national lines, to assure that advantages will accrue to the masses as a whole and not to a few individuals. And above all we must not be lulled, influenced, or conditioned by arguments and scare stories advanced by the holier-than-thou interests of private enterprise in matters relating to political economy.   Practical development of our natural resources must not be impeded by so-called sound private enterprise.[127]

The labor situation was troubled by violent warfare between the so-called 'internationals'—unions affiliated with either the Trades and Labor Congress (A.F.L.) or the Canadian Congress of Labor (C.I.O.)—and the Catholic syndicates. The 'internationals' sought to guard the welfare of their members in English Canada and the United States by organizing French-Canadian labor and achieving equal pay rates, so that Quebec should not become the home of runaway mills and industries. The Catholic syndicates, exploiting French-Canadian group consciousness and nationalist feeling, sought to keep French-Canadian labor under French-Canadian—usually clerical—control, and thus to avoid 'foreign' control of labor as well as of industry. The international unions made the mistakes of not catering to French-Canadian traditional ideals and of advocating violent methods foreign to the tradition of the French-Canadian working class. The syndicates, which had grown up among the old paternalistic small industries, were ill-equipped to bargain on equal terms with national and international industries, since they were generally local and at best only provincial groups. The rivalry between the unions became a serious detriment to Quebec's war effort, first noted when a 1941 strike suspended production of aluminum at Arvida, the world's largest producer of a material which was essential to the Allied war effort.

13

The Lake St. John–Saguenay area of which Arvida is the industrial center provides an admirable social test tube for examining the results of the impact of the industrial revolution upon Quebec and the unrest which resulted. In a little over a century this region passed through the whole cycle of Quebec's economic history. Until well into the nineteenth century the region, which had first been explored by white men in the seventeenth century, remained a preserve for the successive fur-trading empires of the French Crown, the North-Westers, and the Hudson's Bay Company. In 1828, at the instigation of P. Tâché, a former fur-trader, the Quebec Legislature determined to send an expedition to explore the region. The report issued in the following year aroused some interest in the region, but the Hudson's Bay Company, which held a lease on the territory until 1842, managed to discourage any efforts at colonization.

The first settlers in the region came in 1838, and their object was not to clear lands for agriculture—this being forbidden by the fur company—but to cut white pine for William Price of Quebec. Price had come to Canada as an agent of the Admiralty in 1810 to acquire the mast timber which Britain lacked as a result of Napoleon's Continental Blockade, which had cut off the Scandinavian supply. Despite bitter opposition from the Hudson's Bay Company, Price managed to establish two lumber mills on the Saguenay. His river boats brought supplies for the settlers and carried the lumber to Quebec. Price used the same feudal industrial methods as the Channel Island firm of Charles Robin & Co. in Gaspé, paying his labor in script good only at company stores and thus keeping his men constantly in debt to the company. Managers and foremen were English and Scottish, while French-Canadians were never permitted to be anything but hired hands. This exploitation of a subject people and its natural resources by a self-styled 'master race' produced a lasting bitterness against the Price interests, which still exists in Quebec today.

The white pine of the Saguenay was soon gutted by the ruthless lumbering methods of the day and by forest fires, and the industry pushed northward into the Lake St. John region, with its headquarters at Chicoutimi, where the half-breed Peter MacLeod, a former Hudson's Bay employee, had established a mill in 1842. After his death ten years later Price acquired his interests. The region was already sending thirty shiploads of lumber a year to Europe from Chicoutimi, a port at the head of the long fjord of the Saguenay which ocean-going ships could reach with increasing ease as steam came to the aid of sail. Thereafter the lumber industry pushed steadily northward, and by 1868 the Price lumber camps were already ten leagues to the northeast of Lake St. John in the Peribonca country. Overpopulation and soil exhaustion in the old parishes along the St. Lawrence about the middle of the century led to the organization of colonization societies in Charlevoix, Quebec, and Kamouraska, whence colonists were sent to Lake St. John to clear the land and provide the food demanded for man and horse by the expanding lumber industry. Though checked at intervals by the forest fires which accompanied the effort to clear the rich land around the lake in this great natural bowl in the midst of the inhospitable Laurentian Shield, colonization proceeded with extreme rapidity. By 1921 some 250,000 acres had been brought under cultivation and the region had become one of the most prosperous agricultural areas in the province. The original channel of communication by way of the Saguenay, closed for more than five months of the year by ice, was supplemented by three winter roads across the wilderness to the St. Lawrence. A railroad, first proposed in 1854, was finally completed from Quebec to Chambord on the lake in 1888, extended to Chicoutimi in 1893, to Haha Bay at the head of deep-sea navigation on the Saguenay in 1908, and later to Dolbeau, north of Lake St. John.

Meanwhile forest industry had undergone notable changes. By 1871 white pine was beginning to be exhausted and cedar was fast following suit, while the sawmills only occupied some 500 men. Mills on Lake St. John replaced those on the Saguenay, but they lacked the facility and cheapness of transportation which had favored the earlier establishments. After a period of decline from 1880 to 1900, forest industry was rejuvenated by the birth of the pulp industry. In 1897 Alfred Dubuc of Chicoutimi constructed a pulp mill at Chicoutimi, making use of the great waterpower resources of the region and exporting his product to Great Britain and the United States, as well as to English Canada. With the rapid development of this industry the population of Chicoutimi grew fivefold from 1891 to 1921. Many other small mills were established in the region, and it was the pulp industry which established Port Alfred, the new deep-sea port on Haha Bay. But after 1920 the pulp industry suffered from Scandinavian competition, high ocean freight rates, and high railroad rates during the five months when navigation on the Saguenay was closed. Meanwhile another phase of the industry had been launched by Sir William Price, who in 1899 had taken over the tottering forest empire of his grandfather. Benefited by enormous timber limits and large capital resources, he bought the pulp mill at Jonquière, and produced first cardboard and later paper from the pulp it manufactured. Paper was a much more economic product than pulp, since it could be transported easily by rail at all seasons at lower cost. Gradually Price concentrated on supplying the American newsprint market, and his Kénogami-Jonquière establishment became the largest Canadian producer of newsprint.

In 1922 the Price firm controlled nearly three-quarters of the region's 117,000 developed horsepower, but still needed both more power and a more regular supply. Price Brothers then sought American capital and interested the Duke tobacco interests. The Duke-Price Company, which was taken over by Shawinigan Power and the Aluminum Company of America in 1926, began in 1923 to develop the waterpower provided by the outlets of Lake St. John. The level of the lake was raised eighteen feet and eight dams were constructed, while a power-house capable of producing 540,000 horsepower was installed at Ile-Maligne. The village of Saint-Joseph-d'Alma increased its population a hundred-fold in two years, while a new paper mill formed the center of the new company town of Riverbend. This vast program was not carried through without opposition: the farmers of Lake St. John lost land and buildings—15,000 square miles of cultivated land were flooded, while still more was affected—and they complained that the Price company had not compensated them justly; while the importation of workers from Ontario, Finland, Italy, Czechoslovakia, and Poland was resented on nationalist grounds. Port Alfred was linked to the new source of power and became a producer of paper as well as pulp; while a new paper mill at Dolbeau, which had been planned to use local power, was also later connected with Ile-Maligne. Encouraged by this success, a new dam was built at Chute-à-Caron which added 240,000 horsepower to the resources of the region. Plans were already made for developing 800,000 more horsepower at Shipshaw when the 1929 crash brought the project to a halt.

The Aluminum Company of America (later a separate Aluminum Company of Canada was set up) which played the major part in these and later developments, was attracted to the region by the wealth of easily-developed and constant waterpower, the easy access for deep-sea shipping, and by the supply of hardworking, docile, and cheap French-Canadian labor. Cheap power in enormous quantities and cheap labor were the main needs of the aluminum industry, which began work on a great plant and company town at Arvida (named after Arthur Vining Davis, the president of the company) in 1925. It created a great port at Port Alfred, where ocean freighters could bring the vast quantities of bauxite from British Guiana and cryolite from Greenland which were the raw materials of aluminum, and load the finished ingots for transportation to the United States, England, Japan, and the rest of Canada. The Arvida plant had a pre-war capacity of 30,000 tons a year, but plans had already been made for an eventual production of 300,000. The town of Arvida, created out of the wilderness by the company, housed 3,000 people in its individual family houses, each surrounded by lawns and gardens.

With this development the industrial future of the Saguenay-Lake St. John region seemed to be assured of a stability unknown in the forest industries. The lumber mills now employed only a bare hundred workers; while the pulp and paper industry could employ 6,500 when working at full capacity. But the development which had enabled the region in eight years to increase its production of pulp threefold and of paper fourfold, while its power resources were increased eightfold, ended in overproduction before the 1929 crash. Price Brothers began buying and closing down small competing mills in 1927; three years later the company went into bankruptcy itself. In 1932 the region reached the bottom of the depression, with Arvida employing only 300 men in the aluminum industry, Kénogami and Jonquière 1,000 in its pulp and paper plants, Port Alfred 250, and Riverbend half its usual number. Only the small mill at Dolbeau was little affected by the crisis which weighed so heavily upon its giant rivals. Surplus power was used to heat homes and was even transmitted to Quebec. The region rivaled Montreal as that most severely affected by the depression. The agriculture of the region, which was based on supplying food for the industrial centers, was gravely affected by the depression of industry.[128] Public opinion was embittered by the fact that the great 'foreign' industries had revolutionized the life of the region with a high hand, and had left it flat on its back when depression came. Fertile ground was thus provided for the economic nationalism of the 1930's and for leftist schemes of nationalization of industry.

With the coming of the war, however, industrial prosperity returned to a region in which agriculture had already revived, thanks to improved cultivation practices. Lake St. John is one of the few Quebec regions in which large-scale mechanized farming is possible. Arvida soon found itself working at capacity to produce the aluminum so urgently needed by the Allies for airplanes. Its production of aluminum in 1942 equaled the world output in 1939. By 1943 Arvida was employing 15,000 men, while work was carried on night and day on the Shipshaw project, at Ile-Maligne and Chute-à-Caron, and far up the Peribonca at Passe Dangereuse, to increase the developed supply of power, which now amounted to 2,000,000 horsepower—nearly half that of the province as a whole.

This enormous and rapid development had not been accomplished without creating social difficulties. Bad management which disregarded French-Canadian predilections was responsible for the 1941 aluminum strike and for the subsequent struggle between the A.F.L. union and the Catholic syndicate for control of the workers. The aluminum industry became a political football, with the nationalists and Duplessis forces calling for its nationalization, denouncing the Liberals for having sold out to 'foreign' business, and denouncing the Aluminum Company for having ruthlessly undermined the pulp and paper industries of the region. The model industrial city of Arvida was marred by inadequate temporary wartime housing and camps for single men, the latter of which were far superior to the bunkhouses of the lumber trade or to army camp accommodation, but nonetheless introduced into the town a restless and unsettled element. The instinct for the traditional way of life, which had forced the company to remodel along traditional French-Canadian lines its original workers' houses designed by an American architect, led many new workers at Arvida to live in the nearby towns of Kénogami, Jonquière, Chicoutimi, and Port Alfred, whose wretched slums were made still worse by this influx. The ever-growing demand for labor drained manpower from the old agricultural centers all around Lake St. John, and even from the lower St. Lawrence region. Husky farmers were favored as potmen, the highest paid laborers, whose job required a strong back, endurance in high temperatures, and a minimum of brains. Veteran workers sought to transfer from this job, particularly in hot weather when breaking up the crust which formed on the pots as aluminum was produced by electro-chemical process became an arduous job, though the men only had to work about half the time they were on duty in the torrid pot rooms. It was on this crucial department of the industry that the A.F.L. centered its organization drive, since a strike there would cripple the whole plant.

The region had almost the longest record of union history of any part of the province. Chicoutimi had been active center of the Catholic syndicate movement since the foundation there in 1907 by Mgr. Eugène Lapointe of the Fédération Ouvrière Mutuelle du Nord. The syndicates' development had been favored by Alfred Dubuc in his pulp mills, but had been opposed by the English-Canadian and American interests. When the pulp syndicates, representing 85 per cent of the workers in the Price Company, sought a collective contract in 1937, their request was refused. In the following year the internationals intensified their organizational work, and in November signed a contract with the company, despite the fact that they only had a minority of members at Kénogami and only a handful at Jonquière and Riverbend. The syndicates protested and sought to be associated with the minority union in any contract, but their demand was refused. Despite intervention by the provincial minister of labor, the company stood firm by its decision not to deal with unions under clerical auspices, and favored the intensive organizing campaign of the International Brotherhood of Paper Makers (A.F.L.).

The Aluminum Company, however, reversed Price Brothers' labor policies and profited thereby. It recognized the emotional force of French-Canadian particularism and the commercial advantages of dealing with a weak local union rather than a strong international one, which someday would insist upon the same wages being paid in Quebec as in the American and English-Canadian plants of the company.

The *Syndicat national catholique de l'Aluminum*, founded in 1937, won a collective contract from its company that same year. Under this contract, renewed from year to year, potmen's wages were raised 20 to 25 per cent, while workers engaged on a weekly basis received a paid vacation of fifteen days, while those engaged on an hourly basis received paid vacations according to their length of service. The contract was extended to all workers in the plant, and negotiations between the syndicate and the company were in process in October 1942 when the A.F.L. sent an organizer, Philip Cutler, to conduct an intensive campaign for the international union. This organizer, denounced as a Jew and a former Communist, promising staggering wage increases to the workers, while warning the company that 'hell would pop if an agreement was not reached on terms satisfactory to the A.F.L.' The international union succeeded in recruiting 3,000 members, and immediately petitioned Prime Minister King to have the federal ministry of labor exercise its influence on the company to sign a contract with the International Union of Aluminum Workers (A.F.L.) as representative of 'the majority of the employees.' This claim was unquestionably false, since the syndicate represented some 4,000 men while the majority of the 15,000 workers were unorganized, being unwilling to pay dues when they were satisfied with wages and working conditions.

An international meeting at Jonquière on December 1, conducted by Cutler, resulted in a resolution requesting the federal minister of labor to name a conciliator and to order a vote among the workers for their bargaining agent. Rose, a federal labor investigator, began work fifteen days later. This dispatch was in sharp contrast with the procedure followed in 1941, when the syndicate representing two-thirds of the pulp and paper workers at Dolbeau requested a federal conciliator and arbitration of labor difficulties there, and intervention was refused after two months' delay had permitted the company to sign a gentleman's agreement with the international union. Rose was immediately denounced by the syndicate as a Jew and as a former counsel for the international unions, and his decision within two days to recommend a vote at Arvida was violently assailed as evidence of his bias. The provincial minister of labor, who was as favorable to the syndicates as the federal minister was to the international unions, was warned in time, thanks to a syndicate-minded stenographer who supplied a carbon of Rose's report, and immediately protested to Ottawa at this decision to regard the existing contract with the syndicate 'as a scrap of paper.' Rose completed his investigation, declaring that he did not take orders from Quebec, and that he would recommend a vote to the federal authorities. But the vote was not ordered, since the international union could not prove that it represented the majority, and because of pressure from Quebec.

The international union then threatened to call a strike, which would have halted production of a vital war material, already hindered by the long drawn-out struggle. While the syndicates urged the international organizers to 'stay at home as we do' and opposed 'enabling these New York bigshots to live on our money,' the international spokesmen attacked the support given by the clergy and provincial officials to the syndicate, and warned that the day of reckoning would come for them. The local clergy and the Jesuit Père Genest fought the international movement vigorously. When the Jewish Philip Cutler was replaced by an Irish Catholic organizer, 'foreign Catholics' were denounced from the pulpit along with the international union. Public opinion was strongly aroused against the internationals as they continued their drive to organize all the war industries of Quebec. Cutler and a colleague, Claude Jodoin, were finally jailed when they launched another organization campaign at Shawinigan.

The Aluminum Company, which feared an attempt to raise the Arvida wage rates to the level prevailing in its American plants, gave the syndicate discreet support. The international's agitation was unsuccessful because the workers recognized that the company had given them wages, working, and living conditions which were scarcely to be matched in Canada; and because the company made a policy of catering to French-Canadian particularism. Not only were 92 per cent of the Arvida workers French Canadians, but the company employed as many French-Canadian technicians and executives as it could find. Its head chemist and its personnel manager were French Canadians, though its general manager at Arvida was an Englishman and most of the chief executives were Americans. The company, an international cartel, was not afflicted with any such narrow nationalist spirit as had caused Price Brothers so much trouble. It could afford to carry no national flag, and its basic loyalty was to the aluminum empire, with its bauxite deposits in British Guiana, its cryolite deposits in Greenland, its processing plants at Galveston, Massena, Toronto, and Kingston; and its English, Italian, and German subsidiaries.

Since Arvida offered admirable manufacturing conditions, thanks to the largest supply of cheap power in the world and easy access by deep-sea shipping, the company strove in every fashion to make good its position in Quebec. It displayed a paternalism which sometimes misfired and irritated French-Canadian individualism. It revised its model housing plans to suit French-Canadian tastes; it rented or sold houses and land at less than cost; it planted trees and encouraged gardens; it established a vast indoor recreation center for the winter months and sports facilities for the summer ones; it provided a newspaper, a hospital, and schools, and contributed heavily to the building of churches. When the politically-minded French Canadians missed the sport of elections, it added an elected town council to the city manager system it had established. In the industry itself it required its English-speaking employees to learn and to use French; it provided safety devices; it instituted the 48-hour week in a region which had grown up on dawn-to-dusk labor; it had labor relations representatives in each division of the plant, to act as buffers between workmen and foremen and to personalize the company to the individual worker. By prizes for useful suggestions it sought to improve industrial practices and to encourage employee loyalty. It favored the *caisse populaire* and co-operative movements sponsored by the syndicates and established its own pension system.

All these measures proved profitable, since after their adoption the Aluminum Company had less labor trouble than any other war industry. Once the management of the Arvida plant had come into the hands of men who understood and respected French-Canadian ideas after the 1941 strike, there was no further serious difficulty. An indication of employee loyalty was supplied when volunteers responded to a call from the company to spend all of Christmas Day 1943 in unloading a shipment of frozen bauxite from open railway cars in order that the plant might keep functioning without interruption.

Under such conditions the international union could make little progress, particularly after the company had delicately suggested that if the union succeeded in raising wages at Arvida to the American level, the Arvida plant might be shut down in order to keep the American plants running. The anti-Aluminum Company agitation raised in Montreal by nationalist organs was curiously unsupported by similar unrest among the workers at Arvida, although there was a small radical group in the plant which distributed anti-English and anti-capitalist propaganda in parody litany form. Despite all the talk of nationalization from nationalists on the one hand and the C.C.F. on the other, the Aluminum Company was not very frightened on that score for the postwar period, putting its faith in French Canada's deep respect for private property and on its own conviction that public ownership would be unwieldy, more expensive, and less efficient than private enterprise in this industry. The company was much more concerned with the problem of converting to peacetime production and finding outlets for the enormous productive facilities built up during the war. But there was a strong feeling that Arvida had become the most economical place in the world to produce aluminum and that it would continue to do so when other war plants were closed, while the enormous power sources might well be put to other industrial uses if a market for aluminum could not be found.[128]

14

The union situation at Arvida was roughly paralleled elsewhere in Quebec. The internationals were strong only in long-established industries in the old urban centers, and even there were under attack as foreign organizations run in American interests. Management in most of the older industries, if forced to accept unions at all, preferred to deal with the English-speaking internationals rather than with the French clerically-influenced syndicates. A few old industries overcame the racist tradition of industry in Quebec and favored the syndicates, which could be used as company unions under cover of favoring French-Canadian ideas. Such was the policy of the Dominion Textile Company at its Magog plant, where the syndicate chaplain, who received a salary as chaplain of the company-supported hospital and whose father enjoyed a company pension, successfully broke up a C.I.O. organizational campaign.

One notable development of the war was the rise of French-Canadian industrialists, such as the Simard brothers of Sorel, who built ships on the Kaiser plan and also made guns. Two old marine railways which had employed 160 men in pre-war days were converted into a bustling shipyard employing 6,000 men at the peak of production. The latest methods of industrial engineering and management were cleverly adapted for use in Quebec, while the paternalistic relationship between French-Canadian *patron* and French-Canadian labor was preserved. The Simards' enterprises were free of the usual bitterness arising from ethnic division between management and labor which provided admirable openings for agitation in other enterprises, such as the Crown company war industries, which were usually directed by men whom the French Canadians regarded as 'foreigners.' Patriotic propaganda helped to avoid labor trouble in such plants, however, while the syndicates loyally adhered to the attitude that strikes were illegal in wartime, though the internationals did not hesitate to threaten to actually call them.

In the face of the announced intention of Trades and Labor Congress spokesman Robert Haddow to organize first the war industries and later all others in Quebec, the syndicates were forced to become more militant than they had ever been before. Alfred Charpentier, president of the Confédération des Travailleurs Catholiques du Canada which claimed a membership of 53,000 Quebec workers, described the American Federation of Labor as 'Our worst enemy, an enemy who is not afraid to use any means at his disposal to further his aim' at the twenty-second annual convention of the syndicates at Granby in 1944. He accounted for the growth of the C.C.L. and C.I.O. unions by their use of illegal strikes and anti-religious propaganda. Bishop Douville of Saint-Hyacinthe, who attended the convention, warned the workers against following the precedent set by the C.C.L. unions in supporting the C.C.F., which he regarded as communistic. He stressed the fact that support of the internationals was detrimental to French-Canadian interests:

American labor unions, to which certain Quebec workers are affiliated, will logically protect their own before taking care of your welfare. The situation in Quebec must be unique in labor annals, with labor groups here awaiting orders and directives from foreign leaders.[129]

Bishop Douville urged simultaneous development of workers' and employers' syndicates 'as a prelude to the economic corporatism which we consider essential to the future of labor and employers as well.'

The provincial government met this new agitation in clerical and nationalist circles for corporatism by setting up a postwar Economic Council, whose fifteen members included corporatist sympathizers Père Georges-Henri Levesque of Laval, Eugène L'Heureux of *L'Action Catholique*, Esdras Minville of the Ecole des Hautes Etudes Commerciales, and Gérard Picard of the Confédération des Travailleurs Catholiques. The president of the council, however, was Jules Brillant, the able utility magnate of the lower St. Lawrence region. The corporatist movement continued to be strongly supported by the Semaine Sociales, *Le Devoir*, *L'Action Catholique*, and *Le Droit*; while it was bitterly attacked by *Le Jour*, in which Jean-Charles Harvey waged a vigorous campaign in defence of Manchester Liberalism as interpreted by the Canadian Pacific Railway and other big business in the province. It was also violently opposed by the Communists, who regarded it as fascist in inspiration—a view also held by the majority of English-speaking North Americans who had not been inspired by the application of corporatism under Mussolini in Italy and Salazar in Portugal.

Further evidence of the social and economic unrest of French Canada in 1943 was provided by the renewed outbreak of anti-Semitism, with a pro-Pétain French Dominican attacking Jacques Maritain in the Quebec press for having been influenced by his Jewish wife,[130] with the Jews of Quebec City being legally blocked from erecting a synagogue on the fashionable Grande Allée, and with the beating up of several Jews at Plage Laval near Montreal in September. The *Bloc* had revived the old nationalist anti-Semitic tradition in its campaign against Fred Rose; and Paul Gouin's *L'Union* and the Order of Jacques Cartier's *La Boussole* continued to print anti-Semitic propaganda. As Everett Hughes has admirably demonstrated, anti-Semitism in French Canada is largely an attempt to find a scapegoat for dissatisfaction with the economic order: 'The symbolic Jew receives the more bitter of the attacks which the French Canadians would like to make upon the English or even upon some of their own leaders and institutions . . . the Jew in Quebec is the physically present small competitor rather than the hidden wirepuller of high finance and big business.'[131]

Anti-Semitism fulfils an emotional need for the French Canadian, and is as instinctive as the American Southerner's color prejudice. There was a revealing contrast of the two attitudes, when an American Negro doctor, who had been excluded from the dining-room of the Chateau Frontenac and brought a suit against the hotel, was enthusiastically supported by French-Canadian opinion, which deplored such prejudice, while it objected to the number of New York Jews who frequented the hotel. The *Bloc*, which exploited to the full all the popular emotional attitudes of French Canada, did not fail to use anti-Semitism in Montreal, where the Jews have prospered more greatly than the French Canadians in a much shorter time.

The development of the *Bloc* movement continued to be hampered by internal dissension, although its popular appeal was strong, as witnessed by a Canadian Institute of Public Opinion poll in the fall of 1943 which indicated that it was now supported by 33 per cent of the electorate.[132] During Maxime Raymond's illness Edouard Lacroix, the wealthy federal M.P. for the Beauce, took over organization of the movement and alienated the anti-trust radicals. Paul Gouin, Dr. Hamel, Jean Martineau, and René Chaloult conferred together about breaking with the *Bloc*. Hamel and Martineau favoured joining forces with the C.C.F., which had made overtures through Frank Scott's public utterances, while Gouin and Chaloult preferred to revive the *Action Libérale Nationale* movement of the 1930's. On October 16 Dr. Hamel announced in a broadcast the decision of the dissidents to leave the *Bloc*, since it had been taken over by a 'millionaire.' René Chaloult also declared in the legislature: 'We have committed ourselves to fighting the trusts and the financial interests which dominate the lives of French Canadians, and as Mr. Lacroix is himself a millionaire who has made his money by being closely associated with these trusts, we could not in justice to ourselves or to the policy we preach take our place beside him on the hustings.'[133] But there was no hint of the economic reforms dear to the heart of the dissidents, while the Godbout government had already announced its intention of expropriating the Montreal Light, Heat, & Power Co. This step was discounted by Duplessis and the C.C.F. as an electoral measure, but approved by all the French press except *Le Jour*.

No mention of the split within the *Bloc* was made in another radio speech on October 17 in which Raymond outlined the party's provincial program: to champion provincial autonomy, to restore the integrity of the family, and to make Quebec an agricultural province once more. Raymond declared that Quebec must remain French and Catholic, and that the individualism born of the French Revolution must be destroyed. He denounced the injustice of taxes which bore more heavily on large families, and said the *Bloc* would seek to revise the tax laws from a family point of view.[134] Oscar Drouin, leader of the nationalist wing of the Liberal Party, made a bid for support from *Bloc* followers discontented by the defection of the radical nationalists, demanding fair play in the federal civil service for French Canadians and the right for Canada to amend the B.N.A. Act with the consent of the provinces. This utterance, coming after the announcement of the federal plan for family allowances and the provincial plan for nationalization of electricity in Montreal, made evident the Liberal Party's determination to steal the thunder of both the C.C.F. and the *Bloc*.

A bombshell was thrown into the confused political scene by a joint pastoral letter of the Canadian hierarchy in October 1943, which declared the C.C.F. a neutral party for which Catholics were as free to vote as they were for the two old parties. Communism was once more condemned, but the C.C.F. was definitely cleared of the disapproval of the Church. This utterance was a distinct blow to the Liberals and to the nationalists, who sought to belittle its ramifications as much as possible. It was given much fuller attention by the English press than by the French, with the *Canadian Register*, the English Catholic organ of the diocese of Montreal, publishing a lengthy commentary, while *L'Action Catholique* merely printed the text, as did *Le Devoir*, under the disgruntled caption: 'Call it what you like, Communism is still to be condemned.' In an editorial in *Le Devoir* Omer Héroux warned against any 'attempt to read into their statement any more than what it says—neither more nor less.'[135] The Jesuits of the Ecole Sociale Populaire went so far as to distort the clear meaning of the statement in an anti-C.C.F. sense. The Communist spokesman Stanley B. Ryerson deplored the bishops' intervention into politics, while M. J. Coldwell, Frank Scott, and David Lewis welcomed it on behalf of the C.C.F. The utterance cleared from the path of the C.C.F. in Quebec the insuperable barrier of disapproval by the Church.

There remained, however, another major obstacle, the inability of the party to find a representative French-Canadian leader. In the popular mind the party remained 'English,' while the nationalist effort to muddy the clear stream of the bishops' thought offset the original effect of the statement. The semantic confusion of Fabian English socialism with revolutionary and anti-clerical Continental socialism paralleled that of English and Continental liberalism in the previous century, and seemed fated to endure as long. Clarification of the confusion was not facilitated by the subsequent revolutionary utterances of Harold Winch, radical British Columbia chief of the C.C.F., which were duly exploited by the nationalist and clerical opponents of the party in Quebec. In vain Frank Scott and David Lewis sought by statements and speeches to stress the close kinship between the social program of the papal encyclicals and that of the C.C.F., and the party's opposition to imperialism and to racist movements. It was accused by both its French and English opponents of cutting its cloth according to its audience. The newly formed provincial organization of the C.C.F. crumbled as several of its French-Canadian officers resigned under pressure from their compatriots.

The wave of strikes which had afflicted the province in recent months continued, with first the Montreal police and firemen going out, and then the City Hall employees. A similar strike among the municipal employees in Quebec was threatened, while agitation over low wages and consequent poor health and housing conditions mounted ever higher. Faced with general deploring of the situation by the French press and the announced intention of the Communists to profit by it, the Quebec government introduced new labor legislation at the outset of the session in January 1944. The provisions of this bill made it obligatory for employers to recognize any union comprising 60 per cent of their employees and to make collective agreements with them under the supervision of a provincial Labor Relations Board. The bill was based upon the recommendations of the *Conseil Supérieur du Travail*, a provincial body composed of eight representatives of capital, eight of labor, and eight economists. The provincial authorities had hurriedly agreed upon a labor code before Ottawa introduced the proposed federal one. As Premier Godbout stated, the measure would safeguard the autonomy of the province against federal commissions which failed to understand provincial powers under the B.N.A. Act. The first bill was unanimously approved by the legislature. A second bill provided for compulsory arbitration of labor disputes in public service industries, prohibited strikes or lockouts, and denied the right of police or civil servants to join unions. These bills were hailed enthusiastically by the Catholic syndicates. The provincial representatives of the American Federation of Labor, Elphège Beaudoin and Marcel Francq, endorsed the bills, but their endorsement was disowned by officials of the Montreal Trades and Labor Council. The Canadian Congress of Labor which had organized police, firemen, and tramway employees, opposed both measures. The press unanimously approved the legislation.

15

A unanimous reaction such as Quebec had not shown since the plebiscite greeted the Toronto speech of Lord Halifax, British ambassador to the United States, on January 24, 1944, when he proposed a common postwar foreign and defence policy for the Commonwealth. René Chaloult, who had already introduced in the Quebec legislature a resolution deploring Canada's 'excessive' war effort, on January 28 gave notice of the following motion: 'That this House believes it to be its duty to go on record against the new imperialism of Lord Halifax and his dangerous tendencies.' There was a stormy reaction in Quebec, as there was indeed all over Canada, to Halifax's suggestion that a postwar central government for the Commonwealth should be established in London. Godbout and Duplessis followed their federal leaders in keeping silence, but Maxime Raymond echoed M. J. Coldwell's declaration of opposition to the proposal with this statement:

We are for the independence of Canada. The *Bloc* is of the opinion that Canada has an important role to play in world affairs, but it does not consider the British Commonwealth of Nations as the most appropriate organization to allow it to play such a role.

The French press gave wide publicity to the comments of the *Winnipeg Free Press*, deploring the fact that 'Lord Halifax, a member of the British War Cabinet, should make such a speech on Canadian soil and before consulting the Canadian government,' and of the *Toronto Star* that 'The strength of the Commonwealth rests in autonomous association rather than in centralized authority . . . that the units of the Empire must "necessarily speak as one" is too much to expect, and equally so is it that the Dominion should as a matter of course "take the same point of view as the Mother Country."'

Omer Héroux denounced in *Le Devoir* this new imperial federation movement and asserted that 'Canada, a sovereign nation, will not tamely accept either from Great Britain or the United States or from anywhere else the attitude she must take to world affairs . . . Independence will ensure that Canada, like all great peoples, will order her foreign policy according to her own interests and to her geographical situation.' *Le Droit* warned that 'Empire solidarity has limits inevitably fixed by the national interests of each Dominion, and these cannot be overlooked.' *L'Action Catholique* called Halifax's suggestion 'unacceptable' and observed: 'Far better that we should guard our liberty, not to practice an unwise isolationism in international affairs, but to collaborate with those we wish, in the interests of Canada and world peace, keeping in mind the fact we are an American country.' *La Patrie* declared that Canada 'must first of all consider her own interests, and it must not be forgotten that she is an American country.' *Le Canada* found 'something right and something risky' in the proposal, considering that 'the new relationship proposed by Lord Halifax would undoubtedly be a step forward,' but that on the other hand it would seem to many 'an alliance of lamb with the lion' which might drag Canada 'into a whirlpool of Tory imperialism.' *Le Jour* charged Halifax with indirectly furthering the work of the anti-British element in Quebec and regarded Canada's complete sovereignty as inevitable within fifty years. [136]

The speech from the throne at the opening of the federal session contained an indirect reply to Halifax: 'It is only by the general organization in international affairs of peace-loving nations that dangers of future aggression will be removed, and world peace secured.' [137] In proposing adoption of the speech, Léonard Tremblay (Dorchester) said that Mackenzie King would 'stop the imperialistic intrigues of Halifax, just as Chamberlain's imperialism once received a rebuff from Laurier's Canadianism.' [138] The nationalist press warned that the Liberal Party was just as imperialist at heart as the Conservative, and tended to regard this stand as one taken with future elections in mind, like the proposal of family allowances. The Liberal press naturally hailed both policies with delight, devoting particular attention to explaining how Quebec would specially benefit from the family allowance scheme. In the provincial legislature Liberal support was found for Chaloult's anti-Halifax resolution, with Oscar Drouin denouncing 'a concerted plan' to 'put the machine into reverse and set up an Imperial Federation.' Drouin declared: 'We cannot agree to lose what our fathers before us gained, and what was won at the cost of so much strife ... Quebec cannot accept the new imperialism of Lord Halifax.'

The *Bloc* held its first general convention from February 3 to 6 in Montreal. Delegates were invited from all French-speaking centers in Canada. English Canada had been made familiar with the new nationalist movement through *Maclean's Magazine's* publication of an interview with Maxime Raymond. [139] His answers to a series of specific questions, which gave him an opportunity to expose the whole platform of the *Bloc*, were summed up in his final answer to the query as to Canada's future status—'Independence.' But Raymond was unable to attend the opening of the convention, while Gouin, Hamel, and Chaloult were notable for their absence, despite Raymond's earlier appeal for unity. André Laurendeau, who had served as secretary-general and radio spokesman of the group for nearly a year and had been named editor of the new weekly organ

Le Bloc, was nominated as provincial leader, a post almost as important as Raymond's since the *Bloc* could only hope to win power in Quebec. It was rumoured that the elderly Raymond would retire from politics because of ill health, leaving the party in Laurendeau's hands. Though it had been anticipated that Laurendeau's nomination might bring back to the fold the dissidents and their young followers, Laurendeau expressed no eagerness for Chaloult's return when he announced that the *Bloc* would run candidates in every Quebec constituency. And in the first issue of *Le Bloc* Laurendeau rejected a suggested merger of the *Bloc* with Duplessis in the provincial field, with the observation that 'Quebec will punish with a single blow both the guilty: Godbout and Duplessis.'[140]

Paul Gouin, Dr. Hamel, and René Chaloult were immediately reported to be planning a new Liberal-nationalist group, since they would not accept Laurendeau's leadership. On February 14 the dissidents issued an anti-*Bloc* statement which declared that their efforts at reconciliation with the *Bloc* had been rejected, and that they had not been given the assurances they required against a repetition of 1936, when they had been repudiated by M. Duplessis after helping to win the election. Maxime Raymond announced on February 26 that he considered the matter 'ended once and for all,' while on the following day Paul Gouin broadcast a reply to Raymond and an explanation of the split in the party. He asserted that Raymond and Laurendeau had rejected all offers of settlement on a fair basis; that the split was not caused by personal differences between the dissidents and Lacroix, but by a matter of basic principle. He denounced Lacroix's financial control over the Quebec district as 'a return to the policy of the old parties, to the policy of dictatorship by those who handed out the party funds.' He added that Lacroix's financial power had compelled Raymond 'to take sides against the unity and interest of the movement which we had entrusted to him.'

René Chaloult, stating that he was the spokesman of Quebec nationalists, echoed Gouin's charges in the legislature and accused the *Bloc* of refusing to nationalize insurance and credit. He declared:

The only way left to correct the abuses arising from the trusts is to take things over step by step through the agency of expropriation ... It is only by nationalization that we succeed in delivering ourselves from foreign domination, and once again get control of our own wealth. When our government has once more gained possession of our resources, then it will employ French-Canadian engineers, managers, accountants, chemists, etc., to develop them ... So long as we continue to let foreign capitalists exploit against our interests our natural resources, the germs of Communism will inevitably continue to multiply.[141]

Paul Gouin continued to wage a vigorous campaign against the *Bloc* over the radio and through his newspaper *L'Union*. On March 5 he declared that followers of Duplessis had been active in the *Bloc* from the beginning and were now planning a formal alliance, with the *Bloc* leaving the provincial field to Duplessis and the latter aiding Raymond in the event of a federal election.

The Godbout government took heart at these developments and at the enthusiastic reception of its nationalization and labor measures. It was considered possible that the Gouin-Hamel-Chaloult group might make common cause with the Liberals, thus severely weakening the *Bloc*; while Maurice Duplessis' refusal to endorse the nationalization of the Montreal Light, Heat & Power and his anti-labor record made him particularly vulnerable in the current state of public opinion. Though the C.C.L. unions promised to throw their support behind the C.C.F., a Communist-inspired effort to create a united labor political front and the continued confusion within the French-Canadian mind of socialism with Communism weakened the strength of the C.C.F. It was considered likely that the provincial elections would be called in June to take advantage of the disintegration of the opposition parties.

The provincial Liberal Party was strengthened by the declaration made by Mr. King before his departure for the Imperial Conference in May:

> Collaboration with the Commonwealth is being carried out and will continue to be carried out, on a footing of the most specific equality. When sometimes great questions determining peace and war come up for discussion, as well as those on matters of prosperity and depression, such a collaboration cannot be exclusive in its aims and methods. Our undertakings, in connection with these great questions, must spring from a general plan, either worldwide or regional in scope. We look forward, in consequence, to a close collaboration in the interests of peace, not only within the Commonwealth, but also with all friendly nations, whether they be great or small.[142]

French Canada found this program more to its taste than that formulated by Conservative leader John Bracken, who declared: 'I look forward in consequence to Canada, acting as an autonomous power, strengthening the bonds which unite the members of the Commonwealth, and with this end in view, I believe that we should draw up in common a plan of permanent consultation in all matters of common interest.' *Le Canada* likened Bracken's position to that expounded by Lord Halifax. *Le Nouvelliste* held that 'an isolationist policy will not be of any more service to Canada than an imperialist policy will be.' *Le Droit* warned that though they might differ on means, all English-speaking politicians sought greater unification of the empire, and that the conference would 'concern itself only with the methods to be used to ensure such coordination.' *L'Action Catholique* declared: 'We are not isolationists. We want Canada to collaborate with the other countries of the world: the United States, the American republics, the Commonwealth nations, etc; but we ask the Prime Minister of Canada not to take on any new obligation which might prevent us from first considering the interests of Canada ... In international matters let us at last act as a truly autonomous country.' *Le Soleil*, which probably expressed the majority view, urged: 'It is of importance to the British Commonwealth of Nations that their intimate union should be maintained in peacetime as well as during the war. This happy result will be easily obtained by a more generous policy which does not limit in any way the autonomous countries and which encourages the evolution of British Colonies in the democratic framework. Unless she applies this doctrine sincerely, Great Britain will quickly lose the sympathy of free peoples.' *La Presse* lined up with *Le Soleil* in supporting King's insistence on Canadian liberty of action in foreign affairs. *L'Action Catholique* credited Mr. King with 'the idea of playing an important role and with the plan of opposing certain imperialistic policies of Mr. Churchill.' Only *Le Devoir* and *Le Droit* continued to assert that nothing separated King from Bracken, and that once more Canadian sovereignty was 'to be sacrificed on the altar of imperialism.'

Meanwhile the *Bloc* continued to have internal and external troubles. Edouard Lacroix and Dr. Pierre Gauthier were rumored to be on the brink of rupture with Raymond, while in the lower ranks there was a large measure of sympathy for Gouin, Hamel, and Chaloult. Laurendeau's campaign in *Le Bloc* for 'houses before guns' lost some of its effectiveness when the annual May 1 moving day passed without any considerable number of people being left homeless. Duplessis continued to wage violent war on the new movement, while Ernest Grégoire's Social Crediters denounced it as merely one of power-hungry opportunists. The number of *Bloc* public meetings continued to increase, but the question of where electoral funds would come from was raised by Lacroix's prospective departure from the movement. In the Stanstead and Cartier by-elections of the previous year the *Bloc* had sought to exploit the prestige of Henri Bourassa by bringing him out of retirement to speak at its meetings. Bourassa had successfully evoked the old nationalist tradition among the farmers of Stanstead, but carried little weight among the industrial workers of Montreal.

Now, on May 21, Bourassa supported Laurendeau on the platform in his first appearance at a Quebec City political meeting since 1907, when he and Lavergne had been stoned at the Marché Saint-Pierre. After making an appeal to the dissidents to rejoin the *Bloc*, he appalled his sponsors by observing: 'In constituencies where there is no *Bloc* candidate at the next federal elections, true Canadians should vote for the C.C.F. candidate.' He also recommended co-operation between French and English on a basis of equality, observing 'that does not mean we have to shine the shoes of Prime Minister Mackenzie King as Premier Godbout does, or to hold Churchill's cigar as Mackenzie King does.' He reiterated his opposition to imperialism of all kinds, and added: 'When they speak of a crusade for Christianity I cannot forget that our first cooperation with British imperialism at the end of the last century contributed to the extermination of a valiant little nation in South Africa.'[143]

Le Bloc omitted the reference to the C.C.F. in its report of 'the Master's' speech, and a week later urged: 'Let us fight against the imperialistic C.C.F., germ of the Communist revolution!' M. J. Coldwell promptly threw cold water on any prospect of an alliance between the *Bloc* and the C.C.F. René Chaloult in a radio speech expressed admiration for Bourassa, but added: 'That does not mean that I agree with his orders in the field of political strategy.' He urged his hearers to vote for the best man, regardless of party, and named some candidates he favored in all camps. Paul Gouin announced his intention to run as an independent, with the support of Chaloult and Hamel. Both dissidents condemned the Liberals, the *Union Nationale*, and the *Bloc* with equal violence.

On the eve of the long-awaited Allied invasion of Europe, French Canada was in an agitated state. Senator Athanase David's proposal in the Senate that a common history textbook be used in all Canadian schools to promote national unity had aroused violent opposition from the nationalists in May.[144] The nationwide unfavorable publicity aroused by the incendiary fire which destroyed the new synagogue in Quebec in May had irritated Quebec, which considered that much less attention was given to a similar incident shortly afterwards in Toronto. There were streetfights in Montreal in May and June between servicemen and slacker 'zootsuiters,' which received unfavorable attention in the English-Canadian and American press. The Duplessis and *Bloc* forces were evoking anti-war and anti-conscription feeling in the rural districts, while urban labor was agitated by the international-*vs.*-syndicate struggle and by Communist and C.C.F. attempts to form a united labor political front. The Liberal government hastily passed several measures at the close of the session which were regarded as electoral ones: government loans to corporations or co-operatives to aid homebuilding, free textbooks for schools, an 18 per cent cut in Montreal electricity rates, and a prospective cut in the cost of chemical fertilizers.

The news of the Normandy landings burst suddenly upon this troubled scene. After Mackenzie King's announcement of the invasion in the federal House, parliament sang the 'Marseillaise' at the suggestion of Maurice Lalonde (Labelle). *Le Canada* hailed the incident 'as an inspired gesture which once again before the whole world affirms the bi-ethnic character of Canada, and which more-over identifies, with an enthusiasm equal to that of all other parts of the Dominion, the Province of Quebec, from which come the majority of French-speaking members, with the glorious volunteers who have been sent as her representatives at the front.' Minister of Fisheries Ernest Bertrand was the first to speak to the people of France by radio in the name of Canada, urging the Resistance forces to follow the instructions sent them by the Allied High Command, and assuring his listeners of the love for France felt by the French Canadians who formed part of the invading armies. Louis St. Laurent spoke of 'the deep emotion that this dawn of June 6 has brought to each household in Canada—especially in our homes of the Province of Quebec where we speak your language and where everything that is French is so dear and familiar to us. As an answer to the misery of the fatal days of June 1940 there rises the exaltation of this daybreak of June 1944.'

Senators David and Bouchard, Valmore Bienvenue, and Major René Garneau were others who broadcast to France on this occasion. Edmond Turcotte of *Le Canada* evoked Normandy, the birthplace of many founders of French Canada. *Le Soleil* hailed the beginning of the campaign of France: 'May it fulfil our dearest wishes, make us forget the disaster of 1940.' *La Patrie* declared that the invaders were not 'coming as conquerors but as liberators' and would be welcomed by an Allied army of civilians, the Résistance. *L'Evénement-Journal* said: 'The French people are rising with a single impulse and rejoicing in the sweetness of their coming liberation. In this decisive hour when the fate of freedom is being sealed, they have heard the moving appeal of that great patriot Charles De Gaulle, who for four long years has embodied the France which fights, which resists, the France which never gives in.' *L'Action Catholique* published Cardinal Villeneuve's message asking for the prayers of the French-Canadian people, and observed that the secret launching of the invasion indicated that the Allies had carried on the war of nerves with the same ability as the Nazis at the beginning of the war. *Le Devoir* and *Le Droit* remained silent, with the former observing: 'The events taking place in Europe must not make us lose sight of what is going on at home.' *Le Canada*, the Liberal organ which under the aggressive editorship of Edmond Turcotte rarely missed an opportunity to attack the nationalists, commented thus on *Le Devoir's* observation:

On the day when the most powerful armies that free men ever assembled in the history of the world for the defence of their liberty were swinging into action for the liberation of the principal home of Western civilization, a continent completely enslaved by a band of criminals without faith or morals, the editor-in-chief of *Le Devoir* is concerned with two Acadian weeklies, the fate of which is no doubt interesting, but nonetheless somewhat less interesting than the fate of the civilized world for several generations to come.[145]

As in 1917, French Canada had reached the crucial stage of a world conflict in a state of mind increasingly pre-occupied with its own domestic concerns, which led it to show a shocking disregard for what English Canadians, Americans, Britishers, and Frenchmen regarded as the vital struggle for the survival of their common way of life. In its revolt against wartime propaganda and against major alterations in its way of life imposed by Ottawa, French Canada discounted the common danger. The prevailing sense of selfish security was expressed by an old *habitant*, reputed to have the traditional stocking well-filled with savings, who when asked by a war bond salesman how he would like to have the Germans running his village, violating his women, and corrupting his children, replied : 'I wouldn't. I'd vote against them.' Cut off by the war from Rome and Paris, in 1944 French Canada was more isolationist than ever. It was in a disgruntled and uncooperative mood as a result of the brickbats which had come its way for not doing more for the war effort than it had, which in its own eyes was already too much. It was deeply involved in a rapid if relatively peaceful social revolution which had shaken the framework of its society and upset its traditional way of life. It was in no state of mind to respond enthusiastically to the stepped-up war program which English Canadians soon came to demand in a mood of emotional hysteria created by the first heavy losses suffered by the Canadian Army overseas. Once more the conscription question opened a deep rift between the people of Canada, and blighted the limited national unity which had been attained through the common sacrifices of men and women of both stocks.

Notes

[1] The Casa Italiano in Montreal served as a center for propaganda among both French-Canadians and the considerable Italian population of the city. Though after 1939 the conservative French-Canadian sympathy for Mussolini tended to transfer itself to Franco, it was by no means dead. The German State Railways office in Montreal was an unofficial Nazi propaganda center, and paid subsidies to some ultranationalist publications. Some of the nationalist leaders accompanied their German paymasters to Mexico when war came in 1939. On the eve of the conflict, a German firm sought to buy Anticosti Island, in the

mouth of the St. Lawrence, which would have provided an excellent base for the submarine campaign subsequently waged in those waters. Colin Ross, *Zwischen USA und dem Pol* (Leipzig, 1934), a general study of Canada emphasizing the French-Canadian and New Canadian problems, is interesting for the light it sheds on Nazi policy towards Canada.

[2] Florent Lefevbre, *The French-Canadian Press and the War* (Toronto, 1940), 1-8.
[3] *Ibid.*
[4] *Canada, Commons Debates 1939, Special War Session,* 8 Sept., 28.
[5] *Proceedings and Orders in Council passed under the authority of the War Measures Act* (Ottawa, 1940), I, 19-20.
[6] *Montreal Gazette,* 2 Sept. 1939.
[7] *Ibid.,* 4 Sept. 1939.
[8] R. M. Dawson, *Canada in World Affairs: 1939-41* (Toronto, 1943), 8.
[9] *Commons Debates 1939,* 7 Sept., 1.
[10] *Ibid.,* 8 Sept., 12-41, 6.
[11] *Ibid.,* 12.
[12] Dawson, 285-6. For the first time the King declared war for Canada 'by and with the advice of Our Privy Council for Canada.'
[13] *Montreal Gazette,* 8 July 1941.
[14] *Commons 1939,* 8 Sept., 25.
[15] *Ibid.,* 36.
[16] *Ibid.,* 66.
[17] *Ibid.,* 67.
[18] *Ibid.,* 6.
[19] *Ibid.,* 68.
[20] *Ibid.,* 68-9.
[21] *Ibid.,* 69.
[22] *Ibid.,* 70-1.
[23] *Ibid.,* 82, 88.
[24] Lefevbre, 9-13.
[25] *Ibid.,* 13-14.
[26] *Ibid.,* 18.
[27] *Ibid.,* 19.
[28] *Ibid.,* 18-19.
[29] *Ibid.,* 20-1.
[30] *Ibid.,* 21.
[31] *Ibid.,* 21-2.
[32] *Ibid.,* 23.
[33] *Ibid.,* 25.
[34] *Ibid.,* 24-7.
[35] *Ibid.,* 27-8.
[36] *Ibid.,* 29.
[37] *Ibid.,* 27, 28-9.
[38] *Ibid.,* 31-2.
[39] *Ibid.,* 32-5.
[40] *L'Action nat.,* XIV (sept. 1939), 1, 3.
[41] *Ibid.,* 81-3.
[42] *Ibid.,* XIV (oct. 1939), II, 131-2.
[43] *Ibid.,* 141-2.
[44] Dawson, 17.
[45] *Ibid.*
[46] R. Rumilly, *L'Autonomie provinciale* (Montréal, 1948), 120; *Le Soleil,* 2 oct. 1939.
[47] Lefevbre, 36.
[48] *Le Devoir,* 4 nov. 1939.

[49] E. Armstrong, *French-Canadian Opinion on the War* (Toronto, 1942), 6.

[50] W. Churchill, *Blood, Sweat and Tears* (New York, 1941), 297.

[51] Armstrong, 7.

[52] *Ibid.*, 9.

[53] *Ibid.*

[54] Dawson, 41; *Montreal Gazette*, 24 June 1940.

[55] *Ibid.*, 289, text of National Resources Mobilization Act, 1940.

[56] Armstrong, 16.

[57] *Ibid.*, 18.

[58] *Ibid.*, 17–18.

[59] *Ibid.*, 16.

[60] *Montreal Gazette*, 3, 16 August 1940.

[61] Armstrong, 18–19.

[62] *Ibid.*, 19.

[63] *Ibid.*, 20.

[64] *Ibid.*, 22.

[65] *Montreal Herald*, 30 June 1941, 'The Story of French Canada's War Effort.'

[66] Armstrong, 10–13.

[67] *Ibid.*, 13.

[68] G. Vanier, *Paroles de Guerre* (Montréal, 1944), 15.

[69] Dawson, 310–1, text of Ogdensburg Agreement, 18 Aug. 1941.

[70] Armstrong, 23–4.

[71] Dawson, 321–12, text of Hyde Park Declaration, April 20, 1941.

[72] *L'Act. nat.*, XVII (juin 1941), VI, 441–2.

[73] *Ibid.*, 453–4.

[74] *Ibid.*, 455–72.

[75] *Ibid.*, 473–80.

[76] *Ibid.*, 481–99.

[77] *Ibid.*, 500–7.

[78] *Ibid.*, 508–21.

[79] *Ibid.*, 521–33.

[80] *Ibid.*, 534–7.

[81] A. Godbout, *Canadian Unity* (Québec, 1940).

[82] *Montreal Gazette*, 6 June 1940.

[83] *Ibid.*, 23 Nov. 1940.

[84] *Ibid.*, 10 Feb. 1941.

[85] *Ibid.*, 17 April 1941.

[86] Armstrong, 29–30.

[87] *Commons Debates 1941*, 7 May, III, 2637–43.

[88] *Ibid.*, III, 2651–2; Armstrong, 34–5.

[89] Armstrong, 39.

[90] *Report of the Royal Commission appointed under Order in Council P.C.* 411 . . . (Ottawa, 1946).

[91] A. Shea & E. Estorick, *Canada & the Shortwave War* (Toronto, 1942), 14–16.

[92] L. Francoeur, *La Situation Ce Soir*, 1–10 (Montréal, 1941).

[93] *Le Canada Parle à la France* (Montréal, 1944).

[94] M. Raymond, *Politique en ligne droite* (Montréal, 1943), 183.

[95] *Ibid.*, 192.

[96] *Ibid.*, 194.

[97] *The Plebiscite Question* (Ottawa, 1942).

[98] *La Question du plébiscite* (Ottawa, 1942).

[99] *Canadian Forum* (June 1942), F. R. Scott, 'Quebec & the Plebiscite Vote.'

[100] *Winnipeg Free Press*, 24 May 1948, G. Dexter, 'The Colonel.' See *Commons 1942*, June 23, IV, 3553.

[101] *Commons 1942*, June 10, 3236.

[102] Dawson, 95-6. Cardin's letter of resignation & King's reply, *Commons 1942*, May 11, 2280.

[103] Raymond, 209.

[104] *Ibid.*, 213-16.

[105] *Commons 1942*, July 7, IV, 3994.

[106] Abbé A. Maheux, *Pourquoi Sommes-nous Divisés?* (Montréal, 1943).

[107] See note 99.

[108] E. Vaillancourt, *Le Canada et les Nations Unies* (Montréal, 1942).

[109] *Le Devoir*, 29 avril 1943.

[110] *Montreal Gazette*, 17 April 1943.

[111] *Le Devoir*, 20 mai 1943.

[112] Raymond, 225-31.

[113] *Ibid.*, 236.

[114] F. Rose, *Hitler's Fifth Column in Quebec* (Toronto, 1942).

[115] *Life*, 19 Oct. 1942.

[116] *L'Action Catholique*, 25 mai 1943.

[117] *Ibid.*, 9 juin 1943.

[118] *Montreal Daily Star*, 24 June 1943.

[119] S. Ryerson, *French Canada* (Toronto, 1943), 2-4.

[120] *Montreal Gazette*, 10 May 1943.

[121] *Le Canada*, 11 mai; *Le Soleil*, 12 mai; *Le Devoir*, 26 mai, 19 juin 1943.

[122] *Le Canada*, 17 juillet 1943.

[123] *Le Devoir*, 19 juin 1943, 'Depuis bientôt quatre ans.'

[124] *Le Soleil*, 9 sept. 1943.

[125] *Press Information Bureau*, I, 5.

[126] *Ibid.*, I, 1.

[127] *Ibid.*, I, 6.

[128] R. Blanchard, *L'Est du Canada Français* (Montréal, 1935), II, 61-155; Abbé V. Tremblay, *Histoire du Saguenay* (Chicoutimi, 1938). For wartime labor troubles, see E. Laurent, *Une enquête au pays d'aluminium* (Québec, 1943).

[129] *PIB*, I, 5.

[130] *Le Devoir*, 26 mai, 12 juin 1943.

[131] E. Hughes, *French Canada in Transition* (Chicago, 1944), 217-18.

[132] *PIB*, I, 12.

[133] *Ibid.*, I, 11.

[134] *Ibid.*, I, 13.

[135] *Canadian Register*, 17 Oct. 1943; *Le Devoir*, 20 oct. 1943; *L'Action Catholique*, 21 oct. 1943.

[136] *PIB*, I, 42.

[137] *Commons 1944*, 27 Jan., I, 1.

[138] *Ibid.*, 28 Jan., 12-14.

[139] *Maclean's Magazine* (1 Jan. 1944), 'What does the Bloc Populaire Stand For?'

[140] *Le Bloc*, I (12 fév. 1944), 1.

[141] *PIB*, I, 51.

[142] *Ibid.*, I, 67.

[143] *Ibid.*, I, 75.

[144] *Senate Debates 1944*, 4 May, 147-9.

[145] *PIB*, I, 80.

CHAPTER XVI

THE REINFORCEMENT CRISIS
AND ITS AFTERMATH

(1944-5)

THE BEGINNING of the Battle of Europe, with the first heavy losses in the Canadian Army beyond those suffered at Dieppe, opened a rift between English and French Canadians which in the end came perilously near splitting Canada apart on the very eve of victory, after five years of war. Once more, as in 1917, the two main peoples of Canada were opposed by the question of conscription, which meant equality of sacrifice to English Canadians and coercion to serve British and American ends at Canada's cost to the French. All the latent irritations, grievances, and bitterness bred by Canada's effort to maintain a large Army, Navy, and Air Force, as well as to serve as a munition factory, granary, and 'airdrome of democracy,' with a population of only 12,000,000,[1] found expression in the summer and fall of 1944 as the ethnic tension steadily mounted.

I

After the first outburst of enthusiasm at the Normandy landings French Canada's differences with its English-speaking neighbors were once more accentuated. Symptomatic of the long suppressed ill feeling were the street brawls in Montreal between servicemen and 'zoot-suiters.' English Canadians were convinced that the troublemakers were French-Canadian draft-dodgers, who taunted English volunteers, while French Canadians claimed that 'the zoot-suiters are not generally recruited from among French Canadians' and that 'the majority of men in uniform encountered on the streets of Montreal are French-speaking.' The *Montreal Herald* spoke of the threat of mob rule and condemned the lawlessness and racial feeling made evident by the clashes. The incidents produced unfavorable comment in the New York *Newsweek*, and, as always, French-Canadian spokesmen rallied to defend their province from unfavorable outside comment. Justice Minister St. Laurent stated in the House at Ottawa that the Mounted Police were investigating the clashes and that the matter was in no sense a question of racial conflict. Roger Duhamel, president of the Saint-Jean-Baptiste Society of

Montreal, promptly contradicted him in *La Patrie*, but deplored the subsequent clashes between English and French school children with the observation that 'civilized people should have other methods for finding a common ground for their different viewpoints.' In fact, the disturbances seem to have been a natural result of the upsetting social effects of the war upon Montreal's cosmopolitan population.[2]

The Montreal disturbances ceased, but racial feeling had been aroused by them and it continued to grow, particularly among English Canadians as the Canadian forces suffered increasingly heavy losses in Europe. It was generally believed that these losses fell more heavily upon English Canada with its high proportion of volunteers and its small families than upon French Canada. It was impossible to know the facts under the government's policy of avoiding ethnic breakdowns of enlistment figures, and unfounded suspicion probably created a worse atmosphere than the facts would have done.

French Canada's much misunderstood attitude towards France was also once more in question. While no French paper with the exception of *Le Canada* showed as much enthusiasm for the prospective liberation of France as the English press, there was much deploring in the French press of the tension between the Anglo-American high command and the De Gaullist Committee of National Liberation, and relief was felt at the announcement that De Gaulle would visit Washington. *Montréal-Matin*, which with *Le Soleil* and the other Nicol papers had often criticized the State Department, hailed this development with relief and urged that 'a very strong friendship between France and America is indispensable to the maintenance of peace.'[3] Most of the Quebec press made much of the enthusiasm of the liberated people of France for De Gaulle, and deplored American fears of an alliance between Communist Resistance groups in France and Soviet Russia. But *Le Devoir* still failed to smile upon the De Gaullists, and Roger Duhamel in *La Patrie* denounced their 'intransigent' policy. *L'Action Catholique*, however, which had been Pétainist after the fall of France, declared that 'the Algiers group is that most representative of the nation' and urged recognition of the provisional government by London and Washington. For once *L'Action* made common cause with the *Montreal Gazette* and *Le Canada*, both of which came out for recognition of the De Gaullists. Though there had been a brief brush between the French clerical press and the English papers on the eve of the Allied entry into Rome, over the Pope's appeal to the world for a just peace rather than a rigid adherence to the program of 'unconditional surrender,' a June 14 Gallup poll showed that 62 per cent of the French Canadians favored unconditional surrender rather than immediate negotiations for peace with Germany. The liberation of Italy and the establishment of a democratic government there was hailed by *Le Canada*, which had never shared the sympathy felt for Mussolini by French-Canadian nationalists.[4]

2

It was into this troubled atmosphere that Senator T.-D. Bouchard, long a pillar of the Liberal Party in Quebec, dropped a bombshell with his maiden speech in the Senate on June 21, in support of Athanase David's motion for the adoption of a common textbook of Canadian history in the schools of all the provinces. Bouchard opened his speech in French, pointing out that one of the gaps in English-Canadian texts was the failure to note that French was an official language in both the federal and Quebec parliaments. He wished to bring out this fact and to pay tribute to his mother tongue, but he had no desire to impose the study of French upon English Canadians. He declared that 'for their own economic development French-speaking Canadians need to learn a second language more than English-speaking Canadians do,' since English was spoken by 150,000,000 people in North America and French by only 5,000,000.

Then Bouchard repeated his opening remarks and continued his speech in English, since 'it is becoming to speak the language understood by all,' and since he believed that 'speech was given to men to enable them to communicate their ideas to other men rather than to glorify the little corner of the earth where they happened by chance to be born . . . speech is simply the vehicle of thought.' He deplored the fact that he spoke English poorly, because Quebec's teachers had translated Bishop Laflèche's injunction to 'Speak English, but speak it badly' into the maxim 'Teach English, but teach it badly.' He strongly supported the basic aim of the David motion—the furthering of Canadian unity—and speculated as to whether all Canadians were as anxious for unity as members of parliament. As a self-made man of no scholarship, he disclaimed any competence to judge the textbooks used in the English provinces, and declared his belief that it would be best for the citizens of each province to criticize the weaknesses of their own teaching of Canadian history.

Then, after deploring the results of history teaching in Quebec, Bouchard launched his bomb, which shattered the customary calm of the Senate and made him a national figure overnight:

It is by exposing in the open what actually exists in my province, by showing our true history in the making which proceeds from the false history that the past and present generations have been taught in our own schools, that I shall show how urgent it is to make a radical change in this teaching. Canadian history should not serve as a tool of subversive propaganda in the hands of those who are aiming to disrupt Confederation and overthrow our form of democratic government.

Bouchard declared that he would document his charges by citing excerpts from Quebec history textbooks and by describing the 'subversive tendencies . . . created by the way in which Canadian history is taught in our public schools.' Once more he urged that 'laymen in history,' such as himself, 'should restrict themselves to deploring the deficiencies of history teaching in their own lingual realm.' He believed that the David resolution would help to build up a truly Canadian mentality, since 'a manual of basic facts accepted by each province would necessarily smooth the road to good understanding between us all.' But opposed to the modern and North American mentality of those who favored mutual understanding, despite differences of origin and creed, was the old clannish European mentality of those who wanted 'to rebuild in our country one of the small provincial kingdoms we had in France in days of yore,' while others with a colonial complex refused to recognize that Canada had become a true nation. He admitted that there were major sources of friction between Canadians of French and English descent: 'Differences of religion and language are, though they should not be, fertile fields where the sowers of the seeds of discord work day and night, but mostly in the dark,' forgetting the Christian injunction of brotherhood and the French motto of the British coat of arms.

History teaching was one of the main causes of these frictions, and Bouchard declared that since infancy he had been taught that 'everything the French Canadian has to suffer came from the fact that he was of French and Catholic descent.' Only when he went into business did he learn that 'Canadians of English descent were not all cloven-footed and did not all wear horns, but on the contrary entertained the very same good sentiments as did we of French descent.' From the Christian Brothers' elementary text in Canadian history he cited excerpts such as the following: 'The end pursued by the policy of England in the early times of its administration in Canada was to anglicize the French-Canadian nation, to rob it of its religion, of its language and of its national customs.' Bouchard found such teaching 'intended to prejudice young minds against our compatriots of a different tongue and creed.' He denounced it as 'un-Canadian and even un-Christian,' with the observation that 'the founder of Christianity has never preached that one man should rise against another because of differences of race and language.'

Then Bouchard declared that those who taught Canadian history along such lines 'had now attained their ends to such an extent as to imperil our national peace.' There were some French Canadians like himself who thought that the 'time has come—let us pray God that even now it is not too late—to stop a subversive propaganda, intensified by the state of war which has existed for over four years, which tends to bring us before long to mob rule and perhaps to civil war.' He refused to accept the view of those of higher position that it was better to shut one's eyes to such activities, or to lose his belief that 'a large majority of my compatriots love Canada as it is, constitutionally and otherwise, and do not want any change in their allegiance.' He blamed false history teaching for inspiring the nationalist desire for independence, since only the wrongs and none of the advantages of being under British government were stressed. The secessionists had called the forces of religion, race, and greed to their aid in attempting to win the masses to their dream of a 'Catholic, French, and corporative' state in which 'the Catholic and French toiler would be master of his own religious, social, and economic destinies.'

This revolutionary movement was fostered by a secret society, the *Ordre de Jacques Cartier*, with headquarters in Ottawa, which had been founded about 1928 'with the blessing of the Catholic and French clergy,' despite the Church's ban on secret societies:

Prominent French Canadians were induced to join, the avowed practical end of the society being not revolution, but to permit French Canadians to have their fair share of the jobs in the public service. Later on, when the Jacques Cartier Order decided to expand beyond the capital, the strength of the order was to be applied to restraining what was called foreign investment in local trades, when these trades did not belong to French Canadians. Anti-semitism was also called in to aid in the recruiting of members. Finally, the officers of the highest degree gave, in the utmost secrecy, the watchword to invade the political field and to control patriotic societies, governments, and public administrations of every sort.

The invitation has been well received, and nearly all the St. Jean Baptiste societies, Catholic syndicates, city school commissions, municipal councils, and junior boards of trade are under the direct influence of this secret order. It is due to its secret organization that *L'Union Nationale* went to power in 1936, to give us the poorest and most abusive government in the history of the province . . .

This secret society owns its public and secret newspapers. *La Boussole* is the open organ. *L'Emerillon* is the secret publication.

Bouchard considered that this secret society would not have been tolerated if the teaching of Canadian history in the Quebec schools had not 'prepared our population to receive favorably anything tending to dissociate us from our English fellow-citizens.' He declared his firm belief that at least 75 per cent of the 18,000 members were 'good British citizens who do not suspect where they are being

pushed by the fanatics of every description who are the real leaders
. . . Imagine the harm that can be done by these active agents of
destruction in a more or less passive population such as the one
living in my province.' He quoted from a September-October 1937
number of *L'Emerillon*:

Let us note the interlinking of our groups which threatens to shut in
the center of Ontario, and in consequence to choke those who dread,
and rightly, our 'French domination' in a more or less near future.
Our French masses of the north especially will finally weigh so heavily
upon the populations of the center and south of the old Upper Canada
that on each side we shall perhaps think of secession, to the end of creating
a new province which will be French by a great majority.

Not only did the secret order dream of creating a new French
province, but it also proposed to set up an independent Catholic
and French state, as the rise of European totalitarianism in the
1930's gave 'a new impetus to that backward movement tending to
bring us back to the social and economic status of the Middle
Ages.'
   It was not only hot-headed young men seeking public recognition
who epoused such ideas. Mgr. Mozzoni, chargé d'affaires of the
Apostolic Delegation in Canada, had made the following declaration
at the 1937 Sémaine Sociale at Saint-Hyacinthe:

The politicians can talk about the greatness and prosperity of the
country under such and such a form of government; this concerns us but
indirectly. What we do want, and what we shall work to attain by all
our means, is a state completely Catholic, because such a country only
can represent the ideal of human progress, and because a Catholic people
has the right and duty to organize itself socially and politically according
to the tenets of its faith.

Bouchard professed his belief in freedom of thought and of religion,
but asserted that the great majority of the French Canadians 'are
fully contented with their present governmental institutions and do
not ask for a change.' He wanted peace and harmony between
people of different origins, and only cited these words to show that
'there is unrest not only among the masses . . . but also among the
upper classes, and that we have to keep our eyes opened on the
undercurrents producing such apparent eddies on the surface of the
troubled waters of our national life.'
   The situation had gone from bad to worse since 1937: 'More and
more young men have left school with that deformation of the mind
proceeding from the bad teaching of Canadian history, and the
underground propaganda has increased in intensity.' Calling the
Union Nationale administration of 1936-9 the 'first governmental

offspring of the Jacques Cartier Order,' Bouchard deplored its measures shortening the period of English tuition and giving precedence to the French version of the Quebec statutes. He described his personal experience of the campaign against teaching English, which he blamed on members of the clergy. He declared that 'Preventing French Canadians from learning English by any means, to their utmost detriment, is part of the underground work of our isolationists. They do not want us to meet English Canadians, naturally, because when you talk to somebody preventions (*sic*) inspired by propaganda disappear.'

Bouchard cited instructions of the Jacques Cartier Order to infiltrate patriotic and social organizations and to win leadership in them, so that *bonne-entente* policies might be barred; to avoid adopting English methods in business, and anglicization in general. He described the chain of command whereby the watchwords from the supreme council in Ottawa were handed down through the ranks without question. He denounced the recent raising of the '*Drapeau de Carillon*,' favored by the Order, over the new buildings of the Université de Montreal:

Three weeks ago, the war being in full swing, the Order also succeeded in persuading the heads of the Montreal University to consecrate this flag as the real Labarum of the non-existing French-Canadian Catholic state by raising it to the mast of the $10,000,000 building erected with government money, that is, money belonging not only to those favoring the secession of our province, but mainly to Canadians true to their political system, and the British Commonwealth of Nations.

This was done on the top of the mountain overlooking the largest city in Canada, in the presence of thousands upon thousands of citizens brought there by the blessing, by an eminent Catholic priest, of the old flag of Louis XV as the national flag of Canadians of French descent. Evidently there are lots of people who play with fire without knowing it.

He deplored the storm of abuse lavished on Abbé Maheux by separatists and isolationists: 'That most respectable priest was banned as a traitor to the race because he spoke the truth.' He denounced the *Jeunes Laurentiens* as 'one of the most active and open organization of the Jacques Cartier Order,' and cited its president's statement in May: 'This revolution that we want will be practical, efficient, calm, and good, because it calls for pure, fundamentally French and Catholic men. It is the revolution of liberated Spain, of organized Portugal, of France under Pétain.'

It seemed obvious to Bouchard that 'a wrong teaching of Canadian history in our province has already done nearly all the harm that could be desired by those who are in favor of disunion in this country between peoples of different languages and creeds.' He charged that 'their ultimate aim is not only to disunite the people on lingual and religious matters, but also to disrupt Confederation, to abandon the more human North American concept of a large nation composed of people of different religious beliefs and racial origins, and to revert to the old European concept of smaller nations of the same religious and racial descent.' The field was already well prepared for an attack on Canadian political institutions. The old Liberal-Conservative Party in Quebec had been destroyed by 'our hidden Fascists.' The *Bloc Populaire* was 'the open political tool of the Jacques Cartier Order.' Bouchard feared that 'if our liberty-loving people do not open their eyes in good time, they will see to what extent underground work has undermined our free institutions.'

Bouchard anticipated criticism for having frankly given his views on the teaching of Canadian history in the Quebec schools and for showing 'what is going on behind the curtain, where the actors are preparing what many believe will be a farce, but which to my mind will eventually turn out to be a national tragedy.' But he preferred to face the coming storm, and not to be caught unaware by it. He made a final plea for the David motion, and expressed the hope that if provincial autonomy prevented official action, that some progressive association would see to it that 'everything tending to disunite the people of this country shall be eliminated from the textbooks of Canadian history and that only the real and proven facts shall be taught to our younger generation.' His closing words were notable:

We have to build our new generations along different lines from those that have prevailed up to now, and, speaking for my province, I hope the day will come when English and French citizens will realize that they have everything to gain by being at least good neighbors, even if they cannot come up to the evangelical perfection of being good brothers. I must confess that I should like to have painted another picture of the situation in Quebec; but I thought it my duty to present the real situation, being convinced that it has now become dangerous to flatter ourselves regarding things that do not exist. History, past and present, has taught me the hardships of common people during civil wars and revolutions, and it is to preserve my fellow-citizens from their menace that I warn them not to heed the insidious appeals of reactionaries and cheap politicians. Our political institutions and our association with the other nations of the Commonwealth have given us internal peace and prosperity. Let us side with those who are willing to make any sacrifice to preserve them in their integrity. There we shall find safety and happiness.[5]

3

Bouchard's speech, made on the same day as a Eucharistic Congress opened in his native town of Saint-Hyacinthe and three days before the national holiday of French Canada, roused such a storm as Canada had not known since the time of the Guibord affair. Maurice Duplessis, leader of the *Union Nationale* which Bouchard had fought in and out of provincial office, on the following day issued a statement calling the speech 'despicable and reprehensible,' denouncing Bouchard's 'anti-Canadian and anti-clerical tendencies,' and demanding his immediate removal from his new office as head of the Quebec Hydro:

It would be inconceivable and intolerable that the government of the Province of Quebec should keep in its employ, particularly in an important post, a public man who knowingly and maliciously becomes guilty of such treason and such vile calumnies. The immense majority of the population of the province demands insistently the immediate destitution of this unworthy politician.

Premier Godbout, long Bouchard's political colleague, repudiated the speech immediately in these terms: 'I consider these accusations as absolutely unjustifiable and damaging, and I affirm that they represent in no way the opinion of a single member of the provincial government.'

Louis St. Laurent, federal leader of the Quebec Liberals, criticized Bouchard's violence and his loose generalizations, and minimized the importance of the Order of Jacques Cartier, which he said represented one-tenth to one-half of one per cent of the population. He remarked that Bouchard was one of those who believed that a spade should be called a spade, but in the excitement of speaking was sometimes led to call it a steam-shovel or a bull-dozer. Maxime Raymond, leader of the *Bloc Populaire*, denounced the speech as a 'tissue of falsities and calumnies,' 'the despicable act of one who denies and tramples upon all that which has permitted his compatriots to survive and to conserve their language and their faith.' He declared that Bouchard was not worthy of the posts of trust which he occupied. Frédéric Dorion referred in the House to 'this Quebec Quisling, who yesterday satisfied his Masonic hatred against the clergy and religious institutions of Quebec by railing for nearly an hour at those he calls his fellow Catholics and fellow-citizens,' and expressed his belief that Bouchard would be forced to resign from the presidency of the Quebec Hydro. Bouchard was also repudiated by his fellow senators from Quebec. P.-A. Choquette, a stormy petrel of Liberalism in an earlier day, denounced the speech as that of 'a dishonest man or a mad man,' and called upon the Godbout government to oust Bouchard from the Quebec Hydro unless it wished to suffer the consequences in the elections. Cyrille Vaillancourt observed that a decent bird does not dirty its own nest, while the Conservative Thomas Chapais, at a loss to understand

Bouchard's action, referred to it as 'a bad deed which can take a tragic turn.'

Quebec at large, as always when under attack, made a common front against Bouchard. The flood of protests which poured in upon the provincial government, demanding repudiation of Bouchard, was overpowering. The officers of Saint-Jean-Baptiste societies, Catholic syndicates, school commissions, municipal councils, and the junior chambers of commerce denounced Bouchard's charges and demanded his ousting from the Hydro with a singular unanimity which suggested that these bodies were in fact under the orders of the Order of Jacques Cartier, as he had charged. But Quebec's indignation at public attacks upon its clergy and the washing at Ottawa of its dirty linen might have been responsible for the tidal wave of protest. Premier Godbout, a former seminarian as well as the leader of a government which had to face the electorate within a few weeks, bowed to the storm.

In a press conference on June 23 Bouchard refused to withdraw his charges, called for proofs rather than insults from those who denied them, and replied to the charge of anti-clericalism made by Duplessis and others with the observation that he hoped that the people of Quebec would soon realize that 'clericalism is the corruption of religion, as nationalism is the rotting of patriotism.' Of Godbout's statement he observed: 'Mr. Godbout is a man of good faith and if he has formed the opinion which he expressed, it is simply because he has not the information which I possess.' An hour later the radio and press services announced that the provincial government had relieved Bouchard of his duties as president of the Hydro by order-in-council, after a brief cabinet session. Informed personally by Premier Godbout of this action, which the premier announced to the press without comment, Bouchard told newspapermen: 'I am satisfied with the turn of events . . . The circumstances show clearly and definitely to what point these people of the Order of Jacques Cartier have influence . . . The fight has only begun.'

On the following morning Bouchard wired Bishop Douville of Saint-Hyacinthe that he would be unable to be present in his role as mayor at the Eucharistic Congress. That evening Cardinal Villeneuve, addressing the 75,000 people gathered for the Congress, made the following statement:

History has its rights. A shadow was necessary in this resplendent picture which your city offers in these days in which, beside an admirable religious feeling, an old current of anti-clericalism, sometimes open, sometimes latent, betrays itself. And in sharing this evening the piety and pride of the diocese of Saint-Hyacinthe, I feel it is my duty, as one of the spiritual leaders of French Canada, to voice here a solemn protest. Events command it, and you yourselves implore it.

A public man, whom I need not name, has recently before the highest body of the country uttered words as unfair and injurious to our province of Quebec as they are thoughtless and unfounded. They cannot be explained, truly, coming from a man who preaches straightforwardness and justice, and whom for my part I have always tried to understand and interpret with good will. I leave it to others to refute his political and racial accusations. But I openly denounce his insinuations against the Church and the clergy. The words he used carry exactly the same sound and reveal the same corrosive fanaticism as those of another sower of discord whom the great majority of our separated brethren denounce with humiliation. Some time ago, in the House of Commons, the Right Honorable Prime Minister of Canada did not believe it necessary to hide his scorn for such fomenters of national disunity, whom only the grossest ignorance or hereditary madness can excuse. But in the present case the fact that the unfortunate diatribe was made by one of her own sons is what still more enrages and particularly humiliates the people of our province, and with them all those across Canada who share the same blood, the same faith, and the same traditions of Canadian probity and fidelity.

Public opinion will judge this challenge to the national conscience as is fitting.

As for me, I shall avoid committing the episcopate of this province to the movements that our insulter has so little honestly mixed up, in order better to throw his poison. But I ought to reprove publicly this outrage to all that the French-Canadian people holds most dear: its legitimate religious, social, and political aspirations; the authority and mission of its bishops, who are also directly responsible for public education; and finally the teaching of the Sovereign Pontiff and of his very numerous representatives among us. For it is by an unintelligent, not to say perfidious interpretation of the discourse of the secretary of the Apostolic Delegation pronounced in this city in 1937, at the fifteenth session of the Sémaines Sociales, that the orator who at this moment raises such general indignation has wished to throw doubts on the loyalty and diplomatic reserve of this prelate. One can see in the text that in speaking of the integrally Catholic State, the worthy preacher only sought to express the wish that a social doctrine integrally inspired by the Pontifical teachings should be established among us. And who could take umbrage at it, among those who believe in the sincerity and depth of our religious convictions?

And then of what crime must he not accuse the Sovereign Pontiff and the Catholic hierarchy, who wish wholeheartedly that the entire universe become Catholic and under the mandate of Jesus Christ work alertly to that end?

No, truly one is astonished at so much confusion of ideas, so great ignorance about the affirmed facts, and alas so much bitterness in style and word, under cover of independence and high politics.

In the name of my venerated colleagues here present, in the name, I am sure, of all the Catholic hierarchy of the country, in the name of the people that we love and guide, I deny such unworthy denunciations, and

I openly affirm that none of those who follow the teaching of the Church and are faithful to true French-Canadian traditions is no more a danger to Canada than a divisive factor, unlike others who, alas, ignore it.

Repudiated by the highest official of his province and by the highest religious authority, Bouchard issued a statement on Sunday to the press that 'lions are no longer fed upon the flesh of religious reformers, but those who ask only that they be allowed their freedom of opinion on a purely political matter are turned out to die of hunger.' He regretted that Godbout had 'thought it necessary to become the tool of those who dominate our province by exploiting popular prejudice,' but urged support of his government, 'The most progressive by far that we have had since Confederation.' He added: 'It would be national suicide to replace it by the former Duplessis administration or by a reactionary government such as the *Bloc Populaire*.'

Of all the hundred-odd statements[6] from persons of note on the Bouchard speech which appeared in the French press, only two did not denounce him. True to his nineteenth century liberalism Senator Chapais subsequently observed: 'The speech of M. Bouchard is open to criticism, like any other speech delivered in Parliament. Up to a certain point this speech is regrettable, although it has in it certain justifiable elements.' Madame Constance Garneau, president of the League of Woman's Rights, stoutly defended Bouchard:

I should like very much to see an English Canadian denounce his own group in the same way that M. Bouchard has had the courage to do for his. For if we are not deceived, the same thing exists among our English speaking compatriots. As far as we are concerned, it did not befit an English Canadian to put his finger on the sore spot. I should be glad to hear of an English Canadian denouncing those who are anti-French.

The press reaction followed a curious pattern. *Le Devoir* at once reported the speech in full, and represented it as a national tragedy which would bring discredit upon French Canada. Louis-Philippe Roy, acting editor-in-chief of *L'Action Catholique* immediately denounced on the front page of his paper 'the vomitings of T.-D. Bouchard':

Associating himself with Pastor Shields, the Senator has repeated some of the former's hysterical calumnies at a moment of double psychological significance. In St. Hyacinthe, of which city M. Bouchard is still mayor, there is at present being held a great Eucharistic Congress at the opening of which presided His Excellency the Apostolic Delegate. In the Canadian Senate M. Bouchard attacks the Apostolic Delegation and all the Quebec clergy. This reminds us of French Freemasonry at the peak of its anti-Church outbursts under the Third Republic. On Saturday we celebrate the national holiday. Yesterday the Senator attacked our patriotic institutions . . . Could this be a coincidence? One thing is certain: our most fanatical adversaries could never have chosen a more strategic hour to attack us.

Roy went on to demand Bouchard's repudiation by the Liberal Party and his dismissal as president of the Hydro. *L'Action's* Ottawa correspondent, Lorenzo Paré, observed: 'For forty years T.-D. Bouchard has kept on swallowing his anti-clericalism, so that he would not be driven from public life by French Canadians. Yesterday, sure for the rest of his life of senatorial honors, Bouchard spilled forth his spleen, and took a terrible revenge against his compatriots.' And André Roy on the editorial page observed: 'Not content with slinging mud at his compatriots, M. Bouchard used the opportunity of his maiden speech to attack in a most irreverent way the Apostolic Delegation in the person of its secretary, Mgr. Mozzoni.' He added that Bouchard had long served the Liberal Party and done it much harm. If that party did not repudiate Bouchard immediately, it would be eternally ruined in the Catholic and French-Canadian province which it ruled.

The big independent dailies were hesitant in their first reactions, with *La Patrie* preserving a discreet silence and *La Presse* alluding editorially to the speech in a conciliatory way, although it printed many letters of protest. *Le Canada*, the official Liberal organ, kept silent. *Le Soleil* and the other papers of the Liberal Nicol chain published full news stories without editorial comment. *Le Nouvelliste* of Trois-Rivières, however, published on its editorial page *L'Action's* anti-Bouchard blast and the *Montreal Star's* editorial lauding the senator's courage in making the speech. After Godbout's repudiation of Bouchard, *La Presse* observed that the action was 'of a kind to reassure anxious minds and to satisfy the justly indignant French-Canadian and Catholic conscience.' *La Patrie* held that Godbout had given way to popular pressure because the country stood in need of unity among all men of goodwill, and added: 'The action of M. Bouchard could only serve to exaggerate the importance and influence of a society which, to say the least, is an obscure one concerning which nobody among us was much bothered, and to arouse among our English-speaking compatriots unjust suspicions.'

Because of the timing of the speech, the weeklies could not comment on it until the first wave of indignation had calmed down. But Bouchard's action was supported only by his own paper *Le Clairon*, Jean-Charles Harvey's *La Jour*, and *La Victoire*, the French Communist organ. Jean-Charles Harvey devoted two pages of *Le*

Jour to the incident, calling for free men to unite in defence of their threatened liberties. For him Bouchard was the victim of obscurantism and nationalization, and thus the incident aroused his zeal as an apostle of enlightenment and free enterprise: 'The Quebec Hydro, set up on the disastrous socialist principle, is experiencing the worst political interference that could be imagined . . . M. Bouchard is thrown overboard for a purely political reason.' André Bowman, in an article captioned 'The Munich of Quebec,' observed that Bouchard had been sacrificed to clericalism by Godbout as Benes had been sacrificed to fascism by Chamberlain. Emile-Charles Hamel suggested that the time had come for a new party:

By seeing the Liberals becoming the servile tool of the forces of reaction, we are made to wish for a great party, moderately leftist, which would fight for democratic liberties and assure to us the free functioning of the political institutions which we have inherited from Great Britain, the free expansion of those talents of ours which we owe to France. The Bouchard case raises a question of principle going beyond the personalities and the facts at issue. It is freedom of conscience, freedom of speech, freedom of the press which are at stake. It is a question of discovering whether, because of the occult dictatorship of certain secret societies or certain groups working behind the scenes, a person in government employ can be removed from his post for having expressed ideas or written articles which are not contrary to the laws of our land.

The Communist *La Victoire* supported Bouchard and denounced the Order of Jacques Cartier, calling for an investigation by the minister of justice—a step also favored by the Tory *Montreal Gazette* and several labor unions. *La Victoire*, however, reproached the senator with not having made a distinction 'between the Catholic Church as a whole, and that not very numerous minority of members of the clergy who demean themselves by taking part in Fascist and subversive intrigues.' This valid point was obviously made in view of the special line of the Communist Party in Quebec at that moment, for the editorial went on to observe:

The great majority of Catholics are opposed to Fascism and are working to bring about its destruction by the United Nations. It is by the united action of Catholics and non-Catholics that a powerful labor movement has been built up in Quebec, the driving force behind the social and economic reforms initiated by the Godbout government. It would be disastrous if controversies of a religious nature were to spread disunion among the democratic, liberal, and labor forces of French Canada.

Le Bloc devoted half its space to the Bouchard affair. While scarcely recognizing the existence of the Order of Jacques Cartier, it accused Bouchard, whom it called a foe of the clergy, of playing the game of enemies of the Church and of French Canada. *L'Action Nationale* denounced Bouchard as a 'public insulter,' and said he had excluded himself from his nationality. It rested its case on Cardinal Villeneuve's statement, but added: 'The revolution of which Bouchard speaks will be the revolt of all upright spirits against a disgraced regime, a peaceful and constitutional revolution, a democratic and Christian revolution. . . .'[7] *Le Progrès du Saguenay*, a clerical-nationalist weekly, defended the Order of Jacques Cartier: 'The enemy is not the Jacques Cartier Order which the Bouchards and the Harveys are denouncing; it is far more Freemasonry, and the senator from the Saint Lawrence Valley is perfectly aware of the fact.' Bouchard's own organ, *Le Clairon* of Saint-Hyacinthe, stressed the point that the denials of his charges were not supported by facts. It maintained that the senator had not sought to attack the clergy as a whole, but certain facts could not be ignored: 'What is quite certain is that two members of the clergy are directors of the Order, since they themselves signed a document testifying to that effect; what is also incontestable is that each regional command or cell has a spiritual adviser generally belonging to the religious orders, religious communities, or to the secular clergy.'

There was a complete divergence in the attitudes of the English and the French press towards the Bouchard speech. The English press admired his courage in denouncing conditions in his own province before an English audience, while the French press judged it shameful to wash Quebec's dirty linen before a largely English Senate—and in the English language. While the French press howled for and was gratified by Bouchard's dismissal from his $18,000-a-year post as president of the Hydro, the English press was horrified by this drastic penalty for speaking one's mind. It was not Bouchard's charges which gave Quebec a black eye in English-speaking opinion, but the subsequent breach of the sacred doctrine of free speech. The *Montreal Gazette* made this plain on the day following Godbout's action: 'The plain implication of this series of events is that the fundamental right of free speech, even when exercised on the floor of the Senate of Canada, is denied by the government of Quebec to an appointee on pain of dismissal.' The *Gazette*, which as a Conservative organ associated with big business had bitterly opposed nationalization of the Montreal Light, Heat & Power, went on to observe:

The most disturbing aspect of the dismissal is that it tears away any pretense of maintaining the Hydro Commission as an entirely non-political and independent body, which was the avowed basis on which it was established. For the Premier's latest move is inherently political, betraying a panicky weakness in the face of an imminent election and an adverse flurry of reaction to the Senator's speech. It cannot fail but to give the greatest concern to all alive to the full implications of its effects, not only on the Hydro and other provincial government bodies, but upon the plane of political life in this province.

The only French-Canadian reaction of this nature, outside the pages of *Le Jour*, was the announcement on this same day by Hubert Desaulniers, president of the Canadian Civil Liberties Union established in 1937, that the organization was going to resume its activities, which had been suspended at the outbreak of the war.

How little French Canada had ever embraced the doctrine of free speech was revealed not only by the heavy price that Bouchard had to pay for his utterance, but also by two other incidents in June, which saw Tim Buck and other Labor-Progressive leaders prevented from holding a political meeting in Quebec City and escorted out of the city by police, and an assault on the A.F.L. union headquarters in Valleyfield. The *Labor World*, organ of the provincial Federation of Labor, on June 24 observed that 'freedom of speech and of assembly will soon be things of the past in Quebec,' thanks to 'ridiculous and stupid advice given in certain nationalist and ultramontane quarters.'[8] Early in July Bouchard's resignation, 'so as not to cause embarrassment to this association,' as president of the *Institut Démocratique* which he had founded a year earlier was accepted by the governors of the organization, while he also refused to run again as mayor of Saint-Hyacinthe. In the subsequent municipal elections all his followers were defeated.

4

Dominion Day 1944 found French Canada in a mood troubled by the events of recent weeks. *L'Action Catholique* and *Le Droit* used the anniversary to demand more respect for the spirit as well as the letter of Confederation by English Canadians, and to urge such a policy as a better way to promote national unity than the proposed revision of Canadian history-teaching. Even the great independent or Liberal dailies displayed a certain soreness about violations of the British traditions of fair play which led the Ottawa government to treat French Canadians like poor relations and the English provinces to disregard French-Canadian rights. These reactions were reflected in the Gallup Poll taken as the provincial campaign opened, which indicated that the Liberal Party was favored by 37 per cent of the electorate, the *Bloc Populaire* by 27 per cent, the *Union Nationale* by 14 per cent, with the remaining 22 per cent scattered among C.C.F., Social Credit, Communist, and undecided voters.[9] The *Bloc* had gained at the expense of both the Liberals and the *Union Nationale*, making violent attacks upon the old parties as tools of the trusts and imperialists, and upon the C.C.F. as espousing a socialism forbidden to Catholics. The *Bloc* missed no opportunity to exploit popular resentment against the Liberal regimes at Quebec and Ottawa: conscription and the regulations requiring employers to report defaulters, the internment of Camillien Houde, the detention of Marc Carrière, the replacement of French-Canadian workers by English-Canadian ones at the Defence Industries plant at Sainte-Thérèse, the profits of the Aluminum Company, the plea in favor of learning English by Edouard Simard, head of the war-booming Marine & Sorel Industries, the agitation in favor of a single manual of Canadian history, the immigration of Jewish refugees and British subjects, the loans and gifts to Britain—all were grist to its mill. It devoted particular attention to the shooting of Georges Guénette, a young deserter, on May 7 at Saint-Lambert near Quebec City by French-Canadian members of the Mounted Police. Though the campaign against Bouchard, with an effort to identify the Godbout government with him, replaced the Guénette affair as the major interest of *Le Bloc* at the end of June, the *Bloc* campaign speakers continued to make much of the incident, which probably had more effect than any argument in favor of the *Bloc* upon the public. French Canada, which has a great devotion to law and order despite its tendency to verbal violence, was shocked by the shedding of blood in the enforcement of the hated conscription which had been introduced bit by bit at the cost of a steadily growing popular bitterness. Though the *Bloc* devoted most of its fire to the Liberals, it was also notably savage in its attacks on Duplessis and his *Union Nationale*.

Godbout and the Liberals waged an uphill fight to regain prestige for their party in these troubled times. A farmer and a textile worker were named to the cabinet in June, in an effort to give the government greater appeal to the restless masses. In an address on June 21 which set August 8 as the election date, Godbout reviewed the progressive record of his government and proclaimed that the Liberal watchword was '*Notre maître, l'avenir*' ('Our master is the future') in contrast to the *Union Nationale* and *Bloc* devotion to the Groulx slogan of '*Notre maître, le passé*' ('The past is our master'). He lumped the two opposition parties together, though it was clear he attached more importance to the Duplessis forces than to the 'hotheads of the *Bloc*.' He warned that if they came to power, with their 'narrow spirit, opportunism, and fanaticism,' there would be 'a methodical and progressive strangulation of the national culture, which has such abundant possibilities.' He declared his unyielding opposition to fanaticism and hatred: 'My conscience, as a man, a citizen, and a political leader thoroughly aware of his responsibilities, imposes upon me the stern duty to say to fanaticism: "You shall not pass, because you are the enemy of my brothers and the destroyer of the nation.'' '¹⁰ Godbout sought to confine the campaign to provincial issues, urging that his government should be judged on its merits, while the voters would later have a chance to give their verdict on Mr. King's war policy in a federal election. He appointed his most nationalistic and anti-conscriptionist minister, Oscar Drouin, to the Municipal Affairs Commission. But it was already evident that both the *Union Nationale*, with its memories of its 1939 defeat on the federal issue of participation in the war, and the *Bloc*, with its provincial nationalism, would fight the campaign chiefly on the basis of federal issues, with Godbout depicted in the role of a bootlicker of imperialist and centralizing Ottawa.

Godbout's speech was well received by almost the entire French press, which was clearly uneasy over the height to which public feeling had risen in recent weeks. *Le Devoir* had only a few reservations; *L'Action Catholique* argued that partisan passion should not be allowed to suppress reason and urged that 'our political debates should do nothing to raise French Canadians against each other, nor make them lose confidence in authority.' *La Presse* and *La Patrie* showed great sympathy for the speech, while the Liberal press was enthusiastic over it. However, *Le Temps*, organ of the *Union Nationale*, violently denounced Godbout for 'not having spoken a single word about the war, about mobilization, conscription, or autonomy' after having been for five years 'merely the valet, the slave, the marionette of Ottawa.' *Le Bloc* referred to the speech as that of 'one condemned to death' and bitterly denounced Godbout's effort to dissociate himself from Mackenzie King and T.-D. Bouchard, who had been his leaders and political allies since the beginning of his political career in 1935.

Early in July the *Bloc* probably had a good chance to defeat the Godbout government. But its hotheaded young men, drunk on their own eloquence, soon went too far for the moderate French-Canadian masses, angry as they were. The *Bloc* candidate in Maisonneuve, Jacques Sauriol, a thirty-three-year-old journalist with a background of nationalist activity as a supporter of the A.C.J.C. and of Camillien Houde, made an extremely violent speech at Saint-Eustache—with its bitter memories of 1837—on July 2:

I am for the strong method. The former Mayor of Montreal, Camilien Houde, was unjustly arrested. When we of the *Bloc* are in power at Quebec, we will fix that. Wherever he may be, I, Jacques Sauriol, undertake to go and get him on August 9, if he is still the victim of persecution by the federal police . . .

What is important is not to make bombs to destroy the homes of Poles, Ukrainians, and Frenchmen, it is to provide homes for our own people, to build houses for our workmen which will be available to the humblest and to the small wage-earner . . . Five years have now gone by in which we have been told repeatedly of the threat of Fascism and Nazism. Have you yet seen Mussolini in Canada? You have not. But you have seen the King and Churchill. . . .

The *Bloc* in Quebec will defend our young men from the iniquitous selective service. At Ottawa, we of the *Bloc* will break conscription just like that . . . If it is desired that Quebec factories do war work, our young men will have to be released so that they can work in the factories. The British Empire is an institution so wicked and so damnable that it has to have a war every twenty years to keep it going. Federal police or no federal police, we of the *Bloc* are against all foreign wars. We will use every means—and I do not say legitimate means—we will use every means necessary to halt this drainage of our young towards the charnel-house of Europe. . . .

I myself have been threatened by selective service because England has need of an iniquitous war every twenty-five years, because the English soldier is the worst in the world, and it is necessary for Canadians to fight England's battles and be killed in the place of the English in the hell of Caen.

Such incendiary statements bred fear of the *Bloc* in many law-abiding French-Canadian circles which feared that violence worse than that of 1917–18 could be the only fruit of such words.

In addition, the *Bloc* suffered the disadvantage that its youthful urban agitators were distrusted in the country districts, while in the cities the *Bloc* lacked the organization and the means to combat the solidly implanted Liberal machine. The *Bloc* was primarily a youth movement and a class movement, drawing its main strength from the élite of nationalist-minded French-Canadian youth. Older French Canadians, who had outgrown the fervent nationalism of their youth as English-speaking people so frequently outgrow youthful radical sympathies, distrusted the *Bloc's* leadership, which was largely young and unknown, with Maxime Raymond ill; Paul Gouin, René Chaloult, and Dr. Hamel still at odds with the group; and Edouard Lacroix not taking an active part in the campaign. The *Bloc's* campaign meetings provided a safety valve for the venting of Quebec's bitterness about all the irritations, grievances, and conflicts which war had brought upon the province; but the rank and file of French Canada were not ready to support so radical a movement.

Maurice Duplessis and his well-organized *Union Nationale* machine played their cards cleverly. Their attack upon the Liberals was nominally based on provincial rights grounds, with the charge that Godbout had betrayed the province to the centralizers at Ottawa. But it exploited French-Canadian anti-Semitism and anti-war feeling almost as vigorously as the *Bloc*, while it made overtures to the powerful English Conservative interests who controlled so much of Quebec's economic life. While denouncing the expropriation of the Montreal Light, Heat & Power Company in the English press, it published a violently anti-war and anti-conscriptionist campaign sheet in French which held Godbout responsible for all the blood that had been shed by French Canadians at home and abroad. It lavished its attentions upon the rural districts, whose vote outweighed that of the cities where the Liberal strength was concentrated; and upon the *curés*, who were on the whole as opposed to the war and conscription as in 1917 but unwilling to support the *Bloc* extremists. Duplessis' promise to restore the Padlock Law also helped to win him the support of the clergy and of other conservative elements, which were alarmed at the rise of Communism and social unrest in Quebec; though it deprived him of what little support he might expect from organized labor. The *Union Nationale* provided a middle way for moderate French Canadians who had been antagonized by Liberal support of the war and by the Bouchard affair, and who were unwilling to go as far towards reaction as the *Bloc*, or towards radical revision of society as the C.C.F., Social Credit, or Labor-Progressive parties. And despite the repudiation on July 22 by John Bracken, the national Progressive-Conservative leader, of Bona Arsenault, the provincial Conservative organizer who had called Bouchard a 'Quebec Quisling,' the Duplessis forces held the allegiance of traditionally *Bleu* voters whose chief concern was to oust the hated *Rouges*.

Many French Canadians were reminded during the campaign of the battle in 1911 between Laurier and Bourassa. When André Laurendeau announced that the *Bloc* owed its inspiration to the principles formulated by Henri Bourassa in his younger days, Premier Godbout replied:

It would be easy for us to preach hate and discord, but we do not want that kind of thing in Quebec. Perhaps the two greatest minds of their generation were Sir Wilfrid Laurier and the nationalist leader Henri Bourassa. But with his principles of kindliness, respect, and cordiality Laurier is today a world figure, while Bourassa has done nothing but promote discord.

Le Devoir, of course, rallied to the defence of its founder, calling Bourassa 'the great interpreter of Canadian thought and particularly of French-Canadian and Catholic thought':

He has been the champion of educational freedom. He has never sought for discord, but rather for justice, which gives rise to harmony and peace. If he had been listened to in international affairs, our country would not have been dragged, twice in a quarter of a century, into terrible wars which weigh so heavily upon its life. If he had been listened to in national affairs, there would have been more fair play in Canadian life and therefore more chance of a durable peace.[11]

In Liberal circles there was much re-examination of Laurier's speeches to discover how he had overcome in his day the same combination of the Conservative opposition, the nationalists, and the antipathy of the clergy to the Liberals. There was left-wing Liberal talk of founding a more radical or a more democratic party, if the Liberals were defeated in both the provincial and subsequent federal elections. But though many of the young Liberals were inclined to be sympathetic to the C.C.F., the majority were essentially as conservative as the Conservatives themselves, and as fully committed to the preservation of a hierarchical society in which political leaders served as middle men between the French-Canadian masses and the English-speaking economic overlords of Quebec.

Bourassa had the last notable word in the campaign, when in addressing a *Bloc* meeting in Montreal on August 4 he dropped a bombshell with even greater effect than his advice at Quebec in May to support C.C.F. candidates in the absence of *Bloc* ones. No doubt concerned by the support which Duplessis was winning in clerical circles and by growing anti-clericalism, he observed:

In a country which prides itself on being Christian—(Are we really Christian? I do not know)—and in which there are no scruples about using the influence of bishops to buttress a profane cause, we should at least have a little respect for the principles which Christ came on earth to implant and which we mock in our daily lives. The day is not far off, unfortunately, when those bishops who meddled in politics will be derided, and those who use them today will turn their backs against them, once they have served their purpose. No, they have not served their purpose and we still need their spiritual advice. Yes, we respect you, but safeguard your prestige with the people and do not allow yourselves to be made the tools of conscienceless politicians who exploit you.

No one in French Canada had publicly spoken of the hierarchy in such a tone since Laurier fought them on the Manitoba school issue in 1896. The repercussion of Bourassa's speech was great.

It spoke well for Cardinal Villeneuve's discretion that he delayed until two days after the election publication of the following reply:

In his last address in Montreal Henri Bourassa thought fit, as is his custom, to play his habitual refrain against the bishops. We could, of course, pass this off with a smile, but because there are youths who listen to him, that liberty which he takes upon himself periodically of telling the bishops what he thinks of them compels me to say that he is neither a pontiff nor an authorized doctor of the Church. It has always been observed that he better understands a faraway Pope or a dead Pope than living bishops, who embarrass him. In spite of his claim of respect for the hierarchy, he takes every opportunity to treat the bishops with contempt, to display publicly scandalous examples of presumption and disrespect toward the ecclesiastical authorities.

History will recognize his incontestable qualities and his good public service; but without judging for the moment his doctrinal or historical thesis, history will not confirm his pretense of being a lay theologian. It will not make of him a respectful and obedient son of the episcopate. It is time that this ambiguity should cease, and truly Catholic youth must know it.[12]

It is not surprising that Bourassa returned to retirement after this withering blast. The Cardinal's attitude may have played some part in swaying clerical votes from the *Bloc* to the *Union Nationale*; public revelation of it certainly helped to kill the *Bloc*, which found that its effort to exploit Bourassa had backfired.

For one of several surprises in the election results was the fact that the *Bloc* polled only 15 per cent of the vote, though the Gallup Poll of mid-July had given it 25 per cent and many observers were convinced that it was going to make an even more impressive showing because of Quebec's angry mood. The Liberals polled 37 per cent of the vote but won only thirty-seven seats; while the *Union Nationale*, with 36 per cent of the vote, took forty-five seats. With the *Bloc* securing four seats, the C.C.F. one, and René Chaloult returned as an independent, no party had a true majority. It was a question whether the *Union Nationale* would be able to form a government, since one of their members must be named speaker, while another was absent in Normandy with the Army. The Liberals won their popular majority of 45,000 votes on the Island of Montreal, where the upper-class constituencies of Jacques-Cartier, Notre-Dame-de-Grace, Westmount, Outremont, and St. Anne registered their opposition to the *Bloc* and the *Union Nationale* by crushing majorities. In the working-class quarters of Montreal the election was bitterly fought, with brass knuckles, knives, and even revolvers used by hoodlums seeking to terrorize voters.

While the Liberals carried the cities, the *Union Nationale* swept most of the country districts. Though the urban population constituted two-thirds of the population, it elected only one-third of the legislative assembly under the electoral system, which was much criticized on the morrow of the poll. The new parties did better than the four seats won by the *Bloc* and the one by the C.C.F. indicated, since the *Bloc* polled 172,626 votes (about one-third of the Liberal or *Union Nationale* totals); the C.C.F. 33,158, and the Social Credit, Labor-Progressive, and independent candidates together

65,594. It was clear that the new parties had definite appeal for the Quebec voter, since together they won 275,000 votes (two-thirds of the successful *Union Nationale* total). In particular the growth of nationalist sentiment was indicated by the fact that the *Bloc* polled more than four times the number of votes won by Paul Gouin's *Action Nationale Libérale* in 1936.

Though there was some speculation after election day as to whether Godbout would seek to call new elections, the Liberal chief had confessed defeat in a moving broadcast a few hours after the polls closed:

What interests me most is not power in the province, but the future of the province. Whether as leader of the government or chief of the opposition, I shall try to continue to serve and to help the province. I have attempted to serve my province in a loyal manner and I have tried to be honest, not only in the financial domain, but in intellectual and moral fields as well. I have tried to make the people of the Province of Quebec understand what were our principles—the principles for the salvation of our future. Perhaps I was wrong and possibly I was right. I still believe I was right. But I also believed that the province would definitely appreciate that it should aspire to a constructive future on principles of order and peace based on co-operation.

Mr. Duplessis, addressing a crowd of 25,000 jubilant *Bleus*, promised to regain for Quebec the rights ceded to Ottawa by the Liberals:

We shall fight to the limit, to the final victory, for the restoration and respect of our rights. I consider the election result as a punishment inflicted by the province on those who have abandoned its rights.

André Laurendeau, one of the four successful *Bloc* candidates, was clearly pleased with the results of the election, although the *Bloc* had not rallied '*tout Québec*' as its orators had prophesied:

In the short space of two months the *Bloc Populaire* had to form its ranks. It did so. Its standard-bearers were selected and proved to be faithful. I have never witnessed such hope, confidence and faith in the future as that which tonight marks the arrival at Quebec of the first members of the *Bloc Populaire Canadien*.

R.-J. Lamoureux, provincial leader of the C.C.F., declared that his party had assured itself of a wedge for victory in the next federal election, for which the provincial poll had been a rehearsal. He was clearly counting on a preservation and extension of the united front of Montreal labor which had been attained against the *Union Nationale* and the *Bloc*, with the C.C.L. unions voting C.C.F. and the A.F.L. Liberal.[13]

The unexpected outcome of the election was mirrored in editorial comments. The *Gazette* urged Duplessis to 'distinguish between proper preservation of provincial rights and a return to narrow nationalism,' and rejoiced that the *Bloc Populaire Canadien*, 'which was never Canadian,' had proved not to be popular either. *La Presse* prudently distributed congratulations to Duplessis, Godbout, and Laurendeau, and rejoiced that the people had rejected the socialist C.C.F. *Le Devoir*, which along with *L'Action Catholique* and *Le Droit* had supported the *Bloc*, rejoiced in Laurendeau's victory and forecast new elections in the near future. It took note of the popular revolt against the old parties and observed: 'The political face of the province is in full transition.' *Le Canada*, while pointing out that the Liberals had received the greatest support from the electorate, declared that Mr. Duplessis should be called upon to form a government. It took evident pleasure in the poor showing of the *Bloc*, which 'reveals that the population of Quebec is neither separatist nor isolationist as regards Canada's national policy, nor anti-participationist as regards the war.'[14]

5

There was a lull after the electoral storm in Quebec, for the new Duplessis government did not take office until August 30. French Canada's unity was in some measure restored by a speech on August 9 by George Drew, the Conservative Ontario premier, opposing the federal family allowance scheme as a violation of provincial autonomy and as an electoral bribe to Quebec. It became evident that Duplessis was seeking an anti-Ottawa alliance with the Ontario Conservatives, when an inspired statement pointed out that Drew's speech was 'the strongest backing from outside which Mr. Duplessis has received in his fight for provincial autonomy.'[15] Another portent of a federal election was provided by Mackenzie King's statement that he favored a distinctive national flag and 'O Canada' as a national hymn. This gratified a Quebec which had long favored such symbols of nationhood, while English-Canadian nationalism, developed by the war, was now calling for symbolic recognition of Canada's status. There undoubtedly had been an increase in this sentiment since the Gallup Poll of August 1943 which showed a national flag favored by 51 per cent of the population as a whole, with the French Canadians 82 per cent in favor and those of British origin still 58 per cent in favor of the Union Jack. In *Saturday Night* B. K. Sandwell expressed the opinion that English Canadians would favor the adoption of 'O Canada' if the English words did not reflect 'intrinsically Catholic and French inspiration.'[16] English-Canadian loyalty to the Crown was also reflected in the argument that 'God Save the King' was not merely the national hymn of Great Britain but also of all lands over which the King reigned.

Despite all the campaign talk about Ottawa's invasion of provincial affairs, federal intervention in the Montreal Tramways strike was taken calmly by all camps in Quebec, though the *Gazette* pressed for a return to the open-shop principle which had been embodied in the labor code of the Duplessis government in 1938, though not enforced. The federal government made another step towards appeasing Quebec by releasing Camillien Houde after four years of internment for opposing national registration. Houde declared that he was 'only the victim of a political party and a political organization and nothing else,' and threatened to take political revenge. He was given a triumphant reception in Montreal, where it was evident that his political stock was all the higher for his 'martyrdom.' His release had long been sought by the nationalists, but seemingly came as the result of pressure brought to bear on Ottawa by organized labor in Montreal, with both national syndicates and the international unions making common cause. Both dissident Quebec Liberals and newly politically minded labor sought Houde as a popular leader, and his advent in both the federal and provincial fields was widely rumored. But for the time being he refused to commit himself to any course.

The invasion of southern France on August 15 convinced French Canada that the end of the war was in sight. The Quebec press made much of the role of the *Maquis*, but nothing was said of the Communist share in the Resistance, although *Relations* and *L'Action Catholique* devoted much space in August to denouncing international Communism, and particularly to the use of Soviet embassies as propaganda centers, specifically in Ottawa, Washington, and Mexico City.[17] Soviet sympathizers predicted a revival of the 'Padlock Law' when the Duplessis government took office. French Canada had never regarded the Soviet alliance with confidence, and now that the contest in Europe seemed to be drawing rapidly to a close, it expressed its opposition to postwar commercial and cultural relations with Russia. The liberation of Paris on August 25 by Frenchmen unleashed an outburst of joy in Quebec. Justice Minister St. Laurent spoke by radio to the people of Paris in the name of the Canadian government, as did Mayor Raynault of Montreal. The French flag was flown on the public buildings of Montreal, Trois-Rivières, and Quebec, while the Tricolor decorated private houses everywhere. Madame André Simard, now a delegate to the Algiers Assembly just returned from North Africa, told an enormous crowd in Quebec's Place d'Armes: 'By the grace of God who has allowed this resurrection, the heart of France is again beginning to beat.' Then all joined in the singing of the 'Marseillaise', as did a concert audience at the Chalet on Mount Royal in Montreal. *Te Deums* were chanted in churches throughout the province. The press, French and English alike, hailed the liberation of Paris, with the leading business firms using advertising space to swell the chorus.[18]

The swearing-in of the new Duplessis cabinet on August 30 put an end to rumors that a *Union Nationale–Bloc* alliance would be cemented by the offer of a portfolio to René Chaloult or another nationalist. A previous statement by Duplessis, decrying the postponement of redistribution of federal seats, and urging that it be carried through before the next federal election in order that Quebec might not be deprived of its due influence at Ottawa,[19] indicated that the new government would follow a straight provincial autonomy line, rather than a separatist one. The Duplessis cabinet shattered precedent in two respects: its size, with twenty-one ministers out of forty-three *Union Nationale* members; and the fact that the treasury portfolio, traditionally reserved to an English minister, had been given to a French-Canadian one. Jonathan Robinson, the sole English member of the cabinet, was made minister of mines, while Onésime Gagnon, a former federal minister highly regarded both in Quebec and at Ottawa, took the treasury post.

There was no hint of the government's labor policy in the usual Labor Day messages by the new premier and minister of labor shortly after they took office. Both the Liberals and the C.C.F. were engaged in trying to line up the labor vote for a federal election, while the traditional conflict between the national syndicates and the international unions was once more coming to a head. On August 20, the auxiliary bishop of Rimouski, Mgr. C.-E. Parent, expressed the traditional opposition of the clergy to the internationals when in addressing the National Federation of the Wood Industry he said: 'Have nothing to do with neutral unions, albeit they may have made gains in the great cities. Communism glides in their shadow like a snake. It attempts to fish in troubled waters and tries to turn the workers against the employers, as occurred in the last tramway strike in Montreal. Such unions stir up the workers against the employers, against religion, and against the clergy.'[20] On August 6 the CIO United Steelworkers of America announced an organization campaign among the aluminum workers of Arvida. According to the 1943 vote, only 23 per cent of these workers were organized: 17 per cent in syndicates and 6 per cent with the A.F.L. The CIO maintained that Arvida wages were 40–60 per cent below the level prevailing in the aluminum industry in the States, despite 20–40 per cent cheaper production costs. The Lake St. John district was a stronghold of the Catholic syndicates, and the chaplain of the Arvida syndicate, Abbé Bertrand, had recently declared that 'Catholic workers could not in conscience join non-confessional organizations.'[21]

The holding of the second Quebec Conference (September 11–16), concerned with the war against Japan, as the Allied forces stood ready to break into Germany, once more gratified Quebec's pride. *L'Action Catholique* expressed the popular desire for an opportunity to pay tribute on this occasion to both Churchill and Roosevelt, regretting that at the 1943 conference only the British leader had made a brief public appearance. *L'Action* also called for 'a just and durable peace.' Dissatisfaction was evident in the French-Canadian press that France had not been invited to participate in the conference. *Le Bloc* sought to make capital of a rumored conflict between the United States and Britain over policy in India. Barred from reporting the conference by security regulations, the French press devoted much attention at this time to drawing up a balance sheet of Quebec's war effort on the fifth anniversary of Canada's entrance into the war. The English-Canadian and American press were criticized for their contemptuous attitude towards French Canada's share in the war, which was vigorously defended.

L'Action Catholique gave the fullest statement of the French-Canadian position:

For a number of English-language newspapers, there has been only one way to further the war effort: enlist for overseas service. Because young French Canadians have not felt bound to do this in numbers as great as English-speaking Canadians, astonishment has been expressed at our rejoicing over recent Allied victories, notably over the liberation of Paris.

When some of our people show themselves hostile to participation as it is being practised, their ideas are eagerly given prominence as if these persons had spoken in the name of the Province of Quebec. On the other hand, if representatives of religious and civil authority issue directives, some little space is given in the English press, but with all due reserve and without comment. Today Church and State are recommending prayer and rejoicing. The people are exulting because the Allies are triumphing and France is liberated. Our colleagues are scandalized and claim that we should be ashamed.

We are proud of the victory of our arms. We salute the success of the land armies of 1944, just as we saluted the success of the R.A.F. in 1940 and of the Navy in 1941 and 1942. We admire the courage of the French 'patriots' in 1944, just as we admired the morale of the British under the bombs of 1940.

We are not ashamed because we are conscious of having contributed to the triumph of the Allies.

No doubt we have had fewer 'volunteers' and fewer draftees, but we have produced proportionally as many ships and foodstuffs. All the War Loans have succeeded very well indeed, and subscriptions to war charities have on every occasion gone over the top.

We have had fewer soldiers of all branches of the service for very sound

reasons: a greater number of men called up have been rejected for
health reasons (this will have to be explained one of these days); the land
has kept back more men because our agriculture is less industrialized, run
more on a family basis; politics has nourished the phobia of overseas
conscription for twenty-five years; in the different war services we have
been treated as aliens without regard to the antipathy which would thus
be engendered against participation; our drafted men were trained in a
language which was not their own; the scarcely veiled imperialism of
certain clumsy propagandists froze enthusiasm instead of stirring it, etc.

These are some of the causes of the moderate success of voluntary
enlistment in Quebec. But, and this has been stated many times by our
political leaders as well as by those of England and the United States,
the war effort can be effectively supported in other ways than by taking
up arms. In the factory and in the fields the French Canadians have fully
played their part. They have done it generously despite the mockery,
the slanders, the injustices . . . and the official violations of promises of
'voluntary' and 'moderate' participation.

On the other hand Jean-Charles Harvey of *Le Jour*, in a violent
denunciation of the 'anti-British element, anti-participationists,
isolationists, Fascists, pro-Fascists, *Bloc*-ists, and deserters' who had
paid tribute to Camillien Houde upon his release from internment
had earlier pointed out that Quebec's enlistment rate of 22.1 per cent
was half that prevailing in the other provinces, and that the fact
would always be held against Quebec.[22] The heavy Canadian
casualties in the Battle of France had aroused strong emotional feeling
in English Canada against Quebec, which continued to grow. *Le
Canada* sought to refute charges of 'inequality of sacrifice' by pointing
out on the basis of casualty lists that many French Canadians were
serving overseas in English-Canadian units, and that Quebec's part
should not be judged solely on the basis of the French-Canadian
units. *Le Soleil* predicted that Canada would play its due share in
bringing the Pacific War to a victorious conclusion, as it had already
played its part at Hong Kong, the Aleutians, and in the air and on the
sea.[23]

While Prime Minister King took advantage of the Quebec Conference to woo the French-Canadian Liberals to a united front
in the next federal election, the Duplessis government through Paul
Beaulieu, minister of commerce and industry, and its Quebec
organ, *Le Temps*, denounced *Le Devoir*, which was said to have 'done
us irreparable harm,' and the nationalists whose motto was '*notre
maître, le passé.*' A call was made for the union of all men of good will
to maintain the fair name of Quebec and to prepare the way for
prosperity in the postwar world. All the Quebec press, with the
exception of *Le Devoir* and *Le Bloc*, approved Beaulieu's stand.[24]
After the verbal excesses of the provincial campaign, Quebec had

swung back to the innate loyalism and moderation of the great majority of its people. In this process unfavorable publicity abroad and the influence of the Quebec Conference and the subsequent U.N.R.R.A. Conference at Montreal had played their parts.

A significant index of Quebec's return to a calmer mood was the re-election of T.-D. Bouchard to the presidency of the *Institut Démo-cratique*, which had accepted his resignation in the storm which followed his Senate speech. Though virtually deprived of French-Canadian nationality, Bouchard had clung to the ideas he expressed on that occasion, and had re-expressed them in an address at the Couchiching Conference of the Canadian Institute of Public Affairs in August. In his re-acceptance of the presidency, Bouchard said: 'From the testimony you have paid me, I do not infer that you approve the opinions that I uttered in my Senate speech, I simply conclude that you have recognized my right to express them,'[25] and hailed the growth of freedom of opinion and speech in the province.

6

Premier Drew's reflections on Quebec in his August 9 speech against federal family allowances continued to produce bitter reactions in Quebec, which was well aware of the fact that English-Canadian public opinion was mounting against French Canada. There were significant minor incidents which revealed the growing rift. Delegates to an Eastern Ontario Progressive-Conservative meeting at Ottawa protested against the singing of 'O Canada' at the close of a gathering which had been opened with 'God Save the King.' In September Major Connie Smythe, a wounded veteran well known in Toronto hockey circles, charged that half-trained troops were being thrown into the line because of heavy losses and the shortage of reinforcements, which he blamed on Quebec. During October it became common report that there was a shortage of replacements in the Army, while the more popular Navy and the Air Force ceased recruiting, with the latter service discharging men already in training. These men were subject to drafting into the N.R.M.A. home service forces if they did not volunteer for overseas. War correspondents reported that only a small proportion of the troops overseas were prepared to volunteer for service in the Pacific after the European War was over, and that they were bitter about sick and wounded men being sent back into the line, while home defence troops stood idle in Canada. The Conservative press printed anonymous letters to the same effect, allegedly from men at the front. There were calls, chiefly from Conservative sources, for a reopening of the whole manpower question, and the making available of all Canadian troops for service anywhere.

In June, General Stuart, the Army chief of staff in London, had indicated the question would eventually arise of breaking up overseas formations or sending N.R.M.A. conscripts to Europe, in order to meet a heavier call for reinforcements anticipated from October on into 1945. The general informed the government, however, that it could await developments in the war before reaching a decision— he thought there was 'an excellent chance of our being able to finish the war on a voluntary basis'[26]—and he suggested that additional recruiting efforts be made, particularly for infantry. The three defence ministers arranged to slow down Navy and Air Force recruiting for the benefit of the Army. Colonel Ralston brought this situation to the attention of the War Committee of the cabinet in June 1944.[27]

During the first week of August the chief of staff again assured the War Committee of the cabinet that the reinforcement situation was satisfactory.[28] On August 26, however, he reported a shortage of about 3,000 infantrymen in France, which was being met by using men trained for other duties. The estimates for infantry casualties proved too low, however, while those for other branches proved too high. New estimates made in October, when it became apparent that there would be no immediate German collapse and that heavy casualties would continue, indicated a shortage of 2,380 men in the field by the end of the year.

General Stuart then recommended that the trained N.R.M.A. troops should be drawn upon for reinforcements. Defence Minister Ralston concurred after a three-week visit to England and the Canadian fronts in Western Europe and Italy. After warning the prime minister by cable on October 13, Ralston returned to Ottawa with Stuart on October 18, immediately reported to Mr. King, and urged such action at cabinet meetings on the following day and thereafter. When the prime minister showed reluctance to resort to conscription for service overseas, in accordance with his promise in 1942 when Bill 80 was introduced in the House, since it was a step which 'would occasion the most serious controversy that could arise in Canada,' Ralston insisted upon its necessity. He opposed reducing Canada's commitments or breaking up units, and demanded assurance that, if the needed men did not volunteer as a result of a further appeal, N.R.M.A. men would be sent.[29] On October 31 King consulted with General Andrew McNaughton, the man who had built up the Canadian Army and who had retired in December 1943 because of 'ill health,' in which differences with the British were understood to be involved. McNaughton expressed the belief that the necessary recruits could be obtained on a voluntary basis—though only 4,956 men had enlisted for general service during October[30]—and stated his willingness to accept the defence post if Ralston resigned. Confronted with this situation, Ralston resigned at the prime minister's request on October 31, as he had threatened to do since July 1942 if conscription were not adopted if it became necessary.[31] McNaughton was sworn in as minister of defence the following day, while General Montague was appointed to replace General Stuart as chief of staff at Canadian Military Headquarters in London.

One of the most violent political storms in Canada's history then broke loose. It was widely rumored that several other ministers— Navy Minister Angus Macdonald was most frequently named, though Mr. Crerar was seemingly the most conscription-minded minister—would resign in sympathy with Ralston. Conservative forces, the Canadian Legion, army officers, and most English Canadians pressed for all-out conscription, while the French-Canadian press praised Mackenzie King for his faithfulness to his pledge not to invoke conscription, and hailed the shrewdness with which he had replaced a conscriptionist Liberal minister of defence with an anti-conscriptionist Conservative who enjoyed greater personal prestige than any other Canadian. It was evident that many Conservatives sought to make capital of the situation to drive the King government from office. John Bracken, leader of that party, was at odds with the group led by George Drew which was prepared to override Quebec's anti-conscriptionist attitude by force if necessary, although Bracken formally denied any difference of opinion with Drew and that there was an anti-French-Canadian group in his party.

A Quebec speech on November 4 by Justice Minister St. Laurent implied that the cabinet had decided against conscription under any circumstances. On November 5, at Arnprior, McNaughton called for no relaxation of effort on the last hard stretch of the war, and urged the public to encourage volunteers. On the following day at Ottawa he repeated these observations to a hostile Canadian Legion meeting, expressing his conviction that the best hope of solving the reinforcement problem was by the voluntary method, and making an appeal for rational rather than emotional thinking.

The nation-wide agitation continued, however, and on November 8 Mackenzie King made a radio address, announcing that there would be no conscription for overseas service and that National Defence officials were working on plans prepared by General McNaughton to increase volunteering. The prime minister declared that: 'The voluntary system has not broken down,' pointing out that more men had volunteered for overseas since D-Day than had been conscripted. He denied that more than a very few men had failed to receive full training before going into action. The N.R.M.A. forces would continue to be maintained for essential home defence duties and as a source of volunteers for overseas. He revealed that the effective strength of the N.R.M.A. troops at present was 60,000 men, of whom only 25,000 were French-speaking and only 23,000 from Quebec. These figures showed, contrary to popular belief, that the draftees who had refused to volunteer for overseas service were not largely French-Canadian, but were divided into three almost equal groups of French Canadians, English Canadians, and New Canadians in proportion to these groups of the population.

Mr. King expressed the belief that 'without any compulsion or intensification of present methods, a considerable number of these draftees would volunteer. We believe many more can be secured by a special appeal.' He then urged young men, both in the Army and outside it, to volunteer at the present time to meet the present need, warning that very grave difficulties might result from substituting conscription for voluntary service. He paid tribute to Colonel Ralston, regretting the difference of opinion which had led to the minister's resignation, and to General McNaughton, who was determined to give full support to the Army. The prime minister characterized the reinforcement situation as 'not an actual shortage now, but a possible shortage in the next few months.' He implied that while the voluntary system was preferred, the question of compulsion might have to be reconsidered in the light of developing circumstances.

On the following day John Bracken issued a statement accusing the prime minister of betraying his trust and deceiving both the Army overseas and the people at home by failing to disclose Colonel Ralston's report and the reasons for the resignation. He summed up the situation in these words: 'Our army overseas is in dire need of trained reinforcements, in dire need of rest and help, and men must be sent to the entire extent available in Canada. This is an immediate national need.' Bracken reasserted the Conservative manpower policy which called for complete conscription, and declared that the situation now transcended partisan politics.

On November 12 Colonel Ralston, who had been away from Ottawa, also issued a statement in reply to the prime minister's radio address, in which he criticized Mr. King's statement of the position as inaccurate and stressed the urgency of the reinforcement problem. He also made it clear that he had resigned at the request of the prime minister, and not on his own initiative.[32]

7

On November 15 the prime minister bowed to the ever-growing storm and summoned the House to meet in special secret session on November 22 to consider the reinforcement question. After a public statement by Senator Ballantyne, the Senate was also called on

November 17. On November 16 the *Montreal Gazette*, which along with the *Toronto Globe and Mail* and the *Toronto Telegram* had been pressing for conscription, reported that the commanders of all the military districts in Canada had advised General McNaughton that compulsion must be used to secure the necessary number of men. This report was denied by the prime minister and General Mc-Naughton. General L.-R. Laflèche, national war services minister, stated on November 19 that he had taken upon himself the task of finding in Quebec the necessary reinforcements for the French-Canadian units overseas. He added that four French-Canadian regiments—Les Fusiliers Mont-Royal, Le Maisonneuve, Le Chateau-guay, and Le Joliette—had already promised to find men for reserve battalions; and expressed confidence that the reinforcement problem could be solved by the voluntary method.

When parliament met on November 22, the prime minister read and subsequently tabled the correspondence which had been exchanged between Colonel Ralston and himself concerning the defence minister's resignation and the reasons for it. Though he implied that Colonel Ralston had violated cabinet secrecy in his statement of November 12, Mr. King paid tribute to his former colleague's sincerity, personal integrity, and patriotism. He announced General McNaughton's appointment as defence minister, with the observation that 'from the moment of his appointment as commander of the First Canadian Division on October 5, 1939, the name of no man in Canada has been held in higher esteem or commanded more in the way of confidence in the minds of the citizens of Canada or on the part of members of the Canadian Army and their relatives and friends.'[33] Gordon Graydon, House leader of the opposition, pressed for action on the reinforcement question with a 'minimum of talk,' and called for full application of the N.R.M. Act and the immediate sending overseas of all trained home defence troops. His motion to this effect was ruled out of order. The prime minister, urging 'thoughtful consideration' of 'one of the gravest problems that has ever been before the Canadian Parliament for consideration,' headed off a Conservative proposal that the House should sit 'mornings, afternoons, nights, and Satur-days' until the issue was decided.[34] M. J. Coldwell, the C.C.F. leader, suggested a secret session in order that the House might receive every available bit of information. The Conservative leader opposed the suggestion of a secret session, while Mr. King proposed that General McNaughton should make a statement to the House the following day and answer questions. The House agreed to the prime minister's motion.

At a cabinet meeting on the evening of November 22 Mr. King yielded to pressure from those cabinet members who had been pressing for conscription and who had threatened to appeal to a Liberal caucus. The prime minister said that General McNaughton advised him that the appeal for volunteers could not succeed, and felt it necessary to recommend conscription. Mr. King declared that he had reluctantly decided to support this recommendation. An order-in-council was then approved.[35]

When the House met again on November 23 the prime minister tabled an order-in-council (P.C. 8891), passed that day, which on the recommendation of the defence minister and under the Militia Act (Section 67), the N.R.M. Act, and War Measures Act, authorized the sending overseas of 16,000 N.R.M.A. troops 'for the reinforcement of the Canadian forces fighting in Europe and the Mediterranean.'[36] The order left the way open for the later sending of additional men overseas by further orders-in-council. The figure named represented the number of fully or nearly fully trained infantrymen available, and slightly more than the number required to ensure a reinforcement supply. The leader of the opposition expressed dissatisfaction with this partial surrender on the part of the government, opposed a secret session, and gave notice of a motion of lack of confidence and for immediate application of the full provisions of the N.R.M. Act. The government had called for a vote of confidence, while the prime minister left the question of a secret session to the House.

In his prepared opening statement to parliament General Mc-Naughton declared that he differed only in method and not in purpose with his predecessor. In October Colonel Ralston had held that the forces overseas could no longer be maintained by the voluntary method, while McNaughton thought they could, with proper public support. He argued that a change of method would have been dangerous 'until all measures proper to the existing method had been developed to the full and it had become clear and evident to all that they would not suffice.'[37] He stated his own continuing preference for the voluntary method, but did not exclude compulsion if necessary. He reviewed his efforts in behalf of the voluntary system, revealing that the military district commanders had told him they had little hope of meeting requirements in that way, but had loyally agreed to make another effort.[38] He admitted that the results of the drive for overseas volunteers had not been adequate, and that he had been advised that 'there are very many N.R.M.A. men who will not volunteer under present circumstances but who are quite willing to be sent overseas.' He declared that there was no present overall shortage, but 'a possible prospective shortage of fully trained infantrymen' in late January or early February, 1945. He was also greatly concerned about reinforcements for French-Canadian infantry units, but 'promising results' had already been obtained in meeting this situation, thanks to 'our colleagues from the Province of Quebec and others.'

The crux of General McNaughton's statement came in the following words:

> I want to say, quite definitely, that all anxiety would be removed if we are able to find in December a total, above the numbers now arranged, of 5,000 infantry fully trained or in an advanced state of training, a similar number in January and a further 6,000 in the succeeding months.
>
> Every possible economy in the employment of fit general service personnel in home establishments has now been made or is in process, and the men so made available are included in the figures of planned dispatches.
>
> In consequence the only source from which this additional 16,000 can be secured is from the N.R.M.A.[39]

For the future he anticipated siege warfare in both northwest Europe and in Italy, with conditions approximating those of the later phases of the First World War. An increased production of shells and munitions would be necessary, and in this effort might be used 'large numbers of men who have come into the army in Canada, both general service and N.R.M.A., who can never be employed in battle.'[40] He held that many of the functions performed by N.R.M.A. men at present should not 'be done by soldiers to the prejudice of their proceeding overseas.'

McNaughton announced that N.R.M.A. men who did not volunteer would not be released from the Army 'until they can be demobilised without prejudice to the interests of our men returning from overseas.' Those who volunteered would 'become in all respects an integral part of that great band who served Canada by their own free will and whose pride it is to go where duty calls and needs dictate.' Of those who did not convert to general service, 'all men who are physically fit and deemed likely to make efficient combat soldiers' would be concentrated in N.R.M.A. units 'for potential combat duties.'[41] Those not fit for combat duty would be organized in employment companies 'to discharge any requirements for help on works of national importance to the prosecution of the war.' N.R.M.A. men suitable for neither purpose were to be discharged or placed in industry. In conclusion McNaughton stated that it was absolutely necessary to make available overseas 'a substantial reserve of reinforcements,' and that 'the numbers required to make up the reserve that is necessary are larger than could be provided in time by the volunteer conversion of trained and fit personnel of our N.R.M.A. men to general service.' The order-in-council, extending to the European theaters the service of 16,000 N.R.M.A. men, gave the minister power to fill the gap between the requirements and the number of volunteers. McNaughton added: 'This power will be used only to the extent necessary to make up the numbers of reinforcements required.'[42]

The leader of the opposition deferred to Colonel Ralston in opening the questioning of General McNaughton. Ralston expressed the view that a secret session might be advisable for reasons of security, and declared that McNaughton seemed to have adopted the same view he had always held, 'conscription when necessary.'[43] He pressed for information as to the extent of the shortage of reinforcements—this was refused on grounds of security; as to whether the 16,000 to be sent overseas between December and May would be all N.R.M.A. men; and as to whether they would constitute an adequate supply of reinforcements. McNaughton stated that some general service men might be included in the number, and that the reinforcement supply would be adequate.[44] When questioned further by H. C. Green (Vancouver South), as to the use of N.R.M.A. men, McNaughton stated the government's policy thus: 'As long as there are suitable general service personnel available to fill the requirements, it is our intention to use them. We propose to make good whatever deficiencies there are from N.R.M.A. personnel . . . I have no intention of using compulsion except to meet a deficiency, and having regard to the purpose we have of maintaining the strength of our armies overseas.'[45] He denied Mr. Green's efforts to prove that remustered general service men, inadequately trained for combat, would be sent into action while fully trained N.R.M.A. men remained in Canada.

Mr. Hansell (Macleod) brought the afternoon session to a close with an awkward question 'perhaps more directed to the Prime Minister than to General McNaughton': 'Would Colonel Ralston's resignation have been necessary if this order in council had been passed upon his report to the cabinet after his return from overseas?'[46] Mr. King objected to 'almost continuous cross-examination [of General McNaughton] by members of one particular group,' when the Conservative leader had asked that the general's appearance be confined to one day, and expressed the hope that the C.C.F. and Social Credit members would be given a chance. To Hansell's question he gave this answer in his best inscrutable style:

There are some things that can be done or which may be necessary at one time which cannot be done or which may become unnecessary at another, and if the government had attempted to do a month or two ago what at that time did not appear necessary or what has been done to-day, I venture to say that its action would have frustrated the ability of the defence department to give to the men fighting on the other side the reinforcements needed at the time they may be needed.[47]

M. J. Coldwell then took over the questioning, and after queries about leaves and the margin of safety for reinforcements, again paved the way for a secret session. In response to a Conservative interruption, he denied that he had discussed his questions with anyone,[48] though it was rumored that he was co-operating with Mr. King.

That evening, in response to further questions by Mr. Coldwell, General McNaughton stated that 16,000 N.R.M.A. were trained as infantry, and that another 26,000 were of an age and medical category suitable for such training. In reply to Mr. Diefenbaker he gave the following general service enlistment figures: June, 6,282; July, 4,860; August, 5,256; September, 5,318; October, 4,710, which ran about 2,000 higher than the monthly discharge figures.[49] Under further questions from the same source he indicated that he had formed 'the definite opinion' that the N.R.M.A. men 'had been pressed rather than led' to volunteer, and that 'with leadership and persuasion and appeal these men will come forward.'[50] The number of N.R.M.A. men who had gone active from November 1 was given as 734, with the weekly rate steadily increasing.[51] To date, however, the monthly rate was about the same as in July, August, and September, and 50 per cent higher than in October.[52] As the Conservative close questioning continued, using General McNaughton as the butt of an attack on the government, the prime minister intervened several times, and finally threatened to resign.[53] At his suggestion it was agreed to continue the questioning on the following day, partially in secret session if the House so desired, with the debate on the vote of confidence to open on Monday, November 27.

Jean-François Pouliot (Témiscouata), stating that he had to make a choice between his constituents and the present government, crossed the floor of the House at the end of Thursday's sitting, while Wilfrid Lacroix (Quebec-Montmorency) likewise left the government's ranks on Friday afternoon. The prime minister then stated that Air Minister C. G. Power had submitted his resignation, as announced by the press, but that thus far it had not been accepted. Pouliot, declaring that 'the province of Quebec is not at all opposed to a well-balanced conscription where the value of the services of every man who is working in an essential industry is recognized as a help to the war effort,' expressed the hope that 'in the future there will be no politics mixed up with this question.' He urged that General McNaughton be given a free hand to reform the defence department.[54]

McNaughton opened his second day's testimony by a written statement which clarified the previous day's discussion, during which, as a soldier without parliamentary experience, he had become

confused under ruthless cross-examination by veteran parliament-
arians and lawyers:

I expressed a strong preference for our traditional voluntary system,
and also my hope that it might not be necessary to use to the full extent
the powers given to the Minister of National Defence in the order in
council tabled yesterday. In some quarters my remarks have been interpreted as an intention on my part to scrape up men and use our general
service men and to use them first even if they are not as well trained
as N.R.M.A. men. That is not so. What I desired to convey was that I
hoped trained N.R.M.A. men would volunteer for general service soon
enough and in large enough numbers that it would not be necessary
to send them overseas by compulsion. What I wish to make clear is that
if adequately trained men do not volunteer in sufficient numbers the
required numbers will be made up from the best-trained men we have.
These will be detailed for service overseas under the order in council.
    While the order in council extends the locality of service of all N.R.M.A.
personnel, the maximum number the Minister of National Defence is
authorized by the present order to dispatch overseas is 16,000. This
power will be used to the extent that adequately trained men, whether
now in the N.R.M.A. or not, do not come forward as volunteers sufficiently rapidly to meet the numbers required. The maximum was fixed
at 16,000 in order to provide adequate reserves. In addition to giving
the reserves required by the time they are required, these numbers will
also enable increased periods of rest for individuals and will provide the
increased number needed to compensate for the men given leave to
Canada as these proposals develop.[55]

He also revealed that the N.R.M.A. units to provide the 10,000
reinforcements to be sent overseas in December and January had
been selected that morning, and would soon be moved to 'concentration areas in eastern Canada.' Men who wished to volunteer
would be given every opportunity to do so, but 'the whole units,
including those men, would be dispatched on the dates which were
then being arranged.'[56]
    Total enrollments in the N.R.M.A. from 1941 to September 27,
1944, numbered 150,000. Of these 42,000 had converted to general
service, 6,000 had been transferred to other services, and 33,500
had been discharged, leaving a strength of 68,500 of whom 8,500
were on extended leave from their depots for work in the national
interest. Those enrolled in 1942, the peak year, provided over a
third of the present net strength. The largest number of the 60,000
came from the Quebec military districts (22,800), with 15,000 from
the Ontario ones, 13,800 from the Prairies, 4,300 from the Maritimes,
and 4,100 from British Columbia.[57] The leaders of the C.C.F. and
Social Credit parties expressed opposition to coerced conversion
to general service, while Conservative members protested hard cases

of remustered men, wounded men returned to service, and men discharged from the Air Force with less than two years' service who were liable to be conscripted for army duty. At the end of the sitting Coldwell again pressed for a secret session, but the House adjourned over the weekend without settling the question.

When parliament met again on Monday afternoon, November 27, the prime minister announced that he had been unable to persuade Air Minister Power to withdraw his resignation and that it had consequently been accepted. In the correspondence which was read and tabled, Mr. Power stated that he was unable to accept the government's policy on the use of N.R.M.A. men:

I do not believe such a policy to be necessary at this time, nor will it save one single Canadian casualty.

I parted company with Colonel Ralston after the most mature consideration largely on the grounds that the number of troops which he reported as being required was comparatively so small, the means to remedy the situation without placing undue strain on the men at the front so readily available, and the end of the war so imminent that weighing everything in the balance we were not justified in provoking a national scission.

I cannot accept now from a new minister, General McNaughton, a recommendation which I reluctantly felt obliged to reject when made by an old comrade and tried associate, Layton Ralston. [58]

In a speech clarifying his stand, Mr. Power paid tribute to Colonel Ralston's sincerity and conscientiousness, but expressed his own conviction that the Army could have lowered its casualty rate and eliminated the reinforcement crisis by taking 'the men out of the line temporarily to refit, to re-equip, to rest, to recuperate and to refill the gaps in their ranks. . . . If the course of systematic recuperation were taken, then the voluntary system which we have been following, which yielded more men last year than was ever estimated, and which in the words of the present Minister of National Defence (Mr. McNaughton) has not failed, would have sufficed at this stage of the war when by the most authoritative accounts victory is certain.' [59] He felt that 'Neither ultimate victory nor national honour requires that Canadian troops should be in action every hour or every day.' He had been unable to change his convictions on conscription 'in a matter of minutes.' Therefore he, 'for opposite reasons to Colonel Ralston, but following his example,' was also leaving the cabinet in accordance with the doctrine of cabinet solidarity.

As the English-speaking Liberal with the best knowledge of Quebec, Power had this to say:

Conscription may be justified in moments of national crisis and in defence of one's country; and in the discussion of Bill 80 of 1942 I said so. It might have been justified at certain periods and phases of this war when we were on the brink of almost certain defeat. It might have been justified if D-day had been a smashing catastrophe instead of a brilliant success. But these days are now past. We have no right to tear this country asunder at this stage, and in this state of the war.

.   .   .   .   .

A word as to the consequences of this controversy. Millions of honest, decent people in all parts of Canada and of all shades of opinion are in the process of hating and reviling one another. Reason and sincere conviction have given way to hysteria on both sides. Cleavage between classes and between races has been driven deeper and deeper. The most tragic thing of all is the weakening of faith and confidence in public men—not only by the people of one province, but in all provinces; not only amongst those who hold one view, but in men and women of all sides of this unfortunate debate.

As to the cleavages to which I refer, I cherish and hold fast to the ideas of the chieftain under whose aegis I entered this house, Sir Wilfrid Laurier. He could not and would not believe that as a Canadian he could belong to a party of one province only. With him, I cannot and will not subscribe to a purely isolationist provincial standpoint.

It may be that for some time to come the day has gone when men of similar ideas and principles can meet and join in common action across the Ottawa river.

My hope, my prayer is that there will be no such outcome, and that with the advent of external victory and peace, peace and understanding may come within our own country.[60]

Having lost one cabinet colleague because he refused to adopt conscription, and another because he subsequently did so, the prime minister then moved for a vote of confidence, 'That this House will aid the government in its policy of maintaining a vigorous war effort,' and made a long and moving plea for support of his government. He declared that conscription was the real issue, and that the resignations of Power and Ralston for opposite reasons made clear the difficulties which he faced 'in seeking to carry out what has been, above all else, the purpose of my work in public life; the maintenance of unity as far as that might be possible in the government of this country and in the Dominion of Canada itself.'[61] He reviewed at some length the history of the conscription question since September 1939, when parliament had been of one mind that there should be no conscription for overseas service, and since March 1940, when the government received 'a mandate to carry on the war and to carry it on without resort to conscription.'[62] With the fall of France and the threat of invasion of Canada, the N.R.M.

Act, providing for conscription within Canada, had been passed and accepted by the country. An agitation for conscription for overseas then arose, and the government was freed by the plebiscite from its moral obligation not to invoke its legal power to adopt conscription for overseas. Refuting the view that the plebiscite result was a mandate for conscription, Mr. King described the policy of the government under Bill 80 as 'not necessarily conscription but conscription if necessary . . . and to the extent that it might be necessary.'[63] But no such action had proved necessary until the current situation arose.

Mr. King then reviewed the history of the crisis, declaring that although Colonel Ralston 'for a long time has believed that it might become necessary to resort to conscription for service overseas to provide necessary reinforcements,' no such recommendation had been made until October, when Ralston returned from overseas. The prime minister declared that the shortage of reinforcements then anticipated was not expected to arise until 'the beginning of the new year,' and thus 'while the government has been giving this matter all the mature considerations that its great importance and grave significance necessitate, we have been running no risk so far as our fighting men overseas are concerned,'[64] despite Conservative charges. The cabinet had sought a solution of the problem 'which would not involve a break-up of the government itself in a time of war.' He anticipated that in the future the 'organized propaganda for conscription in Canada,' which had created 'a degree of unrest . . . the like of which has not been seen in the history of Canada before,' would be condemned. The cabinet, feeling that everything had been done that was possible 'to make Canada's war effort a total war effort,'[65] had wondered why it was necessary to run the risk of dividing the country on the eve of certain victory. The prime minister himself had been particularly concerned by the effect upon Canada's postwar role in the world of creating division within the country.

The cabinet had accepted the need for reinforcements, but remained divided on the method of obtaining them. A further appeal for volunteers was agreed upon, but no agreement could be reached as to whether its duration should be limited. Ralston 'had not faith' in the success of this appeal, and threatened to resign unless compulsion was used if necessary. Air Minister Power was ill and unable to take Ralston's place as associate minister of national defence. Other ministers intimated that they would resign if Ralston did.[66] King then called in General McNaughton, who expressed his belief that the required number of men could be found by the voluntary method and agreed to enter the government if a crisis arose. The prime minister then so informed the cabinet, and

Ralston resigned and McNaughton took his place, after Ralston and other ministers had refused to take the responsibility of heading the government and putting through conscription.[67]

The prime minister had decided against an appeal to the people—though he had not the least doubt that he would have been returned with a good majority—since an election would have meant a bitter campaign and a delay in sending reinforcements.[68] He declared that until parliament met on November 22, he had thought that the appeal for volunteers would succeed, but at a cabinet meeting that night McNaughton expressed the view, reached 'in conference with his staff,' that 'it might be taking too great a chance not to act immediately.'[69] The cabinet had then chosen the middle course between all-out conscription and no conscription by adopting the order-in-council which guaranteed the necessary reinforcements. Citing Sir John A. Macdonald's description of the 'deadlock and impending anarchy that hung over us' when Quebec and Ontario could not unite to form a strong government before Confederation, Mr. King declared that 'unless this House of Commons can unite in reasonable measure to support an administration that can carry on at this stage of the war we shall have to face the possibility of anarchy in Canada while our men are fighting overseas, giving their lives that we may maintain our free institutions and that we may have peace and concord through the years to come.'[70]

The step taken by the government in this situation was in accordance with the government's stand on Bill 80, as stated many times by the prime minister in the House. But the government required parliament's support in carrying out now a decision which had been taken in 1942. He clarified the scope of the order-in-council in the following words:

That order in council P.C. 8891 applies to all personnel who are serving or who may serve in consequence of having been called up under the National Resources Mobilization Act . . . The order in council authorizes the Minister of National Defence to dispatch overseas a maximum of 16,000 N.R.M.A. personnel. In calculating the number of N.R.M.A. men so dispatched of [sic] reinforcements men will be counted as N.R.M.A. personnel only if they have embarked on board ship without converting to general service. All N.R.M.A. personnel who convert to general service before embarkation will go overseas as volunteers. The additional numbers estimated to be required total 16,000, regardless of their status on leaving Canada.[71]

Mr. King contended that the government had successfully surmounted two crises, Ralston's resignation and the decision on the order-in-council, in which 'the ministry itself might have been obliged as a whole to resign, with what consequences I leave others to contemplate.' Pleading with the House to back the government and thus avoid another crisis, 'a crisis greater than any other that has ever been on the horizon of Canada,' Mr. King declared that 'it will not help the army to defeat the present government and possibly force a general election.'[72] He reiterated the dangers of a wartime election; stated that he would stand or fall with his own party; and asked whether any of his colleagues in the cabinet, or the leaders of the Conservative, C.C.F., or Social Credit parties were prepared to take on the responsibility of government. 'Unless you are, unless you feel that you can present to the country an alternative government worthy of its support at this time, I think you owe it to this administration to support it.'[73]

Addressing his Quebec supporters, he declared that his public acts had always been 'in the interest of Canada as a whole, not in the interests of any particular province,' although he had been often accused of seeking to appease Quebec or to retain its support at all costs. He had sought, however, 'to have the people of Canada understand the province of Quebec.' The other provinces owed something to Quebec for keeping Canada British in 1775 and 1812, and for playing its part ever since in the development of the Canadian nation. He had defended the people of Quebec from 'ruthless, unprincipled and often brutal attacks' from other parts of the country, not merely in the interest of fair play and justice, but because 'Canada cannot be governed unless the rights of minorities are respected.' He stated that the French Canadians did not fear conscription, to which they had submitted under the N.R.M. Act, but that 'they look upon conscription as a symbol of domination by the majority.' Repelling the charge of appeasement, he pointed out that Quebec had accepted the postponement of redistribution at its expense; it had accepted Bill 80, though 'with that measure began the little rift within the lute of the Liberal party'; and now it was being asked to accept partial conscription. He appealed to his Quebec supporters, 'who have trusted me so firmly through the years that have passed to trust me again on this occasion.'[74]

Quoting Laurier's appeals of 1887 to the French Canadians to be Canadians first, and of 1916 to unite with the English Canadians in offering their services, he added the words spoken in 1939 by Ernest Lapointe, 'the closest, the truest and the most devoted friend I have had in my political life,' that: 'No government could stay in office if it refused to do what the great majority of Canadians wanted it to do.' Mr. King then called for a vote of confidence, not as approval of the order-in-council, not as approval of conscription, not as unlimited approval of government policies, but as an indication of willingness 'to support the government in continuing to carry on Canada's war effort at the present time.' A vote against the motion would be taken by the government as a vote 'to have the present administration resign, and another administration immediately take its place.' He concluded with some words of Laurier spoken in 1900, which he wished to use as his own on this occasion and to have 'remembered of me by my fellow-citizens when I also am gone':

If there is anything to which I have devoted my political life, it is to try to promote unity, harmony and amity between the diverse elements of this country. My friends can desert me, they can remove their confidence from me, they can withdraw the trust they have placed in my hands, but never shall I deviate from that line of policy. Whatever may be the consequences, whether loss of prestige, loss of popularity, or loss of power, I feel that I am in the right, and I know that a time will come when every man will render me full justice on that score.[75]

This speech was one of Mackenzie King's most notable efforts and attained the eloquence and feeling which he so often sacrificed to caution and provision against all future eventualities. While its clear reflections of his own opinion that he was indispensable galled his critics, it provided an unsurpassed proof of his extraordinary ability to steer a course for the nation through troubled waters which made allowances for all the currents of Canadian public opinion. It was the masterpiece of an extraordinary figure, who combined the abilities of an idealistic scholar and a highly practical politician.

That evening Gordon Graydon, as floor leader of the opposition, declared that 'This is peculiarly, I think, a parliament of those who fight for Canada, and indirectly of their dependents as well.' He argued that the government could have met and solved the reinforcement crisis, 'had it taken the courage to do so without allowing it to reach the proportions that it has reached or disturbing and distressing our people, both here and overseas, in the long and tragic process.' He urged that party barriers should be let down in the national interest, and that concern should be shown for national unity, 'with no hatred in our hearts for any single section or part of Canada.'[76] The main issue was winning the war, and the war was not yet won despite cabinet statements to that effect. He argued that the public wanted parliament to clean up the situation once and for all, with no more cabinet crises, and no more delays of reinforcements, and so he protested against the order-in-council restricted to 16,000 men and the possibility of future crises when further orders might have to be passed.

The government seemed half-hearted about its policy of 'controlled conscription,' and Graydon thought that 'the question of confidence in the Prime Minister to carry out properly the terms of that legislation was left more in doubt this afternoon by his words than by anything that might be done over here to throw doubt upon it.'[77] He compared the order-in-council unfavourably with that providing for the sending of N.R.M.A. men to the Alaska-Aleutian theater of war, and stated the Conservative opposition 'to the pulling of punches in this last phase of our struggle in the war.' He pressed for one army and an end of this 'piecemeal and appeasement policy' which had produced confusion in the public mind as the government retreated from trench to trench. He urged emphasis on the maximum rather than the minimum requirements for reinforcements, and pressed the question, 'Are those Canadians now serving in the European field of conflict to be asked to go to fight in the Pacific while men drafted under the N.R.M.A. remain in Canada?' He urged more leave for the men about to spend their sixth Christmas overseas. He criticized the prime minister for setting up the cry of 'King or anarchy in Canada.' Arguing that the opposition wanted total war and had not been getting it from the government, he moved an amendment to the motion of confidence:

This house is of the opinion that the government has not made certain of adequate and continuous trained reinforcements by requiring all N.R.M.A. personnel whether now or hereafter enrolled to serve in any theatre of war and has failed to assure equality of service and sacrifice.[78]

M. J. Coldwell, leader of the C.C.F., declared that the issue was reinforcements, not conscription, a matter which had been decided in 1940. He regretted that the government had not seen fit to conscript wealth as well as men under the powers given it by the N.R.M. Act, and had never made a thorough inventory of all resources and allocated man-power to agriculture, industry, and the military services. He had urged that parliament should be summoned after Ralston's resignation because he believed that parliament and not the government alone should know the situation in full detail and take responsibility for what was done. The C.C.F. had taken no part in 'the recent discussion throughout the country based on supposition and rumour,' and had not joined 'the hymn of hate against conscripted men who had not volunteered for service overseas.' Some should have volunteered; others were torn 'between their duty to their country and the necessities of their homes, sometimes involving, too, a consideration of the needs of the country in the production of foodstuffs and other supplies.'[79] He pressed for information about the use of Canadian troops in the Pacific, and declared that too many questions remained unanswered, because of Conservative opposition to a secret session.

Criticizing the order-in-council, Coldwell moved a subamendment, which cancelled the Conservative amendment and added the following words to the government motion:

which in the opinion of this house requires the immediate removal of all distinctions between drafted and volunteer personnel, thus making the entire home defence army available for reinforcements overseas, and requires further the total mobilization of all the resources of Canada, material and financial as well as human, to ensure a total war effort, adequate re-establishment of the members of our fighting forces, and full employment after the war.[80]

He felt no confidence in the government's ability to maintain a vigorous war 'when its proposals in all respects fall far short of obvious requirements.' But he also had no confidence in the intentions or ability of the Conservatives, because of the irresponsibility they had shown in this crisis, their 'really shocking display of political manœuvring. . . . Some of their highly placed friends and a section of the press supporting them have done their best to inflame sectional differences and hatreds.' In conclusion he spoke movingly of his recent visit to the Canadian cemetery at Dieppe:

There was no distinction there of race or creed or colour. They were just Canadian lads who had died for their country. Why, oh why cannot we who are left behind in this country, to enjoy the freedom for which they died, live together? Those who in the midst of war engage in the setting of race against race, creed against creed and colour in this land are in my opinion unworthy of the living and the dead.[81]

J. H. Blackmore, leader of the Social Credit group, dismissed the agitation as 'pure politics' and associated himself with Coldwell's views on the Conservatives, before considering economic issues which he considered of far greater importance.

Then the prime minister took the Conservatives unawares by proposing that the House should meet in secret session on the following day, since Mr. Coldwell, Mr. Ralston, and many members desired further information which could only be given under such circumstances. Mr. Graydon's effort not to exclude the press was overridden on the ground of British precedent. The House met in secret session from 3 p.m. to 11 p.m. on Tuesday, November 28, and the only report of its proceedings was issued by the speaker: 'General the Honourable A. G. L. McNaughton, Minister of National Defence, was present and gave information respecting the Canadian forces.'[82]

8

When the House met again in normal fashion on Wednesday, November 29, a Conservative, R. B. Hanson (York-Sunbury), asked what measures the government was taking to meet the 'mutiny among the men of the home army' on the Pacific coast. The prime minister denied that a 'mutiny' existed and declared that the situation was 'being carefully watched and completely controlled.'[83] Further Ontario petitions for an 'all-out war effort' were received. The prime minister denied that Public Works Minister Alphonse Fournier had resigned. Labor Minister Mitchell made a statement that discharged Air Force or Navy men who had either served overseas or for three years in Canada would not be subject to recall for army service. Their plight had been protested by Conservative members. The speaker ruled that the C.C.F. subamendment was out of order, as the debate on the government's war policy was resumed.

J. A. Johnston (London), a Liberal veteran with four years' active service, defended the government's war effort, citing Churchill's tribute in the British Commons the previous day to 'the magnificent character of the Canadian war effort.' He rejected the possibility of a 'hybrid Union government.'[84] W. Earl Rowe (Dufferin-Simcoe), on behalf of the Progressive Conservatives, made 'an offer of co-operation provided the right leadership is found . . . without any request or suggestion of union government':

The Progressive Conservative party, with the full authority of its leader, John Bracken, and with the unanimous voice of its representation in this parliament, hereby declares that in this hour of national crisis, when the fortunes of political parties must be subordinated to the national weal, it stands prepared to co-operate with any government which, under leadership that will ensure equality of service, offers proof of will and determination to send to our soldiers overseas the reinforcements which our war commitments demand.[85]

He criticized the prime minister's record on conscription, and regretted the resignations of 'two of the most important men in the cabinet.' As he continued with kind words for Colonel Ralston and sharp criticism of General McNaughton, he suffered many interruptions from the government benches, where the cry of 'Tory conspiracy' was raised.

Victor Quelch (Acadia) moved a Social Credit amendment, calling upon the government to give:

1. The unqualified assurance to our men on the battle fronts that they will receive at once ample material supplies, and adequate reinforcements; and the use of all persons in any of Canada's armed services in any theatre of war in which they may be required.

2. The unqualified assurance, backed by appropriate action, that:

(a) Upon demobilization the active service men and women in the armed services, together with their families, will be ensured economic security, together with adequate grants and proper opportunities for training to enable them to re-establish themselves in the country's economic life;

(b) Adequate pensions and free medical care will be given to all persons whose health has been impaired during active service in the Canadian forces from any cause whatsoever;

(c) The dependents of all men killed in action or who have died in active service in the Canadian forces will be provided with economic independence for life.

(d) The foregoing will constitute a first charge on the nation.

3. The assurance to the people of Canada, by immediate action to that end, that following the war the abundant productive resources of the country will be used to the full, and that the resulting goods and services will be equitably distributed to ensure every Canadian economic security with full freedom.

4. The assurance that government wartime controls, bureaucratic regimentation and oppressive taxation will be discontinued as rapidly as possible after the war, and that the peace-time economy will be based on a proper democracy free from state domination of the people's lives.

5. Immediate steps to establish the necessary reforms to our financial system without which the foregoing will be impossible.[86]

Liguori Lacombe reviewed his anti-militaristic record and his prophecies since 1939 of 'the present disaster,' declaring that: 'As a result of Canada's participation in the war, the government has spent sixteen billion dollars; agriculture has lost over half a million workers, male and female; families are broken up, while mothers and daughters are toiling in factories, and thousands of our young men are being sacrificed on foreign soil.'[87] He stated that protests against conscription came 'not only from Quebec but from all sections of the country.' He could not find 'words sufficiently scathing to condemn this new reversal of policy by a government which, at the end of its term of office, imposes this evil and anti-national measure,' and declared: 'Never has a government broken so many pledges. Never has it thus sowed doubt and suspicion.' Since 1939 Canada had reverted to colonialism, but he expressed the hope that 'we may forsake this chaotic situation to unfurl at last a Canadian flag in an independent country, mistress of its own destinies . . . Whether we wish it or not, the deep reactions of the postwar period are bound to bring about the independence of Canada.' The government had inevitably been led into conscription by its decision in favor of participation, and he argued that if conscription was a 'tremendous mistake' in 1917, as Ernest Lapointe had said, it was 'doubly wrong today.' He saw this 'blood tax,' on top of 'too heavy a burden of taxes and loans,' as 'the deferred, but dire results of the military and financial imperialism laid down as a creed by the very people who claimed they were opposing it.'[88]

Fred Rose (Cartier), Communist representative of a working class Montreal district, declared that the Labor-Progressive Party included no N.R.M.A. men and had done everything in its power to support volunteering. He stated his belief that if the character of the War had been properly explained to the people of Quebec at the time of the plebiscite, they would have taken a different view of it. Attention should not be distracted from the issue of reinforcements by raising the questions of conscription of wealth and resources. He urged the House to recognize that Canada was 'a two-nation state,' that the French Canadians had reason to be suspicious of wars because of the past and that they had grievances which had not been corrected. He denounced the press campaign in the other eight provinces against 'Quebec and Quebec zombies' as vicious and un-Canadian. He declared that it was a campaign organized by the leaders of the Progressive Conservative party:

> It started a few months ago on the issue of family allowances. At that time Premier Drew of Ontario said: 'Ontario will not pay for Quebec zombies.' Then came a terrific intensification of this sort of thing in which he nearly broke his neck. He then decided to go overseas and to come back with a new issue, the issue of reinforcements. I am not denying the issue of reinforcements, but I do not like how it came to be raised. Premier Drew came back to this country, and at about the same time Major Connie Smyth came back and in a public statement told the country that untrained men were sent to the front. If I understand military law I should think it would have been more proper for the major to take this matter up with the proper authorities than to go into politics, but that was not done. When N.R.M.A. men parade we hear talk of mutiny, but when officers break every rule nobody says anything about mutiny or treason.[89]

French-Canadian isolationism had been nurtured by English Canadian leaders as well as French-Canadian ones. Rose charged that the Dominion Textile and Aluminum companies had encouraged their workers to join Catholic syndicates, thus isolating them from the rest of Canada and keeping wages lower. Quebec's health and educational levels were lower than in the other provinces; while an English Canadian always held the pursestrings of the province.

Rose declared that the 'poison spread throughout the country against the province' was 'the work of the same Tory elements who have profited in the past by the isolationism of the people.'[90] The people of Quebec had had 'a bigger dose of fascist propaganda than any other people.' Conservative literature in the 1935 general elections had been edited by 'Hitler's aide in Canada, Adrien Arcand,' while 'The Hon. Sam Gobeil, leader of the Conservative party in Quebec, wrote some of the most open pro-Hitler pamphlets written by any politician in this country.' Paul Bouchard, editor of *La Nation*, 'one of the worst Fascist sheets in our province,' had been financed in his campaign in the 1937 Lotbinière by-election by the federal Conservative leader, Maurice Dupré.[91] The paper had received support from Frédéric Dorion, then a Conservative and now leader of the *Groupement des Indépendants*, which Rose implied was a Conservative front. English Canadians had financed Duplessis' 'anti-war machine' in the last provincial election, which had been supported by the 'same *Montreal Gazette* which is now so loudly demanding conscription.' He did not exempt the Liberal party from blame, but he held the Tories chiefly responsible for Quebec's attitude.

Rose defended the French-Canadian record in the services and in war industry, and declared that if Quebec had a lower recruiting record, its people were 'the victims of certain conditions for which, to a great extent, English-speaking Canadians are responsible.' He favoured General Laflèche's methods of getting French-Canadian volunteers over those of M.P.'s 'who sit here and attack, attack, attack every attempt to induce such men to come forward as volunteers.' He deplored the attacks on General McNaughton and on the campaign for volunteers, declaring that the Tories were 'not interested in reinforcements' but 'in bringing down the government, and in having an election so they could ride to power, not for the good of the men who have gone overseas, but so they could bring us back to the old iron-heel Bennett days.' He supported the order-in-council, which he thought should satisfy everybody, 'that is, if he really wants reinforcements and does not want to force an election on the conscription issue . . . The only ones who would gain from such an election would be those whose interest it is to keep us apart. Whenever the English and French people have stood together, all the people have benefitted; whenever they have been torn apart, every one has suffered with the exception of those who wanted them to be torn apart. There must be greater national unity if our men are to get needed reinforcements, and if the people of Canada are to achieve security and peace in the post-war period.'[92]

That evening Colonel Ralston, who had become the key figure in the crisis and was widely spoken of as the potential prime minister of a coalition government,[93] spoke for over two hours, taking issue with the prime minister's version of the whole affair, and with the implication that he himself had violated cabinet secrecy. He returned the compliment on the latter score, with the observation 'What is all right for the Prime Minister of Canada, I am sure he will admit, ought to be quite all right for a humble ex-minister.' He stated that he had mentioned in the cabinet late in September that 'because of heavier infantry casualties' trained N.R.M.A. men might be needed.[94] Though he had never held that the N.R.M.A. men might not have to be used, he had worked just as hard as he possibly could to support the voluntary method. He now felt that it had failed as 'a dependable source for infantry replacements for the army at this stage of the war,' though he still preferred a voluntary army. [95] His version of the prime minister's offer to resign in favor of any other member of the cabinet was that only he and two others had been asked whether they would accept the office, and that they had all refused, taking the question to be 'purely hypothetical.' Mr. King promptly denied both statements. [96]

Colonel Ralston maintained that he had not proposed a new measure, but one which the government had agreed upon in 1942. He made clear that he had no ambition to become prime minister, and that he had resigned on the basis of the cabinet's refusal to accept his recommendation, and not on the question of a time limit for the appeal to the N.R.M.A. men to volunteer. When the prime minister had spoken of General McNaughton's belief that the 15,000 men Ralston had asked for could be got by voluntary means, and had expressed the view that McNaughton should be asked to take over, mentioning Ralston's unwithdrawn resignation of two years' standing, Ralston had resigned. [97] He contradicted the prime minister's statement about a shortage not arising until the beginning of the new year, declaring that when he resigned 'the figures showed that there would be a considerable shortage by the end of December; I mean a shortage in the strength of the units themselves, with no pools whatever.' For this reason he had pressed for immediate action in October, in order that men might be sent overseas in November, without losing another month. [98]

Ralston made a detailed analysis of the reinforcement situation as he had found it in his trip overseas, and reviewed the failure of previous campaigns to get N.R.M.A. men to volunteer. He criticized the course followed by the government after his resignation. But since action was more important than method, he would support the government's motion, rather than risk further delays through the formation of a new government or a dissolution which would result if the Conservative amendment carried, though he favored the principle of making all N.R.M.A. men subject to overseas service. [99] After a closing tribute to the Canadian Army, he called upon the house to see to it that the gaps in the ranks were filled. Ralston was so clearly the dominant figure in the debate thus far that R. B. Hanson moved adjournment until the following day, in order to let his words sink in, after blaming the prime minister and General McNaughton for the delay of six weeks in taking action on reinforcements, and assigning to them the responsibility for any bloodshed that might occur as a result of that delay. [100]

9

When the House met on Thursday, November 30, Daniel McIvor (Fort William) asked Mr. King whether it was not a waste of time and money to continue the debate since the prime minister, Colonel Ralston, General McNaughton, and the leaders of the opposition had spoken. The prime minister expressed a favorable opinion on the question thus raised, though he said he was unwilling to deprive any member of the liberty to speak. When debate was resumed, the Speaker ruled the Social Credit amendment out of order.

Mr. Hanson, speaking as acting leader of the Progressive Conservatives, declared that the offer made in John Bracken's name by Mr. Rowe the previous day still stood, and that it was not 'a mere political gesture.'[101] He denied that there had been any organized campaign for conscription, except on the part of the Canadian Legion, or that there had been 'a conspiracy simply for the purpose of getting rid of the present prime minister.' 'What public opinion outside of this house has done—and expression has been given to it by the great metropolitan newspapers of Canada—is to focus attention on a critical situation which we now know existed, and which still exists and will not be adequately taken care of by the right-about-face policy of the prime minister and those of his cabinet colleagues who have turned face with him.' Hanson took credit for reshaping the government's policy after Dunkirk by helping to evolve the N.R.M. Act, which he regretted had 'a hamstringing limitation that outraged public opinion in Canada.'[102] He sought to prove that Macdonald, Ralston, Ilsley, and Power had favored all-out conscription after the plebiscite, but had yielded in the interest of cabinet solidarity. He asked what confidence could be felt in King and McNaughton, who reversed their policy overnight and adopted one which they had recently condemned, and expressed regret that Colonel Ralston was not 'carrying through' with his case for immediate conscription of all N.R.M.A. men. He resented the prime minister's implication that no one except himself and the 'eighteen old tired men' of the cabinet could carry on the government of the country. After this effective opening Mr. Hanson lost the sympathy of the House by attacking the cabinet ministers one by one in partisan style. He closed by calling for a vote of no confidence because there remained doubt about 'the mandatory authority of the order in council to take every man that is necessary should the occasion arise, and before it arises, to reinforce our men overseas.'[103] But he refused to answer a question as to whether Manchuria, China, Burma, and India were excluded from the terms of the Conservative amendment, as well as Japan as he had stated.

L.-Philippe Picard (Bellechasse) then made the first notable French-Canadian contribution to the debate. Pointing out that 'sanity and reason are seldom present at the birth of great national or parliamentary crises,' he declared the present situation supplied further proof that 'mass emotional outbursts may develop into a situation such as to cause certain steps to be taken in the governings of the nation which may in turn incite other people to react in a way such as to cause friction and unrest.'[104] He briefly reviewed Canada's achievements in the last five years, and pointed out that they had been possible 'because the country was whole-heartedly behind the methods followed by the government up to now.' As he saw it, 'the trouble in Canada started when the conscriptionist elements in the cabinet yielded to the pressure of the Tory press and forced the government to bring in Bill 80.' He declared that 'there was no real urgency in regard to that bill, since two years and four months elapsed after it was passed, over the opposition of myself and quite a number of other hon. members, before further pressure and the threat of a cabinet rupture brought about an order in council applying Bill 80.' All wished to bring the war to 'a speedy and successful conclusion.' The divisive issue was conscription, which had 'split the British nation in 1916,' and in the present war still divided public opinion 'in many, if not all of the British dominions . . . The Tory press, the Orange lodges and the technocracy groups cannot blame the French Canadians or Quebec for the situation which exists in other parts of the empire.'

Considering the historic role of the French Canadians in the making of Canada, Picard objected to the English-Canadian habit of using them 'as a sort of national scapegoat on which to blame everything that goes wrong,' and of blaming the isolationist views of a Groulx or a Laurendeau 'on the whole racial group.'[105] Conscription had been opposed in Britain, Northern Ireland, Australia, New Zealand, and South Africa during this war, yet 'In Canada a question which could remain only the subject of discussion as to the merits or demerits of a principle has become the cause of racial disunity and parochial prejudices.'

After citing opinions on conscription in Britain and the other dominions, Picard turned to the development of anti-conscriptionist feeling in Quebec. He pointed out that from 1898 to 1912 'no encouragement was ever given to anybody of French-Canadian origin in Canada to join the army, for fear he might use unwisely some knowledge he would have acquired.'[106] When the South African War broke out, French Canada had little sympathy for it, an attitude now shared by 'a large proportion of broad-minded British people.' Picard saw a parallel between the position then and the position at the start of the present cabinet crisis, and considered that there began the 'break up of unity in the country on military matters':

> That is the moment the trouble started. You saw Bourassa going around Quebec, spreading trouble, spreading nationalist sentiment and separatist sentiment. You saw this sentiment growing and growing in the elections of 1904, 1908 and 1911. In 1911 they succeeded in destroying Laurier in that province. Some of our opponents say the Liberals are responsible because in Quebec the people are against conscription. I would ask whether or not the Liberals, by keeping for French Canada a political outlet in following a large national party, have not served the country well. If they had not taken the attitude they took in 1917 the whole of the province of Quebec would have gone nationalist and separatist and we French Canadians would have suffered from it. Canada as a whole would have suffered. But due to the broadmindedness and the understanding of Laurier, who gave them an outlet in a national party, French Canadians were kept in a frame of mind which permitted them to collaborate in confederation, and they carried on for twenty-seven years in that fashion.
>
> We are not responsible for conscription. That has been started by the nationalists, and by those people who believe that there should be two countries in Canada instead of one. But we of the Liberal party have fought against it. Laurier maintained national unity. He felt it was his duty to maintain a political outlet by means of a national party for French Canadians. And because of that attitude we were able afterwards to re-establish and re-unite with the rest of Canada in cordial relations, and to play the part which has been played, under this government, from 1921 to the present.[107]

Though the King government had conducted 'an efficient war effort' for five years, 'a powerful machine has been at work trying to undermine public confidence in the Prime Minister . . . and to convince the country that everything would go wrong unless a union government were formed, or unless a Tory administration were in authority':

> A rumour-spreading, lie-whispering, mud-slinging monster has run amok unscrupulously risking to wreck the whole effort of the country . . . No matter how much the welfare of the country would have to suffer, no matter how much the war effort might be hampered, the one question, the only question that was apt to divide public opinion in Canada had to be brought forward and made into a symbol of disunity.[108]

While in English Canada the government was criticized for 'not waging an efficient war effort, and acceding to the views of Quebec in the matter of compulsory service,' in French Canada the same Tory forces, 'masquerading as independents,' accused the government of betraying Quebec.

The Quebec Liberals had backed the war effort wholeheartedly, differing from their colleagues only on Bill 80 and on the order in council sending N.R.M.A. men overseas. Picard declared: 'If I believed that when that order-in-council was passed the security of Canada was at stake unless we sent a few more thousand men overseas, I could have approved it and tried to have it understood in my province. But I cannot believe that, nor can I believe that without these few men the outcome of the war will be changed or even delayed.'[109] He thought 'The whole trouble is that our military experts want to make good the commitments they have made, even if they prove to be too large.' He thought the Canadian forces should have been concentrated on one front, instead of spread out in two theaters, and that thus the reinforcement and recuperation questions would have been simplified. 'If we have taken too large a chunk of the front, let us be sensible and correct our mistake,' since Canada did not have 'the vast reservoirs of men that the Russians or Americans have, and cannot be expected to compete with them.' He urged that Canada, like New Zealand, was justified in relaxing its military war effort if its industrial and agricultural effort were endangered by methods which did not meet with general approval or which would cause more trouble than good. He could not approve of the action of the government in passing the order-in-council.

Picard denounced the 'hysterical panic' which had been 'provoked and kept alive by the Tory press . . . based upon the wrong belief that unless the N.R.M.A. recruits are sent overseas, the sons and relatives of good patriotic Canadians will be incurring more dangers in the battle line.' He sympathized with the government, but believed that it should have given way to another if a change of policy had to be adopted. He made this statement reluctantly, 'because I have more confidence in the Prime Minister than in any other man in public life, and I know that my constituents, except for the passing of Bill 80 and order-in-council 8891, even now have more confidence in the Prime Minister than in any other leader.'[110] He feared that the conduct of a man favorable to the voluntary method but yielding to the pressure of conscriptionist ministers would increase Quebec's distrust of public men, 'while in the rest of the country it will appease but temporarily the worries of those whose attitude on this question has reached a state of hysteria.' He expressed at length his admiration and sympathy for the prime minister, but regretted that Ernest Lapointe was not still associated with him:

His weight in the councils of the nation would have strengthened the will of the Prime Minister to prevent some of the measures which have divided us and at times taken our minds away from Canada's wonderful accomplishments in the war. Never has a man's passing away been so sadly felt, especially when we realize that his presence might have been such an agent of cohesion and of unity.

Picard then moved, seconded by a Western English Canadian, Walter Adam Tucker (Rosthern), an amendment to the amendment: 'That this house will aid in maintaining an efficient war effort but it does not approve of compulsory service overseas.'[111]

Picard's sensible speech failed to sway the aroused conscriptionist English-Canadian members, as was evidenced by Howard Green's (Vancouver South) immediate observation that 'should the amendment be adopted by the House of Commons the effect would be that Canada would be deserting her boys overseas; and neither I nor any other member of the Progressive Conservative party in this house, nor any Tory so-called from coast to coast, has the slightest intention or [of] deserting our lads overseas no matter whatever else may befall.'[112] Green denounced the government measure as 'a political compromise,' and declared that 'this house and the Canadian people must never permit any government to gamble with the lives of our sons.' He called for support of his party's amendment: 'an honest, courageous manpower policy that is in line with the straightforwardness of the Canadian people.'

Walter Tucker, a veteran of both World Wars, criticized the Tories for 'wrapping themselves in the flag' and for breaking their campaign pledges in 1940 against overseas conscription. He supported the Picard motion because 'If we have gone into this war as a partnership on an agreed voluntary basis; if we have done our very best on that basis, and received the support of the whole country on that basis, then nothing short of actual danger to the country's existence, or a loss of the war, would justify our departing from that position.'[113] These conditions did not now exist, with victory assured. Like Picard, he favored solving the reinforcement crisis by the method suggested by Mr. Power, taking the Canadian divisions out of the line for a short time. He thought that the thousands of fully trained aircrew now being discharged could make 'a greater contribution toward the defeat of Germany than two or three times their number of unwilling draftees.'[114] He deplored the attacks upon the French Canadians and upon other Canadians of foreign origin, and cited the situation in his own Saskatchewan riding to prove that under the voluntary policy 'there has been a response from all peoples regardless of their religious beliefs or racial origin.' He condemned Pastor Shield's attacks upon Catholics. Canada's war effort to date could not have been accomplished if disunity had been created at the start by forcing compulsion upon the country.

The campaign for conscription had been started long before the present need for reinforcements arose; it had been intensified at present in an effort to overthrow the government. Tucker suggested that 'the forces of reaction which hate and oppose that great program of social and humanitarian measures which the Prime Minister has laid before Parliament this session saw in this agitation for conscription an opportunity of destroying the greatest Prime Minister Canada has ever seen.'[115] He defended the home defence troops, declaring that they included many Saskatchewan farmers who never should have been called up. Canada faced a troubled world, with the possibility of another situation such as in 1939. He hoped that 'irreparable damage has not been done' to national unity. He considered that conscription in the first war had done more harm than good, and was convinced that history will record once more that 'this attempt at conscription in the present war will have been an equal if not a greater failure.' He closed with a plea for cooperation, 'regardless of racial origin or religious creed, so that we can build up a country worthy of the volunteers who have gone forth to defend us against our enemies.' The speaker then found the Picard amendment out of order.

P.-J.-A. Cardin (Richelieu-Verchères), the veteran minister who had left the cabinet in protest against Bill 80, then spoke, paying tribute to Tucker with this observation: 'It is not very often that we French Canadians hear in this House of Commons an English-speaking voice defending the position that we are taking, expressing views which are similar to those that we entertain and using the same arguments that we ourselves are using in support of our own ideas.'[116] He thanked Tucker for his kindness and frankness in 'an expression of real Canadianism.' He also congratulated Picard, 'who has expressed to a very large extent sentiments which are mine at this time as they were when I debated Bill 80.' The speaker's rulings as to the subamendments also came in for praise, since the effect of these motions was 'purely and simply to becloud the issue and prevent the common people from understanding what is really at stake before parliament.' To Cardin the issue was simply approval or disapproval of the government's policy, which was 'a policy of conscription for service overseas.'[117]

The leaders of Quebec were under attack for creating the present state of mind in that province. He had no apologies to make for his part: 'What I said there was approved by the Prime Minister, with whom I was then associated. What I said there was approved by the leader of the opposition during the last electoral campaign. There was no divergence of view as between Liberals and Conservatives in regard to conscription for overseas service. We all said that this policy was no good for Canada; that it had been a failure

in the past and would be a failure in the future.'[118] Laurier,
Lapointe, and he himself had been true to their duty: 'We have
spoken the truth, and what we have said in the province of Quebec
we have repeated on each occasion and at every opportunity that
has been given us in other sections of Canada, with the same courage,
the same conviction and the same feeling of a real Canadianism.'[119]
Lapointe and he had won Quebec to approval of participation in
1939, in the face of agitation against it. Since then Quebec's leaders
had faced the situation as they found it and argued with the people,
'and there has been no trouble in my province, even though a certain
number of my compatriots felt that they had been unfairly treated,
that they had been insulted, that they were being called zombies by
people who were irresponsible and who never had the courage to
face the electorate in any section of Canada.' This indirect reference
to Mr. Bracken, the titular Conservative leader who had never
sought a seat in parliament, indicated how strong Cardin's Liberal
loyalty was, despite his break with Mr. King. The same was true
of many a French Liberal, for party loyalty is deeply engrained in
the French-Canadian character.

In reply to the charge that Quebec had not furnished as many
soldiers as other sections of Canada, Cardin repeated a statement he
had recently made in Montreal:

We have done more than you English-speaking Canadians of British
descent. You have only obeyed the call of blood. You have answered
the sentiments of your heart and mind. What we have done could only
be done through reasoning, and judging the situation as a judge would
do when deciding a case presented to him. It is not a case of reasoning
with you; it is a case of sentiment, and I understand you. For a moment,
if you wish to understand me and the French Canadians, reverse the
picture if you please. Try to imagine Canada as part of a French empire,
with the descendants of British citizens in the minority. Can you tell
me that if the French empire, of which you would be part, were in danger,
you would be as enthusiastic in defending that empire as would be the
Canadians of French descent? To any man who would say that he would
have the same views and sentiments I would reply that he is not sincere.

Think of the position in which we are placed. Think of the concessions
which the French Canadians and their representatives have been making
to bring about and maintain unity in this great land of ours. I have
no time to enumerate them all, but go over in your minds the concessions that were made by Sir Wilfrid Laurier, by Ernest Lapointe and by
myself, at the risk of losing support and, indeed, with the loss of support
in certain quarters of my province. We are here in the House of Commons, all friends, and as members of a family capable of understanding
the truth. Where are your concessions, you British Canadians, in favour
of the French Canadians? What have you ever done to preserve unity
between the two great races in Canada? Unity has been maintained

owing to concessions made by French Canadians in this House of Commons and elsewhere. These are strong words, but they are the truth and no one can dispute them. The political history of our country is there to sustain my statement.[120]

Cardin argued that there was no more anti-conscription agitation in Quebec than in British Columbia or Nova Scotia, and maintained that the recent British Columbia demonstrations could not be the work of a handful of French Canadians, 'if the soldiers who are there with them did not have the same views, and if the people watching them did not share their views to a large extent.' He agreed with Mr. Howe that the agitation was mostly political, and he regretted that 'this has now become a political issue on both sides.'[121] The debate had made clear that conscription had been the law of the land and had been applied since 1942. He did not think that the volunteers overseas would ask 'that others be sent to help them, through coercion.'[122] He argued that many of the men overseas did not know what they were fighting for, and he believed that beneath the fine words 'most of the countries making up the allied nations are in the end—it may be a secondary consideration—looking after their own interests.'[123]

Cardin criticized the 'extraordinary situation' of a man resigning from the cabinet, 'leaving behind him three or four men who share his views and who, if necessary, will extend the crisis in which we are at the present time.' He declared that the country was entitled to know 'who precipitated the crisis, who caused the change in policy of the government, who brought about the decision which was given to us on November 23.' The ministers who shared Ralston's views should 'stand up and take their responsibility before this house and before the country.' Cardin discounted Mr. King's fear of a wartime election, since one had recently been held in the United States and another in 1917 in Canada, when Laurier fought for his policy and though defeated, emerged 'even greater than he was before.' Cardin remarked bitterly that the prime minister, who had quoted Laurier and Lapointe to justify conscription, should have quoted their words 'in favour of the voluntary system and denouncing the very stand which two or three ministers have forced him to take and who threatened to resign if conscription were not put into effect.'[124]

The Army, the Air Force, and the Navy had competed for recruits, and Canada 'tried to do too much for a country of our size and population.' That was why a need for reinforcements had arisen. Cardin argued that Canada should have followed Australia's course and reduced its armed forces in order to help civilian and war industries. He pressed for an election: 'The sooner we have one, the sooner the clouded atmosphere in which we are now living and have been living for the past five weeks or more will disappear and the sooner we shall be able to follow a policy that will be in the best interests of Canada as well as in the best interests of the allied nations.' He was not afraid of opposition from the party which had long been his: 'I have not ceased to be a Liberal, but I contend that my party, alas, has been moving toward the other side, towards the imperial and Tory spirit.' He paid tribute to Ralston's speech as that of 'a very sincere and trustworthy man, a man who, whatever his opinions may be, deserves the respect and confidence of every member of this house,' but he criticized as 'a bit weak' the former minister's defence of himself against the prime minister's charge that he had been slow in bringing the gravity of the situation before the cabinet.[125]

As the member who had served longest in the House, Cardin made a final plea for the reconciliation of the conflicting opinions of French Canadians, English Canadians, and New Canadians. He appealed to his compatriots of Quebec, 'whatever may be their sentiments, whatever may be their feelings at the present time, to be calm, to take things easy, to reflect before acting, and to remember that they are not only citizens of the province of Quebec but at the same time citizens of Canada as a whole, who desire to see their country in the not distant future, and with the will of all concerned, become a great and independent country.' They had a right to be firm, to be energetic, to freedom of opinion and speech, but they should be careful not to lose 'the advantage of the friendship which we now enjoy to a greater extent than ever before in the English-speaking provinces of Canada.' He urged that men of good will should get together, 'dispense with the military caste, which is a source of trouble,' and think of Canada first.[126]

In a tumultuous House Maxime Raymond, chief of the *Bloc Populaire*, then declared that a government which violated its most solemn pledges did not deserve a vote of confidence. He quoted the prime minister's words in 1942 that the unhappy state of the world was the result of broken pledges, and then recapitulated his pledges against conscription for overseas service.[127] He argued once more that the plebiscite had not relieved the prime minister from his obligations, since his only mandate was to avoid conscription. He charged that the prime minister 'endorses the principle of self-government in his statements and imperialistic tendencies in his acts.'[128] He traced the development of 'camouflaged' conscription since 1942, and urged an end to 'quibbling and dodging' such as the description of conscription under the November order-in-council as 'conditional voluntary service.' He charged that the war effort was already excessive; and questioned the idealistic argument that Canada had gone to war with Germany because it had invaded Poland, when Canada had allied herself with and aided a Russia which had invaded six countries, including Poland. The government's latest action would increase the existing disunion. He held that 'a nation has the right to compel its citizens to fight for its defence but not for the defence of other countries, especially when that nation has already accomplished a war effort of such magnitude.'[129] Confederation was based on the principles of 'provincial autonomy and respect for the rights of minorities, and from a national standpoint, autonomy of Canada with regard to England.' Those who threatened national unity were the 'people who think as imperialists rather than Canadians.' French Canadians were first of all Canadians. 'Too often has the Prime Minister resorted to the argument in favour of national unity, to find justification now in asking for a vote of confidence on a policy most likely to destroy that unity.'[130]

W. E. Harris (Grey-Bruce), a wounded veteran, denied Cardin's statement that the soldiers overseas did not know what they were fighting for. He opposed the Conservative amendment on the grounds that adequate reinforcements had been provided in the past, and that with Ralston and McNaughton in agreement on the present measure, they would be in the future. He denounced the Ontario campaign to make the home defence army, which included 15,000 Ontario men as well as 22,000 from Quebec, a Quebec problem exclusively. He paid tribute to the French-Canadian units with which he had served in Normandy, and to Quebec's 'very considerable' contribution to the armed forces. He closed with a tribute to the prime minister and the government.[131] G. K. Fraser (Peterborough West), made the typical Conservative charge that the King government had 'played favourites with the French Canadians.'[132] F. G. Hoblitzell (Eglinton) showed sympathy for the position of the Quebec members and favored the Conservative amendment, but announced that he would vote for the government motion because the real issue was 'to see that reinforcements are sent overseas without further delay.'[133]

Emmanuel d'Anjou (Rimouski) charged that Quebec had been betrayed, as Premier Godbout and Justice Minister St. Laurent had declared it would be if conscription for overseas service were ever forced upon the country. He saw the order-in-council of November 23 as 'the logical and unavoidable conclusion of the result of the plebiscite,' but declared that the government had no mandate to impose conscription upon Quebec after that province's refusal to free it from its pledges. The government had 'hatefully and brutally deceived' Quebec, and therefore in view of his own promises to his constituents he had quit the Liberal benches and seated himself with the *Bloc* members, 'because that party's platform embodies the ideas and principles for which I have fought since my entrance into public life and to which I intend to remain faithful.' He denounced war profiteers as the advocates of conscription, called for a Canadian flag, and expressed hope that Canada would become independent in the near future.[134] Opening the debate on Friday, December 1, R. W. Mayhew (Victoria, B.C.), supported the government, declaring that 'Anglo-Saxons' were not in favor of compulsion, but 'We adopt it when we have to—and this is one time when we have to.' He denounced the use of the term 'zombie': 'No Canadian who is good enough to wear the King's uniform should be called a zombie,' and defended both the N.R.M.A. men and the general service men serving in Canada.[135] G. S. White (Hastings-Peterborough), in supporting the Conservative amendment, challenged Cardin to put on record in *Hansard* the concessions which French Canadians had made to English Canadians.[136]

Joseph Jean (Mercier), former secretary of Ernest Lapointe, who had resigned that day as parliamentary assistant to Justice Minister St. Laurent, declared his lifelong opposition to conscription and coercion. He believed that 'there has been lack of good will and lack of competence somewhere in using the voluntary system as it should have been used,' when a reinforcement crisis arose after 750,000 volunteers had been sent overseas. He opened a way for members who wished to support the government without supporting conscription by moving an amendment which was seconded by Gaspard Fauteux (Sainte-Marie), to the Conservative amendment: 'That this house is of the opinion that the government has not made certain of adequate and continuous trained reinforcements *by using to the best advantage the general service personnel in Canada and the volunteers overseas without resorting to conscription for service overseas.*' When a question was raised by the leader of the opposition as to whether Mr. Jean had resigned as a parliamentary assistant before making his motion, he declared that he had. The prime minister stated that though there was no reason why a parliamentary assistant should resign before making a motion, both W. C. Macdonald, assistant to Colonel Ralston, and Jean had done so. He expressed the hope that the latter would reconsider his position later on.[137]

L.-T. Tremblay (Dorchester) opened the debate on Monday, December 4, making much of the popular distrust created by the order-in-council, the opposition to the appeal for volunteers from the profiteers who sought to force conscription, and the insults heaped on Quebec N.R.M.A. men in other provinces. He declared:

In a democracy, if democracy is to survive, the majority have not the moral right, though they may have the power, to force upon a minority an obligation which they know this minority is unwilling to assume, especially when that majority, through its authorized and constitutional leaders, have pledged themselves never to impose such an obligation on the minority.[138]

He closed with the question: 'Who has broken the pledge?' Colonel A. J. Brooks (Royal), who had commanded two of the training camps in Canada, made the following statement in reply to Tremblay:

I have had both French and English Canadians in these camps, and I can say truthfully to this house that I do not know of one instance where there was any difference between these two races. They have played together, worked together, drilled together and slept together, and never has there been any trouble between them . . . I know also that overseas our men feel they are all Canadians and that there is no difficulty of the kind the hon. member has mentioned.[139]

In a vehement speech Brooks maintained that the voluntary system had been a 'failure from the very beginning,' and suggested that thousands of the N.R.M.A. men to be sent overseas would go A.W.O.L. He denounced the government's policy as one which was 'even less than half a measure, and in no way meets the requirements of the men overseas,' and had encouraged 'young men in one part of Canada to tear down the flag and to trample it into the dust, to tear down the flag of a country which for one year stood alone.' He called upon French, British, and Jewish Canadians to answer the call of Canadian blood.[140]

Ralph Maybank (Winnipeg South Centre) urged the French Canadians not to 'nurse a persecution complex.' He agreed that English Canadians should try to understand French Canada better, but thought that the French Canadians should also 'try a little harder also to understand us.' He denied that Pastor Shields and the *Globe and Mail* represented English Canada: 'The one is serving some kind of a financial crowd and the other is a mere bigot.' He did not think that a conspiracy had created the crisis, which had arisen from infantry casualties being 50 per cent over estimates, but he did think that once it had arisen it had been exploited by 'the agents of a cabal that wants a chore-boy union government.' He attacked the Conservative leaders, and compared their strategy to that of the Italian Navy.[141] J. W. Noseworthy (York South) declared that the people of Canada did not want a general election, but that they did want 'legislation or an order in council which beyond all shadow of a doubt will provide adequate reinforcements for the future, as well as the present, and legislation which will mobilize all the resources of the country for the further prosecution of the war.' He added that they also wanted 'a ministry in sympathy with that legislation, one upon which they know they can rely to carry it out.'[142] J. R. MacNicol (Davenport) attacked the C.C.F. for having voted against the Conservative motion for an all-out war effort in 1942, and defended Dr. Shields and the *Globe and Mail* before rehearsing the usual Tory arguments. L. A. Mutch (Winnipeg South), a veteran of both wars, supported the government motion.

Frédéric Dorion (Charlevoix-Saguenay), speaking as one 'independent of all political groups,' declared that he wished to associate himself with Mr. Cardin and to congratulate Messrs. Tucker and Harris, who proved that 'in spite of the malicious campaign of the last few weeks there are still in other provinces men of good will who can understand the sentiments of the French Canadians, together with the fundamental basis of Canadian unity.' Attacking the patriotism of Mr. Rose with a veiled reference to his internment in 1939, he denied that the Montrealer had the right 'to speak for French Canadians in this house.'[143] He charged that the debate was unwarranted after the order-in-council had been passed, and that the discussion had served merely 'to provoke a campaign of abuse towards the province of Quebec.' He argued, indeed, that participation and conscription had been settled since the prime minister had visited Hitler in 1937, with the purpose of making it clear that in case of a war of aggression, nothing would keep Canada from Britain's side. He dismissed all the amendments, and declared that the French-Canadian ministers might have avoided the campaign of abuse and the passage of the order-in-council if they had stuck to their guns. He also thought that if the prime minister had maintained his stand for the voluntary system, he would have been returned to office by an 'even larger majority than he has today.' He concluded with the observations that unity did not mean unification, that the two races had different mentalities, and that there could be understanding if the majority did not 'try to overrule the minority and force it to submit to all its wishes.'[144]

Maurice Lalonde (Labelle) supported the Jean subamendment, expressing sympathy for the prime minister but stating that many of his supporters had been placed in an 'unbearable position.'[145] James Sinclair (Vancouver North), an R.C.A.F. officer, declared that he had been converted to total conscription by his experiences in Britain since 1940. He charged that the Army had not made as good use of its manpower as the Air Force, when it had 130,000 general service men and 70,000 conscripts in Canada and a shortage of reinforcements overseas.[146] He had suggested the formation of an R.C.A.F. regiment to serve as infantry, rather than the discharge of surplus airmen. He favored a uniform system of retirement and discharge for all three services, with the use of the whole N.R.M.A. Army on active service, and a 'first-in-first-out' demobilization policy. Though a Liberal, he would vote for the Conservative amendment; if that were defeated, he would support the government motion.

Before the debate continued on Tuesday, December 5, the prime minister in replying to a question stated that in the twenty-six days since November 8, 6,297 men had volunteered for general service, 2,701 from the N.R.M.A. and 3,596 from the general public and the Reserve Army, 'the largest enlistment for a similar period since the outbreak of the war.'[147] J. G. Diefenbaker (Lake Centre) continued the Conservative attack on the order-in-council, arguing that conscription had been the law of the land since Cartier's Militia Act of 1868, and that since 1904, by a provision introduced by Laurier, the militia might be put on active service overseas in case of emergency.[148] He charged that the N.R.M.A. men were being bribed to volunteer. He cited statements of General Laflèche, Justice Minister St. Laurent, Munitions and Supply Minister Howe, Fisheries Minister Bertrand, and General McNaughton, indicating that they favored the voluntary method, as evidence that the government's heart was not in its new policy. He charged that the Jean amendment was designed to allow some members 'to support the government and at the same time remain on friendly terms with their supporters.' He asked whether the prime minister had given any assurance that 16,000 men was the limit, and no further orders would be passed. Mr. King promptly replied that he had 'made no promise to anyone.'[149] Diefenbaker denied that there was any politics in the Conservative amendment. But since reinforcements were on the way, there was no reason why the government should not call an election to see whether or not the people demanded 'equality of service and sacrifice.' A. G. Slaght (Parry Sound) favored the government's course, and charged that the Conservatives were not sincere in moving an amendment in favor of extending the service of N.R.M.A. men to any theater of war, and then excluding Japan as one of those theaters.

Armand Choquette (Stanstead) associated himself with the other *Bloc* members, declaring that their opinions were 'endorsed by the great majority of the Quebec population and by an increasing number of people from other parts of the country.'[150] He charged that political strategy was the cause of the order-in-council: 'The Prime Minister considers himself indispensable and it would seem that, in order to keep him in power, the sacrifice of a few lives and the violation of a few principles are well worth while.'[151] He made an appeal to all Quebec members, from the justice minister down to the lowliest backbencher, to keep their pledges and refuse to support the government policy. He denounced the Jean amendment as inspired by the prime minister. He rejected the idea that the order-in-council was a compromise between two opposing points of view, seeing in it simply an implementation of Bill 80. He defended Canon Groulx and Laurendeau from the charge of isolationism, and associated himself with them in saying that the French Canadians 'do not want to isolate Canada from the rest of the world' or 'to separate Quebec from the other parts of the country':

We are above all Canadians and we wish that Canada as a whole should belong first to its citizens and that it should be the heritage of each and every one of us. We demand complete independence for our country and I do not think that the fact of being supreme masters of our destinies could isolate us from other countries and raise a China wall between ourselves and our neighbours.

Mr. Speaker, those are fables deliberately spread by politicians much more concerned with the unity of their own party than with national unity. We consider the whole of Canada as our motherland ... It should not be an English or a French Canada, but a Canada where both races would enjoy the same rights, the same privileges and the same opportunities, not only in Quebec but also in the eight other provinces of the dominion.[152]

Lt.-Colonel Hugues Lapointe (Lotbinière), the son of the late minister of justice and a veteran who had returned from the front within the last three weeks, censured the criticism which had been directed at General McNaughton. He stated his belief that 'the voluntary system is the only practical system of recruiting an efficient army in the circumstances in which we find ourselves in this dominion. . . . That system has not been a failure, and it can still bring about adequate results if certain individuals and responsible bodies in this country will use it for the purpose for which it was intended and not as an instrument to overthrow the King government.'[153] Parliament was faced with an accomplished fact, however, and in view of the prime minister's declarations in 1942, that members would have an opportunity to express their approval or disapproval if Bill 80 were put into effect, and the introduction of the present motion of confidence, the Jean subamendment offered 'the only way any hon. member may have of expressing his views on or his approval of the order in council.'

Lapointe had first been elected to the House in 1940, because the people of Lotbinière 'believed that the tradition of the Liberal party of which I was the candidate, and the doctrine which had always been preached, rightly or wrongly, was one of no conscription, and they selected me to follow that doctrine.'[154] He believed that he had 'attended as good a political school as any other hon. member in this house':

I have always been taught that politics was not a game of diplomacy, but that it was the most serious task to which any man could devote his talent and ability, and that to represent one's fellow citizens in the House of Commons was possibly the greatest honour and privilege to be vested in any man. I was also taught that pledges and promises once given had to be kept . . . Personally I cannot go back on the word which I solemnly gave to the people whom I represent in this house, especially when I am not convinced that this order in council was necessary for the winning of the war and the security of Canada. Furthermore, as regards this point, I will not permit any man to doubt my sincerity or impute any political motives to my action. It is purely a question to be settled between myself and my own conscience. It may be considered as a selfish attitude to take, but I would rather withdraw from public life than have it be said by any man who placed his faith in me that I had failed to keep the word I had given.[155]

Lapointe did not believe that the sending of N.R.M.A. men would relieve the pressure on the men at the front, because 'they will be swamped among the men who are already there.' He declared that 'you need a man of determination, of character and courage who will go forward under any conditions, in order to fill the ranks of the infantry.' He did not question the courage of any of the N.R.M.A. men, and declared that he had never heard the term 'zombie' until he returned to Canada. 'There is no monopoly of courage on the battle front—although there seems to be some here in Canada.' He criticized the debate and the countrywide campaign which had been carried on of 'playing on the sentiments and emotions of mothers, sisters and wives.'

I ask those people, and I ask hon. members who may have sons in the infantry in the front line to-night: whom would they rather have to-night in a slit trench along the front line, fighting it out, possibly holding back a counter-attack under the most intense conditions; whom would they rather have, the man who is there because he wanted to go there and who will stay there to fight it out and die, if necessary, or the man who is there simply because order in council P.C. 8891 was passed by this government?[156]

Lapointe doubted that draftees would be welcome in the front line, and he was skeptical that the draftees were 'eager to go overseas, and were just waiting for the government to assume its responsibilities,' as certain commanders in Canada had asserted. But to him the important point was not coercion but the loss of public confidence:

In my mind, what is even more important than that possibly 15,000 Canadians will be sent to serve overseas, against their will, in spite of the pledges made by the government, is the fact that for a long time the people of Canada will have lost some of the faith they usually have in their public men . . . It is not the judgment which the electors may pass now, at a time when the country is going through a period of mob hysteria, that is important; it is the judgment they will pass after the war is over, when they can analyze the facts in their true light, in an atmosphere of peace.

Lapointe did not wish to share the responsibility for undermining the Canadian people's faith and confidence in its public men. He expressed great admiration for the prime minister and deep sympathy for his tragic position, and deeply regretted that 'because of the wording of the motion now before the house I am not able to express to him the confidence I have in his ability to run this country during the difficult times through which we are now passing.' He believed he spoke for the people he represented when he told the prime minister that 'there is no one else whom they want to see as the head of the government of Canada, but on the other hand they cannot forget the breaking of a pledge which to them was sacred.' He expressed the hope that 'once the turmoil of this battle is ended, Canadians will realize at last that they should not be separated from one another, that they should not hate one another because of a mere political issue.'[157] He spoke of how men from Toronto, Regina, and New Brunswick had reinforced his company of the Régiment de la Chaudière in the D-day landing when it lost more than half its strength; and how there had been no national disunity at Carpiquet, Falaise, Calais, and Boulogne; and urged: 'Surely if the men at the front can achieve this national unity and attain this spirit of brotherhood the people back in Canada, and especially hon. members of this house, can fight the war on the home front following the example set for them by our Canadian forces overseas.' Otherwise, he felt, and thought he spoke for many of the men overseas, that 'if here in Canada we cannot achieve a community of spirit; if we cannot learn to understand one another better, then the hardships, the miseries and the losses we shall have suffered during this war may well have been in vain.'[158] Clarence Gillis (Cape Breton South) hailed Lapointe's speech as 'a breath of fresh air' before expressing grave doubts about the government's policy and restating the C.C.F. stand.

Mr. St. Laurent, speaking on December 6 as the debate drew to a close, indicated that he had been discussing 'the real truths of the matter' with his fellow members from Quebec. He spoke of the needs of total war and reviewed Canada's contribution, with the observation that 'all has to go on and must be kept in full balance until full victory is achieved.'[159] He had believed that object could be attained by the voluntary system until the evening of November 22, but had accepted the change of policy when it was pointed out that the Canadian Army might be paralyzed by the need of infantry, and that inadequate reserves might affect the morale of men in the fighting line. He realized what the reaction in Quebec might be to his action: 'But I came here to do a war job, and because it was felt by the Prime Minister, rightly or wrongly, that I could be of some help, I feel I must still go on, whatever may be the difficulties of the task, so long as it is made apparent to me that these difficulties arise out of facts which have a bearing on the security of the men who are doing so much more for us than anything we can do for them.' He still felt and hoped that compulsion might not be necessary to secure the needed men, but no chance could be taken, and he had decided to 'stand or fall with the Prime Minister.'[160]

Mr. St. Laurent thought the Jean subamendment was apt to be defeated, and he appealed to those who supported it to accept 'that democratic decision in a democratic way':

I am sure they can do so without accepting the concept of democracy which is sometimes asserted, the concept that it is both a legal right, and a proper exercise of that right, for the majority to assert its will at all times and in all occasions regardless of the feelings and views of the minority and of the reasons for such feelings and views. That is not my concept of the kind of democracy suited to free men; the kind of democracy for which the free nations are waging this war. It is not the kind of democracy which was envisaged by the fathers of confederation; or the kind of democracy which will bring to full fruition the constitution that unites in one nation the various elements which make up our Canadian people.

The will of the majority must be respected and it will prevail. But I trust that, here in Canada, the majority will always, as it is doing in this case, assert that will only after giving due consideration to the feelings and views of the minority and to the reasons for such feelings and views, and then only to the extent to which the minority is sincerely convinced that the general interests of the whole body politic require that it be thus asserted.[161]

He appealed to all members of the House, whether they wished 'to do more or to do less than the order in council provides, to unite and to assert to the men overseas that this nation, from one ocean to the other, stands pledged to a victory that will be decisive and that will endure. . . . Let us neglect nothing that is necessary for victory, but on the other hand let us strive to avoid doing or saying anything that is not really necessary and that might destroy or impair the unity which has made and is still required to make our efforts strong and constant and successful.' Mr. St. Laurent, as titular leader of the Quebec Liberals, rallied many of Mr. King's wavering supporters by his wholehearted and courageous acceptance of the prime minister's decision, which then seemed likely to spell the sudden end of his political career.

10

At the opening of the evening sitting on December 6, the prime minister announced that he had met with the leader of the opposition and the leaders of the C.C.F. and Social Credit groups, and that they had agreed that the debate might be well wound up by the following night, since 'if it were to continue for any length of time it would have an unsettling effect rather than otherwise throughout the country.'[162] It was thereupon agreed to have morning sittings 'until the completion of the current business.'

The Conservative attack on the government motion and the division within the cabinet continued, with H. R. Jackman (Rosedale) pointing out that Mr. St. Laurent was the only minister who had spoken on behalf of the government motion.[163] G. A. Cruickshank (Fraser Valley), a Liberal veteran of the first war, declared that he would vote for the opposition amendment, but if it were defeated would support the main motion, like his colleague Sinclair.[164] Jean-François Pouliot (Témiscouata) explained his departure from the government benches by the observation that the order-in-council was 'the drop of water that made the glass overflow' for him, and that the prime minister had 'since the beginning of the war preferred to take advice from his opponents to taking it from his supporters.'[165] After reviewing his political career, he charged that the Liberal party was dead and the prime minister had killed it.[166] Armand Cloutier (Drummond-Arthabaska) declared that he would vote against the government motion because he was opposed to conscription. He realized that the prime minister was 'the victim of a foul conspiracy hatched by a majority blinded by old prejudices and by new political-military and financial schemes,' and retained confidence in him on other matters than war policy.[167] Similar anti-conscriptionist views, coupled with reluctance to break with their leader, were expressed by other Quebec Liberals. J.-A. Crète (Saint-Maurice-Laflèche), Maurice Bourget (Lévis), and Charles Parent (Quebec West and South), hailed Hugues Lapointe's stand.

On December 7, W. C. Macdonald (Halifax), who had resigned as Ralston's parliamentary assistant, declared he would support the government motion. Colonel Ralston himself for some days past had taken issue with Conservative speakers as the prospect of a coalition under his leadership faded. H.-E. Brunelle (Champlain) bitterly attacked the Conservatives for putting Quebec on trial, and brought out the homely truth that whenever 'there was trouble in our country between the different races it never came from us but because somebody always wanted to interfere with our way of living and our way of thinking.'[168] He saw the current crisis as a repetition of the 1917 one, and quoted the observation of Major David Maclellan of the *Halifax Chronicle*:

As a Canadian with as much British blood as the most energetic flag-waver in the land, it strikes me that English-speaking Canadians may well hang their heads in shame for the stupid, nasty smear campaign against Quebec. Tolerance that has somehow taken root in the Canadian army overseas is, and has been, sadly lacking here. It is a tragedy that many Canadians cannot capture the spirit and resolution which animates their sons and brothers overseas.

Quebec's attitude toward conscription has been no secret for many years, yet, completely ignoring the fact that almost two-thirds of the home defence troops come from other provinces, some Canadians have been vicious enough to pour abuse, all the abuse, on the steadfast, warm-hearted people of Quebec.

For a minority speaking another tongue and subscribing to another faith, the record of cooperation of Quebec residents has been splendid. The record of relations between English and French-speaking Canadians has been blotted repeatedly by the pin pricks, the rude remarks and the stinging insults that have been hurled at Quebec. Regardless of right or wrong, Quebec has every right to be resentful; and the amazing circumstance is that she had not permitted herself to give more forceful evidence of her resentment.

The Canadian voluntary system has worked throughout this war. It can continue to work if given a real chance. One thing is more important than the controversy agitating Canada to-day, and that is the Canadian nation.[169]

Mr. Brunelle retained his confidence in the prime minister but had lost faith in the conscriptionist ministers, and planned to vote against both the Conservative amendment and the government motion.

Sasseville Roy (Gaspé) charged that the debate had been useless, since the prime minister had declared on November 27 in introducing the motion of confidence that it was not a question of approval or disapproval of conscription.[170] He held the Liberal party with its large majority responsible for conscription, and declared that he would vote against both the motion and the amendments. Though he accepted conscription as inevitable, he made a final plea against it: 'If we are Canadians, even if we like England, for God's sake do not let us bring this bitter division into Canada which may do more harm than any good we can ever hope to do by sending a few men overseas.'[171] The prime minister subsequently denied a charge which Mr. Roy had made on the basis of the memoirs of Sir Robert Borden that he had been ready to join the Union Government in the summer of 1917.[172]

Wilfrid Lacroix (Quebec-Montmorency) declared that the Jean subamendment in effect recommended a more vigorous war effort, and asked 'Why we should keep on sacrificing more Canadian lives when Frenchmen, Belgians, and Dutchmen are more than willing to take their revenge?'[173] He called for gradual withdrawal of Canadian troops from the front, and reiterated his opposition to 'every form of participation.' Raymond Eudes (Hochelaga) paid tribute to Canada's war effort, and declared that he would vote against the government motion on anti-conscriptionist grounds, though he backed its policy as a whole and had no wish to favor isolationism, which could 'only bring trouble, worry and misfortune to my fellow-citizens.'[174] Sarto Fournier (Maisonneuve-Rosemont) made a plea for the government to reverse its conscription policy, lest the measure should have the same post-war effects as it had had after the first war.[175] Joseph Lafontaine (Mégantic-Frontenac), the father of three volunteers, favored the Jean subamendment, stating that 'In opposing conscription I am upholding a principle which has inspired all my life; for the French Canadians and for myself what counts above all else is national pride.'[176] D. King Hazen (St. John-Albert), in backing the Conservative amendment in a notably tolerant speech, paid tribute to Mr. St. Laurent's speech as a contribution to national unity, and declared that he had never blamed the French Canadians for their stand. T. V. Grant (Kings), a believer in the voluntary system, favored the government motion as the lesser of two evils. P.-J.-A. Cardin favored the Jean subamendment, despite its 'poor' wording, because it backed the voluntary system and opposed conscription.[177]

The Jean subamendment was lost by a vote of 168 to 43, with 5 English-speaking Quebec members supporting it. The Conservative amendment was lost by a vote of 170 to 44, with George Russell Boucher (Carleton) and Norman Jacques (Wetaskiwin) supporting it.

Stanley Knowles (Winnipeg North Centre), charged that the government motion was admittedly only a vote of confidence in the government 'as a tool to administer a law which is now in effect,' and that it did not present the issue before the country. He moved as an amendment to the main motion the same amendment which M. J. Coldwell had moved as a subamendment on November 27 and which had then been ruled out of order.[178] The speaker again ruled the motion out of order, and the ruling was sustained by a vote of 176 to 20, when Mr. Coldwell appealed it to the House.

Mrs. Dorise Nielsen (North Battleford) opened the debate that evening by endorsing the remarks of Mr. Rose on the position of the Labor-Progressive party, and by agreeing with Leslie Roberts' charge in the *Canadian Mining Reporter* that 'What currently goes on in parliament and press is no political filibuster but sheer political gangsterism, led by men ready to divide and destroy Canada if in the process they can also destroy King.'[179] She declared that the farmers of Saskatchewan sympathized with the French Canadians; that the trades unions supported the government's action; and that the necessity for maintaining unity was generally appreciated throughout Canada. She described the order-in-council as a compromise—'It is more than some French-speaking people feel they should be called upon to support; it is a little less than some English-speaking people feel is necessary'[180]—and called upon all to support it. E. G. Hansell (MacLeod) declared that 90 percent of his constituents whom he had circularized before the special session had favored conscription of the draftees.[181] He was cut off by the speaker before moving a new Social Credit amendment, which was then moved by C. E. Johnston (Bow River):

That this house, while not being requested to support all the policies of the government, will aid the government in sending immediately adequate reinforcements to our men overseas, and will also aid the government at all such times as it wages a vigorous war effort against the totalitarian powers; an effort consistent with Canada's ability and position in the world.[182]

Maxime Raymond challenged Frédéric Dorion's statement that only Liguori Lacombe and Wilfrid Lacroix had voted against participation in the war on September 9, 1939, referring to his own record and that of Mr. Woodsworth. He was contradicted by Mr. Lacombe.[183] The Speaker then ruled the Social Credit amendment out of order, and on appeal to the House was sustained by a division of 165 to 33.

Philippe Picard then moved an amendment in the sense of the rejected Jean subamendment, 'That this house will aid the government in a policy of maintaining an efficient war effort but does not approve of compulsory service overseas,' to clarify the position of those who opposed Bill 80 and the order-in-council.[184] The Speaker ruled the amendment out of order, despite the protests of its seconder, Mr. Tucker, and Mr. Coldwell, who declared that no opportunity was being given opponents of the government to express their views in motions. The latter then moved that the government motion be amended to read: 'That this house will aid the government in maintaining a vigorous war effort,' so that those in favor of a vigorous war effort but not of government policies could support it. The prime minister declared that the amendment was acceptable to him, since it expressed his meaning.[185] The House agreed to the prime minister's motion not to adjourn at 11 p.m. Cardin charged that all the

proposed amendments had beclouded the issue; protested against the
change in wording as meaningless; and declared that he would vote
against 'the motion of confidence now adorned with a few flowers
that have been strewn over it by the leader of the C.C.F. party.'[186]

The leader of the opposition rejected Coldwell's charges that
the Conservatives had tricked those who wanted to oppose the
government, by revising their motions between November 22 and
November 27, and described the Coldwell amendment as 'tanta-
mount to a government amendment moved through the lips of the
hon. member.'[187] He accused the C.C.F. group of making common
cause with the government. Mr. Knowles reviewed the C.C.F.'s
share in the debate. He agreed partially with Mr. Cardin in saying
the government motion as amended was no longer a vote of confidence but 'a pious resolution of the house to the effect that we will
agree to aid the government in maintaining a vigorous war effort,
and then close this session and go home.'[188] He charged the leader
of the opposition with reflecting on those who had contributed
to the war effort, and declared that the Progressive Conservative
party was 'just plain sore' at the failure of their effort to make
political capital of the issue. He felt that 'in the government's
readiness to accept the amendment we have moved at this last
moment we have won, not just for this group but for this parliament
and for the people of Canada, a victory over the crisis through which
we have passed.'[189] Mr. Picard asked whether the government had
again changed its policy, and urged that the C.C.F. amendment
should be declared out of order, since the amended motion had the
same sense as the subamendment which he had earlier moved, and
which had been declared out of order. Mr. Pouliot charged that
there had been an understanding between the C.C.F. leader and the
prime minister, and Mr. Coldwell denied the charge.[190] Jean-
François Pouliot declared that the amended motion was vague,
incoherent, and sullied by the C.C.F.[191] Mr. Blackmore, as leader
of the Social Credit group, then urged support of the government
motion because it provided for reinforcements, which was the
main issue. The C.C.F. amendment was accepted by a division of
141 to 70.

The prime minister made a final plea for support of the fighting
men overseas, and censured the leader of the opposition for concerning himself 'almost exclusively . . . with matters of petty politics
between the different political parties in this country'[192] at such a
time. Restating his opinion that the amended resolution conveyed to
him the same meaning as the original motion, he thanked Mr. Coldwell for his desire to show that the House was 'united and determined
upon having a vigorous war effort in support of our men overseas; a
policy of maintaining a vigorous war effort.' He agreed with Messrs.

Coldwell and Knowles that the government was not asking for an unlimited vote of confidence in all its policies, and urged that the motion 'be carried in no uncertain way.' He declared that Mr. Blackmore had touched the 'real note' with his observation that the eyes of the world were upon Canada, and declared that 'No succour could come to the enemy equal to that he will receive from anything that goes to show that a parliament in any part of the British commonwealth is not united in support of its fighting men, and in its determination to do the utmost that can be done in helping to make a great war effort a complete success.'[193] Referring to the words of Lapointe, his 'young friend and gallant soldier, the son of the truest friend I have ever had in this House of Commons,' he held that the men overseas would be either encouraged or dispirited by the result of the vote. He admitted that it might be difficult for some members to explain their support of the government in its course, but that he had 'more faith than some who have spoken in the intelligence of your electors and in their hearts,' if the situation were properly explained.

With a second cryptic reference to the seriousness of the present and future situations, he urged members and the people of Canada to 'beware of doing anything or letting anything be done that may give those enemies or the people of any land cause to believe that the democracies are weakening, that within and between themselves they are becoming divided with the consequence that in their own eyes the power our enemies, present or future, may possess or come to possess may come to loom much greater than anything they behold elsewhere.' He declared that the day had passed 'when local issues or provincial issues—I might almost say the issues in any one country itself—can be separated from the larger question of how this world is going to hold together in the next few years in a way which will enable men to enjoy liberty, and to preserve their lives and their homes.'[194] As to broken pledges and lost faith in public men, he admitted that he, like the leaders of all parties, had in 1939 given anti-conscription pledges 'to the country as a whole, and not to any province or section of the country.' The result of the plebiscite had freed the government and all parties from these pledges; and Bill 80 had provided freedom to introduce overseas conscription if necessary. He had pledged himself to use that power if necessary, and by invoking it, he felt that he was keeping faith with 'this House of Commons, with the people of Canada, and with the fighting men in Canada's army overseas.'[195]

The amended motion was supported on division, a little after 1 a.m. on December 8, by 143 to 70. Though 32 French-Canadian Quebec members voted against the government, Mackenzie King had won an overwhelming and incredible victory over Tory and nationalist opposition. These two poles of Canadian politics were not brought together in 1944 as they had been to defeat Laurier in 1911, largely thanks to Colonel Ralston's loyal refusal to lend himself to a predominantly Conservative coalition government. The support of the C.C.F. and Social Credit groups offset the defection of Quebec Liberals who broke with Mr. King and Mr. St. Laurent. The result of the conscription debate was an index of the enormous development of Canadian national feeling in a third of a century. It was also a tribute to the consummate political skill of the man who had won a victory out of what had generally been regarded as certain defeat when the special session met on November 22.

II

The Senate was belatedly called on November 17 to meet on November 22, after Senator C. C. Ballantyne had expressed the view in the press on November 16 that it, as well as the House, should assemble. When it met, the government leader, J. H. King, promptly proposed adjournment in order that senators might attend the House debate. Senator Ballantyne, as Conservative leader, approved this course, but regretted that the Senate had not been called at the same time as the House 'in one of the greatest crises through which the world has ever passed.' When the Senate met again on November 24, Ballantyne asked whether the government would send the trained N.R.M.A. men overseas first under the order-in-council announced the previous day. With General McNaughton still under cross-examination by the House, Senator King deferred a statement on behalf of the government until November 28, while charging 'a couple of newspapers published in two of our great cities' with printing editorials inspired by 'the idea of embarrassing the government in its war effort.'[196] The Senate met again on November 28 and 29, merely to adjourn while the vote of confidence debate was carried on in the House.

Finally, on November 30 Senator King defended the prime minister and the war effort, and warned of the danger of arousing public opinion. He decried the use of the term 'zombie' and the conscription cry, which he said had had 'a disastrous effect upon one great political party.' He quoted Meighen's Hamilton and Bagot speeches of 1926, and Dr. Manion's pledge against conscription in 1940. Senator Ballantyne replied for the Conservatives, denouncing the government's manpower policy and its creation of 'two armies.' He made much of the fact that at the Winnipeg Convention of December 9–11, 1942, which had chosen John Bracken as leader, the Conservative Party had pledged 'support to the limit of our resources' to the armed services in 'reinforcements, equipment, and munitions of war.' He declared: 'Not only was that our policy in 1942, but it has been our policy ever since, and it is the policy we shall stand on to the end.'[197] Denying Liberal charges that conscription had been ineffective in the last war and asserting that a striking similarity existed between the situation then and at present, Ballantyne cited official army figures showing that while voluntary enlistments in the ten months preceding the application of the Military Service Act in January 1918 had numbered 51,101, a total of 154,560 men were obtained in the following ten months under the Act.[198] During the subsequent debate Senator Ballantyne, a veteran of the Union government, declared that the bitterness stirred up in 1917 was 'nothing compared to the bitterness that prevails today.'[199]

Senator Chapais, the only French Canadian who took a notable part in the Senate discussion of the issue, reiterated his opposition to conscription under Mackenzie King, as under Sir Robert Borden. He expressed the view that conscription might be justifiable for home defence against aggression, but 'conscription or coercion for the purpose of tearing from their homes the pick of our young men, to send them to foreign countries across the oceans and even to the antipodes, to fight on far-removed fields of battle, is an abusive and tyrannical measure.' He described conscription as foreign to the British tradition, and saw no reason for it with victory in sight. He cited with approval C. G. Power's declaration in the House: 'We have no right to tear this country asunder at this stage, and in this state of the war.' He also quoted several statements of the prime minister to bolster his argument that Canada had attempted too great a war effort, and used Ralston's 1941 statement against conscription in the name of national unity in his concluding protest against 'all those excesses in words or actions which we are now witnessing':

We are going to have conscription, in violation of all pledges and promises. We are going to have that drastic measure which has divided us, which will divide us again, and which we ought to have avoided. . . .[200]

Senator Chapais' eloquence in French was largely wasted on his English-speaking colleagues. It was the only clear-cut expression in the Senate of complete opposition to conscription, although Liberal and Conservative Senators wrangled over the issue largely along party lines, despite the theoretical non-political character of the upper chamber. The most notable speeches made before the Senate adjourned on December 5 were those of J. A. Calder, a Western Liberal and a member of the Union government in 1917, who made a thoughtful and moderate criticism of the government's policy, calling conscription 'a national rather than a purely local issue';[201] and of Major-General W. A. Griesbach, who made an all-out conscriptionist one which expressed the extreme militarist view of his generation of English Canadians. He was the only speaker to oppose English Canada to French Canada:

> We were told that if we wanted national unity, we should have stayed out of this war; and that now we are in it, we should do as little as possible. Honourable senators, that is too high a price to pay for national unity . . . The truth is that a majority of people in this country are fed up with trying to purchase national unity at a price that is too high. We will not pay that price. What we do hope to have in this country is democratic rule by the majority, for a change. We hope that our public men and leaders will have the intestinal fortitude to carry out that policy, let the chips fall where they may.[202]

The Senate served simply as a forum for the expression of the views of the older generation of Canadians during the special session, for it had no official business before it and merely commented on developments in the House.

12

Feeling rose very high in Quebec at the end of November during the early stages of the debate at Ottawa. It was reported that Union Jacks were torn down or burnt at Chicoutimi and Rimouski in response to the slogan launched by Maxime Raymond and echoed by René Chaloult that 'independence is the fitting reply to conscription.' The *Bloc* held mass meetings in Montreal and Quebec and sought to make political capital of the crisis, but the French press of all shades of opinion appealed for calm and minimized the disturbances which were made much of outside the province. Though French Canada was generally united in its opposition to conscription, there was a considerable current of opinion which tacitly or openly favored support of the King government in order 'to avoid a much greater evil.' As feeling rose, the French press turned from defence of Quebec's attitude to attacks on the 'clique of colonels' and on 'St. James Street,' since militarism and big business were thought to be allied in an effort to upset the King government.

In view of the fevered atmosphere, the actual disturbances on November 29 in Montreal and Quebec were somewhat anticlimactic. In Montreal, after a *Bloc Populaire* mass meeting at St. James Market at which André Laurendeau called for 'a united front against conscription' and denounced 'the dictatorship of the majority as being as tyrannical as any Fascism,'[203] a crowd of young men estimated to number 2,000 paraded through the financial district, breaking the windows of the National Selective Service office, *Le Canada*, the Bank of Montreal, the Montreal Trust Company, and other business firms. The *Star* reported that a march against its office and that of the *Gazette* was headed off by the police. On November 30 the *Star* ran a frontpage editorial headed 'This Rioting Must Stop,' which asserted the constitutional right to object to conscription at public meetings, but called for firm repression of outbreaks against law and order. Asserting that 'this country wants no repetition of 1917' and that 'the best elements of Quebec itself want no such repetition,' the *Star* urged 'these young hoodlums . . . to heed the counsel of saner elements who know that Quebec's relationship with the rest of Canada may depend for years to come upon its attitude toward the decisions taken by the people's Government and Parliament.'

Le Devoir, deploring on November 30 the Chicoutimi and Rimouski incidents, recalled its editorial comment on November 27 that 'burning or tearing down flags gets us nowhere, is of no use and can do much harm to the cause it claims to serve,' and added that 'breaking windows is a silly thing to do,' finding both types of demonstration 'equally regrettable.' It cited the *Gazette's* report that 'In the majority of cases, the windows were broken by youngsters out for a lark, who joined the parade as it left the St. James Market Place,' in its protest against giving a false picture of the scenes which had occurred the previous night. In Quebec windows were broken by a mob of young men at the office of the conscriptionist *Chronicle-Telegraph* and at the home of Justice Minister St. Laurent.[204] But after these minor outbursts of popular feeling, which attained no such proportions as the 1917 disturbances, French Canada quickly calmed down and accepted the inevitable with fairly good grace. Fortunately no blood was shed and the demonstrations were wisely put down by local police rather than by troops, although some English Canadians, heedless of the lesson of 1917, had been talking brashly about the advisability of using machine guns to make Quebec accept the will of the rest of Canada.

The reluctant acceptance of a measure abhorrent to the French-Canadian mind was evident in the editorial comments on the vote of confidence in the King government. *Le Soleil* thus expressed the attitude towards Mr. King of the Quebec Liberals, whose federal representatives had mostly voted against the government: 'His former followers of the Province of Quebec are quite willing to believe that the application of a detestable measure will be less cruel under his direction than it would have been under any other government than his; but they feel themselves deceived and wronged by the politician they have trusted for twenty-five years.' *L'Action Catholique*, heading its comment 'A Happy Outcome to a Distressing Crisis,' expressed its continued opposition to conscription and its criticism of King's successive concessions, but added:

We prefer this verdict to an overthrow of the government for three reasons: we like a government that is conscriptionist 'in spite of itself' better than a conscriptionist government angry because compulsion has not been used sooner; we like a government which has reluctantly sacrificed Quebec better than a government which might have sought to sacrifice us still more, if not to be revenged upon us for our anti-conscriptionist stand; we like a government which has approved the recall of French-Canadian recruits to Quebec better than a government which might have cancelled this recall and ordered a repressive discipline very dangerous for peace in military camps and elsewhere.

. . . Just like its representatives in Ottawa, the Quebec electorate prefers the maintenance of the government to an election, but it reproves its policy of compulsion.

La Patrie hailed the vote of confidence as 'a solution which should be acceptable to all those who, opposed to conscription, will stop to reflect what any other alternative would have meant.' It regretted the 'application of a principle which the vast majority of our people reject, as the votes of our members show'; but added: 'It had become evident from the very first hours following the meeting of Parliament that the crisis could not be settled in the absolute way desired by the Province of Quebec, and that it could only end in a compromise.'

Le Canada hailed King's triumph over a 'conspiracy' of Tories and Laurentian nationalists, such as had confronted Laurier a generation before. *Le Devoir* thought Mr. King had won a false if astounding triumph:

He has brought to naught the efforts of all the powerful enemies who were leagued to defeat him . . . The vast plot which was hatched against him brought together the Conservative politicians, almost the whole of the Anglo-Canadian press, numerous conscriptionist elements among the Liberals, the military elements and probably also behind the scenes the big financial interests. The press and the Canadian Legion brilliantly succeeded in arousing public opinion in the English-speaking provinces; the soldiers sabotaged the attempt of General McNaughton to give new life to the voluntary system policy, but those who were chosen as the chief executors of the coup, Colonel Ralston and Conservative Party leaders, failed in ability and decision at the critical moment. Mr. King therefore retains power, but he has won this triumph at the sacrifice of his dignity, at the sacrifice of his friends and those who were faithfully devoted to him, and probably also at the sacrifice of the future of his party and the place it would have been able to occupy in the political history of Canada.[205]

This view of the crisis was generally held in French Canada.

The Montreal mayoralty contest in December between Camillien Houde, campaigning as a victim of arbitrary internment and as an opponent of conscription, and Adhémar Raynault, who proclaimed his belief in order and in full collaboration with the provincial and federal authorities, provided a useful safety valve at this time for pent-up anti-conscriptionist sentiment, which was probably stronger in Montreal than anywhere else in the province. Houde, backed only by *Montréal-Matin*, was re-elected to his old office by a comfortable margin, with French districts voting heavily in his favor and English districts supporting his opponent. When the result was known, *La Presse*, *Le Canada*, and *La Patrie* warned the victor that he had received only a municipal mandate, which was not to be used as a springboard to Quebec or Ottawa.

Premier Duplessis, the other leader likely to exploit Quebec's reaction against Ottawa as a result of the conscription measure, reaffirmed himself a champion of provincial autonomy and of the pact theory of Confederation in an address to the Quebec Saint-Jean-Baptiste Society at this time. Provincial Treasurer Onésime Gagnon, speaking at a Montreal business dinner, made the first statement of the Duplessis government on the expropriation of the Montreal Light, Heat & Power, calling it 'dictatorial,' 'Bolshevist,' and 'a disgrace to our statute books.' He also denounced the C.C.F. Party, likening it to National Socialism, and declared that Quebec would remain as 'a bulwark of security and stability.'[206] Though the Duplessis government had protested officially against the conscription measure, it now seemed evident in the light of these statements that it would be more Tory than nationalist in character. The provincial Liberals, launching their own organ *Le Canadien* to symbolize their break with the federal party on the conscription issue, renewed their bid for labor's support under the influence of the younger members of the party, who sought to halt the gains of the C.C.F. and Labor-Progressive groups at this period when the Quebec masses had largely lost confidence in both of the traditional parties.

The military outcome of the conscription crisis was long shrouded by censorship. The order-in-council of November 23 caused a wave of desertion among the N.R.M.A. soldiers chosen for overseas service when they were moved to eastern camps and given embarkation leave. Wild rumors on this score went unchecked, except by the natural lull after the intense storm of public opinion in November and by the distraction of the Christmas holidays. Finally on January 20, 1945, it was announced that of the 10,000 men warned to report for the sailings of January 3 and 10, 7,800 had been at one time A.W.O.L. or overdue, and that 6,300 were still absent on January 16. There were disturbances in some of the camps, both in Quebec and Ontario, as late as February 24, but absenteeism declined sharply in the case of the third sailing and was nominal in the case of the fourth. Of the total of 14,500 N.R.M.A. men warned for service overseas, 4,082 were still unaccounted for at the end of March, according to the statement of D. C. Abbott, parliamentary assistant to the defence minister, on April 5.[207]

The distribution of absentees by military districts of enrollment was then given as follows:

M.D. 1, 2, & 3 (Ontario)	450
M.D. 4 & 5 (Quebec)	2,400
M.D. 6 & 7 (Maritimes)	100
M.D. 10, 12, & 13 (Prairies)	1,000
Pacific Command	150
	4,100

The number of N.R.M.A. men sent overseas by military districts was then given as follows:

M.D. 1, 2, & 3 (Ontario)	3,466
M.D. 4 & 5 (Quebec)	2,391
M.D. 6 & 7 (Maritimes)	888
M.D. 10, 12, & 13 (Prairies)	3,899
Pacific Command	1,192
	11,836

It was also stated at the same time that 10,279 N.R.M.A. men had converted to active service since November 1—about half in November and December—and over 2,400 former N.R.M.A. men had gone overseas as general service men.[208] In all, 12,908 N.R.M.A. men were sent overseas, the balance of the 16,000 provided for under the order-in-council not being needed. Casualties during November, December, and January proved considerably fewer than anticipated by the October estimate, and reinforcements overseas in April were 75 per cent over the estimates of the secret session.[209] From February until the end of hostilities in Europe 'there was no serious difficulty in keeping our battalions in the field up to strength, and no question of disbanding Canadian formations ever arose,' according to the official history of the Canadian Army in World War II.[210]

In other words, Canada had nearly split itself apart in anticipation of a situation which did not materialize. The reinforcement crisis of 1944 was in great measure an artificial one brought on by the unscrupulous efforts of a party long in opposition to win power at any cost. The stake was not military victory in Europe, which was already assured, or the defence of Canada's reputation and honor, which had already been upheld beyond imputation, but control of Canada in a postwar world full of dangers for the conservative-minded.

The 1944 conscription crisis also provided another example of the periodic clashes of two very different Canadian mentalities. While the French Canadian frequently relieves his pent-up emotions, he does not allow emotion to sway him from following a reasonable course of action dictated by logic, although he may nurse bitterness long afterwards. On the other hand the English Canadian is much less given to emotional reactions, but when he does let common sense and reason yield to them, the outbreak is much more serious, though shortlived. The 1944 crisis was fortunately marked by less violence than the 1917–18 one, and hence its aftermath was much milder and shorter than was anticipated at the time. It is probable that the issue of conscription will never again split the peoples of Canada, who have twice learned the cost of trying to ride roughshod over the deepest emotions of French and English.

The collapse of their effort to win power did not prevent the Conservatives from pressing their case against French Canada's military record by close questioning of Mr. Abbott after his statement on April 5. Mr. Diefenbaker cited the statistics given in the February-March issue of *Canada at War* to show that Quebec had the lowest rate of volunteering and of N.R.M.A. call-ups.[211] George Stanley White, an Ontario member, brought out that the Quebec military districts had the largest number of deserters, 7,800 and 3,713, out of a total of 18,943 for all Canada.[212] On the following day Diefenbaker pointed out that over 50 per cent of the Quebec N.R.M.A. men warned for overseas service had deserted. Abbott protested against 'this blazoning of Canada as a nation of deserters' while Jean-François Pouliot pointed out that the Conservative attacks on Quebec were unfortunate 'because we are bound to live together; we are bound to be in the same boat.'[213] But the Conservative attack on the government with regard to military matters centered at this time on the question of Major-General G. R. Pearkes' resignation from the Pacific Command, first offered on November 26, 1944 and finally accepted by the Defence Department on February 14, which had political implications because of the general's known opposition toward the N.R.M.A. policy and his announced candidacy in the impending general election.

13

Quebec's divided mood in 1945 was expressed by two cultural trends of opposed tendencies. At the beginning of the year a French-Canadian Academy, modeled on the French Academy, was established in Montreal. Of its twenty-four members sixteen represented the liberal arts and eight the moral, political, and religious sciences. Its board was headed by Victor Barbeau and included Léo-Paul Desrosiers and Robert Charbonneau, while other members were Marius Barbeau, Roger Brien, Robert Choquette, Marie-Claire Daveluy, Abbé Rodolphe Dubé ('Francois Hertel'), Guy Frégault, Alain Grandbois, Canon Lionel Groulx, Père Louis Lachance, O.P., Père Gustave Lamarche, O.P., Rina Lasnier, Dr. Philippe Panneton ('Ringuet'), and Robert Rumilly. Eight vacancies were left open to Canadian subjects of either sex, at least twenty-eight years of age, who had produced two published works. The foundation of the Academy was a landmark in the self-conscious development of a French-Canadian culture separate and distinct from that of France. It also was a revolt against the artificial yoking of two distinct colonial cultures in the Royal Society of Canada, whose French-Canadian elder statesmen no longer commanded much respect from the younger generation in Quebec. Many of the members of the new Academy were nationalists who held that French- and English-Canadian cultures were irreconcilable, and that the Royal Society was merely a mutual admiration society of *bonne-ententistes*. French-Canadian art, which had long mirrored the shifting fashions of Paris, returned to native themes while avoiding the sentimentalism of a Henri Julien. Thus a cultural isolationism paralleled Quebec's political isolationism as a result of the reinforcement crisis.

On the other hand, the cartoonist and caricaturist Robert La Palme, a French-Canadian Low, managed to combine the outlook of a citizen of the world with a distinctive French-Canadian spirit. The anonymous *Compagnons de Saint-Laurent* brought new life into the Montreal theater with their stylized productions of Molière, Racine, and Corneille, and modern French, English, and American dramatists. Their director, Père Emile Legault, was a priest who had no use for the Jansenist tradition which had blighted the French-Canadian theater since the days of Bishop Saint-Vallier. 'Fridolin' (Gratien Gélinas), French Canada's beloved dramatic satirist who had espoused the nationalist cause in the early war years, now mocked the *Bloc Populaire* and the Ordre de Jacques Cartier, and resolved the English-French tension by laughter in his annual revue, *Fridolin-nous*, which foreshadowed his first full-length play *Tit-Coq* (1948), which gave poignant expression to the conscription question from a French point of view which was basically Canadian. Another index of cultural maturity was supplied by Roger Lemelin's novel, *Au pied de la pente douce* (1944), which satirized nationalism and mirrored the unrest of the urban workers. The appearance of Lemelin's book and of Gabrielle Roy's *Bonheur d'Occasion* in English drew the attention of the rest of North America to the rapid social evolution of French Canada.

Yet despite these evidences of a growing cultural self-sufficiency, which outstripped English Canada's artistic development, French Canada reached out ever more eagerly for cultural support from Latin America. Cut off from France by the war and with its old sympathy for the mother culture divided and weakened by the Pétain-*vs.*-De Gaulle controversy, Quebec suddenly realized that there were other peoples of 'Latin' culture on a continent which, beyond her limits, she had long considered to be exclusively 'Anglo-Saxon'; and proceeded enthusiastically to cultivate relations with them. Such a course had been urged repeatedly since 1915 by Henri Bourassa, who saw a safeguard against United States imperialism in the development of diplomatic and commercial relations with the South American countries, and had proposed a hemispheric alliance against European aggression in 1916.[214] In the House in 1935 he had urged Canada's entrance into the Pan-American Union, 'in which we would be far more at home than we are in the League of Nations,'[215] arguing that Canada would thus meet 'representatives of those states of South America which, in some respects, are in close understanding with the United States, but in others have the same feelings of diffidence that we have and which are natural in small or weak nations toward a very large one, dominating the continent.' *Le Devoir* had always followed the Pan-American line of its founder, while Emile Bruchési, writing in *L'Action française* in 1922, had described the Latin Americans as 'cousins by blood, by race, by mentality' and had evoked visions of a Latin New World counter-balancing the Anglo-Saxon one.[216] But on the whole French Canada showed little interest in Latin America, aside from a tendency to support Pan-Americanism as an offset to British imperialism, until 1940, when it was challenged by Prime Minister King to assume French cultural leadership, as English Canada sought Latin American markets to replace European ones.

In that year the *Union des Latins d'Amérique* was founded in Montreal by Dostaler O'Leary, a prewar advocate of separatism and of the establishment of a free French state on the St. Lawrence which would embody the cultural tradition of Athens, Rome, and Paris.[217] Although it was suggested that O'Leary's enthusiasm for Latin America was stimulated by racism and the hospitality shown to fascist-minded French Canadians who took refuge there when Canada entered the war,[218] the movement received the sanction of the Université de Montréal, whose rector served as honorary president. Membership, which was restricted to French Canadians, amounted to about 1,500 persons, of whom some 250 took up the study of Spanish. Through discussion groups, exhibits, and addresses the *Union* sought to cultivate the cultural unity of the 'Latins' of America in annual Latin-American Days at the university in 1942,

1943, and 1944. Under its auspices 100 French-Canadian students visited Mexico in 1944, while 50 more went there in 1945 under the auspices of the *Cercle Cervantes* of Laval University.

The war also brought to French-Canadian institutions students from Mexico, Central America, and the Antilles who normally would have gone to France. La Tertulia Club of Ottawa and the Canada-Brazil Committee also arranged for the exchange of students and professors between Quebec and Latin America, while Spanish courses were given in the French-Canadian universities, supplemented at the Université de Montréal and the Ecoles des Hautes Études by courses on Latin America.

Sympathy for Latin America was strongest in nationalist circles, though the theory of strong cultural bonds based upon a common Latin and Catholic heritage was troubled by some awkward facts. Latin America prided itself upon its heritage from the French Revolution, which remained to French Canada a curse which it had happily escaped. Spanish-American Catholicism proved very different from that of French Canada, and was far from universal in the Latin-American academic world, with its old freethinking and anti-clerical traditions and its new Marxism. Latin America was proud of its Indian heritage, while French Canada was ashamed of its Indian blood. Over-enthusiastic expressions of brotherhood by Haitian cultural envoys to Quebec produced in certain French-Canadian quarters the reaction that 'after all, we are not North American Negroes.' An unanticipated development of the Latin-American enthusiasm was the discovery that the French Canadians were more North American than 'Latin' in their ways of life and thought, despite the nationalist teaching of the last quarter century. But the Latin-American movement received widespread support from *L'Oeil*, which stressed a common Latinity, and *Le Bloc*, which saw in Canada's entry into the Pan-American Union a means for Latins to unite against Jewish-American finance.[219]

Not racist-minded like the *Union des Latins* and more concerned with the development of commercial than cultural relations with Latin America, the Pan-American League was founded in December 1943, with a head office in Toronto and an active Montreal branch. The latter conducted in 1944 a survey of the teaching of Spanish and Portuguese in seventeen Canadian universities, and in 1945 a survey of Canada's role in the Western Hemisphere. It was at the instigation of Hector C. Boulay, national director of the League, who had previously written the foreign ministers of Chile, Peru, and Uruguay urging such a step, that the Chilean delegation to the Mexico City meeting of the Pan-American Union in February 1945 moved a resolution that Canada be invited to join the Union.

The French press was notably sympathetic to such a step, although it was generally assumed that Canada would not enter the Union because of United States objections that Canada was not a republic and English-Canadian objections that membership in the Union was incompatible with membership in the British Commonwealth. *L'Action Catholique* spoke of the 'passive but powerful hostility of certain Anglo-Saxons who will not admit that something good may emanate from any other place than London.' *Le Soleil* regretted that 'in Pan-American politics Canadians are still considered as British subjects instead of free citizens of a free country.' *L'Evénement-Journal* deplored the fact that Canada was not officially represented at Mexico City, since 'we must realize that we live in America and that the decisions which will be taken in Mexico interest each and every one of us.'

Le Canada was alone in taking the line that entrance into the Pan-American Union would make Canada subject to a 'strong pressure from Washington' which would be incompatible with Canadian autonomy. This statement clearly reflected the desire of Ottawa, torn between Canada's American and British interests, to defer the Pan-American question until that of regional *vs.* world security systems was discussed at the San Francisco Conference. The English-Canadian nationalism developed by the War was reluctant to increase still further Washington's influence on Ottawa, which had waxed as London's waned during the War, while English-Canadian imperialists sought to restore the old order of British dominance of Canadian foreign policy. On the whole French Canadians were more sympathetic than the English Canadians to Canada's participation in inter-American affairs. The declaration of Malcolm MacDonald, British high commissioner to Canada, in a speech at Quebec at this time, that 'You remain masters of your own destinies,' was used by *Le Devoir* to lecture the imperialists on their outmoded colonialism, while *La Patrie* saw a guarantee for the survival of British institutions in the fact that 'the political structure of the Commonwealth and British Empire is in a state of constant evolution and that it has never become crystalized, fossilized, or mummified, which would have meant its destruction.' *La Patrie* saw as the British goal 'the ever-widening expansion of liberty among all the King's subjects, whatever their color, their race, their creed, or the part of the globe they live in.'[220]

Latin America had commercial as well as cultural charms for a Quebec seeking new markets and anxious to offset 'Anglo-Saxon' dominance of its economic life. After the fall of France, Montreal French publishers were quick to see a market for their wares in Latin America, for whose intellectuals French had always been a common tongue. Latin America was eager for Canadian newsprint, whose distribution had been controlled by American agencies for political purposes. Early in January 1945 Provincial Treasurer Gagnon and Minister of Commerce and Industry Beaulieu set out for Mexico and Haiti, in response to invitations extended the previous year by the Mexican ambassador and President Lescaut during state visits to Quebec. *Montréal-Matin*, the Duplessis administration's organ, hailed Quebec as a liaison agent between Latin America and English Canada, praised the work of the *Union des Latins* in making Canada better known abroad, and commented that 'the signing of [trade] agreements would give an impetus to the business and industry of Quebec and place us in a better position to meet the uncertainties of the post-war period.'[221]

14

The storm aroused in Quebec by the conscription crisis died down rapidly, but the province remained in a sore and sensitive mood. Quebec was once more isolated from the rest of Canada, as in 1918, but this time for the most part it turned outward to the international world rather than in upon itself, while it awaited an opportunity to avenge itself upon the King government at the polls. On January 3, 1945, Cardinal Villeneuve renewed in even more vigorous terms the warning he had given against the worldwide menace of Communism upon his return from his trip to Britain and the battlefronts in the fall. *L'Action Catholique* and *Montréal-Matin* warned that the danger existed at home, with the latter journal urging suspicion of 'all those who seek to sow disunion, agitation and revolt.'[222] The selection of the National Catholic Syndicate as the favored bargaining agent of the Arvida aluminum workers, despite a vigorous four months' campaign by the Canadian Congress of Labor (CIO), was hailed as a victory over 'Communists' and 'American racketeers.'[223] The Yalta Conference, which at first only aroused expressions of regret at France's absence from the deliberations, evoked a storm of vigorous protests from *L'Action Catholique, Le Devoir*, and *Le Droit* as a 'new Munich' containing the germs of a third world war, when it became known that Poland had been sacrificed to Soviet Russia. *Le Canada* and *Le Soleil* defended the Yalta agreements, but a groundswell of sympathy for the seven million Polish Catholics who came under Soviet control in 'the fifth partition of Poland' swept Quebec and reinforced the skepticism of the nationalists about the principles of the Big Three and their peace plans.[224] The arrival in February of Count Jean de Hautecloque, the first ambassador of France to Canada, was warmly greeted by the French press, which hailed his record in the Resistance and expressed the wish that relations between Canada and France might be drawn closer.[225] But the ambassador had hardly arrived in Ottawa before he received a resolution of protest from the Saint-Jean-Baptiste Society against the imposition of the death penalty on French intellectuals accused of collaboration. A group of French-Canadian intellectuals including Edouard Turcotte, Jean-Charles Harvey, René Garneau, and Lucien Parizeau promptly protested against the action of the society.[226]

The Grey North by-election of February 5, in which General McNaughton was defeated by the Progressive-Conservative candidate, with the C.C.F. candidate credited with splitting the anti-Tory vote, was taken as the inevitable forerunner of a general election. *L'Action Catholique* saw the King government as caught between conscriptionist and anti-conscriptionist forces, with Ontario condemning the prime minister for not applying conscription, while Quebec blamed him for doing so. *Le Devoir* thought no party would be strong enough to form a government in the next parliament, and looked forward happily to the prospect of a Quebec group wielding the balance of power.[227] Sympathy for General McNaughton and condemnation of the anti-Quebec sentiment aroused by Conservative speakers was generally expressed in the French press. But Quebec was less sensitive on the score of conscription than it had been in November, since it had become evident that the disorders and absenteeism among N.R.M.A. men posted for overseas were not confined to French Canadians. General McNaughton's announcement that further coercion would not be necessary as the reinforcement situation was satisfactory also eased the tension in Quebec. Popular feeling against conscription last made itself felt in a Saturday night street brawl at Drummondville on February 24, when Mounted Police and Provost Corps officers sought to round up youths whose military papers were not in order. Regret was expressed by the newspapers that disorder had occurred, but more indignation was expressed that the affair had received undue attention in the English-speaking press. Considerable anti-English-Canadian and anti-American feeling had been aroused by the sensationalism with which Quebec's opposition to conscription had been publicized in recent months.[228]

The ethnic solidarity aroused by the conscription crisis and its aftermath sought political expression in both the provincial and federal fields in the early months of 1945. An independent federal group, headed by Frédéric Dorion, Wilfrid Lacroix, Liguori Lacombe, and Sasseville Roy, was launched in the middle of January. Its first aim was to defeat Mackenzie King, and by exploiting anti-conscription and autonomy feeling to bring together all nationalist and anti-government Quebec members in a party which would seek to wield the balance of power at Ottawa. The independents were strongest in the Quebec district; they obviously sought a working alliance with the *Bloc*, which still commanded nationalist feeling in the Montreal district. Dorion, elected as an independent in 1943, was a recognized follower of the *Union Nationale*; Lacroix had left the Liberal Party on the issue of conscription of N.R.M.A. men; Lacombe had been elected as a Liberal in 1940 but had subsequently established a one-man *Parti Canadien*; while Roy was an independent Conservative who had bolted his party. Efforts were made to induce P.-J.-A. Cardin to bring the nationalist wing of the Quebec Liberals into the fold of the new group. *Le Devoir* and *Le Droit* were enthusiastic in their support of a French-Canadian party.

With revolt widespread within the Liberal fold in Quebec, Mr. King gave the province time to cool off by proroguing parliament when it met on January 31, while leaving the date of a general election unfixed. On February 3 *L'Action Catholique* published a Liberal-inspired story that Mr. King would call an election shortly on a platform calling for nomination of a Canadian governor-general, adoption of a Canadian flag, abolition of appeals to the Privy Council, entrance of Canada into the Pan-American Union, and the independence of Canada.[229] Such a program would at once win many allies for the Liberals from the C.C.F. and from Quebec. The prime minister's statement on the result of the Grey North election, referring to 'the splitting of the vote of those who are opposed to reactionary forces,'[230] strengthened the suspicion which had arisen during the conscription crisis that the Liberals would form a working alliance with the C.C.F. in the coming general elections. While the nationalist elements of the C.C.F. program had strong appeal in Quebec, the party's prospects in Quebec were blighted by its emphasis on further centralization of power at Ottawa and by its socialism, which was taken to be of the Continental revolutionary rather than the English evolutionary sort.

The first session of the Quebec legislature under the new Duplessis government opened on February 6, the morrow of the Grey North election. Four days earlier Premier Duplessis had made public a letter to Mr. King in which the Quebec government claimed that the federal family allowance act was unconstitutional, since it invaded the provinces' 'exclusive rights in the domain of family life, education, and civil law.' The statements of Laurier and Sir Lomer Gouin on the inviolability of provincial rights were cited in support of this view. Quebec Liberals made much of the anomalies of a Duplessis-Drew axis, with Premier Drew of Ontario attacking the family allowance measure as an electoral bribe to Quebec which would burden English-Canadian taxpayers with the support of the large French-Canadian families, while Premier Duplessis atacked it as a federal and hence English-Canadian encroachment on Quebec's rights. The Duplessis government promptly proceeded to introduce a provincial family allowance measure which made more liberal provision than the federal measure for families with more than four children. The speech from the throne also announced that a provincial broadcasting system would be set up.

The general spirit of opposition to Ottawa was indicated by the support given by all parties to a resolution of protest against the imposition of conscription for overseas service introduced by René Chaloult, whose previous anti-war resolutions had met short shrift under the Liberal regime. Early in March the premier gave notice of a bill to prevent appeals to the Supreme Court of Canada in Quebec civil cases, but later opposed a *Bloc* resolution to abolish appeals to the Privy Council. A few days later the legislative assembly by an unanimous vote called for redistribution of electoral seats before the federal elections, so as to do justice to Quebec, whose population had increased more largely than those of the other provinces since the last distribution in 1931. On the same day that the provincial radio bill passed its third reading, the premier introduced a measure annulling the agreement made between Quebec and Ottawa in 1942, whereby the province renounced to the federal government for the duration of the war the right to collect corporation taxes.

The tide of anti-Ottawa motions was turned, however, toward the end of March by the misfiring of Chaloult's charge that the federal government was responsible for the corruption of young girls by forcing them to work in war plants. The Liberal press replied to Mr. Chaloult's charges—that half of the country girls engaged in domestic work in Montreal were unmarried mothers, and that half of the female workers in the Quebec Arsenal were in the same plight—by pointing out that Quebec had the lowest rate of illegitimate births of any province.[231] Quebec labor was also quick to protest against the Chaloult charges. In April the premier introduced a bill amending the Quebec Election Act to make 'Canadian nationality' one of the qualifications for voting, instead of the former requirement of being a British subject, born or naturalized. On March 12, as he departed for a conference in Washington with President Roosevelt, Prime Minister King ended the speculation which had been rife since the prorogation of parliament by announcing that there would be no extension of parliament's life, that the cabinet had been revised, and that the opposition would be invited to form part of Canada's delegation to the San Francisco Conference.

When parliament met on March 19, 1945, the speech from the throne announced the government's acceptance of an invitation to participate in the San Francisco Conference on April 25, and called for a joint resolution assuring the Canadian delegation of 'the widest possible support from Parliament.'[232] It was also pointed out that parliament's term expired on April 17, and that a general election would be held shortly thereafter. Meanwhile the House was asked to make provision for the conduct of the war and for ordinary government expenses until the meeting of a new parliament.

15

The motion on the San Francisco Conference, moved by Mr. King and seconded by Justice Minister St. Laurent on the following day, called for endorsement of the government's decision to participate and for recognition that 'the establishment of an effective international organization for the maintenance of peace and security is of vital importance to Canada, and, indeed, to the future well-being of mankind; and that it is in the interests of Canada that Canada should become a member of such an organization.'[233] It also asked approval of the proposals of the United States, the United Kingdom, the U.S.S.R., and China for the international organization. The charter adopted at San Francisco was to be approved by parliament before ratification by Canada, whose delegates were to use their best endeavors in its preparation.

After outlining the proposals, Mr. King dealt with the difficulties and objections which might arise. While approving the predominant role given to the great powers, he urged clarification of 'the constitutional position within the organization of important secondary countries.' He also admitted that 'the obligation to carry out diplomatic, economic and military sanctions at the request of the Security Council raises another difficult question for Canada and other secondary states,' but suggested that 'if the enforcement of sanctions required active aid from a country not represented on the council, its consent would probably be sought.' He urged broad thinking and taking a long view, since 'the benefits which Canada may hope to gain from full participation are immense.' Aside from prestige, 'no country has a greater interest than ours in the prevention of another general war.' He expressed the belief that 'our part in the shaping of peace may be no less urgent and no less effective' than it had been in the achievement of victory. He urged a willingness to give and take in the cooperative effort to organize world security, pointing out that the development of new weapons made no country immune from sudden aggression, and that 'so long as might is made a substitute for right by any nation there can be no security for this, or the next or any succeeding generation of Canadians.' He closed with the observation that the supreme lesson of five and a half years of war was that 'humanity should no longer be made to serve selfish national ends, whether these ends be world domination or merely isolated self-defence.'[234]

The isolationist tradition of French Canada was clearly challenged by the prospect of Canada's participation in a world organization. Gaspard Fauteux(St. Mary), strongly backing the resolution, stressed the aim 'of achieving international cooperation in the solution of international economic, social and other humanitarian problems,' and pointed out the benefit to his compatriots of transforming 'a war economy into a peace economy based on the same principles and the same needs.'[235] But Liguori Lacombe (Laval–Two Mountains) protested that the Canadian delegates would lack a mandate, since the San Francisco Conference would be held after the expiration of the life of parliament; and urged an immediate dissolution of parliament, since the people of Canada had lost confidence in the government. He accused the prime minister of 'sacrificing the friends of Canada to those who are not true Canadians'[236] ever since the N.R.M. Act. He asked why Canada should be represented at San Francisco, when the discussions would turn on questions decided at other conferences at which it had not been heard. He characterized Canada's participation in the League of Nations as useless, and expressed skepticism about the proposed charter, in view of the emptiness of the Atlantic Charter and the dismemberment of Poland. ' It is all very well to set up an international organization to maintain world peace and security, but only through having regard to the rights of all martyred peoples to life, justice and liberty can such an organization build something lasting.' He denounced the 'economic dictatorship' which had dominated Canada since the N.R.M. Act; the government's disregard for the supremacy of parliament in now calling for approval of a decision already made; and warned of a day of reckoning at the polls.

Lacombe charged that under the proposals, 'our air, naval and land forces would be requisitioned at any time by the future league of nations to serve anywhere in the world.' He undoubtedly summed up the attitude of many traditional-minded French Canadians when he concluded:

Parliament can not and should not appoint a delegation entrusted with such powers. I refuse to believe that Canada, once the war is over, should mobilize her resources for the protection of world security. I object to the sending of a delegation of members no longer in office to that conference; it would be contrary to our constitution, to custom, and to law. With many others, I wonder if it would not be more appropriate and reasonable to restore order in our own country, to stabilize our finances, and to prepare our youth for careers worthy of their sacrifice. In short, let us put an end to our international commitments. Let us undertake the rebuilding of our economic structure which is crumbling. Let us think first of our own, of the sons and daughters of Canada who will be returning to this country. They shall have the right to work and to positions worthy of their sacrifices. Up to now, the government has found twenty billions for war purposes. We shall need as much, and maybe more, for works of peace. Peace and national security for Canada should be our greatest worries. To that noble task we should devote all our energy and our resources. Let us use them for our own people and for our country. I know that my call will not be heard. At least I shall have fulfilled my duty to my country and to my people.[237]

L.-P. Picard (Bellechasse), the former secretary of Ernest Lapointe who had taken an important role in the special session, refuted the Conservative charge that the government had displayed a spineless attitude in the past, and made much of the contributions of both French and English to the development of Canadian nationhood, particularly stressing those of Laurier and Lapointe.[238] It was evident from his remarks that the Quebec Liberals had returned to the government fold. Fred Rose (Cartier) endorsed the resolution on behalf of the Labor-Progressive Party, declaring that both French and English Canadians fully shared the determination of 'the world's peoples' to establish peace and economic collaboration. He denounced 'the suicidal isolationism advocated by the Tory-inspired Nationalists, whose programme is both a denial of the realities of the present day world and a betrayal of the true interests of the great French Canadian community.'[239] He urged that labor should be represented in the Canadian delegation.

Wilfrid Lacroix (Quebec-Montmorency) declared that the decisions already taken at Yalta, which he anticipated would be ratified at San Francisco, 'already include the germs of a new war.'[240] He sharply attacked Yalta as another Munich, with its sacrifice of Poland's right to self-determination, and warned: 'We shall see, after this war, communistic influence permeate the whole of Europe and if Canada approves the purposes and principles set forth in the proposals already framed at Yalta, it means for us a war in which we shall inevitably be involved within ten or fifteen years.' He echoed Lacombe's criticism that the government had no mandate to commit the country to any course at San Francisco. He charged that the prime minister had become 'as much of a Tory as the staunchest of the imperialists who sit opposite him,' and declared that in view of Mr. King's record of broken pledges Quebec had lost faith 'in a man who owes it his present standing.' But there could be felt no confidence in the Progressive-Conservatives, because of 'their imperialistic and reactionary doctrines together with their electioneering methods of continuous mud-slinging against the province of Quebec'; nor in the C.C.F., because 'they have never failed to support the views of the Russian government in the field of international politics.' Anticipating that neither of the three parties would have a working majority after the elections, he thought there would be need for 'a group of members strong enough to force the other parties to follow a truly Canadian policy.' Lacroix charged that the Canadian people were again going to be presented with 'an accomplished fact arranged in London and not in Ottawa,' and protested against 'a policy of internationalism and cooperation in the establishment of a programme of world security dependent upon the good will of Stalin, the dictator, or, which would be still worse, of international high finance.'

On March 22 Frédéric Dorion (Charlevoix-Saguenay) protested against the government's undemocratic procedure in asking ratification of its previous decision to participate at San Francisco, and he warned that the independents would not consider themselves bound by any decisions taken by a Canadian delegation without a mandate.[241] Describing the question as 'participation in any future war in the world,' he called the resolution the most important to come before parliament since September 1939. He urged that 'we must first think of ourselves, rather than the world at large,' and asked whether it was 'a crime to stand for Canada first,' as Roosevelt stood for America first, Churchill for Britain first, and Stalin for Russia first. He charged that little had been done by the government for the benefit of the Canadian people, while everything had been done for other nations, 'under the fallacious pretext that we have to save humanity and civilization.' Canada at present was passing through an internal crisis and suffering from disunity, and the government's first task was 'to see to it that a true and lasting peace be established in our own country, before trying to organize the peace of the whole world.' He held that the proposed conference not only offered no better prospects than earlier peace conferences which had failed to avert war, but, because of the Russian dictatorship's role, offered little hope. He blamed wars on international finance and Communism, and deplored the fact that 'the greatest international power in the world, the Vatican' had been ignored in the proposed conference.[242]

J.-A. Bonnier (Saint-Henri) spoke in favor of participation, but strongly urged the Canadian delegates to look after Poland's interests.[243] J.-Emmanuel d'Anjou (Rimouski) expressed the opinion that there had already been too many conferences, since Poland, for whose sake Canada had gone to war, had already been sacrificed at Yalta for the benefit of Russia. He described the League of Nations as 'a colossal fiasco,' and predicted that the new organization would be an equal failure.[244] He quoted motions made by C. G. Power in 1923 for withdrawal from the League and against participation in foreign wars without the consent of parliament, both of which he had then seconded. He declared that the Canadian delegation would have no mandate for committing Canada to participation, that the conference would inevitably involve Canada

in another conflict, and that as in 1923 he still opposed 'participation in empire wars.'[245]

On March 23 Fisheries Minister Ernest Bertrand spoke in favor
of an international organization as a necessity in a contracting
world. Reversing the words used by the Conservative leader that
'Nothing done by this nation at the coming conference or elsewhere
must endanger our close ties with the British commonwealth and
empire,' Bertrand urged thinking in Canadian terms by saying
'Nothing done by the British Empire at the coming conference or
elsewhere must endanger our relations with the nations of the world
with which we are at peace, and we must not be drawn into any
conflict where we would not have an immediate interest.' But he
condemned the attitude taken by the four Quebec independents
in strong terms:

If there is one group of members who should be in favour of creating
an organization to settle disputes and prevent wars, it is that group. If
they are against war they should be in favour of an organization to prevent it. The class of people to whom these gentlemen are appealing have
only one definite article in their programme—the separation of the
province of Quebec from the rest of Canada. That is a programme which
would bring immediate civil war if Quebec tried to enforce it. The
disastrous war that secession brought to the United States would undoubtedly be our lot. So we have a group against all participation in
this war although they would sell, and at very profitable prices, our
agricultural and industrial products to England. This group is against
an organization to prevent war and at the same time it is trying to lead
its own province toward a war of secession.[246]

As for the Polish issue raised by the independents, he pointed out
that 'We went to war not only to defend Poland but to save our own
skins and the skins of twenty-four other nations.' He defended the
Polish boundary and the veto, and closed with the declaration that
'the immense majority of the people in Quebec are in favour of
establishing an international organization which, while it might
not at the start be perfect, could become nearly perfect as the
years go by.'[247]

Maurice Lalonde (Labelle) agreed that the four independents
did not represent the Quebec majority, and expressed the opinion
that 'the efforts of these isolationists who wish that Quebec should
become a sort of reserve, shut out from all the great constitutional
and economic evolutions of our time' would be repudiated.

It is high time that our nationalistic independents should realize the
true situation of our race in Canada . . . We are surrounded by more

than 150 million Anglo-Saxons with whom Providence has decreed that we should live, willy-nilly. It will be of no use to moderate independents, such as the hon. member for Charlevoix-Saguenay (Mr. Dorion) or to extremists of the Chaloult type to preach a provoking resistance. It will be of no use to revolutionists of the Shields clan to threaten us with their thunderbolts. Harmony will be the offspring of an acceptable compromise, both to the honour of the parties in the case and for their future in confederation.[248]

He criticized vigorously those who sought through political opportunism or for the sake of political revenge to keep Canada out of the peace conferences.

The independents came under fire from an unexpected quarter on March 27 when Maxime Raymond, federal leader of the *Bloc Populaire*, took Dorion to task for misinterpreting the motion and for reversing the stand which the independent and *Bloc* members had taken in favor of Canada's participation in international conferences in February 1944. After stating that he and his fellow *Bloc* member, J.-A. Choquette, would support the government motion, Raymond refuted Dorion's arguments, pointing out that the Pope in his Christmas allocution had urged the need of an international organization. Raymond renewed the stand he had taken on international relations in an interview published in *Maclean's Magazine* in 1944,[249] and called for 'an enduring peace based on right and not on might.'[250] He opposed the veto and the make-up of the security council, urging that international trade in armaments be prohibited as a cause of war. But Raymond supported international economic and social cooperation, since 'the peace that is to follow the present war must be more than a clever balance of military powers, it must be founded on real efforts to establish international justice.'[251]

Sasseville Roy (Gaspé) replied on behalf of the independents to Raymond and Bertrand, declaring that he opposed the San Francisco Conference because Canada was not aware of the decisions taken at the Atlantic, Casablanca, Teheran, Quebec, and Yalta conferences and of the nature of the peace which the international organization would seek to maintain. He denied that the independents were separatists and declared they favored 'sound collaboration between the two ethnic elements in our country.'[252] He expressed fear that Canada might be committed at San Francisco to maintaining compulsory military service, and that the prime minister might be once more deceiving the country as he had on the question of participation in the war. He concluded with the observation that the independents were 'in favour of such a conference being held, but what we are opposed to is the wrong way in which our government and the great powers are going about it.' He held that the conference was untimely because peace had not yet been made and because the government lacked a mandate to engage Canada's future.

Armand Choquette reiterated Raymond's argument in favor of a democratic world organization, citing the Pope's Christmas allocution. He criticized the proposals for the security council and the veto. He charged that the decisions reached at Yalta were 'based much more on a brutal policy of force than on a policy of sound justice and right,' and urged that the proposed international organization should eliminate such abuses. Though he had opposed the war measures of the government, he favored their peace measures, so long as Canada participated 'as a free and independent nation, due regard being given to our interests.' To him it was more important that Canada should be represented at San Francisco than at Commonwealth Conferences, 'which unfortunately smack of imperialism.'[253]

Closing the debate on March 28, the prime minister appealed to the Quebec independents 'in the interests of Canada as a whole' to reconsider their intention to vote against the motion, so that Canada might speak with one voice. He urged that they would not be representing the feeling of Canada, or of the province of Quebec, or of their constituencies if they voted against the resolution; and he suggested that they might refrain from voting 'rather than have it broadcast throughout the world that in Canada there were members of her Parliament who felt they were unable to further a great world need.'[254] But Messrs. D'Anjou, Dorion, Lacombe, Lacroix, and Roy remained obdurate, and were the only members to oppose the motion on division. It was noteworthy that the independents did not receive much press support for their stand. *Le Droit* held that Canada must participate in the organization of world peace, while *L'Action Catholique* merely explained the independents' position as the logical consequence of their opposition to Canada's entry into the war.[255] The French press, however, deplored the call for imperial solidarity at San Francisco made by Gordon Graydon, Progressive-Conservative House leader, and denounced 'political colonialism.' *Le Droit* strongly supported Graydon's demand that parliament devote more attention to foreign affairs, and that external affairs should not be a part-time job for 'a very busy Prime Minister.'

Though Mr. King had deplored the concept of the Commonwealth acting as a bloc, the statement made by the prime minister in appealing for Conservative support of the motion, that 'I have done my duty by the British Commonwealth of Nations, by the British Empire, through every hour of the time I have been serving as Prime Minister of this country,' was promptly picked up by Wilfrid Lacroix on April 3 as evidence that Canada would 'continue to be a colony of the empire as heretofore.'[256] On the same occasion Lacroix opposed conscription in any form for the Pacific War on the grounds of cost, of interference with economic reconstruction, and of disregard for the government's promises to Quebec. He also attacked Maxime Raymond's stand on San Francisco and on the N.R.M. Act, though he favored his appointment as a member of the Canadian delegation to the conference.[257] Justice Minister St. Laurent and Senator Lucien Moraud were the only French-Canadian delegates named by the prime minister on April 9, however, while Jean Désy, Ambassador to Brazil, was one of the seven senior advisers who accompanied the delegation. The prime minister's choice was generally approved by the French press, though Le Droit regretted that Maxime Raymond and John Blackmore, as leaders of other parliamentary groups, had not been named.[258] On April 11 Philippe Picard urged that French be an official language at the conference. His stand was strongly backed by the whole French press, with Le Droit taking the lead, although La Patrie feared that the predominance of the United States and Great Britain might cause the elimination of French. The French press was disturbed by the proposal to give several votes to the United States and the U.S.S.R. and its satellites, to offset the six votes of the British Commonwealth nations. Le Devoir used the occasion to call for 'real independence' as a solution for this international difficulty and the problem of national unity as well.[259]

During the discussion of the war estimates, the independents and Bloc members made common cause against continuation of conscription, and particularly against conscription for the Pacific War. The prime minister announced to the House that Canadian participation would be 'strictly limited,' and that only volunteers would go to the Pacific. This stand was approved by the French press, though there was an undercurrent of suspicion which found expression on April 13 when Dorion indicted the government and the Liberal Party for its record of broken promises to Quebec, and moved for repeal of the N.R.M. Act and P.C. 8891.[260] Only nine votes in favor of the amendment were recorded, and with this effort the independent movement, which had sought to create a French-Canadian bloc supplying a balance of power at Ottawa, largely collapsed, though it still talked darkly of the opposition which the prime minister would meet at the polls in Quebec. The last session of the nineteenth parliament closed on April 16, with elections set for June 11.

A Gallup poll early in April indicated that the Liberal Party was barely ahead of the Progressive-Conservatives in the favor of the public, with the prospect of no party commanding an absolute majority.[261] The Quebec Liberals who had planned to take revenge for conscription by voting against Mr. King were faced with the awkward dilemma of thus benefiting either the imperialists in the Tory camp or the socialists of the C.C.F., both anathema to most French Canadians. Anti-King feeling had notably subsided since the previous December, and those who still nourished it were much divided. While the nationalist journals were undecided in their course, *Le Canada*, *Le Soleil*, *Le Nouvelliste*, and *La Tribune* once more lined up squarely behind Mr. King, praising his conduct of the war and his postwar program.[262] A pre-election cabinet shakeup cost the French-Canadians of Quebec one seat, with the retirement of General Laflèche, the Acadians of New Brunswick another, with that of J.-E. Michaud, while the Franco-Ontarians gained two, with the appointment of Paul Martin as secretary of state and Lionel Chevrier as minister of transport. Joseph Jean of Montreal became solicitor-general.

On April 27 P.-J.-A. Cardin announced in a radio speech the formation of the long-rumored anti-King coalition under the name of the National Front. Frédéric Dorion pledged the adherence of his group of independents, while Camillien Houde announced that he had joined forces with the *Bloc Populaire*. *Le Canada* condemned the National Front as having no program other than 'vague grievances,' while *Montréal-Matin* supported it. *Le Droit*, which favored the grouping of all anti-conscriptionists, at first refrained from comment on the new party, as did *Le Devoir* and *L'Action Catholique*.[263] The National Front collapsed within a short time, and those who favored it ran as independents. Alfred Charpentier, president of the Canadian and Catholic Confederation of Labor, supported the non-political tradition of the syndicates in an article in *Le Travail*, though most syndicate members were expected to vote for either the *Bloc* or the National Front. *Labor World*, the provincial A.F.L. organ, came out on May 5 for Mr. King, while the Canadian Congress of Labor was already pledged to the C.C.F. By May 17 there were 294 candidates in Quebec's 65 electoral districts: 72 Independents, 58 Liberals, 29 Progressive-Conservatives, 28 C.C.F., 42 Social Credit, 35 *Bloc Populaire*, and 7 Labor-Progressives.

Le Devoir in a preliminary electoral analysis warned against Conservative candidates disguised as independents; held that the chief issue was Canadian foreign policy; and opposed Canadian intervention in an Anglo-American *vs.* Soviet conflict which it gloomily envisaged as possible within a few years.[264] *Le Droit* continued to regret the absence of a real French-Canadian Front party, while *La Patrie* interpreted the unusual number of candidates as a proof of the vitality of the democratic system and of its complete political freedom. In his opening campaign speech in Montreal Mayor Houde claimed that he had been right in 1938 in warning of a coming conflict and in 1940 in warning of conscription, and predicted that conscription would be invoked again in a new conflict against one of Canada's present allies. He declared that the *Bloc Populaire* favored free enterprise, and defined its position as 'not left of center but right of center.'[265] *Montréal-Matin* also warned of the dangers to Quebec of the demand for the nationalization of its industries, which it termed poor patriotism.[266]

Mr. King's pledge in campaign speeches at Prince Albert and Winnipeg that Canada would have a flag of its own if his government were returned to office was received with great satisfaction by Quebec, where a majority of the French Canadians had long desired such a symbol of Canadian autonomy.[267] Announcement at the end of May by Health Minister Brooke Claxton of a federal health insurance scheme was dismissed by the nationalist press as an electoral maneuver, while *La Presse* urged caution in adopting social legislation which would prove a heavy burden upon the national revenue. *Le Canada* stressed that social measures should be carried out through the cooperation of the federal and provincial governments. Quebec's objections to the family allowance scheme as an invasion of provincial rights had been duly noted by Ottawa.

The Ontario election of June 4, which saw Premier Drew returned to office in a Conservative landslide which cost the C.C.F. twenty-five seats and the Liberals two, made French-Canadian Liberals decide that Toryism was a greater threat than socialism in the federal election scheduled for a week later. Vandalism in the Jewish cemetery at Rivière-des-Prairies, assigned to anti-Semitic nationalists, provided unfavorable publicity for the *Bloc Populaire*, already handicapped by inadequate campaign funds and organization. Only two *Bloc* candidates were elected with Camillien Houde defeated in his stronghold of Montreal-Sainte-Marie. Forty-eight regular Liberals were returned, with six independent Liberals. Only one official Progressive-Conservative candidate was elected, though an independent Conservative also won by a narrow margin. The C.C.F. failed to elect a single candidate in Quebec, while Fred Rose retained the distinction of being the sole Communist member of Parliament. With a political realism which triumphed over appeals to race and class, Quebec remained loyal to the Liberal Party and supplied nearly half its strength at Ottawa.

The Conservative *Montréal-Matin* correctly declared that the King government had been returned to power 'because its policy has been sufficiently elastic to adapt itself to the wishes of the people, while other parties sought to impose their program and doctrines.' It called for a new start in building an opposition party in Quebec. *La Patrie* probably made the most cogent analysis of the electoral verdict:

The variety of groups and the multiplicity of candidates running as independents set a very difficult task in discernment for the electors of our province. There was a serious danger of confusion, which we have been able to avoid. There was likewise the danger of a division of our forces, of the dispersal of French-Canadian representation into irreconcilable groups. Finally, there was the threat of the isolation of Quebec, to which a strong group of the government's opponents invited our province in the name of nationalism, by exhorting the French-Canadian voters to give a negative vote, based on past history. The Province of Quebec has replied to these appeals by a vote which is above all an approval of the doctrine of national unity preached by Mr. Mackenzie King. Our compatriots have understood that they must live united, but that they could not isolate themselves from the majority of the Canadian people and risk stirring up the formation of an anti-French-Canadian parliamentary coalition. After the events of last autumn, the vote which has just been given by our province is an extraordinary demonstration of confidence in the head of the government. The support which Mr. King receives today from French Canadians does not in any way indicate the abandonment of their essential demands; it signifies that our province knows how, as things are, to take account of circumstances and that it wishes, above all, to safeguard the union of the Canadian nation. It has given its approval to a compromise, thus furnishing an example to all Canadians.[268]

Several papers pointed out that Quebec had chosen the middle path between plutocracy and socialism, preferring economic evolution to revolution. Jean-Charles Harvey, who had waged a vigorous campaign against the *Bloc Populaire* in *Le Jour*, proclaimed: 'Our fellow citizens of another language and another faith should know once for all that the Province of Quebec does not march, never has marched, and never will march in the odorous footsteps of the Chaloults, Houdes, Laurendeaus, and Groulx.' For one of the most interesting aspects of the election result was the fact that the *Bloc Populaire* polled only 200,000 votes—some 10,000 more than it had done in the provincial contest of August 1944, and one-seventh of the total— despite the feeling aroused by the imposition of conscription in November and despite the fact that every effort was made to exploit the personal popularity of Camillien Houde and his symbolic value as a 'martyr' in the cause of Quebec's opposition to conscription and to Ottawa's wartime extension of controls over the individualistic French-Canadian way of life.

The federal election of June 1945 extinguished the last hopes of those who sought to unite the French Canadians in an ethnic party which would attempt to play the dangerous game of supplying a balance of power at Ottawa for any national party which would favor its ends. Once more, as in the provincial election of August 1944, French Canada showed its fundamental devotion to the golden mean, after another display of the verbal violence which has so often deceived casual observers, who attach too much importance to the impassioned rhetoric of the nationalist élite and not enough to the inarticulate common sense of the French-Canadian masses. One of the strongest bonds which holds the peoples of Canada together is a fundamental moderation shared by English and French alike. There would be fewer misunderstandings between them if the utterances of extremists on either side of the ethnic fence did not receive so much publicity, in the inevitable emphasis of the popular press on the sensational.

As Quebec repudiated separatism in the postwar election, so English Canada repudiated the Progressive-Conservative effort at the time of the conscription crisis to unite the rest of Canada against Quebec, for only Ontario returned a majority of Conservatives, and a bare forty-eight out of eighty-two at that. Even in that Tory stronghold the Liberals made a notable showing. The C.C.F., the only national group beside the Liberals really accepting Canada's bi-ethnic character, did well only in the Western provinces, long in revolt against the two old parties.

16

The end of the war in Europe on May 8 undoubtedly affected the outcome of the June election. The French press generally agreed that Mussolini met the death he deserved, although Le Droit and Le Devoir expressed admiration for his early achievements and deplored the summary justice dealt out to him.[269] No such sympathy was expressed at the report of Hitler's death, although Le Devoir called him 'one of the principal figures of our time,' and while admitting that he was 'one of the great scourges of mankind,' hailed his achievement in 'embodying the soul of a great country' and 'galvanizing a humiliated people.' Le Canada savagely attacked this utterance, as it had Le Devoir's editorial on Mussolini. L'Action Catholique, in comparing the worldwide sorrow felt at Roosevelt's death with the dishonorable ends of Mussolini and Hitler, stressed the fact that for Hitler: 'Religion, morality, conscience, the Church, God Himself were absolutely nothing outside of the German racial spirit.' Le Droit used the occasion to echo Haile Selassie's words when Italy attacked Ethiopia: 'Those nations which seek peace without justice will find neither justice nor peace.'[270]

French Canada hailed the news of Germany's surrender with unrestrained joy. Flag-decked city and village streets alike were filled with happy throngs, while many gave thanks in the churches. Under the headline of 'La Guerre est Finie' the newspapers expressed relief at the end of six years' war, but all warned that the nation's task was not yet finished, with some drawing attention to the Pacific War and others to the problems of making the peace. *Le Canada*, taking its line from Mr. King's statement at San Francisco, warned that 'we have to conquer fascism and militarism everywhere, as yesterday we conquered it in Germany, and as tomorrow we shall conquer it in Japan. Then, and then only, can we unreservedly rejoice and delight ourselves in a peace which will no longer be threatened.' The Pacific War remained remote from the thinking of most French Canadians, however, and there was more concern for the making of the peace. *La Patrie* urged its readers to 'thank Providence for the great benefit it has accorded us and to ask it to give guidance to the men who are building the peace which is beginning.' *Montréal-Matin* counselled its readers not to forget the men who had given their lives to make victory possible, and *La Presse* said that joy would not be complete until the service men and women returned home, 'so that we can celebrate together the victory and the deliverance in ceremonies worthy of their brilliant deeds.' *Le Devoir* alone struck a discordant note in the general rejoicing:

An illusory victory. Are there many belligerents who can felicitate themselves on the results obtained at the price of incalculable sacrifices? The first of the United Nations went to war to guarantee the integrity of Poland. Poland is today despoiled of nearly half her territory and what remains is subjected to a government imposed from outside. The United Nations went to war especially to prevent a totalitarian régime from establishing its hegemony over Europe and from assuming too big a place in the world. Another totalitarian regime, which relies on populations even more numerous, on natural resources even richer, on sympathies even more efficacious outside its borders, has established its hegemony over all Eastern Europe and threatens to spread to Western Europe. Nazism is dead with Hitler; German imperialism is reduced to impotence; Communism comes out of the conflict stronger than ever. Russian imperialism, supported by the victorious Red Army, is in the process of surrounding itself with a whole string of vassal states and threatens the very independence of the great European nations.[271]

This gloomy view was promptly rebutted by *Le Canada*, which assigned it to *Le Devoir's* disappointment at seeing its fascist idols fall and ultranationalism brought to nought. But once the first reaction to victory in Europe was past, French Canada as a whole faced the postwar world with a greater distrust of Soviet Russia than English Canada, because of its sympathies with Poland, and was less surprised by the subsequent revelations of Soviet espionage operations in Canada under the cloak of a wartime partnership which it had never accepted with good grace.

In the three months that intervened between VE Day and VJ Day, French Canada showed more concern with the making of the peace than with the conclusion of the war. The attitudes it adopted during this period revealed an unsettled mixture of new and old ideas. As in the early 1930's, the provincial government launched a back-to-the-land movement, setting aside $16,000,000 to aid the establishment of colonists, in an effort to develop the remote northern districts of the province and to reverse the wartime movement of population towards the cities. The long neglected North had become Quebec's new frontier, with rich mineral resources as well as some colonization and industrial possibilities. The élite was uneasily aware of the stirring of discontent with the old order among the newly industrialized urban masses. Both the provincial government and the clerical authorities sought by promoting colonization to avoid a possible repetition of the social troubles of the 1930's in the period of postwar depression and unemployment which seemed inevitable, with so many of Quebec's industries wartime creations for wartime purposes. They were also concerned with keeping the new northern industrial districts French-Canadian. The Noranda-Rouyn area in the Abitibi, with its rich copper and gold mines, was becoming a frontier of Toronto rather than of Montreal, under English-Canadian and American ownership and management and with a large element of New Canadian workers. The wartime development of the aluminum industry at Arvida had to a considerable extent internationalized the Lake St. John region, in the past a French-Canadian colonization area. Many other northern districts, notably the North Shore on the lower St. Lawrence, were controlled by American and English-Canadian pulp and paper interests, which overwhelmingly dominated Quebec's largest peacetime manufacturing industry. Quebec was torn between its need for foreign capital and know-how, and the old desire to keep its natural resources for itself. Its leading nationalist economist, Esdras Minville, proposed the decentralization of industry and the integration of part-time manufacturing into the traditional regional economies dominated by lumbering, agriculture, and the fisheries; but such a plan ignored Quebec's close integration into a continental economy based upon concentrated mass production.

French Canada's new interest in international affairs continued to be marked. Quebec took pride in the number of French-Canadians appointed to diplomatic posts abroad, and supported the suggestion that the Ministry of External Affairs should be divorced from the prime minister's duties and given to Mr. St. Laurent. It criticized the San Francisco Charter as imperfect because of its failure to give the middle and small powers any role comparable to that of the three great powers, but largely blamed its faults on Russia's unwillingness to cooperate. The Potsdam Agreement was censured for its secrecy and for its concessions to Russia. The Pan-American movement continued to receive much support from the press. Proposals by Lord Beaverbrook that imperial preference be revived were promptly rejected in favor of the multilateral trade policies adopted at Bretton Woods. The appointment as governor-general of Sir Harold Alexander, who had commanded Canadian troops in Italy, was received with good grace, though French Canada had generally favored the appointment of a Canadian to this office. The success of the Labor Party in the British elections aroused Quebec's waning fear of socialism, but the distinction between British evolutionary and Continental revolutionary socialism was generally made by the press, as it had not been when the C.C.F., modeled on the British Labor Party, was regarded as a serious threat to the old Canadian parties.

Dominion Day and the meeting in August of the first Dominion-Provincial Conference since 1941 evoked once more expressions of Quebec's willingness to collaborate with English Canada, so long as the terms of Confederation were respected and not altered to favor centralization of power at Ottawa, which was repugnant to French-Canadian individualism and regarded as a grave danger to the maintenance of Quebec's language, laws, and customs. The avoidance of an anticipated clash between Prime Minister King and Premier Duplessis on this occasion was greeted with pleasure, and while the conference was adjourned until November for study of the federal proposals, a cry was heard for the immediate end of wartime restrictions, conscription, and taxes.

Japan's capitulation brought tributes to those who had won the victory, calls to make the peace more lasting than that of 1918, and sober reflections on an altered world in which Britain was gravely weakened, France had fallen to minor rank, and the United States and Russia had become the dominant world powers. *Le Devoir* gloomily reflected that, though the fighting was over, the world was far from peace, and stressed the division among the conquerors and the injustice of their settlements.

The news of the trial and condemnation to death of Marshal Pétain, which took the edge off joy at the end of the war, was greeted in various fashions by the French press. *Le Canada* saw it as putting an end to an unfortunate difference between French Canadians; to *Le Devoir* it was 'a fearful blow to France's prestige in the world'; to *L'Action Catholique*, Freemasonry, banned by the Marshal, had avenged itself by preventing a fair trial. There was a general call for commutation of the sentence by General De Gaulle, though *Le Jour* defended France's right 'to condemn those who have tried to assassinate her.'[272]

17

It was a new French Canada which faced the postwar world, though many of its old characteristics had survived the changes brought by the conflict. A minority which had long sought cultural enhancement abroad was now emerging from cultural colonialism and learning to be itself instead of a provincial imitation of France. Quebec was more fully and consciously integrated into both North American and international life, though still determined to assert its Frenchness and Catholicity in the midst of what it regarded as an Anglo-Saxon and Protestant civilization. It still dreamed of being, as Cardinal Villeneuve put it, 'a little Paris and a little Rome.' The war had brought the full impact of the industrial revolution to bear upon Quebec, hastening its transition from a rural agricultural society to an urban industrial one. The profound social changes involved in this process were further complicated by the fact that the industries which were altering the face of the province were largely invaders, owned and operated by men who were cultural and sometimes political aliens to French Canada. The war favored a rapid development of the union movement, particularly the internationals, and made the Quebec worker less willing to accept lower wages, poorer working conditions, and longer hours than those of his English-Canadian or American fellows. He was increasingly eager for the same standard of living as they enjoyed, and for fuller educational opportunities than he had had in the past in French Canada's unbalanced social structure.

To some extent the French Canadian was beginning to turn against his traditional leaders, the clergy and the lawyer politicians, who acted as middlemen between the masses and the English-speaking economic and political overlords. New political and social leaders were rising from outside the old hereditary ruling caste of the élite, while some of the clergy displayed a new democratic outlook more appropriate to their origins than to the institutional conservatism arising from their economic isolation from the changing conditions of the life of the people. Lay leadership in Quebec's wide range of Catholic social movements, notably in the Catholic syndicates, was encouraged to check a growing anti-clericalism and to gratify a desire for more democratic ways. Those French Canadians who had served overseas had lost their traditional fear of the unknown, and were inclined to question the old standing order when they returned home. They sought to meet the challenge brought by the breakdown of the old rural parochial system along lines suggested by French and Belgian experience.

In the postwar period there was to be a clash of two mentalities: a Bourbon-like determination on the part of much of the traditional élite to maintain the old closed world, regardless of changed conditions, the attitude of a frozen mind which had learned nothing and forgotten nothing; and on the other hand a widespread desire among the younger intellectuals and the newly emancipated workers, prompted by recognition of worldwide social changes and particularly of French experience, to evolve a new social order incorporating what the outside world had to offer with the best of the French-Canadian tradition. French-Canadian nationalism was still vigorous despite the crumbling of the old self-centered isolationism, but thanks to the tremendous wartime development of Canadian national feeling there was a better possibility of French-Canadian particularism merging with English-Canadian nationalism into that greater Canadianism for which Laurier stood. National unity remained a probably unattainable ideal, for French and English will never be wholly one in Canada; but the prospects for national union were brighter than in the past, thanks to the wartime achievement of a freer and franker relationship between more English and French Canadians than ever before, and a common pride in Canada's wartime achievements. It remained to be seen whether Canada's new international role, as a leader among the minor powers and a middleman between Britain and the United States, would further the development of that union by common effort abroad, or whether differences on external policy would be added to those inevitable on domestic questions.

Notes

[1] F. H. Soward, *Canada in World Affairs: From Normandy to Paris, 1944-1945* (Toronto, 1950), 32. The quoted phrase is President Roosevelt's.

[2] *PIB*, I, 80.

[3] *Ibid.*, 81.

[4] *Ibid.*, 82.

[5] *Senate Debates 1944-5*, 21 June 1944, 210-18; T. D. Bouchard, *The Teaching of Canadian History* (St. Hyacinthe, 1944).

[6] Ecole Sociale Populaire, *Tout un peuple se dresse* . . . (Montréal, 1944).

[7] *L'Action nat.*, XXII (June-July 1944), VI, 490-1.

[8] *PIB*, I, 86.

[9] *Ibid.*, 89.

[10] *Ibid.*, 86.

[11] *Ibid.*, 92.

[12] *Ibid.*

[13] *Ibid*, 97.

[14] *Ibid.*

[15] *Montreal Gazette*, 17 Aug. 1944.

[16] *Saturday Night*, 17 Aug. 1944.

[17] *PIB*, I, 100.

[18] *Ibid.*, 102.

[19] *Ibid.*, 100.

[20] *Ibid.*, 103.
[21] *Ibid.*, II, 1.
[22] *Ibid.*, I, 142.
[23] *Ibid.*, II, 3.
[24] *Ibid.*, 4.
[25] *Ibid.*
[26] C. Stacey, *The Canadian Army 1939-1945* (Ottawa, 1948), 234.
[27] *Commons Debates 1944*, 29 Nov., VI, 6660.
[28] *Ibid.*, 22 Nov., 6508.
[29] Stacey, 233.
[30] *Commons Debates 1944*, 22 Nov., VI, 6505-6.
[31] *Halifax Chronicle-Herald*, 29 Dec. 1949, Angus Macdonald's statement.
[32] *Winnipeg Free Press*, 24 May 1948, G. Dexter, 'The Colonel.'
[33] *Commons Debates 1944*, 22 Nov., 6510.
[34] *Ibid.*, 6513, 6511.
[35] *Ottawa Citizen*, 6 Jan. 1950, G. Dexter, 'In Defence of Ralston.'
[36] *Commons Debates 1944*, 23 Nov., 6516.
[37] *Ibid.*, 6519.
[38] *Ibid.*, 6520.
[39] *Ibid.*, 6521.
[40] *Ibid.*, 6522.
[41] *Ibid.*, 6522-3.
[42] *Ibid.*, 6524.
[43] *Ibid.*
[44] *Ibid.*, 6524-8.
[45] *Ibid.*, 6529.
[46] *Ibid.*, 6537.
[47] *Ibid.*, 6538.
[48] *Ibid.*
[49] *Ibid.*, 6539.
[50] *Ibid.*, 6540.
[51] *Ibid.*, 6541.
[52] *Ibid.*, 6545.
[53] *Ibid.*, 6559.
[54] *Ibid.*, 6566.
[55] *Ibid.*, 24 Nov., 6568.
[56] *Ibid.*, 6579.
[57] *Ibid.*, 6579-80.
[58] *Ibid.*, 27 Nov., 6591.
[59] *Ibid.*, 6593.
[60] *Ibid.*, 6593-4.
[61] *Ibid.*, 6594.
[62] *Ibid.*, 6595.
[63] *Ibid.*, 6597.
[64] *Ibid.*, 6599.
[65] *Ibid.*, 6600.
[66] *Ibid.*, 6602.
[67] *Ibid.*, 6603.
[68] *Ibid.*, 6603-4.
[69] *Ibid.*, 6605.
[70] *Ibid.*, 6606.
[71] *Ibid.*, 6609.
[72] *Ibid.*, 6610.
[73] *Ibid.*, 6614.
[74] *Ibid.*, 6615.

[75] *Ibid.*, 6617.
[76] *Ibid.*, 6618.
[77] *Ibid.*, 6619.
[78] *Ibid.*, 6622.
[79] *Ibid.*, 6623.
[80] *Ibid.*, 6625.
[81] *Ibid.*, 6626.
[82] *Ibid.*, 28 Nov., 6634.
[83] *Ibid.*, 29 Nov., 6635.
[84] *Ibid.*, 6641.
[85] *Ibid.*, 6642.
[86] *Ibid.*, 6652.
[87] *Ibid.*
[88] *Ibid.*
[89] *Ibid.*, 6654.
[90] *Ibid.*
[91] *Ibid.*, 6654–5.
[92] *Ibid.*, 6657.
[93] *Winnipeg Free Press*, 24 May 1948, G. Dexter, 'The Colonel.'
[94] *Commons Debates 1944*, 29 Nov., 6659, 6661–3.
[95] *Ibid.*, 6663.
[96] *Ibid.*, 6663–4.
[97] *Ibid.*, 6666.
[98] *Ibid.*, 6665–6.
[99] *Ibid.*, 6676–7.
[100] *Ibid.*, 6680.
[101] *Ibid.*, 30 Nov., 6682.
[102] *Ibid.*, 6683.
[103] *Ibid.*, 6690.
[104] *Ibid.*, 6691.
[105] *Ibid.*, 6692.
[106] *Ibid.*, 6693.
[107] *Ibid.*, 6694.
[108] *Ibid.*
[109] *Ibid.*, 6695.
[110] *Ibid.*, 6696.
[111] *Ibid.*
[112] *Ibid.*, 6697.
[113] *Ibid.*, 6701–2.
[114] *Ibid.*, 6703.
[115] *Ibid.*, 6704.
[116] *Ibid.*, 6706.
[117] *Ibid.*, 6707.
[118] *Ibid.*, 6707–8.
[119] *Ibid.*, 6708.
[120] *Ibid.*
[121] *Ibid.*, 6708–9.
[122] *Ibid.*, 6709.
[123] *Ibid.*, 6710.
[124] *Ibid.*, 6711.
[125] *Ibid.*, 6711–12.
[126] *Ibid.*, 6712–13.
[127] *Ibid.*, 6713.
[128] *Ibid.*, 6714.
[129] *Ibid.*, 6716.

130 *Ibid.*
131 *Ibid.*, 6718.
132 *Ibid.*, 6722.
133 *Ibid.*, 6723.
134 *Ibid.*, 6724-5.
135 *Ibid.*, 6728.
136 *Ibid.*, 6734.
137 *Ibid.*, 6734, 6748-9.
138 *Ibid.*, 4 Dec., 6756.
139 *Ibid.*, 6758.
140 *Ibid.*, 6759-61.
141 *Ibid.*, 6763.
142 *Ibid.*, 6768-9.
143 *Ibid.*, 6771.
144 *Ibid.*, 6787.
145 *Ibid.*, 6790.
146 *Ibid.*, 6791.
147 *Ibid.*, 5 Dec., 6803.
148 *Ibid.*, 6806.
149 *Ibid.*, 6809.
150 *Ibid.*, 6817.
151 *Ibid.*, 6818.
152 *Ibid.*, 6820.
153 *Ibid.*, 6829.
154 *Ibid.*, 6829-30.
155 *Ibid.*, 6830.
156 *Ibid.*, 6830-1.
157 *Ibid.*, 6831.
158 *Ibid.*, 6832.
159 *Ibid.*, 6 Dec., 6858.
160 *Ibid.*, 6859.
161 *Ibid.*, 6860.
162 *Ibid.*, 6863.
163 *Ibid.*, 6864.
164 *Ibid.*, 6869.
165 *Ibid.*
166 *Ibid.*, 6872-3.
167 *Ibid.*, 6874.
168 *Ibid.*, 7 Dec., 6891.
169 *Ibid.*, 6893-4.
170 *Ibid.*, 6895.
171 *Ibid.*, 6898.
172 *Ibid.*, 6897, 6901.
173 *Ibid.*, 6900.
174 *Ibid.*, 6902.
175 *Ibid.*, 6907.
176 *Ibid.*, 6909.
177 *Ibid.*, 6911.
178 *Ibid.*, 6914-16.
179 *Ibid.*, 6918.
180 *Ibid.*, 6920.
181 *Ibid.*, 6922.
182 *Ibid.*, 6926.
183 *Ibid.*, 6928-30.
184 *Ibid.*, 6933.

[185] *Ibid.*, 6935.
[186] *Ibid.*, 6939.
[187] *Ibid.*, 6941.
[188] *Ibid.*, 6942.
[189] *Ibid.*, 6943.
[190] *Ibid.*, 6944.
[191] *Ibid.*, 6945.
[192] *Ibid.*, 6949-50.
[193] *Ibid.*, 6950-1.
[194] *Ibid.*, 6951.
[195] *Ibid.*, 6952.
[196] *Senate Debates 1944-5*, 28 Nov., 464-5.
[197] *Ibid.*, 30 Nov., 477.
[198] *Ibid.*, 478.
[199] *Ibid.*, 489.
[200] *Ibid.*, 480-1.
[201] *Ibid.*, 530.
[202] *Ibid.*, 536.
[203] *Montreal Herald*, 30 Nov. 1944.
[204] *PIB*, II, 26.
[205] *Ibid.*, 29.
[206] *Ibid.*, 30.
[207] *Commons Debates 1945*, Sess. I, 5 April, I, 578.
[208] *Ibid.*
[209] *Ibid.*, 577.
[210] Stacey, 235.
[211] *Commons Debates 1945*, Sess. I, 5 April, 584.
[212] *Ibid.*
[213] *Ibid.*, 635.
[214] H. Bourassa, *Hier, aujourd'hui et démain* (Montréal, 1916), 169-70.
[215] *Commons Debates 1935*, 1 April, III, 2287.
[216] *L'Action fran.*, VII (mai 1922), 5, 258-74.
[217] D. O'Leary, *Séparatisme, doctrine constructive* (Montréal, 1937).
[218] *L'Autorite* (Montréal), 19 May 1945.
[219] *Le Bloc*, I (19 Feb. 1944), 2.
[220] *PIB*, II, 50; *International Journal*, III (autumn 1944), 4, 334-48, Iris C. Podea, 'Pan-American Sentiment in French Canada.'
[221] *Ibid.*, 37.
[222] *Ibid.*, 36.
[223] *Ibid.*, 47.
[224] *Ibid.*, 48.
[225] *Ibid.*, 49.
[226] *Ibid.*, 51.
[227] *Ibid.*, 45.
[228] *Ibid.*, 51.
[229] *Ibid.*, 45
[230] *Ibid.*
[231] *Ibid.*, 58.
[232] *Commons Debates 1945*, Sess. I, 19 March, 1.
[233] *Ibid.*, 20 March, 21-2.
[234] *Ibid.*, 29-30.
[235] *Ibid.*, 54-5.
[236] *Ibid.*, 59.
[237] *Ibid.*, 60.
[238] *Ibid.*, 70-6.

[239] *Ibid.*, 100.

[240] *Ibid.*, 101.

[241] *Ibid.*, 25 March, 125.

[242] *Ibid.*, 126.

[243] *Ibid.*, 146.

[244] *Ibid.*

[245] *Ibid.*, 148.

[246] *Ibid.*, 23 March, 159.

[247] *Ibid*, 160.

[248] *Ibid.*, 186.

[249] *Maclean's Magazine* (1 Jan. 1944), M. Raymond, 'What Does the *Bloc Populaire* Stand For?'

[250] *Commons Debates 1945*, Sess. I, 27 March, I, 270.

[251] *Ibid.*, 271.

[252] *Ibid.*, 279.

[253] *Ibid.*, 283–4.

[254] *Ibid.*, 295–6.

[255] *PIB*, II, 58.

[256] *Commons Debates 1945*, Sess. I, 3 April, I, 403.

[257] *Ibid.*, 404.

[258] *PIB*, II, 64.

[259] *Commons Debates 1945*, Sess. I, 11 April, I, 764; *PIB*, II, 61.

[260] *Ibid.*, 13 April, 865–6.

[261] Liberals 36 per cent; Progressive Conservatives 34 per cent; CCF 12 per cent; Independents 12 per cent. *PIB*, II, 62.

[262] *PIB*, II, 65.

[263] *Ibid.*, 68.

[264] *Ibid.*, 73.

[265] *Ibid.*, 74.

[266] *Ibid.*, 76.

[267] *Ibid.*, 79.

[268] *Ibid.*, 1.

[269] *Ibid.*, 69.

[270] *Ibid.*, 70.

[271] *Ibid.*, 71.

[272] *Ibid.*, 100.

CHAPTER XVII

THE NOT-SO-QUIET REVOLUTION:
'MAÎTRES CHEZ NOUS ENFIN?'
(1945-66)

THE POSTWAR struggle between old and new forces in Quebec went unresolved longer than had been anticipated in 1945, thanks to both the force of tradition and the forceful stubbornness with which Premier Maurice Duplessis resisted the ever-mounting tide of change.

The weakening or ending of the federal government's wartime powers strengthened the hand of the provincial government in its opposition to centralization of power in Ottawa, while the unanticipated continuation of the wartime boom until 1957 filled Quebec's coffers. Duplessis posed as the champion of provincial rights, defending the citadel of French and Catholic values against encroachment by a federal government which he accused of being subject to Communistic and atheistic influences. He torpedoed successive federal-provincial conferences, and bitterly fought federal efforts to enter the educational and cultural domains which were constitutionally and traditionally the exclusive preserves of the province. Though for nine of the postwar years before Duplessis' death in 1959 the prime minister of Canada was a distinguished French Canadian—Louis Stephen St. Laurent—who did not neglect the interests of his fellow French Canadians, Duplessis succeeded in convincing the majority of the people of Quebec that he, rather than St. Laurent, was their true champion. Meanwhile the *Union Nationale's* electoral war chest fattened, as non-French-Canadian companies sought and won, at a price, the right to exploit Quebec's immensely rich natural resources, the great pool of unorganized or weakly organized labor accustomed to a lower standard of living than English-speaking North Americans, and the manifold advantages of an accommodating government in an era elsewhere characterized by extensive government regulation of business.

But the rising tide of discontent with the old Quebec order, in which the rich and the politicians received more than their share of the good things of life while the masses found it impossible to satisfy their basic wants, could only be suppressed, not stopped. The forces of change continued to work underground, as they were forced to do by Duplessis' ruthless repression of those who advocated reform. In the end he created an anti-*Union Nationale* coalition of organized labor, the intellectuals, progressive-minded clerics, and even some industrialists who had grown weary of paying tribute to his formidable political machine. Under Duplessis' autocratic leadership the *Union Nationale* had always been a one-man party, and with his death in September 1959 the powerful organization that he had built up splintered and crumbled. Paul Sauvé, son of the leader of the provincial Conservatives in the 1920's and the only Duplessis minister who had dared to differ with 'le Chef', worked himself to death in less than four months, trying to reform the regime and to achieve an overdue accommodation with Ottawa. A Byzantine struggle for power among the rival minor chieftains of the *Union Nationale* then weakened the six months' administration of Antonio Barrette, and on July 15, 1960, the Liberals regained power after sixteen years of *Union Nationale* dominance by a slim margin of 51 seats to the *Union Nationale's* 43—51 per cent of the popular vote to their opponents' 47 per cent. The new Liberal leader chosen in 1958, Jean Lesage, a young Quebec lawyer who had served as federal minister of northern affairs, successfully continued the tactics of his predecessor, Georges-Emile Lapalme, in unifying the widespread opposition to the Duplessis regime under the campaign cry of 'It's time for a change.' His victory owed much to the extraordinary talents of René Lévesque, a radio and television commentator with international experience who represented the views of the progressive intellectuals and knew how to appeal effectively to the discontented urban workers. Another highly influential figure in the new Liberal government was Paul Gérin-Lajoie, Rhodes scholar, constitutional expert, and lawyer, who was to become Quebec's first minister of education and to lead the way in a drastic overhaul of Quebec's outmoded education system.

Though the Duplessis regime had seemed all-powerful in its hey-day, it was unable to check some manifestations of the revolutionary forces of change on which it kept screwing down the lid ever more tightly. The first notable revolt against the regime was the Asbestos strike in 1949, which the government sought to put down by every legal and extra-legal weapon at its command, including an admittedly 'instructed' judge and the use of the provincial police as strike-breakers. Since the striking miners were members of the Catholic syndicates, the hierarchy, under the liberal leadership of Archbishop Joseph Charbonneau of Montreal, Archbishop Maurice Roy of Quebec, and Bishops Philippe Desranleau of Sherbrooke and Arthur Douville of Saint-Hyacinthe, supported the strike, approving a collection at church doors for the benefit of the strikers. Archbishop Charbonneau, president of the Episcopal Commission on Social Questions, declared in a sermon at Notre-Dame-de-Montréal on May 1:

The working class is the victim of a conspiracy which wishes to crush it, and when there is a conspiracy to crush the working class, it is the duty of the Church to intervene.

We wish social peace, but we do not wish the crushing of the working class. We are more attached to man than to capital. This is why the clergy has decided to intervene. It wishes that justice and charity be respected, and it desires that more attention cease to be paid to financial interests than to the human factor.[1]

A settlement of the strike was finally worked out with the aid of Archbishop Roy, although the lay leaders of the strike suffered severe civil sanctions. In the following year the bishops of Quebec issued a notable pastoral letter, which faced the fact that Quebec had become an industrial region and laid down the doctrinal principles that applied to both employers and employees. This document[2] was a landmark in the development of social thought in Quebec, and it revealed an enormous advance on the position taken by the bishops five years earlier, when they had advocated a return to the land as the solution of the postwar social problems, although this well-worn prescription had already proved thoroughly unworkable in coping with the problems of unemployment in the great depression of the 1930's.

This epoch-making statement by the Quebec bishops was but one bit of the mass of evidence that after 1945 French-Canadian nationalism had taken on a new socio-economic orientation, which was far more realistic and applicable to Quebec's problems than the rather sterile provincial nationalism of Henri Bourassa before the First World War, the still more sterile racist provincialism of Canon Lionel Groulx in the 1920's, and the politico-economic separatism of the depressed 1930's which culminated in the fiascos of the *Ligue pour la Défense du Canada* and the *Bloc Populaire* during the Second World War. The new spirit was perhaps most evident in *Le Devoir*, the traditional nationalist journal *par excellence*, which under the editorship of Gérard Filion and André Laurendeau, respectively a former secretary of the Quebec Farmers' Union and the disillusioned former provincial leader of the *Bloc Populaire*, urgently championed social and economic reforms and fearlessly attacked the Duplessis regime. Duplessis and his ministers finally became so irritated by *Le Devoir's* revelations of *Union Nationale* corruption that in 1958 all members of the cabinet brought separate libel suits against the editors, in response to the newspaper's charges of their involvement in the Quebec natural gas scandal.[3] In 1950 the new spirit found expression in the review *Cité Libre*, which under the editorship of Gérard Pelletier, a labor journalist, and Pierre-Elliott Trudeau, a political scientist and labor lawyer, found no cow too sacred to be sociologically anatomized.

The Catholic syndicates made it clear in the Asbestos strike of
1949, and again in the Murdochville strike in 1957 in the new Gaspé
copper mines, that they intended to be just as tough as the international unions in their insistence upon better working conditions and
higher wages. Despite a long tradition of feuding, all the labor unions
in Quebec became united in the demand that wages and working
conditions in the province be raised to the level prevailing in Ontario
and the rest of English-speaking North America. The amalgamation
of the Trades and Labor Congress (A.F.L.) and the Canadian
Labour Congress (C.I.O.) unions into the Canadian Labour Congress in 1956, and the Catholic syndicates' decision in principle that
same year to join the new Congress, reflected a new spirit of cooperation between the three major movements in opposition to Duplessis'
new Draconian labor code, Bill 5, which was defeated in 1949,
though many of its measures were subsequently adopted in Bills 60
(1949), 19 (1954), and 20 (1954). Syndicates and internationals made
common cause in protesting against the government's handling of
the Asbestos strike, and in 1957 the syndicates supported the United
Steel Workers of America (C.L.C.) in the Murdochville strike. The
old *Union Nationale* policy of playing off one labor movement against
another had become unworkable, and the growing political militancy
of labor played a notable part in the popular repudiation of the
regime in 1960. It was Antonio Barrette, the man who had been
Duplessis' minister of labour since 1944, who went down to defeat as
leader of the *Union Nationale* in June 1960. But just as union merger
talks were protracted and desultory after 1956, because of a basic
difference in philosophy between the syndicates and the internationals, the syndicates did not, with some exceptions, endorse the
New Democratic Party, founded in the summer of 1961 as the successor to the C.C.F. with the support of the Canadian Labour Congress.
The N.D.P. did not win much support in Quebec in the 1962 federal
elections, since labor leaders there felt it necessary to back the
Liberals, with their thin margin of advantage over the regrouping
Union Nationale forces and their program of social reforms which included many of labor's traditional aims.

The great surprise of the 1962 federal elections was the capture of
26 Quebec seats by the revived Social Credit forces under the
dynamic leadership of Réal Caouette, a frenetic demagogue who
exploited Quebec's disillusionment with both traditional parties and
the discontent of such underprivileged areas as Lake St. John and the
Abitibi with the existing social order. But it was noteworthy that
Social Credit did not advocate the vocal separatism which attracted
so much attention in 1961 and 1962, both within and without the
province, for while Social Credit exploited Quebec particularism, as
a national party it was as committed to French-English coexistence

as the Liberals and the Conservatives. Caouette's alliance with Robert Thompson's Alberta Social Crediters proved short-lived, for the Quebec version of Major Douglas' gospel had always differed from the Alberta one, and personal difficulties compounded ideological ones. When it became evident after the 1963 elections that Thompson could not muster much support in the rest of Canada, Caouette and his followers split off from their Western allies late in that same year and became *Le Ralliement des Créditistes*. Since there appeared to be no possibility of Social Credit ideas being carried out by the federal government, the *Créditistes*, who had not felt at home at Ottawa, became Quebec nationalists, and early in 1964 issued a program calling for complete provincial control over bank credit, foreign trade, immigration policy, and the collection of taxes. At the party convention in Quebec City in August of that year, this program was ratified and a call made for associate status for Quebec in a new Confederation. The only alternative, in the *Créditistes'* view, was clearly secession.

But the *Créditistes* themselves splintered in shifting from the federal to the provincial field. While their federal representation dropped to 21 in 1963, only 13 followed Caouette in his split with the Alberta group; and they secured only 9 federal seats in the November 1965 federal elections. They also failed to organize a strong provincial party. The spectacular Social Credit success in 1962 appears to have been the result of a conservative protest vote, disillusioned with both old parties, yet unwilling to support the radical separatists. The continuing division of the *Créditistes* was made evident once more in the June 5, 1966, provincial elections, when Laurent Legault, long provincial president of the party, joined with a splinter group from the separatist *Ralliement pour l'Indépendance Nationale* (R.I.N.), headed by Dr. René Jutras, while Réal Caouette remained aloof. The group elected no candidates. Separatism, not Social Credit, was the rising tide among Quebec's newly enfranchised younger voters[4], and recognition of this fact was implied in Gilles Grégoire's subsequent leadership of a merger of provincial *Créditistes* and the R.I.N.

The revival of separatism in the late 1950's and the early 1960's was one of the most striking developments of the period. In the late 1940's and early 1950's the old nationalist dream of a separate French-Canadian state seemed dead, shattered by the facts of geography and economics, subjects far better taught in Quebec at that time than ever before. Despite Duplessis' posturings in defense of provincial rights, it was realized that under the postwar administrations of Mackenzie King and Louis St. Laurent a far better relationship between Quebec and Ottawa had been achieved than since the early years of the Laurier regime. In this improved relationship the traditional federal-provincial wars tended to become minor formal skirmishes, rather than the devastating conflicts that in the past had threatened the continued existence of Canada. Then with the Conservative landslide of 1958 and the pronouncement of Gordon Churchill, one of Mr. Diefenbaker's principal lieutenants, that English Canada did not need French Canada and that it would be possible to form a federal government without French-Canadian support, separatism revived, though chiefly among the traditional lunatic fringe of embittered nationalists and the rising generation of politically naive students. It grew rapidly, as French Canada found itself left without significant representation in an administration to which it had given fifty M.P.'s in 1958, in a revolutionary overturn of the Quebec tradition since 1896 of voting Liberal in federal elections. The unconcealed hostility of Western supporters of the Diefenbaker administration to French-Canadian Catholics, the old spirit of 'down with French domination' which had played its part in creating the largest majority in Canadian political annals, also encouraged the growth of separatism.

So, too, did the gratuitous insults of such unicultural Ontarians as Douglas Fisher of the N.D.P. who killed his party's chances in Quebec in the 1962 elections by declaring at a Laval student congress on separatism in November 1961 that if the French Canadians wanted to leave Confederation, the English would be glad to see them go, since they produced only hockey players and strip-teasers, and their federal representatives were irresponsible do-nothings.[5] Douglas Fisher ignored the truth which René Lévesque, then resources minister of Quebec, proclaimed at the same gathering: English Canada needed French Canada more than French Canada needed English Canada — i.e., that Canada could remain Canada only if it were both French and English; for if it ceased to be both, it would soon inevitably become American. The growing recognition of this truth, which had already been enunciated in 1951 by the Massey Report's stress on both elements in the Canadian tradition, its assessment of the state of Canadian culture, and its recommendations for safeguarding and developing it, and by the subsequent Fowler Report (1957)[6] on broadcasting and the O'Leary Report (1961) on periodical publications, did much to improve French-English relations in the postwar period. The growing English-Canadian appreciation of French Canada's contribution to national life, and English Canada's new willingness to meet French Canada's needs, also tended to bankrupt the old politico-economic nationalism which had traditionally painted a picture of endless conflict between French and English, and which postulated that French Canada's inferior economic position was due to 'Anglo-Saxon' racial discrimination and the abuse of economic power by the ruthless English-speaking overlords of Quebec's economy. With the spread of a better understanding of economics, and with Quebec enjoying a fair share of postwar Canadian prosperity,[7] the French Canadians seemed to realize that their economic lot was bound up with that of the English Canadians and the Americans, whose share in the Canadian economy steadily increased as Britain's declined. The further integration of the Canadian and American economies under the pressures of the Second World War, a process which continued apace in the postwar period, doomed provincial economic nationalism even more finally than it did national economic nationalism. Yet both nationalisms were to become characteristic of the 1960's.

In the immediate postwar period the younger generation of the French-Canadian élite began to take a leading role in the labor movement, after studying economics, social theory, and labor relations in Europe or the United States. This was a far cry from the élite's traditional devotion to sterile exercises in arithmetical nationalism, proving triumphantly that there were two and three-quarters fewer French-Canadian deputy ministers at Ottawa, or ten and a half fewer army officers above the rank of colonel, than French Canada should have in proportion to population — presumably as a result of Machiavellian Masonic intrigues. Notable in the new movement was the Faculté des Sciences Sociales at Laval, headed by the progressive Dominican Père Georges-Henri Lévesque, which became a training school for the lay leaders of the new order, despite Duplessis' efforts to cripple it after charging that it was a hotbed of 'Socialism' and 'Communism.' These efforts finally brought about Père Lévesque's forced retirement as dean of the school, when the provincial government threatened to deprive the university of the customary annual grants upon which its existence depended. Many of the school's graduates who did not enter the educational world or the labor movement went on to serve the federal government, not as mere trained-seal backbenchers in a well-disciplined Quebec bloc, but as top-rank civil servants in Ottawa and abroad. When the Duplessis regime crumbled and the Lesage government took power in Quebec, many of them were called back to serve the provincial government, and these political technocrats must be regarded as the true makers of the' Quiet Revolution,' even if their role has been that of technicians rather than politicians.

Laval's influence also was felt throughout Canada, when its graduates took teaching posts in French institutions outside Quebec or served as visiting professors in English-Canadian universities, several of which established new courses in French-Canadian history, literature, and sociology. There were particularly fruitful exchanges of staff and students between Laval, Montreal, and Sherbrooke on the one hand, and McGill, Toronto, Western Ontario, British Columbia, and Bishop's on the other, which marked a totally new spirit of cooperation between the English and French universities of Canada. It was finally recognized that all Canadian universities had many problems in common, although their traditions, customs, and working language might differ. This recognition was implemented by the formation of the Federation of Canadian Universities (now the Association of Universities and Colleges of Canada), and demonstrated by the common front presented by the French and English universities of Quebec to the provincial government in February 1966, when the Lesage administration proposed to cut the McGill grant while increasing those of the less well-endowed French universities.

Despite the new tendency to make common cause on matters of common interest, the two older French universities continued to be characterized by very different outlooks. Generally speaking, Laval tended to accept the facts of life as they were in Quebec, and to encourage students to adapt themselves to the new industrial order by acquiring competence in the physical and social sciences, as well as in the humanities. Laval maintained much closer contacts with the English-Canadian and American universities than did Montréal, which continued to regard Paris as the only true fount of wisdom and rejected the wisdom of *'les anglais'* as a menace to the preservation of the French-Canadian way of life. The difference was much more marked among the historians of the two universities than among the physical and social scientists, who tended to be less nationalistic and more universal-minded.[8] At the Université de Montréal, far more dominated than Laval by the provincial government because of its lack of private endowment, a group of young disciples of Canon Lionel Groulx, who had received training abroad as scientific historians without losing their master's nationalist spirit, continued to stress the French-Canadian tradition and the irreconcilability of French and English cultures. For Guy Frégault and Maurice Séguin, and to a lesser extent for Michel Brunet, the French period remained the golden age of French Canada, and all Quebec's history since 1760 was one of a decline and fall determined by the Conquest. There was a strong defeatist tendency in this school of historians (described in a Montreal witticism as made up of 'one who thought, one who wrote, and one who shouted'), which tended to encourage separatism as a remedy for frustration. There was also another influential group at Montreal, represented by Jean-Marc Léger, which sought to cultivate the closest possible ties with France to offset the dominant 'Anglo-Saxon' influences. For its part, France stressed cultural ties with Quebec in the postwar years, and both the wealth of fellowships for study in France and modern communications tended to keep Quebec in much closer contact with France than ever before. When it came to office in 1960, the Lesage government recognized the need for closer relations with France by opening a *Maison du Québec* in Paris, and by making efforts to attract French capital to Quebec. To offset English-Canadian and American economic dominance it also established a ministry of cultural affairs, which was specifically charged with assisting the French minority groups in other provinces and in the United States, and a *Conseil des Arts*, which was intended to play the same role for French Canada as the Canada Council did for Canada as a whole. Cultural agreements were concluded directly between the Quebec government and France despite opposition from Ottawa.

A disciple of the Abbé Maheux, Marcel Trudel, postwar director of the *Institut d'histoire et géographie* at Laval, chiefly concerned himself, like Guy Frégault, with the history of the French regime, but unlike his Montreal colleague did not attempt to impose nineteenth- or twentieth-century French-Canadian nationalism upon seventeenth- and eighteenth-century New France. His early major works, *L'influence de Voltaire au Canada* (Montreal, 1945) and *Chiniquy* (Trois-Rivières, 1955), reflect a persistent interest in the history of the Church, which has recently led him to the conclusion that religious intransigence has had much to do with the isolation of French and English Canadians. After devoting himself for some years to immediate post-Conquest history, including a notable volume on the influence of the American Revolution,[9] he has turned to a detailed re-writing of the history of New France which, like Frégault's work, attaches much importance to the neglected economic history of the period. His Laval colleague Jean Hamelin has analyzed the evolution of New France in still more rigorous economic and social terms in 'Economic et Société en Nouvelle-France,'[10] while Fernand Ouellet, perhaps the most influential of the younger Quebec historians, has applied D. G. Creighton's economic interpretation of the period between the Conquest and Confederation to the evolution of Quebec during these years. Ouellet has also been influenced by Freudian and Marxist historiography and has become interested in the revolutionary aspects of the *Patriote* movement, whose causes he finds in a profound economic crisis of Quebec agriculture in the first third of the nineteenth century, and in the development of a conservative professional élite, thanks to the foundation of the *collèges classiques* by refugees from the French Revolution, whose minds were closed to the realities of an emerging capitalist society with more democratic values than the old seigneurial system.

While the School of Quebec refused to accept the Montreal doctrine that the Conquest was the determining factor in French-Canadian history, and that French Canada's grievances were to be blamed solely on the English, the historians of both groups were equally convinced of the importance of economic and social factors, long neglected by earlier writers who were concerned primarily with religious and political history. Both contributed to a more realistic view of the French-Canadian past and of the reasons for French

Canada's present economic inferiority. Like the sociologists, they paved the way for 'La Révolution tranquille,' for history finds a wide audience in Quebec and helps to shape its future. French-Canadian nationalism, while a natural reaction of an ethnic and linguistic minority set apart from the majority by language, religion, and customs, is to a considerable degree the creation of historians, from Garneau to Brunet, and some of the most effective criticism of it has also been by historians, such as Chapais, Lanctot, and Ouellet.[11]

Despite the Montreal School's continuation of the tradition of Canon Groulx, there was a much broader accommodation between French and English Canadians in the postwar period. As a result of the tremendous growth of English-Canadian nationalism during the Second World War and in the postwar period, the much older French-Canadian nationalism tended to blend with it into a common Canadian nationalism, until the revival of separatism in the 1960's. The French Canadians learned that the first loyalty of most English Canadians was not to Britain but to Canada, while the English Canadians learned that their compatriots were not Frenchmen but Canadians.[12] A common pride, born of Canada's distinguished war record and postwar role in international affairs, as well as in Canada's swelling postwar prosperity, tended to make the relations between French and English Canadians better than they ever had been before. It was appropriate that General Georges Vanier, a wounded hero of the First World War and a veteran diplomat of the Second War, should have been chosen to succeed Vincent Massey as governor-general in 1959, and he soon won the respect of all Canadians. The new pan-Canadian nationalism, of which Bourassa had been a premature prophet in the early 1900's, was strengthened by the determination of both elements in the Canadian population to resist American influences, cultural, political, economic, and military, which became ever stronger as the center of postwar power shifted from London to Washington and North American defense and industry became more closely integrated.

One major factor in the development of the new Canadian nationalism was the recognition of Canadian biculturalism in the Report of the Royal Commission on National Development in the Arts, Letters, and Sciences (1951) — better known as the Massey Report, after the chairman of the Commission, Vincent Massey, who in 1952 became the first Canadian-born governor-general. Mr. Massey, born of old Ontario Loyalist stock, first Canadian Minister to Washington from 1926 to 1931, and Canadian high commissioner to London during the Second World War, was devoted to the British tradition and wary of American influences, although recognizing that much that was good had come to Canada from American sources. The vice-chairman of the Commission was Père Georges-Henri

Lévesque, an eloquent and persuasive spokesman for the French tradition, for North Americanism, and for a broad Canadianism. The sympathetic respect shown in the Report for French-Canadian culture and the emphasis placed on encouraging biculturalism caused the Report to be well received in Quebec, despite the political fireworks set off by its recommendations of federal aid for university education, a field constitutionally reserved to the provinces, and jealously guarded by Quebec to ensure French-Canadian cultural survival. In accordance with the Report's recommendations, the St. Laurent government increased its encouragement of cultural dualism through the C.B.C., the National Film Board, and the National Gallery, its chief cultural agencies, while seeking through the same channels to bring Canada's two cultures into closer relations, so that Canadians might become more aware of what they had in common than of their differences. The Canada Council was established in 1957 in accordance with the Report's recommendations, with an endowment of $100,000,000, half of which sum was to be expended in a short-term program of grants in aid to the universities for building purposes, while the interest on the other $50,000,000 was to be devoted to encouraging the arts, humanities, and social sciences. The Council did much to improve the lot of the French-Canadian artist, writer, and scholar, and to further communication between the two cultures by an extensive translation program.

Premier Duplessis refused on constitutional grounds to let the Quebec universities accept the federal grants after the first year of the program, though he promised them equivalent provincial grants at his discretion. In 1958 the university students showed more courage than their elders in going on strike against this policy, after Laval, the most financially independent of the French universities, had failed to win the support of McGill and Bishop's in opposing it. After Duplessis' death in 1959, Premier Paul Sauvé worked out an intricate formula to permit the Quebec universities to receive their share of the federal grants made to all Canadian universities, which had been set aside until they were free to receive them. The availability of federal aid forced the provincial government to provide more generous support for education, and the French universities have rejoiced ever since in unwonted prosperity, which has led to vast expansion of the old universities of Laval and Montréal; the creation of a third, Sherbrooke; and the proposed founding of a fourth at Montreal, to make room for the thousands seeking higher education now that more scholarships are available and the once semi-closed doors of the universities have been opened to all who would learn.

The French-Canadian educational system has been vastly liberalized in the postwar period, and the process is far from ended, as the revolutionary program of the Parent Report (Quebec, 1964, 1966) indicates. Since the French universities are graduate institutions, admission to which was formerly open only to those who had completed the full eight years of the *collège classique* course, many students fell by the wayside, unable, for financial or family reasons, to complete the required preparation. Now it is possible to acquire the baccalaureate degree by taking night courses while earning one's living, and thus win access to the professional training given by the universities. In the *collèges classiques* themselves, laymen are increasingly replacing clerics, and the old tradition that a cleric was entitled to teach merely by virtue of his cloth, without further academic qualifications, has been rejected. The curriculum has been broadened to include more science and economics, though French Canada remains true to its ancient humanistic tradition and takes pleasure in the fact that English-speaking technical institutes, such as M.I.T., are now stressing the importance of such studies in the training of engineers and scientists. The advance of scientific and technical education in Quebec, aided by both federal and provincial funds and scholarships, has been marked. French Canada is now producing scientists, engineers, highly skilled technicians, accountants, economists, and psychologists, whose training fits them to participate in the economic development of the province. They are much in demand among the more intelligently managed 'foreign' companies operating in Quebec, which have realized that the old order of master-race management and subject-people labor is gone for ever.

Cardinal Léger, Archbishop of Montreal, has encouraged the foundation of a lay *collège classique* and has been sympathetic to the establishment of neutral (i.e., non-sectarian) schools for those who are neither Catholic nor Protestant.[13] It is clear that absolute clerical control of the educational world, once so characteristic of Quebec, has become a dead letter, despite the pressures brought to bear upon Paul Gérin-Lajoie, Quebec's first minister of education, by the bishops for modification of his reforms. The Université de Montréal appointed its first lay rector, the distinguished chemist Roger Gaudry, in 1965, and Ottawa became a secular university in 1965. Despite the electoral capital that Daniel Johnson and the *Union Nationale* were able to make in 1966 out of the charge that the Lesage government was 'taking religion out of the schools' (this apropos of the Parent Report, the work of a commission headed by Mgr Alphonse-Marie Parent, former Rector and present Vice-Rector of Laval, and including other progressive clerics), it seems clear that a majority of the population prefer the new order of lay control, as a wise priest did who remarked in the 1940's: 'Today in the Province of Quebec there are only four classes: the clerical clerics, the anti-clerical clerics, the clerical laymen, and the anti-clerical laymen. The second and fourth classes are becoming dominant, and this is no bad thing.' Since 1945 there has been much Catholic anti-clericalism, opposing the traditional extension of clerical authority into non-ecclesiastical fields. Laymen, not chaplains, now dominate the Catholic syndicates. Laymen are taking an increasingly important role of leadership in education, in intellectual life, and even in the religious sphere, with Cardinal Léger calling for wholehearted cooperation between laymen and clerics in the work of the Church. The change has been so rapid and abrupt that it would not be surprising if some old-fashioned clerics should complain of 'lay domination.' The difference in attitude between the younger and older clergy is well depicted in 'Frère Untel's' (Brother Jérome [Jean-Paul Desbiens]) two books, *Les Insolences de Frère Untel* (Montréal, 1962) and *Sous le Soleil de la Pitié* (Montréal, 1965).[14] And the pace of evolution is indicated by the fact that Brother Jérome, silenced by his order in 1960 for criticizing the educational system, is today an official of the provincial Department of Education.

Throughout the postwar years, but more particularly since 1960, French Canada has been a society in full and rapid evolution in all its aspects as its industrial revolution progresses with great strides. The old isolationism has disappeared, with French Canadians serving in the armed forces and civilian services of Canada and the U.N. in many parts of the world. Radio and television reach into the most remote sections of the province, and keep these once isolated regions in touch with what is happening in Greater Montreal, which includes more than half the population of that province. The French Canadian now thinks of all Canada as his country, not just the Province of Quebec, though he retains a special fondness for his *pays*. This development has brought an increasing concern in Quebec with the lot of the French minorities in the other provinces and a demand for full equality of the French and English languages throughout Canada. This concern lies at the root of much of the separatism of recent years. If French Canadians could not be *chez eux* throughout Canada and *maîtres chez eux* in Quebec, many of them were inclined to question the viability of Confederation as its hundredth anniversary approached. But the separatist spokesmen give a distorted picture of sentiment in Quebec, where a majority remains devoted to prudence and *mesure* as rules of life, and deplores the verbal and physical violence of the separatist lunatic fringe. There was a sharp reaction against the terrorism of the *Front de Liberation Québécois* (F.L.Q.) in Montreal in 1963; and while separatism is not dead, its candidates won only 5.6 per cent of the popular vote in the June 1966 elections and failed to take a single seat. In 1964 it was estimated by the *Centre des Recherches Sociales*[15] that 13 per cent of the population was of separatist sympathies. The surprising upset of Jean Lesage's government by a narrow margin (U.N. 55 seats; Liberals 51, with 47 per cent of the popular vote to the U.N.'s 45 per cent) in the June 1966 elections probably reflects Quebec's instinct for the golden mean, when offered a choice between separatism and a somewhat precipitate peaceful revolution which had questioned many of its most cherished traditions. It was also a reaction against *trop de grandeur* on the part of the Liberal leader, who sometimes seemed to have taken General de Gaulle as his model, and in his preoccupation with Quebec's image abroad sometimes forgot the earthy chores of political housekeeping at home. The *Révolution tranquille* cannot be halted by the new Daniel Johnson administration, even if the new regime succeeds in staying in office with its minute majority and inexperienced cabinet; at best the program of change can only be checked. For the spirit of French Canada today is eons removed from that which Louis Hémon noted in his *Maria Chapdelaine* (1912), when he had the voice of Quebec declare: 'Nothing changes in Quebec, and nothing should change.' Today everything is changing, and there is general agreement that it should change. It seems clear that while French Canada is becoming more North American, it is doing so on its own terms, and that Quebec will remain French and Catholic and devoted to its traditions, in the future as in the past.

Notes

[1] *Le Devoir*, 2 mai 1949. For a full account of the Church's role in the strike, see Abbé Gérard Dion, 'L'Eglise et le Conflit,' in Pierre-Elliott Trudeau (ed.), *La Grève de l'Amiante* (Montréal, 1956), 244-62.

[2] *Le Problème ouvrier en regard de la doctrine sociale de l'église* (Québec, 1950).

[3] See Leslie Roberts, *The Chief* (Toronto, 1963), 171-7.

[4] In 1966 those between eighteen and twenty-one were entitled to vote for the first time. Approximately 40 per cent of the population of the province is estimated to fall into the eighteen to twenty-eight age bracket, the element that is most separatist in outlook. These facts explain the attention given by René Lévesque to university audiences, and his observation: 'When I look back over my shoulder, I'm frightened.' The 'Quiet Revolution,' like other revolutions, has outdistanced its first leaders. Gérard Pelletier and Pierre Trudeau, and to some extent René Lévesque, are regarded as old-fashioned and backward by more youthful leaders.

[5] 1ᵉ Congrès des Affaires Canadiennes, *Le Canada, Expérience ratée . . . ou réussie?* (Québec, 1962), 15-16.

[6] 'Canada has travelled a long way over the course of one generation—and at a particularly rapid pace since the Second World War — on the road that leads to the complete English-French reciprocal tolerance and mutual understanding in all parts of the country that now characterize the ancient settlements where English and French have been rubbing shoulders for centuries.' Royal Commission on Broadcasting, *Report*, (Ottawa, 1957), 241.

[7] A striking index is provided by the fact that the number of automobile registrations in Quebec quintupled between 1945 and 1965. The expeditionary zeal of French-Canadian drivers, now that '*Le Canadien errant*' was mounted on wheels, was such that the States of New Hampshire, Vermont, and New York found it advisable to install bilingual highway signs in their northern resort areas. Curiously, such signs are not to be found in New Brunswick or in Ontario. In the latter province, the institution of such signs in a heavily Franco-Ontarian district created such a storm of protest that they had to be taken down.

[8] See F. Dumont and Y. Martin, *Situation de la recherche sur le Canada français;* (Quebec, 1962) and J.-C. Falardeau, *Roots and Values in Canadian Lives* (Ottawa, 1961).

[9] *Louis XVI, la Révolution Américaine, et le Canada* (Québec, 1960).

[10] *Cahiers de l'institut d'histoire*, No. 3 (Québec, 1960).

[11] See Serge Gagnon, 'Pour une conscience historique de la révolution Québecoise,' *Cité Libre*, XVI, 83 (jan. 1966), 4-19.

[12] See J.-C. Falardeau, *op. cit.*

[13] Quebec long had a dual Department of Education, Catholic and Protestant. The large Jewish community in Montreal vainly sought the right to establish its own school system and the Jews remained legally Protestant for educational purposes in Quebec. With the influx of immigrants since 1945, there are now many French-speaking non-Catholics in Quebec, who have a choice of either French-Catholic or English-Protestant education for their children. Their plight was much discussed, and leading French-Canadian laymen called for relief for it.

[14] Published in English as *Brother Anonymous* (Montreal, 1962) and *For Pity's Sake* (Montreal, 1965).

[15] *Maclean's*, 1964.

THE DE GAULLE VISIT

GENERAL de Gaulle's state visit to Canada late in July 1967 disrupted Canada's relations with France, whose reinforcement had been sought by the Pearson government in Ottawa to balance Canada's basically American and Commonwealth orientation, and by both the Lesage and Johnson governments in Quebec to bolster French-Canadian culture against English-speaking pressures. Rejecting the Canadian government's insistence that he, like other heads of state visiting Canada during the Centennial year, come first to Ottawa and then proceed to Expo, the French president accepted Premier Johnson's invitation to visit Quebec first for four days before spending one day in Ottawa. Relations between the federal and provincial governments were thus already strained by protocol disputes before de Gaulle's arrival.

On Sunday, July 23, General de Gaulle landed at Quebec City from the French cruiser *Colbert* in which he had crossed the Atlantic, calling en route at the French colony of St. Pierre and Miquelon, off the coast of Newfoundland, which had been a bone of contention between the de Gaullist movement and the Allies during the Second World War. He was greeted at Wolfe's Cove by the new Governor-General, Roland Michener, Premier Johnson, and External Affairs Minister Paul Martin. The first contretemps of the stormy visit occurred when the dockside crowd hissed and booed "God Save the Queen", which was played in honor of the Governor-General, as the "Marseillaise" was in honor of the French president. Only some 2,000 people gathered for this early Sunday morning ceremony; but 5,000 later greeted de Gaulle with enthusiasm upon his arrival at the Quebec city hall, where the crowd sang the "Marseillaise"; and hundreds more lined the highway to Ste. Anne de Beaupré, where he attended a noon Mass celebrated by Cardinal Roy, the Archbishop of Quebec. In short impromptu speeches during the day de Gaulle stressed the point that Quebec and France had common aims as well as a common heritage and should work together: "What we are doing in France, you are doing here. We will do it a little more together. Whatever is French has its role to play, as always."[1]

That night, at a state dinner given by the provincial government at the Chateau Frontenac, the General declared that not only was Quebec asserting more and more its "popular and political entity", but also was increasingly becoming a "particular economic reality", which wished to govern its own destiny. He promised France's support for Quebec's efforts as the links between them increased, and he urged Quebec intellectuals to participate in French advances. However, he also said that progress for a French Canada that had become master of itself involved cooperation with English Canada to safeguard Canadian independence of the United States. For his part Premier Johnson declared that the question of survival for French Canada no longer existed, and that now it was a matter of "meeting the challenge of excellence" with French aid. He expressed the hope that "the younger generation will look more towards France than we ourselves have been able to do". Federal ministers Paul Martin and Jean Marchand refused to comment on de Gaulle's remarks, which René Lévesque, the uninhibited former Liberal provincial cabinet minister, described as "a masterpiece of inter-Canadian brinkmanship".[2]

The following day, Monday, July 24, the General, accompanied by Premier Johnson, drove from Quebec City to Montreal along the old north-shore *Chemin-du-Roi* (Route 2), whose early settlements were decorated with the French tricolor and the Quebec fleur-de-lis flag, as well as the flags of the French provinces from which the early settlers had come. The absence of the Canadian Maple Leaf flag was noticeable. The General was clearly stimulated by the welcome he received along the way, although the crowds were smaller than had been anticipated by the provincial authorities, who had encouraged decorations and demonstrations in his honor. At Donnacona he told a crowd of 1,000 which had waited an hour in the rain that "Quebec, alive, is on its way to becoming master of itself", and at Trois-Rivières he led the singing of the "Marseillaise" and called on the noon-hour assembly of some 5,000 persons to "be masters of your own destiny" in an age when all peoples were seeking to become themselves, adding "France expects you to do your part." Upon his arrival that evening at the Montreal city hall he concluded a brief extemporaneous address from the balcony to a crowd of more than 10,000 by crying: "Vive le Québec! Vive le Québec libre! Vive le Canada français! Vive la France!" His use of the separatist slogan "Québec libre" ("a free Quebec"), coupled with his observation that on his trip from Quebec City he had found "an atmosphere resembling the liberation" of France in 1944, aroused a storm of protest in Quebec, across Canada, and abroad.[3]

While the French president spent the following day touring Expo, where France's national day was being celebrated, more than a thousand telephone calls and telegrams – over half of them from Quebec – poured into Prime Minister Pearson's office, and the federal cabinet held an all-day meeting to determine what attitude to take towards this flagrant intervention into Canadian internal affairs by a visiting head of state. The Liberal member for Notre Dame de Grace, Warren Allmand, expressed a widely held English-Canadian view when he urged External Affairs Minister Martin to cancel the remainder of the General's tour and to insist upon his immediate departure. Opposition Leader Diefenbaker declared: "However great a respect Canadians have for General de Gaulle, his comments on domestic affairs are an inexcusable intrusion." Dr. Eugene Forsey, a well-known constitutional expert, observed: "General de Gaulle and M. Daniel Johnson appear to believe that Quebec is France's Sudetenland."[4] While the English-Canadian press generally exploded in anger, the Montreal *Star*, as well as *La Presse* and *Le Devoir*, was at first defensive about the General's remarks and tried to explain them away as "emotionally charged reactions to an emotionally charged situation."[5] Claude Ryan observed in *Le Devoir* that "the worst error English Canadians can commit would be to remember only the words "Long live a free Quebec" and to forget the rest"[6] – the need for English and French Canada to settle their immediate joint problems by direct dialogue and negotiation rather than by having recourse to foreign support. *Le Soleil*, the Quebec City Liberal organ, sharply attacked de Gaulle for having divided Canada and France rather than bringing them together, and observed: "If the visit of de Gaulle should lead to another rise of independence fever, the great majority of the Quebec population that is not separatist will know how to place the blame on those responsible, the government of Quebec."[7] Réal Caouette, leader of the *Créditistes*, declared that de Gaulle had done Canada a very bad service by trying to please "a handful of irresponsible separatists", while Gilles Grégoire rejoiced that the General had given an international character to the idea of an independent Quebec.[8]

On Tuesday evening Prime Minister Pearson issued the following statement, which was described as "pussyfooting" by Mr. Diefenbaker and "too brutal" by some of the French-Canadian press:

I am sure that Canadians in all parts of our country were pleased when the President of France received such a warm welcome in Quebec.

However, certain statements by the President tend to encourage a small minority of our population whose aim is to destroy Canada, and, as such, they are unacceptable to the Canadian people and its Government.

The people of Canada are free. Every province of Canada is free. Canadians do not need to be liberated. Indeed, many thousands of Canadians gave their lives in two World Wars in the liberation of France and other European countries.

Canada will remain united and will reject any effort to destroy her unity.[9]

The Prime Minister went on to stress how much importance Canada attached to its special relationship with France, "the motherland of so many of her citizens", and expressed the hope that his scheduled discussions with General de Gaulle would foster a friendly relationship. But late that night, after declaring at a dinner at the French pavilion (which was boycotted by the federal ministers and Premier Robichaud of New Brunswick) that "There may have been some difficulty . . . but if the President of the French Republic has helped the French of Canada, he will rejoice and so will France, I assure you,"[10] de Gaulle decided to cut short his visit and return home from Montreal the following day, without visiting Ottawa. When informed of his decision, the Canadian government issued the following statement: "General de Gaulle's decision to cut short his visit to Canada is understandable under the circumstances. But those circumstances, which are not of the Government's making, are greatly to be regretted."[11]

On Wednesday July 26 Mayor Jean Drapeau of Montreal, an ultra-nationalist in his younger days, made himself a hero in Canada from coast to coast by an extemporaneous speech at a city-hall lunch for the French president by telling him how Canadian the French Canadians were:

For more than two centuries the French Canadians have had to reconcile themselves to living alone and to learning to survive by themselves. . . . Our roots are here. . . . We have had to assume, for a long time, the role of guardian of French culture and life in America. . . . May the renewal that Quebec is presently experiencing find support in lasting friendships which arise from the same spirit that inspires the General, so that French Canada may better serve Canada as a whole and the North American continent by realizing itself.

Our dream is to play in Canada and in North America a role analogous to that which France plays in Europe and in the family of nations. . . . As for us, we are profoundly attached to our immense country, and we consider that this is the best way to serve French life and culture.[12]

In a following speech the General declared that he felt that he had been able to get to the root of things during his visit, and called for a tightening of the ties between France and Quebec and the development of all manner of exchange programs, despite the storm that had arisen. But a somewhat chastened president ignored the cry of "de Gaulle au balcon" from several dozen separatists when he emerged from the luncheon. He was seen off at the Montreal airport that afternoon only by Premier Johnson, Mayor Drapeau, and Ambassador Lionel Chevrier, delegated to represent the Canadian government for all state visitors during the Centennial year.

What might have been a mere temporary tempest in a teapot, enlivening the journalistic midsummer dog-days for French-Canadian and English-Canadian press alike, showed signs of turning into a continuing deterioration of Franco-Canadian and French-English relations in Canada when upon his return home de Gaulle made no apology for his conduct and instead reasserted and amplified the position he had taken in Canada, despite a mounting wave of criticism in France itself and abroad. Although one of his own cabinet ministers had characterized his conduct as "a little gross" and several other French political leaders censured his intervention in Canadian affairs, the General's return to Paris was promptly followed on July 27 by an official statement distributed by Agence France-Presse, which asserted: "There is no de Gaulle problem but a Canadian problem", and went on to say:

By going to Canada, General de Gaulle deliberately attempted to help the French Canadians in their thrust. . . . General de Gaulle's trip, authorized circles feel, will exercise a definite influence on the evolution of French-Canadian personality. France will continue, and will develop, its cooperation with the French Canadians on the cultural level, since this is of capital interest to us.[13]

This inspired declaration was followed on July 31 by a 600-word statement by de Gaulle himself, in which he said that the French Canadians, after "a century of oppression," were still not assured of "liberty, equality, and fraternity in their own country." He promised them France's help in achieving "the liberationist aims that they have set for themselves".[14] On August 1 the Canadian government issued another statement: "It has already made its position clear on the unacceptibility of any outside interference in Canadian affairs and has nothing to add in the present circumstances."[15] Ottawa intimated that it would seek clarification of the French position in private rather than indulging in diplomacy by press release. An opportunity for such clarification was afforded by the opening of long-scheduled Franco-Canadian discussions of St. Pierre and Miquelon's offshore mineral rights.

Then on August 10, in a long television address defending his foreign and domestic policies, General de Gaulle said that "Frenchmen of Canada" had displayed a "unanimous and indescribable will for emancipation" during his visit, and that France, "without disavowing in any way the friendship that it has for the Anglo-Saxon nations", was taking an "appropriately French" position on this as well as other current questions.[16] On August 23 the French cabinet approved a considerable increase in cultural, economic, and technical aid to Quebec, "to help the French of Canada to maintain and develop their personality", despite the fact that a recent French public opinion poll indicated that 45 per cent disapproved of de Gaulle's Canadian policy, while only 18 per cent approved.[17] On September 13, during a visit to Quebec City,

French Minister of Education Alain Peyrefitte announced a ten-fold increase in Franco-Quebec cultural exchanges for 1968-70.[18]

While the long-range results of de Gaulle's visit cannot be assessed so shortly after the event, some conclusions can none the less be drawn. Certainly the affair helped to reinforce the old persistent English-Canadian delusion that the French Canadians are "Frenchmen" more attached to France than to Canada, despite Mayor Drapeau's eloquent declaration to the contrary. It was divisive in that some French-Canadian leaders, notably Premier Johnson, tended to welcome de Gaulle's intervention, while English Canadians generally deplored it. On July 28 the Quebec government declared that the province had not been shocked by the General's "courageous and lucid" remarks, and deplored the federal government's yielding to "extremist pressures" in issuing the statement that forced his departure.[19] The Canadian press, which in recent years has made notable progress in more fairly reporting English and French Canada to each other, was also divided, with a considerable group of French-Canadian journalists charging their English colleagues with biased reporting and comment.[20] For its part, the French-Canadian press was clearly more sympathetic to the General. The Quebec Federation of Saint-Jean-Baptiste Societies, on behalf of its 300,000 members, regretted the "incomprehension of the Canadian government" and its attitude towards General de Gaulle. It added that the government's declaration was "cavelier" and "unacceptable to the French-speaking population as well as to Quebec's guest".[21]

The aftermath of the de Gaulle visit also involved an escalation of the debate within Quebec about its future, and some shifting of political allegiances. After charging that Premier Johnson had used de Gaulle's visit to bolster his shaky administration, Opposition Leader Jean Lesage challenged him to declare whether the *Union Nationale* was separatist or not. This statement caused the resignation from the Liberal Party of François Aquin, former Quebec Liberal Federation leader, who subsequently espoused separatism. The influential former Liberal minister, René Lévesque, later made a proposal for the independence of Quebec, while conserving its economic ties with the rest of Canada. After stating in an interview at the provincial premiers' conference at Fredericton that he favored cultural exchanges with France, but "we can settle our own political problems in Canada",[22] Premier Johnson subsequently denied this statement and hailed de Gaulle as a catalyst of French Canada's problems. At the final session of the Quebec legislature on August 12 Johnson said that he would have liked to introduce a motion of thanks to General de Gaulle for his visit and one of blame for the federal government for having prevented the completion of his trip. Lesage promptly associated himself with Johnson in expressing "our gratitude to General de Gaulle for having come to visit us as he did", describing him as "worthy of Quebec's reception which he merited because of all that he has said and done for Quebeckers".[23] Separatist spokesmen generally were jubilant at the General's espousal of their cause.

On balance, the immediate net effect of de Gaulle's visit to Quebec would appear to have been a setback to the process of accommodation between English and French Canadians which must continue if Canada is to survive, and an increase in the division within Quebec concerning future goals. Far from helping the French cause in Canada and the world, de Gaulle may have hurt it. For if the French Canadians should ever despair of maintaining their culture and achieving equality in Canada, they might opt for integration into the United States, according to Premier Johnson.[24] But Prime Minister Pearson remained confident that "Canadians all together will manage to make . . . separatism unnecessary and impossible".[25]

Notes

1 *New York Times*, July 24; *Le Devoir*, July 25.
2 *New York Times*, July 25; *Le Devoir*, July 25.
3 *Ibid.*
4 *Globe and Mail*, July 26.
5 *Montreal Star*, July 25.
6 *Le Devoir*, July 26.
7 *Le Soleil*, July 25.
8 *Le Devoir*, July 26.
9 *New York Times*, July 26; *Le Devoir*, July 26.
10 *Globe and Mail*, July 26.
11 *New York Times*, July 27.
12 *Le Devoir*, July 27.
13 *New York Times*, July 29.
14 *Globe and Mail*, August 1; *Le Devoir*, August 1.
15 *Montreal Star*, August 2.
16 *Globe and Mail*, August 11.
17 *New York Times*, August 24.
18 *Le Devoir*, September 14.
19 *Montreal Star*, July 29.
20 *Globe and Mail*, July 31.
21 *Montreal Star*, August 2.
22 *Ibid.*
23 *L'Evangéline*, August 14.
24 *Paris-Match* interview, *L'Evangéline*, August 18.
25 *Globe and Mail*, August 22.

SELECTIVE BIBLIOGRAPHY

General Works

The standard reference guide, now badly out of date, is R. G. Trotter, *Canadian History: a Syllabus and Guide to Reading* (Toronto, 1934), which is supplemented by Robin W. Winks, *Recent Trends and New Literature in Canadian History* (Washington, 1959). *The Cambridge History of the British Empire*, Vol. VI: "Canada and Newfoundland" (Cambridge, 1930); Justin Winsor, *Narrative and Critical History of America* (8 vols., Boston, 1888-9); and R. G. Thwaites, *The Jesuit Relations and Allied Documents*, Vol. LXXI (Cleveland, 1901) offer guidance to the earlier literature. G. Lanctot, *L'Oeuvre de la France en Amérique du Nord; bibliographie sélective et critique* (Montreal, 1951); Philippe Garigue, *A Bibliographical Introduction to the Study of French Canada* (Montreal, 1956); and F. Dumont and Y. Martin, *Situation de la recherche sur le Canada français* (Quebec, 1963) are the most recent bibliographies. There is much useful guidance in H. P. Beers, *The French in North America: a Bibliographical Guide to French Archives, Reproductions, and Research Missions* (Baton Rouge, 1957) and *The French and British in the Old Northwest: A Bibliographical Guide to Archive and Manuscript Sources* (Detroit, 1964). F. M. Staton and M. Tremaine, *A Bibliography of Canadiana* (Toronto, 1934) covers up to 1867. The *Bulletin des recherches historiques* (Quebec), the *Review of Historical Publications Relating to Canada* (Toronto, 1897-1919), and the *Canadian Historical Review* (Toronto) deal with recent publications, as does the *Revue de l'histoire de l'Amérique française* (Montreal).

L.-M. LeJeune, *Dictionnaire général du Canada* (2 vols., Ottawa, 1931); C. Tanguay, *Dictionnaire généalogique des familles canadiennes* (7 vols., Montreal, 1871-90); W. S. Wallace (ed.), *The Macmillan Dictionary of Canadian Biography* (3rd ed. rev., Toronto, 1963); Norah Story, *The Oxford Companion to Canadian History and Literature* (Toronto, 1967); and J.-J. Lefebvre, "Le Canada; L'Amérique-Géographique, Historique, Biographique, Littéraire", Supplément du *Larousse Canadien Complet* (Montreal, 1955) are useful reference works.

Chapter XI (1911-16)

Allen, P. *et al. La Pensée d'Henri Bourassa* (Montreal, 1954).

Armstrong, E. H. *The Crisis of Quebec, 1914-18* (New York, 1937).

Asselin, O. *Le Sou de la pensée française* (*Feuilles de combat III*, Montreal, 1913).

——"*L'Action Catholique*," *les évêques et la guerre* (Montreal, 1914).

——*Les Evêques et la Propagande de "l'Action Catholique"* (Montreal, 1915).

——*Pourquoi je m'enrôle* (Montreal, 1916).

——*Pensées françaises*, pages choisies (Montreal, 1937).

Barber, Marilyn. "The Ontario Bilingual Schools Issue," *CHR* XLVII, 3 (September 1966), 227-48.

[Borden] H. Borden (ed.). *Robert Laird Borden: His Memoirs* (2 vols., Toronto, 1938).

Bouchette, E. *Emparons-nous de l'industrie* (Ottawa, 1901).

——"Evolution économique dans la Province de Québec," *TRSC 1901*, I, 117-44.

Bourassa, H. *Why the Navy Act Should Be Repealed* (Montreal, 1912).

——*Pour la justice* (Montreal, 1912).

——*Le Spectre de l'annexation / The Spectre of Annexation and the Real Danger of National Disruption* (Montreal, 1912).

——*La Langue française et l'avenir de notre race* (Quebec, 1913).

——*Ireland and Canada* (Montreal, 1914).

——*French and English Frictions and Misunderstandings* (Montreal, 1914).

——*Le Canada à Lourdes* (Montreal, 1914).

——*La Politique de l'Angleterre avant et après la guerre* (Montreal, 1914).

——"Foreign Policy", *Contemporary Review* (September 1914).

——*The Duty of Canada at the Present Hour* (Montreal, 1915).

——*Le 5e Anniversaire du* Devoir (Montreal, 1915).

——*Hier, aujourd'hui, demain* (Montreal, 1916).

——*Le Devoir et la guerre: le conflit des races* (Montreal, 1916).

——*In Memoriam: Paul-Emile Lamarche* (Montreal, 1919).

Bruchési, Mgr. P. "Le Dualisme Canadien", *TRSC 1915*, App. A, xlvi-xlvii.

Dantin, L. *Emile Nelligan et son oeuvre* (Montreal, 1903).

Desaulniers, G. *Les Bois qui chantent* (Montreal, 1930).

Falardeau, J.-C. (ed.). *Essais sur le Québec contemporain / Essays on Contemporary Quebec* (Quebec, 1953).

Gagnon, M. *Olivar Asselin* (2 vols., Montreal, 1962).

Gérin, L. "Notre mouvement intellectuel", *TRSC 1901*, I, 169-70.

Groulx, Lionel. *L'Enseignement français au Canada*, II (Montreal, 1933).

——*Nos luttes constitutionnelles* (Montreal, 1916).

Laurendeau, A. "Henri Bourassa", in McDougall, R. L. (ed.), *Our Living Tradition*, IV (Toronto, 1962).

[Laurier] A. DeCelles (ed.). *Discours de Sir Wilfrid Laurier*, II (Montreal, 1920).

Lavergne, A. *Trente ans de vie nationale* (Montreal, 1934).

Michel, J. *La Participation des Canadiens-français à la Grande Guerre* (Montreal, 1936).

Routhier, A. "Le Problème des races au Canada", *TRSC 1915*, I, 5-11.

Rumilly, R. *Histoire de la Province de Québec*, XVI-XXI.

Sellar, R. *The Tragedy of Quebec* (Toronto, 1916).

Sissons, C. B. *Bilingual Schools in Canada* (Toronto, 1917).

Skelton, O. D. *Life and Letters of Sir Wilfrid Laurier*, II (Carleton Library, Toronto, 1965).

Tucker, G. N. "The Naval Policy of Sir Robert Borden, 1912-14", *CHR* XXVIII, I (March 1947), 1-30.

Wade, M. "Olivar Asselin" in McDougall, R. L. (ed.), *Our Living Tradition*, V (Toronto, 1965).

Weir, G. M. *The Separate School Question in Canada* (Toronto, 1934).

Chapter XII (1916-19)

Armstrong, E. H. *The Crisis of Quebec, 1914-18* (New York, 1937).

[Borden] H. Borden (ed.). *Robert Laird Borden: His Memoirs*, II (Toronto, 1938).

Bourassa, H. *Le Problème de l'Empire: Indépendence ou Association Impériale / Independence or Imperial Partnership* (Montreal, 1916).

———"Letter to A. R. McMaster," *Le Devoir*, 5 August, 1916.

———*L'Intervention américaine: ses motifs, son objet, ses conséquences* (Montreal, 1917).

———*L'Emprunt de la "Victoire"* (Montreal, 1917).

———*Conscription* (Montreal, 1917).

———*Le Canada apostolique* (Montreal, 1917).

———*Le Langue, gardienne de la foi* (Montreal, 1918).

Cook, Ramsay. *The Politics of J. W. Dafoe and the Free Press* (Toronto, 1963).

Curtis, Lionel. *The Problem of the Commonwealth* (London, 1916).

Dawson, R. M. *William Lyon Mackenzie King: A Political Biography, 1874-1923* (Toronto, 1958).

[Laurier] A. DeCelles (ed.). *Discours de Laurier*, II (Montreal, 1920).

Ferns, H. S. and Ostry, B. *The Age of Mackenzie King* (London, 1955).

Graham, Roger. *Arthur Meighen:* I, *The Door of Opportunity* (Toronto, 1960).

Hawkes, A. *Canadian Nationalism and the War* (Montreal, 1916).

Hughes, S. H. S. "Sir Sam Hughes and the Problem of Imperialism", *CHAR 1950*, 30-70.

Hutchison, Bruce. *The Incredible Canadian, a Candid Portrait of Mackenzie King, his Works, his Times, and his Nation* (Toronto, 1952).

McGregor, F. A. *The Fall and Rise of Mackenzie King: 1911-1919* (Toronto, 1962).

Our Volunteer Army (Montreal, 1916).

"Patriote" (Abbé D'Amours). *Où allons-nous? Le Nationalisme canadien. Lettres d'un "Patriote"* (Montreal, 1916).

Papineau, T. "Letter to Henri Bourassa," *Montreal Gazette*, 28 July, 1916.

[Power, C. G.] Norman Ward (ed.). *A Party Politician: The Memoirs of Chubby Power* (Toronto, 1966).

Roy, F. *L'Appel aux armes et la réponse canadienne-française* (Quebec, 1917).

Rumilly, R. *Histoire de la Province de Québec*, XXI.

Savard, A. and Playfair, W. E. (trans.). *Quebec and Confederation: A Record of the Debate of the Legislative Assembly of Quebec on the Motion proposed by J.-N. Francoeur* (Quebec, 1918).

Sissons, C. B. *Bilingual Schools* (Toronto, 1917).

Skelton, O. D. *Life and Letters of Sir Wilfrid Laurier*, II (Carleton Library, Toronto, 1965).

Stacey, C. P. *The Military Problems of Canada* (Toronto, 1940).

"Vindex, J." (R. P. Hermas Lalande, S. J.). *Halte-là "Patriote"* (Rimouski, 1917).

Chapter XIII (1920-39)

Borden, R. L. *Canada in the Commonwealth* (Oxford, 1927).

[Borden] H. Borden (ed.). *Robert Laird Borden: His Memoirs*, II (Toronto, 1938).

Bourassa, H. *Le Canada, nation libre* (Montreal, 1926).

Brebner, J. B. *North Atlantic Triangle* (New Haven and Toronto, 1945; Carleton Library, Toronto, 1966).

———"Canada and the Anglo-Japanese Alliance," *Political Science Quarterly*, L (March, 1935).

Corbett, P. E. and Smith, H. E. *Canada and World Politics* (London, 1928).

Dawson, R. M. *William Lyon Mackenzie King, a Political Biography, 1874-1923* (Toronto, 1958).

Dewey, A. G. *The Dominions and Diplomacy* (2 vols., London, 1929).

[Dominicans]. *Notre Américanisation, enquête de "La Revue Dominicaine"* (Montreal, 1937).

Eayrs, J. *In Defence of Canada*: I, *From the Great War to the Depression* (Toronto, 1965).

———*In Defence of Canada*: II, *Appeasement and Disarmament* (Toronto, 1965).

Ewart, J. S. *Canada and British Wars* (Ottawa, 1922).

Graham, Roger. *Arthur Meighen*: I, *The Door of Opportunity* (Toronto, 1960).

———*Arthur Meighen*: II, *And Fortune Fled* (Toronto, 1967).

Groulx, Lionel. *Directives* (Montreal, 1937).

Lower, A. R. M. *Canada and the Far East, 1940* (New York, 1940).

———*Canada: Nation and Neighbour* (Toronto, 1952).

Ludecke, K. G. W. *I Knew Hitler* (New York, 1937).

McInnis, Grace. *J. S. Woodsworth, a Man to Remember* (Toronto, 1953).

McNaught, K. W. *A Prophet in Politics: A Biography of J. S. Woodsworth* (Toronto, 1959).

Montpetit, E. *Reflèts d'Amérique* (Montreal, 1941).

Neatby, H. B. *W. L. M. King*: II, *The Lonely Heights, 1924-32* (Toronto, 1963).

Neuendorf, G. *Studies in the Evolution of Dominion Status* (London, 1942).

Pickersgill, J. W. *The Mackenzie King Record*: I, *1939-41* (Toronto, 1960).

Ross, Colin. *Zwischen USA und dem Pol* (Leipzig, 1934).

Rumilly, R. *L'Autonomie provinciale* (Montreal, 1948).

Soward, F. H. *et al. Canada in World Affairs: The Pre-War Years* (Toronto, 1941).

Stacey, C. P. *The Military Problems of Canada* (Toronto, 1940).

Chapter XIV (1920-39)

L'Action française. *Notre avenir politique: enquête de "l'Action française," 1922* (Montreal, 1923).

———*Les Canadiens-français et la Confédération Canadienne: enquête de "l'Action française"* (Montreal, 1927).

Asselin, O. "L'Industrie dans l'économie du Canada français" (Ecole Sociale Populaire, no. 296, Montreal, 1938).

———*L'Oeuvre de l'abbé Groulx* (Montreal, 1923).

Barbeau, V. *L'Oeuvre du chanoine Lionel Groulx* (Montreal, 1964).

Bouchette, E. *Emparons-nous de l'industrie* (Ottawa, 1901).

Brunet, M. *Canadians et Canadiens* (Montreal, 1954).

Falardeau, J.-C. (ed.). *Essais sur le Québec contemporain / Essays on Contemporary Quebec* (Quebec, 1953).

Gouin, Paul. *Servir*: I, *La Cause nationale* (Montreal, 1938).

Groulx, Abbé Lionel. *Nos luttes constitutionnelles* (Montreal, 1916).

———"Les Patriotes de 1837" (Montreal, 1917).

———*La Confédération canadienne* (Montreal, 1918).

———"La Naissance d'une race" (Montreal, 1919).

———*Les Lendemains de la conquête* (Montreal, 1920).

———*Vers l'émancipation* (Montreal, 1921).

——— *L'Appel de la race* (Montreal, 1922).

——— *Dix ans de "l'Action française"* (Montreal, 1926).

——— *Au Cap Blomidon* (Montreal, 1932).

——— *Orientations* (Montreal, 1935).

——— *Directives* (Montreal, 1937).

——— *Pour bâtir* (Montreal, 1953).

Hughes, E. C. *French Canada in Transition* (Chicago, 1943).

——— "Industry and the Rural System in Quebec," in *French-Canadian Society*, I (Carleton Library, Toronto, 1964) 76-85.

Laurendeau, A. *L'Abbé Lionel Groulx* (Montreal, 1939).

Marshall, H. *et al. Canadian-American Industry* (New Haven, 1936).

Montpetit, E. *Pour une doctrine* (Montreal, 1931).

——— *Les Cordons de la bourse* (Montreal, 1935).

——— *D'Azur à trois lys d'or* (Montreal, 1937).

——— *La Conquête économique* (1938, 1940, 1942).

——— *Reflèts d'Amérique* (Montreal, 1941).

——— *Souvenirs* (3 vols., 1944-54).

Perreault, A. *et al. Soirées de "l'Action française"* (Montreal, 1926).

Truesdell, L. E. *The Canadian-Born in the United States* (New Haven, 1943).

Zimmern, A. *The Third British Empire* (London, 1926).

Chapter XV (1939-44)

Armstrong, E. H. *French-Canadian Opinion on the War* (Toronto, 1942).

Blanchard, R. *L'Est du Canada français* (Montreal, 1935).

Dawson, R. M. *Canada in World Affairs*: 1939-41 (Toronto, 1943).

——— *The Conscription Crisis of 1944* (Toronto, 1961).

Francoeur, L. *La Situation ce soir*, 1-10 (Montreal, 1941).

Godbout, A. "Canadian Unity" (Quebec, 1940).

Groulx, Abbé Lionel. *Pourquoi nous sommes divisés* (Montreal, 1943).

Hughes, E. C. *French Canada in Transition* (Chicago, 1943).

Laurendeau, A. *La Crise de la conscription, 1942* (Montreal, 1962).

Laurent, E. *Une Enquête au pays de l'aluminium* (Quebec, 1943).

Lefevbre, F. *The French-Canadian Press and the War* (Toronto, 1940).

Lingard, C. C. and Trotter, R. G. *Canada in World Affairs: 1941-44* (Toronto, 1950).

Maheux, Abbé A. *Pourquoi sommes-nous divisés?* (Montreal, 1943).

Pickersgill, J. W. *The Mackenzie King Record*: I, *1939-44* (Toronto, 1961).

——— *The Plebiscite Question / La Question du plébiscite* (Ottawa, 1942).

Radio-Canada. "Le Canada parle à la France" (Montreal, 1944).

Raymond, M. *Politique en ligne droite* (Montreal, 1943).

Rose, F. *Hitler's Fifth Column in Quebec* (Toronto, 1942).

Rumilly, R. *L'Autonomie provinciale* (Montreal, 1948).

Ryerson, S. *French Canada* (Toronto, 1943).

Scott, F. R. "Quebec and the Plebiscite Vote," *Canadian Forum* (June 1942).

Shea, A. and Estorick, E. *Canada and the Shortwave War* (Toronto, 1942).

Tremblay, Abbé V. *Histoire du Saguenay* (Chicoutimi, 1938).

Vaillancourt, E. *Le Canada et les Nations Unies* (Montreal, 1942).

Vanier, General Georges. *Paroles de guerre* (Montreal, 1944).

Chapter XVI (1944-5)

Bouchard, T.-D. "The Teaching of Canadian History" (St. Hyacinthe, 1944).
————*Mémoires* (3 vols., Montreal, 1960).
Bourassa, H. *Hier, aujourd'hui, demain* (Montreal, 1916).
Dawson, R. M. *The Conscription Crisis of 1944* (Toronto, 1961).
Ecole Sociale Populaire. "Tout un peuple se dresse" (Montreal, 1944).
Gélinas, Gratien ("Fridolin"). *Tit-Coq* (Montreal, 1950).
Laurendeau, A. *La Crise de la conscription, 1944* (Montreal, 1962).
Lemelin, R. *Au pied de la pente douce* (Quebec, 1944) / *The Town Below* (Toronto, 1948).
Minville, E. *Notre Milieu* (Montreal, 1942).
————*Le Citoyen canadien* (2 vols., Montreal, 1940).
————*Invitation à l'étude* (Montreal, 1943).
O'Leary, D. *Séparatisme, doctrine constructive* (Montreal, 1937).
Podea, I. C. "Pan-American Sentiment in French Canada," *International Journal* III, (Autumn 1944).
[Power, C. G.] Norman Ward (ed.). *A Party Politician: The Memoirs of Chubby Power* (Toronto, 1966).
Raymond, M. "What does the *Bloc Populaire* Stand For?" *Maclean's* Magazine (1 January, 1944) 8-10, 35.
Roy, Gabrielle. *Bonheur d'Occasion* (Montreal, 1944) / *The Tin Flute* (Toronto, 1959).
Soward, F. H. *Canada in World Affairs: From Normandy to Paris, 1944-1946* (Toronto, 1950).
Stacey, C. P. *The Canadian Army, 1939-1945* (Ottawa, 1948).

Chapter XVII (1945-66)

Archevêques et évêques de la Province de Québec. "Le Problème ouvrier en regard de la doctrine sociale de "l'Eglise" (Quebec, 1950).
Ballantyne, M. G. "The Catholic Church and the CCF," *Canadian Catholic Historical Review*, 1963, 33-45.
Barbeau, Raymond. *J'ai choisi l'indépendence* (Montreal, 1961).
————*Le Québec est-il une colonie?* (Montreal, 1962).
————*Le Québec bientôt unilingue?* (Montreal, 1965).
Barrette, Antonio. *Mémoires*, I (Montreal, 1966).
Borduas, E. "Refus global" (Montreal, 1948).
Brunet, M. *Canadians et Canadiens* (Montreal, 1954).
"Le Canada Français," *Esprit* (Paris), August-September 1952.
Cathelin, J. and Gray, G. *Révolution au Canada* (Paris, 1963).
Chaput, M. *Pourquoi je suis séparatiste* (Montreal, 1961) / *Why I am a Separatist* (Toronto, 1962).
Cohen, R. I. *Quebec Votes* (Montreal, 1965).
Crepeau, P. A. and Macpherson, C. B. *The Future of Canadian Federalism/L'Avenir du fédéralisme canadien* (Toronto and Montreal, 1965).
Dansereau, Pierre. *Contradictions & Biculture* (Montreal, 1964).
Desbarats, Peter. *The State of Quebec* (Toronto, 1965).

Desbiens, J.-P. (Brother Jérôme). *Les Insolences du Frère Untel* (Montreal, 1960)/ The Impertinences of Brother Anonymous (Montreal, 1962).

———*Sous le soleil de la pitié* / *For Pity's Sake* (Montreal, 1965).

Desprès, J.-P. *Le Mouvement ouvrier canadien* (Montreal, 1956).

Dion, Abbé Gérard. *Le Communisme dans la Province de Québec* (Quebec, 1949).

Dion, Gérard and O'Neil, Louis (Les abbés). *Political Immorality in the Province of Quebec* (Montreal, 1956).

———*Le Chrétien et les élections* (Montreal, 1960).

Elie, R. (ed.). *L'Ecole laïque* (Montreal, 1961).

Falardeau, J.-C. (ed.). *Essais sur le Québec contemporain/Essays on Contemporary Quebec* (Quebec, 1953).

———*Roots and Values in Canadian Lives* (Toronto, 1961).

Filion, G. *Les Confidences d'un commissaire d'école* (Montreal, 1960).

Faribault, M. and Fowler, R. M. *Ten to One: The Confederation Wager* (Toronto, 1965).

Fowler Report. *Report of the Royal Commission on Broadcasting* (Ottawa, 1957).

———*Report of the Committee on Broadcasting, 1965* (Ottawa, 1965).

Gagnon, S. "Pour une conscience historique de la révolution québecoise," *Cité libre*, XVI, 83 (January 1966), 4-19.

Garigue, P. *Etudes sur le Canada français* (Montreal, 1958).

———*L'Option politique du Canada français* (Montreal, 1963).

Gauldrault, R. P. "Non-confessionalité et le mouvement ouvrier" (Ottawa-Montreal, 1946).

Gérin-Lajoie, P. *Pourquoi le bill 60* (Montreal, 1963).

Graham, G. and Chaput-Rolland, S. *Dear Enemies* / *Chers ennemis* (Toronto and Montreal, 1963).

Guindon, H. "The Social Evolution of Quebec Reconsidered," in *French-Canadian Society*, I (Carleton Library, Toronto, 1964) 137-61.

Hamelin, J. and M. *Les Moeurs electorales dans le Québec de 1791 à nos jours* (Montreal, 1962).

Institut canadien des affaires publiques. *L'Eglise et le Québec* (Montreal, 1960).

———*Le Rôle de l'Etat* (Montreal, 1962).

———*Nos Hommes politiques* (Montreal, 1963).

———*Le Canada face à l'avenir* (Montreal, 1964).

———*L'Utilisation des ressources humaines* (Montreal, 1965).

———*Disparités régionales d'une société opulente* (Montreal, 1966).

Julien, Claude. "Le Canada, peut-il survivre?" *Le Monde* (Paris), October 10-14, 1967.

Kierans, Eric. *Challenge of Confidence: Kierans on Canada* (Toronto, 1967).

Lamontagne, M. *Le Fédéralisme canadien: évolution et problèmes* (Quebec, 1954).

Lapointe, R. *Mgr. Joseph Charbonneau* (Montreal, 1962).

Laporte, P. *Le Vrai visage de Duplessis* (Montreal, 1960).

Laurendeau-Dunton Commission. *A Preliminary Report of the Royal Commission on Bilingualism and Biculturalism* (Ottawa, 1965).

Laval Congrès des affaires canadiennes. I. *Le Canada, expérience ratée . . . ou réussie* (Quebec, 1961); II. *L'Economie canadienne: où allons-nous?* (Quebec, 1962); III. *La Dualité canadienne à l'heure des Etats-Unis* (Quebec, 1965).

Massey Report. *Report of the Royal Commission on National Developments in the Arts, Letters, and Sciences* (Ottawa, 1951).

"Mercer, John". *The Squeaking Wheel* (Montreal, 1965).

O'Leary Report. *Report, Royal Commission on Publications* (Ottawa, 1961).

Parent Commission. *Report of the Royal Commission of Inquiry on Education in the Province of Quebec* (5 vols., Quebec, 1963-6).

"Quebec Today", *University of Toronto Quarterly* (April 1958), 305-412.

Quinn, H. F. *The Union Nationale: A Study in Quebec Nationalism* (Toronto, 1963).

Rioux, M. and Martin, Y. *French-Canadian Society*, I (Carleton Library, Toronto, 1964).

Roberts, Leslie. *The Chief* (Toronto, 1963).

Rumilly, R. *La Conspiration gauchiste au Canada-français* (Montreal, 1956).

——*Le Problème national des Canadiens-français* (Montreal, 1961).

Saint-Jean-Baptiste Society of Montreal. *Le Fédéralisme, l'acte de l'Amérique du Nord britannique et les Canadiens-français* (Montreal, 1964).

Savoie, C. *La Véritable histoire du F.L.Q.* (Montreal, 1963).

Scott, F. R. and Oliver, M. (eds.). *Quebec States her Case* (Toronto, 1964).

Sloan, T. *The Not So Quiet Revolution* (Toronto, 1965).

Tremblay Commission. *Report of the Royal Committee of Inquiry on Constitutional Problems* (Quebec, 1956).

Trudeau, P.-E. (ed.). *La Grève de l'amiante* (Montreal, 1956).

——"Some Obstacles to Democracy in Quebec," *CJEPS* XXIV, 3 (August 1958), 297-311.

——"The Conflict of Nationalisms in Canada," in Scott and Oliver, *Quebec States her Case*, 57-69.

Wade, M. (ed.). *Canadian Dualism/La Dualité canadienne* (Toronto and Quebec, 1960).

INDEX TO VOLUMES ONE AND TWO